AMERICAN CONSPIRACY FILES

G000044485

The Stories
We Were
Never Told

Peter Kross

Adventures Unlimited Press

For Suzanne and Greg:
To New Beginnings.

Books by Peter Kross:

Tales From Langely
The Secret History of the United States
JFK: The French Connection
Spies, Traitors and Moles
The Encyclopedia of World War II Spies
Oswald, the CIA and the Warren Commission

AMERICAN CONSPIRACY FILES

The Stories We Were Never Told

Peter Kross

American Conspiracy Files

by Peter Kross

ISBN 13: 978-1-939149-50-3

Published by:
Adventures Unlimited Press
One Adventure Place
Kempton, Illinois 60946 USA
auphq@frontiernet.net

www.adventuresunlimitedpress.com

TABLE OF CONTENTS

Chapter 1) The Lost Colony of Roanoke   11

Chapter 2) The Treason of Benedict Arnold   19

Chapter 3) The Doctor Was a Spy   27

Chapter 4) Ben Franklin's Wayward Son Page   31

Chapter 5) Thomas Jefferson's Secret War   35

Chapter 6) How Did Davy Crockett Die?   41

Chapter 7) Jesse James   47

Chapter 8) Butch Cassidy and the Sundance Kid   55

Chapter 9) What Happened to Zachery Taylor?   61

Chapter 10) The Search for Hitler's Gold   67

Chapter 11) The Murder of Judge John Wood   75

Chapter 12) Operation Northwoods   81

Chapter 13) Who Was Jack Ruby?   89

Chapter 14) The Woman Who Tried to Kill Castro   99

Chapter 15) The Zimmerman Telegram   107

Chapter 16) What Happened to the USS Maine?   115

Chapter 17) The Walker Family Spy Ring   123

Chapter 18) The Lincoln Assassination   129

Chapter 19) DeMorenschildt and Oswald   141

Chapter 20) The Robert Hanssen Spy Case   151

Chapter 21) What Was Majestic 12?   159

Chapter 22) J. Edgar Hoover's Private War ... 169

Chapter 23) The FBI and the Day of Terror Plot ... 177

Chapter 24) Oswald's Doubles ... 187

Chapter 25) The U.S. Navy-Mafia Alliance ... 199

Chapter 26) The Saudi-9-11 Connection ... 209

Chapter 27) The Case of Alger Hiss ... 219

Chapter 28) The Oklahoma City Bombing ... 229

Chapter 29) The Plumbers Target Torrijos ... 239

Chapter 30) The Plot to Kill Jack Anderson ... 247

Chapter 31) The Rosenberg Spy Case ... 257

Chapter 32) Was Oswald an Agent? ... 265

Chapter 33) The Atom Bomb Spies ... 277

Chapter 34) Nazi Spies Invade America ... 285

Chapter 35) "DeepThroat" Revealed ... 291

Chapter 36) The Dallas-Watergate Connection ... 303

Chapter 37) Booth or Boyd? ... 315

Chapter 38) The death of Frank Olson ... 323

Chapter 39) William Sebold—Double Agent ... 331

Chapter 40) The Pentagon Papers ... 339

Chapter 41) The October Surprise ... 349

Chapter 42) Did Hitler Live? ... 359

Chapter 43) The FBI and the "Phoenix Memo" ... 369

Chapter 44) Who Killed Bobby?   377

Chapter 45) What the Warren Commission Got Wrong 391

Chapter 46) The Reason for the Watergate Break-In   405

Chapter 47) Oswald in Mexico City   419

Chapter 48) Spies in the Roosevelt Administration   435

Chapter 49) The Spy in the Pentagon   449

Chapter 50) Nixon and the Vietnam Peace Talks   459

Chapter 51) Searching for the Octopus   471

Chapter 52) Who Killed Martin Luther King?   479

Chapter 53) The LBJ Connection   493

Chapter 54) What Happened to Marilyn?   509

Chapter 55) The Vatican Bank Scandal   519

Chapter 56) America At War with Itself   535

*It's no wonder that truth is stranger than fiction.
Fiction has to make sense.*
—Mark Twain.

INTRODUCTION

Conspiracies have been part of our hidden history from the beginning of time, not just a creation of our modern world. This concept is not a new phenomenon and traces its roots back to biblical times when the Moses sent his spies into the Promised Land to "spy the land." One of the earliest conspiracies in recorded history is the assassination of Julius Caesar by members of the Roman Senate. Espionage is also not a new concept and there are stories in the bible that tell of various accounts of skullduggery being perpetuated in ancient Israel by the tribes who inhabited that land.

Then why are so many conspiracy theories not taken seriously or debunked by many people, especially those in the academic community who brush aside all potentially credible accounts that they don't believe in? The answer is simple. If you are a tenured professor in a major college or university and speak out in favor of such conspiracy theories, then your budding professional career is in jeopardy. No one wants to listen to a kook.

Conspiracy theories have found much more favor in Europe than in the United States. There is no concrete reason for that idea except to say that European nations have had more of a written history than that of the infant United States. Right after the Kennedy assassination, while most Americans believed the original findings of the Warren Commission, a majority of Europeans believed that Lee Oswald did not act alone in killing JFK. Even French President Charles de Gaulle believed that the president's death was part of a right-wing conspiracy. Today, 50 years after the murder of John F. Kennedy, a majority of American's still believe that Oswald did not act alone that he had may have had confederates who helped him in the events of November 22, 1963. There are a number of conspiracy theories surrounding the 9-11 attacks, some of which are plausible, some of which are not.

And then there is Benghazi. Need, I say more?

This book, *The American Conspiracy Files: The Stories We Were Never Told*, gives the reader some historical perspective on the major conspiracy theories in American history beginning in the American Revolution and ending in our modern day. There is an historical connection between espionage and conspiracy and this book will also tell these stories as well.

We will explore such events as the disappearance of the English settlers in the Roanoke Colony, the treason of Benedict Arnold, a real American hero (before changing sides), the Culper Spy ring, the mysteries surrounding the deaths of such American legends as Davy Crockett, Jesse James, Butch Cassidy and the "Sundance Kid," tales of World War II espionage, the plot to kill President Lincoln, cold war intrigue, who was "Deep Throat," the plot to kill journalist Jack Anderson, red spies in the Roosevelt administration, the deaths of Martin Luther King, Marilyn Monroe, and Robert Kennedy, ending with the mysterious events of our recent past.

Conspiracy theories, per sé, are not a dirty word. They are part of our history, a topic that is not taught in college or high school, whether we like it or not. So, get ready. Here's the history you were never taught.

Peter Kross
North Brunswick, NJ

Chapter 1
The Lost Colony of Roanoke

As the modern day sailor plies the beautiful waters of the Chesapeake Bay, one can only look at the shoreline with its abundant trees, wildlife and breathtaking scenery and not think back hundreds of years ago when the same land lay in stark contrast to what we see now. If we close our eyes, we can picture a pristine land, populated by Native Americans and the few white settlers who managed to arrive on those shores. If we look a little deeper, we can see a settlement of English settlers who arrived on those shores, the first wave of what would become a permanent English colony in the new world. This settlement, called Roanoke, would soon become one of the most intriguing mysteries of early American history and the fate of its colonists is still debated today.

The participants in this drama were the noted British adventurer, Sir Walter Raleigh, the Queen of England, a painter named John White (who would later play an important role in the search for the lost colonists), a Portuguese ship captain named Simon Fernandez (a privateer and adventurer himself), and the almost 130 people who sailed from England to make a new life across the sea.

At the time Sir Walter Raleigh set sail for what was to become America, almost 20 years before John Smith established the first permanent English settlement at Jamestown, Virginia, Great Britain was the most important sea power of the day. Britain, in her dominant position as a world power, saw the unexplored eastern seaboard of the New World (United States), then a vast unexplored area, a land ripe for its influence. The British saw in the area, around the as yet unexplored Chesapeake Bay, a land that could serve as a base camp for a permanent British colony. It was with this in mind that the Queen of England took the first step toward colonizing the area for the Crown.

The British were not the only ones interested in settling the land across the ocean. The Spanish had colonized what would now become Florida, establishing settlements in such places as St. Augustine and other parts of Latin America. The Spanish and the British were old-time adversaries, and the Spanish would have liked nothing more than to be the first to settle the area of what was now the Carolinas and Virginia, in place of the British.

In 1584, a British flotilla that was funded by Sir Walter Raleigh left England for America and the Chesapeake Bay. Queen Elizabeth issued an order allowing Raleigh to "discover, search, find out and view such remote heathen and barbarian lands, countries, and territories, to have, hold, occupy and enjoy." Philip Amadas and Arthur Barlowe headed the expedition and they made shore off the coast of North Carolina on July 13, 1584. On board one of the ships was John White, a man who would later play an important part in the search for the lost colonists. Another man who played a paramount part in the first expedition was Ralph Lane, a military man by training. One of the reasons that the first expedition failed was that Lane did not have the requisite civilian skills to organize and supervise what was an expedition of discovery, not a military affair.

White was a renowned painter who took his considerable talents with him to the New World. When he arrived with the other settlers, White began his own explorations of the area. He captured the flavor of the region, painting and making a detailed survey of the new land. He drew maps, painted the wildlife and the occasional Native American he met. He also wrote a detailed chronicle of all he saw.

White's activities were on the present site of Roanoke Island, and it was here that the British decided to make their home. As White began to explore the bay, he went further inland, often leaving camp for days on end. Much to his surprise, White met a group of Native Americans called the Lumbees, who spoke English. How, or who, taught them English, White never learned. He befriended the Lumbees and learned their ways. Other native tribes near the English settlement were the Algonquin's, who kept their distance. A native called Manteo from the Algonquin tribe soon was befriended by the colonists and was later baptized and made Lord of Roanoke on August 27, 1587.

To the settlers' chagrin, life was hard at the Roanoke settlement. The leaders of the colony decided to send a ship back to England for supplies. By now, White had become the Governor of the colony and he waited long enough to see the birth of his daughter Eleanor's child, Virginia Dare. Virginia was the first English child born in America. White was part of the group that left Roanoke bound for England. It was to be three long years before they returned. Before their departure for England, White told the remaining settlers that if they had to leave for any reason, they should write the name of the place they were going to on a stone near their settlement. On the stone they were to place a cross as a sign of danger.

Upon arriving back in England, Walter Raleigh met with the Queen and told her of his discovery. He also told her that he had named the land he found Virginia in honor of the Virgin Queen.

Walter Raleigh was born into a well-to-do family in 1552. His family lived in Devon, England. He attended Oxford University for a while, then saw battle against the Huguenots in France and later returned to his studies in London. In 1580, Raleigh went to Ireland where he fought to end an uprising in Munster. His actions soon gained the attention of Queen Elizabeth that same year, and he was knighted and appointed a Captain of the Queen's Guard in 1587. He later entered politics and was elected to Parliament in 1584 and was given extensive lands in Ireland.

In what would turn out to be a bad break for Raleigh, the Queen found out that he was secretly married to one of her maids of honor, Elizabeth Throckmorton, and both were imprisoned in the Tower of London. After their release Raleigh tried to win back the Queen's favor by embarking on an expedition to find the fabulous treasure of El Dorado, or "Golden Land," which was supposed to have been located in or near the Orinoco River in Guiana (today's Venezuela).

Now back in England, Raleigh made plans to return to the New World in an effort to re-supply the remaining colonists. However, political and other impediments got in the way, including a war between Spain and England in which Raleigh took part.

In 1580, White and a two-ship convoy left England aboard the ships, the *Moonlight,* and the *Hopewell.* For Raleigh, the long voyage was one of personal torture. It had been a few years since his departure from the island and he had no idea what to expect. Was his family still alive or had something unforeseen happened to them?

As they made landfall off the coast of Roanoke Island after their long voyage, they observed no activity along the shore. After dropping anchor, White and his men returned to their settlement only to find it deserted and all the people gone. Their homes were taken down and to their surprise defensive works were erected. As they walked around the deserted area they came upon markings on a tree with the letters CRO. As they approached what was left of their prior homes (they were all taken down), they found the name "Croatoan" carved on a stone near the empty ground, but there was no cross on the rock. The name Croatoan was the name of an island to the south. Was this the place where the settlers went? What led to the abandonment of the Roanoke colony, and what was the fate of the inhabitants?

The Croatoans were a Native American tribe who lived along the coast of the Chesapeake Bay. Old maps of the area place Croatoan Island in various locations including Cape Hatteras, North Carolina, Cape Lookout, or directly opposite Roanoke Island. Did the lost colonists go there?

After the discovery of the abandoned settlement, Sir Walter Raleigh sent five expeditions in search of any survivors. Intermittently for 10 years, scouts plied the waters of the Chesapeake Bay looking for any trace of life, until giving up the search in 1602.

Desperate to find his family, White asked Simon Fernandes, one of the ship's pilots, to take him to Croatoan Island. Fernandes, who was serving as his own pirate in search of any passing Spanish ship to plunder, turned down White's request and instead sailed for the West Indies.

The first real search for the answers to the riddle of the Roanoke colony came after the Jamestown colony was settled. Various accounts by people who lived in the area gave tantalizing clues as to their fate.

A man named George Percy, who lived in the Jamestown settlement, said that he saw an Indian with yellow hair and white skin, not traits noticeable in dark-complexioned Native Americans.

John Smith, of the famous love affair with the Indian beauty Pocahontas, wrote in his chronicles of his life in Virginia, that he met a Native American who told him that she had met certain men who were dressed like Smith at a place called "Ocanohonan."

There were other reports by various people of seeing stone homes built atop each other in the style that Europeans of the time constructed. If this was correct, who built them? There were also reports from people at the time laying blame for the disappearance of the lost Roanoke colony on Chief Powhatan, the father of Pocahontas. According to this tale, the Roanoke settlers came to live along the Chesapeake Bay, not far from the Chesapeake Indians. In time however, Powhatan declared war on the English after the Jamestown fort was established, and killed all the settlers.

One of the possible sites that the colonists might have gone to was Croatoan Island. John White described the area as, "the place where Manteo (a Native American whom the colonists befriended) was born, and the savages of the land our friends." These were later called the Hatteras Indians who were on good terms with the colonists. However, this might not be true. When John White first left the colony he wrote that the people "were prepared to remove from Roanoke 50 miles into the maine." Fifty miles would put them well past Croatoan Island. It is also possible that the colonists broke up into two separate groups, each heading in a different direction with the hope of meeting up at some future date. It is even possible that the settles were killed or captured by the Spanish, who had designs on the region, but without historical proof of that taking place. Another theory is that the colonists somehow sailed back to England. However, there is nothing in any written records that they came back home, and if they did, then there would have been such a hue and cry about their return that someone would have written down the facts of their arrival.

One possible answer to the mystery of the lost colony of Roanoke may be found in old historical records in Robeson County, North Carolina. Lumbee Indian records note that in the U.S. census of 1790, 24 lost colony surnames were found in Robeson County. Historical records state that of the 120 colonists in the first Roanoke settlement, 41 were listed as being Native Americans living in Robeson County.

Another clue to Robeson County as being the home of the people of the lost colony is the fact that land grants were issued in 1732 to Henry Berry and James Laurie, two Lumbee surnames belonging to the lost tribe.

Undocumented stories also point to the North Carolina area as being the place they fled to. In 1704, Reverend John Blair, a missionary in the Albemarle settlement, told of hearing of a tribe of 100,000 who lived with the English and were "civilized."

In 1790, John Larson, an early historian of North Carolina, explored the Pamlico Sound. He says that the Hatteras Indians, who were a part of the Croatoan tribe, told of their ancestors being able to read and write English. Larson was also told that some Native Americans had gray eyes, leaving open the possibility of intermarriage between some Indians and whites.

If we don't know the fate of the lost colonists of Roanoke, we do have information on the other players in the drama. Sir Walter Raleigh returned to England and found to his chagrin that the trust given to him by the former ruler, Queen Elizabeth was not returned by the current monarch, King James 1. Raleigh spent 12 horrible years in the Tower of London before being released in 1616. In that year, he mounted an expedition to South America in search of new treasures and was killed.

As for John White, it was said that he made his way to Ireland and died there in 1606.

Virginia Dare, the first English child to be born in the New World, is now just a footnote in our early history. However, in 1937 a discovery made by a man looking around his field would make a connection to Virginia Dare and add more mystery to the whereabouts of the lost colony.

In that year, Louis Hammond found a stone with strange markings on it, which he could not make out. He took the stone to Dr. Haywood Pearce, a history professor. Dr. Pearce said the writing was of Elizabethan English. Part of the writing on the stone reads as follows:

Ananias Dare & Virginia went hence vnto heaven 1591.
Anye Englishman, shew John White, Govr Via.

"Father soone After yov goe for Englande we cam

16

hither/ onlie misarie & warretow yeare "Above halfe
DeaDe ere tow yeere moore from sickenes beine fovre
& twentie/ salvage with mesage of shipp vnto vs/ smal
space of time they affrite of revenge rann al awaye/ wee
bleeve yt nott you/ soone after ye salvages faine spirts
angrie/ suddiane mvrther al save seaven/ mine childe
ananias to slaine wth mvch misarie/bvrie al neere fovre
myles easte this river vppon smal hil/ names writ al ther
on rocke/ pvtt this ther alsoe/ salvage shew this vnto yov
& hither wee promise yov to give great plentie presents
E W D

Over the next four years, a total of 46 stones called the Dare
Stones, were found from Edenton, North Carolina to Atlanta,
Georgia, along the Chattahoochee River. The Dare Stones, if they
are correct, say that the Roanoke settlers split up and were helped
by native tribes and many were killed along the way. Dr. Pearce
said that in his opinion, the stones were legitimate. But are they?

Modern day archeologists are still looking for clues as to the
fate of the lost colony of Roanoke, and in August 2015 a new,
tantalizing clue was found near a location called Site X, near Merry
Hill, North Carolina. A group headed by Nicholas Luccketti with
the First Colony Foundation, which has been excavating a site near
the waters of the Albemarle Sound made some interesting finds.
Speaking about his new discovery, Mr. Luccketti said, "I'm trying
to make sure that I say this correctly. We have evidence from this
site that strongly indicates that there was Roanoke colonists here."

The first clue came in 2012 when the British Museum re-
examined a copy of John White's costal map for the First
Colony Foundation. Using x-ray spectroscopy and other imaging
techniques, they found that a patch hid a four-pointed blue and red
star on the western end of Albemarle Sound which corresponded
to White's reference to a site 50 miles inland that he mentioned to
friends in England after his return from the New World.

The site of the new discovery was located in Bertie County
and the land was supposed to have been developed for 2,000
condominiums. Mr. Luccketti's company was called in to survey
the land before it was to be developed, but when they were digging

they came up with some interesting finds, including many Native American artifacts, which Mr. Luccketti says were left by European settlers. They also found artifacts such as a food-storage jar called a baluster, a hook used to stretch hides, a buckle and pieces of gun flintlocks, called priming pans, which were consistent with the type of guns used by Europeans at the time.

Other recent excavations have taken place at other sites along the coast at Hatteras Island, which also revealed other important finds. British archaeologist, Mark Horton, who led an excavation at that location, found items like a rapier hilt, late 16th century hardware and part of writing table. Mr. Horton speculates that certain members of the lost colony made their way south to Hatteras Island around 1590 and may have intermingled with the Native Americans they found in the area. "I don't necessarily see that what we've found on Hatteras rules out their site, or vice versa," Mr. Horton said.

These new clues only add mystery to the legend of the lost setters of Roanoke and what might have happened to them. Maybe someday the sands of time will finally unearth its secrets. (Information on this new aspect of the case was found in the *New York Times,* dated August 10, 2015 under the title *"The Roanoke Island Colony: Lost, and Found?* By Theo Emery).

Chapter 2
The Treason of Benedict Arnold

One man's name stands out in the annals of American history as being this country's most notorious spy, that being Benedict Arnold. Benedict Arnold, before his decision to abandon the revolutionary fight for independence, was one of the most gifted officers in the American army and a personal friend of General George Washington. So it was with the greatest shame that Washington learned of the treason of Benedict Arnold when he decided to offer to sell West Point and the surrounding area to the British in September 1780. What made this hero of the revolution turn traitor, abandoning the country that he fought for?

Benedict Arnold was born on January 14, 1741 in Norwich, Connecticut. He came from a dysfunctional family whose father was often times drunk and could not provide for his family. After a struggle to make ends meet, Benedict's mother sent her son off to work for two local druggists, Daniel and Joshua Lathrop. Arnold did not take well to learning the business and he ran away to take part in the French and Indian Wars. His mother found out where her son was and with the help of the Lathrop brothers, brought him home. Benedict did not linger and promptly ran away again. He re-joined the ranks but once again grew tired of the military discipline he was subjected to and again deserted. However, the war ended and he suffered no further punishment.

Once home in Connecticut, Arnold opened his own business and soon was a prosperous man, trading his goods in the West Indies and Canada. He ran a pharmacy, as well as running a bookstore in New Haven. In time he became one of the wealthiest men in the area and was a respected man in the community. About this time, he asked his sister, Hannah, to come and help him run the business while he engaged in other endeavors. In December 1774, he joined the Connecticut militia and received the rank of Captain. In 1767 he married Margaret Mansfield who was from New Haven. Arnold was then 26 but found that being home was not all it was cracked up to be. Even though they had three sons,

Arnold went to sea, leaving Margaret alone to raise the children.

When the colonists began to actively oppose the harsh taxes that the British were imposing on the colonists, Arnold once again took up arms. He was elected to be a militia captain and he led his men to Lexington and Concord in April 1775 to fight the British. Arnold soon learned that there were 80 cannons to be found at Fort Ticonderoga in New York that had been abandoned by the British after the end of the French and Indian War. Arnold, now a Colonel, decided to personally go after the guns and began preparations to seize them. Arnold told of his plans to seize the guns to Colonel Samuel Parsons, who promptly told his superiors. The Connecticut Assembly then asked Ethan Allen and his Blue Mountain Boys to capture Fort Ticonderoga. Shortly before arriving at the fort, both Allen and Arnold met, and they had a verbal confrontation as to who would take the fort. After much bickering, they decided to pool their forces and successfully mounted a raid and took over the fort. In a grueling march that lasted days, they were able to bring the cannons back to Boston and put them in the hands of Henry Knox, who used them successfully in the defense of the city.

After his campaign at Fort Ticonderoga, Arnold sailed to Lake Champlain in upstate New York and took over a British fort at St. John's Ontario. Despite his victory in the Lake Champlain campaign, Arnold was disappointed that the rulers of Massachusetts for whom he was working, did not reimburse him for the money he expended in the battle. This was not to be the first or the last time that Arnold felt snubbed by men of higher authority. The next time this happened to him, it would lead to his change of heart in working for the revolutionary cause.

Things continued to go wrong for Arnold during the period after his victory in the Lake Champlain campaign. His young wife died suddenly, leaving him grieving and unsure of where his future would lie.

By now, George Washington had been made Commander in Chief of the Continental Army and Arnold was, by now, a proven commodity in Washington's eyes. Arnold met with Washington and persuaded him to mount an invasion of Canada, which Washington approved. During the winter of 1775-76, Arnold, along with Richard Montgomery, led an expedition to Quebec with a total of 2,200 men. Accompanying them was the noted fighter, Daniel Morgan, and his sharpshooters. Arnold brought his men up through the woods of Maine, before arriving in Quebec, near the mighty fort that housed the majority of the British troops. On December 27, 1775, Arnold and Montgomery split up their forces and attacked the citadel. During the fierce fighting, Arnold was wounded in the leg and would suffer that infliction for the rest of his life. Morgan carried the wounded Arnold off the field of battle where the soldiers planned their next move. The Americans were eventually thwarted by the arrival of a regiment of British troops and had to withdraw. After the campaign was over, the Continental Congress once again snubbed him for promotion to the rank of major general after five other officers were given increases in rank.

Arnold now ran afoul of certain members of the Continental Congress who did not like his brash, self-serving ways. However, he still had an important friend in Washington who came to his defense. Washington now made him a major general and sent him on his next assignment. He was sent to Trenton, New Jersey to block an attack by General William Howe and his 20,000 men. Arnold made a great defense of the area, using his 5,000 men as a diversion and making General Howe believe that he had twice as many men on hand as he really did.

After his successful battle against General Howe, Arnold again petitioned Congress to pay him back for the expenses he had given out for the previous military campaigns. Once again he was turned down and he resigned his commission in a huff (Congress eventually paid him £2,700). However, he did not have much time to ponder his fate. General Washington soon asked him to come back to military service and he accepted.

At this time, the British were making a move toward the strategically important Mohawk Valley under the command of General Johnny Burgoyne and his Native American allies. Arnold joined up with the forces under the command of General Philip Schuyler, and together through grit and strength (as well as good military luck), were able to throw back the larger British force in the Mohawk Valley with the aid of another army led by General Horatio Gates (whom Arnold loathed). During the battle, Arnold suffered a fractured leg, adding to his serious military wounds. After the battle, General Gates, who really took little action, told everyone that he was the one responsible for the victory, earning Arnold's everlasting animosity toward him.

In 1778, Arnold was no longer fit for military duty and Washington promoted him to the position of military governor of Philadelphia, then the seat of American government. It was from here that Arnold, now a bitter man, would hatch the plot that would make him the most despised man in America. Arnold tried hard to improve the condition of the city but he ran his operation like a business, trying to make a profit instead of doing well for the citizens of Philadelphia. He sold staples for a profit and pocketed a large percentage of the money for his own personal account. It was also in Philadelphia that Arnold was to meet a beautiful, young woman named Peggy Shippen, whom he would eventually marry. If anyone was to aid in his later treachery, it was Peggy Shippen.

Peggy Shippen came from a very well to do family in Philadelphia and unlike other women of the day, was immersed in the world of politics from a young age. She was soon one of the most sought after young women in the city and it was not too long before Arnold and Peggy became romantically involved. Another person whom Peggy was acquainted with, and would later play an important role in Arnold's treachery, was Major John Andre of the British army, who was the intelligence chief for General Howe. Arnold and Peggy were married on April 8, 1779; she was only 19 years old. Their marriage caused heads to roll in the city, as the Shippens were loyal Tories. Just what was Benedict Arnold, the top man in Philadelphia, doing being married to an enemy of the revolutionary cause? It's not too much to say that Peggy was relaying information on nearly a daily basis to Major Andre who was passing it along to General Howe.

At the time of his marriage to Peggy, the Continental Congress charged Arnold with stealing money and began court-martial charges against him. At this point, even George Washington was unable or unwilling to stick his neck out for Arnold. It was now that Arnold decided to give up the revolutionary cause and throw his lot in with the British. Using Peggy as a go-between, she arranged a meeting between Arnold and Major Andre, who was by now on the staff of General Clinton in New York. Over time both men wrote each other using invisible ink in regular letters that could only be read when using the proper liquids to reveal the writings. Even Peggy got into the act, having been paid by the British, £350 for "her services, which were very meritorious."

After his court-martial, Washington relieved Arnold of his post in Philadelphia. He was now a man adrift, unwanted by the Americans, not yet trusted by the British. In order to placate Arnold, Washington appointed him as the commander of the strategic fort at West Point, on the Hudson River. Whoever controlled West Point controlled the river traffic heading south into British-controlled New York City. With the command of West Point in his pocket, Arnold contacted Major Andre and told him that for a price he'd turn over West Point to the British. The price for his treason was £10,000 plus expenses. He soon asked for double that amount and offered to surrender the fort once he took control. As their communications grew, Arnold asked that he be given the rank of brigadier in the British Army. He also stipulated that if his plan to turn over the fort failed he was to be paid an additional £10,000 and be allowed to keep his rank. Andre agreed and the plot was now taking shape for his ultimate betrayal. In his letters to Major Andre, Arnold as "John Anderson," a name that would later play an important role in Arnold's capture, knew him. Arnold used the alias of "Monk" or "Mr. Moore."

John Andre was the right man to serve as Arnold's intermediary. At 27 he served in the important post as intelligence chief for General Clinton whose job it was to find the nest of spies that Washington had infiltrated into New York. Andre secreted a woman by the name of Ann Bates into Washington's headquarters but was never able to unravel the Culper network run by Benjamin Tallmadge, which operated right under his nose.

Arnold wanted to find out the names of all the spies who were employed on the American side. He asked Washington to provide him with these names but Washington did not know them. Washington was most interested in keeping the secret of the Culper Ring to himself, (the Culpers were a ring of spies located in New York and Long Island, who operated throughout the war and were instrumental in tricking the British at every point).

With the approval of General Clinton, Andre agreed to meet with Arnold on neutral ground and was asked by Arnold to wear his British uniform when they met. Andre agreed to the first condition, but not the last.

On September 20, 1780 Major Andre boarded the British ship the *Vulture,* which sailed up the Hudson to the town of Haverstraw, New York, near the town of Stony Point. It was here Andre met up with Joshua Hett Smith, a Tory friend. Early the next morning, Arnold appeared and both men formally agreed to Arnold's terms about turning over West Point to the British. Since it was too late for Andre to return to New York, he spent the night at Smith's home. The next morning, the Patriots, leaving Andre unable to return to New York, attacked the *Vulture*. Arnold proceeded to write a note to Andre under the name of "John Anderson," giving him safe passage back to the city.

On the morning of September 23rd, Andre left Smith's home and headed back to New York. He was now wearing civilian clothes, a mistake that would cost him dearly. As he passed the neutral ground en-route to New York, three men stopped him for questioning: John Paulding, Isaac Van Wart and David Williams. Andre told them that he was a British officer who was heading toward New York. The men toyed with Andre, at first making him believe that they too were British subjects, before revealing to Andre their true identities. They were suspicious of Andre and began searching his person. They asked him to take off his boots and found the papers hidden inside. Upon reading the papers they were astonished to find the notes that Arnold had given Andre regarding the fortifications of West Point. Andre tried to bribe his way by offering them money, but they refused.

The men took Andre to Patriot headquarters at North Castle for interrogation by Lt. Colonel John Jameson. Upon reading the papers in Andre's possession, Jameson knew that he had a potential spy on his hands. He sent a courier with Andre's papers to General Washington at a fast pace. Andrew identified himself as John Anderson, the name that Arnold had written on the papers in his pocket. By now, Benjamin Tallmadge, the head of the Culper ring found out that Andre/Anderson had been captured and he remembered that Arnold told him to expect a man named John Anderson to arrive in the area on his behalf. Tallmadge wanted to see Andre, but when he arrived at North Castle Andre had already been transferred to Arnold's headquarters.

On September 24th Washington arrived at West Point for a meeting with Arnold. Arnold was not there so Washington took a tour of West Point without his presence. Later, Washington arrived at Arnold's home and still did not find him. However, a rider came to Arnold's home with a message for Washington. It was the parcel of letters taken from Major Andre at North Castle. Reading with astonishment, Washington now had proof that Arnold was trying to sell West Point to the British. He felt betrayed and angry with his one-time friend.

Arnold soon learned of Andre's capture and made plans for his escape. Arnold returned home and told Peggy what had occurred. He rushed up to his room, hastily packed a bag, kissed his wife and left for the *Vulture,* which was not far away. He was taken to New York where he was put under the protection of the British.

Major Andre, however, did not fare so well. After a plan to swap prisoners in order to get him back failed, he was put on trial. He was convicted as being a spy and was sentenced to death by hanging. He was hanged at Tappan, New York on October 2, 1780.

While in British-held New York, Washington devised a plan to capture Arnold and bring him back for trial. The raid was to be led by Sgt. John Champe, but Arnold left New York shortly before the raid took place.

Arnold was given the rank of brigadier general in the British army and took part in raids in Virginia and Connecticut. In December 1781, both Arnold and Peggy went to England, where they lived out the rest of their lives in obscurity. He was never able to return to America and died in England on June 14, 1801, a man mostly forgotten by his fellow countrymen.

Chapter 3
The Doctor Was a Spy

The most notorious spy of the Revolutionary War that no one ever heard of was Doctor Benjamin Church, who, like Benedict Arnold, was a confidant and friend of General George Washington. If Washington were keeping score at the time, he would have wondered why so many men he trusted had turned their allegiance away from the cause for independence and decided to cast their lot with the enemy.

Benjamin Church was born on August 24, 1734 in Newport, Rhode Island. He went to the Boston Latin School from 1745-1750, and then graduated from Harvard in 1754. He then attended the London Medical School, married an English lady and moved back to America to begin his medical career. Around 1768 he moved to Raynham, Massachusetts, where he started his practice, going out into the rural community, seeing patients and earning the trust of his neighbors.

As the British began their harsh treatment of the people of Massachusetts by putting taxes on their goods without representation, closing off the port of Boston to traffic which inflamed the local population, and made a huge crimp in the daily lives of the people, Benjamin Church decided it was time to take action in opposition to the British. He entered a secret group of men called the Committee of Correspondence and also joined Paul Revere in his secret group of spies that began operating in Boston. Paul Revere was a noted silversmith in Boston and would later be immortalized in history for his "midnight ride" across Boston warning that the "British were coming" to attack the rebels in the city (actually, there were two other people who took part in the ride with Revere, William Dawes and Dr. Joseph Warren).

Revere called his group the "mechanics," which grew out of The Sons of Liberty, taking shape after the Stamp Act that imposed a tax on all written material such as paper, legal notices, etc. that people used every day. The job of the mechanics was to gather as much intelligence on the British as possible and funnel it to the proper patriot authorities. By 1774-75, there were about 30 men in Revere's spy ring who, according to Revere, "frequently took turns, two and two, to watch British soldiers by patrolling the streets all night."

While Dr. Church was siding with the patriot cause, there was another, darker side to him. He contributed articles to the Whig press, British affiliated newspapers in and around Boston. He was also a noted poet and he had a wide following among certain people who liked his style. His brother-in-law, John Fleming, was a Tory printer and he probably worked for him at some point.

It is not really known just when Dr. Church began his clandestine work for the British, but some historians put the year at 1774 when he began correspondence with Thomas Hutchinson, the Royal Governor of Massachusetts, and later with Gen. Thomas Gage, the British Commander-in-Chief. It is said that Dr. Church told General Gage the colonists had stored arms and ammunition in Concord, which led to the battles of Lexington and Concord. A few days after the battles of Lexington and Concord, Dr. Church met with General Gage to cement their covert relationship and make arrangements for further visits.

Dr. Church was soon appointed to the position of chief surgeon of the Continental Army and took care of the wounded at each major battle, including Bunker Hill. He also took part in secret meetings with Paul Revere and his mechanics, which often times took place at the Green Dragon Tavern with the likes of John Hancock, John Adams and Doctor Warren. It was at these meetings the most important discussions took place regarding military/political decisions involving the future of the revolutionary cause. At one point, Revere was told by one of his is informants that General Gage had a spy in the Sons of Liberty and knew everything that went on in the meetings. There were even stories that someone had seen Dr. Church leaving the headquarters of General Gage and that Dr. Church looked "more like a man that was acquainted than a prisoner." However, there was no concrete information linking him directly to the British at that point.

Church's brother-in-law then made an unusual request. He asked Dr. Church to renounce his loyalty to the revolution and side with the British. He asked him to reply via a British officer named Captain James Wallace who was attached to the ship, the *Rose,* in Newport, Rhode Island. Dr. Church could not go himself to Newport so he asked his mistress to intercede on his behalf. The mistress then went to her boyfriend, Geoffrey Wenwood, and asked him to contact Captain Wallace. Wenwood told her that he could not get in touch with the British officer and asked her to give him the letter; he'd take care of it. Wenwood left the letter in his drawer for some time and forgot it was there. Sometime later, Wenwood found the letter and took it to a friend. Both men opened it and found the letter written in some sort of code, which they could not read. Out of the blue, Church's mistress called, asking Wenwood why the letter hadn't been delivered. Wenwood, a patriot, smelled a rat and took the letter to General Nathaniel Green's headquarters, delivered it to George Washington who read it with consternation.

Washington had the unlucky girl brought to his headquarters where he questioned her thoroughly about who had given her the letter. She finally told her it was Dr. Church. Washington was horrified at the news. Dr. Church, a fellow patriot, was corresponding with the enemy. Did he have another Benedict Arnold affair to deal with?

Washington then took two actions: He brought Dr. Church in for questioning and had two men with knowledge of secret writing come see if they could decipher the letter. Dr. Church told Washington he was the sender of the letter but that it was nothing but personal correspondence and he had done nothing wrong. When asked why he did not use regular words in his letter he could not answer to Washington's satisfaction. When the letter was finally deciphered, it put the blame straight on Church's shoulders. The letter said he had been in Philadelphia at the same time that Congress was meeting. Church met with his handler and gave him information on the condition of the Rebel Army. The letter also contained the number of men in Washington's force, as well as secret plans for an invasion of Canada. When confronted by Washington, Dr. Church said he was only trying to fool the British, not side with them. However, the evidence against him was overwhelming and Church was arrested while the proper authorities decided what to do with him.

General Washington convened a council to decide his fate. At the time, there was no penalty for espionage. Under the so-called "Articles of War," the only punishment was to give the offender 39 lashes and take away two-month's pay. Soon, the Continental Congress passed a new espionage statute, but it did not affect Church's case.

Dr. Church was imprisoned in a jail in Norwich, Connecticut, but was soon moved to Massachusetts where he was put under guard and told not to leave the colony. In 1790, it was decided that the best course of action would be to expel him from the colonies for everyone's benefit. He was put aboard a ship bound for the West Indies, but fate intervened once again. The ship he was on was lost at sea, never to be found.

The conspiracy hatched by Dr. Church was a blow to the revolutionary cause but it did not deter the fight for victory. Church's treachery would continue by those whose loyalties would outweigh their devotion to country.

Chapter 4
Ben Franklin's Wayward Son

The old saying, "like father like son," certainly could not be more applicable than it is in the case of William Franklin and his famous father, Benjamin Franklin. Though they ended up on opposite sides of the Revolutionary War, they were both men who remained highly partisan and rigid in support of their various causes. One wonders how these two brilliant, educated men of the same blood could arrive at such opposite beliefs.

William Franklin was the illegitimate son of Benjamin Franklin and his common law wife, Deborah Read. William never knew who his mother was and Ben never told him. A friend of Benjamin's, named George Roberts, said that she was "a low woman" whom Franklin had an affair with. Roberts wrote that "'Tis generally known here his birth is illegitimate and his mother not in good circumstances." No one really knows just how much his illegitimacy affected his youth, as he was quite reluctant to talk about his circumstances. Throughout his rise in politics, his many opponents would often time attack him for his low standing whenever possible. Even John Adams, one of the elder Franklin's contemporaries in the Continental Congress, called William, then the Governor of the New Jersey colony, "an insult to the morals of America, the elevation of the government of New Jersey of a base born brat." If those comments affected William, he never said anything in reply.

Ben and his wife, Deborah, whose relationship with William is really not known, raised him. Soon, another child named Francis Folger was born and he now had to share his half-brother with Ben. It is not known how the two siblings got along, but it is not too complicated to say that they were rivals from the beginning. In 1736, Frankie, as he was called, died of smallpox, casting a shadow over the family.

Ben Franklin saw to young William's every need, giving him a proper education, taking him on his many scientific endeavors (probably even his historic kite flying experiment), and gearing him in the trade of politics that would later dominate his career. At one point, young William tried to run away from home to join a privateering expedition. When Ben found out about his son's plans, he nipped them in the bud.

"Young Bill," as he was called, had an adventurous spirit that took him away from his native Philadelphia. With his father's blessings, William left home in 1740. For the next eight years, he set out to find himself in new areas of the American frontier.

He joined the Pennsylvania Company and went to Albany to fight the French, who, in the mid-1700s, had come to the United States to seek new trade routes. He rose to the rank of Captain. Ben asked a printer friend of his to send William maps of the area to better acquaint him with the skills needed in battle and prepare him for life as a soldier. Gaining experience in battle, William then moved on to the wild Ohio country as an assistant to an Indian trader called Conrad Weiser. In his contacts with the local Indian tribes and the settlers in the Ohio Valley, young William learned valuable lessons in diplomacy that he would later use as governor of New Jersey.

After years of exploring the new territories, he returned to Philadelphia to become the city's postmaster. In 1751, William took over the job of Clerk of the Pennsylvania Assembly, the job his father once held. There, he helped to mediate a dispute with the powerful Penn family over taxation of proprietary lands they owned.

Franklin's influence on his son was overpowering and William obeyed his father's wishes. Franklin wanted his son to become a lawyer and William studied under a Philadelphia attorney named James Galloway. When Ben rounded up horses and wagons for General Braddock's ill-fated campaign against the French in 1775, William went along as his chief agent.

In 1757, a new adventure opened up for William. In that year he accompanied his father to London where Ben acted on behalf of certain Pennsylvania business interests to settle a dispute regarding their refusal to pay taxes on certain proprietors, as well as looking into charges that London was not giving enough rights to the people of Pennsylvania. There was another reason for Ben's taking William with him. It seems that he had fallen in love with a girl named Elizabeth Graeme, whose wealthy family did not like

William consorting with their daughter. For William, London was an adventurous and lively city, a place where he could study new people and see new things. He was instructed in the politics of London and took away a political philosophy that was good for the American colonies. It was from these political beliefs that lead to his decision, once the revolution started, to side with the British. While in England, the two men visited Ben's extended family and were greeted warmly wherever they went.

Ben's actions in London were a failure and he came back to America with a feeling of hopelessness that an amicable solution between Britain and the colonies could be worked out. The elder Franklin now knew the only reasonable solution for the colonies was to secure independence from England.

By 1760, now home in America, William began one of the most important parts of his career, and the beginning of his break with his father.

Like his father, William sired an illegitimate son, William Temple. Grandfather Ben understood his son's behavior and he doted on the child. Two years later, on September 4, 1762 he married Elizabeth Downes of Barbados, whom he met in London. With a new wife in tow, William broke with his father politically and openly sided with the British.

Shortly after his marriage, William was elected as the governor of New Jersey. The political watchers in the colony did not take his appointment lightly. Many people in the government considered him unfit for the job because he had no experience and, to a lesser degree, because of his illegitimate birth.

William and his allies countered by highlighting his knowledge of military affairs and influential friends in both the colonies and in England. He was liked by the people of New Jersey and often visited their towns listening to their complaints.

But where William deviated from his father was in his loyalty to the British Crown, which had appointed him to the office.

At the beginning of the British occupancy of the colonies, William was directly confronted with the will of his constituents. He reluctantly carried out the Stamp Act, which imposed taxes on an assortment of paper goods, actively working to stem the tide of the revolution by sending news of the independence movement to

London. Both Ben and William tried in vain to persuade the others into changing their minds, but to no avail. Despite their growing political differences, there was no personal animosity between them. However, Ben used his influence to prevent William from getting the post as governor of Barbados in 1772. Another strike against William, as far as Ben was concerned, was that his son was also the head of the Associated Loyalists, a pro-British party that conducted guerilla war against the colonies.

But William was lucky as governor, because New Jersey was spared the bitter internal turmoil of the other colonies. William blamed his partners in government for his troubles. At one point he had a heated argument with William Coxe, the provincial stamp distributor, who, as a trusted advisor, didn't tell the governor how to deal with the bad publicity surrounding the Stamp Act, which Coxe had to execute. Franklin's performance during the Stamp Act crisis was the result of his inexperience and ignorance of British colonial politics.

In 1775 Ben Franklin parted from his son. They were not to meet again until the war was over.

Back in New Jersey, William took on another domestic enemy, the Presbyterians. He wanted to take control over their main institution, the College of New Jersey at Princeton. When they refused to relinquish control, William got a charter from the legislature to open a competing school in New Brunswick, called Queen's College, later named Rutgers.

With American resisting stiffening and William's motives now openly challenged, the people of New Jersey took action against him.

On January 8, 1776, he was captured in Perth Amboy. In July he was sent to jail in Lebanon, Connecticut. Three years later he was exchanged for John McKinley, the former President of Delaware.

October 1778 found William living in British-occupied New York City, where he worked to suppress the rebellion. On September 18, 1782 (20 years after being appointed governor of New Jersey), he set sail for England and permanent exile.

Ben Franklin never forgave his wayward son who had so deeply dishonored his family. There were some who called William Franklin a traitor, others a patriot. We will never be sure which, patriot or traitor, he felt himself to be.

Chapter 5
Thomas Jefferson's Secret War

Since the beginning of the Reagan administration, American foreign policy has been mostly focused on events in the Middle East. The advent of Muslim terrorism has shifted our 21st century foreign policy perspective toward combating various terrorist groups that seem to spring up with regularity. America has fought a number of wars in the region beginning with the 1991 Persian Gulf War. The United States, and its coalition partners, threw the troops out of Kuwait under the direction of Iraq's brutal leader, Saddam Hussein. The Clinton administration attacked Iraq with limited air strikes after a provocation by Hussein. In 2003, President George W. Bush attacked Iraq over the threat Iraq may have had weapons of mass destruction supposedly to be used in a possible attack against the United States (there were none). President Obama has used American air power in its current attack against the forces of ISIS (Islamic State of Iraq and Syria) in both Iraq and Syria.

However, it was during the administration of President Thomas Jefferson that the young United States began its first attempt at regime change in the Middle East. That enemy was the Arab states of the Barbary Coast in the Mediterranean Sea, namely Tripoli, Tunis, Morocco and Algiers. These North African nations had been taking American seaman off ships, demanding ransom from the U.S. (which we paid) and creating havoc for the U.S. By the time the Barbary War was over, President Jefferson would mount a secret expedition to overthrow the ruler of Algiers and use one of our most experienced and colorful military officers, William Eaton to lead the expedition.

The object of our wrath was the so-called Barbary Corsairs who roamed the seas of North Africa with impunity. They were a most formidable fighting force that scoured the Mediterranean and North Africa from the 17th to the 19th centuries. They were out for plunder from whatever nation they could find and the major powers of the day did little to stop them. The Barbary States compromise the nations of Morocco, Libya, Algeria and Tunisia today. These states were once under the direction of the Ottoman (Turkish) Empire before being granted their freedom. In order to prevent their ships from being attacked, nations along the Barbary Coast paid tribute in cash to the Corsairs. This was pure and simple bribery, but it was paid nevertheless.

These pirates also raided American and European ships, some capturing people and selling them as slaves.

Before gaining our independence after the Revolutionary War, the United States was protected from piracy by Great Britain. All that stopped after the war ended and we had to fend for ourselves. In 1784, the Congress appropriated $80,000 in bribe money to be paid to the Barbary States in order to protect our ships. We sent two of our most able negotiators, John Adams and Thomas Jefferson, to act on our behalf. In July 1785 things changed for the worse. In that year the Algerians captured two American ships and the Dey (ruler) held their crews for a ransom of $60,000.

Minister Jefferson opposed paying any tribute and urged the United States to form a coalition of nations to oppose the Algerians. He wrote, "The object of the convention shall be to compel the piratical States to perpetual peace." Jefferson asked the nations of Portugal, Naples, Venice, Denmark and Sweden to go along with the plan. He wrote to President John Adams saying, "I acknowledge I very early thought it would be best to effect a peace through the medium of war." The only way that America could block the Arab would be by investing in a large American Navy whose power could be sent overseas. In the end the United States decided it would be better to pay than to fight. In years to come, that option would change.

All this was transformed in 1801 when Tripoli declared war against the United States. In 1803, the American ship *Philadelphia* sailed into the harbor of Tripoli to try and blockade the port. Unfortunately, the *Philadelphia* ran aground and her crew, over 300 men, was captured. President Jefferson devised a covert mission to destabilize the government of Tripoli and get the crew of the *Philadelphia* back in one piece.

The ruler of Tripoli was Yusuf Karamanli, who issued an ultimatum to the United States: if the Jefferson administration would not pay further tribute to his government, he'd declare war on the United States. In response, President Jefferson sent a U.S. naval squadron to the waters off Tripoli to show the flag. However, Jefferson decided not to tell Congress of his actions. This action by President Jefferson set a precedent that would be carried out by future presidents in the coming decades.

It took four years for the Navy to subdue the states of Algiers, Morocco and Tunis until they decided not to ally themselves with ruler Karamanli. However, Tripoli decided not to cooperate with the other states and continued its hostile aggression against the U.S.

The captain of the *Philadelphia* was William Bainbridge, 29 years old, from New Jersey. He was a ruthless disciplinarian who was harsh to his men when it came to handing out punishment. When the ship got into the harbor of Tripoli, she gave chase to a blockade-runner, and as the confrontation went on, she was stranded on a reef and eventually captured.

Back in Washington, President Jefferson decided that a covert campaign to overthrow the government of Algiers was necessary. The man he chose for the assignment was William Eaton, a soldier who served in the Revolutionary War and a man that had a reputation for taking no prisoners. He was a graduate of Dartmouth College, a schoolteacher, and served as a clerk in the Connecticut legislature. He married the widow of his late commanding officer, and had a run-in with his superiors. He was court marshaled on unspecified charges and was given a two-month suspension. Eaton had, however, made a friend of Secretary of State, William Pickering. Pickering chose Eaton to look out for any French and British spies in the United States.

Despite his past record, he was appointed to the post of "United States Navy Agent for Several Barbary Regencies." He had also seen previous work as an agent for the State Department when he investigated the treachery of Senator William Blount of Tennessee. Blount had conspired with the British to attack Louisiana and Florida.

Eaton's job was to go to Tunis and negotiate a treaty with the bey for better terms with his country for the payment of American tribute to free our ships and crew. Eaton spent two fruitless years in talks with the bey and came away empty handed. He returned to Washington and recommended war as the only way out of the conflict.

While in Tripoli, Eaton negotiated with the leader of that nation, Ahmed Pasha. While the two men did not see eye to eye on most matters, Pasha took a liking to Eaton, and they continued to respect each other's points of view.

Eaton served as a presidential agent, one of many men who would work in that job in the future. Eaton had to deal with Tripoli's stern and vicious leader, Yusuf Karamanli, who did not like America, or Eaton, and made negotiating with him a chore. Karamanli had his older brother killed and drove his younger sibling, Hamet into exile. Hamet would later play an important role in Eaton's attack on Tripoli. Many historians have compared William Eaton with the fabled Lawrence of Arabia (T. E. Lawrence). The two men fought over the same territory in the sands of Arabia, almost 150 years apart.

While meeting with Karamanli, he demanded more American tribute to be paid to his government and threatened hostilities if his requests were not met. Eaton met with James Cathcart, who was the American counsel to Tripoli. Both men agreed that the United States should not agree to Karamanli's blustering and asked that the U.S. send troops and ships to the region. Without the consent of Congress, President Jefferson ordered a flotilla comprised of three frigates and one sloop to set sail. On board was a contingent of Marines who would be used in ground fighting. Karamanli's forces continued to raid American shipping and in April 1802 President Jefferson ordered another six ships to join the original squadron.

While the ships were en-route to Algiers, Eaton took matters in to his own hands. He arrived in Egypt where he met with Hamet, Yusuf's exiled brother. Eaton told him what had been happening in Algiers and asked if Hamet would consider mounting an overland expedition to oust his brother. Eaton wrote to Jefferson asking for money and equipment for such a force. He was turned down. Eaton raised a small amount of money on his own and he got Hamet to persuade others tribes in the region who were loyal to him to join his band. Eaton also asked Commodore Samuel Barron if he would allow the use of U.S. frigates for his invasion. Barron did not like Eaton and he too turned him down.

In time however, Eaton and Hamet were able to assemble a rag-tag contingent of 300 Arab mercenaries, as well as 10 United States Marines. They picked up along the way a number of Christians who fought alongside them, and with 1,000 camels, headed for Tripoli.

Their first attack came against the city of Derna, the second largest city in the country. Eaton and Hamet split up their forces with Eaton's men attacking the harbor fortress while Hamet's men stormed the town's wall. Eaton's cannons bombarded the city, causing major damage. Lt. Pressley O'Bannon of the Marines raised the American flag over the city and Hamet's forces took control. In the battle, one Marine died and Eaton was wounded in the wrist.

The assault of Derna was successful, and the government of Yusef Karamanli finally agreed to release the captured Americans being held. In the end the treaty signed by the U.S. and Tripoli left a bitter aftertaste in Eaton's mouth. The United States abandoned Hamet, whom the Jefferson administration backed during the uprising. Yusef Karamanli remained in power until 1815, when the American naval force, under the command of Commodore Stephen Decatur, burned Tripoli harbor finally putting to an end to Arab blackmail. As history has shown, this was not the last the United States would see of the conflict in the Middle East.

An engraving of Davy Crockett.

Chapter 6
How Did Davy Crockett Die?

Anyone of the baby boomer generation is familiar with the story of Davy Crockett, "the king of the wild frontier." The legend of Davy Crockett was provided to a certain generation by Walt Disney, who produced for television a three-part miniseries called *Davy Crockett. King of the Wild Frontier,* starring Fes Parker, as Davy Crockett. The show was so successful that a generation of kids began wearing coonskin caps and leather coats, just like Davy did. Fess Parker became a national star and he was on his way to celebrity status. The story of the battle of the Alamo was put on the large screen with the movie of the same name starring John Wayne and an all-star cast. Moviegoers saw the heroic Davy Crockett swinging his famous rife called "Old Betsey," clubbing the attacking Mexican troops as they came over the walls of the Alamo. In most recent times, the Alamo story was once again put on the big screen starring Billy Bob Thornton and Dennis Quaid. The story was the same, except this time we saw Davy on the top of the Alamo, fiddle in hand, playing a lonely tune.

History has written that the real Davy Crockett died at the hands of the invading Mexicans as they poured into the Alamo. Davy was seen clubbing as many Mexican soldiers as he could, before being killed. He was our iconic heroic figure, dying for the liberty of Texas. But is that the real way he died?

In recent years the standard story of the death of Davy Crockett has changed dramatically. Some writers, and Crockett researchers, say that Davy did not die inside the walls of the Alamo, but was taken alive by the Mexicans, along with a few other survivors, and killed after the garrison surrendered. If that is so, then our fundamental idea of the Alamo story, and in particular the death of this great American hero, has to be revisited.

David Crockett was born on August 17, 1786 in Greene County, Tennessee. His parents were John and Rebecca (Hawkins). The elder Crockett ran a tavern on the road from Knoxville to Abingdon, Virginia. As young Davy grew up he was sent to work

41

for a man named Jacob Siler helping him drive cattle in parts of Virginia. Siler wanted to keep Davy with him after the cattle drive ended, but Davy headed home. He did not like school and soon ran away, doing jobs such as working on a wagon, and any task that came along. He returned to the Crockett homestead after two years.

In August 1806 Davy married Mary (Polly) Finley in Jefferson County, Tennessee. They stayed there for five years before moving (now with two sons, John Wesley and William), to Lincoln County, Tennessee. They later moved near the border of Alabama, where Davy named his home Kentuck.

When a massacre of 36 white settlers took place at Fort Mims in Alabama, in August 1813, Davy left home and joined the local militia. He worked as a scout during the Creek War of 1813-14 under the command of General Andrew Jackson. In later years both their paths would cross again in national politics.

In 1815, Davy's wife died from malaria the summer after giving birth to their daughter, Margaret. He soon married Elizabeth Patton, who had two of her own children. Davy moved in with his three children and they began a new life together.

The Crockett family now moved to Shoal Creek in Lawrence County where Davy entered local politics. He was elected as a magistrate, justice of the peace, town commissioner, and a colonel in the local militia. In 1821 he was elected to the Tennessee state legislature and in 1827 was elected as a congressman from Tennessee. When he entered congress, he associated himself with the policies of President Andrew Jackson with whom he had served in the Creek War. Both men came from similar backgrounds: they were frontiersmen, who aligned themselves with the common man instead of past presidents who were beholden to the land holders and Virginia aristocrats who ran the country until that time.

While in the congress, Crockett was something of an amusement to his fellow legislators. He did not have the educational background many of his colleagues had and his reputation as an Indian fighter and frontiersman was well known. While he supported most of President Jackson's policies, he split with him when it came to the president's Indian policies. Jackson proposed a bill called the "Indian Removal Bill," which would have proposed moving the

Indians then living in the southeastern regions to reservations in Oklahoma. The bill would take them from what their ancestral homes were to places they had never lived before. Despite having fought the Native tribes for years, Crockett believed the bill to be against the best wishes of the tribes and opposed Jackson on the measure.

Crockett served three terms in the congress, 1827-1831 and 1833-1835, having passed no meaningful legislation. His heart was not really in politics and he soon realized that a change in his life was needed.

Alexis de Tocqueville, the noted French writer, took notice of Davy while in Washington during a tour of the country. When he saw Crockett, he couldn't believe what he saw. He wrote years later of his encounter, "Two years ago, the inhabitants of the district of which Memphis is the capital sent to the House of Representatives in Congress an individual named David Crockett, who has had no education, can read with difficulty, has no property, no fixed residence, but passes his life hunting, selling his game to live, and dwelling continuously in the woods."

Hucksters however, saw in Davy a moneymaking machine and a play was shown in New York called *The Lion of the West,* which was seen by hundreds of people. The star character was Colonel Nimrod Wildfire, a man who was modeled after the real Davy Crockett. When the show came to Washington, Congressman Crockett was in the audience, having a wonderful time.

In time, books were written on Crockett's exploits, including his autobiography called *Life of David Crockett of the State of Tennessee,* which was ghostwritten and released in 1834. Another book was called *Davy Crockett's Almanack of Wild Sports of the West*, and *Life in the Backwoods*, issued 50 editions, which was a huge success.

In 1835, he was defeated for re-election, his short political career over. While campaigning, Davy told the people that he'd serve to the best of his ability, and if they weren't so desired, "You may go to hell, and I will go to Texas." That is exactly what he did.

In the 1830s, the province of Texas was under the control of Mexico, headed by its president, Antonio Lopez de Santa Ana. A steady stream of Americans headed for Texas where land was cheap and plentiful. Americans made up to 75 percent of the Mexican population and Santa Ana took steps to stem the flood of "gringos" heading for his nation. He banned slavery in Mexico and put restrictive customs duties on the settlers coming into Mexico. Sam Houston, leader of the Americans in Texas, declared their independence from Mexico on March 2, 1836 forming their own government and further inflaming Santa Ana's hostilities against the United States.

In November 1835 Davy Crockett and three other men left Tennessee, headed for Texas. He hoped to bring his family there once he got settled. The men arrived in San Antonio de Bexar in early February 1836 and he soon introduced himself to two of the most influential men in the Texas government: Colonel William B. Travis and Sam Houston. Santa Ana arrived in San Antonio on February 23, 1836 with over 2,400 men, along with powerful cannons and cavalry. Col. Travis had 183 men at his disposal at an old fort called the Alamo. Houston ordered Travis to blow up the fort, but Travis ignored his order. The Americans, including Davy Crockett, took up defensive positions inside the fort, awaiting the arrival of Santa Ana. A few days later, 32 men arrived at the Alamo from Gonzales, bringing the total amount of men to 200. Also inside the fort was the noted American fighter, Jim Bowie. Travis asked the assembled men if they wanted to leave. Only one left. The battle for the Alamo was about to begin.

The battle of the Alamo was a foregone conclusion before the first shot was fired. The brave defenders didn't stand a chance against the overwhelming Mexican force. The Alamo defenders fought bravely and the climactic battle took place on June 6, 1836. Santa Ana's forces besieged the Alamo with wave after wave of troops and cannon fire, which destroyed the fort, killing most of its defenders. About 20 non-combatants were allowed to leave the fort, including Joe, who was Travis's slave and Mrs. Susanna Dickinson.

According to all accounts, Davy Crockett was killed inside the Alamo holding "old Betsey." But is that what really happened?

Accounts by some Mexican observers say that a number of Alamo defenders were taken out of the fort alive and were later shot by an enraged Santa Ana. One of those men was Crockett.

Jose Enrique de la Pena, who was a lieutenant in the Mexican Army, told that account. De la Pena said that Crockett was a "naturalist" who just happened to be in San Antonio when Santa Anna showed up and took refuge inside the fort. He wrote in a diary, which was published in English in 1975 by Carmen Perry, that the Mexican soldiers "fell upon these unfortunate, defenseless men just as a tiger leaps upon its prey." The so-called de la Pena diary is the paramount account that still exists and purports to show that Crockett did not die inside the walls of the Alamo, but was instead executed outside its walls.

De La Pena was assigned to the command of Colonel Duque at the Alamo and was previously in the Navy. After the battle ended, de la Pena returned to Mexico where he was arrested for taking part in a revolt against the government.

The de la Pena story was used by Dan Kilgore, who was a former president of the Texas State Historical Association, in his book called *How Did Davy Die?* The book caused a huge stir in the mainstream historical community, with many saying the diary was a fake. However, the paper on which the diary was written was said to have been in use in Mexico at the time. James Crisp, a North Carolina University history professor who studied the diary said, "Everyone knew that the paper is old." Crisp also said, "the army was using the paper for pamphlets and the like and de la Pena had access to it. I don't know if this will satisfy others, but my position is that I welcome another test because it would be one more test that the diary would pass."

Another account of Davy's death is the so-called Dolson letter, which was published by a Detroit newspaper in September 1836. It is an account by Sgt. George Dolson who served in the Texas army at the time the incident took place. An unidentified Mexican soldier who had been captured told the story to him. The Mexican soldier told Dolson that Crockett surrendered and was subsequently killed. The Crockett surrender story was also told in a book called *The Life of Colonel David Crockett,* written by Edward Ellis, which was published in 1884. What Ellis does not say is whether or not Davy was killed after the battle, just that he was captured.

Another story regarding the Crockett death incident came via a woman named Andrea Castanon Villanueva who was said to have been an Alamo survivor. In 1899 a newspaper in San Antonio wrote an article based on her recollections of the event. She said that Crockett died fighting a column of Mexican soldiers, swinging his rifle after his last round had been fired. She said that the Mexican soldiers attacked Crockett with their swords but did not say where the incident took place (inside or outside of the Alamo).

So where do we stand? Was Davy Crockett killed fighting bravely with his comrades inside the Alamo as depicted by history? Or has the story as we know it been changed with the passage of time? Americans need their heroes, and no matter the way Davy died, he still fits the bill. Let Davy rest. Only he knows—and he's not telling.

A portrait of Jesse James.

Chapter 7
Jesse James

The mourners attending the service at Mount Olivet Cemetery in Missouri stared attentively as the coffin of their long-deceased loved one was raised from the cold, wet ground. They watched in anticipation as the coffin was brought to the surface after so many years. Also in attendance were doctors, as well as the eager press, who were also waiting to see history unfold. The person they were taking out of the ground that day was not your ordinary man. He was an American legend whose story was told and re-told throughout the years. The person of interest was none other than the notorious outlaw, Jesse James. Although James died in 1882 at the hands of his so-called friend, Bob Ford, the circumstances of his death, as well as the identity of the person in the grave, was in doubt. The purpose of the exhumation was to positively identify the remains in the coffin. That would take three days. But for Jesse James, whether outlaw or Robin Hood, as many people of the day regarded him to be, the story was not that simple.

The James family settled in Kearney, Clay County, Missouri on a 275-acre farm. His father was Robert Sallee James, a Baptist preacher, who graduated from Georgetown College in Kentucky in 1843. His mother was Zerelda Elizabeth Cole, whom his father met at a revival meeting. The couple was soon married and began a family. Four children soon followed: Alexander (Frank) on January 10, 1843; Robert, who only lived for 33 days; Jesse Woodson on September 5, 1847; and Susan Lavina on November 25, 1849.

Jesse's father was a well-known man who founded two churches and saw to the spiritual nourishment of the community. He spoke at revival meetings and also found time to establish a college. Despite all his faithfulness, he owned slaves that he brought with him from Kentucky. In 1850, the Rev. James abruptly left the homestead and started off on a wagon train that was heading for the gold region of California. Why he left home is anyone's guess, but he probably departed in order to seek a fortune for himself and his family. He never returned, dying in a camp in Placerville, California on August 18, 1850.

Zerelda James soon re-married but her husband was killed in 1852. She was married once again to Dr. Ruben Samuel who took an active interest in her children and raised them as his own. By 1855 the conflict that would soon erupt six years later (the Civil War) was spreading across Missouri. Zerelda James was an ardent southerner and Frank James also joined the cause. He enlisted in the Confederacy after the war broke out and served under the command of General Sterling Price. He later joined a band of Confederates lead by a notorious man named William Quantrill whose only purpose was to kill as many people as he could, even if they were not combatants. One of Quantrill's men, Thomas "Cole" Younger, would later take part in the gang run by Jesse and Frank James. Jesse too joined the Quantrill gang and took part in their robbery and murder spree.

Frank James took part in one of the worst atrocities of the war. Quantrill and his men raided the town of Lawrence, Kansas. The town was looted and burned, resulting in the deaths of 150 people (most were non-combatants). A few months before the raid on Lawrence, Union troops arrived at the home of Jesse's father, Dr. Samuel, looking for information on Quantrill's whereabouts. In the ensuing incident, Dr. Samuel was attacked and Jesse was hit repeatedly.

Jesse was so enraged by the incident that he joined a band lead by William "Bloody Bill" Anderson, a noted outlaw in his own right. Jesse took part in Anderson's brutal attack on the town of Centralia, Missouri on September 27, 1864 where 25 unarmed Union troops were killed. It was reported that during the incident, Jesse killed Union Major A.V.E. Johnson, whose men went after the Anderson gang.

By the time the Civil War was over, Jesse had seen action in campaigns with Colonel Joe Shelby's unit in Arkansas, at Cane Hill, and at Big Cabin in the Creek Indian Territory. His final engagement came in the spring of 1865 when Jesse tried to surrender to Union forces in Lexington, Missouri and received a bullet wound for his troubles.

After the war ended, he went back to Kansas City, Missouri,

recovered from his wounds, and met and married his cousin Zerelda Amanda Mimms. With the war now over, Jesse wondered what his next move would be. There was no talk of just standing around doing nothing. He needed action, so he, Frank and the Younger brothers, decided to merge their talents and formed the so-called "James-Younger" gang that would terrorize the west for the next decade. On February 13, 1866 the gang (with or without Jesse is not known), robbed a bank in Liberty, Missouri called the Clay County Savings Association Bank. At least $60-70,000 was taken in the first daylight bank robbery in U.S. history. During the robbery, a young college student named George Wymore was killed. The head cashier, Greenup Bird, said the robbers looked familiar, but out of fear for his life, could not positively identify the robbers.

After the heist, both Frank and Jesse traveled to California and eventually headed back to Missouri to meet up once again with the Youngers. Soon they were back on the trail, this time robbing two more banks in Missouri of around $14,000. During the period from 1868-69, Frank and Jesse headed for Nashville, Tennessee posing as grain dealers. While in the area, they used the aliases John Davis Howard (for Jesse) and Ben Woodson for Frank.

By 1875, both Jesse and Frank had returned to their old stomping grounds in the Midwest (Iowa), where they branched out robbing banks, holding up stagecoaches and trains, shooting and killing an engineer. From 1869-1881, the James and Younger gangs roamed the Midwest, sometimes acting as a team, and also independently. One robbery by the James boys turned personal. In December 1869, they robbed a bank in Gallatin, Missouri of only $700. However, during the robbery Jesse killed a bank teller named John Sheets who was involved in the chase for Bill Anderson. After the robbery, a $3,000 reward was placed on the James brothers. Jesse and Frank now had a reputation as noted criminals, although some newspapers began to write about them as modern day Robin Hoods, stealing from the wealthy (but not giving to the poor). After stealing a box of cash at the Kansas City Fairgrounds in September 1872, where a little girl was accidentally shot, one newspaper called the robbery "a feat of stupendous nerve and fearlessness that makes one's hair raised to think of it."

The success of the James-Younger Gang caused the authorities to take action against them. They called in the famous Pinkerton Detective Agency, headed by Alan Pinkerton, to bring them to justice. Pinkerton headed the National Detective Police during the Civil War and helped the Union track down Confederate spies during the conflict. On June 3, 1871 the gang robbed a bank in Corydon, Iowa and stole $6,000. One member of the gang, Cell Miller, was captured a year later by Pinkerton detectives. Despite their early success, the Pinkertons failed to locate the entire gang. Some unfortunate Pinkertons that tried to infiltrate the gang were recognized and killed in retaliation. Jesse is credited with killing one Pinkerton man named James Whicher in 1874. They got a hot tip that the brothers were planning to visit their mother at her home in Kearney so they snuck up to the house to await their arrival. No one is exactly sure what happened next, but the Pinkertons attacked the house, dropping an incendiary device into the farmhouse, which exploded. In the ensuing melee, Jesse's half-brother, Archie Samuel, was killed. Neither Jesse nor Frank was at the house that night. After the incident, public opinion rallied to the side of the James boys and they continued to sow havoc, unmolested.

The James-Younger Gang was now ready for one last spectacular mission. On September 7, 1876 Jesse, Bob Younger and Charlie Pitts (one of their friends), rode into the town of Northfield, Minnesota in order to rob the First National Bank. They posed as cattle buyers and mingled with the town's folk who had no idea who they were. The three men entered the bank while the rest of the group took up positions outside. Announcing the holdup, a number of people in the bank fought back. One of the patrons was wounded but managed to leave the bank and spread the word that the bank had been robbed. Jesse killed the unlucky cashier who happened to be at the wrong place at the wrong time. Fleeing the bank, two members of the gang, Cell Miller and Bill Chadwell, were killed by local residents. Both Frank and Jesse managed to escape during the firefight. Others in the gang were also wounded, including Cole Younger, who was shot in the shoulder. His brother Jim was shot in the face.

A posse was immediately formed and a 10-day chase ensued,

but Jesse and Frank made their way to the Dakota Territory. However, the other members of the gang were not so lucky. The Youngers were eventually captured and Charlie Pitts was killed. Frank and Jesse James were now the most wanted men in the west. They fled to Mexico for a while before coming back to Nashville, Tennessee. It was during this time that Jesse began to use the alias "Howard," which he would use over again.

With the Youngers now out of the picture, Jesse formed a new team and robbed a train in Glendale, Missouri in 1879. Two years later they robbed a train in the Rock Island line and killed a man named Frank McMillan. During the robbery, Jesse shot and killed the conductor, William Westfall, who he had been targeting. One of the new men in Jesse's troupe, James Andrew "Dick" Liddil, had enough of the gang's murderous ways and broke with them. He then went to the authorities and told them about his knowledge of the James men killing McMillan and Westfall. By now the James Gang had broken up. Many were killed or went their separate ways. Missouri Governor Thomas Crittenden put a $10,000 reward on Jesse's head. His time was now running out.

In 1879, Jesse, his wife Zee and their son moved to Kansas City, Missouri under the alias Thomas Howard. Jesse now had two new gang members, Charley and Bob Ford. They were not as well trusted as the Youngers, but at this point Jesse had no real choice.

On April 3, 1882 Jesse and the Ford brothers were in St. Joseph, Missouri at the Ford home where they were discussing plans to rob a nearby bank. After their discussion, Charley Ford left the room, leaving his brother Bob alone with Jesse. Jesse saw that his mother's picture had fallen down, went over to fix it, his back turned. The rest of the story has been debated over the last hundred or so years. Bob Ford took out his gun and shot Jesse below the right ear. His evil deed done, Bob Ford fled the house where he met up with brother Charley, who asked him what happened. Bob Ford said the shooting was an accident. Why did Bob Ford kill Jesse James? Some say for the reward money offered by Governor Crittenden. He might have believed he was doing the country a service in response to Jesse's decade-long spree as an outlaw and killer.

Shortly after the murder of Jesse James, the Ford brothers

came back to the scene of the crime. The police were called and a cursory investigation took place. No sooner had Jesse been buried than Bob Ford was awarded the $10,000 bounty that was put on Jesse's head by Governor Crittenden. Zee James (Jesse's wife) told the sheriff her husband was not Jesse James, but Tom Howard. Jesse's body was sent home for burial and it seemed that the saga of Jesse James, the West's most feared and fancied outlaw, had come to an end. Frank James surrendered, but the law had a hard time making a case against him and the charges were dismissed. He died on February 18, 1915.

As the years passed, there were some in the country who did not believe that Jesse had been killed. They believed in a vast conspiracy involving the Ford brothers and Governor Crittenden. Many people came forth claiming to be Jesse James. One was a man named John James, who killed a man in Illinois in 1926. While he was in jail, he told an amazing story of a man named Charley Bigelow who was supposed to have carried out various robberies and said they were the work of the James Gang. He said Bigelow was present at Jesse's home on the night of the assassination; that Jesse killed him, dragged his corpse away and put the body in James's home. Jesse's wife, Zee James, then smeared blood on her clothing and had Bob Ford fire a shot into the wall, leaving Charley Ford the job of calling the sheriff. Jesse then went to Argentina where he lived for a while, eventually returning to the United States where he changed his name to John James. John James then toured the country, telling anyone who would listen, that he was the real Jesse James, making a profit along the way.

The "real" Jesse James re-appeared in 1948 under the name of J. Frank Dalton. Dalton was now over 100 years old. His story was picked up by a noted reporter of the day, Robert Ruark, who worked for the *St. Louis Globe-Democrat*. Ruark interviewed Dalton and his reporting was written up in the popular magazine of the time, *The Police Gazette*. Dalton went on national radio to promote his story and for a time he was believed to be the real deal. On September 5, 1950, a curious event took place at the Meramec Caverns where the James-Younger Gang used to hide out. On hand were J. Frank Dalton (then 103) and James Davis (106), who said he was Cole Younger (Younger was said to have died in 1916).

Also on hand was John Trammell (age 110—did they all really live that long?), who said he was a cook for the gang. No one really believed the story but it was fun while it lasted. J. Frank Dalton, AKA Jesse James, died on August 15, 1951 in Granbury, Texas.

Many conspiracy theorists have put a new spin on the life and death of Jesse James and it's quite a story. They say that Jesse James did not die at the hands of Bob Ford, and instead was the assassin of John Wilkes Booth, who died at the Grand Avenue Hotel in Enid, Oklahoma in 1903. Theorists say that Jesse James became a member of a secret society called the Knights of the Golden Circle (KGC), which was formed in the 1850s. The purpose of the KGC was to conquer Mexico and certain parts of the Caribbean in order to make those areas safe for the advancement of slavery. The leader of the KGC was George Washington Lafayette Bickley, a man with a rather checkered past, who founded the group in Lexington, Kentucky in 1854.

The KGC fostered the secessionist movement prior to the Civil War. They had many different chapters with each person having a certain rank and duties, like the Masons. When the Civil War started, the KGC offered their services but were turned down.

Jesse James was supposed to have been a member of the KGC and the story goes that he was responsible for hiding a vast amount of gold that the group had accumulated and hidden in various locations across the south. The reason Jesse was given such a high honor was that he was one of the top men in the KGC and thus given added responsibility by the leadership. Jesse was also supposed to have been a 33rd degree Freemason, as well as a member of the KGC.

James was appointed the treasurer and comptroller of all the gold and bullion in the possession of the KGC and he paid John Wilkes Booth (who survived the shoot-out at the Garrett Farm), $3,600 with the proviso that he never discussed his role in the Lincoln assassination. The story goes that Booth landed in Enid, Oklahoma under the name of David George and began bragging about his sordid past. The KGC had no other option but to silence him, and Jesse James was given the job. He met with Booth at an Enid bar and put poison in his drink. Booth subsequently died and the deed was done.

Still, as time went on, the story and legend of Jesse James did not die. In 1995 the descendants of Jesse James had their illustrious relative exhumed from Mt. Olivet Cemetery. Over several days, DNA testing was done to verify the body entombed in the grave was indeed that of Jesse James. After a thorough examination by a team of highly professional scientists, the results were in. The man in the casket was the "real" Jesse James.

While testing for the positive remains of Jesse James, a reporter from the *Kansas City Star,* Kelly Garbus, wrote the following, "Jesse Woodson James, 34, of St. Joseph, died April 3, 1882, of a gunshot wound to the head. He will be buried Saturday—for the third time—in Mount Olivet Cemetery in Kearney." Jesse would have been pleased.

Chapter 8
Butch Cassidy and
the Sundance Kid

In 1969 moviegoers flocked by the thousands to see the new film released by 20th Century Fox called *Butch Cassidy and the Sundance Kid*. No one really knew what to expect except for the fact that two of the biggest movie stars of the day, Robert Redford and Paul Newman, were starring in the film. When the film came out, not many people ever heard of Butch Cassidy and the Sundance Kid, outlaws who roamed the West in the late 1800s, robbing banks and having a jolly good time doing it. However, the film was a Hollywood success, making the two men (Butch and Sundance) right on par with Jesse James in notoriety. The song from the movie, "Raindrops Keep Falling On My Head," was played on national radio shows, which also became a hit. Butch and Sundance were now ready for historical prime time. The exploits of Butch and Sundance were the background for a movie called *The Great Train Robbery*, which came out in 1903. Like Jesse James, there has been a debate among western historians that Butch and Sundance did not die in Bolivia, rather they went on to adopt other aliases and lived to a ripe old age. But who were they, and how did their story go unnoticed for so long?

Like the James Gang, the antics of Butch and Sundance made them out to be heroes among certain members of the population who saw their criminal activities in parts of Utah and Wyoming as stealing from the rich to give to the poor. That was not accurate, as the money they robbed went into their own coffers. But it didn't matter; they were what the people wanted them to be and nothing more.

Butch Cassidy's real name was Robert LeRoy Parker who was born in Beaver, Utah on April 13, 1866. His parents were Mormons who came to the United States from England in 1856. They settled in Circleville, Utah. As a young man, Robert Parker worked as a ranch hand in order to make money for his family.

Things did not go so well for the Parker's and soon young Parker was rustling cattle. As a young man, he joined a gang that was run by a man named Mike Cassidy. No one knows what really happened to Mike Cassidy, but he disappeared one day, never to return. With Mike gone, Robert Parker made himself head of the gang and adopted the last named of Cassidy in honor of his friend. For whatever reason, he also changed his first name to Butch and Robert LeRoy Parker was now known as Butch Cassidy.

The Sundance Kid's real name was Harry Longabaugh. The name Longabaugh did not sound right for an outlaw, and while serving an 18-month sentence in a Wyoming jail, he decided to change his name to that of the county seat where he was incarcerated (Sundance). He was born in Mont Clare, Pennsylvania in 1870 and in the 1880s he was involved in the rustling of cattle in Sundance, Wyoming. His life of crime did not end at that point. He teamed up with a man called Harvey Logan to rob a bank in Belle Fourche, South Dakota on June 27, 1897. They were captured but managed to escape from jail three months later. Sundance joined Cassidy's Gang in 1899, a full 12 years after Butch began his career as an outlaw. There is some discrepancy as to just what Sundance's real name was. In 1977, Lula Parker Betenson, Cassidy's sister, said that Sundance's real name was Elzy Lay. Records show however, that his real name was William Ellsworth.

The gang's first robbery took place against the San Miguel Valley Bank in 1889, getting them a nice sum of $20,000. Like the James Gang, Butch, Sundance and their men robbed banks as far away as Denver and Telluride, Colorado and the Rio Grande Express in Grand Junction, Colorado. They bribed local ranchers to pay them protection money with the provision that the gang wouldn't steal their cattle.

During one robbery, Cassidy was wounded by the local sheriff and was taken to jail. He served a two-year sentence in the Laramie Penitentiary before being released. Then a strange thing happened—one that had to be seen to believe. Governor William Richards visited Cassidy in jail and made a proposal to him. If he renounced any more attempts to rob banks and go straight, he'd commute his sentence. Looking a gift horse in the mouth, Butch agreed and was released. Unfortunately for Governor Richards, Butch failed to keep his word.

It was at this point Butch Cassidy and his team started calling themselves the Wild Bunch. Its members included Butch, Sundance, Ben Kilpatrick, Harvey Logan, William Carver, George Curry and Bob Meeks. Butch and his gang made their headquarters in a very remote part of Wyoming that they called the Hole-in-the-Wall country, located in Johnson County. This area was one of the most remote areas in the West, one that was hardly ridden by outsiders. It was rocky and inhospitable, a perfect place to hide. The area was made up of a 55-mile gap in the Bighorn Mountains, near the Middle Peak of the Powder River. This area was home to the Cheyenne and Arapaho Indians. It had only one entrance from the east, which made it a perfect place to watch for any attackers or people looking for them. Butch and his gang lived in the Hole-in-the-Wall country during the time of his bank robberies.

From this rugged area, the gang robbed banks in such states as Utah, Idaho and South Dakota. One of their most daring robberies took place on the Denver and Rio Grande train in Castle Gate, Utah. Before the robbery took place, Butch rode into town and managed to get a job working on the train station. He was in the perfect spot to notice the time and schedules that trains arrived and more importantly, when the various payrolls were delivered. At the appointed time, both Butch and Frank Caffey entered the paymaster's office and walked out with the sum of $8,000.

As the new century arrived, Butch and Sundance robbed the Union Pacific train at Tipton, Wyoming. Their next heist was the First National Bank in Winnemucca, Nevada in September 1900. They got away with $32,640, a huge amount for that time. In 1901 they robbed a Great Northern train near Wager, Montana of $65,000.

However, their luck did not last. Sheriff Jesse Tyler killed one member of the group, George Curry, on April 17, 1900. The next year William Carver was killed and Ben Kilpatrick was taken prisoner in Sonora, Texas but escaped before finally being captured in St. Louis with another member of the group.

Butch's new spree of bank and train robberies attracted the

notice of Governor Richards, who only a few years back had let him go with the proviso that he would stop his lawless ways. When Butch ignored their deal, the governor called in the Pinkerton Detective Agency to look for them. This was the same route that authorities took in regard to Jesse James and his gang. The Pinkertons did manage to capture Elzy Lay who was captured in New Mexico. The Pinkerton's chase of Cassidy's Gang garnered the attention of the major newspapers of the country. It was now the early 19th century and the days of the wild and wooly west were gone forever. Industrialization was now taking over the country with modern changes in machinery and transportation, making the United States a new and world-developing nation. So when readers learned that there was one Wild Bunch still on the loose, they took interest.

It was at this point that Butch and Sundance dismantled the gang. They went on the lam and for a long time no one quite knew where they were. Were their days as the nation's number one outlaw gang finally over? The story goes that that they went to Fort Worth, Texas where Sundance met a woman named Etta Place. The trio then headed to New York City where they stayed for a short while, no one knowing their true identities. On February 29, 1902 they boarded a ship, the *Soldier Prince,* en-route to South America. They then moved to Argentina where the story goes they bought land in the province of Chubut and became farmers. After living in perfect obscurity for four years, and yearning to relive their outlaw ways, they robbed a number of banks in Argentina. Not wanting to overstay their welcome, they went to Bolivia. No one knows just what reality and fiction are regarding the last days of Butch and Sundance. It was reported that after robbing tin mines in the country, they were trapped in the town of San Vicente and were killed in a shootout with Bolivian soldiers. The soldiers were not able to identify the bodies so we aren't sure if it was Butch and Sundance who really died in the incident. Other accounts said that Longabaugh (Sundance) escaped Bolivia and wound up back in the United States, where he died in Casper, Wyoming in 1957.

Now legend really took shape. Butch was supposed to have sailed to Europe where he took on the alias "William Phillips."

He then settled in Michigan where he married a woman named Gertrude Livesay in 1908. They went to Arizona where, it was said, Butch fought with Pancho Villa (why not), then moved to Spokane, Washington and founded his own company. He supposedly died of cancer on July 20, 1937.

The parallels of the stories of Butch Cassidy and the Sundance Kid, and that of Jesse James, are striking. They both were supposed to have survived their deaths and taken on new identities in other places, living to a ripe old age. There is also a parallel with the de La Pena diary, which said that Davy Crockett did not die in the Alamo. A rare book expert named Brent Ashworth and author Larry Pointer recovered a 200-page manuscript that was dated in 1934 called: *Bandit Invincible: The Story of Butch Cassidy,* which was written by Butch's alias, William Phillips. The theory is that Butch fled Bolivia and arrived in Paris, France where he underwent facial surgery to alter his appearance. He then returned to the United States where Butch reunited with his old love, Gertrude Livesay. The couple were then married in Michigan in 1908 and moved to Spokane, Washington in 1911. Butch then died in 1937 at the age of 71.

Larry Pointer then elaborated on Butch's life in his own book called *In Search of Butch Cassidy,* which was published in 1978 by the University Press of Oklahoma.

In an interview conducted in 1977 with Butch's sister, she said that Butch had come to visit her at her home in Circleville, Utah long after he was supposedly killed in Bolivia. His sister was quoted as saying of her brother, "Butch was chased all his life, and so when we got the news that he was dead, and we decided he would be chased no more. He had good table manners, great regard for ladies, and always left a fancy tip. But he was sure death on banks and railroads."

So, did Butch Cassidy live to be an old man like Jesse James? Or is real life more believable than fiction. As of now, there are still no answers.

Zachary Taylor, the 12th President of the United States.

Chapter 9
What Happened to
Zachary Taylor?

If you ask most American's who the first president to be assassinated was, the answer would be Abraham Lincoln (the others being William McKinley, James Garfield and John Kennedy). There have been other attempts on the lives of presidents, including Andrew Jackson, Theodore and Franklin Roosevelt, Harry Truman, Ronald Reagan and Gerald Ford. What if I told you that an earlier resident might have met the same fate as the one's mentioned above. That man might have been the 12th president of the United States, Zachary Taylor. The name of Zachary Taylor might not be recognized by most American's because he only served a mere 16 months in office before dying suddenly. However, there is circumstantial evidence that President Taylor might have been poisoned, and thus the first president to be killed while in office.

Zachary Taylor was born November 24, 1784 in Virginia and his family soon moved to Kentucky where he was raised on a plantation. His father was in the American Revolution and served under George Washington. He graduated from Harvard College and then went into business. As a young man he worked raising cotton, later moving to Baton Rouge, Louisiana and then to Mississippi where he owned a home. Even though he lived in the South, he was not an advocate of slavery and those sentiments got him in trouble with his neighbors.

Taylor joined the army on May 3, 1808 and received the rank of first lieutenant in the Seventh Infantry Regiment with the help of his cousin, James Madison. He served in the Indiana Territory and was promoted to captain in November 1810. He was also the commander of Fort Knox until 1814. During the War of 1812, he defeated the Indian Chief Tecumseh in a major battle. He also fought in the Black Hawk War in 1832 against the Seminole Indians. Now, holding the rank of Brigadier General, he was promoted to the commander of all American troops in Florida.

When Texas became a state in 1845, President James K. Polk assigned Taylor to the Texas-Mexico border where tensions with Mexico over Texas statehood were growing. He was in charge of all U.S. troops under the Army of Occupation. When hostilities began, Taylor led his troops to victory in the battles of Palo Alto and Monterey. The climactic battle of the war was Veracruz in which Taylor and General Winfield Scott defeated the Mexican's under the command of General Lopez de Santa Anna (Santa Anna would later be the victor against the men at the Alamo). After the Mexican defeat at Veracruz, Taylor was heralded as one of the greatest military leaders of the day and it was the start of his later political career.

In 1848 the Whig party asked Taylor to be their candidate in that's year's presidential election. Taylor had never had an interest in politics, nor had he voted in an election. However, he agreed and ran against the Democratic candidate, picking Millard Fillmore as his Vice President. Despite the fact that Taylor owned 100 slaves, he was opposed to any thought of secession by a state in the union over the question of slavery.

As President, Taylor had to confront the question of the expansion of slavery into any new state or territory that might come into the union. He opposed any expansion of slavery into the new western territories and believed that the president should not interfere in the legislative process. With California and New Mexico seeking statehood, President Taylor proposed the people of those territories decide for themselves whether or not they wanted to be slave or free. Since both were not in favor of slavery, Taylor got in trouble with his fellow Southerner's in congress. In February 1850 President Taylor had a contentious meeting with many Southern leaders on the slavery question. He told them if any state left the union, he'd use the army against them. He said of the threat of secession, "Persons taken in rebellion against the Union, would be hanged with less reluctance than he had hanged deserters and spies in Mexico." President Taylor was thus able to defuse a potential secession problem, 11 years before the start of the Civil War.

For 16 months President Taylor kept the Union together without any further bloodshed, with little or no major accomplishments in his presidency. However, circumstances then changed dramatically on July 4, 1850 when he left the White House to celebrate the National holiday. He attended a program at a Sunday school and attended a groundbreaking ceremony for the upcoming construction of the Washington Monument. After the ceremony was over, the president took a walk along the Potomac River and then returned to the White House. It was then things began to go horribly wrong.

That particular day the weather in Washington was very hot. When he took his walk along the Potomac, the president ate green apples, a large bowl of cherries and drank cold water and milk. Part of the ceremonies that day was the laying of the cornerstone of what was to be the Washington Monument. That night, he did not feel well and went to bed. In the morning he felt even worse and began to have diarrhea, some of it bloody. The doctor diagnosed the problem as cholera and treated it with calomel and opium. It is even possible the doctor bled the president, which was a common treatment in those days. After suffering for four long days, President Taylor finally succumbed to his illness. He was 64 years old. "Old Rough and Ready," as he was called, was the first president to die in office. But what was the exact circumstance and was it foul play?

Over the years, people have speculated as to why the president died. Modern day doctors say that President Taylor might have succumbed to a bad case of salmonella poisoning. It was possible that the food he ate, the apples, cherries or the milk had been somehow naturally tainted. Or was it possible that the president had some illness that no one knew about? The official case of death was gastroenteritis (I guess they didn't have Tums back then).

Soon after the president's death, people began to talk that perhaps he was the victim of foul play, i.e., assassinated. Some people, including members of the Republican Party, believed that he was killed by some faction of the pro-slavery movement who did not like his anti-secessionist policies. An historian going through the Lincoln Papers at the Library of Congress came upon a letter from a supporter of Taylor from Ohio who referenced the death of President Taylor. The note said, "Taylor was a vigorous man, of good habits and accustomed to active live and trying duties, and that he should fall a solitary victim to cholera, in a time of health, after eating a little ice cream is quite unsatisfactory." One person even believed the sordid Borgia family of Italy was responsible for the president's death.

Taylor's death was investigated by John Bingham who was a lawyer that took part in the prosecution of President Lincoln's assassins. This inquiry took place after the Lincoln assassination verdict had been handed down and he came up with a bombshell. Bingham said that President Taylor had been poisoned and the culprit was Jefferson Davis, the President of the Confederate States of America. It is also interesting to note that Jefferson Davis was Taylor's son-in-law from a previous marriage. An author, who wrote an article on the Bingham claim, went through Bingham's papers at the Library of Congress and could not find any reference to Bingham's interest in the conspiracy angle to President Taylor's death.

That theory is taken to task by Eugene Genovese, who was a distinguished professor in residence at the University Center of Georgia. He said of a possible Southern conspiracy surrounding Taylor's death: "For the life of me, I can't imagine any Southern personalities who would have been involved in such a conspiracy. But there is always the possibility that there were some nuts that had access to him and did it."

In the 1990s, a professor named Clara Rising, while doing research on a book about President Taylor, postulated that Taylor might have been poisoned with a lethal dose of arsenic by persons unknown. Ms. Rising contacted the coroner in the jurisdiction where President Taylor was buried, Dr. Richard Greathouse, telling him of her theories on the death of the president. Dr. Greathouse agreed to do an exhumation of President Taylor's remains. In her negotiations with Dr. Greathouse, Ms. Rising agreed to pay the sum of $1,200 in costs for the exhumation. Dr. Greathouse was assisted in the examination of the president's remains by William Maples, a forensic anthropologist at the University of Florida in Gainesville, who was an authority in doing such procedures.

In June 1991 the remains of President Taylor were removed from his crypt and the forensic analysis began. They concluded that while there were traces of arsenic in Taylor's body, there was not enough of it to prove that the president had been murdered.

So many years have passed since the death of President Zachary Taylor that it will be impossible to verify whether he was poisoned or not. Was the amount of arsenic found in his body enough to kill him? If so, the perpetrators are long dead and there is no "smoking gun" to verify any findings of conspiracy. Like Roger Maris's 61 home runs in 1961, historians might have to put an asterisk next to his name as possibly the first U.S. president to be killed while in office.

Gerneral George S. Patton.

Chapter 10
The Search for Hitler's Gold

On the morning of February 3, 1945 a massive allied air attack comprised of 1,000 bombers from the 5th U.S. Army Air Force attacked Berlin. As the unsuspecting American bombardiers let loose their powerful explosives against their targets below, neither they or anyone else, could know that by their actions that winter day, one of the greatest conspiracies of World War II would be set in motion.

The prime target of the air raid was the Tempelhof marshaling yards in Berlin where all that was left of the German armaments was stored. Other important targets were the Reichstag, the Reich Chancellery, Goering's Air Ministry and the Propaganda Ministry. Another building that was destroyed, and the one that is the most important as far as this story goes, is the Reich bank, the depository of the German government. The Reichsbank took 21 direct hits, but amazingly the 5,000 employees who huddled in the basement survived.

The Reichsbank was the leading bank in Germany, holding vast amounts of gold and currencies belonging to Germany and other conquered nations. With it in flames and allied troops on the edge of Berlin, the president of the bank, Dr. Walter Funk, knew he had to take drastic action to save his precious reserves. At a meeting in Hitler's bunker, it was decided to take as much of the Reich gold out of the city as possible to a safe location in the Bavarian Alps. They removed 450 sacks of paper marks, but left 500 sacks buried in an abandoned mine shaft in the city of Merkers. This was the first of two trips that would be made to hide Hitler's gold.

On March 22, 1945, the U.S. Third Army, led by Lt. Col. George Patton, crossed the Rhine River and on April 6th two military policemen from Patton's command received information from two displaced women who said that certain amounts of gold were hidden in the Kaiser's mine.

A half-mile below ground, Patton's men found 550 sacks of

German paper currency, totaling a billion Reichsmarks stacked along the walls of the main passageway. General Dwight D. Eisenhower, the allied commander-in-chief, decided that the gold had to be moved to a safer place. On April 14, 1945 the treasury of the Third Reich was taken to the Reichsbank in Frankfurt, which was now in American hands.

Information relating to the Merker's mine was relayed to the members of the so-called "Monuments Men," a section of the U.S. Third Army under General Patton (the story of the Monuments Men was shown in the recent film of the same name starring George Clooney, Mat Damon and others). Two members of the Monuments Men team, Robert Posey and Lincoln Kirstein, arrived at Merker's to make an inspection. As they approached the mine, it was guarded by a ring of steel, hundreds of soldiers carrying automatic weapons, tanks and machine guns formed a huge circle near the mine. As the elevator took them deeper in the mine shaft, they were subjected to a sight that startled them to the bone. Beyond a blasted door, the found a Nazi treasure room about 150 feet long and 75 feet across. Inside was a railroad track that the Nazis used to bring and remove gold from the mine. On the floor of the mine lay thousands upon thousands of bags of gold. Inside the shaft was Room 8, another treasure trove of stolen Nazi loot. But what they found was more extraordinary. Inside was box upon box of stolen art works, some of the most important and valuable pieces of art, which were stolen from the homes of the victims of the Holocaust. Also discovered were Ancient Egyptian papyri in metal cases, Greek and Roman decorative art, ancient rugs and mosaics. They also found 8,198 gold bars, 711 bags of U.S. $20 gold pieces, 1,300 bags of other gold coins, hundreds of bags of foreign currencies and $2.76 billion German Reichsmarks.

In a massive undertaking, the U.S. began a massive removal of the looted gold and artwork that were taken away for cataloging and safe-keeping. Not all of the gold was removed, and in that dark pit a half-mile below ground, the great Reichsbank robbery began.

Unknown to the Americans, the job of removing the gold was given to Friedrich Rauch, Hitler's personal security officer. Hitler's personal hideout in the Alpine Forest, the Berghof, was where the gold was hidden.

It was decided to ship the gold and currency south in two separate convoys to protect it from falling into the hands of the Americans. Two trains, codenamed Adler and Dohle, were loaded on the nights of April 13th and 14th and headed for Munich where the money would be distributed. After a hazardous journey over war-torn Germany, the gold finally arrived at the small town of Mittenwald in the Bavarian Alps; but not all of it.

The man in charge of the Reichsbank evacuation, Director Hans Alfred von Rosenberg-Lipinski, diverted 25 bags of bullion for his own use.

The job of burying the remaining gold fell to the hands of Colonel Franz Pfeiffer, the commander of the famous Mountain Infantry School in Mittenwald. It was up to Colonel Pfeiffer to move the $15 million-worth of foreign notes and gold, and he did so with pure professionalism. He had the gold taken up into the mountains, two-and-a-half miles north of Mittenwald to the Forest House owned by Hans Neuhauser Sr., the Chief Forester of Walchensee.

When the job was done, seven caches of Reichsbank currency as well as ammunition and gold were buried in at least three separate holes. As the 10th Armored Division reached Germash, the closest town to the buried gold, Col. Pfeiffer used a public phone to arrange his surrender.

The Americans, in their confusion while occupying the area, forgot about Colonel Pfeiffer's catch of gold and an investigation team was sent up the mountain where they found guns, but no trace of any money.

It was now up to the United States military to mount a full-scale investigation and an English officer, Michael Waring, was chosen. The first thing that Waring did was to arrest Frederich Will and George Netzeband, two Reichsbank officials. Netzeband spilled the beans to Waring and on June 6th took the Americans up the mountain where they found 364 bags with a total of 728 bars of gold, valued at 10 million dollars.

Later, a myth would grow out of the discovery of the 728 bags of gold, with people calling it the greatest robbery in history. A theft of great proportions did take place, but it didn't concern the

728 bars that have been described. Diverted by the Americans, the money disappeared into thin air and nobody was every arrested.

After being on the run for several weeks, Col. Pfeiffer finally surrendered and led his captors, once again, up his mountain where he exhumed a small amount of his hidden assets. He turned the money over to the army who shockingly refused to accept it. Instead the money was given to the German Military Government, which was run by the United States.

To answer these questions, Brigadier Waring turned to a man who was to loom very large in the gold rush, Captain Fred Neumann. Neumann was General Patton's interpreter, a German Jew and an intelligence officer. Neumann met with the principles in the Reichsbank robbery case, including Col. Pfeiffer, who handed over $400,000 to Neumann. Immediately after signing for the money, Captain Neumann got into his car and was never seen again.

In what was beginning to look like another inquiry in an endless cycle, the matter was handed over to the U.S. Army's Criminal Investigation Division, along with the FBI. Captain Neumann was the only real suspect investigated in the robbery of the Reichsbank and that probe would take investigators from the Bavarian Alps to United States.

Frederick Siegfried Neumann was born in Hersfeld, Germany to a Jewish family in January 1912. His family came to the United States in 1930 where Frederick was naturalized in 1937 and married an American girl in 1942. At age 31 he was commissioned as a lieutenant in the U.S. Army Field Artillery at the end of 1943 and transferred to Military Intelligence due to his fluency in German. One of his first assignments was as a Prisoner of War Interrogator with a "secret" clearance with the Sixth Army. Then from June 1944 to September 1945 he served with the Third Army as a special Counter-Intelligence Officer. He was then assigned to be General Patton's interpreter.

A man named Hubert von Blucher, who knew Fred Neumann, told an incredible tale about him. One day Captain Neumann was at von Blucher's home in Germany for dinner. At the dinner table Captain Neumann said the Jewish people had suffered tremendously in the war and they needed a homeland for themselves. His plan was to send the Reichsbank money to von Blucher's home in Garmisch as a donation to the Jewish state. Neumann further stated that an elaborate plan had been prepared to take the money to Palestine. He said that a flying boat from the International Red Cross in Switzerland would land at Lake Walchen and would then take the money to Palestine, which would be appropriated to the Zionist leaders.

Writing about the meeting years later, von Blucher said, "It never occurred to me for a second that Neumann might perhaps have put up this idea in order to keep the money for himself. The last six months had been so filled with realities that were so utterly improbable that there was really nothing improbable left that could happen."

In August 1945 U.S. Military authorities found $50,000 hidden in von Blucher's garden, which was transferred to the Military Government Detachment in Munich. In an astonishing move, Captain Neumann returned to the von Blucher's home and ordered a more thorough search of the property be conducted. Soldiers found a pot filled with 100 bills. Just why Captain Neumann took it upon himself to order a search of the von Blucher's home is questionable in itself. Was he there to collect the money and abscond with it a proper time? In all, $404,000 was taken from the von Blucher's home and Captain Neumann got a signed receipt for it.

After the war was over, the investigation of Captain Neumann took on another twist. In September 1947 the FBI mounted "Operation Garpeck" and reopened the Neumann case. The Bureau traced him to California where steps were taken to interview him. Fred Neumann had been working for a coin-operations company near San Francisco by then. In that month, CID officer, Agent Howard Hyatt, arrived in California where he contacted the FBI regarding the Neumann case. On September 19th, the local office sent a memo to FBI headquarters in Washington stating, "A Special Project of CID has been established in Garmisch-Partenkirchen, Bavaria, to determine, among other matters, the ultimate disposition of some $404,840 and £405, allegedly receipted for on August 24, 1945 by Captain Neumann, CIB, Third Army. In this connection, investigation has been undertaken by CID to determine if Neumann may have misappropriated funds turned over to the Army by captured prisoners of war."[1]

Federal agents were not able to find Neumann and no formal investigation was ever undertaken. Fred Neumann died of tuberculosis in the National Jewish Hospital in Denver, Colorado.

But one more curious dimension was now added to the already growing confusion surrounding the CID's probe in the American zone. What made the American zone different from the other allied areas of conquered Germany was the enormity of criminal activity that occurred there. It was like the Old West reincarnated with drugs, prostitution and black market racketeering taking place.

The man who finally blew the lid on the Reichsbank robbery was Guenther Reinhardt. Reinhardt was a member of the CIC (Counter Intelligence Corps) in Bavaria who had made the right contacts wherever he went. During his travels, Reinhardt met two newspaper reporters, Ed Hartrich and Tom Agoston whose articles on the Reichsbank robbery had been suppressed by the military government.

When his superiors discovered that he had met with the two reporters and was ready to talk, they quickly ordered him to stop his inquiry and threatened to have him arrested.

Reinhardt sailed home and while on board wrote a 55-page report detailing the track of the lost gold from the bombing of the Reichsbank to its mysterious disappearance in the Bavarian Alps.

Thus, the famous Reinhardt memorandum, as it was called, was about to write the final chapter on the Reichsbank robbery.

He took his report to Assistant Secretary of the Army, Gordon Gray, who in turn gave it to the top brass in the Pentagon and finally to General Lucius Clay, the Deputy Military Governor in the American zone in Germany.

And as the Christmas season of 1947 came and went, official Washington learned of the systematic corruption and conspiracy in the American zone of Germany.

It was up to General Clay to finally put the cover-up into high gear. He appointed Orville Taylor, Special Assistant to the Secretary of the Army, to file a report on Reinhardt's charges. The Taylor report rebutted Reinhardt's memorandum, calling it the

1 Sayer, Ian and Botting, Douglas, *Nazi Gold,* Congdon &Weed, New York, 1984, Page 295.

work of an over-imaginative writer who had no solid facts to go on.

And that was the end of the investigation. Nobody in official Washington ever looked into the missing gold and currency allegedly stolen from the Reichsbank. Nobody investigated the massive corruption in the American zone of Germany, and more importantly, nobody was ever prosecuted for one of the most far reaching crimes in American history.

Federal Judge John H. Wood.

Chapter 11
The Death of Judge John Wood

On May 29, 1979 as Federal Judge John Wood was leaving his home for work, a gunman fired one shot from a .240 caliber rifle, mortally wounding him. He was swiftly taken to Northeast Baptist Hospital where he died.

What followed was one of the largest manhunts in the history of the FBI. During their investigation of the murder of Judge Wood, authorities would uncover certain leads connecting underworld crimes, drug smuggling and most tantalizing, a possible link to the assassination of President John F. Kennedy.

Judge John Wood, called "Maximum John," because of the stiff sentences he handed down, especially in drug cases, made a lot of enemies on the bench.

On February 26, 1979 Jamiel "Jimmy" Chagra, a drug dealer and gambler with links to organized crime, was indicted in a Midland, Texas court on narcotics and conspiracy charges. His trial date was set for July of that year with Judge Wood presiding.

Shortly before the trial began, an assassination attempt was made against James Kerr, the Assistant U.S. Attorney who was prosecuting the Chagra case before Judge Wood. He survived the attempt on his life, despite being wounded.

Chagra was linked to the murder attempt on James Kerr and was accused of hiring a crook named Jimmy Kerns to carry out the hit. It is believed that Chagra paid Kerns $45,000 for the Kerr contract.

By August 1979 a new judge, William Sessions (later to become Director of the FBI), took over as the presiding judge in the trial of Jimmy Chagra.

A jury convicted Chagra of "having engaged in a continuing criminal enterprise" and was handed down a 47-year sentence.

Jimmy Chagra was born Jamiel Chagra in El Paso, Texas and was the middle son of a Lebanese-American drug dealer. A friend called him "the bad penny" of the family. His two brothers, Joseph and Lee were well-respected lawyers in El Paso and were well-known in the legal community. His brother Lee was often the lawyer for a string of drug dealers who had no resistance in taking on such cases. Lee Chagra was killed in a 1978 Christmas Eve robbery in his law office. A total of $450,000 was taken during the robbery/murder and the money was supposed to have been cash Jimmy owed to mob boss Joe Bonnano, Sr. for a drug deal gone bad.

Jimmy's younger brother, Joe Chagra, who was also a lawyer in El Paso, was sentenced to six-and-a-half years in prison for his alleged role in the assassination of John Wood.

Jimmy started out running his father's carpet business, but it soon went bankrupt. He then made a sudden job change as a high-powered gambler in Las Vegas. He lived the good life at Caesar's Palace, where he lived under the alias "Jim Alexander." He was a high-stakes roller, often times winning or losing millions of dollars at a time on cards or craps. He then went into the drug smuggling business, transporting loads of marijuana from Columbia to the United States.

His illegal narcotics dealings caught the attention of the Justice Department, opening a case against him. He was indicted from two different grand juries in 1979 and arrested in Las Vegas and was scheduled to be tried in Judge Wood's courtroom.

With Jimmy Chagra now behind bars, the FBI mounted a nation-wide manhunt for Judge Wood's killer. The investigation was headed by John Lawn, who would later serve as the Director of the Drug Enforcement Agency (DEA).

While there were no eye-witnesses to the actual slaying of Judge Wood, a number of people in the vicinity of the crime saw a man leaving the scene. Later, under hypnosis, they were able to identify the suspect.

The man named as the prime suspect in the death of Judge Wood was an ex-con named Charles Harrelson. Harrelson had also been linked to a secret, and violent, gang in the South and, more importantly, to the events of November 22, 1963.

Charles Harrelson was born in Huntsville, Texas on July 23, 1938. He had four wives, worked as an encyclopedia salesman in California and was a professional gambler. As an adult, he served in the Navy from 1956-59 and trained for Naval Intelligence.

While in the Navy, he served in Key West and learned demolition work. His first arrest came at age 21 and began his first jail term at age 35.

In 1968 he was tried for the murder of Alan Harry Berg and was defended by the noted criminal lawyer, Percy Foreman. After a jury trial, Harrelson was acquitted in Angleton, Texas.

The Berg trial was not the only time Harrelson was accused of murder. In 1968 he was tried for killing Sam Degelia, Jr., a grain dealer who lived in Hearne, Texas. Degelia was killed in McAllen, Texas and Harrelson was charged with the murder. His trial ended with a deadlocked jury, but a co-defendant, Pete Scamardo, was found guilty of being an accomplice in Degelia's murder. He was sentenced to seven years in jail. In 1973 Harrelson was retried and found guilty, sentenced to 15 years in jail. In 1978 he was released on good behavior.

Charles Harrelson is the father of the noted actor of television and movies, Woody Harrelson. The younger Harrelson got his start in television when he played Woody Boyd in he hit series *Cheers*. He also played in movies such as *Kingpin* and *Natural Born Killers*.

Charles Harrelson was arrested by the FBI on September 1, 1980 and charged with the murder of Judge Wood. At the time of his arrest he was high on drugs. While in police custody, he admitted to the Wood slaying and, in an unexpected move, said that he had a hand in the assassination of President Kennedy.

In the investigation of Harrelson, the FBI uncovered his links, not only to the Chagra brother's criminal enterprise, but more importantly, to that of the Louisiana crime boss, Carlos Marcello. Joseph Chagra, Jimmy's brother, accepted a plea deal and agreed to testify against Harrelson. He pled guilty to conspiracy in return for a 10-year prison sentence and did not have to testify against Jimmy. The prosecutors in the case said that Jimmy had paid Harrelson $250,000 to kill Judge Wood.

While Harrelson was safely tucked away in prison, the feds began a wire-tap program against Jimmy Chagra, also serving time. They secretly worked with a fellow convict, Jerry Ray James, who was in the same jail as Chagra. James befriended Chagra and soon won over his confidence. What Chagra didn't know was that

Ray was wired.

Chagra provided details of his past criminal activities to Ray, including the details of the Judge Wood murder. Based on the wiretaps, the FBI, with warrant in hand, searched Chagra's home in El Paso finding a map of an area near Dallas where the murder weapon in the Wood case was said to be buried.

With Chagra's admissions on tape, he was indicted and later pleaded guilty of working with Kearns in the plot to kill U.S. Attorney James Kerr. In a related development, Jimmy's brother Lee was found dead in his office. It has been speculated that Lee Chagra was involved in the drug trade in the Southwest.

As the investigation of Charles Harrelson began, the FBI came up with tenuous links with members of organized crime. They discovered he had ties to the so-called "Dixie Mafia," an organization who had members from Tennessee to New Mexico. Through their information, the FBI learned that Jimmy Chagra "hired" the Dixie Mafia to kill Judge Wood for one million dollars.

Harrelson has also been associated with an underworld group, "The Company" (also the nickname of the CIA), which consisted of a few hundred mercenaries and outlaws. The Company is said to own ships and planes, and to have participated in drug smuggling shipments to South America.

More importantly, the brother of Mob Boss Carlos Marcello of New Orleans was also indicted along with Harrelson in the murder of Judge Wood.

In 1961, Marcello was deported from the United States to Guatemala on direct orders of Attorney General Robert Kennedy. He harbored a deep hostility to both Kennedy brothers and is believed, especially by the House Select Committee on Assassinations, that Marcello played a direct role in the president's death.

When he finally got around to discussing the JFK assassination, Harrelson had quite a story to tell. He said the Warren Commission was wrong in its conclusion that Lee Oswald was the killer of the president. He believed that Oswald was a "scapegoat," and the shots that killed the president came from the famous grassy knoll.

Harrelson had been the subject of considerable debate, possibly being one of the three "tramps" who were arrested in

Dealey Plaza in Dallas, Texas following the assassination of JFK. Harrelson always denied he was one of the tramps, even though he admitted in an interview there was a resemblance between him and one of them. He told a reporter that he was having lunch with a friend in Houston when the assassination took place saying, "I did not kill John Kennedy." When viewing the pictures of the three tramps, a forensic anthropologist said there was a 90 to 95% chance that Harrelson was one of the tramps. The three tramps were taken off a railroad car near Dealey Plaza in the aftermath of the assassination. They were later identified as Gus Abrams, 53; John F. Gedney, 38; and Harold Doyle, 32. After questioning by police, the three men were released.

When he was arrested, Harrelson had in his possession a business card of Russell Mathews, a close friend of Jack Ruby, the man who killed Lee Harvey Oswald. The House of Representatives Select Committee on Assassinations (HSCA) said Matthews was "actively engaged in criminal activity since the 1940s."

In 1981 Harrelson gave an interview to Dallas reporter Chuck Cook. When talking about the JFK assassination, Harrelson replied, "If and when I get out of here [jail] and feel free to talk, I will have something that will be the biggest story you ever had." When asked what he meant by that statement Harrelson said, "November 22, 1963. You remember that?"

On July 4, 1995 Harrelson and two other convicts, Gary Settle and Michael Rivers, attempted to escape from the Atlanta Federal Penitentiary by using a rope. Their effort failed and Harrelson was sent to the Supermax prison in Florence, Colorado, one of the most secure facilities in the nation. He died in prison on March 15, 2007 of an apparent heart attack. He never was able to reveal to reporter Cook what the "biggest story you ever had" was.

Jack Ruby with some of his strippers.

Chapter 12
Operation Northwoods

In December 2014 the Obama Administration reversed the United States' 50-year policy of non-negotiating with the Castro regime in Cuba and took steps to restore full diplomatic and commercial relations. In the ensuing 50 years, the United States recognized many of its one-time adversaries like Vietnam and China, while Cuba was left in limbo, a relic of the old Cold War.

With the thaw in diplomatic relations in place, newly released files dating back to the 1960s reveal a secret plan to invade Cuba. It was hatched by the Joint Chiefs of Staff to instigate a war with Cuba in order to remove the Castro government from power. The plan was the brainchild of JCS Chairman, Lyman Lemnitzer, which was passed along to Secretary of Defense Robert McNamara, where it died a natural death. But the plan as scheduled would have made Cuba the fall guy in a plot to kill many Americans and cause a preemptive American invasion of Cuba.

Dwight Eisenhower was president of the United States at the time Fidel Castro took over leadership of Cuba. At first, the Eisenhower Administration took a cautious look at Castro and tried working with him, after the corruption of the Batista era. But as time went on it became obvious Castro was not the democrat he proclaimed himself to be. Soon after taking over, Castro began to nationalize certain foreign-owned industries, closed down lucrative mafia casinos run by American gangsters and the final straw, as far as the Americans were concerned, began to make overtures to the Soviet Union. Something would have to be done as far as Castro was concerned, and to that extent, the first covert moves by the Eisenhower Administration began.

A secret group called the Cuba Task Force was formed in 1959 by the Eisenhower Administration that began the United States' first efforts to topple Castro from power in Cuba. Its original mandate was to design ways of overthrowing the Castro regime without any apparent U.S. involvement. The first formal meeting took place on March 9, 1959. One of the participants in the meeting was J.C. King, the head of the CIA's Western Hemisphere Division. King told the assembled men that unless Castro, his brother Raul and their most trusted lieutenant, Che Guevara were not eliminated soon, possible U.S. military intervention would be needed against Cuba. He also said there was a plot to attack the U.S. naval base at Guantanamo Bay in Cuba (this was one part of Operation North Wind). In reality there was no attack on the base, yet in that meeting, the seeds of future American clandestine intervention against Castro were set in motion.

On March 17, 1960 President Eisenhower signed a secret National Security Council Directive giving "A Program of Covert Action Against the Castro Regime" the green light.

The administration ordered the CIA to begin covert training of a number of Cuban exiles in the jungles of Guatemala under agency tutelage. Soon, a number of American military officers and staff were covertly sent to Guatemala to train the ragged, but eager, troops for an eventual invasion of their homeland. The seeds that were planted in 1960 in the jungles of Guatemala were the forerunner of the 1961 Bay of Pigs invasion.

During the summer of 1960 two assassination plots against Fidel Castro and his brother Raul were approved by the CIA. During the summer of 1960, at the time of the presidential campaign between Senator John F. Kennedy and Vice President Richard Nixon, the first CIA-Mob contacts were initiated using Robert Mahue as the go-between. The CIA-Mob trio of John Roselli, Sam Giancana and Santo Trafficante, Jr. would eventually become the contacts to try and kill Castro.

The seeds of Operation Northwoods were flouted in the last days of the Eisenhower Administration. The president told General Lemnitzer that he'd like to invade Cuba before John Kennedy was inaugurated president on January 20, 1961 if the Cuban's gave him the excuse he needed. If Castro did not provide one, then maybe the United States "could think of manufacturing something that would be generally acceptable." What the president was discussing was an attack on the United States by the United States that would instigate war fever in the country. Cooler heads prevailed and no attack was launched.

When John Kennedy was elected president in November

82

1960, his election was not cheered by many members of the top brass of the United States military. The Joint Chiefs were more accustomed to having Dwight Eisenhower in the White House. After all, Ike was a decorated military man who was the Supreme Commander of allied forces during the D-Day invasion of Europe in June 1944, and a West Point graduate. They understood Ike and he understood them. To them, Kennedy, despite his heroism in saving his crew of PT 109 after it was struck by a Japanese destroyer in the Solomon Islands campaign, was an upstart, not anywhere in Ike's league, despite the fact President Eisenhower had warned about the dangers of the "military industrial complex" in his farewell address to the country (apparently they weren't listening). The members of the Joint Chiefs were of one mind; that communism was inherently evil and it had to be eliminated at all costs.

The Chiefs also held JFK personally responsible for the failed invasion of Cuba at the Bay of Pigs in April 1961. The Bay of Pigs invasion had its beginning in the last days of the Eisenhower presidency and was carried out under Kennedy, despite his misgivings. The operation was run by the CIA over the objections of the Chiefs. In the aftermath of the botched invasion, JFK fired two top members of the CIA's hierarchy, Director Allen Dulles and General Charles Cabell who was the deputy director of the CIA at time of the invasion. After the Bay of Pigs invasion, JFK made this comment about the JCS to one of his aids, "Those sons-of-bitches with all the fruit salad just sat there nodding, saying it would work." He also told his friend and advisor, Arthur Schlesinger Jr., that in the future he would be "overawed by professional military advice."

Whether the president knew it or not, certain U.S. Army generals were actively working to undermine his leadership. In Germany the main opponent of the president was General Edwin Walker, a right-winger in his politics and a frequent critic of the new administration. General Walker was stationed in Augsburg, West Germany and commanded the 24th Infantry, one of the most efficient units in the army. Prior to the 1960 election, he provided the troops under his command with "guidance" in how they should vote, a clear violation of the military chain of command. He also gave to his troops material from the ultra-conservative John Burch Society, which hated Kennedy in particular, and liberals of all stripes. He was an ardent segregationist and opposed the integration of the public schools in Little Rock, Arkansas. He even made a slur against Kennedy's old college, Harvard University, calling it a place that bred communism.

General Walker was not the only top military man who was scheming against the new president. Added to the list was JCS Chairman Lemnitzer, Chief of Staff of the Army, General George Decker and the Chief of Naval Operations, Arleigh Burke, all of whom made derogatory comments about JFK behind his back.

General Lemnitzer was in favor of a United States backed military invasion of Cuba in order to get rid of Castro. He did not back the CIA funded Bay of Pigs operation, believing correctly that it would fail. The only way to get rid of Castro, in his mind, was a full-scale American invasion of Cuba. So what to do? In a secret meeting held at the Pentagon days before the new administration came into office, General Lemnitzer and the other members of the Joint Chiefs decided to take drastic action. What they approved was a plan to carry out an attack against the U.S. naval base at Guantanamo Bay, Cuba and blame the raid on Castro. With the "successful" attack against the Americans, the public would demand an invasion of the island in retaliation, thus precipitating a full-scale war against Cuba. On January 19, 1961 one day before John F. Kennedy was to take office as the 35th president of the United States, General Lemnitzer gave his approval of the idea. Unknown to the new president, his top military advisor was planning a war with another nation behind his back. This was the genesis of Operation Northwoods. Soon Operation Northwoods would morph into more than just an attack on Guantanamo—it would include attacks on American soil, the proposed downing of American aircraft, and other nefarious schemes, all with the purpose of going to war with Cuba.[1]

Before Operation Northwoods could take effect, the Kennedy Administration took one more effort to remove Castro from power. It was a CIA-run plan called Operation Mongoose, which would be overseen by Attorney General Robert Kennedy. Operation

[1] Bamford, James, Body of Secrets: *Anatomy of the Ultra-Secret National Security Agency*, Doubleday, New York, 2001, Page 71.

Mongoose was an all-purpose administration effort to remove Castro from power, including State, Defense, the Army, CIA, and The Voice of America among others. Newly released documents on the Kennedy era, show that Defense Secretary McNamara urged Castro be removed even if it meant killing him. The top man in the army responsible for Mongoose was General Edward Lansdale, who was a pioneer in the arts of guerilla warfare from his days in World War II. On January 19, 1962 the "Special Group," as they were called, met in Robert Kennedy's office to discuss the operation. Bobby urged its members to "spare no time, effort or manpower toward the overthrow of Castro's regime."

The CIA set up its covert operation's headquarters in Miami, Florida and called it JMWAVE. Soon JMWAVE would include the most elaborate paramilitary operation since the creation of the CIA in 1947. Working out of an abandoned site on the University of Miami complex, JMWAVE took on a life of its own. Some 400 agents, subagents and others began plotting the demise of Fidel Castro.

Heading JMWAVE was an ex-FBI agent named William Harvey, one of the CIA's top guns. Disliked by the Kennedy brothers, he was the one man capable of getting rid of Castro. JMWAVE soon had its own air force, navy, foot soldiers, radio communications apparatus, banking operation, etc. Harvey began sending teams of agents into Cuba to sabotage sugarcane fields, attack Russian and Cuban ships in port, and create as much havoc as possible.

After the end of the Cuban Missile Crisis in October 1962, the Kennedy Administration conducted a two-track foreign policy as far as Cuba was concerned. On the one hand, Operation Mongoose was "officially" ended, but separate exile raids against targets in Cuba continued. The other track was a secret outreach to the Castro government to see if hostile relations between the two nations could be reduced.

While all this was going on, the Senate Foreign Relations Committee wrote a secret report on right wing extremism in the military. The report dealt with the Joint Chiefs distrust of the new Kennedy team because of their liberal, internal policies and in their view, communist-leaning influences. In a chilling part of the report, the senators wrote of the dangers of a military takeover of the United States. One part of the report reads as follows: "Military officers, French or American, have some common characteristics arising from their profession, and there are numerous military fingers on the trigger throughout the world."

The Senate report paid particular attention to the right wing views of General Lemnitzer and other members of the JCS team. He told his fellow generals and admirals he had no faith in the civilian leadership, meaning JFK, saying "the problem was simply that the civilians would not accept military judgments."

In his last days as president, Dwight Eisenhower flouted a plan that was just like Operation Northwoods. He told General Lemnitzer he wanted to strike Cuba before Kennedy was inaugurated only if Castro provoked him. If Castro did not provide that excuse then maybe the United States "could think of manufacturing something that would be generally acceptable." The last straw, as far as Lemnitzer was concerned, came on February 26th when Robert Kennedy told him to stop all remaining attacks against Cuban targets because they were ineffective.

Soon Operation Northwoods was laid out in detail with the only caveat that any U.S. action "continues to hold good only as long as there can be reasonable certainty that U.S. military intervention in Cuba would not directly involve the Soviet Union." According to a Memorandum for the Chief of Operations, Cuba Project was "the desired resultant from the execution of this plan would be to place the United States in the apparent position of suffering defensible grievances from a rash and irresponsible government of Cuba and to develop an international image of a Cuban threat to peace in the Western Hemisphere."

One of these outrageous plans involved the liftoff of astronaut John Glenn on February 20, 1962 into space. General Lemnitzer's plan said if Glenn's spacecraft suffered a malfunction and was destroyed on liftoff, it would be blamed on the Cuban government. Lemnitzer wrote that "the objective is to provide irrevocable proof that the fault lies with the Communists, et al Cuba." This would take place "by manufacturing various pieces of evidence which would prove electronic interference on the part of the Cubans."

Other actions called for military incidents to be taken inside and outside the Guantanamo Naval Base. This included the blowing up of ammunition inside the base, starting fires, burning aircraft on the base, lobbing mortar shells from outside the base causing major damage, capturing bogus assault teams coming from the sea, capturing bogus militia groups inside Guantanamo, and destruction of a ship in harbor, like the incident that destroyed the USS *Maine* which started the Spanish-American War and blaming the Cubans,

The most outrageous of these plans was a series of terror campaigns inside the United States, including Florida and Washington, D.C. "The terror campaign could be pointed at Cuban refugees seeking haven in the United States. We could sink a boatload of Cubans en-route to Florida. We could foster attempts on lives of Cuban refugees in the United States to the extent of wounding in instances to be widely publicized. Exploding a few plastic bombs in carefully chosen spots, the arrest of Cuban agents and the release of prepared documents substantiating Cuban involvement also would be helpful in projecting the idea of an irresponsible government."[2]

Another aspect of Northwoods was "attacks" by Cuba on an ally of the United States in the Caribbean area. The proposed targets were Haiti, the Dominican Republic, Nicaragua or Guatemala. Staged raids against targets in the Dominican Republic called for attacks by "Cuban" forces against the Dominican Air Force, attacks by Cuban aircraft on Dominican sugarcane fields, the bogus shipment of Cuban arms to Guatemala which would be found.

Other fake incidents included, "the use of KGB-type aircraft by U.S. pilots could provide additional provocation. Harassment of civil air attacks on surface shipping and destruction of U.S. military drone aircraft by MIG-type planes would be useful as complementary actions. An F-86 properly painted would convince air passengers they saw a Cuban MIG, especially if the pilot of the transport were to announce such fact."

"It is possible to create an incident which will demonstrate convincingly that a Cuban aircraft has attacked and shot down a

---

[2] Report By The Department of Defense and Joint Chiefs of Staff Representative on the Caribbean Study Group to the Joint Chiefs of Staff on Cuba Project. March 9, 1962.

chartered civil airliner en-route from the United States to Jamaica, Guatemala, Panama or Venezuela. The destination would be chosen only to cause the flight plan route to cross Cuba. The passengers could be a group of college students off on a holiday or any grouping of persons with a common interest to support chartering a non-scheduled flight."

The CIA would use a plane which would take off from Eglin AFB in Florida and be painted with the exact numbers and identification markings as a real passenger plane. "At a designated time the duplicate would be substituted for the actual civil aircraft and would be loaded with the selected passengers, all boarded under carefully prepared aliases. The actual registered aircraft would be converted to a drone."[3]

These covert plans hatched by the JCS were both treasonous and highly illegal and if they had ever been brought to the attention of the public it would have made Watergate and the Iran-Contra scandal look like child's play. The Kennedy Administration would have been rocked to its knees and there is no telling how far it might have gone, possibly even destroying the fabric of the nation. The proposed action of carrying out terrorist attacks on American soil reeks with insanity, yet that was a major portion of Operation Northwoods. In the end, the plans were scuttled before they ever took place. Operation Northwoods is a precautionary tale as to just how far certain segments of the American military were willing to go in order to start a war with Cuba. That almost happened in October 1962 with the onset of the Cuban Missile Crisis which almost precipitated a world war with the Soviet Union. In the end, cooler heads prevailed and both the United States and the Soviet Union retreated from the brink of total nuclear war.

---

[3] Ibid.

Chapter 13
Who Was Jack Ruby?

On Sunday, November 24, 1963, two days after the assassination of President John F. Kennedy in the hot afternoon sun of Dealey Plaza in Dallas, Texas, another assassination was about to take place. Lee Harvey Oswald, the president's alleged assassin, was being transferred to the county jail from Dallas Police Headquarters where he had undergone interrogation since his arrest for the alleged murder of DPD officer J. D. Tippit. Throngs of newspaper and television reporters, along with their cameras, were zeroed in on Oswald and the two officers escorting him to a waiting car. The scene was being televised to the stunned nation who was just beginning to get a grasp on the murder of their president. As Oswald came into camera range, a reporter in the room was heard to shout out, "here comes the prisoner." Out of the corner of the crowd, a man wearing a suit and fedora hat lunged in front of Oswald and his escort and began firing at point- blank range. Oswald was hit in the stomach and collapsed in a heap. The assassin was quickly wrestled to the ground by police and taken into custody. Oswald was quickly put in an ambulance and taken to Parkland Hospital where President Kennedy had died, only two days before. The doctors were unable to save his life and he died, the case against him seemingly closed.

When the Warren Commission began its investigation into the Kennedy assassination, one area they looked into was the connection between Lee Oswald and Jack Ruby. When the investigation was over, the commission said that there was no relationship between both men, nor was there any connection on Ruby's part to members of organized crime in the United States. The jury is still out on the first charge, even though there had been reports over the years of Ruby meeting with Oswald at his nightclub on a few occasions. However, on the organized crime front, the Commission got it all wrong. Ruby was well connected to many members of organized crime since his days as a runner for Al Capone in Chicago. He also had connections with many members of the Mob who were associated with major crime bosses in the United States, including Jimmy Hoffa, Carlos Marcello and Santo Trafficante, all of whom were linked one way or another with the assassination of President Kennedy. He also had close ties to the underworld in Cuba, serving as a gunrunner to the anti-Castro Cuban operations and made a number of documented trips to Cuba.

Jack Ruby, born Jacob Rubenstein on March 19, 1911 was the fifth of eight children. His father, Joseph, immigrated to the United States from Poland, as well as Jack's mother, Fannie. Jack's early childhood was in Chicago, where the young Ruby children learned quickly to survive on the city's mean streets. Both parents argued frequently and finally separated. At age 11, the local Jewish Social Service Bureau sent Jack to the Institute for Juvenile Research because of his unruly behavior. In 1942, he and two siblings were sent to foster homes. He attended Chicago public schools, while getting into as many fights as he could.

In 1933 he and a few friends went to Los Angeles and San Francisco looking for work, but soon found themselves back in Chicago. Ruby became active in Local 20467 of the Scrap Iron and Junk Handlers Union. For three years, Ruby worked as a union organizer. On December 8, 1939 John Cook, the union's president, shot Leon Cook, the local's financial secretary. A jury on the grounds of self-defense acquitted him. Ruby's name was mentioned in the minutes of a union meeting on February 2, 1940 in which Ruby was quoted as saying he wanted to take over the union following Cook's demise. Following Cook's death, Ruby left the union.

In 1941 Ruby and associate Harry Epstein started a novelty business, which sold candy and gambling devices. While he was not a success in any of his business ventures, he did make friends with heavyweight boxer Barney Ross and attended many of his bouts.

In September 1941 Ruby joined the Army Air Forces and besides his routine training, continued to sell merchandise shipped to him from Chicago to his service buddies. After his discharge from the Army, Ruby came back home and went into business with his three brothers, but this venture also went bankrupt. It was at this time Ruby made a decision that was to change his life forever. He moved to Dallas, Texas in 1947, where almost 20 years later, his name would forever go down in history.

Jack went to Dallas to help his sister, Eva, run a nightclub called Singapore. Upon coming to Dallas, Eva Ruby met a man named Paul Roland Jones. Jones was in hot water with the law for the attempted bribery of the new sheriff of Dallas, Steve Guthrie. Jones was associated with the Chicago Mob that wanted to take over its share of gambling profits if he would look the other way. Guthrie said that Jack Ruby's name came up in his bribery investigation of Jones but nothing came of it. Ruby's first establishment of his own in Dallas was called the Silver Spur Club, which was the home away from home of various Chicago Mobsters including Paul Roland Jones. Later, Ruby would take over the Vegas Club. He later took control over the Carousel Club, which he managed with Ralph Paul. It was at the Carousel Club that many people say Ruby and Oswald secretly met.

While in Dallas, Jack made friends with both the local police and certain members of the Mafia, mostly from Chicago. Dallas Police Officers would frequently come into the Carousel Club, watch the strippers do their thing, have a few drinks and schmooze with Ruby. Ruby also met a man, Lewis McWillie, who was closely associated with the Mob, and its considerable ties to Cuba. McWillie would later become Ruby's best friend and introduced him to illegal gun running activities in Cuba. The Federal Bureau of Narcotics had observed Ruby's reputation in Dallas, and in 1956 Ruby became an undercover informer for them as a "contact for a large narcotics set-up operating between Mexico, Texas and the East." He also served briefly as an informer for the FBI, but supplied little significant information.

Ruby's considerable Cuban connections on behalf of the American Mob actually began in 1958, while Cuban dictator Batista was still in power. Before Castro took over power in Havana, the American Mob was supplying Castro with small arms and ammunition to fight his revolutionary battle against Batista. The Mob was having it both ways, still loyal to Batista, who was allowing them to continue their lucrative casino business in Cuba, while seeing the writing on the wall as far as how long the hated

Batista was to remain in power. Ruby served in the gunrunning organization of crime boss Norman "Roughhouse" Rothman, who also served Tampa Mob boss, Santo Trafficante. Rothman managed the popular Sans Souci Casino in Havana, which was run by Trafficante.

Ruby's most influential friend, as far as his Cuban activities were concerned, was Lewis McWillie. McWillie moved from Las Vegas to Havana in 1958 and immediately became intertwined with the Mob's gunrunning and anti-Castro activities. While in Havana, McWillie worked in various casinos and was associated with both Meyer Lansky and Santo Trafficante. The Warren Commission looked into the Ruby-McWillie connection and said, in their opinion, Ruby, who by then had formed a close friendship with McWillie, had only made one trip to Cuba to visit him in 1959. But a closer examination by the HSCA and other researchers postulates that Ruby made at least three trips to Cuba during that time period. The HSCA, looking at tourist cards from the Bureau of Immigration and Naturalization, point out that Ruby entered Cuba on August 8, 1959 and departed on September 11th. He re-entered Cuba on September 12th and left the next day. After his return to the United States, Ruby made two trips to both New Orleans and back to his home in Dallas.

The House Select Committee on Assassinations (HSCA), concluded that, "Ruby most likely was serving as a courier for gambling interests when he traveled to Miami from Havana for one day, returning to Cuba for a day, and then flying to New Orleans. The committee also deemed it likely Ruby met various organized crime figures in Cuba, possibly including some who had been detained by the Cuban government. In fact, Ruby told the Warren Commission that he was later visited in Dallas by McWillie and an Havana casino owner and they discussed the gambling business in Cuba."[1]

Another person who gave testimony to both the Warren Commission and the HSCA detailing Ruby's Cuban gunrunning connection was a Texan named Robert McKeown. In 1959 McKeown was arrested along with former Cuban president, Carlos Prio Socarrás, who lived in Dallas. McKeown told the FBI in 1959

---

[1] *The Final Assassinations Report*, Bantam Books, New York, 1979, Pages 184-185.

he received a call from a stranger named "Rubenstein" who lived in Dallas. Rubenstein told McKeown that he would offer him $15,000 if he could get three people released from Cuban jails. One of these individuals was most likely Santos Trafficante, who had been kept in prison by Castro after the fall of Batista. He also said that Ruby talked to him about the sale of jeeps to certain unnamed people in Cuba. In its report, the HSCA said that if McKeown's reports were true, Ruby was not in Cuba for vacation purposes as McWillie said he was. The HSCA also said when McKeown testified before the panel in executive session that, "McKeown's story did not seem credible, based on the committee's assessment of his demeanor."

While Ruby was in Cuba, there were persistent rumors he met with Mob boss Santos Trafficante who was in a Cuban jail. According to the HSCA's report, "The committee developed circumstantial evidence that makes a meeting between Ruby and Trafficante a distinct possibility, but the evidence was not sufficient to form a final conclusion as to whether or not such a meeting took place."

What are the facts in the case? The answer to this question came from a statement on November 26, 1963, four days after the assassination of the president. It came from a British journalist, John Wilson-Hudson, who had been in the same jail as Santos Trafficante. Wilson-Hudson said that he saw an "American gangster-type" named Ruby who visited Cuba in 1959. Wilson-Hudson said while in jail he met another American gangster named Trafficante, whom he got to know. Wilson-Hudson said Ruby frequently visited Trafficante while he was in jail. The CIA got wind of the report and decided Hudson's allegations were unworthy of a follow up. His reports never reached the Warren Commission, which never looked into Ruby's Mobster or Cuban connections very seriously. Unlike the Warren Commission, the HSCA did verify that Wilson-Hudson was in jail at the time Trafficante was incarcerated.

On June 6, 1959 Santos Trafficante was arrested by Cuban authorities for his illegal gambling activities and sent to detention at the Trescornia prison.

Lewis McWillie also testified that while Ruby was in Cuba

visiting him he, McWillie, made a visit to the Trescornia camp and saw the Mobster there. He said it was possible Ruby went to the prison but couldn't verify it.

When Santos Trafficante testified before the HSCA he said, "there was no reason for

Dallas. I never had no [sic] contact with him. I don't see why he was going to come and visit me."

The HSCA concluded the following regarding the alleged Ruby-Trafficante meeting and its implications: "The importance of a Ruby-Trafficante meeting in Trescornia should not be overemphasized. The most it would show would be a meeting, at that a brief one. No one has suggested that President Kennedy's assassination was planned at Trescornia in 1959. At the same time, a meeting or an association, even minor, between Ruby and Trafficante would not have been necessary for Ruby to have been used by Trafficante to murder Oswald. Indeed, it is likely that such a direct contact would have been avoided by Trafficante if there had been a plan to execute either the President or the President's assassin, but, since no such plot could have been under consideration in 1959, there would not have been a particular necessity for Trafficante—to avoid contact with Ruby in Cuba."

It was during this same time period (1959) that Jack Ruby contacted the FBI in Dallas saying he would be willing to provide the Bureau with information on Cuba on a "confidential basis." FBI agent Charles Flynn met with Ruby and opened a "potential criminal informant" file on Ruby, or PCI. Both Agent Flynn and Ruby met eight times between April and October 1959, which was the same time period that Ruby was in Cuba, meeting with Lewis McWillie and who knows what else. On November 6, 1959 Agent Flynn closed Ruby's PCI file because the information he gave was not particularly helpful.

Why Jack Ruby, if the evidence of his covert dealings on behalf of the Mob in Cuba is correct, would want to volunteer information to the FBI or the CIA would find useful, is hard to reconcile. When questioned by the HSCA, Agent Flynn said Ruby never discussed Cuba with him. Ruby, it seems, probably wanted to establish a certain relationship with the FBI for his own reasons, in the hope that sometime in the future he could use his informant contact as possible leverage with the Bureau in case he got into trouble with the feds.

For all of Ruby's Mob contacts, the most intriguing, as far as federal sources are concerned, is his supposed link to Mobster Johnny Rosselli. Rosselli was one of three Mobsters hired by the CIA to kill Fidel Castro. After Rosselli's mysterious death, federal sources in Florida, who were in on the investigation of Rosselli's passing, identified two Miami hotel rooms, which were said to be the places both Ruby and Rosselli met. These supposed meetings took place in the two months before the assassination of JFK.

Also, according to columnist Jack Anderson, Rosselli said he knew Ruby and that Rosselli said Ruby "was one of our boys." Rosselli, according to Anderson, also referred to Ruby as "the crazy Jew."

What is known for sure is that in the month prior to the assassination of JFK, Ruby was in constant phone contact with many members of organized crime, notably Dusty Miller. Miller was head of the Teamsters Union Southern Conference This was the same Teamsters Union headed by Jimmy Hoffa; Paul Dorfman; Irwin Weiner, a senior Teamster member who had close ties with the Chicago Mob headed by Sam Giancana; and Barney Baker, described by Robert Kennedy as "Hoffa's roving ambassador of violence." Also talking with Ruby during this time was Dave Yaras, a tough Cuban gunrunner, also a member of the Chicago Mob. He was also a close friend of Joseph Campisi, who ran a number of restaurants in Dallas, which was linked to the crime family of Carlos Marcello of New Orleans. Ruby's sister, Eva Grant, said that Campisi "was one of Ruby's closest friends." Campisi told the FBI he had been in contact with Ruby on the day before the president's assassination and had visited him in jail on November 30, 1963. Another Mob friend of Ruby's, Joseph Civello, was the representative of the Mob in Dallas and had known Ruby for 10 years.

Another Mob-related man, known to Ruby in one way or another, was Russell Mathews, who had ties to Joseph Campisi and Santo Trafficante. Ruby placed a call to Matthew's former wife on October 3, 1963 from Ruby's Carousel Club. Lenny Patrick was also called by Ruby sometime in late 1963. Federal authorities called him "a high ranking associate of the Chicago Mob." Patrick was also associated with Sam Giancana of Florida.

The Warren Commission, if it wanted to, had plenty of opportunity to examine Ruby's Mob ties. However, they chose not to do so and missed many opportunities to find out just why Ruby was having so many conversations with Mob related people in the months prior to the Kennedy assassination. The Warren Report said, "The Commission believes that the evidence does not establish a significant link between Ruby and organized crime."

On June 7, 1964, Chief Justice Earl Warren, Commission member Gerald Ford and staff lawyers interviewed Ruby in his jail cell. Ruby pleaded to Chief Warren to take him back to Washington because he did not feel safe in Dallas. He said he wanted to tell his story but did not want to do it in Dallas. Before the commissioners left, Ruby told them, "Well, you won't ever see me again. I tell you that a whole new form of government is going to take over the country, and I know I won't live to see you another time." While in prison, Ruby said he was involved in a conspiracy to kill Kennedy and the trail led to high government officials. He also feared that his gunrunning activities related to Cuba would become public knowledge.

When Jack Ruby was going to have his day in court, his first lawyer asked him if there was any person who could do him harm at trial. He mentioned a man named "Davis," a gunrunner to the anti-Castro Cubans. Davis turned out to be Thomas Eli Davis, who was active in the anti-Castro cause, a bank robber who was known to federal law enforcement authorities. At one point Davis met Ruby at his club and an association began.

When the president was killed, Davis was in North Africa and later arrested in Tangier, being held in relation to the Kennedy assassination. Moroccan authorities found in Davis' possession, "a letter in his handwriting which referred in passing to Oswald and the Kennedy assassination." Reports over the years have said that Davis was released from jail due to the intervention of a CIA asset known only as QJ/WIN, who was part of the CIA's Executive Action Project, an assassination plan that was run by CIA agent William Harvey.

The Warren Commission never looked into the alleged Ruby/

Davis connection to find out if their relationship went any further. Davis died in 1973 by electrocution while cutting a power line during a robbery.

On October 5, 1966 the Texas Court of Criminal Appeals overturned Ruby's conviction and ordered a new trial. He never got one. On December 9, 1966 Ruby was transferred to Parkland Hospital after complaining of coughing and nausea. He was diagnosed as having lung cancer that was inoperable. He died on January 3, 1967 taking with him his reasons for killing Lee Harvey Oswald and forever robbing the country of his knowledge, or lack thereof, in the murder of John F. Kennedy.

Fidel Castro.

Chapter 14
The Woman Who Tried
to Kill Castro

On a hot February day in 1959 the German liner *MS Berlin* made its way through the Straits of Florida and docked at one of the many piers along the Havana waterfront. As the bejeweled passengers watched the old city from the *Berlin's* railing, they noticed a small boat making steady progress toward the liner. When the boat became more visible they were astonished to see a number of men wearing fatigues, some carrying guns, dock next to the ship and climb aboard. Thinking they were about to be attacked, the high-strung passengers, some wearing their best gowns and suites, made a beeline toward the safety of their cabins.

The captain of the ship, Heinrich Lorenz, stood his ground as the boarding party arrived on deck. Captain Lorenz was astonished to see a number of bearded men walking toward him. He was more astonished when the leader of the group introduced himself as Fidel Castro, the new leader of Cuba. Castro told Captain Lorenz not to worry. He was a friend of America and only wanted to say hello to the newly arrived passengers. Temporarily mollified, Captain Lorenz offered them his hospitality and showed them around the ship.

Later that day, as the men joined the captain in his stateroom for dinner, he introduced Fidel to his lovely 18-year old daughter, Marita, who had accompanied her father on the journey. That innocent introduction began one of the most bizarre plots devised by the American government to kill Fidel Castro involving one of the men, Frank Sturgis, who later was arrested in the Watergate break-in.

Castro took immediate liking to Marita and before leaving he ship asked Captain Lorenz if Marita could stay in Cuba and work as his private secretary. Captain Lorenz said no and the ship sailed to New York.

As far as Marita was concerned, she soon forgot about the bearded men who came to visit her father's ship. But Fidel Castro had other plans for this lovely young girl and he set wheels in

99

motion that would bring her back to his arms in Havana.

Marita Lorenz was born on August 18, 1939 in Bremen, Germany. Her father was a German citizen and her mother an American. Unknown to Marita, Castro's agents in New York had been following her around and knew where she was living. One day a few of Castro's men arrived at her brother's home in New York and asked her to come back to Cuba, where Fidel needed her to work as his personal secretary. Just why Marita agreed to return to Cuba with Castro's agents is not known, but years later Marita said of her decision, "I was very idealistic then. I was going on an adventure and to my first job. I was going to help the new government. Instead, I became Castro's plaything."

She left New York on a Cubana Airline plane that had been sent especially for her return. She was escorted to the 24th floor of the Havana Hilton Hotel where she would stay. She had no real freedom in Havana and was essentially a prisoner in her room, guarded by armed soldiers who stood outside her door. She passed the time by learning Spanish and looking out at the blue Caribbean. If this was what being Castro's secretary meant, Lorenz probably regretted her decision to return to Cuba more than once.

As time went on Marita became pregnant with Castro's child. She asked her father to contact the American Embassy to intercede on her behalf, but they could do nothing.

During a time when Marita was at the Riveria Hotel in Havana, an American who said he could help her get out of Castro's clutches approached her. He told her he was with the American Embassy and a meeting was arranged. That man was Frank Fiorini, a.k.a. "Frank Sturgis." That introduction was the beginning of a clandestine relationship between Marita and Sturgis. The connection would take both of them into the murky world of international espionage, deception and into the middle of the CIA's undeclared war on Fidel Castro. It would also bring Marita Lorenz into the seamy world of the plots to kill President John Kennedy.

As time went on, Marita was able to steal a number of files from Fidel's safe, giving them to Sturgis. She met with Sturgis about five times while in Cuba. What she did not know was that Sturgis was working as an Air Force officer for Castro.

Marita's pregnancy was not going well and Sturgis arranged for her to be flown to New York City for medical treatment. After her recovery she met with Sturgis at the FBI's New York office on East 69th Street. During her congressional testimony, Ms. Lorenz had this to say about that meeting at the FBI's headquarters:

"This meeting, we had a long discussion in the private office and they asked me to return to Cuba to take whatever papers I could from Fidel Castro's suite. Since I had the uniform and the Cubana Airlines were still running at the time, it was early enough for me to get back in and I agreed to go. I wanted to talk to Fidel anyway but they timed it such where I would have access to the suite while he was at a different part of the island."[1]

According to Lorenz, it was at that time she was brought into the world of U.S. intelligence, working for the CIA, FBI and the NYPD. Marita believed, wrongly it turned out, that Castro was bent on killing her and for revenge she agreed to take on undercover operations for the CIA, including providing guns for the Cuban underground. In time she would be thrust right into the CIA's secret plans to assassinate Castro, a plan that she readily agreed to take on.

The CIA's plan was to have Marita return to Cuba and resume her relationship with him. However, her main purpose was to assassinate Castro by placing poison capsules in his drink. She was given assurances by the Agency that once the deed was done she would be safely taken out of Cuba.

The two men who recruited Marita for the Castro assassination hit were Frank Sturgis and Alexander Rorke, whom she believed worked for the CIA. It was Frank Sturgis who provided her with the poison pills, which were placed in a bottle of cold cream, which she carried in her luggage. She was to put these pills in Castro's food or drink at an appropriate time.

After getting the poison pills form Sturgis, Lorenz boarded a Cubana Airlines plane in New York and landed safely in Havana, unrecognized. She entered Castro's office and found him gone. She then began rifling through the files, taking what she thought

[1] Marita Lorenz Testimony. # 180-10118-10129.

was the most interesting material. Before she was able to leave the hotel, Castro returned and asked her why she left Cuba. She said she wanted to visit her family. A while later Castro fell asleep and Marita retrieved the poison pills and was ready to place them in Castro's mouth. She went into the bathroom to find the pills, but was shocked to see that they had dissolved and were now useless. She left the sleeping Castro and hurriedly left the hotel, her first mission as a CIA assassin, over.

Years later, when Castro learned of her attempt to kill him he asked Marita, "You couldn't kill me. You would never do that would you?" She told him she could not have carried out the plan.

In late December 1960, Lorenz arrived in Florida where she contacted both Frank Sturgis and Alexander Rorke. An FBI informant was watching them and wrote a memo saying, "Rorke and Lorenz were going to join the anti-Castro movement of FIORINI (Sturgis), a de-naturalized American citizen who lost his citizenship for spying in the Cuban Revolutionary Army of CASTRO. (The informant) stated that Lorenz was reportedly in the protective custody of the FBI."

Marita Lorenz was now right in the middle of the anti-Castro activities that were sprouting up in South Florida as the secret CIA-Mob efforts to kill Castro got underway. She worked alongside Frank Sturgis and Gerry Hemming, a soldier of fortune that had his own private mercenary for hire business. Also joining the anti-Castro cause were other men who would, years later, be associated with the break-in of the Watergate building; Howard Hunt, Bernard Barker and Eugenio Martinez.

While in Florida, Marita conducted an interview with Paul Meskill of the *New York Daily News*. In the April 20, 1975 edition of the paper, Miss Lorenz gave the fullest accounting of her role in the anti-Castro plots at this time. She told the journalist there were many discussions about killing Castro in the pre-Bay of Pigs days and talk of how to carry out the deed was rampant among the exiles. When asked if a plot was hatched to kill Castro she said, "Sure, we all did. We were going to bomb him during one of his speeches. We were going to fly over and drop it right on top of him. We had the bomb, the plane. I was going to go along. We were all set, but it was called off. Somebody stopped it. That's all

I know."[2]

Over a decade later, when the anti-Castro plots had faded into the background, and with John Kennedy dead, Paul Meskill of the New York *Daily News,* broke the story of Lorenz's part in the Castro plots by writing a story with the incredible headline, "CIA Sent Bedmate to Kill Castro in 60." The article was picked up by many of the leading papers in the country and when Marita saw it, she went ballistic. She blamed Sturgis for aiding Meskill in his stories and said that she feared for her life.

Lorenz now turned for help to Gaeton Fonzi, a former newspaperman who was then working as a staff investigator for the Senate committee investigating the assassinations of President Kennedy and Martin Luther King. Fonzi's specialty on the committee was to look into the Cuban angle to the president's murder. Lorenz asked Fonzi, whom she knew from her days living in south Florida, to ask the Justice Department if they could provide protection for her. To her relief, that protection was granted.

Despite the wealth of information that Marita had concerning the anti-Castro activities during the early 1960s, the HSCA did not find her story credible and failed to call her for testimony.

Later however, Marita was called to testify before the HSCA and what she told committee members was nothing but sensational. Her story went like this: One week before the president's death, Lorenz claimed that she, along with Frank Sturgis, Lee Harvey Oswald, Gerry Hemming, anti-Castro leaders Orlando Bosh and Pedro Diaz Lanz, left Miami in a multi-car caravan bound for Dallas. She asserted that the members of the group were a radical organization called Operation 40, an assassination squad that was then operating against Castro. Now Lorenz' story got even better. She said while the group was in a Dallas hotel they were met by two men whose names would play an integral part in the Kennedy assassination drama, E. Howard Hunt and Jack Ruby. Hunt, according to Lorenz, came with an unspecified amount of cash, which he left with them. Shortly before the assassination, Lorenz returned to Miami, where a few days later, she heard the news that JFK had been killed. She further said Sturgis told her she "missed" the big time, meaning the assassination of the president. In her

---

[2] Meskill, Paul, "American Mata Hari Who Duped Castro," *N.Y. Daily News,* April 20, 1975.

testimony before the committee, she said that Lee Oswald was not a full-fledged member of the CIA, but called him an "associate."

The claim made by Marita that Oswald was involved with other, anti-Castro mercenaries in Florida prior to 1963, has never been fully verified, although second-hand rumors putting him in Miami were widely publicized after the president's assassination.

In her testimony before the HSCA, Miss Lorenz said she met Oswald in Miami in early 1961 and that Sturgis was running the training of his cadre. Sturgis shot down her recollections of meeting Oswald at that time, according to an FBI document on the event. Sturgis heard of Oswald's visit to Miami from a newspaper reporter named Jerry Buchanan, who worked for various newspapers in south Florida such as the *Daily News* of Fort Lauderdale and the *Sun Sentinel* of Pompano Beach. The document regarding Sturgis' comment on the Buchanan allegations reads as follows:

> It was pointed out to Mr. Fiorini (Sturgis) that according to Jerry Buchanan, Lee Harvey Oswald was one of the members of the FPCC who was engaged in the fight in Bayfront Park, and further, that Oswald was again in Miami as of March 1963 distributing pro-Castro literature.
>
> Mr. Fiorini stated that he considered these allegations by Jerry Buchanan as ridiculous and without any foundation in fact. He said that as head of the International Anti-Communist Brigade, he would certainly have learned of such incidents at Miami from other members of the Brigade. Mr. Fiorini stated that this was the first he had heard that Jerry Buchanan claimed that Oswald had been engaged in a fight with members of the Brigade in Bayfront Park, Miami.[3]

Lorenz's testimony before the HSCA was contentious to say the least. A number of congressmen who questioned her found her testimony rather hard to believe, to put it mildly. She touched a raw nerve among the committee members, describing her participation in the poison pill plot to kill Castro, her involvement with Operation 40, her allegations that she participated in a caravan to Dallas one week before JFK was killed and most astonishing, her claim she

[3] Commission Document 1020, 11 May 1964: Re-Oswald-Russia/Cuba.

met and trained with Lee Oswald in Miami.

None of her audacious allegations were ever authenticated, but her story makes good reading. What is undeniable is that the CIA used Marita Lorenz in a plot to kill Fidel Castro, all of whom failed to live up to their attended goal.

Chapter 15
The Zimmermann Telegram

Throughout its history, the United States has gone to war through different routes. In March 1770 British troops fired upon a crowd of people in Boston, setting the fire that would become America's War of Independence. On December 7, 1941 Japanese warplanes attacked the United States Naval base at Pearl Harbor in Hawaii killing over 2,000 people. On January 16, 1917 a coded message sent by German foreign minister, Arthur Zimmermann, via the German ambassador in Washington to the German minister in Mexico City, the unknowing impetus that would allow the then neutral United States war with Germany and its allies. This so-called Zimmermann Telegram hatched by Germany had far-reaching and unintended consequences for the outcome of World War I and the rest of history during the 20th century.

When World War I began with the assassination of Archduke Franz Ferdinand, the heir to the throne of the Austria-Hungary Empire, by Serbian Nationalists on June 28, 1914, the United States did not partake in the war and would not do so until three years later. While millions on both sides died in the blood-soaked trenches of the Western Front, the United States remained out of the conflict. In 1916 President Woodrow Wilson was elected to a second term in the White House on the slogan, "He kept us out of war." The British, with their far-flung navy, managed to blockade its ports, thus, effectively protecting Britain from defeat. In February 1917, fearing the worst, Germany broke its restrictions on submarine warfare, the so-called Sussex Pledge, and began attacking allied ships. In response the United States broke off diplomatic relations with Germany. All this took place after German U-boats sunk the unarmed French boat, the *Sussex* in the English Channel in March 1916. President Wilson threatened to sever diplomatic relations with Germany (which we eventually did) unless the German government stopped attacking all passenger ships and allowed the crews of enemy merchant ships to abandon their vessels before any attack took place. On May 4, 1916 Germany temporarily accepted Wilson's terms.

By its resumption of unrestricted submarine warfare, the German government unwittingly began the process of its eventual defeat when the United States entered the war in 1917. To that effect, on January 31, 1917 the German ambassador to the United States, Count Johann von Bernstorff gave Secretary of State Robert Lansing a letter stating the new German naval policy.

When the war started, the British had a distinct advantage over the Germans as far as code breaking was concerned. The British had a well-established espionage system that went back to Elizabethan times. At that time, all cable messages from Europe to the United States went through trans-Atlantic cables that passed under the English Channel. The British used their knowledge of these cables to snoop on the secret diplomatic messages sent from Berlin to its ambassador in Washington, D.C. In order to gain a step on the Germans, the British used a cable ship, the *Teleconia,* to sever five of the cables carrying secret messages under the channel. These secret messages were now passed on to British code breakers who now had a distinct advantage over their German counterparts in Berlin. The Germans now had to send their messages by radio from their wireless station in Nauen, near Berlin. The British code breakers from unit MI8 now had access to their once secret message.

The unit that worked to crack German codes was called Room 40, which was located in the Old Admiralty Buildings in Whitehall. The Royal Navy used the offices of Room 40 to decipher German codes, but soon expanded in other directions as well. The Royal Navy asked the director of naval education, Sir Alfred Ewing to take on the task of making Room 40 its primary code breaking service. Through hard work the analysts were able to break the German codes, giving them a distinct advantage. Their first real break came with the destruction of a German cruiser, *Magdenburg,* on October 13, 1914. Found on the boat was a codebook containing hundreds of pages of columns with five digit and three digit groups, which were a substitution code, used by the Germans. Another windfall came when the British captured a codebook from a German merchant ship near Melbourne, Australia. This was especially important because the

British now had a second key that enabled them to decipher all German naval communications. By November 1914 Room 40 analysts broke the German Navy code and were able to read all their secret communications.

Overseeing Room 40 was Admiral Sir William Hall, called "Blinker" because of his nervous tick. He was Director of Naval Intelligence from 1914 to 1917. The information culled from Room 40 under Hall's direction, was used in espionage operations during the war and he melded the unit into a first-rate intelligence gathering operation. Room 40 was such an invaluable tool that in time they were able to decipher almost all the messages sent by the German Navy to their surface ships, as well as their submarines, along with their overseas consulates and embassies. This was instrumental in picking up the Zimmermann Telegram when it was sent. Analysts at Room 40 were also able to read messages going to the United States, a fact that was not shared with their American allies.

On January 17, 1917 analysts at Room 40 intercepted a coded German diplomatic message from Foreign Secretary Arthur Zimmermann to Count von Bernstorff, the German ambassador in Washington. They were able to intercept this message in an unusual way. Sweden, which was neutral in the war (but really pro-German), was transmitting messages for Germany. However, the British were able to tap into the Swedish cable traffic to South America where it then passed by England. Zimmermann sent his cable via this passage to the German ambassador in Buenos Aires, Argentina with instructions to send it to its final destination, the German embassy in Washington. As the telegram was being sent in this way, the code breakers in Room 40 managed to get their hands on it.

The message was sent a second time via an unusual route. Arthur Zimmermann sent it to the American ambassador in Berlin, via telegraph, to the State Department in Washington, which then gave it to the German embassy. This strange routing took place because President Wilson allowed German diplomatic cables to be sent to Washington when the German government made a fuss, because they were then unable to send secure messages to the United States. This was done because President Wilson, at the time, was trying to mediate an end to the war and wanted to give the Germans a small olive branch. This second message went to Copenhagen, Denmark, then to London, and finally to Washington. Instructions were given that the message was then to be forward to Mexico City.

In Room 40 in London, two of their most efficient code breakers, Reverend William Montgomery and Nigel de Grey, began to decipher the telegram. They noticed at the top of the telegram a series of numbers, 13042, that was a variation of another code group numbered 13040. This was a diplomatic code that Room 40, having gotten hold of the German codebook 13040, was now able to read. As they began reading the message they noticed a few words that kept cropping up: Germany, Japan and Mexico, although they had no idea what that meant. As they began to crack the missive, they became more and more concerned at what they were reading. Part one of the message revealed that Germany was now going to resume "unrestricted" submarine warfare against shipping in the Atlantic beginning on February 1st. This now allowed Germany to attack any ship, even from the neutral nations they encountered at sea. On February 3rd, the American ship, the *Housatonic,* was attacked at sea with no prior notice. In 1915 the Germans attacked the luxury liner, *Lusitania,* which killed over 1,000 passengers, including 114 Americans. President Wilson did nothing after the sinking of *Lusitania* and his patience was now running out.

This was a dangerous maneuver on Germany's part. The United States, while still neutral, were sending supplies to Britain via sea. The Germans had to know if they sank any American ships they risked the chance that the U.S. would now enter the war on Britain's side.

Just what Arthur Zimmermann meant in the message about Mexico still baffled the code breakers. Was Germany giving Mexico secret instructions to take military actions against America?

Admiral Hall was given access to the message but he didn't want to immediately hand it over to the American's. He was reluctant to do so because he didn't want Washington to know that Room 40 was reading the intercepts. Hall pulled strings and had a contact in the Mexico City telegraph office give him a copy of the encoded message sent from the German embassy in Washington. By using confusing information on the top of the message, the British were able to alter some of the headings before sending it on to Washington. When the State Department finally got a copy of the Zimmermann Telegram, the Americans were now convinced the message had come from Mexico, and Germany had also had been notified to that effect.

Two weeks later, on February 22nd, the British gave the Zimmermann Telegram to American ambassador Walter Page. The British told Page they had no objection to the message going public but that they didn't want its source (them) to be revealed. Ambassador Page gave his okay and sent the note to President Wilson.

The Zimmermann Telegram reads as follows:

"We intend to begin on the first of February unrestricted submarine warfare. We shall endeavor in spite of this to keep the United States of America neutral. In the event of this not succeeding, we make Mexico a proposal of alliance on the following basis: make war together, make peace together, generous financial support and an understanding on our part that Mexico is to reconquer the lost territory in Texas, New Mexico, and Arizona. The settlement in detail is left to you. You will inform the President of the above most secretly as soon as the outbreak of war with the United States of America is certain and add the suggestion that he should, on his own initiative, invite Japan to immediate adherence and at the same time mediate between Japan and ourselves. Please call the President's attention to the fact that the ruthless employment of our submarines now offers the prospect of compelling England in a few months to make peace." Signed, ZIMMERMANN.[1]

The Associated Press then published the Zimmermann Telegram and gave it to the major papers of the day. The public was not aware of the secret way the telegram was decoded or how

[1] TeachingAmericanHistory.org. The Zimmermann Note to the German Minister to Mexico, January 19, 1917.

the United States got it. The culprit was indeed Germany and the public outrage of the news went viral.

War fever gripped America and on April 6, 1917, the United States Congress declared war on Germany and its Entente allies. America was now in the war and its outcome would never be in doubt.

The German government conducted an investigation on how the Americans had gotten the Zimmermann Telegram, not realizing that the code breakers in Room 40 had broken their codes. One of the suppositions they made was that some person might have broken into the safe in the German embassy in Washington and stole the code from the safe where it was kept. The report noted that the combination lock, which hadn't been changed since 1902, was old and worn and that an intruder could have easily figured out the combination. However, they noted that no break-in at the embassy had taken place during this time. The report also said it was possible that someone in the embassy had helped unauthorized, unknown persons steal the code. Only 12 people had access to the code room until the fall of 1916.[2]

The German investigation posits the leak might have come from someone inside the consulate in Mexico City. They pointed the finger at 12 mid-level employees who worked in the consulate as possible culprits, although they were never named. The report states:

> "The perpetrator would then have either sold the copy or a translation to a foreign agent or, without negative intentions, have given it to an acquaintance who for his own part betrayed it. The dispatch is also so short that someone with a good memory can certainly remember the text after one reading. The perpetrator could have communicated the final section of telegram no. 157 at the same time. In so doing he would have erroneously given the date as January 17. This date was of no special interest, while the date of the Mexico dispatch was significant in order to be able to verify the message through comparison with the enciphered telegram that had been sent"[3]

[2] The Zimmermann Telegram, Cryptologic Quarterly, Unclassified.
[3] Ibid, Page 51.

The German report of the leaking of the Zimmermann Telegram is like any other investigation where events have decidedly gone wrong. They concluded that it was impossible to believe that anyone in the chain of command could have been responsible for leaking of the document.

The success of the code breakers in Room 40 in deciphering the Zimmermann Telegram is the real heroes in the drama that played itself out. The Germans were so sure that their codes were so secure that no one could break them (the same fallacy was displayed again in World War II when the German Enigma code was broken). Their huge miscalculation in devising a scheme that would bring Mexico into the war with the United States was never a reality. Instead, the unmasking of Arthur Zimmermann's telegram brought the United States into the conflict and ensured Germany's defeat.

Chapter 16
What Happened to
the USS *Maine*?

One of the lingering mysteries in American history is what happened to the battleship USS *Maine,* which sank in Havana Harbor on the night of February 15, 1898. In the ensuing years following the sinking of the ship, three investigations took place attempting to find out exactly what happened that fateful night. Did a mine, or an internal or external explosion cause the ship's destruction? Was sabotage involved in the disaster and if so, who was responsible? Whoever was responsible for the sinking of the USS *Maine* could not have known the consequences of their actions. Like the events following the release of the Zimmermann Telegram by British code breakers in Room 40 in London, which caused the United States to become involved in World War I, the result of the sinking of the USS *Maine* thrust the U.S. into the Spanish-American War. The United States defeated Spain in mostly naval battles in the Pacific. The outcome of the war made the United States an up-and-coming world power that would shape the history of the 20ᵗʰ century.

What led up to the USS *Maine* being in Cuba? Cuba was ruled by Spain for over 400 years and governed the island nation with an iron fist. Human rights for the native population were not one of their prime interests and the people soon began a guerilla campaign to resolve their differences. The United States backed the guerillas but did nothing materially to help them. Their revolt however, did attract the attention of the so-called "Yellow Press," which covered the revolt in detail. The New York *Journal* and the New York *World* reported the revolt with screaming headlines, blaming the war directly on the shoulders of Spain. The owner of the New York *Journal,* noted publisher William Randolph Hearst, saw a good story in the making and coverage of the Cuban rebellion caused his circulation to soar as they continued reports on the ever-growing conflict. After the sinking of the *Maine,* the headline in the New York *Journal* cried, "Remember the Maine!

To hell with Spain!"

Inside Cuba the situation was going from bad to worse. The Governor General, Valeriano Weyler, started the Reconcentration Policy, whereby by huge numbers of the Cuban population who lived in the country, were brought into the cities to live. They were not allowed to bring food or their livestock and were restricted as to where they could, their movements also hindered. The situation grew from bad to worse, as the Cuban authorities were unable to handle the ever-deteriorating conditions on the ground. People began to die by the hundreds, food ran out and soon the failed policy was rescinded. This resulted in the resignation of Governor Weyler who was replaced by a more moderate man, Governor General Ramon Blanco. Blanco eventually rescinded Weyler's harsh policy, which only allowed the rebels in Cuba to increase their rebellion against Spanish rule. All this was reported in the American newspapers and American sympathy soon swelled to the rebels' side.

In Washington, President Grover Cleveland took measures to alleviate the situation, as far as Cuba was concerned. He ended the policy of sending American warships to Cuba, in part, to try and calm the situation in that country.

The top American diplomat in Cuba in 1897 was consul general Fitzhugh Lee. Lee was concerned about the safety of the large number of Americans who lived in Cuba, fearing for their lives as the insurrection grew. Many of the Americans were involved in the sugar trade, which was a large source of income for American companies. Consul Lee cabled Washington saying the rebels were burning sugar cane fields owned by American companies and urged the new McKinley Administration to consider military actions against Cuba. He urged Washington to reverse the ban on naval visits to Cuba in order to show the flag and support the rebels.

At the time these events were going on in Cuba, the USS *Maine* was stationed in Key West, Florida in order to be ready for any possible deployment to Cuba. The captain of the *Maine* was Charles Sigsbee who commanded a total of 354 men. The USS *Maine* was not Sigsbee's first command. In 1886 he was the officer in charge of the USS *Kearsage*. After complaints the ship was not in proper working order, an investigation accused him of not properly carrying out naval regulations. The *Maine* was part of the Navy's North Atlantic Squadron and soon sailed for their winter base at the small island of Dry Tortugas at the end of the Florida Keys. They were to wait there for any request to go to Cuba if ordered to do so. When Captain Sigsbee arrived in Key West he had an order directing him to sail to Havana on a "friendly" visit. It is not known exactly why Sigsbee was ordered to Havana, but one reason was most likely to show the American flag and to ostensibly protect the American's who lived in Cuba.

While all this was going on, it seems Captain Sigsbee and Consul Fitzhugh Lee were in secret communication with each other. If Lee sent a message that read "two dollars," the *Maine* was to be put on immediate alert to sail for Cuba in two hours. If Lee sent a further message that "Vessels might be employed elsewhere," Captain Sigsbee would depart Florida at once. While this was going on, riots spread across Cuba and Fitzhugh sent the second message to Captain Sigsbee. The riots, it turned out, were not directed toward the Americans living in Cuba, but carried domestically by people who were turning against the government.

The *Maine* arrived in Havana harbor at about 10:00 a.m. on January 25, 1898. No one was more surprised at the arrival of the ship than Fitzhugh Lee, who had no idea the ship was coming, despite his secret communications with Captain Sigsbee. John Caldwell who worked for the New York *Herald* told Consul Lee only that morning of the ships arrival. Caldwell came up with a cockamamie story in which he said the *Herald* should send the needed cartridges for his revolver to him because he could not get them in Cuba. He sent a message to the paper saying, "Camera received but no plates; please rush by next steamer." Caldwell said the paper decoded the message incorrectly, believing it to mean "U.S. Consulate under attack." Caldwell later said he believed this message was sent to Washington and believed by higher authority. The answer Caldwell got back was, "Send report Cuban cane crop. Want for main section," which meant that the *Maine* be sent to Cuba.[1]

Nothing untoward happened to the ship and crew of the *Maine*

[1] McSherry, Patrick, *USS Maine-Mission in Havana,* Maine at Havana, worldwide web.

for the next three weeks. The men enjoyed the sunshine while Captain Sigsbee met with Consul Lee to work out what to do next. That all changed dramatically on the night of February 15, 1898 when a huge eruption cascaded over the ship. One minute all was quiet, the next all was bedlam. Men and machinery were tossed around like children's toys being thrown by unruly toddlers. At the time of the explosion, Captain Sigsbee was in his cabin writing a letter to his wife when he heard a sound he described as, "a bursting, rending, and crashing sound or roar of immense volume, largely metallic in character." Men frantically dived off the ship while the rest turned into a hot configuration. Of the 354 men on board, 266 died.

Once safely on shore, Captain Sigsbee hurriedly sent a cable to Washington telling what had happened. Privately he believed his ship was sunk as a result of sabotage, but he wrote saying, "Public opinion should be suspended until further report." The Hearst newspapers failed to heed Sigsbee's warning and blasted the news on its front pages. That sentiment was further echoed in Washington as the Assistant Secretary of the Navy, Theodore Roosevelt, said in pubic, "the *Maine* was sunk by an act of dirty treachery on the part of the Spanish." The headline in the New York *Journal* blared, "Destruction of the Warship *Maine* Was the Work of an Enemy. The Spanish, it is believed, arranged to have the *Maine* anchored over one of the harbor mines." When William Randolph Hearst first learned about the sinking of the *Maine,* he asked one of his editors if he heard the news. The man said no and Hearst immediately told him what happened and instructed him to print the story in bold type. Hearst later told a friend after hearing the news, "Please spread the story all over the page. This means war." The next day's edition of the paper carried seven pages about the circumstances surrounding the sinking of the ship. Since news was scarce, Hearst had his reporters made up wild-eyed accounts of what they believed happened. The Hearst writers speculated loudly that a mine was responsible for sinking the ship without any proof.

In that regard, Philip Alger, a professor at the U.S. Naval Academy, told a reporter for the Washington *Star,* "No torpedo such as is known in modern warfare can of itself cause an explosion as powerful as that which destroyed the *Maine.* We know of no instances where the explosion of a torpedo or mine under a ship's bottom has exploded the magazine within."[2]

Alger went on to say he believed the ship was sunk by accident. He pointed out the coal bunker on board the ship was right next to the gun powder magazine on the *Maine,* and that an unintentional spark might have ignited the powder and set off the explosion.

President William McKinley was more cautious. He said of the ship's destruction, "We must learn the truth and endeavor, if possible, to fix the responsibility. The country can afford to withhold its judgment and not strike an avenging blow until the truth is known." Teddy Roosevelt replied in kind: "The president has no more backbone than a chocolate éclair." Theodore Roosevelt was the Assistant Secretary of the Navy at the time of the *Maine* explosion and was one of the main proponents of war against Spain. Roosevelt wanted to protect the Navy at all costs and it was not in his interests if it was determined there was a fatal flaw in the design of the ship that led to its destruction. Shortly before the incident, Roosevelt had on his desk a copy of a letter from Lt. Commander Richard Wainright, the executive officer on the ill-fated ship. He wrote to Roosevelt saying the Navies of France, Germany and England took precautionary measures, and Italy insulated their powder magazines from any fire that might accidentally erupt on their ships, including a spark from the coalbunkers. Roosevelt did nothing about the warning. His boss, Secretary of the Navy John Long, was well aware of the potential trouble that could be caused from an accidental spark coming from the gun powder room and told others about his concerns.

The government of Spain initially wanted to have joint investigations into the cause of the sinking of the ship but Washington rejected the offer. Instead, the Navy appointed a board of three officers to look into what happened in Havana Harbor. Roosevelt tried to silence Alger who said the ship was sunk by accident. Roosevelt wrote a letter to Captain Charles O'Neil, Chief of the Bureau of Ordnance, saying, "Don't you think it inadvisable for Prof. Alger to express opinions in this way? The fact that Mr. Alger happens to take the Spanish side, and to imply that the

[2] Thomas, Evan, *The War Lovers: Roosevelt, Lodge, Hearst, And The Rush to Empire, 1898,* Little Brown & Co., New York, 2010, Page210-211.

explosion was probably due to some fault to the Navy, has, of course, nothing to do with the matter." When the court of inquiry met to gather the facts, Professor Alger was not called to testify.

The Spanish government did their own investigation of the affair and came up with their own conclusion. They wrote that if a mine had destroyed the ship, witnesses would have heard a dull concussion rather than a loud bang. They also said the absence of dead fish in the vicinity of the wreck meant that a mine did not cause the explosion.

When Secretary of the Navy Long took ill, Roosevelt temporarily took on his duties. Roosevelt saw an opportunity that wouldn't come again. He took immediate steps to make the Navy ready for war against Spain, even though Congress had not voted on war resolution. He ordered that ammunition and stores be immediately sent to warships in harbors across the nation and they should be ready for action if ordered. He sent a cable to Admiral George Dewey in Hong Kong telling him to have his fleet all coaled up and to make plans to bottle up the Spanish fleet if it set sail. While Roosevelt was publicly blaming the Spanish, he had misgivings, which he kept to himself. He wrote a letter to his brother-in-law, Doug Robinson, saying the opposite. Talking about the coalbunkers as a possible cause of the accident he said, "With so much loose powder round, a coal may hop into it at any moment." In the end, the board concluded the keel of the ship had wound up on an inverted V shape and said the explosion had been caused by an underwater mine. Shortly after the verdict was handed in, the United States declared war against Spain.

In the ensuing years, the U.S. Army Corps of Engineers set up a cofferdam around the wreck and pumped out the water engulfing the ship. Parts of the ship were raised and towed out to sea and sunk with honors. The bodies of the sailors found in the wreckage were buried in Arlington Cemetery.

In 1911, a second probe of the destruction of the *Maine* began. The commission convened in Havana and was comprised of four Naval Officers and an Army Officer. Rear Admiral Charles Vreeland headed the board, and using photographs taken after the *Maine* sunk, and other physical evidence, came up with its own conclusions. They said that while they basically agreed with the 1898 finding that the ship was sunk from a mine, they were unable to determine who the perpetrators were. In 1974 there was another probe into the sinking of the *Maine.* This was a private investigation conducted by Admiral Hyman Rickover, one of the most controversial Naval Officers of this day. Rickover served 63 years in the Navy and was considered to be the father of nuclear powered submarines. He retired from the Navy in 1982 under orders from Secretary of the Navy, John F. Lehman, Jr. Rickover read an article in a newspaper on the sinking of the ship and asked an engineer from the Naval Ship Research and Development Center, and a physicist from the Naval Surface Warfare Center, to look into the matter. Two of the men that worked on the project were civilian engineers working for the Navy, Ib Hansen and Robert Price. Both men studied all the material from the two previous investigations and their research, which was published under the title "An Examination of the Technical Evidence Bearing on Its Destruction," was published as an appendix to Rickover's 1976 book called *How The Battleship Maine Was Destroyed.* All three men determined that the ship had sunk as a result of an internal accident, not an act of war (a mine attack).

The Rickover account put the blame partially on the shoulders of Captain Sigsbee, saying he was lacking in security on the ship before the explosion took place. He also said that the 1898 and 1911 Boards did not want to blame the Navy for the explosion due to political considerations of the day.

So, who was to blame for the sinking of the *Maine?* Was it a conspiracy hatched by the Spanish government? Spain had no real reason for attacking the ship. They had more than their share of trouble with the rebels in Cuba, who were demanding their independence. Realistically, they did not want war with the United States, a potential conflict they were not sure they could win. The rebel groups in Cuba, on the other hand, had every reason for wanting a war between Spain and the United States. If the two nations went to war, the obvious winners would be the Cuban rebels who might gain their freedom with an American victory. Could they have planted the mine? Certainly William Randolph Hearst wanted a war and he did everything in his power to ferment one, after the fact. One of his illustrators, Frederick Remington was in Cuba shortly before the ship exploded. He asked to come home and was told by Hearst via cable, "Please remain. You furnish the pictures and I'll furnish the war." Time and tide have pushed the tragedy of the sinking of the *Maine* into history. The result of the Spanish-American war started as a result of the sinking of the ship, expanded American power in the Pacific, and put the United States on the world map, as the new power to be reckoned with. The war lasted only 113 days and ended via the Treaty of Paris. The United States got the former Spanish colonies of Puerto Rico, the Philippines and Guam, and took control over the process of independence for Cuba that was completed in 1902.

Chapter 17
The Walker Family Spy Ring

On August 30, 2014 there appeared in the nation's newspapers an obituary for John A. Walker, Jr. For the younger reader, the name John Walker probably doesn't ring a bell. For over a decade, John Walker ran one of the most successful and damaging spy rings operating in the United States on behalf of the Soviet Union at the height of the Cold War. In time, John Walker recruited his son, brother and best friend, and tried to bring his daughter into his scheme. By the time of his arrest, on May 20, 1985, Walker had passed on to the Soviet Union some of the most sensitive and important naval secrets the United States possessed.

John Walker was a Navy Communications Specialist with high-level access to the crypto/communications keys of the U.S. Navy's Atlantic Fleet based in Norfolk, Virginia. From 1968, until his arrest in 1985, John Anthony Walker, along with his son Michael, his brother Arthur, and their navy buddy, Jerry Whitworth, passed along to the old Soviet Union vital U.S. Navy cryptographic intelligence on the inner workings of the nuclear submarine fleet; information that led to the North Vietnamese interception of U.S. bombing missions over North Vietnam, important naval tactics and airborne training scenarios, among other vital information. Along with other high-profile spies such as Aldrich Ames, who worked for the CIA, and Robert Hanssen, a long-time FBI agent, both of whom worked secretly for the KGB for decades, Walker's justification for his espionage career was money. While Walker was not an employee of the CIA, he gave the information to the Russians over a 20-year period, blew the cover on many important CIA operations and compromised many of its personnel.

Vitaly Yurchenko was a KGB officer who briefly defected to the United States in 1985 before taking a flyer and evading his CIA handler in a Washington restaurant. He said the activities of Walker and his family of spies allowed the Soviets to decipher a huge number of coded messages including, "If there had been a war, we would (the Soviet Union) have won."

Secretary of Defense Casper Weinberger, who was at the helm at the time of Walker's espionage activities, said the information he gave the Soviet Union "made significant gains in naval warfare that were attributable to Walker's spying. His espionage provided Moscow access to weapons and sensor data and naval tactics, terrorist threats and surface, submarine and airborne training, readiness and tactics."

John Walker was born in Scranton, Pennsylvania in 1937. He came from a troubled family where abuse was the order of the day. His father worked for a Warner Brothers film marketer and soon turned to alcoholism, leaving little time for his family. The family soon filed for bankruptcy and young John went to work delivering newspapers, sold home products door to door and worked as a movie usher. As a teenager he turned to petty crime and only escaped a jail sentence when the judge agreed to drop the charges if John entered the Navy. He enlisted in the Navy in 1956 and worked as a radioman and served on board a destroyer escort before joining the crew of the aircraft carrier USS *Forrestal*. His duty assignments included tours on a nuclear powered submarine, land duties at the bustling Charleston and Norfolk Naval Bases, and a stint as the assistant director of the radioman's school at the Naval Training Center in San Diego. While serving on board the *Razorback,* he received his top-secret cryptographic clearance; an important part of what became his later spying career.

In 1962, Walker served as a radioman on board the new SSBN *Andrew Jackson,* a nuclear ballistic missile submarine, which was in the latter stages of being built. In 1965 he was assigned to the SSBN *Simon Bolivar,* where he served as Senior Chief Radioman and got his official top-secret clearance for the first time. Now he was in the rarified air of the Navy's best-kept secret, something he relished. He'd finally made it to the big time and wasn't about to give it up. While the *Bolivar* was stationed in Charleston, South Carolina, his wife told the FBI her husband first began spying for the Soviet Union. It is possible that he actually began his clandestine work some years before.

As a radioman, Walker was one of the most important members of any ship's crew. Radiomen were the jack-of-all trades, posting information as harmless as the daily schedule, to the transmissions and decryption of classified information that came in from land stations to ships at sea. He had access to the sailing schedules of most of the ships in the fleet; important information that if put in the wrong hands, could severely disrupt the flow of supplies and men.

Walker was a warrant officer, just one step down from a commissioned officer. He specialized in radio communications and knew all the ropes in the naval pecking order. He was in a position to trade useful (unclassified) information to other warrant officers, just like the old barter system was used in the Middle Ages.

While in the Navy, John Walker married Barbara Crowley, and soon began raising a family. Barbara and the children followed John from base to base, never complaining of the disruptions of Navy life. Later on in their marriage, Barbara would take to drinking, and it was under the influence of alcohol that she would eventually contact the FBI regarding her husband's espionage work for the Russians. Her information was greeted with suspicion because of her drinking problems.

By the time of his decision to work for the Soviet Union, John Walker was a watch officer for the Atlantic Fleet submarine force. In this highly classified position, Walker knew all the locations of the U.S. submarine fleet, learned of their operational plans, received their secret communications and was privy to the positions of the Soviet Navy, whose ships were stationed out in international waters, not far from the big U.S. Naval bases in Norfolk and Charleston. All in all, the information possessed by John Walker was a potential intelligence bonanza to any foreign power that could get their hands on it. John Walker, now almost broke, his marriage on the rocks, would be the man who supplied the secrets.

Walker moved his family into an old concrete blockhouse near the Charleston Naval Base. It wasn't much of a home, but Walker soon expanded to make it a snack bar where he got a license to sell fast food such as burgers and pizza, which he cooked over a gas grill, and cold sandwiches. The place became popular with both the locals and the seamen who were stationed on the various ships in port. Walker was soon able to buy a nice MG sports car that he drove around the city. He named the place the Bamboo Snack Bar and soon made a name for himself and briefly thrived. However, the bar soon went bust and Walker, now seeing his once large bank account down to zero, decided to contact the Russians and sell the information he had accumulated while working in the Navy.

At the same time Walker was having troubles with his bar, his marriage to Barbara was on shaky ground. They had been fighting for some time and the constant tours of duty away from home for long periods of time were finally causing trouble. It is not sure exactly when John Walker contacted the Soviet's, but some people in the know said that it might have taken place while he ran the bar in Charleston. It was a fact that Soviet agents were in attendance in and around the vast Norfolk Naval Shipyard and knew many of the sailors who frequented the bars, especially Walker's Bamboo Snack Bar. Walker was an outgoing man and it is not out of the realm of possibility that a Soviet agent might have been a customer of his and talked to him about his duties.

On December 18, 1967 John Walker made the fateful decision to contact the Soviet's and offer to spy on their behalf. On that day he entered the gates of the Soviet Embassy in Washington, D.C. and asked to see someone in the security office. In spy parlance, he was a "walk in," a person who offers to give information to the enemy without prior notice. Walker was taken to the office of Yanis Lukashevich. He told the Russian, "I want to sell you top secrets." The Soviet officer was wary of the man who came to see him. Was he a plant sent by the CIA or FBI to act as a double agent against the Soviet Union? Walker gave him a top-secret key list for the KL-47 cipher machine, which was used at the Navy's Atlantic submarine fleet headquarters. He was asked why he was selling information and he replied by saying, "purely financial." He was paid an initial $1,000 by the Russians, but was soon earning up to $5,000 per handover of classified materials.[1]

In September 1969 Walker was transferred to San Diego, California where he was the director of the Navy's basic radioman school. Being so far away from Washington led to a drop in his espionage activities and he was only able to make two drops per year. It was at San Diego that Walker was to meet another

[1] Glasser, Jeff, *Secrets Cheap: John Anthony Walker,* US News & World Report, January 27-February 3, 2003, Page 68.

radio instructor, Jerry Whitworth, whom he would enroll in his espionage ring.

The number of radio instructors was few and Walker soon found Jerry Whitworth to be a man with common interests. During their many hours and days together, Walker was able to persuade Whitworth to join him in his espionage activities and it was in San Diego the two men decided to work together. Walker made his official pitch to Whitworth in 1974 and told him he was selling information to the Mafia and other interested parties and he'd share the profits with him. At no time did Walker tell his friend he was working for the Soviet Union. After the FBI arrested Whitworth they found out he received at least $338,000 during his spying career. The largest single payment was in the amount of $100,000 in June 1980, and he received two more $100,000 payments in 1981 and 1982. Both men often times met in San Francisco where they were both stationed. Whitworth left the Navy for two months in 1974 then reenlisted. In 1976, he served as the chief radioman on the USS *Constellation* where he had knowledge of U.S. nuclear attack plans and defensive tactics against Soviet submarines.

In 1975 Walker officially retired from the Navy, but that did not prevent him from continuing his espionage activities. He recruited his brother, Arthur, as well as his son Michael. Arthur Walker was also in the Navy and he supplied his brother with classified materials that he was privy to. He also tried to enlist his daughter, Laura Walker Snyder, who was serving in the Army while her father's espionage activities were taking place. She refused to go along with her father's request.

During his retirement, John Walker opened up a private detective agency called Confidential Reports, Inc. in Norfolk, Virginia, and a company that removed bugs—surveillance equipment for commercial customers.

John traveled to Hong Kong, Vienna, Austria and the Philippines, as well as various cities in the United States to meet with his Soviet controllers. Walker was well protected by the Soviets for his decades-long work for them. According to Oleg Kalugin, the former KGB Chief of Counterintelligence, only 12 high-ranking Soviet officials knew of Walker's espionage activities for them. Walker's Soviet handler was Yuri Linkov who knew more about Walker's espionage than almost any other Soviet intelligence officer at that time.

In November 1974 Barbara Walker, who had previous knowledge of her husband's espionage activities, contacted the FBI and told them of her husband's spying activities. At first the FBI agents with whom she talked did not believe her because of her drinking problem. However, after a number of face-to-face meetings with her, the Bureau finally took her allegations seriously and began an investigation of him. Her story was backed up when Jerry Whitworth came forward and told the FBI that he too had been part of John's spy ring.

On numerous occasions, Barbara Walker accompanied her husband on his routes where he picked up and dropped off secret material at dead drop sites in the surrounding neighborhoods where they lived. These sites included areas along the dark roads of Virginia and Maryland. He used this age-old bit of tradecraft, using light poles, bridges and any other natural areas of ground to leave garbage bags filled with documents. The Russians, in turn, would put his money wrapped in bundles of newspapers or other packing materials behind pre-determined rocks or trees for pick up.

The FBI was now closing in on the Walker spy ring and FBI agents arrested John Walker on May 20, 1985 at a motel in Rockville, Maryland after servicing a dead drop. He told the FBI agents that arrested him he was working for the French, doing industrial espionage. On May 28th, federal authorities arrested Michael Walker on board the USS *Nimitz* and brought him back to the United States. Hidden in Michael's footlocker were 15 pounds of pilfered classified documents. On May 29th, Arthur Walker was brought into custody and arrested. On June 3rd, Jerry Whitworth was arrested, bringing an end to the largest spy ring to operate in the United States thus far.

John Walker died in prison in 2014. Arthur Walker was sentenced to life imprisonment and fined $250,000. He is eligible for parole in 2015. Jerry Whitworth was also sentenced to life in jail. Michael Walker was released from a Boston halfway house on February 17, 2000 after serving 15 years of a 25-year sentence.

Chapter 18
The Lincoln Assassination

Abraham Lincoln was the first president to be assassinated while in office. Lincoln is regarded as the best president the United States ever had serving in a time that tore the country apart. From 1861 to 1865, a bloody Civil War pitted brother against brother, father against son, and almost changed the course of history, as we know it. Only days after the war ended, and a new beginning about to start, one more violent and senseless act took place. On the night of April 14, 1865 while attending a play at Ford's Theater in Washington, Abraham Lincoln was shot and killed by the noted actor, John Wilkes Booth. Booth fired one shot into the president's head, mortally wounding him. For the next 12 days Booth and his accomplice, David Herold, evaded the largest manhunt ever assembled in United States history. They were finally captured at a farmhouse owned by Richard Garrett, where Booth was killed and Herold captured. In the aftermath of the Lincoln assassination, a trial was held for his accomplices and four of his co-conspirators were hung. The trial brought forth evidence that placed the Confederate government squarely in the middle of the plot to kill President Lincoln, with John Wilkes Booth at its epicenter.

John Wilkes Booth was born on May 10, 1838 near the town of Bel Air, Maryland. Booth was the second youngest of 10 children. His father was the noted actor, Junius Brutus Booth, and his mother was Mary Ann Holmes. He was named after John Wilkes who was an 18th century English political agitator. The family home was called Tudor Hall, which housed a barn, stables and quarters for the slaves who lived on the property. His father was born in London and came to the United States in 1821. Over time he would become one of the greatest actors in the country. His brother Edwin Booth was soon to replace his father as the country's greatest tragedian. His brother, Junius Brutus Jr., was also an actor and the three Booth brothers acted together on several occasions. He adored his sister, Asia, and would confide in her things he would never tell his parents and brothers. Later in life, John's betrayal would severely wound Asia and she would never forgive her brother for killing the president.

As a youngster, John attended the Milton Boarding School for Boys and later St. Timothy Hall in Maryland. While he was attending St. Timothy Hall he would meet another student, Samuel Arnold, who would later become part of Booth's attempted kidnapping plot against President Lincoln.

John Wilkes Booth was a handsome lad and his acting ability soon bloomed. At age 17 he made his acting debut in Baltimore, with a role in a production of Shakespeare's *Richard III* at the Charles Street Theater in Baltimore. His reviews were not so good and he determined to pave his own acting path calling himself "J. Wilkes" in future productions. By 1858 Booth was employed as an actor with the Richmond Theater making 11 dollars a week. He was now beginning to come into his own as an actor and reviews got better with each performance. He made his New York acting debut in 1862, playing the lead role in *Richard III*. One paper called him a "veritable sensation." Booth later described his goal as an actor saying, "I am determined to be a villain." Late in 1863 he suffered from a respiratory condition and had to take time away from acting.

Booth was in Richmond when John Brown and his anti-slavery raiders attacked the Union armory at Harpers Ferry, Virginia. Booth was able to get an appointment with the local militia and was on hand when John Brown was executed on December 2, 1859. John Wilkes Booth was an ardent Southern sympathizer, believing the white race was superior to the Blacks and that the latter should have no political rights in the country.

From 1861 to 1864 Booth became a national star. He was now one of the finest and most respected actors in the country and was soon making thousands of dollars a year. He toured the country, playing in every major city and town, to lavish reviews and sold-out crowds (many years later, a theater in New York would be named after him). While Booth was an ardent Confederate sympathizer he decided it was not worth it to join the Confederate cause once the war broke out. Instead, he began smuggling medicine and information from the North to the South and did a little spying in his spare time. He was, in effect, a spy for the South. He once remarked to a friend, "My brains are worth 20 men, my money worth a thousand. I have a free pass everywhere; my profession, my name is my passport." Later, he would become more. Booth's sister, Asia Booth Clark, in a book she wrote called *The Unlocked Book,* regarding her brother said, "I now knew that my hero was a spy, a blockade-runner, a rebel! I set the terrible words before my eyes, and knew each one meant death."

During the war, Booth traveled to such cities as Baltimore, New York, Philadelphia and Montreal, Canada, meeting with Confederate agents. Booth confided to his actor friend, Samuel Chester, in New York that he was planning to kidnap President Lincoln and asked if he would like to join in (he refused). Booth further told Chester that he had at least 50 persons allied with him.

What is not in doubt is that John Wilkes Booth had meetings with certain members of the Confederate Secret Service in Montreal, Canada during the war. In the spring of 1864 the Confederate government decided to send agents to Canada where they would plot strategy against the Union. President Jefferson Davis chose Jacob Thompson of Mississippi to head the operation, and sent Clement Clay as his assistant. One million in gold was authorized to fund the operation, which came from a special secret service fund that only Jefferson Davis and Judah Benjamin, the Secretary of State for the Confederate States of America (CSA) could access. They set up shop in Toronto, as well as other cities in Canada. The man in charge of the Montreal office, Patrick Martin, gave Booth letters of introduction to Dr. Samuel Mudd in Bryantown, Maryland. Another person who aided the Confederates in Canada was George Sanders, who was an advocate of political assassinations and a Lincoln hater.[1]

Booth arrived in Canada on October 18, 1864 and registered at the St. Lawrence Hall Hotel, a hotbed of Confederate Canadian operations. Booth had various meetings with Patrick Martin and George Sanders and it is not out of the realm of possibility that the Confederate plots to either capture or kill President Lincoln were

[1] Steers, Edward, Jr., *The Lincoln Assassination Encyclopedia*, Harper Books, New York, 2010, Page 171.

discussed.

While in Montreal, Booth was able to use money set up for him in the Ontario Bank in the amount of $455 Canadian dollars. He traded in $300 in gold coins for 60 pounds sterling and bought an exchange for $455. This money was most likely supplied to Booth by the Confederate commissioners who were then living in the city. Immediately after leaving Canada, Booth came to Washington where he obtained a room at the National Hotel and made deposits in a bank owned by Jay Cooke.

A check was written on November 16, 1864 on the account of Jay Cooke and Co., a bank in Washington, in the amount of $100. It was payable to Matthew Canning, a long- time friend and theatrical agent of Booth. A total of seven checks were drawn on the account, the $100 to Canning, a $150 check cashed by Booth on January 7, 1865, and another one for $25, also cashed by Booth on March 7, 1865. What makes these transactions interesting is that Booth made these deposits in Cooke's bank just after he made his covert trip to Montreal.[2]

When Booth was killed at Garrett's Farm, soldiers found a Canadian bill of exchange on his body. This "paper trail" is just one of many things that tie Booth to the covert activities of the Confederate Secret Service and its relationship to the assassination of the president. When federal detectives searched the room of George Atzerodt, one of Booth's accomplices in the kidnap plot, after the assassination, they found Booth's bankbook with the $455 amount duly recorded.

Booth was never far removed from his associations with the members of the Confederate underground, if not its leaders. One year after his Canadian sojourn, Booth and his accomplices devised a plan to kidnap the president when Lincoln was to attend a performance at the Campbell Military Hospital, about two miles from the Capitol. The date for the abduction plan was March 17, 1865. The performance was at the Soldiers Home and was to benefit some of the wounded Union troops who were now recuperating. Booth and his men waited on the road back from the hospital, where their plan was to capture Lincoln, and spirit him

[2] Kross, Peter, *Spies, Traitors and Moles: An Espionage and Intelligence Quiz Book, Illuminet Press, Lilburn, Ga., 1998, Page 43-44.*

south and use him to ransom the thousands of Confederate troops languishing in Federal prisons. Much to their consternation, the president abruptly canceled his trip in order to attend a ceremony at the National Hotel in Washington, in which a Confederate flag would be presented to Oliver Morton, the governor of Indiana. In a bit of irony, John Wilkes Booth had a room at the National when the ceremony was going on.

The members of the unsuccessful kidnapping plot were all Booth's friends: Samuel Arnold, Michael O'Laughlen, John Surratt and George Atzerodt. Another person enlisted in the plans to kill the president was Dr. Samuel Mudd (who did not participate in the kidnap plot). Dr. Mudd was an ardent Southern sympathizer during the Civil War, who at times helped shelter a Confederate spy named Walter Bowie at his Charles County home. When Booth was in Montreal, he was given letters of introduction from Patrick Martin to Dr. Mudd and Dr. William Queen. In November 1864 Booth traveled to Bryantown, Maryland where he met with both Drs. Queen and Mudd. He returned once again in December and it was at this time he brought both men into his plans to kidnap the president. Thus Booth and Dr. Samuel Mudd began a covert relationship long before their paths crossed again, in April 1865. It has also been verified that while he was in Bryantown, Dr. Mudd introduced Booth to Thomas Harbin, a well-known Southern agent. It is believed they discussed a possible plot to kidnap President Lincoln. Harbin agreed to join in the plot and if it was successful, the plan called for both men to whisk the president to Richmond. [3]

Another person having close ties to both Booth and the Confederate government in Richmond was John Surratt Jr., whose mother, Mary, owned a boarding house in Washington in which many of the Lincoln conspirators met (including Booth). Mary Surratt owned an inn in Surrattsville, Maryland that was a way station for Confederate agents as they passed through Washington. Surratt was a dispatch runner between Richmond and Confederate agents in Canada. Surratt was in Richmond in March 1865, one month before the president was killed. He left Richmond on April 1, 1865, after meeting with Confederate Secretary of State Judah Benjamin and possibly President Jefferson Davis returning

[3] Steer, Edward, *The Lincoln Assassination Encyclopedia*, Pages 264-65.

to his mother's boarding house with a large amount of cash. He then left for Montreal where he met with the members of the CSA that were working in that city. Surratt was briefed on the Lincoln kidnapping plot and on April 10th he got a letter from Booth telling him the kidnapping plot had been changed and he should return to Washington. After the president was shot, John Surratt was in Elmira, New York and later made his way to Canada where he was given shelter. He later fled to Italy, joined Papal Zouaves, fled to Egypt where he was finally caught and returned to the United States for trial. He would face the same charges as that of his mother, Mary (who was hung for her role as a Lincoln co-conspirator), but the jury could not come to a verdict and the charges were dropped.[4]

So what do we make of the events surrounding John Surratt's trip from Richmond to Canada, back to Washington, then hence to Europe? From the above story it is not inconceivable that Surratt was given money and orders from someone high up in the Confederate government, i.e., either Davis or Benjamin to give to Booth, who in turn killed the president on April 14, 1865. The assassination attempt on the president was not a one shot deal. The plan was to decapitate the core leaders of the federal government in Washington with Booth as the ringleader.

By the middle of April 1865 the Civil War was all but over. Richmond had fallen, and on April 9th Confederate troops under the command of General Robert E. Lee had surrendered to General Grant at Appomattox. The cause that Booth had worked so hard to win was now over and he felt bitter and cheated over the Confederate surrender. His abortive kidnap plot was over and Booth now changed strategy, devising a bold and desperate last plan against the president. His new plan was to assassinate the president, as well as two other high officials in the Union government, Vice President Andrew Johnson and Secretary of State William Seward.

Earlier on April 14, 1865 Booth found out the president was to attend a play at Ford's Theater that night. The play was *Our American Cousin*, a farce staring Laura Keane. Booth visited the

[4] Fazio, John, C. *Confederate Complicity In the Assassination of Abraham Lincoln-Part 3*, The Cleveland Civil War Roundtable, 2008.

theater earlier in the day, making mental notes about how and when he was going to carry out the assassination. At 8:00 p.m. Booth assembled his hit team at the Hendron House just around the corner from Ford's Theater. On hand for the fateful meeting were Lewis Powell, David Herold and George Atzerodt. Booth told them of his new plans, and except for George Atzerodt, all the men accepted the job. Atzerodt balked, but Booth told him that if he did not carry out his assignment he would tell the authorities of his complicity in the earlier kidnapping plot. The plan called for Atzerodt to kill Vice President Andrew Johnson in his room at the Kirkwood Hotel. David Herold and Lewis Powell were to kill Secretary of State William Seward at his home. Powell would do the actual murder, while Herold would wait outside Seward's home and take Powell out of the city after the murder. Booth was to kill the president at Ford's Theater. The plan was to be carried out at the same time, 10:00 p.m.

That night the plot went into fruition. Atzerodt arrived at Vice President Johnson's hotel, went into the bar for a few drinks and lost his nerve. While the Vice President slept, Atzerodt slipped out of the hotel and made his way out of the city. Lewis Powell arrived at the home of Secretary Seward and told the man who answered the door that he had medicine for the secretary and he was to personally give it to him. When he was told to go away, Powell barged into Seward's home, attacked Seward's son and made his way to Seward's room. The secretary had been recuperating from a carriage accident and both his neck and head were in a brace. Powell slashed Secretary Seward numerous times, cutting his cheek and chin, but not mortally wounding him. As Powell fled the house, he yelled, "I am mad."

Booth had slipped into the room outside the box where the President, Mrs. Lincoln and their guests, Major Henry Rathbone and his date, Clara Harris, were attentively watching the play. The guard who was stationed outside of the president's box, John Parker, had left his post and was nowhere to be found when Booth entered, unnoticed. At the precise moment that Booth had chosen during the play, he quietly slipped into the presidential box and fired one bullet right into the president's head, mortally wounding him. He then vaulted onto the stage below, caught his leg on the flag on the railing and broke it. Once on stage, with gun in hand, Booth shouted, "Sic Semper Tyrannis," the Latin phrase for "Thus always to tyrants."

Booth was a master manipulator and took pains to implicate not only himself, but also his co-conspirators. Before he assassinated the president, he sent a letter to John Matthews and was told to give it to the *National Intelligencer* newspaper after the event. The note read as follows:

> For a long time I have devoted my energies, my time, and money, to the accomplishment of a certain end. I have been disappointed. The moment has now arrived when I must change my plans. Many will blame me for what I am about to do; but posterity, I am sure, will justify me.
>
> Men who love their country better than gold or life, John W. Booth, Payne, Herold, Atzerodt.[5]

After fatally shooting President Lincoln, Booth and Herold fled the chaotic city over the Navy Yard Bridge and headed for the safety of Maryland, an area that Booth knew very well. They stopped briefly at the tavern at Surrattsville owned by Mary Surratt.

Booth, with his leg broken and in pain, needed a doctor to treat his wounds and he and Herold made their way to the home of Dr. Samuel Mudd in Bryantown, Maryland. Booth knew Dr. Mudd from his previous meeting with him, several months before. At his home Dr. Mudd set Booth's leg and let them stay for the night. One important question was whether Dr. Mudd recognized Booth when he came to his home that night. As the story goes, Booth had his face covered by a shawl the entire time he was in Dr. Mudd's home. But the men had met before, with Booth spending a night at Dr. Mudd's home. Is it conceivable that he did not recognize Booth whom he had met not only in Washington, but also at his own home? After a while both Booth and Herold left Dr. Mudd's

---

5   Swanson, James, *Manhunt: The 12-Day Chase For Lincoln's Killer,* William Morrow & Co., New York, 2006, Page 29.

residence heading for safer ground near the Potomac River, where they hoped to cross the river into Virginia and safety. Before leaving Dr. Mudd's home, Booth wrote the following note, "Until today nothing was ever thought of sacrificing to our country's wrongs. For six months we had worked to capture [and abduct the president unharmed]. But our cause being almost lost, something decisive and great must be done."

Dr. Mudd was later arrested by Union troops after questioning him regarding possible sightings of Booth in Herold in the Bryantown area.

After a massive 12-day hunt by hundreds of Union troops, Booth and Herold were trapped at the home of Richard Garrett in Virginia on April 25, 1865. Booth and Herold were in Garrett's tobacco barn when troops of the 16th New York Cavalry under the command of Lt. Edward Doherty, who had been sent to the area by Lafayette Baker, head of the National Detective Police who was leading the hunt for the assassins. Along with Lt. Doherty in command, Lt. Colonel Everton Conger was the de facto leader of the 25-man group. Booth and David Herold were trapped in the barn and Herold surrendered after much shouting and hollering. The story goes that one of the members of the unit, Boston Corbett, shot Booth inside the barn when he thought Booth was pointing his gun at one of his fellow soldiers. Corbett's shot hit Booth on the right side of his neck, paralyzing his spinal cord. Booth was taken out of the barn and was made as comfortable as possible in his last hours of life. He died shortly thereafter.

Many questions lingered about the circumstances surrounding the events at the Garrett farm. Why did a force of 25 men not take Booth alive? It they had done so and Booth was taken back to Washington, he could have testified about the possibilities of a larger conspiracy that might have been afoot. In a diary that was taken from Booth's body, there was a cryptic entry that read, "I have almost a mind to return to Washington and clear my name, which I feel I can do." What did he mean by that? Did Booth have knowledge of other participants in the plot to kill the president? General Ben Butler, one of the members of a congressional committee that was set up to look into the circumstances of the assassination, wrote, "How clear himself? By disclosing his accomplices? Who were they? If we had only the advantage of all the testimony, Mr. Speaker, we might have been able to find who, indeed were all the accomplices of Booth."

After his death, the officers found the diary Booth had been keeping. The diary was kept secret from the public for two years before it was disclosed. The diary was taken to the War Department under the direction of Lafayette Baker. Baker later resigned, but wrote about the diary in his book, *The History of the Secret Service.* He was later called to testify before the House Judiciary Committee. In his testimony he said, "the diary had been mutilated since it had been taken from the body at Garrett's farm." General Butler said, "That diary, now produced, has eighteen pages cut out, the pages prior to the time when Abraham Lincoln was massacred, although the edges as yet show they had all been written over. Now, what I want to know was that diary whole? Who spoiled that book?"[6]

The diary was also in the possession of two other important federal officials, Edwin Stanton, the Secretary of War and General Joseph Holt, the Judge Advocate General from 1862-1875, and the chief prosecutor of the conspirators in the Lincoln assassination trial. The contents of the diary were never introduced as evidence in the trials of Dr. Mudd, Samuel Arnold, George Atzerodt, David Herold and Lewis Paine (Powell).

When Lafayette Baker testified before the trial of the Lincoln conspirators he told the court he had read portions of Booth's diary and said he believed there was more to the diary than he saw. "In my opinion," said Baker, "there have been leaves torn out of that book since I saw it." Since the diary belonged to Booth, it is reasonable to assume that the assassin himself cut out the leaves, but for what purpose we don't know.

In the 150 years since the assassination of President Lincoln, there has been speculation other people might have had a hand in the president's murder, including Vice President Andrew Johnson, Lafayette Baker and William Stanton. But in that intervening time, there have been no "smoking guns" as to their possible

[6] Eisenschiml, Otto, *Why Was Lincoln Murdered?*, Grosset & Dunlap, New York, 1937, Page 140.

involvement in the crime.

What is not in doubt is the number of Confederate agents and spies who played a role in aiding Booth and Herold out of Washington after the assassination. These included Dr. Samuel Mudd, Thomas Harbin (a Confederate agent who lived in Charles County, Maryland) and a friend of Dr, Mudd's. Harbin was part of the kidnap plot and took his orders directly from the government in Richmond. Thomas Jones, a member of the Confederate Signal Corps, aided Booth and Herold after their escape from Washington. Jones cared for both men when they were hiding in the pine thickets. He made arrangements for their escape south, and Samuel Cox, a low-level courier for the Confederate government, passed them on to Thomas Jones and Thomas Nelson Conrad, a member of the Confederate Secret Service, who was to take part in the Lincoln kidnapping plot. Judah Benjamin directed the plot, and said he received two letters from CSA President Jefferson Davis and Secretary of War James Seddon transferring him to the secret service and providing him with money for the mission.

The longstanding historical myth that John Wilkes Booth and his lonely band of miscreants plotted and killed President Abraham Lincoln has been debunked. Much evidence has come forward over the past two centuries pointing the finger directly at the high officials in the Confederate capital of Richmond and their direct involvement in the plots to kidnap the president, as well as facilitating Booth's escape from Washington to the South. Sometimes history takes a little longer to get the story right.

Lee Harvey Oswald (center) handing out leaflets in New Orleans, 1963

Chapter 19
de Mohrenschildt and Oswald

When Lee Harvey Oswald returned to the United States with his wife and new baby, after spending two and a half years in the Soviet Union, they settled in the Dallas-Fort Worth area, which had a large Russian-American community. Among the group there was one man who, for whatever reason, befriended the Oswald's and took them under his wing. That man was George de Mohrenschildt. It was a decision that would change his life.

George de Mohrenschildt was born in Baku, in Mozyr, Russia, on April 17, 1911. He told varying stories as to his exact place of birth; sometimes it was St. Petersburg, Russia or Poland. He came from an aristocratic family, an urbane and well-educated man, and the opposite of Lee Harvey Oswald. His father, Sergius von Mohrenschildt had once served as the governor of the Province of Minsk during the reign of the Czar (where Lee Harvey Oswald lived while in Russia) and served for a time as the vice-president of the Nobel Oil Company. Upon assuming power, the Bolsheviks took over the oil company and he was arrested for a time. After escaping from jail, Sergius and his family arrived in Poland. According to author Joan Mellen, in her book, *Our Man in Haiti,* Sergius worked for Allan Dulles, who operated the Bern, Switzerland office of the OSS (Office of Strategic Services) during World War II. She writes that he was one of many people the OSS used after the war and that he had been "a spy reporting on the Bolsheviks for the Abwehr, the German intelligence services."

George's older brother, Dimitri von Mohrenschildt, who was born in 1902, was a member of the OSS and later the CIA. He would help create the CIA's Radio Free Europe and later was a professor at Dartmouth College. If his father and brother were part of the intelligence services, George too wanted a place in that covert world. In later years, he would be accused of being a Nazi spy and had many associations with people in the CIA.

Young George got his education at the Polish Cavalry Academy and the University of Belgium. He was a troubled youth and in

141

1931 he was arrested in Antwerp, charged with drunkenness, using a false name and resisting arrest. He served eight days in jail and paid a fine. At age 27, on May 13, 1938 he came to the United States money borrowed from his family. He changed his name from "von Mohrenschildt" to "de Mohrenschildt" in order not to sound German. He invented a new persona for himself, telling people made up stories about his past in order to impress them. He rarely worked, but managed to stay afloat using money borrowed from friends or relatives and staying at other people's homes. An FBI memo on him reads, "He always seemed to associate with very fine people and moved about in high social circles."

In 1938 or 1940, while he was living in New York City, George began working for Pierre Fraiss, the head of French intelligence in the United States, as a salesman. Fraiss used the name Shumaker Company, a fabric business, as the cover for his company. Fraiss hired de Mohrenschildt to "collect facts on people involved in pro-German activity." In his capacity with Fraiss, de Mohrenschildt traveled across the United States contacting oil companies regarding selling oil to the French in competition against German suppliers during the war. When George later applied for a job with the U.S. government, Pierre Fraiss recommended him as a trustworthy man and called him fit "for a position critical from the standpoint of the national security." However, he would not say exactly what kind of intelligence work de Mohrenschildt did for him.

During this time period, the FBI put a watch on him having him followed on a regular basis. The Bureau speculated that he did undercover work for the Nazis in the United States. At one point, he was spotted sketching a scene that included a U.S. naval installation. George's FBI file contains the following note: "to determine if the person posed a security threat." The FBI contacted the U.S. Department of State regarding the actions of de Mohrenschildt and they placed a "refusal," or "lookout" notice, in his passport office file. This meant that when a person applied for a passport an investigation would be conducted to determine if the person posed any security threat to the United States. The reason for the "lookout" notice being filed is that he was "Alleged to be Nazi agent. Refer any application to Fraud Section."

At one point, George met a lovely Mexican woman, Lilia Larin, and they both went south of the border for a trip. They first stopped at a beach in Corpus Christi, Texas before heading to Mexico where their behavior attracted the attention of U.S. government agents. While at Corpus Christi, George made drawings of people fishing near a U.S. Coast Guard Station and in another bit of strange behavior (sometime in 1941), he was seen taking pictures and sketching a Coast Guard Station and ship channel near Port Aransas, Texas. The feds accused him of being a Nazi spy, searched his car and finally let the couple go.

In 1942 George was deported from Mexico carrying a $6,000 letter of credit issued by the Chase Manhattan Bank of New York that was owned by the Rockefeller family. U.S. Intelligence authorities now took an active interest in de Mohrenschildt's activities and said he was interested in getting a job with Rockefeller's Inter-American Affairs organization. The Office of Naval Investigation now opened a file on him that would be kept active for years to come.

The FBI also took an interest in de Mohrenschildt's activities when he teamed up with a known German agent, Baron Konstantin von Maydell, in a company run by him called "Facts and Film." In June of 1941 the FBI intercepted a letter from von Maydell to de Mohrenschildt stating he was trying to get credentials from Nelson Rockefeller, who was then the coordinator of information for Latin America, to distribute films in that region of the world. Maydell's work ended in September 1942 when he was arrested by presidential warrant for being a "dangerous alien." The FBI also found that de Mohrenschildt was trying to get in touch with German agents through Saburo Matsukata, the son of former prime minister of Japan who, it was believed, was spying inside the U.S. No one really knows what game de Mohrenschildt's was running or for whom he was really working. Henry Doscher, who served as his attorney, said George told him he was working for "the British Intelligence Corps during World War II."

In 1942 he applied for a wartime position in the OSS, which was denied because of his tainted past.

In 1957 he applied for a U.S. passport and received one, despite the fact he had been under surveillance for years by the

OSS and ONI. However, the State Department placed a notation in his passport file regarding his past "lookout" notation.

In 1944 he attended the University of Texas and received a master's degree in petroleum engineering. But it was in the 1950s and early 60s that de Mohrenschildt began a new, and sometimes murky, part of his life, one that led certain people to believe he had some intelligence-related connections. He worked for a time as a petroleum engineer in Colorado, inflating his resume to make him look more experienced than he really was. In 1957 he traveled to Yugoslavia through the U.S. government as a geologist and once again was noticed by the CIA. A CIA report on him states:

> De Mohrenschildt appears to be a dubious character. In 1942 he was considered a Nazi sympathizer and possible intelligence agent; he spent a good deal of time in Mexico where he was suspected of possible subversive activities; and at the University of Texas, where in 1944, he was said to have Communists tendencies.[1]

In the 1950s de Mohrenschildt went to Texas where he worked in the oil business. While there, he soon began to have ties with certain oil people and companies who had connections to the CIA. Among these were Brown and Root, Schlumberger Oil Well Drilling Company and William Buckley Sr. at the Pantepec Oil (Venezuela). The Schlumberger Company would later become involved with anti-Castro operations in Louisiana and would act as a CIA front company for many years. Another person George knew during this time who was connected to the CIA was James Duce who worked for ARAMCO oil. The CIA knew all about these connections regarding de Mohrenschildt while he lived in Dallas and his activities were monitored by the Army's 66th Military Intelligence Group (MIG), reporting to "90 Deuce," the 902nd MIG, a top-secret military organization.[2]

After his return to the United States from Yugoslavia, George met with J. Walton Moore, who was in charge of the CIA's Dallas

---

[1] Epstein, Edward, Jay, *Legend: The Secret world of Lee Harvey Oswald,* McGraw Hill Books, New York, 1978, Page 182.

[2] Mellen, Joan, *Our Man in Haiti,* Trine Day Publishers, Walterville, Or., 2012, Page 37-38.

office. Moore waned to find out about his European trip and the Agency generated at least 10 different reports in that regard. This meeting was not to be the last time both men would meet. A number of years later they would get together once again to chat about a Russian defector, an ex-Marine, who returned to the Dallas-Fort Worth area, Lee Harvey Oswald and his young Russian bride.

In the early months of 1961, George and his wife, Jeanne, went on a 7,000 mile "walking tour" of Central America and by happenstance, managed to be near the secret training camps in Guatemala that were being used by the CIA to train the anti-Castro Cubans for what was to be the Bay of Pigs invasion of Cuba (coincidence or not?).

Upon their return to Dallas, both George and Jeanne resumed their lives and shortly met Lee and Marina Oswald. George and Lee had a father-son relationship despite their vastly different backgrounds. Why would de Mohrenschildt give his friendship and loyalty to Oswald?

De Mohrenschildt's views of Oswald were contradictory at best. He saw two different sides of Oswald, telling different versions about the ex-Marine to anyone who would listen. Yet both George and his wife took care of the Oswald's, even giving Marina money to live.

In his long talks with Oswald, George emphasized his close relationship with the Bouvier-Kennedy family. To Lee, the fact that his best friend, and mentor, knew the wife of the president of the United States was nothing but astounding.

George was Oswald's intellectual mentor and was also able to sway Oswald's mind around to his own political philosophy. He told Lee of Major General Edwin Walker, a member of the John Birch Society and a rightwing former Army general who had been fired by the Kennedy Administration for spouting rightwing propaganda to his troops while on active duty. It is believed that Oswald tried to kill General Walker, but there is no concrete proof he actually took part in the attempt on his life.

The most important question asked by assassination researchers was why de Mohrenschildt befriended Oswald and if he had any connections to U.S. intelligence agencies. The answers are still contradictory, yet fascinating to think about.

When George first met Oswald he didn't know what to make of him. He found Oswald most intriguing, yet didn't seek out his friendship right away. He didn't want to get involved with Oswald until he checked him out. Interestingly enough, the man George turned to in order to find out about Oswald was his friend, J. Walton Moore, a CIA agent in the Domestic Contacts Division stationed in Dallas. Moore reassured him he wasn't under any FBI surveillance because of his association with Oswald. De Mohrenschildt asked Moore if Oswald was dangerous in any way. Moore replied that Oswald was a "harmless lunatic" and was of no concern to the CIA, despite the fact he had lived in the Soviet Union for over two years and no one really knew what he was doing there. Thus, with Moore's assurance, de Mohrenschildt began to cultivate Lee Harvey Oswald.

The CIA files on de Mohrenschildt and Moore are contradictory. It seems that a reference to a possible Oswald-CIA connection was made on a local television station, WFAA-TV, in Dallas that alleged the CIA employed Oswald and Moore knew Oswald. The memo states that Moore is quoted as saying that by his records, the last time he talked with de Mohrenschildt was in the fall of 1961. Moore further said at no time did he speak with George regarding Oswald. Moore also said he only had two talks with de Mohrenschildt, one in the spring of 1958 regarding China, and in the fall of 1961 when de Mohrenschildt and his wife returned from their tour of Central America.

As time went on, many writers began to place their own interpretation on the Oswald-de Mohrenschildt connection. Author Michael Eddoes, in his book *The Oswald File,* believed there was a so-called Dallas Triangle consisting of Jack Ruby, an imposter Oswald and de Mohrenschildt, who plotted to kill Kennedy. He points out that in 1956 Ruby and George lived within 100 yards of each other. Eddoes also said de Mohrenschildt was told to befriend Oswald, to get him a job at Jaggers-Stoval and help him introduce Marina to Ruth Paine, who made the call to the Texas School Book Depository where Oswald got a job.

George Evica, in his book *And We Are All Mortal,* takes this conspiracy theory one step further. He asks whether de Mohrenschildt was ordered, possibly through his oil or intelligence connections, to spy on Oswald to see if he was on any covert operation on behalf of the U.S. government.

A partial answer to de Mohrenschildt's possible intelligence connections can be found in his relationship with President Duvalier of Haiti.

One of his worldwide contacts was Clemard Charles, President of Banque Commercial d'Haiti. Clemard Charles was soon to become a target of the CIA and would be on their radar for some time to come. The reason for this interest was Charles' close association with President "Papa Doc" Duvalier of Haiti, whom the U.S. government did not trust. Both the CIA and military intelligence would place Charles under close surveillance, including a request from the 902nd Military Intelligence Group to the FBI that they place a check on Charles' business dealings in Miami.[3]

In May 1963, Colonel Sam Kail, a U.S. Army intelligence officer working out of Miami, contacted Dorothe Matlack of the Office of the Army Chief of Staff for Intelligence. She served as Assistant Director of the Army's human source collection and was the liaison with the CIA. Kail told de Mohrenschildt to meet with Charles to get information on President Duvalier.

In a related development, Joseph Dyer of Palm Beach, Florida told the HSCA that he knew de Mohrenschildt in Haiti in the 1950s and 1960s. He related that George and Charles met with a woman named Jacqueline Lancelot who owned a restaurant in Haiti. Lancelot was supposed to have given U.S. Intelligence agents, who worked in the American embassy in Port au-Prince, information on President Duvalier. Dryer stated he heard hearsay information from Lancelot that after Kennedy's death, de Mohrenschildt got $200,000-$250,000, which was deposited in his Port Au-Prince bank account.

Mrs. Matlack used her intelligence connections to arrange a meeting with both George and Jeanne, along with Charles in May 1963 with Tony Czajkowski of the CIA's Domestic Contact Division, whom she introduced as a professor from Georgetown University. Charles asked Mrs. Matlack to use her influence with the Army to ask for an American invasion of Haiti to overthrow President Duvalier. Mrs. Matlack did not know that George and

[3] Ibid. Page 69.

147

his wife were to attend the meeting and when George told her he and Charles were in the jute business together, she did not believe him. She later said of the Charles-de Mohrenschidt relationship, "I knew the Texan wasn't there to sell hemp." She later told a friend in the FBI, Pat Putnam, of the meeting because she was sure there was something not right about it. It turned out that from this meeting, the CIA began a longstanding relationship with Clemard Joseph Charles because of his close connection with President Duvalier and the secret information he could bring. They also were now in a position to monitor George de Mohrenschildt who was very close to Charles in their various business dealings in Haiti.

De Mohrenschildt had an intuitive sense of his friend, Lee Oswald, and his possible associations to U.S. Intelligence. It had been rumored that Oswald was either an FBI plant or someone who had links to the CIA. In his book, *I Am A Patsy,* written for the HSCA, George wrote, "It never occurred to me that he (Oswald) might be an agent of any country, including the U.S.—although he might have been trained in Russia for some ulterior motive."

Shortly before his mysterious death, George had a conversation with journalist Edward Jay Epstein, which related a talk he had with the CIA's J. Walton Moore in late 1961. He said while the two men were having lunch, Moore told him the CIA was aware of Oswald who was then in the process of returning to the U.S., and said the agency had "interest" in him. Moore then suggested to George that he befriend Lee Oswald to find out more information about him upon his return to the U.S. Moore later denied that he ever told de Mohrenschildt to contact Oswald. [4]

Whatever the truth about de Mohrenschildt and Oswald, can never be known. George de Mohrenschildt, like many other witnesses to the Kennedy assassination, died under mysterious circumstances. Events prior to his "suicide" are as strange as his life. On March 1, 1977 he went with Dutch writer William Oltmans to Holland, where for one week he disappeared. On March 14th, he returned to New York. The next day Oltmans, under questioning from the HSCA, told them that Oswald acted with the knowledge of de Mohrenschildt when he killed President Kennedy. George returned to Palm Beach to visit his daughter, Alexandria. He

[4] Russell, Dick, *The Man Who Knew Too Much,* Carroll & Graf, New York, 1992, Page 274.

was to have met with members of the House Select Committee on Assassinations to discuss his relationship with Oswald, but in one final desperate act, George committed suicide (Or so goes the official story).

The Oswald-de Mohrenschildt relationship is fraught with mystery and intrigue and is a part of the aftermath of the Kennedy assassination that still begs answers.

Robert Hanssen.

Chapter 20
The Robert Hanssen Spy Case

With the arrest of Aldrich Ames in February 1994, the U.S. Intelligence Community believed they had finally uncovered the traitor responsible for the disruption of covert operations behind the Iron Curtain and the untimely deaths of at least 10 moles working for the United States inside the Soviet Union. That fallacy prevailed in both the CIA and the FBI for the next seven years. No major spy case dominated the headlines as the American public read about other, major events: the impeachment of President Clinton, the war in the Balkans and the breakup of the Soviet Union. That all changed on February 18, 2001 when the FBI announced it had uncovered another mole inside their own organization. A 20-year veteran, a religious man, who wore dark suits to work, never joined the boys at the local strip clubs in the D.C. area, Robert Philip Hanssen. While Robert Hanssen was not a member of the CIA, where many of the previous moles had been uncovered, his espionage activities uncovered major covert agency operations, which would have devastating effects after the fiasco of the Ames case.

Robert Hanssen was born in Chicago, Illinois on April 18, 1944. His father was a Chicago police officer who lived with his wife, Vivian. As a youngster, he attended Chicago's Taft High School in the Norwood Park area. One of his friends at Taft High was Jack Hoschouer, who would later become a decorated army officer and a friend for years to come, who he would try to enlist as a fellow spy for the Russians. Bob Hanssen came from a very religious family and was brought up as a Lutheran, but later converted to Catholicism at the urging of his wife. After graduating from Knox College in Illinois, he briefly attended dentistry school at Northwestern University. In 1971 he changed his major and got his MBA degree in accounting from Northwestern. He joined the Chicago Police Department in an undercover capacity, connecting with a unit that went by the title C-5. Little has been written about the goings-on regarding C-5, but it was supposed to be one of Chicago PD's most elite units. Part of C5's job was to investigate police corruption and run sting operations. It was reported that at one point in his training, Bob Hanssen was sent to a secret counterintelligence school to learn to install listening devices and other, hi-tech equipment. He soon left the force after three years and joined the FBI on January 12, 1976 working in both the Indiana and New York City offices. Hanssen also worked at FBI headquarters where he tracked white-collar criminals. With his expertise in computer technology, Hanssen organized a complete database on all foreign diplomats who worked in the United States. Hanssen was so good with computers that in 1992 he told two fellow FBI agents, Ray Mislock and Roger Watson, that their internal computer system was not safe from hackers and that he could penetrate their system. Mislock, who was the chief of the Soviet Intelligence Division, and Watson, the Division's Deputy Assistant Director, both said it couldn't be done. Hanssen disappeared into his own office for a brief period of time and hacked into Mislock's computer, downloading all the classified material on the computer.

In the years between joining the CPD (Chicago Police Department) and the Bureau, Hansen married Bernadette Wauck, known as Bonnie. Bonnie, like Robert, came from the Chicago area and her father was a Navy veteran and a clinical psychologist. One of the most important parts of Bob Hanssen's life was his religious belief, and he stood out among the streetwise agents in both Washington and New York. He was politically conservative, no friends of liberal democrats, and in a city like Washington, with its liberal majority, he was like a fish out of water. Hanssen repeatedly rejected offers from his colleagues to attend stag parties or have drinks after work. He was not one of the boys and also held a deeply anti-communist view of the world. Hanssen's Bureau colleagues often times referred to him as "The Mortician," or "Dr. Death," because of the dark suits he always wore. His social skills were also lacking and one incident in particular almost got Hanssen in deep trouble with the FBI. He had an altercation with a woman named Kimberly Lichtenberg who worked for the FBI in the National Security Threat List unit. After a meeting, Mrs. Lichtenberg decided to leave the meeting early, which enraged

Hanssen to no end. Hanssen grabbed her by the arm and in the process she fell to the floor. She was bruised from the incident and Hanssen was suspended for five days without pay.

Despite his personal problems, the FBI saw Hanssen as a valuable agent and in 1979 he was transferred to New York City where he was to head the Bureau's foreign counterintelligence operations, based in Manhattan. The Hanssen's moved to a nice home in suburban Scarsdale, Westchester County, less than an hour's ride from New York.

Hanssen had access to the most sensitive, top-secret material coming out of the FBI. He served as Deputy Director of the FBI's Intelligence Division's Soviet section, gaining him total access to all counterespionage operations inside the United States. He was later put in charge of the Bureau's Soviet analytical unit working as the FBI's foremost representative to the U.S. State Department.

Like Aldrich Ames, Robert Hanssen found it difficult to make ends meet. With a large family to support, he realized he could not afford to keep his family financially sound on his $46,000 FBI salary (unlike Rosario Ames, Bonnie Hanssen did not know of her husband's espionage and did not take part in any of his activities).

Within a two-week period of joining the FBI's New York office in 1985, Hanssen contacted the Soviet GRU (Military Intelligence) and sold classified materials to them in return for $100,000. His double life as a Soviet spy had begun.

One day while Robert was in the basement of his home, writing a letter to his Soviet contacts, Bonnie Hanssen came in and saw what he was doing. She confronted her husband and he admitted he was working for the Soviet Union. He told her that he was really fooling the Russians, giving them outdated information that was worthless. In reality, Hanssen did not give the Russians outdated information. Instead, he provided them with the identity of a U.S. mole working as double agent against the Soviet's, General Dmitri Polyakov, who was working inside the Soviet military. The CIA dubbed Polyakov "Top Hat" and in time, he would be one of the most important moles U.S. intelligence would place inside the bowels of Soviet intelligence. In an ironic twist, General Polyakov would be unmasked by Aldrich Ames and executed in 1985. After Bonnie's confrontation with Hanssen, she was told he'd never spy for the Russians again.

A number of his fellow New York FBI agents would later have different opinions as to why Hanssen spied for the Russians. Some said that since he was not part of the inner circle of decision makers, he decided to play his own, personal game. One colleague, Jim Ohlson said, "Although Hanssen was involved with, and fascinated by, CI and Soviet operations, he was never in the core group that actually conducted them. He may have felt excluded, his skills unappreciated. He had longed to be involved in spy work—so he turned to another government to do it. Hanssen had a great respect for the KGB and its professionalism. They're the only target I want to work against. They're the one enemy worth fighting. So he was drawn to the KGB."[1]

The Hanssen family belonged to a Catholic organization called Opus Dei whose followers adhere strictly to church doctrine and principles. Opus Dei members are supposed to attend mass on a daily basis and take confession regularly. Critics in the Catholic Church say members of Opus Dei have used more than persuasive powers to lure other Catholics into the church and have alienated mainstream Catholics with their intensive pressure. Records indicate Hanssen gave $4,000 in donations to the organization.

When Bonnie Hanssen found out her husband was spying for the Russians, she insisted that he see a priest from Opus Dei. The Hanssen's had joined the church in 1978 out of a "study center" located in New Rochelle, New York. The priest, Father Bucciarelli, saw them together for a private session. At that meeting, both of them told Father Bucciarelli that Robert was spying for the Russians and he urged him to turn himself in. However, he then changed his mind and told Robert Hanssen to give whatever monies he had received from the Soviet's to charity. Robert later told his wife that he set aside a certain amount of cash each month to give to Mother Teresa. He now temporarily halted his spying activities because of Bonnie's discovery, but this would not last long. By October 1985 he would once again contact his Russian handlers.

This time, Bob Hanssen opened communication with Victor Cherkashin, the KGB's chief of counterintelligence in their Washington, D.C. embassy. Hanssen devised a number of "fire

[1] Wise, David, *Spy: The Inside Story of How the FBI's Robert Hanssen Betrayed America,* Random House, New York, 2002, Page 274.

walls" in order to keep any possible FBI surveillance from him. He wrote a cryptic note to Cherkashin, never revealing his true identity, or the intelligence agency he worked for. "My identity and actual position must be left unstated to ensure my security," he wrote to Cherkashin. He gave his new controller a little bit of information on himself saying, "Please recognize that there are a limited number of persons with this array of clearances. As a collection they point to me. I trust that an officer of your experience will handle them appropriately."

In order to contact his Russian friends, Hanssen would use "dead drops," secret places known only to himself and the Russians, where money and classified materials would be exchanged. It was in one of these dead drop sites, a park in Vienna, Virginia, close to his home, that Hanssen would be arrested. He also used codenames in his exchanges with the Russians, calling himself "B", "Ramon Garcia," "Jim Baker" and "G. Robertson." The name Ramon Garcia was someone he had known as an exchange student in school in the late 1980s.

While Hanssen took large sums of money from the Russians, his primary motive for his espionage was ego. He believed he was smarter than his fellow FBI agents, and wanted to show them up at all costs. At one point in his correspondence with the Russians, Hanssen wrote, "As far as funds are concerned, I have little need or utility for more than the $100,000. It merely provides a difficulty since I cannot spend it, or invest it easily without tripping 'drug money' warning bells. Perhaps some diamonds as security to my children and some goodwill so that when the time comes, you will accept by (sic) senior services as a guest lecturer. Eventually, I would appreciate an escape plan (Nothing lasts forever)."

As part of his espionage, Hanssen revealed the names of three of the top Americans double agents working for U.S. Intelligence inside the Soviet Union: Valery Martynov, a KGB officer who worked in the Soviet's Washington Embassy since 1982, Sergi Motorin, a prime source regarding Soviet counterintelligence operations since January 1985 and Boris Yuzhin, an American agent who worked undercover as a Soviet journalist from 1978-1982. Both Martynov and Motorin were executed, while Yuzhin served a prison sentence and immigrated to the United States in 1992.

Sergi Motorin had the dubious distinction of being unmasked by two CIA double agents, Aldrich Ames and Robert Hanssen. He returned to Moscow in January 1985 on normal rotation and was arrested later that year. He was executed in February 1987.

Valery Martynov returned to Moscow on November 6, 1985, arriving with Vitaly Yurchenko, a Russian spy who decided to return home after escaping from his CIA handler at a Washington restaurant. Hanssen had written a letter to his Russian handlers telling them that Martynov had been spying for the U.S. The unlucky Martynov was kept as a prisoner by the KGB and was executed on May 28, 1987. If Hanssen had any remorse for the deaths of Martynov and Motorin, he did not say.

While the cases of Robert Hanssen and Aldrich Ames intersected, there is no concrete evidence that either man knew each other. The Russians probably never informed either of their top double agents of the other's identity in order to protect them in case either one was uncovered.

Evidence has come to light that Hanssen was protecting the identity of Felix Bloch, a State Department diplomat who was spying for the Soviet Union for many years. Bloch worked as the deputy chief of mission in Vienna up until 1987. Hanssen told the Soviet's that French counterintelligence had spotted Bloch meeting in Paris on May 14, 1989 with Reino Gikman, a known KGB officer, and that the U.S. knew of the meeting. Eventually, Bloch was recalled to Washington, relieved of his job and retired to private life. In the end, Bloch was never charged with any crime. Referring to him, Hanssen said, "Bloch was such a schnook. I almost hated protecting him."

During his time as a Russian spy, the so-called family man, the devoted church going parishioner, was living a secret life (besides being a spy). Often times, Hanssen would invite a friend, Jack Hoschouer, to his home having him watch while he and Bonnie had sex. He also inadvertently met a very attractive woman, Priscilla Sue Galey, at a strip club he attended. What attraction brought these two very different people together is a story in itself, but over time a bond developed between them. Hanssen said he never had sex with Galey and the point is now moot. However, Hanssen tried to pry her away from her life of sex and booze, attempting to show her how God-fearing, Christian people live. At one point he had her come to his church service, but when she saw Hanssen with Bonnie and the children, she fled.

Hanssen also gave her lots of money, a Mercedes Benz and an American Express credit card to pay for the car's expenses. He also brought Galey with him on an FBI sanctioned trip to Hong Kong. When Galey used the card for gifts for her family, Hanssen flew into a rage. He tailed Galey to Columbus, Ohio in 1991 where she was visiting relatives saying he could never see her again. In time, Galey returned to her former life and became a crack addict.

In the aftermath of the deaths of Martynov and Motorin, the Bloch case could not be attributable to Ames. The discovery of the espionage of FBI agent Earl Pitts (who spied for the Russians from 1987 to 1996) the FBI assigned Robert "Bear" Bryant, head of the National Security Division, to look into the damage caused by the Pitts case. They wanted to determine if more moles were secreted inside the FBI. Bryant, in turn, handed the investigation to Thomas Kimmel, who reported back that he believed another mole was inside the FBI. Further investigation pointed the finger at a second mole hidden in the CIA. During his interrogation, Pitts said he thought there was another mole inside the FBI, but he could give no clue as to the person's identity. The Kimmel investigation reached the desk of FBI Director Louis Freeh who gave him carte blanche to find the mole. In time, Kimmel reported to Director Freeh that he believed there was another spy inside the Bureau.

The break in the Hanssen case came in the year 2000 when a new, highly-guarded FBI plan enticed new Russian agents into defecting awarding them huge amounts of cash in return for information bore fruit.

This unnamed SVR (the successor organization to the KGB) agent gave the Americans a huge packet of information regarding a valuable spy working for the Russian Federation. The documents contained physical evidence from drop sites in the Virginia area that the agent used in his espionage. U.S. authorities also got their hands on computer disks and other electronic materials that the hitherto unnamed spy had compiled over the years. Matching fingerprints taken from the physical evidence, the FBI was able to put a name to the untellable spy, Robert Hanssen.

On Sunday, February 18, 2001 FBI agents arrested Robert Hanssen as he was servicing a dead drop site in a nearby Vienna, Virginia park.

Prior to his arrest, Hanssen was beginning to think he might have gained the attention of the FBI. For some time, his Taurus was making sounds he never heard before. There were crackling noises coming from his radio and static that began to alarm him. He was right to be concerned. The FBI had planted listening devices in his car as the investigation into his possible espionage activities gained ground.

In one of his last notes to his Russian handlers, Bob wrote:

> "Life is full of its ups and downs. My hope is that, if you respond to this constant-conditions-of connection messages, you will have provided some sufficient means of re-contact besides it. If not, I will be in contact next year, same time, same place. Perhaps the correlation of forces and circumstances then will have improved."

In the probe of the damage caused by Robert Hanssen, U.S. Intelligence was able to ascertain the extent of the damage of his espionage activities. Hanssen's deception led to the deaths of two highly placed U.S. double agents. Divulging the inner workings of the U.S. double agent program, giving up a study on the recruitment efforts of the KGB inside the U.S., FBI counterintelligence techniques and methods appeared compromised. The "Continuity of Government Plan" was implemented in the event of a successful nuclear strike or terrorist attack that would wipe out Congress and/ or the executive branch of government. The CIA and the National Security Agency had built a secret tunnel under the Soviet embassy in Washington, D.C. It is not known exactly when the tunnel operation began, but it cost millions of dollars to operate and was shut down in 1995.

In the final analysis, Robert Hanssen gave the Soviet Union 6,000 pages of secret documents in a period covering 15 years. In exchange for his work, he received $1.4 million. Like Aldrich Ames, Robert Hanssen will never see the light of day.

Chapter 21
What Was Majestic 12?

What does the United States Government know about UFOs (Unidentified Flying Object) and what are they hiding? That question has been hotly debated for the past 60 plus years since the so-called Roswell Incident in New Mexico in 1947 where a supposed UFO crashed on a farmer's ranch, causing a national stir as to what exactly happened that spring day. Did the mysterious crash contain alien bodies, and if so, where did they go? Did the government cover up the incident or was it just a weather balloon that came down that day on the ranch owned by William "Mac" Brazel?

In the late 1940s and 1950s there were a slew of reports from the United States and around the world of UFO sightings. This was at the height of the Cold War, with the United States and the Soviet Union staring each other down the barrel of nuclear war. Were these unexplained sightings part of preparations for the launching of nuclear weapons by both sides?

The first event in the modern UFO era (except for the WW II phenomenon of foo fighters) took place on June 24, 1947 in the remote skies over Mt. Rainier in Washington State. While flying his private plane, pilot Kenneth Arnold saw several objects in his immediate vicinity. He later described these objects as looking like geese and moving "like a saucer would if you skipped it across the water." Many national and regional newspapers picked up the Arnold-Flying Saucer story and it soon became a national dinnertime point of conversation.

This was not the first time unexplained events took place over America. On the night of February 25, 1942 air raid sirens started to go off and the skies over Los Angeles suddenly were ablaze with anti-aircraft fire. It was only a few months before that the United States entered the war against Japan after the attack at Pearl Harbor, Hawaii and tensions were high in the country. Was this an attack by hostile powers against the homeland? Radar had reported sighting unidentified blips about 120 miles west of

L.A. Troops on the ground began firing into the air at an enemy they could not see. After the incident was over, six people on the ground were dead (caused by car accidents). No enemy bombs were dropped, no military personnel were hurt and over 1,400 rounds of ammunition were expended. Word of the so-called "attack" soon spread to Washington, where Navy Secretary Frank Knox said, "as far as I know, the whole raid was a false alarm and could be attributed to jittery nerves."

However, reports by numerous people on the ground tell a different story. Observers in the L.A. area saw red or silver objects in the sky accompanied by larger, slower targets, some of which hung suspended in the sky before taking off again. One witness, Peter Jenkins, who worked for the *Los Angeles Evening Herald Examiner,* said, "I could clearly see the "V" formation of about 25 silvery planes overhead moving slowly across the sky toward Long Beach." Another witness, Long Beach Police Chief J.H. McClelland said, "An experienced Naval observer with me using powerful Carl Zeiss binoculars said he counted nine planes in the cone of a searchlight. He said they were silver in color. This group passed along from one battery of searchlights to another, and under fire from anti-aircraft guns, flew from the direction of Redondo Beach and Inglewood on the land side of Fort MacArthur, and continued toward Santa Ana and Huntington Beach."[1]

To this day, no one really knows what was in the nighttime sky over Los Angeles that caused the army to begin firing into the sky. Was it a weather balloon or some sort of atmospheric anomaly?

Fast forward 37-years to 1984 when a series of papers came to light that supposedly told exactly what happened that night in Roswell on Mac Brazel's farm. These documents were called The Majestic 12 Papers, the contents of which have been hotly debated in the UFO community since its publication. Are the Majestic 12 Papers forgeries or is there some truth to them?

The origins of The Majestic 12 papers are an interesting one. On December 11, 1984 UFO researcher Jaime Shandera received a package in the mail, something he was not expecting. When he opened the package he found a roll of 35-millimeter Tri-X black-and-white film. Shandera showed the film to his friend and fellow

[1] Marrs, Jim, *Alien Agenda,* Harper Collins Publishers, New York, 1997, Page 63.

researcher, William Moore, which they then developed. When the film was developed they found documents and photos of what was supposed to be eight pages from a November 18, 1952 "Briefing Document" prepared for President-elect Dwight Eisenhower concerning "Operation Majestic 12." The top and bottom of the page were stamped TOP-SECRET/MAJIC EYES ONLY.

The Majestic 12 papers listed 12 important men who were members of that organization. It went on to say that Majestic 12 was a "TOP SECRET Research and Development /Intelligence operation responsible directly and only to the President of the United States" who were to deal with information concerning UFOs. The document went on to talk about the incident that took place near Roswell and what was found. It said a "secret operation" was put into motion on July 7, 1947 to recover the wreckage of a disc-shaped object which was located about 75 miles from Roswell Army Air Base. In the wreckage were "four small human-like beings who had apparently ejected from the craft" and were found dead a few miles from the crash site. Regarding the crash, the papers said, "Civilian and military witnesses in the area were debriefed, and news reporters were given the effective cover story that the object had been a misguided weather research balloon."[2]

The documents went on to describe more incredible information coming from the recovered craft. They said the beings recovered from the wreck were, "Extra-Terrestrial Biological Entities" (EBEs), who probably came from Mars (how it was determined they came from Mars is not mentioned) and the military were unable to decipher strange writing found on the craft, nor were they able to determine its method of travel. The papers then went on to say, "A need for as much additional information as possible about these craft, their performance characteristics and their purpose, led to the creation of Air Force Projects Sign and Grudge." Also, this startling information was given to two people from the Intelligence Division of Air Material Command to look into the matter further. The papers ended by saying, "Implications for the National Security are of continuing importance in that the motives and ultimate intentions of these visitors remain completely unknown." They also went on to say this information had to be kept secret in order not to create mass panic in the general population if

[2] Ibid. Page 108.

the news ever became public.

The names of the members of Majestic 12 were:

*Admiral Roscoe Hillenkoetter, the first director of the CIA when it took effect in 1947. After his retirement from government service, he founded a private UFO group called the National Investigations Committee on Aerial Phenomena, and believed that UFOs were real.

*Dr. Vannevar Bush, a noted scientist who worked on research and development of the first U.S. atomic bomb.

*Secretary of Defense James Forrestal, who served in that position until March 1949. One month after his resignation, Forrestal committed suicide by jumping out a window at the Bethesda Naval Hospital. There has been considerable speculation as to the exact circumstances surrounding the death of Secretary Forrestal and his death remains a mystery to this day.

*General Nathan Twining, the Commander of the Air Material Command based at Wright-Patterson AFB. Twining was heavily involved in the government's investigation of the UFO situation and wrote many controversial reports about the phenomena. In a letter written September 23, 1947 regarding UFOs he said, "The phenomenon reported is something real and not visionary or fictitious." While admitting that some UFO sightings had rational explanations, he said the operational capacities of these craft, "lend belief to the possibility that some of the objects are controlled manually, automatically or remotely." UFO researchers speculated that General Twining had more information about the Roswell crash than he ever revealed publicly.

*Dr. Detlev Bronk, a noted physiologist and biophysicist who chaired the National Research Council and was a member of the Atomic Energy Commission.

*Jerome Hunsaker, an aircraft designer, and the Chair of the Department of Mechanical and Aeronautical Engineering at MIT.

*Sidney Souers, a retired Navy admiral who became

the Director of the CIA in 1947.

*Gordon Gray, Assistant Secretary of the Army in 1947 and later its secretary. He was also an advisor to President Truman on national security affairs.

*Dr. Donald Menzel, a noted astronomer who worked at the Harvard College Observatory and later a debunker of UFO's.

*General Robert Montague, the base commander at the Sandia Atomic Energy Commission facility in Albuquerque, New Mexico, and

*Dr. Lloyd Berkner, who worked as the Executive Secretary of the Joint Research and Development Board under Vannevar Bush.

It is interesting to note that almost all of the above mentioned men had some sort of connection to the U.S. Intelligence Community, including two later directors of the CIA, Souers and Hillenkoetter. In the decades to come, the CIA would take an active interest in covering up the possibilities that UFOs were real and had their own secret agenda in doing so.

In the 1950s the UFO investigation went under the direction of the Pentagon in its Directorate of Intelligence, which joined with the Air Force at Wright-Patterson AFB to serve as a clearinghouse for information on UFOs. Soon, there was a deep division between Air Force officers as to whether or not the UFO phenomena were real or not. By the early 1950s a consensus among Air Force officers and the military had concluded that UFOs were not a real threat to national security, but if information about them were made public it would have a deep psychological effect on the public at large. The disagreements between the Pentagon and the Air Force led to the creation of Project Blue Book, which was given the job of investigating the many UFO reports that had been coming into public view for some time. The people who ran Project Blue Book compiled an index of all the reported sightings of UFO activity in the United States, and its mandate was to "satisfy public curiosity" about UFOs. Blue Book closed down operations in December 1969 and was replaced by Project Aquarius under the operation and control of "NSC/MJ12."

163

Project Aquarius was created in 1959 by President Eisenhower and was run by the National Security Council and MJ 12. According to author Jim Marrs in his book, *Alien Agenda,* Project Aquarius was funded by money provided by the CIA. Its prime objective was to "collect all scientific, technological, medical and intelligence information from UFO/IAC (Identified Alien Crafts), sightings, and contacts with Alien Life forms." If one can believe the facts surrounding Project Aquarius, here is a whopper for you. The Project Aquarius papers say that in 1949 another alien craft crash landed in some part of the United States and was recovered intact by the military. The craft contained a live alien creature called "EBE." This being was from a planet in the Zeta Reticuli star system, which is located about 40 light years from earth. This EBE lived until June 18, 1952 when it died of some strange illness.[3]

According to more material from Project Aquarius, in 1947 the U.S. Air Force began a number of projects to determine if aliens posed a threat to the national security of the United States. Three of these projects morphed into names such as Blue Book, Sign and Grudge. They came to the conclusion that up to 90% of the reported sightings were explainable, i.e., hoaxes, natural phenomena, or astronomical conditions, while the other ten percent were described as "legitimate" Alien sightings and/or incidents."

Other parts of Project Aquarius say "MJ12 feels confident that Aliens are on an exploration of our solar system for peaceful purposes but it was decided to observe and track the aliens in secret."

As we read the information from Project Aquarius, the most important question to be asked is are they real or fake, made up by an over-eager imagination. To answer that question we have to look into the career of UFO researcher William Moore. While time and space do not permit a full description of his UFO connections, a brief summary is in order. Moore was a former English teacher who wrote a best-selling book, *The Philadelphia Experiment* (later turned into a not-so-good movie), with author Charles Berlitz. Moore said a man called "Falcon" eventually recruited him into government service. The mysterious Falcon said he wanted to get the truth about UFOs out to the public and he, in turn, had Moore

[3] Ibid. Page 112.

contact a man, Master Sgt. Richard Doty, who was then stationed at Kirkland AFB in Albuquerque, New Mexico. Moore was given an assignment to look into a man named Dr. Paul Bennewitz, who owned an electronics firm in the city. Dr. Bennewitz told Moore that he had been monitoring alien transmissions from equipment he designed. He told Moore there were two kinds of aliens living on earth: peaceful "white" or "blond" aliens who were friendly and "grey" aliens, those who were no friend of mankind

Using Doty as an intermediary, Moore said people associated with an organization that Bennewitz ran, the Aerial Phenomena Research Organization, had been feeding him false information for many years regarding UFO contact. The kicker in the story is that it was Moore, who, in February 1981 gave Bennewitz a paper relating to the Majestic 12 project called "Project Aquarius Telex." Moore said he had retyped some of the documents and added a date stamp. Later, the Air Force investigated the Project Aquarius Telex and said they were forgeries, based on how they were written.

Another debunker of the authenticity of The Majestic 12 project was Philip Klass, who studied the UFO phenomena for years. He said that some of the members of Majestic 12 had no knowledge of UFOs landing in the United States because most of them expressed public doubt about whether UFOs ever existed.

To muddy the waters even more regarding the authenticity of Majestic 12, there appeared another group of supposed papers related to the project in April 1954 called "Majestic-12 Group Special Operations Manual."

The person receiving The Majestic 12 manual was Dr. Bruce Maccabee who ran a group called the Fund for UFO Research. The manual states that Operation Majestic 12 was started by a presidential order dated September 24, 1947 on the advice of Defense Secretary James Forrestal and Dr. Vannevar Bush. Its object was to "recover and study all materials and devices of a foreign or extraterrestrial manufacture, as well as entities or remains of entities not of terrestrial origin." The information in the manual went on to say that a number of bodies of these beings were found in the wreckage of these crashes and were being studied at an undisclosed location.

The authenticity of the so-called Majestic 12 documents has been hotly debated since their existence was made public decades ago. Among the debunkers were Philip Klass and UFO author Kevin Randle, who co-authored a book with Donald Schmitt called *The Truth About the UFO Crash at Roswell.* Randle said that in his opinion, Moore fabricated The Majestic 12 papers for his own reasons.

On the other side of the coin were believers like Stanton Friedman and Timothy Good, a British writer who said the papers had some validity. Good wrote that during his research into MJ12, he believed the MJ12 panel did exist and the documents were real. He wrote, "Unfortunately, all the members are now deceased and my questions addressed to a former director of the CIA, as well as two ex-Presidents, remain unanswered, which is hardly surprising."

In a remarkable twist, the FBI decided to initiate an investigation to see if The Majestic 12 papers were real or not. The instigator of the investigation was Philip Klass, who, in 1987 persuaded the Bureau to officially look into the matter to see if the papers were stolen government documents. At the end of their probe, the FBI was unable to decide if any person or group was willing to admit that they stole The Majestic 12 papers from the United States government or if they were a forgery.

So, the controversy regarding whether or not The Majestic 12 Project is real goes on, years after they were brought to life. There is no one alive to confirm or deny the validity of The Majestic 12 program. It is a good story, but that is all we have. Even though the controversy regarding MJ-12 continues, there are too many credible UFO sightings around the world to explain them away. UFO sightings go back hundreds of years and all of them can't be hoaxes. For example, when Columbus was nearing the new world, he and his crew saw unexplained lights in the sky, which they had never seen before. Television shows such as *Ancient Aliens* are well watched and give important information relating to sightings of unexplained phenomena dating back to biblical times. The world is full of unexplained events that we can't understand and they all shouldn't be lumped into one category, whether true or false. Until ET comes home, we'll still have to argue the point.

Chapter 22
J. Edgar Hoover's Secret War

Throughout his long tenure as the Director of the FBI, J. Edgar Hoover was the master of his own house. His orders were followed without the blink of an eye, and lord help the hapless agent who disregarded even the slightest edict from Hoover's office, be it the length of one's hair, or the color of his shirt. In the last decade of his life, Hoover conducted a number of highly illegal operations, some of which were sanctioned by the president at the time. Others were his private vendettas against his enemies, public or otherwise. While he was the lord of his fiefdom, there was one man in Hoover's executive department who had the guts to question Hoover's decision. William Sullivan (Sullivan would later die in mysterious circumstances while hunting with friends. Some researchers speculate that his death was other than the official finding of a "hunting accident") was liked more by his CIA contacts than some in his own department. Finally, a man who ultimately broke ranks with Hoover's long-held beliefs on the communist menace inside the United States.

William Sullivan joined the FBI in 1941, at age twenty-nine. He rose rapidly in the ranks and caught the attention of Hoover over the years. In 1961, Sullivan was appointed head of the Bureau's Domestic Intelligence Division. He would serve in that vitally important position until he quit the department in disgust in 1971.

As head of the Domestic Intelligence Division, Sullivan had a perfect view in which to follow the ever-growing radical underground that was sweeping the country in the 1960s and 1970s. He saw the growth of such organizations as the Weather Underground, the activities of the Civil Rights Movement and its possible ties to the Communist Party, and the Bureau's subsequent program called COINTELPRO, in which the FBI tried to disrupt the radical fridge that was mounting a campaign of terror across the country. From his perch, William Sullivan also watched the development of such radical groups as the Ku Klux Klan and the

Socialist Workers Party.

Unlike other FBI agents who adhered to Hoover's every wish, Sullivan was a maverick. He disobeyed the Bureau's strict dress code, had close ties with the Washington press corps that he cultivated, giving them tidbits of classified information. He made many friends and many enemies, especially two of the top members of Hoover's inner staff, his aide and best friend, Clyde Tolson (and possibly his lover), and Cartha "Deke" De Loach.

William Sullivan, despite his go-it-alone mentality, was one of the most knowledgeable men in the nation as far as American communism was concerned. He had studied the party since his days as an agent in World War II, collecting a personal library of over 3,000 books on the subject. He often times met with scholars, and to Hoover's deep dislike, even members of the Communist Party itself to learn more about the enemy. Hoover used Sullivan's encyclopedic mind to devise ways to disrupt the so-called communist menace inside the country, even going so far as to discredit the Rev. Martin Luther King as being a tool of foreign communists, who, Hoover was certain, were backing the Civil Rights Movement.

Sullivan's interest in looking into the possible ties between King and the CPUSA (Communist Party of the United States) came in the person of Stanley Levinson, a New York lawyer who was a long-time friend of King's. Levinson counseled King, while at the same time accused by the FBI as being a member of the communist party, but may have left the organization in 1955. The Bureau followed Levinson on one of his rounds, wiretapped his conversations, and bugged his home. Still, if a pro-communist was now working for the Rev. King then according to the FBI's thinking, King, by association, was also a communist.

In light of all of Sullivan's discourses on the threat of the American Communist party, it must have come as a monumental shock to Hoover's psyche when, on August 23, 1963 Sullivan dropped a bombshell on Hoover's desk. In a 67-page report, Sullivan debunked any link between the Communist party and their so-called efforts to intrude on the Civil Rights Movement, or to influence individual African-Americans. As Hoover read Sullivan's report, the angrier he got. While the narrative said, "Time alone will tell," the exact relationship between the CPUSA and the Black movement, Hoover was still not swayed. The pertinent sentence in Sullivan's report said, "There has been an obvious failure to the Communist Party of the United States to appreciably infiltrate, influence, or control large number of American Negroes in this country."

Hoover wrote a scathing letter back to Sullivan saying, "this memo reminds me vividly of those I received when Castro took over Cuba. You contend that Castro and his cohorts were not communists and not influenced by communists. Time alone proved you wrong. I for one can't ignore the memos as having only an infinitesimal effect on the efforts to exploit the American Negro by Communists."

Sullivan's memo regarding the CPUSA and the American Negro community set both men on a collision course that would culminate in a very surprise move by Sullivan, only one week later.

Sullivan's dramatic memo to Hoover sent his fellow agents inside the Domestic Intelligence Division into an uproar. All the work they had done linking the Communists to the Civil Rights Movement, and King in particular, was now down the drain. They couldn't understand why Sullivan had changed his mind. Unexpectedly, Sullivan sent a new, different memo to Hoover changing his position on the subject. Instead of ridiculing any relationship between the two parties, he now laid out a case that tied the CPUSA to King and his campaign.

Part of Sullivan's long memo reads in part, "The director is correct. We were completely wrong about believing the evidence was not sufficient to determine some years ago that Fidel Castro was not a communist or under communist influence. On investigating and writing about communism and the American Negro, we had better remember this and profit by the lesson it should teach us. Personally, I believe in the light of King's powerful demagogic speech yesterday, (the "I have a dream" speech); he stands head and shoulders above all masses of Negroes. We must mark him now, if we have not done so before, as the most dangerous Negro of the future in this nation from the standpoint of communism, the Negro, and national security. We greatly regret that the memorandum did not measure up to what the director has a right to expect from our analysis."

Hoover did not know what to believe from Sullivan and he shot back a harsh memo of his own: "No, I can't understand how you can so agilely switch your thinking and evaluation. Just a few weeks ago you contended that the Communist influence in the radical movement was ineffective and infinitesimal. This, notwithstanding many memos of specific instances of infiltration. Now you want to load down the field with more coverage in spite of your recent memo depreciating CP influence in the radical movement. I don't intend to waste time and money until you can make up your minds what the situation really is."

Hoover couldn't have been more upset when he learned that *Time* magazine had named Rev. King as "Man of the Year" in its January 3, 1964 edition. Now the kid gloves were off as far as King was concerned, and the FBI went on a full court press to bring down King and his Civil Rights Movement.

Hoover got an unexpected ally in his private war against King in the person of Attorney General Robert Kennedy. While there was no love lost between the two men (and also President Kennedy), Hoover persuaded RFK to place a wiretap on the phone of King's friend and political ally, Stanley Levinson, in 1962. Hoover went one step further in his war against King. He began to send derogatory information on King gleamed from "the raw intelligence reports about King, Levinson, the Civil Rights Movement, and Communist subversion" to the president, Robert Kennedy and certain of his allies in congress. In time, King scaled back his relationship with Levinson, but Hoover kept sending off memos accusing "King of a leading role in the Communist conspiracy against America."

After King's "I have a dream speech," Robert Kennedy authorized full electronic surveillance of King. Hoover's agents placed bugs in King's hotel rooms when he traveled and at his own home in Atlanta. The FBI was now able to listen in on King's policies regarding the Civil Rights Movement as well as more, juicer information; that King was having sexual relations with other women.

Hoover exacerbated the situation regarding King when, in a press conference, he called King, "the most notorious liar," and "one of the lowest characters in the country," in response from King's attack on the FBI that it did not have enough African-American agents.

In January 1965, Coretta King, Martin's wife, found a letter in her mailbox. She opened it and found an unsigned note that was a bombshell. It read in part:

> Look into your heart. You know, you are a complete fraud and a greater liability to all of us Negroes. White people in this country have enough frauds of their own but I am sure they don't have one at this time that is anywhere near your equal. You are no clergyman and you know it. I repeat that you are a colossal fraud and an evil one at that. King, like all frauds your end is approaching. You could have been our greatest leader but you are done. King, there is only one thing left for you to do. You know what it is. There is but one way out for you. You better take it before your filthy fraudulent self is bared to the nation.[1]

This fraudulent letter was the work of the FBI. It was made up entirely by the FBI in order to smear the reputation of Rev. King. The recording tape that accompanied the letter was from a number of speeches made by Rev. King over the years and put together at the FBI's laboratory. William Sullivan sent one of his most trusted FBI agents, Lish Whitsun, to go to Florida with the package and mail it to Mrs. King.

Using a wiretap on King, Hoover was able to hear King's reaction. King said, "They are out to break me, out to get me, harass me, break my spirit." Talking with Ralph Abernathy, one of his most trusted aids in the Civil Rights Movement, King replied by saying, "We are not going to let Hoover and the FBI turn us around."

In the firestorm after Hoover's "liar" remark, a mad and defiant Hoover met with King on December 1, 1964 on orders from President Lyndon Johnson.

Hoover's vendetta against Martin Luther King did not begin during the administrations of John Kennedy and Lyndon Johnson.

[1] Summers, Anthony, *Official and Confidential: The Secret Life of J. Edgar Hoover,* G.P. Putnam, Sons, New York, 1993, Page 360-361.

In 1959, when King was still a relatively unknown Negro preacher, the FBI broke into the headquarters of the Southern Christian Leadership Conference in order to gather personal information on Rev. King and to put in wiretaps to record their conversations. Early in the Kennedy Administration, Hoover ordered all of his Special Agents in Charge (SACs) around the country to compile as much dirt on Rev. King as they could find. He put his assistant, Deke DeLoach in charge of gathering up all this information. As mentioned before, Robert Kennedy ordered a wiretap to be placed on King at the insistence of Hoover. Bobby did this reluctantly for a number of reasons. One was the fact that Hoover had a huge file on JFK regarding his assignations with several women during his White House years, including Marilyn Monroe and Judith Campbell Exner. Both JFK and RFK knew about Hoover's knowledge regarding the president's affairs and they could not afford to make an enemy of Hoover who would have, in a minute, released the files to the public, virtually ending Kennedy's Administration. Hoover also was aware that Judith Exner was also having an affair with Sam Giancana, who as the Mob boss of Chicago. Giancana was also part of the CIA's secret plot to kill Fidel Castro of Cuba.

Besides the possible blackmail of JFK regarding Miss Exner, Hoover also had another bombshell he could have released regarding one of the president's mistresses. She was an East German beauty, Ellen Rometsch, who came to the United States in 1961 with her husband who was a West German Army sergeant assigned to the West German mission in Washington. Rometsch met with Bobby Baker who was the secretary to the Senate Majority Leader, Lyndon Johnson. In time, Baker used his contacts to arrange a clandestine meeting with the president, which ended in an affair. Hoover soon learned of the assignation and had another chip to use against the Kennedy's if needed. An FBI memo on the affair reads as follows:

> Information has been developed that pertains to possible questionable activities on the part of high government officials. It was also alleged that the President and the Attorney General had availed themselves of services of

playgirls.

Before any further scandal could erupt, Miss Rometsch was expelled from the United States and the story was soon forgotten in official Washington.

The author, Taylor Branch, who wrote a best-selling book on Martin Luther King called *Parting The Waters,* said of the Hoover-Robert Kennedy relationship, "It was a trap. Hoover would possess a club to offset Kennedy's special relationship with the President. How could Kennedy hope to control Hoover once he had agreed to wiretap King? There was a Faustian undertow to Kennedy's dilemma, and he did not feel strong enough to resist."

During the Kennedy Administration both the president and his brother met with King to tell him about the FBI's surveillance regarding his associations with Levinson and Jack O'Dell, a King aide who had leftwing and communist associations. Both brothers told King that for his own good he should fire both men, but King refused. At one point in his presidency, JFK had a meeting with King in which they took a walk in the White House Rose Garden. The president told King, "I assume you know that you're under close surveillance." Speaking of O'Dell and Levinson, the president told King, "They're Communists." He said, "O'Dell was the Number Five Communist in the United States." The president told King that his old friend Levinson was "so high up in the party (communist) hierarchy "that he couldn't discuss the matter further. The president further told King, "Both were agents of a foreign power." King told the president he wasn't concerned with either man but that he would take his information under advisement.

In 2010, information became public concerning a brazen move by the FBI to place a mole inside the inner circle of Dr. King. Information provided under the Freedom of Information Act revealed that King's photographer and trusted aide, Ernest Withers, was working as a double agent for the FBI. This information was released to the public via the *Commercial Appeal* newspaper in Memphis, Tennessee. Withers was with Rev. King through some of the most turbulent times in the Civil Rights Movement, including the murder of Emmett Till in 1955 and the Little Rock school integration incident. Withers worked for the FBI in King's retinue taking pictures of major events of the movement beginning in 1968, as well as spying on King's activities, all of which he reported back to Washington. Withers also spied on other civil rights leaders besides King and also Catholic priests who were involved in the Civil Rights Movement. Andrew Young, one of Rev. King's most trusted advisors, said of Ernest Withers, "I always liked him because he was a good photographer. And he was always around. I don't think Dr. King would have minded him making a little money on the side."

While Withers was working with Rev. King, he was not immune to the physical violence that many members of the group had to endure by white racists, as well as local sheriff's departments in the South. He was shot at, beaten and put-upon by, like many of the other members of the Civil Rights Movement in those turbulent times.

On April 4, 1968 Martin Luther King was shot and killed while in Memphis, Tennessee as he stood on the balcony of a hotel where he was staying. After an intense manhunt that led to England, a smalltime crook named James Earl Ray was arrested in King's murder. Ray was extradited back to the United States where he stood trial, was found guilty and sentenced to 99 years in jail. When the news of King's death reached Hoover, one can only imagine the relief on his face. His number one nemesis was dead and there would be no mourning at FBI headquarters. The day after King's death, Hoover went to the races. Soon after his conviction, Ray recanted his guilty plea and later died in jail.

Over the years, many people believed there was a conspiracy in King's death and a congressional investigation would formally look into the matter (see later chapter on the King assassination). Ralph Abernathy, one of King's most trusted friends, said that the Ku Klux Klan might have been behind the assassination. He also theorized that the FBI was behind the event. He said that King had been killed, "by someone trained or hired by the FBI and acting under orders from J. Edgar Hoover himself."

In 1988, Ray gave an interview to a TV station from his prison cell. He stated he made his original confession because of pressure from the FBI because the Bureau threatened to put his father and brother in jail. Ray said he was framed in order to cover up the

FBI's involvement in the King assassination.

William Sullivan, Hoover's other bane of existence found his career on a second track. In the summer of 1970, despite being at loggerheads with Hoover over his comments on the communist party, Sullivan was appointed to the number two position in the FBI as assistant to the director, after the resignation of Deke DeLoach, who took a job as an executive with PepsiCo. Hoover would lament of his decision to appoint Sullivan to that position as "the worst mistake I ever made."

Chapter 23
The FBI and the
Day of Terror Plot

On February 26, 1993, a massive explosion took place at the World Trade Center in New York City blowing a four-story crater down the B-4 parking level of the massive structures. The blast killed five people, injured over 1,000 and caused billions of dollars of damage to the iconic buildings. This horrible event brought terrorism to the gates of the United States and its story would culminate, eight years later when al-Qaeda terrorists hijacked four planes and crashed them into the sides of the World Trade Center, turning them into rubble, and at the Pentagon in Washington, D.C. Not known at the time of the 1993 bombings was the incident could have been averted except for the massive intelligence failure on the part of the FBI and other law enforcement agencies in the United States. There people in particular, an FBI agent named Nancy Floyd, a decorated NYFD officer named Ronald Bucca, and an FBI informant, Emad Salem, had put the pieces of the puzzle together but their collective information was not heeded in time to prevent the attack.

As international terrorism began to affect American citizens around the world, the FBI's New York office was designated as the originator for all Islamic terror cases. In order to facilitate better cooperation between local and federal law enforcement authorities, the FBI and the NYPD began intelligence sharing arrangement called the Joint Terrorism Task Force or JTTF. Their goal was to share pertinent information between the two agencies that would better enable them to do their jobs more effectively. More often than not, cooperation lasted until the front door, with deep distrust between the two rival agencies taking center stage.

The FBI's Special Operations Group (SOG) had the job of watching a number of Middle Eastern men called ME's who attended the Alkifa Center at the Al-Farooq mosque in Brooklyn, New York. The mosque was a hotbed of anti-American, pro-Islamic activity and was the place where the radical blind Sheik,

Omar Abdul Rahman, held forth. Not known to the FBI in 1989 was that a little known Saudi millionaire was bankrolling Sheik Rahman named Osama bin Laden.

In July 1989, the SOG team watched as a number of MEs left Brooklyn in a car and traveled along the Long Island Expressway to a shooting range in Calverton, Long Island. Parking near the shooting range, the FBI agents saw the men practice with AK-47 rifles at stationary targets. They followed the men on four different occasions during July and took numerous pictures. While it was not a crime to fire AK-47's at a public rifle range, it did perk the FBI's interest. Unfortunately, no law had been broken so the SOG team had no probable cause to arrest them. If they had been a little more diligent in their investigation of the ME's at Calverton, they would have been shocked at what they would have found.

The Calverton shooters had direct links to the blind Sheik and were all identified as being cell members in the 1993 bombing of the WTC, the assassination of the radical Rabbi, Meir Kahane, and the so-called "Day of Terror " plots to destroy tunnels and landmarks in New York City.

The men the SOE followed were:

*Mahmud Abouhalima, an Egyptian who was a known associate of the WTC planner, Ramzi Yousef, and a New York cabby.

*El Sayyid Nossair, another Egyptian who worked in the Manhattan Civil Court building as a maintenance man. Nossair would later kill Rabbi Meyer Kahane.

*Mohammed Salameh, born in Jordan, who was a member of Ramzi Yousef's team that struck the WTC in February, 1993.

*Nidal Ayyad, a Kuwaiti who attended Rutgers University in New Jersey. He would buy the chemicals that were used by Yousef in the WTC attack.

*Clement Rodney Hampton-El, an American citizen, Black Muslim who was later to be convicted in the plots to blow up New York City landmarks.

*Ali Mohammed, a man with a both military and terrorist backgrounds whose presence among the other ME's should have made the FBI look deeper.

Ali Mohammed was an Egyptian army officer and a member

of the Egyptian Islamic Jihad. He was linked to the assassination of President Anwar Sadat of Egypt but was not prosecuted because he was in the U.S. at the time of the 1981 assassination attending the Army's Special Warfare Operations School at Fort Bragg, North Carolina. In the aftermath of the WTC bombing in 1993, police found a large amount of classified material in the New Jersey home of one of Yousef's accomplices. That top-secret material belonged to Ali Mohammed. In time, Mohammed would become a "contract" agent for the CIA. As the feds began an investigation of him they found out that he was linked to the Middle Eastern terror group Hezbollah, and was placed on a State Department "Watch List" of people who were to be denied entry into the United States.

If the FBI had decided to put forth a full court press and bring in for questioning the men who made up the Calverton shooting cell, who knows how far they would have gone in possibly cracking the February 1993, WTC bombing before it took place.

The convoluted story that led up to the first WTC attack that would prove to be a major black mark on the ability of the FBI to get inside the radicals surrounding the blind Sheik, is full of twists and turns. It is a tale steeped in petty jealousies, turf wars, and most of all, ego on the parts of certain high level FBI agents.

The narrative revolves around two individuals, Nancy Floyd, a Texas born FBI agent and her informer in the camp of Sheik Rahman, Emad Salem, an ex-Egyptian army officer, and Floyd's friend and confidant.

Nancy Floyd attended the University of Texas at Arlington where she got her B.S. in criminal justice in 1982. After graduation she was accepted into the FBI. Her first assignment was in Savannah, Georgia before coming to work at the New York office. She got a choice assignment, working at 26 Federal Plaza in downtown New York. She worked in the FBI's Foreign Counter Intelligence Division. Her unit was tasked with the job of following the members of the GRU-Soviet military intelligence-who mostly worked undercover as members of the Soviet delegation to the United Nations.

Nancy Floyd and Emad Salem first met in 1991 when she was carrying out her job at a Manhattan Hotel as part of the FBI's

Hotel Asset Program in which she spoke to the various hotel managers, and discreetly asked them to keep an eye out for any Soviet diplomats who might have ran afoul of the law. Salem had come from Egypt, was a naturalized American citizen, and was eager to help the United States any way he could. He worked at an undisclosed hotel as a guard and she and the Egyptian soon hit it off. Over time, Salem did surveillance work for Floyd, turning in a number of illegal aliens, and building up his bona fides with her. Salem began telling Floyd about the different people he'd come across in the city, one of whom was the blind Sheik, Omar Abdel Rahman and his anti-American exhortations at the Jersey City mosque he preached in. Floyd was intrigued with Salem and his wide connections and she persuaded her bosses to bring Salem on as an "asset." He was paid $500 a week and went to work infiltrating the Sheiks cell. Emad Salem would now join the Sheiks inner circle, and provided an abundance of real time information on the illegal activities going on in Brooklyn and Jersey City.

Two other FBI agents, John Anticev and his associate, Detective Lou Napoli, also began tracking the whereabouts and activities of a number of men associated with the Calverton shooters. They began putting the pieces together regarding the shooting of Rabbi Kahane, as well as the activities of his killer, El Sayyid Nosair. They also ran down leads associating Mohamed Abouhalima with the killing of Mustafa Shalabi, the man who once ran the Alkifa Center in Brooklyn, a hot bed of Islamic agitation in New York. In time, the investigations of Floyd, Napoli and Anticev would intertwine.

Emad Salem had been in the United States for five years before meeting Nancy Floyd. He was raised in Cairo, and attended a technical college. He also served in the Egyptian army and held the rank of major. He told Agent Floyd that he was trained in intelligence work while in the army. He also told her that his unit had been responsible for the protection of Egyptian President Anwar Sadat.

In his conversations with Nancy Floyd, Salem brought her up to date on who Sheik Rahman really was-that he was the leader of the radical al Gamma'a Islamiya, an Egyptian terror group with a long history of violence in that country. For days on end, Salem drilled Nancy Floyd with the history of the Middle East and the various radical groups that plied their deadly trade.

Salem's first job as an "asset" was to identify an Egyptian U.N. officer whom the FBI believed might be acting undercover. Not only did Salem name him and shocked them by reporting that the same person was working for the CIA.

After passing the test, Floyd introduced Salem to her colleagues, Anticev and Napoli. Salem told them that he knew that Abouhalima, whom they were trying to locate. Salem also told them that the red headed Abouhalima was a currently the driver for Sheik Rahman. Salem was now to become the FBI's first informant inside the cell run by Sheik Rahman whose office also proved to be the home to many of the men who would blow up the WTC in 1993, and was being secretly funded by Osama bin Laden.

Salem was now ready to go undercover for the FBI but under one condition. He did not want his identity to be revealed. He said his wife and children were still living in Egypt and that he wanted them safe from any reprisals. He also said that he would agree to be wired but that he needed a promise from the FBI that he would not have to testify about his activities in court. His demands were met and in FBI parlance, Salem was now considered to be an "intelligence asset."

In the paperwork done before he went undercover, it was agreed that Nancy Floyd would be Salem's contact officer, while Napoli and Anticev would evaluate the material he provided.

Using his connections in the New York Egyptian community, Salem managed to get an introduction to Sheik Rahman and he soon became a familiar presence at the Brooklyn mosque, a spy in the lion's den.

As the FBI watched the nightly news, they could not have been happier with what they saw. Standing arm in arm with the blind Sheik was Emad Salem. As Salem grew familiar with the Sheik and his religious order, Sheik Rahman asked Salem to issue a fatwa, or religious decree, putting in motion an assassination attempt on the life of Egyptian President Hosni Mubarak.

After the conviction of El Sayyid Nosair in the Kahane murder, Nossair was sent to the maximum-security prison in Attica, New

York. Often times, Salem would visit Nossair in jail and gained his trust. It was during one of these visits that Nosair asked Salem to put out a hit on the judge who sentenced him to jail, as well as a contract on the life of a New York politician from Brooklyn. More disturbingly, Nosair wanted Salem to form a plot to destroy twelve "Jewish locations" centered on the diamond district in Manhattan. All this information was passed along to Nancy Floyd and her FBI bosses. No follow up was ever done regarding the possible plot to bomb the "Jewish locations."

During his nightly sessions with the men from the Brooklyn and New Jersey mosques, talk of bringing the jihad to the United States was the paramount topic of discussion. Soon, two other men would join the group, Ahmed Sattar, a U.S. postal employee, and an Egyptian named Ahmed Amin Refai, an accountant who was employed by the New York Fire Department. Often times, Refai was seen on television with Sheik Rahman but neither the NYPD nor the JTTF sought to open a file on them until much later.

At one point, Salem met with a man called "Dr. Rashid," a.k.a, Clement Rodney Hampton-El who told Salem that he would be able to provide the Sheik's cell with automatic weapons. As Salem listened, he now realized that the Brooklyn cell headed by Sheik Rahman were planning a major terrorist attack against Jewish locations in the city, as well as the planned assassinations of a number of public figures. All of this information was passed along to Floyd, Napoli and Anticev, as well as their superiors at 26 Federal Plaza. Despite the explicit warnings by Salem that something big was about to take place in New York, nothing was done to interrupt the blind Sheik's plans.

Soon, internal politics at the FBI would intervene to change Salem's situation for the worse. At the time that he went undercover, a new management supervisor directing the Floyd-Salem mission took over. The new head of the New York office was Carson Dunbar, a former New Jersey State Trooper with limited field experience. Working with Dunbar was SA John Crouthamel, a new branch supervisor responsible for terrorism activities.

Without bringing Nancy Floyd into the picture, Crouthamel met with Salem, Napoli, and Anticev. The gist of the conversation was to have Salem work with the two agents, leaving Nancy out of the picture entirely. From that point on, the top brass at the New York FBI terrorism unit did all they could to drive Nancy Floyd from her job, and in the process, remove the only lead they had into the growing terror cell in New York led by Osama bin Laden and Sheik Rahman.

Salem's undoing came after he was given a polygraph test that Nancy did not know about. Dunbar met with Salem without Nancy's permission. He gave Salem an ultimatum, "Either you wear a wire or agree to testify, or I don't want to see you anymore." It was obvious that Dunbar did not like Salem and he wanted to control him at all costs. Despite the fact that Salem was the only plant inside the Sheik's terror cell, Dunbar had the nerve to say of Salem, "We don't know if *they* would trust him. He was not believable to us." With that mind set in place, it is no wonder that the FBI failed to connect the dots linking a number of men working out of the blind Sheik's mosque with the February 1993 WTC bombing with the information being provided to them by Emad Salem.[1]

Believing that he was being double crossed, Salem refused to go along with Dunbar's demand and quit his job. The FBI was now left out in the cold as far as getting useful information regarding the terror cell organized by Sheik Rahman. The decision to let Salem hung in the wind would later come to haunt the FBI.

During the early 1990s, Emad Salem was not the only person interested in cracking the den of thieves headed by Sheik Rahman. A lone, New York City Fire Department Fighter, Ronnie Bucca, would mount a one-man crusade to stem the tide of Islamic fundamentalism that he saw as a threat to New York City. Like Salem, the FBI would not invite Bucca to the dance, leaving him a lone wolf, operating outside the system.

Besides being a member of the FDNY, Ronnie Bucca was a member of the U.S. Army's 242nd Military Intelligence Battalion, with the rank of sergeant. His reserve unit was associated with the secret Defense Intelligence Analysis section located at Bolling AFB in Washington. This unit was part of the super-secret Defense Intelligence Agency. Bucca read all the classified materials that he could find regarding international terrorism, especially as

[1] Lance, Peter, *1000 Years For Revenge,* Regan Books, New York, 2003, Page 93.

it related to the Middle Eastern conflict. The more he read the more convinced he became that the U.S. would become a target of radical Islamic terrorism. What he didn't know, but would soon learn, was the group he feared were only a few miles away.

Ronnie Bucca worked in the elite unit of the NYFD called Rescue One, which was responsible for calls in the borough of Manhattan. However, in July 1992, he put in for a position as fire marshal with the FDNY's Bureau of Fire Investigation. While attending his meetings with his intelligence division he learned that the Feds had put an informer inside the blind Sheik's inner circle (Salem), and that he was subsequently, let go.

As he dug deeper into the intelligence gleamed from his top-secret clearance, Bucca was able to lay out the evidence against Ramzi Yousef (who was mastermind of the 1993 WTC attack), and the blind Sheik. The information he collected led him to believe that the followers of Yousef would try again to topple the twin towers.

Bucca decided to apply for a position with the JTTF but there were no positions available. Undeterred, he set out on a one-man crusade to follow the connecting dots linking all the Calverton shooter suspects to the blind Sheik and his Day of Terror Plots.

In 1999, almost by chance, Bucca would come across a man who worked for the NYFD as an accountant, a U.S. citizen of Egyptian heritage, Ahmed Refai. Bucca learned that Refai told his supervisor that he had lost his FDNY ID card and was applying for a replacement. Using surveillance films, Bucca knew that Refai was lying. Ronnie talked to Refai's supervisor, Kay Woods, who gave him the most astounding information. It seems that Refai, an insignificant accountant, asked for, and was given the blue prints for the World Trade Center.

Digging deeper, Ronnie found out that Refai had been seen walking with Sheik Rahman at various times. Refai also served as the Sheik's translator at an immigration hearing and that he also attended the al-Salaam mosque in Jersey City frequented by the Sheik. Ronnie gave his information on Refai to the FBI but they, once again, refused to follow up because Refai had committed no obvious crime.

On 9-11, 2001, Ronnie Bucca responded to the inferno that

was the twin towers. His body was later found amid the rubble.

The seminal event in the lives of Ronnie Bucca, Nancy Floyd, and Emad Salem took place on February 26, 1996 when Ramzi Yousef and the Calverton shooting range suspects set off a bomb that was secreted inside a Ryder Van near Room 107 on the B-2 level beneath the WTC. Suffice it to say that with the attack on the WTC, all bets were off as far as the FBI was concerned. If they didn't have proof positive that Emad Salem was telling the truth about the men associated with Sheik Rahman, they did now. In a hastily called meeting, the FBI reinstated Salem as their prime source inside the cell and agreed to pay him not the five hundred a month that he previously received, but a total of $1.5 million.

Salem returned to the field, convinced the mosque members that he was free of FBI surveillance and borrowed back deep inside the cell. In a matter of luck and sheer perseverance, Salem was able to interrupt a wave of terror attacks dubbed the Day of Terror plot in which Sheik Rahman and a number of his followers were arrested. Their deadly scheme included the bombings of the Lincoln and Holland tunnels, the U.N. building, and the George Washington Bridge.

The events after the WTC bombing were bittersweet for both Salem and Floyd. Salem lambasted the bureau for not believing him in the first place regarding the goings on at the Brooklyn mosque, saying that if the feds had put their trust in him from the beginning, the WTC attack may have been prevented. Salem was subsequently put in the Witness Protection Service.

Nancy Floyd also did not fare well. The FBI opened up an OPR, or internal affairs investigation of her that would last five years and effectively end her FBI career. In an article in the *New York Post* of March 11, 1994, it was alleged that Nancy was having an affair with Salem, a charge that was false. In the end, Nancy Floyd was found innocent of all charges.

On 9-11, 2001, as Nancy Floyd was driving into New York she saw the billowing flames shoot up from the WTC. All of her years of work with Emad Salem had come full circle.

Chapter 24
Oswald's Doubles

When the accused assassin of President John F. Kennedy, Lee Oswald was arrested, the Dallas Police Department had a hard time figuring out just whom they had in custody. Oswald was arrested about an hour after the assassination in Dealey Plaza when he was captured in the Texas Theater for allegedly killing DPD Officer J.D. Tippit in the Oak Cliff section of Dallas. The police and the Secret Service interrogated Oswald for two days and the police of what he told them took no official record. He related the basic facts of his life. He was born in New Orleans in 1939, his family moved frequently to various cities in the United States; he joined the Marines at age seventeen, and in 1959, traveled to the Soviet Union where he lived for over two years. He said he married a Russian woman and wanted to become a Soviet citizen but decided not to do so and returned to the U.S. with his wife, Marina and their young child. They lived in New Orleans for a while and then the Oswald's returned to Texas, moving to Dallas.

Shortly after the assassination, the Dallas police found a rife on the sixth floor of the Texas School Depository building where Oswald worked as a book handler. On the floor were three spent cartridge shells, presumably coming from the rifle. The gun was a 6.5 Mannlicher-Carcano, Italian made rifle that was used in World War II, serial number C-2766. Later, the FBI said they found a palm print on the rifle that matched Oswald's.

The next day, the FBI called Klein's Sporting Goods Company in Chicago and asked them to check their files for any gun sold with the serial number C-2766. Soon, a positive match was found. They had sold the rile on March 20 to a customer named A. Hidell at Post Office Box 2915 in Dallas, Texas. "A. J. Hidell" signed the order form.

The Dallas police now had incriminating evidence on Oswald. His handwriting matched the mail order form for the rifle from Klein's and his palm print matched those found on the gun. But what they couldn't figure out was why Oswald was carrying a fake identity card with the name of "A.J. Hidell" on his person. Was Oswald his real name or was he "A.J. Hidell?

Under interrogation, Oswald said that he used the alias "Hidell" and began using it while he was living in New Orleans in the summer of 1963 while passing out Fair Play for Cuba Committee literature on the streets of the Big Easy. He later told the police that he never used the name Hidell and got angry when they pushed him into accounting for the name.

It seems however that Oswald knew someone who had a name similar to his alias, "Hidell." This man was John Rene Heindel who served in the Marines with Oswald. He later said that while in the Marines he was often times called "Hidell" by his fellow Marines because he sounded a lot like the name Rydell. He said, "This was a nickname and not merely a mispronunciation." Heindel said that he served with Oswald at Atsugi Base in Japan where Oswald was a radar operator and monitored the secret U-2 planes that flew secret missions across the U.S.S.R. and China. The U-2 program was run by the CIA. Heindel also said that he lived in New Orleans, the same city where Oswald was born and lived in the summer of 1963, doing all sorts of shady activities.[1]

The Warren Commission's investigation of the Kennedy assassination did not really look into the possibilities that another person was using the alias of Hidell because it did not fit in with their preconceived notion that Oswald was the lone killer of the president. John Rene Heindel was never called as a witness to testify before the commission in this matter.

When Oswald was arrested after the assassination, the police found in his wallet a draft cared with the name "Hidell". Why did he have it and was it a real name? If the police did not have any clue as to who "A.J. Hidell" was, the United States Army sure did.

When the Warren Commission began their investigation of the assassination, they had no idea that the U.S. military had any files of Oswald before the assassination with the possible exception being Oswald's personal military records. As a routine part of their work, they wrote to the Army requesting any such records and were told that none existed. The military did indeed have an extensive file on Oswald but did not produce it.

[1] Summers, Anthony, *Conspiracy,* McGraw Hill & Co., New York, 1980, Page 90.

On the day of the assassination, Army intelligence officers were slated to be part of the security detail in Dealey Plaza. This is standard operating procedure for the military to augment the Secret Service. On November 22, 1963, the 112th Army Intelligence Unit at Fort Sam Houston was ready to travel to Dallas to aid the security detail. At the last minute they were told to stand down. Why? The unit's commander, Colonel Maximilian Reich, objected to the "stand down" order but was overruled.

But if the entire 112th M.I. detachment did not proceed to Dealey Plaza there were a number of men linked to military intelligence on the ground. Army agent James Powell was in Dealey Plaza during the assassination and had with him a 35mm. Minox camera. After the shooting, agent Powell was in the Book Depository Building and said he helped the sheriff's department to seal up the building. But what was he really doing there?

Lt. Commander George Whitmeyer, the commander of the local military intelligence unit was riding with the police in the motorcade. An unidentified member of Army Intelligence spent some time on the morning of the 22nd with FBI agent James Hosty. Oswald had Hosty's name and car license plate number in his address book.

After word had been received that a suspect, Lee Harvey Oswald had been arrested in the president's death, word went out to the various intelligence agencies of the United States. The 112th M.I. unit searched its files and came up with a startling piece of information. They had a file on Oswald, along with the fact that he used an alias, A.J. Hidell. His name was listed because he was a "possible counter-intelligence threat."

Oswald's file was listed under both his real name and his alias, A.J. Hidell. The file contained all the critical information on Oswald's background including his stay in Russia, his marriage to Marina and his return home. In an interesting twist, the 112th M.I. had a file on Oswald listing his name as "Harvey Lee Oswald" living at 605 Elsbeth Street in Dallas. Oswald lived there late in 1962 and early 1963.

Lt. Colonel Robert Jones, the operations officer of the 112th M.I., had more interesting things to say about the Oswald file in their possession. He said that the military had information on

Oswald's time in New Orleans, as well as his stay in Russia. When Jones testified before the HSCA he told the investigators that the army file on Oswald had been opened in mid-1963 under the names Lee Harvey Oswald and A.J. Hidell. Col. Jones, after hearing about the assassination, passed this information on to Gordon Shanklin, the Agent-in-Charge of the FBI's Dallas office. When the HSCA was conducting its probe of the Kennedy assassination, they asked the army for any relevant files they had on Oswald. The army replied that all the files on Oswald had been destroyed as a matter of "routine." Why?

Lt. Col. Jones said that the name Hidell was an Oswald alias, but Oswald did not use that name while he was living in New Orleans in the summer of 1963. The only time Oswald factually used the alias Hidell was when he ordered the rifle from Klein's Sporting Goods Company. This leaves the possibility that some segment of the U.S. Army was watching Oswald's movements in New Orleans in the summer of 1963 for some unknown reason.

Another interesting fact to be discussed is why Oswald ordered a rifle through the mail when he could have bone into any gun shop in Texas and ordered one with no questions asked. There were none of the rigorous conditions that we have now in place to buy a gun and by doing so, Oswald opened up a clear paper trail for anyone to find, and find the FBI did after the assassination. Did he have a reason to buy a gun in this manner? Oswald also bought a .38 Smith and Wesson revolver, which he purchased from Seaport Traders of Los Angeles in March 1963 through a mail order coupon. This was another over the counter gun purchase, which left a paper trail.

Another person who was affiliated with the CIA, Richard Case Nagell told author Dick Russell who wrote a huge book on him called *The Man Who Knew Too Much,* said that at one time he used the alias Alek Hidell, the same last name as Oswald's. Nagell said that he used the Hidell alias on two different occasions as part of his undercover work. Author Russell writes that the alias Hidell might have been part of an intelligence operation "derived from the last three letters of Nagell's name," possibly linked to an operation conducted by the South Korean government.

In the run up to the president's assassination, there were a number of Oswald sightings in and around the Dallas area, some of which were credible, others which were not. One of the most curious parts of this story date back to 1959, long before John F. Kennedy was even elected president of the United States. On June 3, 1960, an FBI memorandum that contained the signature of J. Edgar Hoover warned the State Department "there is a possibility that an imposter is using Oswald's birth certificate." This was during the time that the real Oswald was in Russia. Why was Hoover so interested in an obscure Marine who defected to the Soviet Union whom no one had heard of?

This incident is of interest for the following reason. After the assassination, the FBI got a letter from the manager of a Ford Motor Company dealership in New Orleans with some intriguing information. The manager, Oscar Desclatte, said that he remembered the name Oswald and checked his files. He found paper work that revealed that in 1961, two years before the assassination, that a customer arrived at his place and wanted to buy Ford trucks. Desclatte told the FBI that he remembered the man who said he was Oswald was with a Cuban looking man and that they both tried to purchase the trucks on January 20, 1961 (the day of John Kennedy's inauguration). Desclatte said that the men asked him to give them a deal on the trucks because, "We're doing this for the good of the country." This was the time when the U.S. government was beginning its preparations for the invasion of Cuba that would take place at the Bay of Pigs in April 1961. Desclatte said the man who was going to buy the trucks said that his name was "Joseph Moore" but asked that the name of "Oswald" be put on the official documents. Oswald, Desclatte was told was handing the trucks for his anti-Castro organization and that the money would come in some time later. When Desclatte saw a picture of Lee Oswald, he could not identify him as the man who came to his dealership two years previously. The crux of the matter is that while "Joseph Moore" was trying to buy Ford trucks under the Oswald name, the real Lee Oswald was living in Russia. Why was someone using the name of Oswald in 1961 when he was in Russia? Was he being set up *then* for some future use?

On September 25, 1963, a man calling himself Harvey Oswald came to the Selective Service Headquarters (the infamous draft board) in Austin. Texas. He told the person in charge that he had been discharged from the Marines under "other than honorable conditions" and wanted to see if his status could be changed. The woman who Harvey Oswald saw, a Mrs. Lee Dannelly, checked her files and could not find anyone by that name. The young man told her that he was living in Fort Worth and she told him to go to that office. On that date, the real Lee Oswald was however, on his way from New Orleans to Mexico City where he would engage in all sorts of mischief. Were unknown persons setting him up again?

On November 24, 1963, two days after the assassination, the DPD got an anonymous call from the Irving Sports Shop saying that Oswald had a rifle sighted a few weeks before. An employee of the shop said he found a customer ticket for work being done from November 4-8. The name of the person who left the rifle was named "Oswald." After checking other gun shops in the area, no other trace of any person with the name Oswald having repairs done on a rifle was ever found. What "Oswald" wanted to have done on the rifle was to drill three holes for a telescopic sight mounting. The gun found in the Book Depository had the same three holes bored on the rifle.

Another Oswald sighting came on November 16, 1963 at the Sports Drome Rifle Range. This story comes from a doctor named Homer Wood who was at the range that day with his young son. Dr. Wood told the FBI that he and his son were talking with a young man who was in the booth next to them, also shooting. Dr. Wood said the man told them he was using an Italian made rifle with a four-power scope. After the assassination, they told authorities that the person in the next booth was Lee Harvey Oswald. The FBI tried to persuade the Woods to change their story but they refused to do so.

Another double Oswald sighting took place on November 9, 1963 when a man calling himself Lee Oswald arrived at a Lincoln Mercury car dealership in Dallas. Lee Oswald talked with salesman Albert Bogard who took the customer on a harrowing, 70 mile an hour test-drive around the city. Oswald said that he did not have the money that day to buy the car but he would have it in a few weeks. What makes this incident interesting is that the real Lee Oswald did not have a driver's license and did not know how to drive. Once they were back in the dealership, another salesman, Eugene Wilson, tried to get Oswald to buy the Comet that very day. Oswald grew belligerent and said something to the effect that, "Maybe I'm going to go back to Russia to buy a car."

Another impersonation of Oswald comes from Robert Vinson, at the time (1963), a U.S. Air Force sergeant who was attached to the North American Air Defense Command (NORAD). This event is right out of a spy novel coming from the likes of the late Robert Ludlum and Tom Clancy. It is a story that even Hollywood would have a hard time getting its hands on. Sgt. Vinson claims that he was on a CIA plane that took off from Dallas right after the assassination with Lee Harvey Oswald on board. On November 20, 12963, Sgt. Vinson was en-route to Washington, D.C. to discuss with his superiors his promotion that he thought the deserved. He had an exemplary military record, having served for sixteen-years. On November 21, 1963, one day before the president was scheduled to go to Dallas, Sgt. Vinson was meeting with a Colonel Chapman at his office in the Capitol Building, when the phone rang at Col. Chapman's desk. Sgt. Vinson heard the officer tell the person on the other end of the line that he thought it would be ill advised for the president to make his trip to Dallas the next day "because there had been something reported" (what that was something is not known).

Col. Chapman told Sgt. Vinson that he would refer his promotion recommendation to the Pentagon and said he'd do all he could to speed it up. The next day, Sgt. Vinson was at Andrews AFB to catch a plane back to Colorado where he was stationed. After waiting a while, he boarded a C-54 cargo plane, which had no military markings or serial numbers visible. The only thing that was on the plane was markings on its tail. As he sat down, two other men came aboard, saying nothing to Sgt. Vinson. Sgt. Vinson did not have to sign any flight manifest as to his being on the plane (neither did the other two men).

A few hours into the flight, the pilot announced the death of the president over the intercom and the plane then made preparations to make an unscheduled landing in Dallas, Texas. The C-54 landed not an airport but on a stretch of sand near the Trinity River. Soon after the plane landed, two men got onboard without saying a word to Sgt.. Vinson. One man was white, about 5'7 to 5'9 while the other man looked Latin and was about 6 feet tall. Both men wore workers clothing. On the weekend of the assassination, Sgt. Vinson made a startling discovery while watching the news. The shorter man who came on board the plane looked identical to Lee Harvey Oswald. A few hours later, the plane landed and the two men who got on in Dallas suddenly left the plane, as clandestinely as they had arrived. Years later, Vinson said of the strange goings on, "That was very strange, very strange. I couldn't understand why they were in such a rush. They just bailed out."[2]

When the plane landed, Vinson was informed that he was in Roswell, New Mexico, not Denver. On Saturday, he managed to get a military flight home to Colorado Springs. He later told his wife about his strange encounter and told her about the man on the plane who looked like Oswald. He had no idea what had happened but he knew it wasn't kosher. He was later asked by his superior officer to sign a secrecy agreement and the FBI regarding the Vinson's questioned his neighbors.

On November 25, 1964, Sgt. Vinson found himself at CIA headquarters going through a number of tests. He was asked to work for the CIA but he refused. Three months later, Sgt. Vinson was in Las Vegas speaking again to a CIA officer. Without his knowledge, he had been transferred by the Air Force to the CIA and was now working as Nellis AFB, or Area 51. He also worked in the super-secret Blackbird spy plane project run out of Nellis. One day at Nellis, Vinson saw the same unmarked C-54 with the distinctive tail markings as the same plane he was on that fateful November weekend in 1963. A fellow Sergeant told him that the plane belonged to the CIA.[3]

In 1993, Robert Vinson broke his silence regarding the mysterious plane ride he'd taken on the weekend of November 22, 1963, giving an interview to a news anchor at KAKE-TV channel 10 in Wichita. What Robert Vinson took part in, he believed, was a CIA effort to get the "Oswald double" out of Dallas at the time of the assassination. While we don't know if the "real" Oswald was on the C-54 or his double was killed in the basement of the

---

[2] Douglas, James, *JFK And The Unspeakable: Why He Died & Why It Matters,* Orbis Books, Maryknoll, New York, 2008, Page 299-300.

[3] Ibid. Page 302.

DPD by Jack Ruby is still open for question. But the intriguing circumstances of that weekend beg for answers, a C-54 without markings, an unscheduled stop in Dallas from Washington where two men, one looking like Lee Oswald got on board right after the president was shot, and the transfer of Robert Vinson to the CIA a few years later (most likely to keep him quiet), is all more than coincidence. Robert Vinson summed up his feelings on the subject when he said, "Every time I see an article on the assassination, I stop and wonder if I have the answer to this puzzle. Could this small piece of information fit into the larger picture to help us learn what happened?"

Another unsolved incident involving an Oswald double took place on September 26, 1963, that still perplexes and confounds Kennedy assassination researchers as to exactly what happened that particular day and how it connects in the long run to the president's assassination.

On that day, three men came to the Dallas home of Sylvia Odio, an influential person in the anti-Castro community. Her father was Amador Odio, one of the wealthiest men in Cuba who owned the largest trucking business on the island. When Castro first came to power, the Odio's were supporters of his revolution, but as time went on, they began to sour on how Castro was running the country. Amador Odio joined with Manolo Ray to form a large, anti-Castro organization, JURE. While in Cuba, the Odio's were arrested by Castro's forces and put in jail. Sylvia was then living with her two sisters, Annie and Sarita and they too were to be brought into the strange events that took place later that day.

On that day, three men came unannounced to her house. Neither Sylvia nor her sisters had ever met the men before and were wary of letting them in. Instead, Sylvia spoke to them with the latch still on the door. According to Odio, two of the men were Cuban looking, one with more pronounced Mexican heritage than the other. The third man was an American, who did not say very much. He was introduced to them as "Leon Oswald."

One of her guests introduced himself as "Leopoldo" and the other man as "Angel." They said they were friends of Manolo Ray and that they also knew her father. They said that "Leon Oswald" was interested in joining their cause but did not elaborate further.

They said that they had just arrived from New Orleans and hoped that Sylvia would help them to obtain funds for JURE's activities, and asked if she would write a letter to certain anti-Castro businessmen who might be able to help. Sylvia was noncommittal and asked the men to leave. That, as far as Sylvia Odio was concerned, was the end of the matter. Or so she thought.

A few days later, Sylvia received a call from Leopoldo, one of the men who had been at her home. He began by telling something Sylvia did not expect. He said that "the American (Leon Oswald) had been in the Marines and was an excellent shot and that the American said that the Cubans don't have any guts because President Kennedy should have been assassinated after the Bay of Pigs, and some Cubans should have done that, because he was the one that was holding the freedom of Cuba actually." Leopoldo also said that Leon was "loco," kind of nuts." He asked her if Oswald had made any impression on her and Sylvia replied that she never gave it much thought.

After that phone call, Sylvia did not hear from the two men again. However, she did write a letter to her father who was still imprisoned in Cuba, telling him of the incident. Amador Odio replied that he didn't know the identities of the three men and told Sylvia to be careful with any other suspicious visitors.

Both sisters forgot about the incident until the afternoon of November 22, 1963. Upon seeing the picture of the man accused of killing the president, both Annie and Sylvia tried to remember where they had seen the face of Lee Harvey Oswald before. They both remembered that the man in question was "Leon Oswald," the man who had been to their home two months before. Upon seeing Oswald's picture, Sylvia had a fainting spell and wound up in the hospital.

The FBI learned of Miss Odio's run in with "Leon Oswald" through a third party and she was interviewed by them shortly thereafter. The Bureau then relayed their interview with Sylvia Odio to the Warren Commission. The Commission found Odio's allegations about an Oswald visit credible. However, if what Sylvia and Sarita said were true, the whole basis of the Warren Report of Oswald being the lone assassin might have been put in jeopardy.

The FBI first interviewed Sylvia Odio on December 12, 1963. In August 1964, shortly before the final draft of the report was issued, J. Lee Rankin, the Chief Counsel of the Commission sent the following note to J. Edgar Hoover, "It is a matter of some importance that Mrs. Odio's allegations either be proved or disapproved." The incident did not go away when Staff Counsel Wesley Leibeler wrote in a memo, "There are problems. Odio may well be right. The Commission will look bad if it turns out that she is. There is no need to look foolish by grasping at straws admitting that there is a problem."

And what was that problem? The Warren Commission said that at the time of the Odio visit, the real Oswald was in New Orleans on September 26 or 27, 1963, and furthermore, that Oswald was then en-route by bus to Mexico City at the same time. Therefore, Oswald could not have been at the Odio residence as she claimed. But if the real Oswald was at their home in the company of anti-Castro people, then a possible connection between Oswald and anti-Castro, and possibly anti-Kennedy people could be ascertained.

In September 1964, the Warren Commission members came up with the names of three men whom they said were at the Odio home; Loren Eugene Hall, Lawrence Howard, and William Seymour.

The Warren Commission had a real quandary on their hands. Should they take Sylvia Odio at her word and put a huge monkey wrench into the report? Or should they ignore it as being too uncomfortable and let it drop? In the end, the Commission said that while the FBI report was not complete, they concluded that Oswald was not at Mrs. Odio's home in September 1963.

The Odio incident is just one more piece of evidence that Lee Oswald was being impersonated in the months leading up to the Kennedy assassination by persons unknown in order to be set up as the patsy in the assassination of the president on November 22, 1963.

Chapter 25
The U.S. Navy-Mafia Alliance

As the year 1942 began, the United States was in the war for only a few months, but already the tide of battle was shifting away at a terrible rate. Along the Atlantic coast of France, German U-boats headed away from their docks and entered the teaming sea lanes toward the open Atlantic where convoys of allied ships, many coming from the United States were ferrying much needed supplies to beleaguered England. From the period of January to October 1942, 541 allied ships were sunk by the marauding U-boats that swarmed in wolf packs against the unsuspecting merchant ships. All along the east coast of the United States, from North Carolina to New Jersey, ships were sunk at a steady, dangerous rate with nothing the U.S. could do to stop them. In May 1942 alone, 102 ships were sunk. June was not much better with 11 going down.

In order to ameliorate the ever-growing bad situation on the New York docks, an ingenious plan was hatched by the Office of Naval Intelligence to use certain members of the Mafia who just about ran the dock workers union in New York, to see if they could use their influence to try to stop the threat of Nazi penetration of the docks, and thus, stop any sabotage that the Nazi's were planning. By the time that "Operation Underworld, " the codename that was given by the ONI in their secret alliance with the Mafia was over, a hidden pact between the highest members of the U.S. Navy, the Roosevelt administration, and the power brokers in New York State would cement an alliance that would have roots far beyond the immediate threat.

The man whom the U.S. Navy turned to in order to quell the ever-growing threat to the New York docks was Joseph "Socks" Lanza who ran the highly lucrative Fulton Fish Market in lower Manhattan, the place where all the fish that was caught in the New York area was taken for sale by the hundreds of retailers who manned the large warehouses. Lanza was one of the most powerful men in the local Teamsters Union, and even other, tough New Yorkers learned to stay away from him when he got mad. He ran the Fulton Fish Market like his own personal fiefdom, taking a percentage of each sale.

Lanza was well connected with the crime family of Charles "Lucky" Luciano, a major figure in Operation Underworld. As a young man, Lanza worked at the Fish Market, earning $12 a week. Now, years later, he was a multi-millionaire, doing the same, dirty work that he'd done as a youngster. However, he was now in charge of the entire operation, and god-forbid anyone who crossed him.

Lanza's luck ran out in the decade of the 1930s, when he was sent to federal prison for a two-year sentence for the violation of the Sherman Anti-Trust Act. However, while in jail, his minions still extorted money from the Teamsters Union, making his reputation as a "made man" even that much more durable.

The U.S. Navy officer who was to be chosen as the intermediary between the Navy and the Mafia was Lt. Commander Charles Haffenden who was then in charge of the Third Naval District's investigation section, located in Manhattan. Haffenden said of his task to find allies in the mob to undertake this rather unorthodox mission by commenting that, "I'll talk to anybody, a bank manager, a gangster, the devil himself, if I can get the information I need. There is a war. American lives are at stake. It's not a college game where we have to look up the rulebook every minute, and we're not running a headquarters office where regulations must be followed to the letter. I have a job to do."

If Commander Haffenden was the operations officer involved in running Operation Underworld, the brainchild was Captain Roscoe MacFall, the Chief Intelligence Officer of the Third Naval District, which included New York and New Jersey. It was Captain MacFall's idea to contact members of the mob in order to see it their plan could work. Captain MacFall got the go ahead from his superior officer, Admiral Carl Espe, Director of Naval Intelligence.

The man whom Captain MacFall turned to in the pecking order was Lt. Anthony Marsloe, who worked for the Third Naval District. Before joining the Navy, Lt. Marsloe worked for the New York District Attorney's Office under the supervision of Thomas Dewey (Dewey would play an active role in the upcoming events).

In a meeting on March 7, 1942, between Captain MacFall

and Frank Hogan, the Manhattan DA, the rudimentary plan to use the mob was put in place. Also at the meeting was Murray Gurfein, who had been in charge of the DA's office that ran the Rackets Bureau. DA Hoganbeen working hard investigating the role of organized crime on the New York waterfront and he had an abiding interest in putting an end to the practice. Their discussion turned towards the threat that fishing boats off New York, posing a threat to the city, would refuel German submarines. Hogan said that the Mafia sometimes had advance warnings on all manners of illegal activity on the waterfront; maybe they could help in the war effort?

When the meeting broke up, all agreed to work with each other in trying to see if they could entice the mob to help. Gurfein was given the job of acting as the representative of the DA's office with Commander Haffenden. In subsequent meetings, it was Gurfein who recommended they meet with Socks Lanza.

A few days later, both Lanza and Gurfein met to work out details of their new arrangement. In the weeks that followed, Lanza gave Gurfein the names and telephone numbers of his top men on the waterfront that he enticed to go along with their plan. As time went on, Lanza's fishing boat captains kept a watchful eye for any German submarines or other unusual naval traffic that they encountered on their regular fishing trips. They even communicated with the Navy via ship-to-shore radios provided by Commander Haffenden.

Lanza was not only working for the Navy in his new position. He also kept his two most important mob contacts, Meyer Lansky and Frank Costello up to date on what he was doing.

While Lanza was having a great deal of support from most of his assets, many of the Italian's whom he'd been talking to were not cooperating. He then came up with an idea that changed the entire picture. He suggested to his Navy buddies that he be able to contact Charles Luciano, then serving time in a New York prison for help in the project. This was a risky decision, one that might not go down well with the major players in the game, especially the Navy brass who were supervising the entire show. Reluctantly, the ok was given to make direct contact with Luciano.

Charles "Lucky" Luciano was the most prominent Italian

mobster in the United States at the time he was recruited by the Navy in Operation Underworld. He was the Godfather of the modern American Mafia, even bigger in stature than the notorious hoodlum, Al Capone. He, along with Meyer Lansky, who was the moneyman behind the modern mob, were arguably the two most important Mafia figures of the time.

He was born Salvatore Luciana in Palermo, Italy and came to the United States in 1906. In his early years, he gravitated to a life of low-level street crime and met another youngster who would become his life-long friend in crime, Meyer Lansky. By 1920, Luciano was a permanent member of the Five Points Gang and was a suspect in a number of murders. By the time the decade was over, he was a major figure in the bootlegging rackets and made friends with some of the most notorious criminals of the day, Vito Genovese, Frank Costello, among others.

In the late 1920s, Luciano had joined the gang that was run by Giuseppe "Joe the Boss" Masseria, who was the head of the biggest crime family in New York. When open warfare broke out between the factions belonging to mobster and rival of Masseria, Salvatore Maranzano, which left dozens of bodies strewn across the streets of the city, Luciano stayed of the sidelines, waiting for the carnage to end.

Masseria's bloody end came in 1931, when men associated Luciano rubbed him out in a Coney Island restaurant. Maranzano was now the undisputed head of the Mafia and he made Luciano one of his top lieutenants. Unknown to Luciano, Maranzano had other ideas. He made secret plans to have Luciano killed, but Charles "Lucky" found out before hand and had Maranzano rubbed in his own office.

With the death of Maranzano, Luciano and Meyer Lansky now took effective control of the Mafia in the United States and broadened the scope of the Mafia into areas such as narcotics, loan sharking, gambling, labor racketeering, and prostitution.

In 1936, the tide turned dramatically for Luciano. He ran square into the powerful grip of Thomas Dewey, an ambitious New York prosecutor (Dewey would later become Governor of New York, and ran for president against Harry Truman in 1948— he lost). Luciano became Dewey's main target and he was able to have a jury convict him on "compulsory prostitution" charges. He was given one of the harshest sentences ever seen in New York criminal history, 30 to 50 years behind bars.

At the time that Sox Lanza and the Navy Department decided it was worth its while to contact Luciano, he was serving time in one of the most notorious prisons, Dannemora, in upstate New York.

In April 1942, Murray Gurfein got in touch with a man named Moses Polakoff, who served as Luciano's attorney in his trial for prostitution. Gurfein and Polakoff met and Gurfein pitched the story that the Italian community was interfering in the Navy's efforts to stop Nazi infiltration of the docks, etc. Could he use his good graces to seek Luciano's help? Polakoff called Luciano's good friend, Meyer Lansky, and told him of the Navy's offer. Much to his surprise, Lansky offered whatever help he could give.

In a most unusual meeting, Gurfein, Lansky and Polakoff met in New York and discussed the Navy's predicament. Luciano's name came up and Lansky proposed that he and Polakoff meet with Luciano in Dannemora. Lansky said that he'd take no money; he, after all, was a patriot.

At the Astor Hotel in New York, Lansky and Polakoff met with Commander Haffenden. Haffenden explained to Lansky the predicament that the Navy was in. German spies were infiltrating the New York docks and the entire waterfront was in danger. He then told Lansky a secret; a convoy of U.S. troops would soon be heading overseas and the number one priority was the safety of the convoy. He also told Lansky about the U-boat threat and asked if there was anything Lansky could do. Lansky agreed and put out the word to Lanza and Frank Costello to put the squeeze on any pending danger on the docks.

While all these secret dealings were going on vis-a-vis the New York docks, another secret arrangement was being implemented to get Lucky Luciano transferred out of Dannemora. With the intervention of Commander Haffenden and the Navy, New York prison authorities reluctantly agreed to transfer Luciano to another prison, Great Meadow. This was still a maximum-security jail but the conditions were better for Luciano than being stuck in the hellhole that was Dannemora.

During the time period between May 15 and June 4, 1942, Lansky and Polakoff visited Luciano. As soon as they sat down, the two men briefed Luciano as to the purpose of their visit. After listening intently to what they had to say, Luciano said that he'd cooperate—however, there was caveat.

As soon as he heard their proposal, Luciano knew he might have the government over a barrel. There was always a quid pro quo in life and Luciano was now ready to play his trump card. He realized that by helping with the war effort, he'd only be aiding his own cause, which was now, a dire one. If he didn't help, he would not be released until 1965, an incredibly long time.

For Luciano, the fact that he was not a citizen of the United States hung over his head like a lead balloon, one that might fall at any time. There was also a deportation order waiting for him when he was eventually freed. He had no certainty where he'd be sent after leaving the United States, and he didn't want to take the chance that he'd be sent to a country that would not be favorable to him. Luciano made his secret deal with the Navy and he now began the process of delivering on his part of the bargain. Lucky passed the word to all his Mafia friends along the east coast that from then on, they were to cooperate with the Navy, no questions asked.

According to the Herlands Report, which told the complete story of the Luciano-Navy agreement, Luciano gave the following orders to the dockworkers. "There'll be no German submarines in the Port of New York. Every man down there who works in the harbor—all the sailors, all the fishermen, every longshoreman, every individual who has anything to do with the coming and going of ships to the United States—is now helping the fight against the Nazis."[1]

According to the Herlands Report, there were at least twenty meetings between Luciano, Polakoff, and Lansky during the time period of May 15, 1942 and August 21, 1945. Luciano even conducted meetings in the warden's office at Great Meadow with his pals on the docks.

Meyer Lansky proved to be the main intermediary between Commander Haffenden and Luciano during the duration of

[1] Newark, Tim, *Mafia Allies,* Zenith Press, St Paul, Minnesota, 2007, Page 105.

Operation Underworld. Lansky also persuaded his friends who owned restaurants in the predominately German speaking Yorkville section of New York to hire German U.S. Navy men to serve as waiters. Their job was to listen in on any unusual conversations that they might pick up while serving a meal.

The covert dealings between the U.S. Navy and the mob, led by "Lucky" Luciano, proved to be a success. During the time that Operation Underworld was in effect, there were no attacks by German submarines or any sabotage along the New York docks. Unmistakably, this was a marriage of convenience, one that ultimately aided both parties. While it was a fact that the Germans were able to successfully infiltrate two teams of men along the east coast of the United States—one in Florida and the other in Maine—they were all captured—there was no sabotage along the New York docks.

In 1946, Thomas Dewey, now Governor of New York, paroled Charles Luciano for his secret wartime service for the United States. He was deported to Italy and then fled to Cuba where he established himself as one of the major drug kingpins of the time.

However, the Mafia's involvement in the war effort was not over with the shutdown of Operation Underworld. There was still another area where they'd aid Uncle Sam—in Sicily.

In a summit meeting between President Roosevelt and Winston Churchill, it was decided that the allies would mount an invasion of Italy called Operation Husky. The navy chose men from the Third Naval District in New York, veterans of the deal with Luciano, to aid the project. One of the men they turned to was Lt. Anthony Marsloe, one of four men who were going to be sent undercover to North Africa in May 1943 as a prelude to Operation Husky, as the Sicilian operation was dubbed. The other men who'd be working with Lt. Marsloe were Lt. Joachim Titolo, Lt. Paul Alferi, and Ensign James Murray.

Commander Haffenden once again turned to Meyer Lansky for help and Lansky passed the word around to the New York Italian community to work with the Navy without questions asked. Lansky's informants provided the Navy with invaluable information from various snitches and the regular population in the city. He also brought into the picture, Socks Lanza who once again proved invaluable in providing intelligence. In a show of bravado, Luciano offered to parachute with American forces once the invasion began (he was turned down).

As preparations for Operation Husky began, the OSS, Office of Strategic Services, got in to the act. Their main objective was to recruit as many covert operatives into Sicily as possible, locate targets for sabotage, and find as many Anti-Fascist's on the island as possible who'd aided the troops once they landed. In March 1943, an eleven-man OSS team commanded by Colonel William Eddy, arrived in North Africa.

Operation Husky began on July 9-10, 1943, when over 160,000 allied troops began disembarking from their landing crafts on the southwestern shore of Sicily. The landing force consisted of troops from both the United States and England, commanded by Lt. General George Patton and his opposite, General Bernard Montgomery.

Accompanying the troops into Sicily were members of Lt. Marsloe's Naval Intelligence team who linked up with people whose names were provided by Lansky back in New York.

One of the most colorful stories coming out of Operation Husky took place on July 14, when an American plane flew over the village of Villalba, a center of Mafia power in Sicily. According to the story, the plane dropped a canvas sack that was addressed to "Zu Calo," who went by the name of Don Calogero Vizzini. Vizzini was the man to see in Mafia circles in Sicily and for all intents and purposes, was the head of the Sicilian Mafia. Inside the sack was a silk scarf with a black letter L printed on it. The "L" was supposed to have stood for Lucky Luciano and when Don Calogero Vizzini received it, he automatically knew who sent it. Luciano was born in the town of Lertcara Fridi, a mere fifteen miles from Villalaba.[2]

According to local custom, the use of a silk handkerchief was used as a symbol of greeting. While one can assume that Luciano was not in contact with Don Carlo Vizzini while he was serving his time in his New York prison cell, it is safe to assume that his influence made it safely to his old hometown.

On July 22nd, the Americans captured the strategic town of Palermo, a major success in winning the battle for Sicily. But the

[2] Ibid. Page 159.

price of victory did not come cheap. The U.S. lost 9,213 killed and wounded. The British and Canadian's lost over 12,000 men.

The success of the Sicily invasion was the first step in the conquest of Germany. Once Italy had fallen, the allies spent the next two, bloody years advancing further into Germany proper, finally seizing Berlin in May 1945.

War makes strange bedfellows, and the United States, in the form of a secret alliance with the Mafia headed by men like Meyer Lansky, Charles Luciano, Socks Lanza, and Vito Genovese, made a precedent that they'd use as World War II ended and the cold war began.

Chapter 26
The Saudi/9-11 Connection

Fourteen years after the attacks on the World Trade Center and the Pentagon, there are many unanswered questions as to just what happened that beautiful September morning. Among the points of contention are the possible connections between the hijackers and the government of Saudi Arabia. Of the nineteen men who hijacked the planes that hit the WTC and the Pentagon, fifteen were Saudi nationals. There had been a long connection between al Qaeda and Saudi Arabia dating back to the 1990s when the Russians invaded Afghanistan and the Taliban morphed into a position of strength in Afghanistan. Saudi Arabia was one of but a few nations who gave diplomatic recognition to the Taliban. In the months leading up to the attacks of 9-11 there were a number of covert meetings between two of the 9-11 hijackers, Khalid al-Mihdar and Nawaf al-Hazmi and persons connected with the government of Saudi Arabia. This is a convoluted story that has many parts, including meetings with Saudi agents in the United States and some of the highest ranking Saudi diplomats then in residence in Washington, as well as a confession by the "20th" hijacker, Zacarias Moussaoui who implicated certain members of the Saudi Royal family in the 9-11 attacks.

In 2002, a joint House-Senate panel investigated the 9-11 attacks and came up with a number of interesting facts that were later further looked into by the National Commission on Terrorist Attacks Upon the United States, or the 9-11 Commission, among which were reference to a missing 28 page section on al-Qaeda's "specific sources of foreign support," much of which has been classified (more about that later in the chapter). To this date, Neither the Bush nor Obama Administrations have sought fit to release the entire contents of the 28 pages, only making the interest in what is in those pages more enticing. The 9-11 Commission report said that it "found no evidence that the Saudi government as an institution or senior Saudi officials individually funded the organization," meaning al-Qaeda.

The 9-11 Commission described the lapses in intelligence sharing between the FBI and the CIA which might have prevented the attack s from taking place, as well as telling the story of the activities of these two men in the San Diego area without the knowledge of the either the CIA or the FBI.

This story revolves around two of the 9-11 hijackers, Khalid al Mihdar and Nawaf al Hazmi who arrived in the United States in January 2000. Both men settled in San Diego and in April 2000, al Hazmi took flying lessons at the National Air College in San Diego. One week later he received $5,000 from an unnamed person located in the United Arab Emirates. In May 2000, both men enrolled in flight training in San Diego, Later in May, al Mihdar went to Oman and didn't return to the U.S. until July 2001.

Al Hazmi stayed in the San Diego area until December 2000 and then moved to Arizona with another 9-11 hijacker, Hani Hanjour.

At the time that al Hazmi and al Mihdar lived in San Diego, they were in constant contact with an unnamed FBI informant who provided the Bureau with information on them. This unnamed informer only knew the first names of both men and relayed that information to his FBI controller. The informant told his FBI handler that they were "good Muslim Saudi youths" who were in America to attend flight school.

In an intelligence blunder on the parts of the FBI and the CIA, the CIA did not inform the FBI that the two men had previously attended an Al Qaeda summit in Malaysia in which planning for the 9-11 plot was hatched. Adding to the CIA's sin, it wasn't until August 2001, that the CIA asked that the two men be placed on a watch list in order to prevent their entry into the United States.

According to the Senate/House report, "During a debriefing in the summer of 2000, the informant told me (his FBI hander) that the informant met two individuals described as good Muslim Saudi youths who were legally in the United States to visit and attend school. According to the informant, they were religious and not involved in criminal or political activities. At some later point, but before Sept 11, the informant told me their names were Nawaf and Khalid. The informant did not tell me their last names prior to Sept. 11, 2001."

The FBI report said they had problems with the informant's bona fides and tried to block his appearance as a witness and give his testimony. The FBI objected when the committee tried to interview the person and he never did attend any of the committee's sessions.

After 9-11, FBI agents had numerous interrogations sessions with the unnamed source and he repeatedly told them that he was kept in the dark about 9-11 an did not know the real reason why the two men were in the United States. The informant also told the FBI in the days after 9-11, the identities of a number of men who al Mihdar and al Hazmi had been in communication with in San Diego. Four of these people were of operational interest to the FBI.

In his congressional testimony, the FBI handler said that the informant did not mention that al Hazmi was taking flight training until after the attacks. "The handling agent said that none of the information provided by the informant about the hijackers before September 11 raised concerns. The fact that the two individuals were Saudi was not a concern before September 11 because Saudi Arabia was considered an ally."

The FBI, according to the Joint Congressional account, did not believe the informant when he said he did not recognize the other 9-11 hijacker, Hani Hanjour when he visited al Hazmi in San Diego.

The failure of the CIA to inform the FBI that it was aware that al Mihdar had obtained a U.S. visa and was seen in California in March 2000 was an intelligence offense of the first order. If both agencies agency's had been able to track al Mihdar and al Hazmi in August 2001, they might have been able to break up the 9-11 plot.

However, the story of which al-Hazmi and al Mihdar were associated with once they entered the U.S. has grown murkier as events unfolded. It was originally believed that both men had little contact once they entered the United States. That assumption is now in doubt thanks to information that has been become public since 9-11.

Prince Turki al-Faisal, the Saudi intelligence minister reported that in the months before 9-11, that the Saudi external intelligence service told the CIA that Nawaf al-Hazmi and Khalid al-Mihdar were placed on a Saudi terror watch list. Another person whom they were tracking was Nawaf's brother, Salem. Two other senior Saudi officials, Saeed Badeeb, Turki's chief analyst, and Nawaf Obaid, a security consultant to the Saudi government, backed up Turki's claims regarding the two men, however Turki reneged on his claim about the two hijackers when he became the Saudi ambassador to the U.S.[1]

One of the men whom they made contact with was a murky Saudi named Omar al-Bayoumi. Al-Bayoumi, who lived in San Diego, is said to have had links to Saudi intelligence, and was possibly keeping track of the large Saudi contingent of college students in the area. While in Saudi Arabia, he worked for the large Saudi Minister of Defense and Aviation. His "cover" while living in San Diego was that of a "pilot" or "student."

Al-Bayoumi became a target of interest by the FBI's office in San Diego who began compiling a large dossier on him. While the FBI did not find any illegal activities being carried out by him, they noted that he had "access to seemingly unlimited funding from Saudi Arabia." One FBI report said that al-Bayoumi paid $500,000 in cash given to him by the Saudi government in order to buy a mosque in 1998. Despite his shadowy life style, the FBI stopped their investigation of him by 1999. In his book called *The Terror Timeline,* author Paul Thompson says that a classified section of the 9-11 report notes that payments to al Bayoumi increased dramatically just after he made contact with al Hazmi and al Mihdar in early 2000.

But the al-Bayoumi story does not end there. When al-Hazmi and al-Mihdar arrived in Los Angeles, they met with al-Bayoumi in a restaurant. Shortly after their lunch date, both of the future 9-11 hijackers moved to San Diego, possibly on the recommendation of al-Bayoumi. Al-Bayoumi helped both men move into an apartment near where he and his family were living, and he even co-signed the lease on their apartment, putting down $1,500 for their initial month's rent and their security deposit.

Al-Bayoumi also introduced another of the 9-11 hijackers, Hani Hanjour to al-Hazmi and al-Mihdar and all three would soon

[1] Complete 9-11 Timeline: CIA Hiding Knowledge of Alhamzi and Almihdar, History Commons.

live together.

Instead of living covertly in San Diego, both men blended in with American society. They used their real names when conducting business, were listed in the 2000-2001 phone book, hand banks accounts, and valid driver's licenses.

In the summer of 2000, while living in San Diego, Khalid al-Mihdar made a phone call to an al-Qaeda safe house in Yemen, which belonged to his father-in-law. The NSA monitored this call. However, the NSA did not realize that the person known as "Khalid" was calling from the United States.

If the FBI bungled in not knowing that al-Hazmi and al-Mihdar were living openly in the U.S., they were to face another lost opportunity when it was revealed that both men were living in the same apartment with an FBI "asset" named Abdussattar Shaikh. Shaikh only told the FBI the first name of his roommates, never revealing their last names. If he had told the FBI their full names, they both would have popped up on the Watch List, which now had them in their database.

Abdussattar Shaikh's FBI handler was Steven Butler. Butler's informant gave him their first names, but nothing more. He further told Agent Butler that both men are no menace to society, were in the U.S. for school, and were not associating with any known radicals. Nor does he mention the fact that the men are taking flying lessons.

The 9-11 Commission disbelieved Shaikh's story that he had no prior knowledge of the 9-11 attack, and wrote in their final report that if the FBI had been more proactive in its relation with Shaikh, "it would have given the San Diego FBI field office perhaps the Intelligence Community's best chance to unravel the September 11 plot."

By the spring and summer of 2001, the hijackers moved about the country without being noticed. In March 2001, both Hani Hanjour and Nawaf al-Hazmi moved to Falls Church, Virginia form Phoenix. Others would settle for a time in New Jersey and other places along the east coast. In a bit of bad luck for U.S. intelligence, Nawaf al-Hazmi was issued a speeding ticket in Oklahoma on April 1, 2001. However, his name did not come up on any criminal list. He was given a ticket and the matter is dropped.

On the day that Khalid al-Mihdar and Nawaf al-Hazmi are put on the government's Watch List (August 24-25, 2001), they purchased their 9-11 tickets by credit card. The FAA and the domestic airline carriers were not told of the men being added to the Watch List, and their ticket purchases are not looked up.

Another person associated with the Saudi's was Osama Basnan who was living in California (1998) at the same time as al-Mihdar and al-Hazmi and befriended both of them. Omar Basnan wrote a letter to Saudi Prince Bandar bin Sultan and his wife, asking for financial help because his wife was in need of money for a thyroid operation. Prince Bandar's wife, Princess Haifa sent upwards of $73,000 over a period of three years to Basnan for his wife's medical treatment. Medical records state however that Basnan's wife was treated for her condition in April 2000, two years after the money was first sent. Basnan, it is alleged, funneled some of this money to al-Mihdar and al-Hazmi but the FBI could not positively say this happened.[2]

If there was one Senator who believed that the government of Saudi Arabia was implicated in the 9-11 attacks it was Florida's Robert Graham. Graham, a Democrat, served on the Senate Intelligence Committee investigating the 9-11 attacks and said that he believed there was "a direct line between the terrorists and the government of Saudi Arabia." Senator Graham was one of the panel members who read the secret 28-page report that the Bush administration refused to release to the public and as he sat in a secure part of the capital beneath the visitor's center in a sound proof room, he was more determined to get to the truth of what happened that day. The secret 28-page report contained classified information revealing the relationship between the Saudi "spies" as Graham called them and the terrorists who hit the WTC. While there was no direct link between the members of the Saudi Royal family and 9-11, Senator Graham, and other members of the panel, believed that a number of lower level Saudi diplomats were associated with al-Qaeda, possibly members of the Islamic Affairs Ministry who were in touch with the 9-11 hijackers.

Senator Graham was a maverick as far as his allegation that

[2] Thompson, Paul, *The Terror Timeline*, Regan Books, New York, 2004, Page 158.

the Saudis were involved, as well as his belief that the Bush administration were trying to cover up Saudi involvement in the attack because of their close ties to the Saudi Royal family, as well as the continuing need for Saudi oil. He was also a harsh critic of the way the FBI conduced their investigation, pointing blame directly on the hand of the new FBI Director, Robert Mueller.

Two of the committee's staffers who were most involved in digging up the information regarding the Saudi connection 9-11 were Eleanor Hill, the commission's staff director and Michael Jacobson, a former FBI lawyer and expert on counterterrorism matters. Jacobson found damming material concerning al-Hazmi and al-Mihdar in the files of the FBI office in San Diego, as well as in the FBI's Washington office. Jacobson learned of their relationship with Omar al-Bayoumi and his associations with the Saudi regime. As Senator Graham read the classified material, the more he came to believe that the Saudi's were connected to al-Qaeda prior to the 9-11 attacks and that the Bush administration did not want that information to come to light.

Members of the committee were investigated by the FBI in June 2002 when CNN received classified information, possibly coming from the committee, which was sent by al-Qaeda members referring to the upcoming attacks by saying, "Tomorrow is zero day. The match is tomorrow." This message was intercepted by the NSA but not translated from Arabic until after the attacks took place. At the urging of the Bush administration, the FBI began interviewing members of Senate panel as well as their staff to find out who the leak was. Senator Graham was furious at the Bush administration's hard tactics toward his colleagues and believed that the actions taken against them were made in order to stifle any further investigation of the 9-11 attacks.

It was Michael Jacobson who wrote the 28-page summary revealing the possible Saudi relationship to the 9-11 hijackers, which the Bush administration refused to release.

Another 9-11 committee staffer who was not intimidated by the bright lights was Dana Lesmann who joined Jacobson on the staff. Lesmann had previously worked for the Justice Department before coming to the committee and took a skeptical view of the FBI and its practices regarding their investigation of the events before 9-11.

Lesmann asked Philip Zelikow, the 9-11 commission's executive director for permission to interview 20 people, including some FBI agents, but he only allowed her to see ten. She also requested to see a copy of the 28-page report but that demand was refused. On her own, Lesmann got a copy of the 28-page report by other means, leaving Zelikow out in the cold. Zelikow got the last word and fired Lesmann on the spot for going behind his back regarding her possession of the 28 page secret report. After her firing, the top members of the 9-11 staff did not leak the firing of Dana Lesmann or why she was let go to the press, thus, covering up a matter that would have put mud on their faces if the real reason for her dismissal was ever revealed.

In recent years, two other congressmen who read the 28-pages also put the onus on the government of Saudi Arabia. Walter Jones, a Republican from North Carolina said, "It's about the Bush administration and its relationship with the Saudi's." Stephen Lynch, a Massachusetts Democrat, told author Lawrence Wright that the document "is stunning in its clarity, and that it offers direct evidence of complicity on the part of certain Saudi individuals and entities in al Qaeda's attack on America. Those 28-eight pages tell a story that has been completely removed from the 9-11 Report." Another unnamed congressman who read the pages also backed up both Lynch and Jones. This law maker said the evidence against the Saudi government support for the 9-11 hijacking is "very disturbing, and that the real question is whether it was sanctioned at the royal-family level or beneath that, and whether these leads were followed through."[3]

Both Lynch and Jones sponsored a resolution requesting that the Obama administration to declassify the pages.

For their part, the Saudi government has also asked that the 28 pages be released. Prince Bandar bin Sultan, who was the Saudi Ambassador to the States at the time of the 9-11 attacks said, "Twenty-eight blanked –out pages are being used by some to malign our country and our people. Saudi Arabia has nothing to hide. We can deal with questions in public, but we cannot respond to blank pages."

In 2004, a lawsuit was brought forth on behalf of the victims

[3] Wright, Lawrence, *The Twenty-Eight Pages*, The New Yorker September 9, 2014.

of the attacks, along with some insurers who paid claims to the families of those who died in the strikes. The suit alleges that some Saudi charities, banks, and certain persons were involved in the attacks. In 2005, the government of Saudi Arabia was dismissed from the suit on the ground of sovereign immunity, but in the U.S. Supreme Court reinstated the Saudi's as a defendant. In a statement by the families of those lost on 9-11, they said, "The redaction of the 28-pages has become a cover-up by two Presidents, and cover-up implies complicity."

Philip Zelikow, the man who fired Dana Lesmann called the 28-eight pages "an agglomeration of preliminary, unvetted reports" concerning the Saudi regime. "There are wild accusations that needed to be checked out," he said.

The members of the 9-11 Commission were never able to make a direct connection between the Saudi government and the hijackers. One person who worked on the commission warned that if the pages were released it would set back U.S.-Saudi relations in the extreme.

In an interview with journalist Lawrence Wright, the 9-11 Chairman, Thomas Kean, the former New Jersey governor, had much to say about the 28-eight pages. He said that while reading the pages in the basement of the capital, he had someone standing over his shoulder. He said that most of the material he read "should never have been kept secret." He also said in relation to the pages that, "a ton of stuff" (documents) is still classified, including the Commission's interviews with George Bush, Bill Clinton, and Dick Cheney. "I don't know of a single thing in our report that should not be public after ten years," he said.

The single most important person involved in 9-11 who accused the Saudi's of being complicit in the attacks is Zacarias Moussaoui, a 9-11 co-conspirator who took flight-training courses in the U.S. in 2001 and was arrested by federal authorities that year. Moussaoui said that members of the Saudi Royal family helped finance al-Qaeda prior to 9-11. In a court deposition, Moussaoui said that he was told by al-Qaeda officials in Afghanistan in either 1998 or 1999 to create a digital database of donors to his group. Some of these donors were Prince Turiki-al-Faisal, then the Saudi intelligence chief, Prince Bandar Bin Sultan, and the ambassador to the U.S., Prince al-Waleed bin Talal, a prominent billionaire investor, and others. He said that Osama bin Laden wanted to keep a record of who donated to al-Qaeda. He also said that he was a courier from bin Laden to important Saudi leaders, taking them important messages.[4]

Naturally, the Saudi government refuted Moussaoui's allegations, calling him a "deranged criminal whose own lawyers presented evidence that he was mentally incompetent. His words have no credibility. His goal in making these statements only serves to get attention for himself and try to do what he could not do through acts of terrorism—to undermine Saudi-U.S. relations."

While the 9-11 Commission found no credible link by the Saudi regime to the attacks, they did say that, "al-Qaeda had fertile fund raising ground in Saudi Arabia" including from corrupt charities and wealthy individuals.

The information provided in this chapter gives a lot of circumstantial evidence that links the government in Riyadh to the 9-11 attacks. Sometimes in a court of law, circumstantial evidence is enough to convict.

---

[4] No author, *Saudi Arabia and the 9/11 Terrorist Attacks,* The Wire, February 6, 2015.

Chapter 27
The Case of Alger Hiss

Alger Hiss was one of this country's most respectable diplomats, serving in Washington in since the 1930s. For members of that generation, the name of Alger Hiss invokes memories of a time when the communist threat seemed to be just around the corner.

The fallout from the Hiss case pitted liberals and conservatives against each other. Now, almost 80 years after the espionage trial of Alger Hiss, new revelations may finally put to rest the question of whether Hiss was an agent for the Soviet Union during and after World War II.

Hiss was a graduate of the prestigious Johns Hopkins University and Harvard Law School. He was a protégé of Supreme Court Justice Felix Frankfurter, one of the most competent jurists in our legal history. He also worked as a law clerk for Associate Justice Oliver Wendell Holmes.

In 1933, Hiss joined the new administration of Franklin D. Roosevelt and worked in the Agricultural Adjustment Administration, and was a member of the Nye Committee, which looked into corruption in the munitions industry. He also worked for the Justice Department in 1936 and the State Department in 1944. It was his work in the State Department that would set off the controversy surrounding his alleged espionage against the United States.

In the summer of 1944, Hiss was a member of the Dumbarton Oaks Conference, the organization that created the United Nations. As a trusted member of the State Department, Hiss went to Yalta for a meeting of FDR, Joseph Stalin, and Winston Churchill. The Yalta Conference divided post-war Europe into spheres of influence between the western powers and the Soviet Union. Hiss was appointed temporary secretary general of the newly founded United Nations, a post where he would have worldwide political power. By 1947, with a strong UN, Hiss was appointed Chairman of the Board of Trustees of the Carnegie Endowment for International Peace. According to Whittaker Chambers, Hiss was a member of the Soviet secret service during this time.

Whittaker Chambers brought the communist/espionage charges against Hiss. Chambers had gravitated to the world of American communism at Columbia University, espousing Marxist ideology. By 1937, however, Chambers had grown disillusioned with Stalin and had broken away from the party. He became a devout Christian and fervent anti-communist.

Prior to taking the Carnegie job, Hiss was quietly dismissed by the Truman administration because there were rumors that he was associated with Soviet agents and posed a security threat if he remained in his job.

Whittaker Chambers was born Jay Vivian Chambers into a dysfunctional family. His father was bi-sexual, who made his way from partner to partner, often ignoring his wife and child. His passport out of this environment was his brilliant mind and he soon accepted at Columbia University. He changed his first name to Whittaker and soon gravitated to American Communism, espousing the proposition that the Marxist ideology was the only way the world could be saved.

Chambers soon began a homosexual relationship with a number of students on campus. He was a brilliant poet, but was soon forced out of the university after writing a "blasphemous" play. He then got a job at the New York Public Library, but was fired after he was accused of stealing books. In 1925, he joined the Communist Party and worked for two of their most important newspapers, the *Daily Worker* and the *New Masses*. By 1932, he was doing undercover work for the party and became a trusted agent.

In 1934, Chambers met a man named Harold Ware who was one of the most important members of the Communist Party in the United States. Ware worked for the Department of Agriculture, but on the side, he was recruiting many of the New Dealers who flocked to the new Roosevelt administration. Ware was the head of a covert Communist cell in Washington, D.C., which had infiltrated the Roosevelt administration. Josef Peters, a Hungarian, and veteran of World War I headed ware's group. He was a member of the Communist Party and was sent to the U.S. to aid Ware in his work. In the summer of 1934, Peters introduced Chambers to

Ware in New York and he was soon recruited to work undercover for the Communist Party. Ware met Chambers in Washington and his assignment was to "learn the set-up of the Ware group and then separate out some members of the group, forming a parallel operation that would eventually penetrate the upper levels of government."

Chambers settled in Washington and was assigned a Soviet handler called "Bill" who was an Estonian. "Bill" took Chambers with him to England were Chambers would assist Bill in setting up an intelligence operation in that country.

After a while, Moscow assigned Chambers a new handler, Boris Bykov, a GRU (Russian military intelligence) officer whose job in America was to supervise the entire Russian underground network. They had a not so easy relationship, but wound up working together for a common purpose. Under Bykov's tutelage, Chambers now took on mainly espionage assignments, traveling to such cities as Baltimore, New York, meeting with agents, picking up information at dead drops, doing everything a spy would do. He was now a full-fledged member of the Communist apparatus and did his job well.

By 1937, however, Chambers had grown disillusioned with Joseph Stalin's massive purges in Russia and he broke away from the party. He now turned to the Christian religious belief and fervent anti-communism.

By 1947, a federal grand jury in New York was hearing testimony from undercover FBI agents on allegations that members of the federal government secretly belonged to the Communist Party. However, no solid cases of espionage could be proven and the probe seemed futile. At FBI headquarters, J. Edgar Hoover wanted to place blame and leaked information to Congress to restart the case. Hoover sent one of his most trusted agents, Assistant Director Louis Nichols ("Hoover's ghost"), to Capitol Hill to give confidential information to Congress on supposed communists in government.

One of the Senators to be given this FBI intelligence was Homer Ferguson, a Republican of Michigan who considered Hoover's material a blessing. He was a member of the Senate Investigations Subcommittee who played along with Hoover's request. He turned this material over to his counterpart in the House of Representatives whose House Un-American Activities Committee (HUAC) would lead the hearings on agent Nichols' charges. The main accuser was Whittaker Chambers.

The initial charge against Hiss came not from Chambers but from a sensitive source. In 1945, a Soviet military intelligence officer named Igor Gouzenko, who was a cipher clerk in the Soviet embassy in Ottawa, Canada, defected to the West. He brought with him hundreds of documents supporting the fact that the Soviet's had been spying in Canada during World War II, at the same time they were supposed to be our ally against Germany. The Canadians immediately brought this information to the attention of the FBI. One of the most important pieces of data revealed that an American who was an assistant to the Secretary of State was a Soviet agent. Gouzenko's charge was corroborated to American courier, Elizabeth Bentley. That man was Alger Hiss.

In 1945, Bentley had a change of heart and told a grand jury about her wartime work. She also said that Whittaker Chambers was part of her organization. Bentley told the FBI that Alger Hiss was part of a secret Soviet spy apparatus called the Perlo Group.

It was now Chamber's turn in the national spotlight, and he relished his new status. He told the HUAC committee that Hiss was a secret member of the Ware group, a Soviet network based in Washington (of which he was a member), headed by Harold Ware. Chambers did not accuse Hiss of being a spy, only a communist. Hiss publicly denied Chambers charges and even denied knowing him. At first, the press believed Hiss's denials, but eventually his story wore thin.

One of the members of HUAC who did not believe anything Hiss had to say was Congressman Richard Nixon of California. Nixon had been privy to Hoover's leaked material, and he persuaded the rest of the committee to investigate Hiss's relationship to Chambers.

The scene now shifted to New York, where HUAC was in special session. Chambers testified that Hiss's wife Priscilla was a Communist and that the Hiss family knew him by an alias, "Carl." He told the members the layout of the Hiss house, that they owned a Ford roadster, and a Plymouth. Chambers said that Hiss donated his old Ford to the Communist Party. But there were segments of Chambers' testimony that were not correct concerning Hiss. He said that Hiss did not drink (he did), that Hiss was shorter than he actually was, and that Hiss was deaf in one ear (another falsehood). He also correctly said that the Hisses told him that he had seen a rare bird, called a "prothonotary warbler" along the banks of the Potomac River.

On August 16th, the committee brought in Alger Hiss to respond to Chambers' allegations. Hiss said, when shown a picture of Chambers that he "had a certain familiarity." His further testified that he had known a man matching Chambers' description as an acquaintance who went by the name of George Crosley. He said that at one time he sublet his apartment to Crosley and that Crosley was an unkempt man who sometimes wrote articles for magazines (Chambers was a freelance writer). Hiss said that he gave the old Ford to Crosley and was given an Oriental rug in return. At an August 25 hearing, Nixon brought Chambers and Hiss face to face. Hiss said that Chambers was George Crosley.

Responding to Hiss' charges, Chambers appeared on *"Meet the Press,"* then a radio program, and said, "Alger Hiss was a Communist and may be now." One month later, Hiss filed his lawsuit against Chambers for his comments. Chambers commented, "I do not minimize the ferocity or the ingenuity of the forces that are working through him."

At the trial, Chambers promised to bring forth evidence that would confirm Hiss's espionage. Chambers said he kept documents made up of 65 pages of typewritten copies of secret material, four pieces of paper with Hiss's handwriting on them, two strips of developed microfilm of State Department documents, three rolls of undeveloped microfilm and other assorted papers.

In what was to become the most controversial part of the case, Chambers turned over to the committee microfilm that he said he had hidden at his Maryland farm in a hollowed out pumpkin. These became known as the "pumpkin papers."

After looking at all the evidence, a grand jury, which took testimony from Hiss, indicted him on December 15, 1948, for perjury, accusing him of lying when he said he never turned over State Department information to Chambers. Hiss, however, was never charged with espionage.

The trial began in New York Federal Court on May 31, 1949, for perjury and lasted for six weeks. The state based much of its evidence on an old Woodstock typewriter that was owned by Hiss and his wife and was reportedly used by them to type the State Department materials.

The defense responded by saying that Chambers had lied when he said he had hidden the film in 1938; the company that made the film, Eastman Kodak, said that the film was originally manufactured in 1948. After an angry call from Congressman Nixon to Kodak headquarters, the company quickly changed its story and said that the film was indeed made in 1938.

The defense also brought forth as a character witness on Hiss' part, Supreme Court Justice Felix Frankfurter, Gov. Adlai Stevenson of Illinois, among others. They claimed that Chambers was a liar and a thief and insisted that the documents were faked by Chambers to implicate Hiss. They told the jury that a man named Henry Julian Wadleigh, a State Department economist, another Soviet agent, admitted that he had passed classified material to Chambers. They said Wadleigh was the man responsible for stealing this material.

It has been revealed that shortly before Hiss was to appear before HUAC, Congressman Nixon and a number of other committee members went to Chambers' home for a strategy session. This was a brazen act on Nixon's part, if not an illegal action.

The trial ended in a hung jury. Another trial was set for November 17, 1949 at which time Hiss was found guilty and was given a 44-month prison term.

Defenders of Hiss believe that he was a victim of those who wished to portray the Truman administration as weak on communism.

However, a number of years ago, the National Security Agency released once top-secret Soviet intelligence cables that were intercepted by the United States during World War II. A number of these cables implicated Hiss who went to by the name of "Ales." A March 30, 1945 message from Washington to Moscow concerning Ales said, "Ales is probably famed State Department official Alger Hiss." The VENONA files also report a meeting between a KGB

(Soviet intelligence) officer and a GRU intelligence officer whose source in Washington was Ales.

The headquarters of the Venona Project was a remote cite in Virginia called Arlington Hall. It was from here that code breakers worked on the thousands of pages of cables being intercepted from Soviet diplomatic missions around the world.

Venona analysts were able to match the cover names originating from the Soviet cables to real people and places. For example, "Kapitan" was FDR, "Antenna and Liberal" were Julius and Ethel Rosenberg, "ENORMOZ" was the Manhattan Project (the American effort to build an atomic bomb), "Babylon" was San Francisco, and "Good Girl" was Elizabeth Bentley.

By the time the Venona Project ended, more than 3,000 letters from the Soviet Union to their personnel in the United States had been read. The Freedom of Information Act led to the opening up of the Venona files, and it was in 1995 that the world learned fully of its contents.

Another file linking Hiss to Soviet intelligence comes from a cable to Moscow from its agent, "Vadim," Anatoly Gorsky, the station chief of the NKVD (the forerunner of the KGB), in which he reports a conversation between agent "A" and Ales. The Venona files say that A was Iskhak Akhmerov, one of the most important Soviet spies operating in the United States during the war. This same intercept states that Ales had been working for the Soviets since 1935 and continued to work for the Soviets even after Chambers left the party in 1938.

The files buttress the Hiss/Russian relationship in that "Ales functioned as the leader of a small group of neighbors probationers, for the most part consisting of his relations. " In the Venona papers, "Neighbors" refers to members of the American Communist Party. The tapes also say that "Ales" went on a separate trip to Moscow after the Big Three meeting at Yalta. The record proves that Hiss went to the Soviet capital on the plane carrying U.S. Secretary of State Edward Stettinus, along with two other career diplomats.

More startling information linking Hiss to Soviet intelligence comes from a former high-ranking Soviet intelligence (KGB) officer named Alexander Vassiliev, who had access to a huge amount of information on Soviet documents from the Stalin era on Soviet operations against the United States. This information was put in a book called *Spies: The Rise and Fall of the KGB in America* by John Earl Haynes and Harvey Klehr. Alexander Vassiliev, while living in London, brought with him notebooks of transcribed documents from Moscow, which he accumulated. These notebooks make up much of the material in *Spies*.

According to Vassiliev, Hiss worked for the GRU (Soviet military intelligence), beginning in the 1930s and continued into the next decade. He went by his real name, as well as cover names such as "Jurist," "Ales," and "Leonard."

In the 1930s, Hiss, while working in Washington, tried to recruit Noel Field who worked in the Department of State as a Foreign Service officer. Soon, Field was recruited as a Communist agent by a woman named Hede Massing, herself a member of the communist party. Field had been feeding the Soviets classified State Department information beginning in 1935 but did not know that Hiss was working secretly for the Soviets. Both Hiss and Field had become friends while in Washington and in 1936, Hiss tried to enlist Field to join the cause. One day before Field was to go to Europe, Hiss approached him for a private meeting. "Hiss informed him that he is a Communist, that he has ties to an organization working for the Soviet Union; and that he is aware that he has ties as well, however, he fears that they are not robust enough and that his knowledge is probably being misused." Hede Massing then told Hiss that he was indiscrete when he tried to recruit Field and said, "When I pointed out to him what a terrible lack of discipline he had shown and what a danger he had created for the value of his use for the whole enterprise by linking three people with each other, he acted as if he did not understand.[1]

By trying to enlist list Noel Field, Hiss had made the Soviet's mad because Field now knew that he was working for the GRU, something that Moscow Center did not want to happen.

Later, Field explained his version of Hiss' try at recruiting him. "Alger Hiss wanted to recruit me for espionage for the Soviet Union. I did not find the right words and carelessly told him that I was already working for the Soviet intelligence. I knew, from

[1] Haynes, John, Klehr, Harvey, and Vassiliev, Alexander, *Spies: The Rise and Fall of the KGB in America,* Yale University Press, New Haven, Ct., 2009, Page 6-7.

what Hiss told me, that he was working for the Soviet service. I drew the conclusion that Chambers was Hiss's upper contact in the secret service, too. Later it became certain, first when in Chambers' flat they found the secret material obtained by Hiss, and then when Chambers' testimony made it clear that he knew of the conversation between Hiss and myself, when Hiss tried to recruit me into the secret service."[2]

Another Soviet agent who knew about Hiss was Michael Straight who was recruited by the Soviet's out of Cambridge University in London. Hiss met Straight in Washington but Straight was told not to go near Hiss for fear that there might be another incident like that of Noel Field.

The Vassiliev papers, along with the Venona material, point to a direct connection between Alger Hiss and Soviet intelligence dating back to the decade of the 1930s and into the 1940s.

It is clear, with historical hindsight, that the Hiss case was just the opening gun in the rise of two of the most important events in the history of post-war America—the rise of Joseph McCarthy and his red baiting witch hunts that poisoned a generation, and the rise to national prominence of an obscure congressman from California, Richard Nixon.

Partisans on both sides of the political spectrum will still find fault with the newly released documents, and it is a sure bet that the controversy surrounding Alger Hiss will not fade.

---

[2] Ibid. Page 10-11.

Alger Hiss, testifying.

Chapter 28
The Oklahoma City Bombing

In the years prior to 9-11, most Americans felt safe from international terrorism. Sure, there was the isolated terrorist attack against U.S. targets, but they were all overseas. But all that changed in February of 1993 when again, a bunch of Arab extremists made their most daring attack on U.S. soil: the bombing of the World Trade Center in New York, the nerve center of America's financial interests. That was followed by the arrest of a group of Muslim and American militants who were planning to blow up landmarks in New York and assassinate prominent politicians (the day of terror plots).

The attack on the WTC finally brought home to Americans the unmistakable fact that we were vulnerable to outside hostilities and that we had better be prepared for what could follow. What happened next was the April 19, 1993 Oklahoma City bombing, in the heartland of America where these things weren't supposed to happen.

In the years since the destruction of the Alfred Murrah Federal Building, the landscape of America has certainly been changed as far as how we as a nation view international terrorism. 9-11 was the next target, this time not perpetuated by homegrown militants but foreign-born terrorists who brought their jihad to American shores.

The prime suspect in the Oklahoma City Bombing was a 27 year old, ex-Army veteran, an outwardly innocent looking man, yet one with an inner rage that had been penned up for many years, Timothy McVeigh. McVeigh grew up in upstate New York in the town of Pendleton where he graduated from high school in 1986. He lived with his father and sister, his mother having left home a few years before. After graduating from high school he got a job as a security guard with an armored car company near Buffalo called Burke Armor Inc. One time, McVeigh came to work carrying a sawed-off shotgun and bandoleers over his chest, a little overkill, for a guard taking money to and from banks. But that didn't pan out and McVeigh decided to join the army. Maybe there he could find himself. He joined up in 1989 and was sent to basic training at Fort Benning, Georgia. Once in the army, McVeigh proved to be a model soldier, often taking unpopular duties that other men in his unit wouldn't touch. But after duty hours were over, McVeigh preferred his own company, hardly ever going off base with his buddies. Instead, he stayed in his barracks, cleaning his rifle and reading extremist literature that he subscribed to. One of the men whom McVeigh befriended was the oldest man in his unit, Terry Lynn Nichols. This odd pair would soon begin a deep friendship, which would take them far beyond their small worlds of military action, and saluting officers they couldn't stand.

After basic training the entire unit moved out to the flat plains of Kansas where they were divided into two companies, McVeigh to Charlie Company and Nichols to Bravo Company, 2nd Battalion, 16th Infantry Regiment of the First Infantry Division, also-called the "Big Red One."

After a short period of time, Terry Nichols, for reasons we still do not fully understand, was given a discharge form the army and he returned home to Michigan. Both men were to keep in touch and would reacquaint themselves after McVeigh's discharge three years later.

McVeigh trained as the operator of a Bradley Fighting Vehicle and he would later be at the wheel of the Bradley when his unit was shipped out to the sands of Saudi Arabia to fight in the Gulf War. By 1990, he was now Sergeant McVeigh, still the same lonesome young man who joined the army three years earlier. But now, it seems, he had finally found himself. His identity as an up and coming soldier of fortune had finally been established. And there were better things to come. In March 1993, while his unit remained in the Gulf, Sgt. McVeigh flew home to carry out his dream; he would try out for the elite Army Special Forces.

For 21 days, McVeigh and the other potential recruits pushed themselves to the breaking point, both mentally and physically. But in was finally the psychological testing of McVeigh that caused his dream to come crashing down. He failed his psychological test and left the program deeply depressed and resentful of authority. After all, hadn't he given over one hundred percent to the Army these past three years? And this was how they treated him?

Deeply depressed and resentful, McVeigh returned to his old unit back at Fort Riley Kansas. But subtle changes were now taking place. He began to carry guns with him at all times. Friends said that he began to talk against the government and said that he was going to get ready for the approaching "apocalypse."

McVeigh and two other soldiers moved off base to a rented house in Herington. His roommates said that McVeigh's room was covered with guns and military equipment. He also joined the National Rifle Association but dropped out of the organization. After one of his roommates got married, McVeigh made one of the most important decisions of his life; he quit the army.

It is not known precisely what McVeigh did after he left the army but from the pieces of the puzzle that we do known about, this period of time only solidified his antagonisms against authority, in this case, the United States government.

It is possible that he spent some time with Terry Nichols at the latter's Michigan farm. He also went to Kingman, Arizona where he lived in a trailer park where it seems, the only thing he liked to do was shoot at targets and get the neighbors so riled up that he was evicted. While living in Kingman, McVeigh was often seen in the company of another ex-army buddy, Michael Fortier.

But what is known during this time is that McVeigh went the burnt out ruins of the Branch Davidian compound in Waco, Texas. It was here that dozens of people were killed in a violent confrontation with FBI and ATF agents. The massacre at Waco, according to McVeigh, was solely the fault of the government, restricting the people's right to bear arms. In his own mind, he was now at war with his own government.

For a short period of time, McVeigh returned to his upstate New York home. He joined the New York National Guard and took on a security job. He even had time to write a letter to his hometown newspaper, the *Lockport Union & Journal,* bitterly complaining of high taxes, and said that bloodshed might have to be spilled in order to change the government.

McVeigh now left New York and spent some time in Kingman, Arizona. But he soon tired of the hot sun and traveled to the Decker, Michigan home of his old army buddy, Terry Nichols and his brother James. In the rural area surrounding the Nichols farmhouse, McVeigh and the Nichols brothers would build bombs made out of fertilizer. It was a fertilizer base bomb that would be used in the Oklahoma City attack. While staying with the Nichols brothers, McVeigh would attend meetings of the underground and often violent Michigan Militia whose verbal attacks against the federal government were legendary. Their number one enemy was the Bureau of Alcohol, Tobacco and Firearms whose agents were the spearhead in the attack at Waco. For McVeigh and Terry Nichols who now came to be close, personal friends, both men decided that something big had to be done to change the way the country was going.

After the bombing, and with McVeigh and Terry Nichols in custody, Federal officials were able to track down the trail that led them to the Alfred P. Murrah Federal Building. In the months prior to the bombing, both McVeigh and Nichols focused their activities on the lonely stretch of highway along U.S. 77 in Kansas. Their route took them from Fort Riley, to Junction City were they made preparations for the attack.

In September 1994, they were seen in the small Kansas town of Herrington where at the same time, someone stole 299 sticks of dynamite and 500 blasting caps from a rock quarry nearby. While the duo were making their way across U.S. 77, a number of unsolved bank robberies were taking place in Kansas City, Mo, and the Midwest. From January 30, 1994 to March 1995, two men wearing ski masks robbed various banks. During this time period, members of the Aryan Republican Army (ARA) were robbing banks across the mid-West. The group's leader was Peter Langan, a.k.a. Commander Pedro, who, with their cohorts, robbed around 19 banks between 1993 and 1996 netting $250,000. According to Langan, there was a connection between the ARA and both Nichols and McVeigh. Both men were in the same locations during the robbery spree and people have argued that both men were part of the ARA. The FBI, however, could not find a connection between the ARA and Nichols and McVeigh. In an interview with Timothy McVeigh's sister she said that Timothy told her he was involved with some bank robbers and had given her some cash from the proceeds to launder.[1]

[1] No author, Q&A: What really happened. *BBC News/Programs/Conspiracy Files*. March 2, 2007.

In the days before the bombing, Mr. McVeigh paid cash for various items he purchased. The FBI believed that it is possible that the two men financed their attack with the proceeds stolen from bank robberies. On April 16th, Nichols drove McVeigh from Oklahoma City to Junction City where McVeigh says that "something big" is going to happen. On April 17th, McVeigh and as yet unidentified man called "John Doe," rented a Ryder truck from Elliot's body shop. Both men now were in Herrington, Kansas, and the home of Terry Nichols where McVeigh drove the Ryder truck to a rental shed where unidentified materials were probably taken and placed into the truck. It was at this time that McVeigh is to have told Nichols, "If I don't come back in a while, you'll clear out the storage shed." Clearly, from McVeigh's perspective, something was about to happen.

On April 19th, according to federal authorities, McVeigh and other unnamed co-conspirator's drove to Oklahoma City where they set off a huge explosion, which killed over one hundred innocent people.

The FBI said that only McVeigh and Terry Nichols were involved in the OK City attack. However, there were other witnesses who saw McVeigh with other people on the day of the bombing. Over two dozen people saw McVeigh with "persons unknown" on the day of attack. The FBI called one of these mysterious people as "John Doe 11." A man named Mike Moroz said that McVeigh stopped him on the day of the attack asking for directions to the Murrah Building. McVeigh knew where the building was located from previous trips to the city. The Oklahoma Grand Jury, which looked into any possible conspiracy in the attack said they could not find one but said, "We cannot finally put closure to the question of the existence of John Doe 11 and are confident that if any new evidence come to light, they (the FBI) and other law enforcement agencies will pursue these leads. (No governmental agency ever did).

Another person who made inquiries about the possible identity of John Doe 11 was a Salk Lake City lawyer named Jesse Trentadue whose brother, Kenny, a one-time bank robber, died while in federal prison under mysterious circumstances. It seems that Kenny Trentadue had multiple cuts and bruises over his body (including his throat) at the time of his death (the official cause of his death was that he hanged himself while in jail). After doing the autopsy, the Oklahoma City's medical examiner said of the death of Mr. Trentadue that, "very likely he was murdered." His brother was never able to find out exactly how he died but the family received a $1.1 million settlement for "emotional distress."

The case did not end there. In the spring of 2003, Jesse Trentadue got a call out of the blue from an Oklahoma newspaper reporter named J.D. Cash. Mr. Cash said that Kenney looked like John Doe 11, who might have been the second OK bomber. Cash said that Kenny and John Doe 11 looked like Richard Lee Guthrie who was a member of the Aryan Republican Army whose group carried out 22 bank robberies across the Midwest, getting $250,000 for their raciest cause. Was it possible that Kenney Trentadue was Richard Guthrie and that Guthrie was John Doe 11? Conspiracy theorists say that it is possible that the FBI had a feeling that Kenney was Guthrie and might have been in cahoots with McVeigh in the Murrah building bombing.

By then, the FBI had closed down the OK bombing case and Jesse Trentadue was left hanging. He filed a FOIA request and received documents that revealed the FBI was investigating a possible link between the OK bombing and Guthrie's ARA.

The FBI focused on a remote site called Elohim City in Oklahoma's Ozark Mountains where right wing extremists lived. The FBI did in fact have informants hidden inside the Elohim City complex and one document said, "That the bureau was interested in any connection between McVeigh and the ARA immediately before the bombing, and that Guthrie himself was in Pittsburg, Kansas—some 200 miles from Oklahoma City—three days before the attack. In addition, the memos indicate that the FBI received reports of McVeigh calling and possibly visiting Elohim City before the bombing, at one point seeking to recruit a second conspirator."[2]

The FOIA documents also reveal that a source said that McVeigh had a "lengthily relationship with someone at Elohim City, and that he called that person just two days before the bombing."

[2] Ridgeway, James, *Did` the FBI Bury Oklahoma City Bombing Evidence?*, *Mother Jones*, July 21, 2011.

In the end, Jerry Trentadue got nowhere fast with the FBI and the Justice Department who refused to look further into his charges regarding his brother and any connection to John Doe 11.

Ninety minutes after the bombing of the Murrah building, an Oklahoma State trooper stopped a speeding car along an isolated stretch of highway in Perry, sixty miles from the blast. In a bit of luck, the person in the car was Timothy McVeigh. While in custody, the Perry police received a photograph of prime suspect over their teletype. That person was McVeigh (although how they figured that piece of evidence out so fast was not known at the time).

The aforementioned Jesse Trentadue also found evidence of a phone call that was made to the FBI the day before the OK bombing took place and that they tried to reach a deal with Terry Nichols to take the blame for the attack in order to be spared the death penalty. Mr. Trentadue said he believed that the bombing was an inside job by the FBI who was handling Timothy McVeigh. "What that indicates," said Mr. Trentadue, "to me, there is a record of that phone call and the FBI needs to explain it. If the call was from one of their informants with McVeigh, clearly, they had knowledge of the bombing and didn't stop it."

While in jail, Nichols received a visit from an attorney named Michael Selby who said he was working for the government. He further said that if Nichols aided the feds in their investigation of the explosion, he'd be spared the death penalty if he'd go along with the fact that the FBI covered up the attack. In response, Nichols filed an affidavit with the U.S. District Court in Utah in which he said, "This was the first I had heard of such a telephone call having been made. And I told Mr. Shelby that as well as the fact that I had not made that telephone call."

Shelby also tried to get Nichols to reveal the location of a box of explosives that the FBI failed to find when they searched Nichols' home in 1995. In time, the FBI did locate the box of explosives hidden in Nichols' home and took possession of it. On the box were the fingerprints of both Nichols and McVeigh, as well as fingerprints of at least two other people whose names were redacted by the FBI. Jesse Trentadue said of this incident, "When you look at these documents, that this was being monitored, this search for the box of explosives at the highest levels within the Department of Justice, right up to and including the White House, I think, I mean, this wasn't your local FBI office handling this. This was being run out of the main justice in Washington, D.C."[3]

Once McVeigh and Nichols were arrested, the government settled the case, saying they were the only two men responsible for the attack. However, as time went on, the fingers began to point to "others involved" in the attack.

One person to question the official result was Carol Howe who worked as an informant for the ATF. Ms. Howe told federal authorities that Murrah building was a target of extreme right wing groups in the U.S. She zeroed in on members of the radical group in Elohim City and a man called Andreas Strassmeir who lived there. Elohim City was a white separatist, Christian Identity settlement in the Ozark Mountains in Oklahoma, far from federal control (although on their radar). Howe said that months before the attack, she warned the ATF that members of Strassmeir's group were, "preparing for war" and that Robert Millar—a leader of the Elohim City community, had "brought forth his soldiers and instructed them to take whatever action is necessary against the US government." She said that Strassmeir was a very dangerous man who advocated political assassination as way of life. The FBI investigated Strassmeir and his links to Elohim City but found no credible evidence to link him to the attack.

Conspiracy theorists say that there is more to Andres Strassmeir than meets the eye. He was known in many circles as, "Andy the German," and that he was really a German secret agent sent to the United States to monitor the activities of the American right. Some researchers believe that he was an "agent provocateur" who was sent to America to ferment right-wing action against the U.S. government. He was not questioned by the FBI after the OK bombing and was only questioned nine months after the attack by phone after he left the country. Strassmeir met with McVeigh at a gun show in Tulsa, Oklahoma 1993, and McVeigh had tried to call him on April 5, 1995.

Despite all these possible leads, the federal government ended its probe of the Oklahoma City bombing attack, concluding that

[3] Watson, Paul Joseph, *Confirmed: FBI Got Warning Day Before OKC Bombing*. Alex Jones' Infowars, February 8, 2011.

Timothy McVeigh and Terry Nichols were the only perpetrators.

On August 10, 1995, Timothy McVeigh and Terry Nichols were indicted by a Federal grand jury in Oklahoma City on charges that they blew up the Federal building on April 19, 1993. Another bombing suspect, Michael Fortier plead guilty to lesser changers in the bombing plot. At trial, Nichols and McVeigh were convicted of their participation in the OK building attack. Timothy McVeigh was put to death in his jail cell at the Federal Correctional Complex in Terre Haute, Indiana. Terry Nichols is serving life in prison. If there are others unknown in the Ok bombing plot, they are still at large.

Chapter 29
The Plumbers Target Torrijos

When the Watergate scandal hit the news, the American people were introduced to a secret group of people who worked out of the White House under the direction of President Richard M. Nixon called the Plumbers. The Plumbers were called in to stop the leaks coming out of the Nixon administration but they soon took on rather dubious actions such as the break-in at the office of Dr. Lewis Fielding, the psychiatrist who was the doctor of Daniel Ellsberg who leaked the Pentagon Papers, and broke into the Watergate building which led to the resignation of President Nixon. However, it seems that they were also interested in a foreign target, the President of Panama, Omar Torrijos and might have taken part in a plot to kill him. What made this reported incident most interesting is the fact that the hit did not involve the CIA, but may have been instigated by Richard Nixon's infamous "Plumbers," headed by Howard Hunt and Frank Sturgis. While there is no solid proof that an assassination attempt was actually carried out by Nixon's men, the circumstantial and other evidence makes the case that a Torrijos hit was actively being planned.

The focus of the Nixon administration's interest was the President of Panama, Omar Torrijos. During this period of time (early 1970s), the United States and Panama were beginning discussions for the eventual return to Panama of the Panama Canal Zone, which remained under United States sovereignty.

But more importantly to our story were reports by the United States Drug Enforcement Agency (DEA) that President Torrijos and certain members of his administration were heavily involved in the heroin trade coming out of Latin America. President Nixon made the war on drugs one of the main topics of his administration. There were even reports that a covert action team made up of an ex-spook, and former CIA clandestine warrior, Lucien Conein, were under orders from the Nixon camp to begin preparations for the murder of the top drug lords then operating in South America. Conein, along with Howard Hunt, would be involved in a scheme to fabricate false cable traffic that would have the Kennedy administration deeply involved in the murder of South Vietnamese President Ngo Dinh Diem in early November 1963.

The Church Committee investigators first got wind of the Torrijos plot in a March 4, 1972 newspaper article by nationally known investigative reporter, Jack Anderson. Anderson heard of the story from Rep. John Murphy's House Panama Canal Subcommittee, which was then referred to the House Merchant Marine Subcommittee. The report said that "high ranking Panamanian officials were deeply involved in the world heroin trade. American narcotics agents have implicated the foreign minister of Panama and the brother of Panamanian dictator Omar Torrijos in a scheme to smuggle hundreds of pounds of heroin into the United States." Anderson wrote that Panamanian Foreign Minister Juan Track and Moises Torrijos, the President's brother, were the principal ringleaders of these drug shipments.

In the wake of the Anderson story and others (The *New York Times* also reported on it), Panama expelled two U.S narcotics officers who were employed in the American embassy in Panama City, It seemed to both countries that the alleged drug involvement of the top leaders of Panama were about to derail the delicate negotiations over the future of the Canal Zone.

When the Church Committee began investigating an alleged Panama/Torrijos hit, staff members interviewed E. Howard Hunt on February 25, 1977.While little documentation exists from that meeting, what can be learned is that when questioned about the Panama plan, Hunt said that there was talk among people in the Nixon White House about such an assassination plot but that no firm date or any hard plan was put into effect.

But what has fascinated investigators during the ensuing years is the timing in which the Torrijos plot was hatched.

It was at this time that the Nixon administration was being rocked by the newly released Pentagon Papers affair by a then little known figure by the name of Daniel Ellsberg. Ellsberg was a minor government official who had worked in Vietnam for the CIA's infamous "pacification" program during the 1960s. Early on, Ellsberg considered himself a "hawk," believing in the Johnson/Nixon positions concerning the U.S. role in Vietnam.

Ellsberg returned to the United States embittered about what he had seen and done in Southeast Asia. His political thinking had reversed itself and he was now opposed to Nixon's Vietnam policy. When he came back home, Ellsberg taught at MIT, and later worked for Henry Kissinger in the White House at the start of the Nixon presidency. He also did a stint as a staffer at the RAND Corporation.

Ellsberg began copying the top-secret "Pentagon Papers," a highly critical report on how the United States got involved in Vietnam. To Nixon, the leaking of the Pentagon Papers to the *New York Times* on June 13, 1971 was nothing but treason. Both Ellsberg and the other papers such as the *Washington Post,* which printed major excerpts, (along with the *Times),* had to be stopped at all cost. To that end, Nixon team took legal action to stop the *Times* from publishing any further portions of the report. Eventually, the Supreme Court ruled against the administration and the full Pentagon Papers was made public.

The geneses for the creation of the Plumbers were put into effect in a White House meeting on July 2nd between the President, John Ehrlichman and Bob Haldeman. Nixon wanted to be able to control the fallout over the Ellsberg/Pentagon Papers affair and the only way to do that without running into any outside interference, i.e. Hoover's FBI or the CIA, was to command the investigation at the White House level. Nixon and Ehrlichman decided that David Young, who was then working as an assistant to National Security Advisor Henry Kissinger, would head up part of the new unit.

On July 17, Ehrlichman appointed his own man to head the Plumbers. He appointed Egil Krogh, a White House aide who was director on the president's domestic council. Krogh was to head the Special Investigations Unit, a.k.a. the Plumbers, while Young would serve as its staff director. When taking on the job as head of the unit, Ehrlichman told Krogh that he would have direct contact with the president at any time. Another job of the new SPU was to take over the investigation of Ellsberg from the Justice Department and concentrate it in the White House.

As the Plumbers operation was getting organized, Krogh began his search for people of a certain caliber who would be totally loyal to Nixon. One of the first recruits to come on board

241

was a former FBI agent, Gordon Liddy. After leaving the FBI, Liddy served as an assistant district attorney in Poughkeepsie, New York, was totally opposed to any type of gun control, and harbored harsh right-wing political views. In 1968, he ran against Congressman Hamilton Fish in the Republican primary contest but lost the race. When Nixon won the election for president over Hubert Humphrey, Liddy was given a job in the Treasury Department but he didn't last long. After getting into one too many scrapes with his boss, Liddy was transferred to the White House, working for Attorney General John Mitchell where he specialized in "narcotics, bombing and guns." For Liddy, the Plumbers assignment was manna from heaven.

The other person that was to play a part in the Watergate & Torrijos affair was a former CIA agent, whose shadowy past would bring him right smack into the investigation of the assassination of President John Kennedy, E Howard Hunt. A detailed description of Hunt's background is not needed here as most researchers familiar with both the Watergate scandal and the Kennedy assassination are by now most familiar with Hunt's resume. Suffice it to say that Nixon staffer Charles Colson introduced Hunt to the Plumbers. Hunt, working out of a secure spot in the Executive Office building opposite the White House was to gather as much dirt on the president's potential Democratic opponents as he could find.

In this time period, when the Plumbers were beginning to carry out their covert action plan, the Jack Anderson article concerning the Torrijos heroin connection hit the stands. It should also be noted that during this time, Gordon Liddy had proposed an assassination plot against Anderson. As the government report on this phase of the Torrijos affair states:

> In setting forth this March 1972 period as a likely period in which the alleged Panama Assassination plan was initiated by the Nixon men, one should bear in mind that other Plumber assignments were later revealed to have been set in motion by a single news Report, such as Anderson's March 1972 column on Torrijos. Thus, the Plumbers plot against Torrijos (if in fact one did exist), might quiet reasonably be traced to these March 1972

disclosures about the heroin trade.

By the spring of 1972, the CIA had hard evidence concerning the use of Panama as a shipping and receiving point for the sale of drugs throughout the Latin American region. In the Anderson article the columnist reported that the CIA had in hand, a 20-page document detailing the Torrijos connection, and that this report was being circulated to other interested governmental agencies.

With regard to this plot the government report states:

> That some low level White House officials at one point considered assassinating Panama's head of government. Dean's story is that the administration suspected High Panamanian government officials of being involved in the flow of heroin from Latin America into the U.S. and was also concerned about strongman Omar Torrijos' uncooperative attitude toward renegotiating the Panama Canal treaty. Thus, in Dean's Telling, some officials found a Torrijos hit doubly attractive. The contract, he said, went to E. Howard Hunt later a ringleader in the Watergate break-in. Hunt, according to Dean, had his team in Mexico before the mission was aborted.

It is interesting to note that John Dean, wrapped up as he was in the unfolding of the Watergate scandal, did not make any mention in a public forum on the alleged Panama hit. The story was not confirmed until *four years later* when Hunt testified to it in February 1977.

As in many other areas of Howard Hunt's professional life, his involvement in the Panama hit remains a mystery (Hunt is now dead and can't tell what he knew—Note: the Ervin Committee investigators have said that they called in Hunt regarding the Torrijos hit and that he denied any involvement in such a scheme. Yet, after Hunt's release from jail for his participation in Watergate, he confirmed, in a February 25, 1977 interview, that a Plumbers plan to kill Torrijos was in the works. Which story is true?).

Another interesting person who was associated a possible Panama hit was Bernard Barker, another man how was arrested in the Watergate break-in.

On June 1, 1974, *ABC* news reporter David Schoumacher aired a report stating that, according to his sources—Hunt had sent a Torrijos murder team to Mexico in preparation for the attack. The plan was subsequently aborted. Hunt, the report said, had made frequent secret trips to Mexico using the alias, "Edward J. Hamilton." Interestingly, Watergate evidence also establishes the fact the Watergate burglar, Frank Sturgis, had also apparently traveled to Mexico in 1972, during the same period of time in which he was working on various assignments for the Hunt/ Liddy team. Following his arrest in the Watergate break-in, and the extensive news coverage devoted to him, it was reported that Sturgis had applied for and received a Mexican visa in early 1972. The Sturgis visa was good for January 7th to April 6, 1972—dates, which once again falls within an interesting time period.

The House proceedings in which this chapter is based, reported a secret trip made by Hunt to Nicaragua in the time period covering January to April 1972. What Hunt was doing in Nicaragua is still unknown but it is speculated that he was there on the behest of the Nixon re-election committee. During the time of Hunt's alleged trip to Nicaragua, Howard Hughes, a secret contributor to Nixon's presidential campaign, was living in that country.

If the Howard Hunt story that he was in Mexico to plan the Torrijos hit is true, this opens up a whole new area of investigation; it leads right up to the "smoking gun" tape of June 23, 1972 between President Nixon and his top aides. During that meeting, both the president and Haldeman talk about the White Houses' effort to have the FBI call off their investigation of the "Mexico connection" to Watergate (the money funneled to the burglars was laundered through Mexico by Liddy). After the meeting, the president's men had CIA Director Helms order FBI Director L. Patrick Gray to halt the FBI's investigation into covert activities in Mexico. What is still not known is what was going on in Mexico at that time.

The testimonies of two of the principal players in the CIA/ Watergate affair spell out an intriguing aspect of this "Mexico connection." When CIA Deputy Director Vernon Walters testified about the June 23rd White House meeting, he said "that Haldeman warned that there is concern that these investigations—this investigation in Mexico, may expose some covert activities of the CIA."

Even more interesting is the statement by ex-CIA Director Richard Helms to the Ervin Committee concerning the same June 23rd meeting. Helms stated:

> At this point the references to Mexico were quite unclear to me. I had to recognize that if the White House, the president, Mr. Haldeman, somebody in high authority, had information about something in Mexico which I did not have information about, which is quite possible—the White House constantly has information which others do not have—that it would be a prudent thing for me to find out. This possibility always had to exist. Nobody knows everything about everything.

Many questions still remain concerning the possible Torrijos assassination plot, if indeed there really was one. Knowing what we now know about the character of the Watergate Plumbers during the Nixon administration, it is not out of the realm of possibility that some sort of plot against Omar Torrijos was planned. But this strange episode is just one more riddle from the vast, illegal network that dominated the Nixon years. NOTE to readers. This information came from an article I wrote in my magazine, *Back Channels,* in the issue dated Volume 4, Number 1, 1995. This information is available at the National Archives in their vast Watergate collection.

Chapter 30
The Plot to Kill Jack Anderson

On December 18, 2005, an obituary was reported in many of the nation's newspapers concerning the death of one of the most well known reporters in Washington and the United States, Jack Anderson. For readers of a certain generation, Jack Anderson's name was recognized as one of the preeminent muckrakers of the world of journalism, taking on powerful politicians and revealing many of the most important events in the decade of the 1960s and 1970s. Over his long career in journalism, Jack Anderson would team up with Drew Pearson and the two men would soon become household name to millions of daily readers. During his long and distinguished career, Jack Anderson would report on events like the Keating Five congressional scandal, revelations regarding President Reagan and the Iran-Contra scandal, the U.S. government's shift away from India toward Pakistan in international relations, for which he received the Pulitzer Prize in 1972, the CIA-Mafia assassination plots against Fidel Castro during the Kennedy Administration, the Dita Beard-ITT scandal which linked the settlement of a federal anti-trust suit against the International Telephone and Telegraph Company, revelations against Howard Hughes, and the Watergate affair. Not known to many Americans during those tumultuous years is that President Richard Nixon planned an assassination attempt against Anderson, who had become one of his harshest critics, using one of his Plumbers, G. Gordon Liddy to do the deed.

Jack Anderson was born on October 19, 1922 in Long Beach, California. His grew up in a strict Mormon family where religion was part of every-day life. The family soon moved to Utah at 12 years of age where Jack Anderson got the bug to become a writer. While he was still in high school he worked for the *Salt Lake City Tribune* and continued working there when he attended the University of Utah. He dropped out of college before graduating and headed south where he did his missionary work. In 1943 he joined the Merchant Marine but in 1945 he abruptly left the

Merchant Marine without permission and soon wound up in China as a freelance reporter affiliated with the *Deseret News*. He covered the Chinese Nationalists who were battling the Japanese and soon found himself covering the Communist leader Chou En-Lai who would later, become the leader of Communist China. He also got hooked up with the military run *Stars and Stripes* newspaper and began broadcasting news from Shanghai.

In 1947, Anderson was back in Washington, D.C. where he got his first break in journalism. Drew Pearson, then one of the most influential newspaper reporters in the country, hired him as a researcher or "leg man". *Time* Magazine called Pearson, "the most intensely feared and hated man in Washington." Pearson's column ran in hundreds of papers nation-wide and his was as influential as any senator or congressman. Pearson's column was called "The Washington Merry-Go-Round", and was must reading for anyone in power in Washington at the time.

In the late 1940s, Anderson became friendly with Senator Joseph McCarthy who was then investigating allegations that there were communists operating in the American government. Drew Pearson however, refused to publish any of these stories as he did not trust McCarthy. He also exposed secret Ku Klux Klan ties to a congressman and would up testifying before a congressional committee on what he found.

For the next two decades, Anderson and Pearson covered every major and minor news story in Washington, becoming a dynamic duo among the legion of newsmen who worked in the city.

Pearson got his first real break in 1969 when Richard Nixon was elected president. When Nixon took office, he installed two of his aids, John Ehrlichman and Bob Haldeman to be his top men in the White House. Nixon's long-time friend and political hatchet man, Murray Chotiner who had been with Nixon since the beginning of his (Nixon's) career, was now pushed to the side. Chotiner, without Nixon's approval, contacted Anderson and said that the White House would like to have a good relationship with Pearson and Anderson. Anderson was skeptical but met with Chotiner, nevertheless. In order to get back at Nixon, Chotiner told Anderson that there was a homosexual ring operating out of the White House consisting of Bob Haldeman and John Ehrlichman, along with Dwight Chapin, and that the assignations took place at Haldeman's Watergate apartment. In order to verify the story, Anderson sent members of his staff to follow the men but in the end, they found nothing incriminating. Chotiner had pulled a fast one on Anderson and Pearson.

On June 11, 1969, Anderson showed up at the office of Deke DeLoach, the deputy director of the FB I. Anderson told DeLoach about the possibility of a sex ring operating out of the White House and an official investigation by the FBI was started. J. Edgar Hoover personally interviewed Nixon's men under oath in the White House and after a long investigation, did not find anything out of the ordinary concerning Nixon's men. In an interesting note, Hoover sent Mark Felt, later to be unmasked as Watergate's "Deep Throat," to transcribe the notes of Hoover's meeting.

Anderson did not write anything about the alleged sex ring in his column, waiting for a better and more reliable story to come his way. Anderson would later say about the mind of Richard Nixon by writing, "Other president's looked out the windows of the White House and saw the world. Richard Nixon looked out those windows and saw his own troubled reflection staring back at him."[1]

As time went on, the Nixon administration began a new phase in its relations with Jack Anderson; they used the CIA to spy on him. The surveillance on Anderson began in early 1972 and it was called "Project Mudhen." According to its charger, the CIA was not allowed to spy on domestic targets, but in the Anderson case, the rule went out the door. One CIA report on Anderson says he was, "as opinionated, self-righteous, ambitious and highly envious toward anyone in a position of power, especially "Establishment types." Another document says that, "Anderson's politics are not known; however, it is generally conceded that he is a first class liar."

Actual physical surveillance began in January 1972 and included some of Anderson's employees like Less Whitten, whom the CIA said, was a bad driver who "operates his personal automobile in a fast, impatient manner and will deviate from

---

[1] Feldstein, Mark, *Poisoning The Press: Richard Nixon, Jack Anderson, And The Rise of Washington's Scandal Culture,* Farrar, Straus and Giroux, New York, 2010, Page 106-111.

normal routes in order to avoid minor traffic delays." The CIA also followed Anderson and his wife and family as they did their daily chores, failing to find anything of interest. They also followed him to work, to television interviews, to universities where he made speeches, etc. Once, when Anderson had an interview with CIA Director Richard Helms in a restaurant, CIA officers bugged the conversation while agents sat at other tables observing the entire engagement.

While the CIA was surveilling Anderson, he turned the tables on the Nixon administration by having his own people watch the activities of Assistant Attorney General Robert Mardian who was conducting his own investigation on Anderson (it seems that everyone was following everyone). Anderson had one of his intern's follow Mardian on his daily tasks, letting him know in no uncertain terms that he was being followed. Mardian told the FBI who put Mark Felt (Deep Throat) on the case. In what proved to be a brazen act on Anderson's part, he hired well-trained agents to spy on the CIA, tracking certain members across the city in a game of "I got you."

In April 1972, the CIA ended its investigation of Anderson, saying, "the surveillance failed to establish the existence and/ or identity of any individual who might have been supplying Anderson with classified data."

Anderson was now officially an enemy of the Nixon administration, one that was reciprocated on the reporter's part.

In 1969, Drew Pearson died, leaving the" Washington Merry-Go-Round" column to Anderson. After a rough period of time, Anderson was able to continue the column, and hired a new staff that included Brit Hume and Less Whitten.

In the summer of 1969, Anderson took aim at Senator Edward Kennedy after he and a young woman, Mary Jo Kopechne, were involved in a car crash in Massachusetts on the island of Chappaquiddick. Kopechne drowned in the car, while the senator unsuccessfully tried to save her life. Anderson was able to get hold of the sealed deposition transcripts of those who testified in the aftermath of the tragedy. In a series of newspaper columns, Anderson blasted Kennedy for his actions in the aftermath of the incident, much to the delight of the Nixon administration. In the

Chappaquiddick incident, Anderson saw a good story, even if all of what he wrote was not right. He now added Edward Kennedy to his list of people who did not like him, but in his line of work, it all came with the territory.

Over the next decade, Anderson was the bet noir of the Nixon administration. It seems that Anderson was right there whenever Nixon made a blunder and he was ready to pounce at every opportunity. He covered all the scandals from the Dita Beard-ATT Affair, the US tilt toward Pakistan over India, the earlier CIA-Mafia plots to kill Castro on behest of the CIA, the CIA's secret relationship with the mobster, Johnny Rosselli who took part in the CIA-Mafia plots to kill Castro, stories in the national press regarding Lee Harvey Oswald and the CIA in the Kennedy assassination, and much more. Anderson was now officially on Nixon's "enemies list" and it wasn't too long before there was talk in the White House about dealing with the irascible Anderson permanently.

President Nixon's hatred of Jack Anderson went back to the 1960 Presidential election against John Kennedy. Drew Pearson wrote a scathing article in the middle of the campaign that linked Donald Nixon, the Vice President's brother, of receiving a $205,000 "loan" from the reclusive billionaire, Howard Hughes. When the IRS found out about the loan they reversed a prior ruling that granted tax-exempt status to Hughes's shady "medical institute." Nixon at first denied that Donald had done anything wrong but he soon had to distance himself from his brother. Donald Nixon used the money to start a chain of "Nixon-Burger" franchises that soon went bust. Richard Nixon blamed Pearson-Anderson for creating a diversion during the campaign, and for contributing to his loss to Kennedy.

Once in office, Nixon ordered his men to investigate Anderson in a questionable land deal that went nowhere. In his paranoia, Nixon told his aides that Anderson, who was a Mormon, was being fed classified information by fellow Mormon's inside the government (not true).

The one event that caused Nixon to go bonkers regarding Anderson was a report he wrote that revealed that the U.S. was arming Pakistan in its military clash with India in December

251

1971, despite the fact that the administration said it was going to be neutral in the conflict. The root of the problem was that the Bengalis in eastern Pakistan wanted to form their own nation and revolted against the Pakistani government. Pakistan's brutal ruler, General Agha Muhammad Yahya Khan, set out to destroy the Bengalis by murdering them. Nixon decided to back Pakistan while the Russians backed India. On December 3, 1971, Pakistan invaded India to the utter condemnation of the world. Nixon broke US neutrality and used other nations to funnel military equipment to Pakistan. As the conflict grew in scope, the U.S. sent the navy's Seventh Fleet to the Bay of Bengal that included nuclear weapons. The conflict was now getting to the point where a possible US-Russian conflict was near.

Anderson had a source high up in the national security hierarchy and is a series of clandestine meetings, the source gave Anderson classified material regarding the US military shift toward Pakistan.

Anderson began writing a series of articles on the U.S. shift toward Pakistan starting on December 13th, using top-secret, classified Pentagon reports that should never have seen the light of day. The articles showed just how much the Nixon administration lied to the public in its pronouncements of neutrality in the India-Pakistan conflict.

The source for the Anderson blockbuster articles was Charles Radford, a Navy yeoman who had been working as a military aid inside the White House and had previously worked as a clerk at the U.S. Embassy in New Delhi, India. Radford worked for Admiral Robert Welander and he was questioned by Navy officials and hotly denied he was the source of Anderson's articles.

Anderson further enraged the administration by writing an article saying that his aide, Brit Hume, had gotten hold of memo written by a Washington lobbyist tying a $400,000 political contribution to help underwrite the 1972 GOP National Convention to the Justice Department's decision to drop an antitrust investigation of the ITT Company.

The Nixon administration's plan to get back at Jack Anderson now entered high gear. At a White House meeting on March 18, 1972, H.R. Haldeman, Nixon's chief of staff, said, "Don't we have some spurious stuff we can give to Jack Anderson?"

Charles Colson, a top Nixon aide, said, "We got a whole plot concocted yesterday." Haldeman asked if what Colson had on Anderson was false and he replied, "Oh, I got just the scheme for that." Both men had a plan to plant bogus information saying that Anderson was gay in order to ruin his reputation. The president replied by saying, "Anderson, I remember from year ago, he's got a strange, strange habit out of—I think Pearson was homosexual, too. I think he and Anderson were." At one White House meeting, Nixon's counselor, John Dean said, regarding Anderson, "To take us off the defensive. It is not enough just to react to each of his stories one at a time, after the fact, by discrediting the allegations in his column." Hunt said that the goal was "to diminish his reputation, personally and professionally. The White House sent one of its investigators, Jack Caulfield to interview Anderson's family and friends but came up with no derogatory information. The also used the services of a private investigative agency called Intertel which was staffed by retired FBI and CIA agents to probe Anderson's background. Whatever information culled by Intertel was forwarded to the Justice Department as well as the White House, which was then given to the Nixon's reelection campaign, and Republican Party Headquarters.

At one point, the White House planted a spy inside Anderson's office, Lou Russell. Russell had once been an investigator for then Congressman Nixon and they remained friends. Russell soon was incased in the "Merry-Go-Round" office and he began doing odd jobs for Anderson. Russell gave his information to Nixon's security chief, James McCord who would later be arrested in the Watergate break-in. After a while, Russell was let go and nothing out of the ordinary was discovered.

In a prelude to Watergate, *Washington Post* reporter Bob Woodward wrote an article in the September 21, 1975 edition, saying that an unnamed White House aide gave Nixon's chief spy, E. Howard Hunt, "the order to kill Anderson." The assignment was to be carried out by two of the Watergate Plumbers, Howard Hunt and Gordon Liddy. Both men followed Anderson around town and they were to get poison that could not be traced from a CIA physician. Woodward wrote that the plot to kill Anderson came from a "senior official in the Nixon White House." According to the story, both Hunt and Liddy had a lunch date at the Hays Adams Hotel in Washington with a retired CIA doctor in which they discussed ways to kill Anderson by putting poison in his medicine cabinet or by putting a large amount of LSD on the steering wheel of his car. The poison would then be absorbed in his skin and which would result in a car crash.

The name of the doctor whom Hunt and Liddy met that day was Dr. Edward Gunn. No names were mentioned in that meeting but in an interview with him many years later, Dr. Gunn said that the target was someone of Scandinavian descent. Dr. Gunn further stated that Hunt and Liddy "asked for something that would get him out of the way, make him look foolish." The doctor said that at no time was murder even mentioned in their conversation and that he advised them to use alcohol as the best means to do the job. When Liddy pressed Dr. Gunn to take part in the Anderson assignment, he said no because he had retired from the CIA and thus, had no access to any hallucinogens. For his service, Dr. Gunn was paid one hundred dollars for his time. The money came from the coffers of the Committee to Re-elect the President, the infamous CREEP. In a book on Anderson by author Mark Feldstein called *Poisoning The Press, Richard Nixon, Jack Anderson, and the Rise of Washington's Scandal Culture,* he writes that in an interview with Hunt before his death, he said that Charles Colson had ordered them to "locate Anderson's home and examine it on the outside for vulnerabilities. This was high on Chuck Colson's list of things to do, Hunt said. That was when the idea of putting a drug-laden pill in a bottle that Anderson was taking medicine from. Liddy had an idea that by wiping poison on a man's wrist that could kill him that way." Hunt said, "The more that Colson knew about Anderson, the more resolved he was to end it by whatever means. He regarded it as a protective function in terms of the president, get rid of this thorn in his side, one way or another, with hallucinogens or not."[2]

Colson denied any knowledge of any plot to kill Anderson, while Liddy said he knew about the plot and took part in discussions regarding its implementation. In his autobiography called *Will,* Liddy said that both he and Hunt were given the task of "stopping "Anderson, and wrote, "We examined all the alternatives and very

[2] Isikoff, Michael, Nixon plot against newspaper columnist detailed, NBC News 9/13/2010.

254

quickly came to the conclusion the only way you're going to be able to stop him is to kill him, and that was the recommendation." Years later, when Liddy met with Anderson, he told the journalist that, "The rational was to come up with a method of silencing you through killing you." Liddy said that in his meeting with Hunt at the Adams Hotel that the talk was "hypothetical" and that Anderson's name per say was not mentioned.

Both Hunt and Liddy also discussed the possibility that they use members of the Plumbers to stage a street robbery against Anderson. These were some of the Cuban's who would later enter the Watergate building with Hunt and Liddy in 1972. When it was mentioned to Liddy that higher ups in the White House would find the death of Anderson distasteful, Liddy said, "If necessary, I'll do it."

In an ironic twist to the story, Liddy told Jeb Stuart Magruder who was appointed by H.R. Haldeman to run CRP, the Committee to Re-Elect the President, of his plans to kill Anderson. Magruder was so incensed by Liddy's proposed actions that he took the highly unusual step of going to Anderson to apologize for Liddy's proposed actions.

No one knows if the plan to kill Jack Anderson was just macho talk or there was something else to the story. In later interviews, Hunt said that Anderson was the "enemy" in the Nixon White House. "Colson just hated him," he said. "And the more that Colson knew about Anderson, the more resolved he was to put an end to it by whatever means." Hunt said that in the final analysis, any order to kill Anderson had to come from the president himself. "If Nixon said, Chuck, I want you to do this, he would do it or he would find people to do it for him."

One thing is clear. Nixon held grudges, and had done so since he came to fame on the national stage in the late 1940s. He took no enemies, and had an opponents list, which he was proud of flaunting. He saw demons at every turn, real or imagined. The historian, Stanley Kutler, who wrote two books on Watergate called, *Abuse of Power: The New Nixon Tapes* (1997) and *The Wars of Watergate: The Last Crisis of Richard Nixon, (1990),* said of how Nixon operated in the White House, " Nixon tells Colson, Colson orders Hunt. Hunt executes. Thus, Colson fed off Nixon.

Haldeman realized for if there were no Nixon, there would have been no Colson in the White House. When it came to the darkest crimes of his Praetorian Guard, Richard Nixon commanded the patrol and dictated its missions."

Chapter 31
The Rosenberg Spy Case

It has been six decades since the June 19, 1953 execution of Julius and Ethel Rosenberg in Sing Sing prison on espionage charges for their involvement in stealing America's atomic secrets during World War II. The case against the Rosenberg's still creates passionate debate over their death sentences, and to what extent Julius and Ethel were involved with the Soviet Union's espionage operations. Like the case of Alger Hiss, new information has come forth that helps to explain their role in the stealing of America's atomic secrets and the exact role Julius played in the recruitment of a number of spies into his secret ring.

In the ensuing years, their now-grown sons, Michael and Robert Meeropol (they took on the names of their adoptive parent's after the execution), have spent their lives trying to clear their parent's name. With the end of the cold war, America's most prominent code-breaking service, the National Security Agency, as well as former Soviet intelligence officials who knew the Rosenberg's well, have shed new light on the role they performed for the Soviets during the war.

Julius Rosenberg was born on May 12, 1918 in New York City. His parents had immigrated from Poland at the turn of the century and raised five children. Julius attended school in New York and graduated from Seward Park High School at age 16.

He attended City College of New York and joined the Young Communist League where he would meet a number of other young men who shared his political views and would later become part of the Soviet espionage apparatus: Morton Sobel, William Pearl, and Joel Barr. Julius studied electrical engineering, instead of rabbinical studies that his father asked him to pursue.

Ethel Greenglass Rosenberg was two years younger than Julius and fancied herself going into the performing arts or a career in music. She, too, had radical political ideas. They met at a rally and were married in 1939.

In 1940, Julius went to work as a civilian employee for the

U.S. Army Signal Corps and in 1942 attained the position of inspector. While he was working for the army, both joined the Communist Party USA (CPUSA). In time, he served as the chairman of Branch 16B of the Party's Industrial Division. However, in 1943, Julius left the Communist Party to purse active espionage for the Soviet Union.

There have been conflicting accounts over who originally recruited Julius Rosenberg into the Soviet espionage orbit. The two leading candidates were Semen Semenov, a KGB agent who worked out of the Soviet trade organization called Amtorg, or Gaik Ovakimian, the NKVD's top agent in New York City.

Whatever the case, Julius began active spying in 1942. In 1943, Semenov returned to the Soviet Union, after it was discovered that he was under tight FBI surveillance. With Semenov gone, Rosenberg was assigned a new controller Alexander Feklisov, then a promising agent working in the Soviet consulate in New York. In time, Feklisov would also work closely with two other people whom Julius had recruited, his sister Ruth Greenglass and her husband, David. Feklisov was a busy man at that particular time, also having run another spy in the Manhattan Project (the U.S. project to build an atomic bomb), a British scientist named Klaus Fuchs.

Through his Russian contacts in New York, Julius was put in touch with a member of the intelligence apparatus working out of the Russian consulate, Anatoli Yakovlev (he also went by the last name of Yatskov). Yakovlev's aim was the theft of America's atomic bomb secrets. One of the men whom Yakovlev employed was Julius Rosenberg.

Julius used his brother-in-law, David Greenglass, a soldier assigned to the top-secret Los Alamos Laboratory in New Mexico, as his conduit for the transfer of material to the Russians. Greenglass worked for the Manhattan Project, the most sensitive project undertaken by the United States during World War II.

On October 15, 1942, General Leslie Groves appointed J. Robert Oppenheimer as head of the Manhattan Project, or Project Y. Oppenheimer was sent to Los Alamos, New Mexico where critical work on the bomb was taking place. Over the years, it has been alleged that Oppenheimer might have been working for the Soviet Union during that time. However, no concrete evidence linking him to Soviet intelligence at Los Alamos was found.

Not known to the United States was that the Russians had infiltrated the Manhattan Project with their own spies (many of whom were linked to the Rosenberg's). They received their first reports on U.S. atomic bomb research from John Cairncross, a member of the infamous Cambridge Spy Ring. Cairncross worked as a secretary for Lord Maurice Hankey, the chairman of the British governmental organization studying atomic bomb theory. The Soviet's top nuclear spy in the heart of the Manhattan Project was a British subject named Klaus Fuchs. Fuchs came to Britain in 1933 from Germany. He was a brilliant physicist, and also a member of the German Communist Party. Fuchs was put in contact with a Soviet agent whom he would pass his top-secret material. That man was given the codename "Raymond." In reality, "Raymond" was Harry Gold, a courier for the Soviet intelligence spy ring operating in the United States.

Julius arranged for Harry Gold to go to New Mexico and bring back information supplied by Greenglass. In 1945, while on leave, Greenglass arrived at Julius's apartment in New York and gave him a picture of a lens mold used for the detonation of the atomic bomb.

Julius was partly responsible for the recruitment of his sister and her husband into the Soviet orbit. By September 1944, the Soviet intelligence service began an active interest in taking on both of them. Ruth's first job was to act as a courier between her husband who worked at Los Alamos. The Soviet's gave them cover names, "Wasp" for Ruth, and "Bumblebee" for David, and recommended that they be handled by Harry Gold. In a conversation Julius had with Ruth and Ethel, Julius asked Ruth how she felt about the Soviet Union and her feelings regarding Communism in particular. She told him that it would be an honor to work for the Soviet Union because she believed in the cause. When he asked her if David would also be willing to work for the Russians, she said she believed her husband would also be interested. "Julius then explained his connections with certain people interested in supplying the Soviet Union with urgently needed technical information it could not obtain through the regular channels and impressed upon her the tremendous importance of the project in which David is now at work. Julius then instructed her that under no circumstances should they discuss any of these things inside a room or indeed anywhere except out-of-doors and under no circumstances to make any notes of any kind. She was simply to commit to memory as much as possible. Ethel here interposed to stress the need for the utmost care and caution in informing David of the work in which Julius was engaged and that, for his own safety, all other political discussion and activity on his part should be subdued."[1]

While Julius was active in the transfer of the atomic bomb intelligence, he also was involved in other facets of spying. He helped recruit a number of people in the American electronics industry who provided the Russians with highly technical data coming from U.S. factories. One of his major coups was the revelation to the Soviets of a working model of the so-called proximity fuse, which was used to shoot down aircraft without a direct hit. Julius was able to secure this device from his new employer, the Emerson Radio Company in New York.

Throughout the time that Julius was working for the Russians, the FBI had been intercepting an enormous amount of enciphered messages to and from the Soviet consulates in New York and Moscow. His NKGB controller, Feklisov, feared that the FBI was tracking Rosenberg and did everything in his power to keep him safe. It was now until after the war in 1947 that the messages were turned over to the Army Security Agency. In years of painstaking work by a crack team of cryptanalysts, U.S. code breakers were able to piece together the story. What they found shocked them to the core. They discovered that the Soviets had penetrated the Manhattan Project and that the prime leader was Klaus Fuchs. The British took Fuchs into custody, and he admitted his Los Alamos espionage activities. Fuchs in turn, gave the British and the Americans, the name of his cut-out in the operation, Harry Gold. Gold turned in David Greenglass, and he was arrested. The circumstances of what happened next are still unclear. When questioned by the FBI, Greenglass told them that his sister, Ethel, and her husband Julius, had recruited him into their Russian-controlled spy ring. On June 17, 1950, Julius was arrested on suspicion of espionage. Ethel was

[1] Weinstein, Allen, and Vassileiv, *The Haunted Wood: Soviet Espionage In America-The Stalin Era,* Random House, New York, 1999, Page 199.

arrested shortly thereafter.

At their trial, which lasted from March-April 1951, Julius and Ethel were convicted of espionage. The other two defendants, David Greenglass and Morton Sobell, received a 15- and 30-year prison sentence.

Julius and Ethel were taken to Sing Sing Prison in New York, while their appeal process went on. Despite an uproar from numerous prominent world leaders, the two were executed on June 19, 1953 (Ethel was the second woman in American history to be put to death for wartime espionage. The first was Mary Surratt who was hanged for her alleged participation in the plot to kill Abraham Lincoln).

In the 1990s, decades after their deaths, and after the end of the Cold War, new information relating to the Rosenberg's played during that time has come to light.

The U.S. intelligence agencies used the Venona Project to spy on the Soviets during World War II. It was run out of Arlington Hall and taken over after the conflict ended by the newly created National Security Agency. The Venona decryption revealed Julius Rosenberg's role in Soviet wartime espionage.

By the time the Venona analysts made headway breaking Soviet traffic, the war was won. But what they did learn in the early 1950s was that the Soviet Union had penetrated the Manhattan Project in which U.S. scientists developed the atomic bomb.

The Russians gave Rosenberg two codenames: "Antenna" and Liberal." From 1944 to 1945, the Venona analysts picked up 21 cables referring to Julius. What they learned was that by May 23, 1944, Rosenberg's network in New York was flourishing. Julius recruited Alfred Sarant, a classmate at CCNY who had previously worked for the Signal Corps laboratory at Fort Monmouth, New Jersey. After working for the Soviet's, he fled the U.S. in July 1950. The early Venona materials report that the Russians provided Julius with his own camera in order to copy stolen documents at his home.

At the height of his work, Julius Rosenberg had one of the most valuable intelligence networks operating clandestinely in the United States for the Soviet Union. The men he recruited were five engineers, Nathan Sussman, Joel Barr, Alfred Surant, and Morton

Sobell. These men worked in such industries as leading electronic firms that produced advanced military radio, radar, sonar, and other equipment of a military nature. William Perl worked for a firm that was working on the development of America's first jet fighter, and David Greenglass who worked in the bowels of Los Alamos as Julius's number one mole.

In late 1944, the FBI gave the Army information that Julius Rosenberg, who was then employed as an engineer-inspector by the Army Signal Corps, that he was a Communist. He was fired from that sensitive job in February 1945. When Moscow Center found out that their prized agent ahd been outed, they made plans to protect him. A message in that regard reads as follows:

> The most recent events with L (Liberal) Rosenberg are extremely serious and require us, first of all, to properly evaluate what happened, and secondly, to make a decision about L's role in the future. In deciding the latter we should proceed from the fact that we have a loyal man whom we can trust completely, a man who in his practical work over the course of several years has shown how strong his desire is to help our country. Besides this, in L, we have a talented agent who knows how to work with people and has considerable experience recruiting new agents.[2]

While the FBI did have information that Julius was a Communist, they did not know he was then running a large scale Soviet spy ring in New York. Julius was then able to get a new job at the Emerson Radio Company, despite the fact that he was branded as a Communist. The Venona papers reveal that Julius stole a complete set of a new, highly secret proximity fuse used for the military while he was at Emerson. For his action, he received a $1,000 incentive.

In the fall of 1945, a major blow to the Soviet espionage establishment in the United States took place. A woman named Elizabeth Bentley, a high-ranking Soviet agent in the U.S., defected to the FBI and reported that the Soviet's had a major spy-ring operating in the country. She was recruited into the Soviet orbit by

[2] Haynes, John, Klehr, Harvey, and Vassillev, Alexander, *Spies: The Rise And Fall of The KGB in America,* Page 341.

her lover, Jacob Golos and after Golos's death, Bentley took over the ring. One of the men whom the Russians had recruited, said Bentley, was Julius Rosenberg.

A retired Russian spy who was close to Julius and Ethel during the war, Alexander Feklisov, provided more information on their wartime espionage activities. In 1997, Feklisov gave a number of interviews to American news organizations regarding his knowledge of the Rosenberg espionage case.

Feklisov said that he met with Julius in the summer of 1946 in a New York restaurant. At that meeting he gave him $1,000 expense money. Prior to that date, Feklisov said that between 1943 and 1946, he met with Julius Rosenberg in New York more than 50 times, helping him to establish his espionage network.

He emphatically told his interviewers that while Ethel Rosenberg was aware of her husband's work for the Russians, she had no direct contact with any members of Soviet intelligence. Of Ethel Rosenberg, the Venona papers say that she "knows about her husband's work, but is in delicate health and does not work." When questioned about Julius's role in stealing America's atomic secrets, he said that he played only a minor role in the affair (He alluded to the fact that Klaus Fuchs was the main participant in the theft of the Manhattan Project's secrets).

During his tenure for the Soviet Union, Julius would meet with Feklisov at such places as Madison Square Garden, at Child's Restaurant, and other public places. The ex-Russian spy said that Julius once told him that, " I calculated the risks very carefully, What I was risking was only one-hundredth of what a Red Army soldier risks when he attacks a tank."

The new information supplied via the Venona Project and Alexander Feklisov's revelations, adds new details to the case. Their trial came at a time in American history when the Cold War hysteria and McCarthyism were at their height. The Korean War had just begun, and Americans were looking for scapegoats. Whether they were the first victims of the Cold War, or pawns in a larger game of Soviet-American tension's, is still debatable. History, in the Rosenberg case, is still ongoing.

Chapter 32
Was Oswald an Agent?

One of the many lingering mysteries of the Kennedy assassination is whether or not Lee Harvey Oswald had any connection to U.S. intelligence, i.e., the FBI or the CIA. In the story of Lee Harvey Oswald's brief life, there are numerous tangential links to one intelligence agency or another, both here at home and overseas. The more one looks into the evidence, most, if not all of it, not looked into by the Warren Commission, point to some sort of intelligence training of Oswald and his possible association of both the FBI and the CIA, (and possibly with the Office of Naval Intelligence) with the alleged presidential assassin.

In December 1958, Lee Harvey Oswald ended his tour of duty with the Marines in the Pacific, and was transferred back to the United States, winding up at the El Toro Marine base in California. His new duty assignment was the Marine Air Control Squadron 9 in Santa Ana, California. He was part of a ten-man unit that would study radar operations. Oswald's CO at El Toro, John F. Donovan, later testified to the Warren Commission that his unit's job was "basically to train both enlisted men and officers for later assignments overseas." All of the men in the unit had to have a "Secret" clearance, including Oswald. This seems rather strange considering that Oswald was charged with various crimes, including being court-martialed while stationed in Japan.

Oswald was considered a rather odd character by his fellow Marines, many of whom began calling his "Comrade Oswald-sko-vitch." In his spare time, he leanred Russian, and tended to keep to himself. Oswald's military record says nothing about his officially learning Russian but the Warren Commission had other ideas. In a Warren Commission executive session that was declassified in 1974, chief counsel J. Lee Rankin said of Oswald's possible training in the Russian language, "We are trying to find out what he studied at the Monterey School of the Army in way of languages." Most members of the armed forces who are taught a foreign language usually go into some sort of intelligence work. Was Oswald slated for this kind of operation that we are not aware of?

Over the years there have been constant rumors about whether or not Oswald attended the Monterey Language School. It is interesting to note that when Marina Oswald met Lee in Minsk she thought he was Russian because of his fluency in that language. While the verdict is out as to Oswald's attendance at the Language School, it is certain that he did more in Monterey than take the 17 Mile Drive.

One man who knew Lee Oswald and was himself a part of the anti-Castro-mercenary world of the late 1950s and early 1960s was the late Gerry Patrick Hemming. In the late 1950s, Gerry Hemming was part of an anti-Castro group in Florida called the Intercontinental Penetration Force, a.k.a., Interpen. As a young man, Hemming joined the Marines in 1954, after enlisting while still under age. He took basic training at Jacksonville, Florida and later was selected to work as an air controller serving in duty stations in Kansas, El Toro, California and Hawaii. (Oswald's unit would later be assigned to the top-secret Atsugi Air Base in Japan which monitored the secret U-2 spy planes that flew over Russia and China. Oswald would serve as one of these operators). While actually serving with the ONI (Office of Naval Intelligence), Hemming was approached by them shortly before his discharge.

This writer met Hemming in the early 1990s at the Assassination Archives and Records Center in Washington that is run by attorney Jim Lazar. Jerry was a talkative man, regaling me with stories of his time in the mercenary world and the people he came to know. One of these was Lee Harvey Oswald. He told me the following story. Hemming was approached by them shortly before his discharge. "They were interested in what I was doing with Castro's Cuba, supplying them with guns. They wanted to get some information about security violations at Guantanamo where some time previously some Naval and Marine personnel were captured by Raul Castro." Hemming said that at this time some of the Americans at the base were supplying guns and ammunition to the rebels.

Hemming had a long history of gunrunning and it was in this business that he met with Lee Oswald. One day, as Hemming was working at the Cuban Consulate in Los Angeles, he was told by a Cuban "that there was an American looking for me. I went out and there was Oswald standing there. "Oswald said he wanted to join the group. Hemming was abrupt with him and ran him off."

"The next morning over at the consulate," continued Hemming, "Oswald was seated inside the ante-room." Hemming asked the Cuban what Oswald was doing there. They (the Cuban's), thought Oswald was a friend of Hemming because Oswald had asked to speak to "the American." According to Hemming, Oswald was still on active duty with the Marines and was livid that the Cuban's would invite an American military man into the building. Hemming feared an "international incident" should Oswald be discovered. At that point, Hemming took Oswald aside. "What is it you want?" he asked, thinking that the young Marine was some sort of a plant. Oswald replied, "I want to go to Cuba and join the revolution."

According to Hemming, Oswald who had never met him before, began using military code words describing where he was stationed (LTA Base), what kind of work he did, and knew of Hemming's military background. "Marines don't talk to civilians and use that slang. They would only say it to someone who they knew was a Marine. He's a snitch, or somebody sending me somebody and now he's going to tell me about me," said an incredulous Hemming. As they departed, Oswald said to Hemming, "I'll find you there (in Cuba). I know how to find people."

Hemming also said that he met with Oswald on another occasion when his Interpen group was arrested at No Name Key in Florida in December 1962. Hemming said that Oswald was trying to infiltrate his (Hemming's) group at a motel where they were being detained.

Hemming was a storyteller extraordinaire and there is no way to ascertain the validity of his claims about meeting Oswald in Los Angeles.

In September 1959, Lee Oswald abruptly left the Marine Corps because he said his mother had taken ill and needed his help. Instead of going back to Fort Worth, he applied for, and received a passport in record time and headed to the Soviet Union. He was supposed to have attended the Albert Schweitzer College in Zurich, Switzerland but he never showed up. He made his way to France and then he went on to the Soviet Union. Once in Russia, he went to the American embassy where he met with the Consul Richard Snyder and Vice Consul John McVickar and told them that he was renouncing his U.S. citizenship and pledged allegiance to the Soviet Union. He told them of his work as a radar operator in Japan and offered to give them whatever information he had on the U-2 spy plane. While he was in the Soviet Union, U-2 pilot Francis Gary Powers was shot down over Russia. After his capture, Powers said that the information Oswald gave the Soviet's might have been responsible for his shoot down. Prior to his departure for Russia, Oswald did not have enough money to afford the trip but he somehow made it to Russia, even though there was no commercial means of transportation that could have gotten him there in the time he arrived. This leaves open the possibility that he took some sort of military transport to Europe and then made his way to Russia.

Once in Russia, Oswald was packed off to the city of Minsk where he worked in a radio factory, lived high on the hog and married a pretty Russian woman named Marina. His two and a half years in Russia are still a huge mystery to this day and the debate lingers as to just what he was doing in Russia in the first place. Some people have speculated that Oswald was part of a covert U.S. false defector program that was sending U.S. intelligence operatives into Russia to gather information of the Soviet Union. In the eighteen months prior to 1960, two former Navy men, five Army personnel stationed in West Germany, and two employees of the National Security Agency changed sides. Joan Hallett, who was married to the Assistant Naval Attach' and worked as a receptionist in the embassy, told author Anthony Summers that Counsel Snyder and a security officer "took him (Oswald) upstairs to the working floors, a secure area where the Ambassador and the political, economic, and military officers were. According to Hall, Oswald came to the embassy several times in 1959."

If Oswald was just a low-level defector, then why did the Navy change all the aircraft call signs, codes, and radio and radar frequencies at the last base that Oswald was stationed at? Did they fear that he would give that information to the Soviet's? After his "defection," the Navy did not conduct a "formal damage assessment" on what Oswald might have given up. This was done in the two previous cases where U.S. military men defected to Russia. [3]

It's possible that Oswald was used by the U.S. government as an unwitting false defector to see how much the Soviet's would debrief him and what information Oswald could bring back with him.

A former Chief Security Officer at the State Department, Otto Otepka, said that in 1963 that his office was working on a program to study American defectors that included Oswald. Otepka said that in the months before the Kennedy assassination, the State Department did not know if Oswald "had been one of ours or one of theirs."

When Oswald returned to the United States with Marina from Russia, he was not charged with desertion by the Navy. Why? By defecting to the Soviet Union, Oswald should have been considered a traitor but there was no disciplinary action taken against him. The Office of Naval Intelligence told the FBI that they had no intention of taking any further action against one of their own. Once back in Texas, the FBI opened a "security case" on him because of his defection and the FBI sent agents to interview him and found him to be "cold, arrogant, and difficult to interview." Since they FBI did not have any evidence that Oswald had given any secrets to the Soviet Union, they left him alone.

After the Kennedy assassination, the FBI would learn that Oswald had brought a note into its Dallas office. There is no way to know for certain just what was in the note Oswald delivered because it was destroyed after Oswald was killed by Jack Ruby. Conspiracy theorists say that Oswald was delivering a note to warn the Bureau of the impeding assassination because he was working for them as an agent. Both the CIA and the FBI denied any link to Oswald.

Before Oswald arrived in Russia, he was in Helsinki, Finland for a brief time. It was there that Oswald got a visa to travel to Russia in days instead of the usual one week time period. We know about this via a CIA memo from the vice consul/CIA officer named William Costille called REDCAP/LCMPROVE. During this time period, Costille met with his Soviet counterpart, Gregory Golub and they began to trust each other, swapping stores, among

[3] Summers, Anthony & Swan, Robin, *Lee Harvey Oswald: A Simple Defector?*, wordpress.com, 11/19/2013.

other things. According to CIA records, REDCAP was "originally designed in 1952 to deal with the results of uprisings in the Soviet satellites, with a special focus on defectors and refugees." One CIA member said of the REDCAP mission," First priority went to recruit Soviets as sources or, as the Redcap sloganeers put it, to encourage them to defect in place. Failing that, those who insisted on defecting outright, would be brought to the West, where their intelligence knowledge could be tapped."[4]

The information we have on the REDCAP/REDSKIN program might have something to do with Oswald's "defection" to the Soviet Union. This information is given in a memo written by the CIA's Deputy Director of Plans, Richard Bissell on 9/2/59, days before Oswald left the U.S. for Russia. In the memo, Bissell wrote that the CIA needed to expand its efforts by the Clandestine Service against Russia and that, "One way was to monitor the activities of Soviet personnel and installations (REDCAP) and to negate their activities outside the USSR, and the other was all the operations aimed inside the USSR itself, including REDSKIN."

It is very possible that Oswald was to be part of the REDSKIN program. The State Department listed Oswald was a "tourist" when he made out his application to go to Russia. In the late 1950s, there were at least twenty REDCAP agents sent to the Soviet Union. It is not out of the realm of possibility that Oswald was part of the REDCAP program in order to send him to the Soviet Union in order to find out as much information on the Soviet Union as he could.

It is now known that the CIA had a longstanding interest in Lee Harvey Oswald, much of which was not shared with the Warren Commission. Almost immediately after the president's assassination, the CIA began its own, internal investigation of the events on Dallas. The man put in charge of the operation was John Whitten, a.k.a, "John Scelso." John Whitten worked for the CIA for twenty-three years as an officer in the clandestine operations organization. At the time of President Kennedy's assassination, Whitten was chief of a branch responsible for operations in Mexico and Central America, including Panama. His branch was called WH-3, or Western Hemisphere 3. Through the release of thousands of

---

[4] Simpich, Bill, *Lee Harvey Oswald's First Intelligence Assignment*, World-wide-web, September 25, 2010.

pages of Kennedy assassination related information via the JFK Records Act, the 188-page so-called "Scelso" report was declassified, and tells the story of the CIA's probe into the Kennedy assassination.

For a lone nut that the Warren Commission made Oswald out to be, the CIA had a keen interest in him. New information shows that four important CIA officials kept track of Oswald prior to the assassination. These four people read a lot of information on Oswald and by October 1963, all of them said that he was "maturing." The names of these four people were Jane Roman, William Hood, Tom Karamessines, and John Whitten. These individuals were responding to a cable that they received from the CIA's Mexico City station about Oswald. They told their colleagues in Mexico City that they were aware of Oswald's defection to Russia and his return to the U.S. in 1962. They said that Oswald stay in the Soviet Union had a "maturing effect on him." If they knew that his stay abroad had a "maturing" effect on him, what did they know about him before his trip to Russia?

Jane Roman was the senior liaison officer on the Counter-intelligence Staff of the CIA at Langley headquarters. The Oswald file was handled by James Angleton's Counter-intelligence Staff, one of the most secretive parts of the CIA. The Counter-intelligence Staff was the mole hunting group at the CIA and when Oswald returned home the agency did not know if he was an agent of the Soviet Union or just a disgruntled American who had seen the light. When she was interviewed by John Newman and Jefferson Morley, two writers who were serious Kennedy assassination researchers, they showed Roman a sheaf of files that the FBI had on Oswald, including some material on his stay in New Orleans in the summer of 1963, Some of these files came from the Directorate of Plans, then the covert division of the CIA." Is this the mark of a person who's dull and uninteresting," asked Newman. "No, we're really trying to zero in on somebody here," said Roman.

When asked to comment on the Oswald paper trail and all the people who read it, Roman said, "The only interpretation I could put on this would that the SAS (Special Affairs Staff) group would have held all the information on Oswald under tight control." Roman said of the CIA's interest in Oswald via its paper trail. "To me it's indicative of a keen interest in Oswald held very closely on the need to know basis. There wouldn't be any point in withholding it (the current information on Oswald). There has to be a point for withholding information from Mexico City." She also said that, "Oswald was the subject of great interest to both the CIA and the FBI before November 22, 1963."

The second officer was William Hood whose name has not previously been associated in any way with the Kennedy assassination. In 1963, William Hood served in the job as the chief of covert operations in the Western Hemisphere Branch. During that time, the CIA, under JFK, was running a number of covert operations against Fidel Castro in order to overthrow him, (Operation Mongoose). In an interview, Hood said that the CIA had no operation at that time that involved Oswald. When asked why he said that Oswald was "maturing," he said I would like to think that 80 percent of CIA cables would be more competent. I don't find anything smelly in it."

Thomas Karamessines was the assistant to the deputy CIA director, Richard Helms and was aware of the Oswald paper trail. When asked about his reaction to the cable, he gave a rather convoluted and meaningless answer. "I read the message. It concerns a Marine defector who apparently according to the incoming message to which this was a response, was trying to get in touch with some Soviet's or Cubans in Mexico. That would be the extent of my interest in it at the time." He had no rational answer to his statement that Oswald was "maturing."

The last person of interest was John Whitten whom I have written about above. He did a complete study for the CIA on the Kennedy assassination right after November 22, 1963, but was not given all pertinent information for his study that the agency had in its possession. He also criticized James Angleton for not sharing with him the information about Oswald's time in New Orleans in the summer of 1963 when he was passing out Fair Play For Cuba Committee leaflets and associating with such rabid anti-communist and anti-Castro people like Guy Bannister and David Ferrie, both of whom were probably associated with the Kennedy assassination in some way. Whitten also said that in his opinion, the U.S. government should have looked into the possibility that William

Harvey, who ran the CIA's Executive Action/ZR Rifle assassination program, should have been investigated as a possible participant in the president's assassination.[5]

If Lee Harvey Oswald was not some sort of intelligence operative for the U.S. government (wittingly or unwittingly), why then were there so many important people in the CIA interested in his whereabouts and actions? He associated with various people in Dallas (George de Mohrenschildt) and New Orleans in the summer of 1963 (Ferrie, Banister and Clay Shaw) before his return to Dallas. Then there is his mysterious trip to Mexico City in late September-early October 1963 when he tried to get a visa to return to Russian via Cuba. The CIA knew that someone was impersonating Oswald while he was in Mexico City and in an interesting development, the pictures of people entering the Cuban and Russian embassies when Oswald was supposed to have been there were, quite by accident, disappeared.

There were rumors that Oswald may have been an informant with the FBI and the Warren Commission took a look into that possibility. That possibility came up on January1, 1964, during the Commission's Executive Session. The Commission's legal counsel, J. Lee Rankin started the conversation by telling his fellow commissioners the following story. He said that he had a telephone conversation with Waggoner Carr, the Attorney General of Texas that Oswald was an FBI informant and was given the designation Number 179. Oswald was supposed to have been paid two hundred dollars a month from September 1962 to the time of the assassination. When asked by Rankin how Carr had gotten the information, he said that the news had been given to the defense team for Jack Ruby. Rankin said that he immediately told Chief Justice Warren and that Warren broached the possibility of bringing Carr up to Washington for further testimony.

During their session, the commissioners talked among themselves as to the possible ramifications of such a fact being true. Rankin said that," Now it is something that would be very difficult to prove out. There are events in connection with this that are curious, in that they might make it possible to check some of it out on time. I assume the FBI records would never show it, and if it

[5] "4 CIA officers who made a lethal mistake about Lee Harvey Oswald." JFK Facts in the Mary Ferrell Foundation website.

is true, and of course we don't know, but we thought you should have the information."

Commission member John Sherman Cooper asked Rankin if it would be possible to absolutely prove that Oswald was or was not an FBI informer. Rankin responded by saying, It is going to be very difficult for us to be able to establish the fact in it. I am confident that the FBI would never admit it, and I presume their records will never show it, or if their records do show anything, I think their records would show some kind of a number that could be assigned to a dozen different people according to how they wanted to describe them. So that it seemed to me if it truly happened, he (Oswald) did use postal boxes practically every place that he went, and that would be an ideal way to get money for anything that you wanted as an undercover agent, or anybody else that you wanted to do business with without having any particular transaction."[6]

Commission member Allan Dulles, the former head of the CIA whom Kennedy had fired after the botched invasion of Cuba at the Bay of Pigs in April 1961 that he oversaw, took up the next question. He asked rhetorically concerning Oswald by saying, "What was the ostensible mission? I mean when they hire somebody they hire somebody for a purpose. It is either. Was it to penetrate the Fair Play For Cuba Committee? That is the only thing I can think of where they might have used this man. It would be quite ordinary for me because they are very careful about the agents they use. You wouldn't pick up a fellow like this to do an agent's job. You have got to watch out for your agents. You really got to know. Sometimes you make a mistake."

Commissioner Hale Boggs had many lingering questions about Oswald being the killer of the president and he posed this question.

"Of course it is conceivable that he may have been brought back from Russia you know."

Dulles replied, "They (the FBI) have no facilities, they haven't any people in Russia. They may have some people in Russia but they haven't got any organization of their own in Russia. They might have their agents there. They have some people, sometimes American Communists who go to Russia under their guidance and

---

[6] Warren Commission Executive Session 1/22/64, 5:30-7PM.

so forth and so on under their control."

It is evident from this conversation that the members of the panel were concerned enough about Oswald's stay in Russia and the possibility that he might have been sent under the auspices of the FBI in some undercover capacity. If Dulles knew about any relationship Oswald might have had with the CIA in Russia (or anywhere else), he never would have mentioned it in open session.

There is a large amount of circumstantial evidence that point to the fact that Lee Oswald was in fact a member, one way or another, with some branch of U.S. Intelligence. The CIA and the FBI took an active interest in him while he was in Russia and upon his return to the U.S. He actively associated with both pro and anti-Castro organizations and people in New Orleans in 1963 and the CIA knew of his travels to Mexico City where someone impersonated him. Four important people in the CIA's hierarchy kept track of him and knew his every move. For someone unimportant, he had a lot of eyes on him.

Chapter 33
The Atom Bomb Spies

Of all the secrets of the Second World War, the greatest was the development of the atomic bomb by the United States and England. Both Germany and Japan tried to develop an atomic bomb but had no success. Working under the strictest conditions, allied scientists harnessed the atom and changed the art of warfare as we know it. In one of the ironies of the war, members of the industrious spy operation that infiltrated the Manhattan Project leaked the development of the atomic bomb to the Soviet Union. The fallout of this affair would be felt in the early days of the Cold War, and changed the way post-war presidents dealt with Joseph Stalin's Soviet Union.

The concept of developing an atomic bomb dates back to the years before the war began. The most eminent scientists of the day knew about the theoretical process of nuclear fusion and fission but lacked the tools to connect them. Two of the best minds of the era, Leo Szilard and Albert Einstein, drafted a letter to President Roosevelt, which explained the possible role of atomic weapons in wartime.

Their letter was sent on October 11, 1939, and hit a nerve in the White House. Ten days later, the president ordered an Advisory Committee on Uranium (also-called the "Briggs Uranium Committee) to look into the matter of producing atomic weapons. Nothing was done, however, and in time, the United States turned to Great Britain for help.

In February 1940, two British scientists, Otto Frisch and Rudolf Peierls, made the first technological breakthrough in the development of fission U-235. They designed a "roadmap" from which other men of science would use to successfully build an atomic bomb, as well as a hydrogen bomb.

Soon, American scientists like Philip Abelson, Glenn Seaborg and Arthur Wahl, would make important discoveries in the enrichment of uranium and the critical use of plutonium in building a bomb.

These developments were so productive that Prime Minister Winston Churchill, on September 3, 1941, ordered his Chiefs of Staff to begin development of an atomic bomb.

In the United States, work on a bomb was begun under the direction of an organization code-named S-1, headed by Arthur Compton (S-1 would later be renamed the Manhattan Project).

During this time period, President Roosevelt had a discussion with his science advisor, Vannevar Bush in which Bush told him that a program then underway to develop atomic bombs was proceeding rapidly, and that it was now out of the laboratory stage and proceeding into the industrial phase.

On September 17, 1942, official work on the Manhattan Engineer District was under way. The man appointed to supervise the project was General Leslie Groves. General Groves had previously been responsible for the construction of the Pentagon outside of Washington, D.C. Under extreme secrecy, Groves purchased 1,250 tons of fine-grade uranium from the Belgian Congo, which was sent to its new facility at Oak Ridge, Tennessee. In time, other locations were established in which British and American scientists would labor to build the bomb. They were in Los Alamos, New Mexico, and Hanford, Washington, on a site near the Columbia River. Work in the bomb project was conducted in such places as the University of Chicago, as well as labs at the DuPont and Kellogg Corporation.

On September 15, 1942, General Groves appointed J. Robert Oppenheimer as head of the Manhattan Project, or Project Y. Oppenheimer was sent to Los Alamos, New Mexico, where critical work on the bomb was taking place. Oppenheimer was a professor of physics at Berkeley and worked with other scientists on the S-1 program. His family was also linked to communist front organizations, and his wife was a former member of the Communist party (Over the years, it has been alleged that Oppenheimer might have been working for the Soviet Union during this time. However, no concrete evidence linking him to Soviet espionage at Los Alamos was found).

In 1944, the United States government put a huge amount of resources, both men and money, into the Manhattan Project. It now rivaled that of the largest privately owned company. It was decided by the Manhattan Project scientists to shelve plans for the construction of a proposed plutonium gun, and instead, concentrate on the implosion theory, a chain reaction of fissionable material that made up the bomb. Working around the clock for months on end, the scientists at Los Alamos, Hanford, and Oak Ridge were able to make huge strides in the construction of the world's first atomic bomb. The first test of the new weapon was approved in October 1944, and scheduled for the Alamagordo Bombing Range in New Mexico that same year.

The last piece of the puzzle was in place with the successful introduction of the explosive lens used in the implosion bomb. In February 1945, the enriched plutonium arrived in Los Alamos from Hanford, and in a military decision, the island of Tinian was chosen as the loading point for the completed bomb.

It was now that another unexpected development in the story of the Manhattan Project began; the infiltration of a number of Soviet spies right in the middle of Los Alamos.

The Soviet Union received its first reports on U.S. atomic bomb research from John Cairncross, a member of the infamous Cambridge Five Spy Ring. Cairncross worked as a secretary for Lord Maurice Hankey, the chairman of the British governmental organization studying the atomic bomb. Another member of the Cambridge Spy Ring who passed information to Moscow on the atomic bomb project was Donald Maclean. In another related development, the United States and Britain ceased publishing journal articles on atomic fission. Georgi Flerov, a young Soviet physicist who, in April 1942, passed this information along to Soviet Premier Joseph Stalin, noticed this change.

The Soviet's would soon give a codename to the Manhattan Project called "ENORMOZ." This codename would later be revealed in the Venona project that was undertaken by the U.S. Army when it broke Soviet codes the latter part of World War II. Soviet intelligence had a number of assets hidden inside the various American research institutes who dealt with the Manhattan Project and asked them to provide as much information as possible. The FBI got wind of this operation and in February 1943, they learned of a Soviet attempt to contact certain physicists working at the "Rad Lab" at the University of California, Berkeley. These scientists were put under surveillance and some of them were drafted into the military in order to prevent them from contacting Soviet agents. One scientist in the Rad Lab was caught passing information to the Russians and he was immediately dismissed.

The Soviet's top nuclear spy right in the heart of the Los Alamos complex was a British subject named Klaus Fuchs. Fuchs came to Britain in 1933 from Germany. He was a brilliant physicist, and also a member of the German Communist Party.

After serving time in a Canadian jail for supposed Fifth Column activities, Fuchs came to England, where despite his communist roots, he joined British scientists responsible for building the atomic bomb. In December 1943, Fuchs was sent to the United States with a large British delegation assigned to the bomb project. He worked at the Oak Ridge plant with other members of his team. Fuchs was put in contact with a Soviet agent whom he would pass his top-secret material. That man was called "Raymond." In reality, Raymond was Harry Gold, a courier for the Soviet intelligence spy ring operating in the United States. Fuchs worked in the bomb research and development section at Los Alamos. He also took part in the Theoretical Division at Los Alamos where he passed his information to his Soviet contacts.

Gold passed along the high-grade intelligence concerning the bomb to his Soviet contacts in New York, who gave it to Moscow. By 1950, Fuchs had returned to England, where he worked in developing that nation's own atom bomb. That same year, Fuchs, after being interrogated by MI-5, broke down and confessed his role as a Russian spy. He turned in David Greenglass, a soldier who worked at Los Alamos, as well as Harry Gold. Their arrest led to charges being brought against Julius and Ethel Rosenberg for their activities in the atomic spy ring. Fuchs, Gold, Greenglass, and the Rosenberg's were the main players in the Soviet's atomic spy ring during the war.

Another deep cover Soviet agent inside the Manhattan Project was Theodore "Ted" Hall whose identity was revealed via the Venona Project. The Soviets recruited Hall at age 18, right out of Harvard University. He was a communist but that did not prevent him from being sent to Los Alamos. He was directed to Camp 2 in Santa Fe, New Mexico, where he was put in charge of a small group of scientists, and worked on nuclear implosion techniques in the Experimental Physics Division. This process was instrumental in how the bomb exploded.

In time, Hall gave the Russians a detailed report on the "Fat Man" plutonium bomb, the one later dropped on the Japanese city of Nagasaki. The Fat Man bomb was also tested in the New Mexico desert outside of Los Alamos. One of the scientists who worked with Hall in the G (Gadgets) section of Los Alamos was Klaus Fuchs. When Hall went on a two-week leave, he arrived in New York where he met with his Soviet contact, Sergei Kurnakov and passed along his secret information stolen from his lab. By the early 1950s, with the Red Scare dominating the headlines, the FBI had been investigating Hall for two years. An FBI memo on Hall reads: Hall has been identified as a Soviet espionage agent while at Los Alamos." Former FBI agent Robert Lamphere, leader of the Hall investigation, claimed the bureau got its first hint of a spy inside the Los Alamos facility from the Venona Project. An FBI memo written by the Chicago field office stated that although the FBI doubted Hall's guilt as the "unknown subject," both Hall and his friend, Saville Sax were still "associating with known Communists." The memo also said that they doubted Hall was still working for the Soviets.

Two other atomic spies in the Manhattan Project were Allan Nunn May and Bruno Pontecorvo.

Allan Nunn May was a British nuclear physicist who spied for the Soviet Union in Canada. He was a secret communist and was recruited at Cambridge University, along with Kim Philby, Donald MacLean, and Guy Burgess. He joined the British –sponsored Tub Alloys project (the codename for Britain's bomb-making program) in 1942 and worked at Cambridge. While in Canada, he was recruited by Colonel Nikolai Zabotin, the military attaché' at the Soviet embassy. May detailed the fruitful test of the atomic bomb at Alamagordo, New Mexico, as well as handling over parts of the Uranium 235, a complex component of the bomb. Scotland Yard officers arrested May on March 4, 1945 after a long surveillance. He was released from jail in 1952.

Bruno Pontecorvo was an Italian scientist who worked closely with Klaus Fuchs on atomic research. He was educated at Rome and Pisa Universities and later went to work with Enrico Fermi, one of the best minds in the field of science. In 1943, he worked with the Anglo-Canadian atomic research group at Chalk River in Ontario, Canada. It has been alleged, but never proved, that during the six years he worked at Chalk River, Pontecorvo provided the Soviets with documents relating to his duties. After the war, he returned to the Soviet Union where he was an important member of a scientific team at Harwell, the location of Great Britain's nuclear research facility. Because of his checkered past, British officials transferred Pontecorvo to a teaching job at Liverpool University in January 1951. When Pontecorvo failed to show up at Liverpool, many questions began to be asked. In 1955, he surfaced in Moscow, saying that he had defected to Russia three years before. For many years, he worked on the development of Russia's first atomic bomb. He died in 1993.

While the Venona files provide a number of names of people who worked for the Russian's at Los Alamos, there are still a number of them who were not revealed. One scientist was called FOGEL (later changed to PERSEUS). This man was offered a job at Los Alamos but he turned it down. Another source was called MAR who began spying for the Russians in 1943. In October of that year, he was transferred to the Hanford Engineer Works. In an interesting twist, a man came to the Soviet Consulate in New York unannounced and left a package at the receptionist desk. The package contained a number of secret documents relating to the Manhattan Project. No one knows who this man was. Two other unidentified people, an Englishman codenamed ERIC, passed along details of the atomic bomb research in 1943, along with an American source codenamed QUANTUM, who provided information relating to gaseous diffusion in the summer of 1943. Again, it is not clear who these people were.

In recent years, charges have been leveled against Robert Oppenheimer, Enrico Fermi, Niels Bohr, and Leo Szilard, as being factors in the Russian spy ring operating out of Los Alamos. The man making these allegations is Pavel Sudoplatov, in his book called *Special Tasks: The Memoirs of an Unwanted Witness—A Soviet Spymaster.* Sudoplatov states that he saw documents linking these men as Soviet spies based on information he read when he was the intelligence director of the Special Committee on Atomic Problems from 1944 to 1946.

He further says that Oppenheimer and his wife met twice with Gregory Kheifetz, a Soviet resident (intelligence officer) in Berkeley, California in December 1941. He also said that Bruno Pontecorvo met with a Soviet agent in 1943 and that Enrico Fermi was going to provide information on the workings at Los Alamos, as well as Oak Ridge.

Pavel Sudoplatov's detractors are many and they point out discrepancies in his account. Most of the atomic intelligence the Russians received came in 1945, not before. The information they did get prior to 1945 came almost exclusively from Klaus Fuchs, who had unlimited access to Los Alamos. Also, by the time (1945) when Sudoplatov claims these spies were hard at work, most of the Russian espionage nets in the United States had been shut down with the defection of Elizabeth Bentley.

On July 6, 1945, the first test of the atomic bomb was carried out at the Trinity site in New Mexico desert.

On August 6, 1945, the 509th Composite Bomb Group commanded by Lieutenant Colonel Paul Tibbets, in his specially designed bomber, the *Enola Gay,* dropped the first atomic bomb on the Japanese city of Hiroshima. On August 9th, a second bomb destroyed Nagasaki. Days later, Japan surrendered, ending World War II. The top-secret work begun by FDR almost six years earlier was finally revealed.

The information shown by the cadre of Soviet spies operating inside the Manhattan Project, (Fuchs, Gold. Greenglass, etc.), gave the Soviet Union a lead-time in the construction of their own atomic bomb. It is estimated that these spies allowed the Russians to get their own bomb about 12-18 months earlier if they hadn't had these men burrowed inside the Los Alamos complex. The Russians exploded their first atomic bomb on August 29, 1949. Their bomb was almost the exact replica of the one that was dropped at the Trinity test site four years previously.

Chapter 34
Nazi Spies Invade America

In 1942, the war that was so far in the distance came home to the shores of the United States. It was not an invasion of large armies or a fleet of ships bombarding our shores. Instead, it was a small group of Nazi soldiers who landed on the shores of Long Island in a mission that had no chance of success in the first place. This mission impossible was called Operation Pastorius, the codename of a detailed Nazi plot to wreak havoc and sabotage inside the United States. Admiral Wihelem Canaris, who was responsible for the training and execution of the plot, also conceived it. Operation Pastorius was the first attempt by the Germans to infiltrate directly into America and by the time the mission was completed, Canarias's future would be in doubt, the plot to blow up American factories, a dismal failure.

On the dark night of June 13, 1942, 21-year old coastguardsman John Cullen, was patrolling the silent beaches off Amagansett, Long Island, some 105 miles from New York City. The stretch of Atlantic beach that Cullen was working was far from the battles raging a continent away. Or so he thought. Out of the darkness, Cullen heard the rustle of noise and men's voices coming his way. Cullen spotted four men, the leader walking directly toward him. He confronted the stranger, not knowing what to expect. The man said he was a fisherman from Southampton whose boat had run aground. The fisherman said that his name was George Davis.

John Cullen, growing suspicious of the four men who emerged from the sea, asked Davis if he would come with him to the coast guard station to file a report. Davis refused. He then offered Cullen a bribe of $300.00 if he would forget he ever saw them and threatened to kill him. Cullen was in no position to take any action, and he watched as the four men headed inland. They would later be seen at the Amagansett train station of the Long Island Railroad boarding a train for New York City.

Cullen went back to his station and reported on what had just transpired. Cullen, along with a number of coastguardsmen, returned to the spot where the encounter had taken place. What they found corroborated his story. Strewn across the dunes were German marine uniforms, cigar boxes, boxes of explosives, bombs made out of clay, and other German-related items.

Just as they were about to leave, their attention was turned to the sea and the sight of a conning tower of a German submarine diving beneath the waves. What the coastguardsman saw was the German U-boat 202, which had just dropped off Davis and his men.

Immediately after the incident took place, the coast guard at Amagansett called the New York office of the FBI, who took over the investigation, and more importantly, the search for the German agents.

In reality, George Davis was George Dasch, a 39-year old German who had previously lived in the United States from 1922 to 1941. Dasch was the leader of an undercover mission called Operation Pastorius, named after Franz Daniel Pastorius, the leader of one of the early groups of German settlers to immigrate to the United States during the early 1600s.

Preparations for Operation Pastorius lay in the hands of Colonel Erwin von Lahousen, the director of the Abwehr's sabotage unit. Colonel Lahousen chose Lt. Walter Kappe to find suitable men who were fluent in English and who knew American customs for their planned sabotage operation inside the United States. Kappe had previously lived in the States from 1925 to 1937. After an exhaustive search conducted by the DAI, "Deutsches Ausland-Instiut," eight men were selected. They were then sent to the Abwehr sabotage school located at Quenz Lake Farm, outside the city of Brandenburg. For several months, they were trained in demolition, the use of explosives, and the study of American magazines and newspapers to catch up on the latest news and information coming from the States. They were given false identities, including genuine American social security cards and selective service (draft) cards.

Shortly before their training was completed, they were given their targets in the United States: the Aluminum Company of America plants in Tennessee, Illinois, and New York. Other secondary targets were the Philadelphia Salt Company's plant in Philadelphia, as well as the disruption of Newark, New Jersey's railroad terminal, the locks around the Ohio River, and the vital reservoirs supplying water to New York City. With the final preparations for Operation Pastorius completed, each team leader was given $50,000 in U.S. bills to cover expenses.

Newly released documents (93 pages) from the British Security Service MI5 files, fill in the story of Operation Pastorius. A report written by Victor Rothschild was sent to the United States by the British government to be informed of the incident. The report covered the actions by Dasch and his men while on American soil. The British report said, in part, "The task of the saboteurs was to slow down production at certain factories concerned with the American war effort. The sabotage was not to be done in such a way that it appeared accidental. The saboteurs were however told that they must avoid killing or injuring people as this would not benefit Germany."

It was decided by the Abwehr that two targets of opportunity would be selected for operations inside the United States. To that end, the team left by submarine from the German naval base at Lorient, France. The first group, led by Edward Kerling, departed by sub on May 26, 1942 bound for Ponte Verda, Beach, Florida, 25 miles from Jacksonville.

Kerling, then 33, had lived in the United States, working as a chauffeur and other odd jobs. He returned to Germany in 1940 and got a job as a translator for English language broadcasts.

The U-202, carrying Dasch and his team, set out to sea on May 28, 1942. Kerling's team arrived off the Florida coast on June 17, while Dasch's U-202 reached shore off Amagansett on June 13.

George Dasch was born in Speyer-am-Rhein, Germany in 1903 and came to Philadelphia in 1922. For many years, he shuttled between New York, Miami, Los Angeles, and San Francisco, working as a waiter. He married Rose Marie Guille in 1930. Once the war started, however, Dasch and his bride returned to Germany, where he took up the Nazi cause. Once home, Dasch met Lt. Walter Kappe, who worked for the Abwehr. Kappe got Dasch a job tracing American broadcasts in Germany (the same job as Kerling), and it was through Kappe that George Dasch was assigned to Operation Pastorius.

The other men who took part in Operation Pastorius besides Dasch and Kerling were Ernst Burger, a native of Augsburg; Richard Quirin, who lived in Berlin before arriving in the U.S. in 1927, and worked in upstate New York as a mechanic; Heinrich Heinck, born in Hamburg in 1907, an illegal immigrant to the U.S. in 1926; Herman Neubauer, also from Hamburg, who worked in the U.S. as a cook and in the hotel industry, going back to 1940; Werner Thiel, born in Dortmund in 1907, who lived for a time in Philadelphia and Los Angeles and joined the Bund in the U.S., and was given an all-expenses paid trip to Germany in 1939; Herbert Hans Haupt, who lived as a youth in Chicago and worked making eyeglasses. All these men took training at the Abwehr run Quentz Lake facility.

After making their getaway from Amagansett, the raiders arrived in New York City and divided themselves into two parts. George Dasch found himself with Ernest Burger. They checked into a hotel under assumed names. Then, the most unlikely and still unresolved event took place. George Dasch called the FBI on June 14, saying that he was "Franz Daniel Pastorius" and that he had information he could give only to J. Edgar Hoover, the Director of the FBI.

The FBI man thought the call was a prank, but Dasch said that he would come to Washington to personally give his information to the director. Dasch arrived in Washington on June 18 and checked into the fashionable Mayflower Hotel It was from there that he called FBI headquarters once again. This time, though, the bureau was aware of the incident on Long Island, and agents were at Dasch's hotel within minutes. He was taken into custody and told his story.

Dasch confessed the history of the Abwehr plan to infiltrate the United States, testified about the second landing party in Florida, and gave the names of his accomplices. Within days, all eight Germans were arrested and proceeded to stand trial.

The declassified report written by Victor Rothschild gives a summary of why Dasch turned himself in:

> It is abundantly evident that the leader of the first group of saboteurs, George Dasch, had every intention of giving himself up to the American authorities and compromising the whole expedition, probably from the moment that it

was first suggested to him in Germany that he should go to the USA on a sabotage assignment. DASCH's character is difficult to fathom. He was a strong left-wing supporter in the USA and both the FBI and the writer independently had the idea that he might be more than just a Supporter of the Left.[1]

Victor Rothschild's report is a no nonsense narrative of just what happened and he minces no words about blaming certain people at the start of the German landings on Long Island.

The submarine which landed one of the groups got into difficulties during the landing operation and went aground. It was only owing to the laziness or stupidity of the American coastguards that this submarine was not attacked by USA forces. The submarine went aground because it came in close to the shore to prevent the rubber boat containing the bulky sabotage supplies having to be rowed too far. It is believed that a decision has been reached not to send submarines on pure sabotage expeditions in future, but to include one or possibly two saboteurs among the normal crew of a submarine going on an operational trip.

It is almost certain that a third group of German agents landed in the USA at about the same time as the PASTORIOUS groups, and is still at large. It is not certain with which type of German Secret Service activity this group is concerned, though indirect evidence suggests Naval espionage. The German Secret Services definitely intend (and still intend) to send further groups of saboteurs to the USA. Apart from their function of committing sabotage, the PASTORIUS groups had the duty of laying the foundation for a much larger sabotage organization in wireless communication with German headquarters. [2]

The Germans were put on trial on orders from President Roosevelt on July 8, at the Justice Department Building in Washington,

---

[1] World War II: German Saboteurs Infiltration of America-British Intelligence MI5 Files.
[2] Ibid.

D.C. the proceedings were kept secret form the public, with only a few in the administration aware of it. Attorney General Francis Biddle and the army's Judge Advocate General (JAG), General Myron Cramer, headed the prosecution. Colonel Carl Ristine was Dasch's attorney, while Colonels Casius Dowell and Kenneth Royall represented the other defendants.

The defense attorneys tried to petition the court for a change of venue, i.e., that no overt act of espionage was committed and that the trial should not be held in a military court. Defense Counsel Royall, in a highly unusual move, managed to get the members of the Supreme Court, who were all on summer break, to reconvene in an emergency session to deliberate on the issue of whether or not the military should have jurisdiction over the case. The Supreme Court judges agreed that the Germans were indeed an invasion force and let the military commission stand.

The trial took less than a month to make a decision. On August 3, 1942, they sent their decision to the president. Five days later, FDR's decision regarding what action to take was carried out.

On August 8, 1942, Edward Kerling, Richard Quirin, Herbert Haupt, Heinrich Heinck, Werner Thiel, and Hermann Neubauer were executed in an electric chair in the District of Columbia jail. Their bodies were buried in a potter's field called Blue Plains in the Anacostia region of Washington.

The military tribunal, however, asked that the death penalty be waved in the cases of George Dasch and Ernst Burger, because of their cooperation in exposing the case to the FBI. Burger was given a life sentence, while Dasch was sentenced to 30 years.

Both men served only six years of their prison term. In April 1948, President Harry Truman commuted their sentences, and both men were sent back to Germany, now an ally of the United States.

It was not until years later that the American public was told the entire story of the landings at Amagansett and Jacksonville, Florida. What was obvious in that summer of 1942 was that the United States was now directly in the line of fire, its people and industries ripe for invasion. Hitler's secret conspiracy to invade America ended not with a bang but with a bust, known only to the United States government and the people in Berlin who started this ill-fated assignment in the first place.

Chapter 35
"Deep Throat" Revealed

On the night of June 17, 1972, five well-dressed men in suits with walkie-talkies were arrested by local police in the headquarters of the DNC, the Democratic National Committee in the posh Watergate apartment building and hotel in Washington, D.C. What just started as a routine break-in tuned out to be the tip of a very large iceberg that finally toppled the presidency of Richard Nixon and changed the way the American people looked at their politicians for years to come.

One of the lingering historical mysteries surrounding the Watergate scandal was the identity of Bob Woodward's source who funneled him with on-going, and important information regarding the developing scandal. That man was dubbed "Deep Throat." Bob Woodward, who worked for the *Washington Post* at the time the scandal broke, and his colleague, Carl Bernstein, were given the job by their editor, Ben Bradlee, to investigate the burglary at the DNC over more experienced *Post* reporters. Little did they know that when they began their investigation, there reporting would eventually end the presidency of Richard Nixon and make their names household names across the country.

The name of Woodward's source, "Deep Throat," was first revealed in Woodward and Bernstein's national bestseller called *All The President's Men*. The revelation of Deep Throat's involvement in their investigation of the Watergate affair made a rather ordinary book into a best-seller, igniting the imagination of the public as to just what happened that night at the headquarters of the DNC. Woodward kept the identity of his source confidential in the book and the readers were left wondering who this person really was.

A few years later, *All The President's Men* was made into a blockbuster movie starring Robert Redford as Bob Woodward and Dustin Hoffman as Carl Bernstein. In one of the iconic scenes of the movie, there is a meeting in the office of the *Washington Post* with Bernstein, Woodward, Ben Bradlee and other *Post* editors, discussing the Watergate investigation. In one of the scenes, a newspaper official notes that Woodward has been meeting with his unnamed source at various, secluded places in the Washington D.C. area and refers to him as "Deep Throat," the name of a popular porn move that was playing at the time. He also calls him "Woodward's garage freak." There is laughter in the room before the men return to business.

In *All The President's Men,* Deep Throat is played by the noted actor Hal Holbrook who meets with Woodward/Redford in a parking garage in Rosslyn, Virginia, in the dead of night to pass along information regarding the on-going Watergate scandal (the parking garage is slated to be torn down in the near future). In their hushed conversations, Woodward's source is never identified but you know that he is in the loop, guiding Woodward down the dangerous path of Watergate. At one point, Throat tells Woodward that, "the FBI badly wanted to know where the *Post* was getting its information." Woodward, who immediately after the break-in had cultivated Deep Throat as a source, told him that he had gotten a clue from Watergate burglar, Bernard Barker's seized note book that Howard Hunt who then worked in the White House, may have been involved in the break-in, and said that things were going to "heat up." Throat also told Woodward that the FBI believed that Hunt was involved in the burglary. At one point, Throat told Woodard and Bernstein "to take care when using their telephones," and that they might be followed. The Holbrook description of Deep Throat is one of the most important parts of the movie, one that made the film all the more interesting. But who was he?

Over the years there had been a cottage industry as to the real identify of Deep Throat. Some pundits speculated that he was White House Chief of Staff General Alexander Haig, National Security Advisor Henry Kissinger, Leonard Garment who worked in Nixon's law firm and later served as special consultant to the president on domestic policy from 1969 to 1974. He later served in the job of Counsel to the President after the resignation of John Dean. Some people said that Deep Throat might have been a compilation of various people, either in the White House or the FBI, not just one.

In a later conversation that Leonard Garment had with Bob Woodward, the latter told Garment that by 1972-73, Deep Throat had become a "public persona." From that meeting, Garment believed that Throat was one person, not a composite of many (Garment himself would also be viewed as a possible Deep Throat candidate). In his 2000 book on Watergate called *In Search of Deep Throat,* Garment wrote that in his opinion, Throat was in reality, John Sears who worked in the 1968 Nixon presidential campaign, and for a short time, worked in the White House. Of course, Sears did not turn out to be Deep Throat but the book is worthwhile to read for its Watergate information.

In *All The President's Men,* Woodward did not mention who his source was or what position he held. He wrote that this person worked in the executive branch of government, but said he had quite a bit of knowledge of what was going on behind the scenes as Watergate was unfolding. He said that Throat had his own sources of information in the White House, the Justice Department (FBI), and the Committee to Re-elect the President (CRP). Whoever Deep Throat was, he knew quite a lot of inside information regarding the president's inner circle, among them, the president himself, Attorney General John Mitchell, Charles Colson, and presidential aides H.R. Haldeman and John Ehrlichman.

In the time period of June to early September 1972, Woodward and Bernstein wrote more than twenty Watergate related articles for the *Post,* based on information gathered from various, confidential sources. By the summer of 1972, the Nixon White House suspected that Bernstein and Woodward's informer might have come from the FBI although they had no idea whom that might be. In their stories, both writers said that they had "sources close to the investigation," or "federal sources." Federal sources left out the CIA as they were not a law enforcement gathering agency. However, as the Watergate scandal unfolded, the CIA would become intricately involved in the secret machinations of the scandal, especially to the tracing of the money that the burglars got that was funneled through a Mexican bank, along with the fact that a number of the burglars had ties with the agency.

As far as Bob Woodward was concerned, he always felt obligated to his source not to reveal his identity as long as he remained alive, even after the resignation of Richard Nixon and the end of the Watergate affair. A promise was a promise, one that he would live up to.

Woodward and Bernstein's closely held secret was kept under the tightest wraps for thirty years until June 2005, when in a highly unusual set of circumstances, the real identity of Deep Throat was revealed. In July of that year, *Vanity Fair* magazine published a block-buster article in the manner of Woodward and Bernstein in which they finally revealed the true identify of Deep Throat. That man turned out to be W. Mark Felt, who at the time of the Watergate scandal, was the third highest ranking member of the FBI, right under Director J. Edgar Hoover, his long-time confidant, Clyde Tolson. Tolson was a very sick man at that time and in reality, Felt assumed most of the work that Tolson could not do. The *Washington Post,* and for Bob Woodward and Carl Bernstein, who for thirty years had kept their greatest secret under wraps, was now scooped in the biggest story in decades. Shortly after the *Vanity Fair* article came out, both men backed up their story and one of the deepest secrets in American history was suddenly out for all to see. But who was Mark Felt and how did he become Deep Throat?

Mark Felt was born in Twin Falls, Idaho on August 17, 1913. After he graduated from the University of Idaho in 1935, he worked for James Pope, the Democratic senator from Idaho. Mr. Felt later studied at the George Washington University Law School taking night classes while he worked in Washington and graduated with his law degree. In 1938, he married his college sweetheart, Audrey Robinson in Washington in a ceremony conducted by the chaplain of the House of Representatives. They later had two children, Joan and Mark. He joined the FBI in January 1942, and spent most of the war tracking German spies. After a tour of duty in Washington, Felt was assigned to the FBI office in Seattle, Washington, New Orleans, and Los Angeles. He was then named the special agent in charge of the Salt Lake City and Kansas City offices in the late 1950s. Due to his hard work, his name was recognized at bureau headquarters and he oversaw the training of FBI agents and conducted internal investigations as chief of the Inspection Division.

By the early 1970s, Mr. Felt was third in line in the Bureau's hierarchy after J. Edgar Hoover and William Sullivan. On July 1, 1971, Hoover appointed Felt to deputy associate director a powerful position in the FBI at the time. During this time, both Hoover and his long-time assistant Clyde Tolson were in poor health and Felt took on added responsibilities at headquarters. With the retirement of Clyde Tolson (who was rumored to have been Mr. Hoover's lover), and the death of J. Edgar Hoover, Felt saw his path to the directorship in his grasp. However, that was not to be. President Nixon left Felt out in the cold and appointed L. Patrick Grey as the new acting FBI Director. Felt later wrote about his being denied the FBI Directorship post by saying, "It did not cross my mind that the President would appoint an outsider to replace Hoover. My own record was as good and I allowed myself to think I had an excellent chance." Grey resigned from the Navy in 1960 to work for then Vice President Richard Nixon during that year's presidential race against John Kennedy. Felt was not impressed with the way Grey was running the FBI and considered retiring but changed his mind. He was sent out to visit many FBI field offices to get away from his weariness of being in Washington.

When Alabama Governor George Wallace, who was running for president, was shot on May 15, 1972 by Arthur Bremer, Felt got an unexpected call from President Nixon because Patrick Grey was not in town. Nixon wanted to know about Bremer's condition because he had been attacked by bystanders after the shooting. Nixon told Felt, "Well, it's too bad they didn't rough up the son of a bitch. I hope they worked him over a little bit more than that." President Nixon was so obsessed with Wallace that on the night that Wallace was shot, Charles Colson, one of Nixon's top aids, ordered Howard Hunt to break into Bremer's apartment in Milwaukee to find out if he had any connections to any left wing political groups or politicians. After the Wallace shooting, an investigation was conducted which showed no connection between Bremer and Nixon or the Nixon campaign.

After the intense interest that developed in the public's mind after Mr. Felt was disclosed at Deep Throat, the people forgot that he took part in illegal proceedings against radical groups in the United States while he was in the FBI. In 1966, J. Edgar Hoover decided not to continue the use of break-ins without warrants-"black bag jobs," which the Bureau had been conducting for over forty years. The Nixon White House then began using their own, private undercover operatives to do their dirty work. This group would later become known as the Plumbers who took on illegal jobs on the behest of the Nixon White House. It is an interesting historical note that the Watergate break-in took place six weeks after Hoover died. White the Watergate affair was in full swing, Felt ordered break-ins at the homes of friends and members of the Weather Underground, a violent left-wing splinter group. These raids were conducted without legal warrants between 1972 and 1973. These raids were conducted to find any persons involved in the anti-Vietnam War effort and see if they were linked to any outside country. In 1980, Felt was convicted on unrelated charges of authorizing government agents to conduct these illegal activities. He was pardoned by President Reagan for these actions.

In his book, *The Secret Man: The Story of Watergate's Deep Throat,* Bob Woodward writes that he first met Mark Felt while he was a full lieutenant in the Navy. Woodward was then working in the Pentagon as a watch officer overseeing worldwide Teletype communications for the chief of naval operations, Admiral Thomas Moorer, (Moorer would later become involved in a spy scandal in his office for the leaking of certain classified material). Woodward had top secret clearance and had access to what was then called SPECAT, Special Category Crypto messages of "unusual sensitivity." He also oversaw the communications of the chief of naval operations, the secretary of the navy, the Navy staff and personal communications among the various admirals who worked in the Pentagon. He writes that one evening he was sent to the West Wing of the White House near the Situation Room where the members of the National Security Council Staff met to discuss important matters. The date of this meeting was 1970 and as he was waiting to meet the person he was to see, he saw a man dressed in a nice suite, age about 40, sitting near him. With nothing to do, Woodward began talking to the stranger, introducing himself and telling him what he was doing in the Navy and what his career path he wanted to pursue. In time, the man introduced himself as Mark Felt and that he was an assistant director at the FBI. Before leaving, Felt gave Woodward his phone number at the FBI.

Woodward soon got a writing job at a small Maryland newspaper called the *Montgomery County Sentinel,* after deciding not to go to Law School. In time, he was hired by the *Washington Post,* having been rejected by Ben Bradlee sometime before. Little did Woodward know that he and the *Post* would soon be snarled in the biggest story of their lives.

When Woodward and Bernstein were given the assignment to look into the Watergate break-in, Woodward remembered his meeting with Mark Felt and called him to ask if he could aid them in their investigation. Felt agreed under certain conditions which were clearly spelled out to them. In his talks with Felt, Woodward came to realize that Felt was no fan of the Nixon administration. He called them "corrupt, sinister and a cabal." Woodward says that Felt had these feelings about Nixon prior to the break-in. Another person who shared Felt's feelings about the Nixon team was none other than James McCord who was a former security chief at the CIA who led the break-in at the Watergate. McCord had a conspiracy theory that said that the Rockefeller family was trying to take control of the government's national security functions, using the Council on Foreign Relations and using the efforts of Henry Kissinger who was the National Security Advisor to Nixon.

Felt agreed to help Woodward and laid out the following conditions. If Woodward wanted to talk with him, Woodward would move a flowerpot planted with a red flag on the balcony of his apartment on P. Street. If Felt had a message to deliver, he'd put an inked circle in Mr. Woodward's issue of the *New York Times* on Page 20. Woodward would then leave his apartment by the back door and take a series of taxis to an underground parking garage in Rosslyn, Virginia. It was in this setting that Felt would give Woodward whatever information he had on the FBI's investigation of Watergate and would steer him in the right direction. Both men would have seventeen conversations regarding the investigation between June 1972 and November 1973. Woodward even met with Felt once at Felt's FBI office, once at Felt's house, and once at a bar in Prince George's County, Maryland, once in an undisclosed location, and six times in the Roslyn garage.

The Watergate story seemed to fizzle out when indictments were handed down to the five burglars, plus Howard Hunt and Gordon Liddy. In a meeting with Felt after the indictments were delivered, Felt told Woodward that he "could go much stronger" with his reporting. He told Woodward to look into "other intelligence gathering activities" beyond Watergate. He told Woodward that the money for the burglary was controlled by top assistants to former Attorney General John Mitchell, who was then Chief of the Nixon re-election campaign. Carl Bernstein later found out that a secret campaign fund was managed by two top campaign aides, Jeb Magruder and Herbert "Bart" Porter, along with G. Gordon Liddy. Woodward called Felt who told him not to call again but confirmed Bernstein's findings. In what would become one of the most important parts of the Watergate investigation, Felt told Woodward to "follow the money."

On October 9, 1972, Woodward met with Felt in the parking garage and Felt told him about a large amount of "dirty tricks" coming out of the Nixon administration. He told Woodward that John Mitchell was involved in dirty tricks and that, "Only the president and Mitchell know" the extent of what was going on. According to Felt, "Mitchell learned some things in those ten days after Watergate, information that shocked even him. If what Mitchell knows ever comes to light, it could destroy the Nixon administration." He further told him that President Nixon's aide John Ehrlichman ordered Howard Hunt who was arrested in the Watergate break-in, to leave town. Felt added that there were four major groups inside the Nixon presidential campaign. One was called "The November Group" which handled campaign advertising. Another group handled political espionage and sabotage for both the Republican and Democratic National Conventions. A third "primary group" did the same for the campaign primaries, and a fourth called "The Howard Hunt group," a.k.a., the Plumbers, who worked under Hunt. Felt called the Plumbers the "really heavy operations team." The Plumbers reported to Charles Colson, Nixon's special counsel. "Total manipulation-that was their goal, with everyone eating at one time or another out of their hands. Even the press."[3]

Felt told Woodward that the indictments of the break-in team did not go far enough and that evidence of political espionage or illegal campaign finances were not considered. He said that the investigation was plagued by witness perjury and evasions.

In one meeting inside the parking garage, Woodward grows

[3] History Commons, *The Nixon Administration and Watergate-"Deep Throat."*

298

weary of Felt's uncooperative behavior. Woodward lashes out and says that he is "tired of their chickenshit games." Felt responds by saying, "Okay. This is very serious. You can safely say that 50 people worked for the White House and CREEP to play games and spy and sabotage and gather intelligence. Some of it is beyond belief, kicking at the opposition in every imaginable way. You already have some of it."

While Felt was not specific in everything he supplied to Woodward, both he and Bernstein now had a huge amount of information regarding the illegal machinations going on inside both the Nixon administration, and inside CREEP. The later stories would blow open the break-in from a "third rate burglary" as said by Nixon's press secretary, to a full blown scandal, which engulfed the entire Nixon White House.

One of the most important developments in the Watergate investigation was the gaps in one of the presidential tapes that was revealed after the scandal broke. Nixon's secretary Rose Mary Woods said she accidentally erased one of the tapes while transcribing them. No one really believed her story and the press had a good laugh when the news broke. Woodward says that in early November 1973, Felt told him about the gaps, saying that it was probably done on purpose. We don't know how Felt found out about the erasers, nor do we know that answer to that vexing question. Carl Bernstein asked his sources inside the White House about the erasures and four of them backed up Felt's story.

The leaks coming out of the White House were getting more numerous and the administration was eager to find out who it was. On October 19, 1972, the president met with H.R. Haldeman in the Executive Office Building and Haldeman told the president that he learned from a source that the leaker who was providing Woodard and Bernstein worked in the highest echelons of the FBI and that he had good reason to believe it was Mark Felt. Haldeman urged caution in revealing Felt's name, "If we move on Felt, he'll go out and unload everything. He knows everything that's to be known in the FBI." John Dean said there was nothing legally they could to regarding Felt and if they did, "Felt will go out and get him network television. Nixon, in anger says regarding Felt, "You know what I'll do with him, the little bastard. Well, that's all

I want to hear about it." Nixon then wants to know if Felt wants to be named FBI Director and asked if he was a Catholic. Haldeman says that Felt is Jewish and says, "Christ, put a Jew in there?' Nixon then replies, "Well, that could explain it too." In early 1973, L. Patrick Gray told Felt about the White House's suspicion of him which made him even angrier.

Woodward was now trying hard to connect Haldeman to the Nixon administration's "slush fund" but Felt was not giving him any further information on that front. Woodward and Bernstein wrote in an article in the paper that Hugh Sloan, the treasurer of Nixon's secret campaign fund, said that Haldeman was the instigator of the fund. This turned out not to be the case, however, later, Sloan would later confirm that Haldeman was indeed in charge of the secret fund, but he never testified to that fact. Felt told Woodward that he was disappointed with his reporting, saying You've got people feeling sorry for Haldeman. I didn't think that was possible. You've put the investigation back months. It puts everyone on the defensive-editors, FBI agents, everybody has to go into a crouch after this." In a later article, Woodward writes that Haldeman did control the secret fund and quoted Felt, saying he was "one source," something he told Felt he'd never do.

In February 1973, Felt met Woodward in a bar in Maryland and told him that the Nixon administration was out to get him and the *Post,* any way they can. He describes Nixon as "wild" and "shouting about the idea. He thinks the press is out to get him and therefore is disloyal." They can't stop the real story from coming out. That's why they are so desperate. The flood is coming, I'm telling you. He told Woodward that the nomination of Patrick Gray was a result of blackmail on Gray's part-"name him FBI Director or, all hell could break loose."

Patrick Gray resigned as acting director of the FBI on April 27, 1973 after it was disclosed that he had destroyed papers from the White House safe of Howard Hunt. Felt now became deputy director under William Ruckelshaus. Felt left the Bureau in June 1973.

He later wrote a book called *The FBI Pyramid: Inside the FBI,* with Ralph de Toledano. Toledano said that Felt swore to him that he was not Deep Throat and that he had never leaked information to Woodward or Bernstein. The book did not last long and was soon removed from stores because of poor sales.

In the years to come, there was a full court press to find out who Deep Throat really was. A few writers, including Ronald Kessler in *The Bureau: The Secret History of the FBI,* James Martin in the *Atlantic Monthly,* Jack Limpert in the *Washingtonian,* said he was the elusive Throat. A young man named Chase Culeman-Beckman, 17 years old, wrote a paper for his high school in 1999 that Felt was Throat. He said that at 8 years old he was told of Deep Throat's identity by Jacob Bernstein, the son of Carl Bernstein. The young man's history teacher did not believe him (why would he?). [4]

On the 25th anniversary of Nixon's resignation in 1999, Felt told a reporter that it would be "terrible" if someone in his position at the FBI had been Deep Throat. "This would completely undermine the reputation that you might have as a loyal employee of the FBI. It just wouldn't fit at all." It seems from that quote that Felt was somehow rejecting the fact that he was Woodward and Bernstein's source. Did he not want to remember those times and the role he played in the scandal?

Mark Felt retired to his home in Santa Rosa, California in 2001. Sometime later, he was felled by a stroke which took much of his memory with him. However, before getting sick, Felt told his daughter Joan that he was indeed the mysterious Deep Throat. He was quoted as telling his daughter that, "I don't think being Deep Throat was anything to be proud of. You should not leak information to anyone. If you know your government is engaging in illegal and/or immoral acts, then, you have an obligation to speak out that overrides confidentiality agreements and secrecy laws. It's never wrong to inform on serious criminal acts no matter who is perpetrating them."

Felt managed to keep his secret for thirty years but there were a number of high-level persons inside the Nixon White House who had an inkling that Felt was Woodward's source, among them, Bob Haldeman, John Dean, John Mitchell, President Nixon, Alexander Haig, and Richard Kleindienst.

After Felt's name was confirmed as Deep Throat, Woodward said that both he and Bernstein had other sources that aided them

[4] Mark Felt-American History-Watergate at Spartacus educational.com.

in their Watergate investigation and that Felt was not their only source.

Shortly before his death, Woodward went out to California to see Felt who was then in failing health. He was happy to see his old friend but when he asked Felt if he remembered what he had done in the Nixon years, he said he only had a vague recollection.

Mark Felt died from heart failure on December 18, 2008 at a nursing facility in Santa Rosa, California. Sometimes it takes a long time for history's mysteries to come to light. In the case of Deep Throat, Mark Felt, it was worth the wait.

Chapter 36
The Dallas-Watergate Connection.

The two most seminal events of the decades of the 1960s and the 1970s, were the assassination of John F. Kennedy on November 22, 1963 in Dallas, Texas, and the break-in of the Watergate building in June 1972. To the untrained eye, there should be no connection between both events. But if one looks more closely into the circumstances behind both affairs, a commonality becomes visible. A number of people associated with both the assassination of the president and the Watergate break-in are tied together. Howard Hunt, Frank Sturgis and Bernard Barker who were arrested in the burglary of the DNC (Democratic National Committee Headquarters) were also part of the assassination plots to kill Cuba's Fidel Castro in the early 1960s. It has been rumored throughout the past fifty years that Hunt played a role in the assassination of the president and before his death he made a confession that linked both him and Frank Sturgis to the plot. Hunt also played a part in the events leading up to the CIA's failed invasion of Cuba at the Bay of Pigs in April 1961. The release of the Watergate report and the files from the JFK Records Act, shed new light on all three men's participation in both events. The chain of events that link both Watergate and the Kennedy assassination is Cuba, although at the time that both events took place, no one knew of the connection. Here then, in the story.

When the Church Committee began operation in January 1975, they soon leaned the shocking fact that the CIA had begun a secret project, beginning in 1960, to assassinate certain heads of state who were not popular with the U.S. Among those targeted for assassination were Patrice Lumumba of the Congo, Rafael Trujillo of the Dominican Republic, President Ngo Dinh Diem of South Vietnam, and Fidel Castro of Cuba. In 1975, just as the HSCA (House Select Committee on Assassinations) was winding down its business, Senator Richard Schweiker persuaded Senator Church to allow him to form a separate subcommittee to investigate the Kennedy assassination. Joining him on the panel was Senator

Gary Hart, Democrat of Colorado.

As their investigation got under way, Senator Schweiker was persuaded that Fidel Castro might have had a role in the president's assassination. In time, Senator Hart too became obsessed with the possibility that Castro had something to do with the events in Dealey Plaza. He was intrigued by all the secret goings-on that linked Lee Oswald, the man accused of killing JFK, with various CIA and other para-military people and organizations operating of out Florida during the early 1960s. One of these people was Frank Sturgis who was running his own private military company in Florida and who fancied himself as a member of the CIA (he wasn't).

In the early part of the Eisenhower administration, the first attempts to kill Fidel Castro were put in place and would soon evolve into crazy schemes to poison him, put an exploding shell in the water where he dived, and soon involved members of organized crime, the Mafia, including Sam Giancana, Johnny Roselli, and Santo Trafficante. These efforts continued into the administration of John F. Kennedy with the creation of Operation Mongoose, a CIA inspired, covert effort to overthrow Castro (it was a miserable failure). In time, men like Frank Sturgis, Howard Hunt, and Bernard Barker would join the cause.

Howard Hunt was a veteran of World War II, a pulp-fiction writer doing spy novels, and a world-class spy. In the 1950s, he served in Europe for the CIA and may have played some role in the CIA's super-secret U-2 spy plane program.

In 1956, he was assigned to Montevideo, Uruguay where Hunt was to take on the job of CIA Station Chief. His main duties were to keep an eye on the large Soviet legation in the capital city and follow their agents as they made their way across the city. Hunt drove an MG sports car, as well as a Cadillac which was provided to him by the CIA.

Hunt returned to Washington in the spring of 1960 to take on another, top secret assignment, one, that would dominate his time for the next several years. He was given the job of "Chief of Political Action" in the Eisenhower administration to remove Castro from power. Hunt was given the job by his boss and friend, Tracy Barnes. He told Hunt that his job was to create an alliance among the various Cuban exile leaders into one, cohesive group. These men would constitute a new provisional government in waiting who would take control of the government in Havana once Castro was gone.

In his memoirs, Hunt wrote that his immediate boss in the Cuba Project, told him, "The only question raised about you is whether you're too conservative to handle guys like these. A lot of them are way to the left of you, socialists, labor leaders, and so forth. Hunt's reply was that, "My own political views, whatever they may be, don't enter into it." Those words would soon come back to haunt Hunt as the Cuba Project unfolded.

Hunt's other supervisors were Colonel J.C. King, the chief of the Western Hemisphere Division at the CIA, the Project Chief known as "Jake" who was really Jack Esterline, and a German-American named Gerry Droller, whose real name was Frank Bender. The CIA sent Hunt to help Bender baby sit the Cuban's whom the administration wanted to see in power once Castro was gone. Hunt and Bender never got along, with each man trumping the virtues of their own favorite Cuban's. Hunt even went so far as to have Droller banned from taking part in Agency operations in Miami. But Bender/Droller showed up anyway.

Despite Hunt's assurances that he would work with the myriad anti-Castro leadership, he never felt comfortable in his daily tasks. He left after spending one year trying to reconcile all the different anti-Castro groups into one cohesive force. After leaving the Cuba operation, Hunt was sent to Spain where he told his friends he was going to write his books. However, one of his assignments was to try and recruit the Cuban Military Attache, Colonel Ramon Barquin. Colonel Barquin told Hunt that he still believed in the Cuban revolution and turned down the offer.

Hunt wrote of his impressions of his trip to Cuba by saying, "If I had doubts about the wisdom of our Cuban project, they were resolved… and I determined to dedicate myself to ridding Cuba of Castro and his henchmen, regardless of personal cost and effort."

One of these efforts was Hunt's plan to kill Fidel Castro. At CIA HQ, Hunt held a series of meetings with various agency and Eisenhower administration officials on his trip to Cuba. His recommendation that caused the most controversy and head scratching was an eye-popping plan to assassinate Fidel Castro.

This was two years from the start of the CIA-Mafia plots to kill Castro and Hunt's idea was met with more than a certain skepticism among the top brass at the CIA. There was no hint of any plans at the time by the Eisenhower administration to even contemplate any assassination attempt on Castro's life. At that time, the US still had not run its course with Castro and there was still some men in Washington who believed that an accommodation with Castro could be achieved. All that would change, but not for now, Hunt's idea was quickly strangled in the bud.

Writing about this early idea about killing Castro, Hunt said, "As the months wore on I was to ask Barnes (Tracy Barnes, a top CIA official in the Castro plots) repeatedly about any actions on my principal recommendation, only to be told that it was "in the hands of a special group." So far as I have been able to determine, no coherent plan was ever developed within CIA to assassinate Castro, though it was the heart's desire of many exile groups."

In the spring of 1960, Hunt had a meeting with Jack Esterline and Brigadier General Cushman who was the military aide to Vice President Richard Nixon. As that meeting, Hunt expressed his opinion to the general that Castro should be killed. Hunt also said that if Castro were eliminated, then he, Hunt, was willing to help the new government in exile set up shop in Havana and act as their point man with the American administration.

During his testimony before the Church Committee in the 1970s, Hunt was asked by Mr. Baron, one of the panel members about his recollections of any plans to kill Castro, he replied, "No, I did not." He further expanded on his testimony in relation to any talk about killing Castro by saying, "Well, I'll answer your question no. I will then go on to say that in the exile milieu in which I was living in Miami, for those many months, and also traveling as frequently as I had into Mexico and Guatemala, that you could hardly draw a breath or smoke a cigarette without hearing about some project. And people would come up to you and say, so and so will do the job if he can just get the necessary. What they did on their own outside office hours I felt was up to them. But I never encouraged anyone to do it because as I say, Bissell had assured me that the matter that I had recommended was in the hands of a special group. So I thought no more about it."

Hunt's testimony runs contrary to his offer to the CIA to kill Castro in the months before the invasion of the Bay of Pigs. So what we have here is either Hunt's purposely lying about his views on killing Castro or we can chalk in up to a fact that he had a rather, faulty memory when it came to such important matters as the killing of a head of state.

What Hunt did not know in 1959 when he made his recommendations to the CIA regarding the possible assassination of Castro was that the United States government, only a few years later, would propose just such an official plan. The name of the proposed assassination scheme was called ZR/RIFLE, a.k.a, "Executive Action" which involved the use of two highly trained assassins, codenamed QJ/WIN and WI/ROGUE. Despite all the preparations at the CIA in regards to the operational nature of "Executive Action," this program was never directly used against Castro or Cuba.

Another man who offered to kill Castro in 1958 was Frank Fiorini, a.k.a., "Frank Sturgis," an ex-Marine, soldier-of-fortune, a man who, on more than one occasion, boasted that he had worked or the CIA, Sturgis was closely associated with many of the top Mafia figures who lived and worked in Havana during the reign of Fulgencio Batista, including Lewis McWillie who was a friend of Jack Ruby's, and who worked for the powerful mob boss, Meyer Lansky, and Santos Trafficante Jr.

Frank Fiorini/Sturgis arrived in Cuba in 1958 in Oriente Province working for the anti-Batista resistance. He also had a double life, working as an asset, (not an employee) of the CIA. Sturgis became attracted to the Cuban cause after going to Miami in the early 1950s and met Carlos Prio who was the former Cuban President. Frank Sturgis left for Cuba and eventually teamed up with Castro before his successful revolution toppled Batista. Castro appointed Fiorini as the Air Force's Director of Security. While in Castro's good graces, Sturgis met and befriended Pedro Diaz Lanz who was named chief of the Air Force. He also served for a time as Castro's chief security officer for the casinos in Havana. Almost one year after Castro took power in Havana, both Sturgis and Lanz gave up the cause and fled to the U.S.

The CIA knew of Sturgis' Cuban connection and made its first contact with him in 1958 while he was still working for Castro. While there was not actual job offer by the CIA to Sturgis, he worked hand in glove with the CIA during its whirlwind efforts to kill Castro. He flew various missions with other anti-Castro exiles, oftentimes dropping leaflets over Cuba.

Castro grew to trust Sturgis like his own son and called him his "favorite Yanquis." It is not impossible to visualize how Castro would have reacted if he had known that his "favorite Yanquis" was secretly working for Uncle Sam.

Speaking about his early time with Castro, Sturgis said, "The July 26th Movement, since 1957, I was in it. That's why, last year, Fidel said I was one of the most dangerous agents the CIA ever had." Sturgis was arrested in 1958 by Batista's Secret Police and was accused of being a courier for Castro. Help came from the US embassy in Havana who was alerted to Sturgis' real agency association.

As well as taking on the job of Security for the Air Force under Castro, Sturgis also held the position of Minister of Games of Chance in Havana. He was now able to connect with many of the top names in the American mob who operated the casinos and many friendships developed between Sturgis and the crime bosses.

By 1960, Sturgis made a complete break with Castro, deciding that Castro had betrayed the revolution by turning towards the Soviet Union. He fled the island in a stolen plane and made his way to Miami where he began his militant anti-Castro crusade.

Once in Miami, he met with the FBI on various occasions to tell them what he knew about Castro and his revolution. They listened with increasing skepticism and said they'd get back to him if needed. The FBI wrote in its closing paragraph in one of its meetings with Sturgis by saying, "Havana is requested to submit its comments and recommendations in this matter as to the development of Fiorini as a possible source. There is no objection to Havana accepting any information the subject may volunteer. However, caution should be exercised in dealing with the subject in view of his position with the Castro Government and his background."

The FBI was keeping a close watch on Sturgis and his associates and wrote in a report, "Fiorini has a reputation as a braggart and liar and appears more adventurer than dedicated political extremist."

What we have here is a prominent role played by Frank Sturgis in the anti-Castro activity in 1959 and 1960. But the question to be asked during this hectic time period before the "official" CIA-Mafia plots to kill Castro began, was what role did Frank Sturgis play in the early, non-CIA sanctioned attempts against Castro's life.

While still living in Cuba, Frank Sturgis (1958) was working with the U.S. Consular mission in Santiago de Cuba. He was smuggling arms to Castro's forces in the hills and the Americans wanted to know what he was doing. Sturgis said that he made contact with an American named Park Wollam who was the U.S. Consul in Santiago de Cuba. According to Sturgis, Wollam approached him and asked if he could supply him with information on rebel movements, and other military related items for pay. Sturgis said he'd cooperate but refused payment. Wollam was not a member of the CIA but was Sturgis's cut out when the latter got him information on Castro's forces. He also worked with Robert Wiecha, a CIA officer operating out of the consulate.

When Castro took power in Cuba, Sturgis was one of his most trusted aides and he was now in a position to give the CIA a large amount of information on what Castro was doing, including his political thinking. Sturgis was then close to Pedro Diaz Lanz, the rebel air force commander and soon Sturgis was posted to Havana where he cooperated fully with the CIA in giving them as much information on the Castro revolution as he could. While not officially on the Agency payroll, Sturgis was as much a CIA employee without having to sign a contract. Sturgis said he didn't want to sign a contract with the CIA because he didn't want to take orders from them.

Sturgis soon found himself in Havana after leaving Santiago de Cuba and he now met up with a new set of American handlers at the U.S. Embassy, the Air Attache ',Colonel Erikson Nichols. Sturgis met with Colonel Nichols in various locations across the city, giving him the intelligence he found. The other person whom he worked with at the embassy was Major Van Horn. Both Major Van Horn and Colonel Nichols had some relationship with the CIA, if not being outright employed by them. At one point in time Sturgis made a brief trip back to Miami where he met with his friend Bernard Barker who was working at the CIA's JMWAVE station doing psychological warfare operations. Barker would later be arrested with Sturgis and Hunt at the Watergate.

Other CIA people whom Sturgis worked with in Havana were "Jack Stewart," and "Jim Knowles." Jack Stewart was James Noel who was the chief of the CIA Station in Havana. "Jack Stewart" was in reality, David Phillips, who worked in the CIA's psychological operation department and whose name would come up in the Kennedy assassination investigation as the elusive "Maurice Bishop," who may have met with Lee Oswald in Dallas before the assassination.
[5]

In 1975, the CIA wrote in a memo regarding Sturgis's role with the CIA that, "I am convinced from my review of the files that Sturgis never worked for us-he did associate with people who did work for us."

Sturgis talked with his rebel comrades about the idea of assassinating Castro. His plan was to arrange a conference that would take place at Camp Libertad in which all the top commanders would gather. "I was going to station gunners on the roofs to set up crossfire. I would have wiped out Fidel, his brother Raul and all the top pro-communist military commanders in 30 seconds." Sturgis said he broached the subject of assassinating Castro with Colonel Nichols in February 1958 and that the Colonel gave him the green light to proceed. Sturgis had various locations in which the attempt to kill Castro would take place but it never materialized.

Sturgis liked to boast to all who would listen that he was a hired operative for a decade prior to 1960. He told associates that, "he was in contact with some of the CIA Cuban employees in the Miami area, but had no direct relationship with the Agency." That statement is in variance with what we have learned about Sturgis via the writings of John Newman in his new book, *Where Angles Tread Lightly.*

[5] Newman, John, *Where Angles Tread Lightly: The Assassination of President Kennedy Volume 1*, 2015, Pages 83-88.

When the CIA wrote their internal report on the CIA-Mafia attempts to kill Castro, they had an interesting account of what possible role Sturgis may have played in these early Castro plots. "The IGR recognizes that Sturgis, through his gambling activities and relationship with various casino owners may quite possibly have known Orta (Juan Orta, the Office Chief and Director General of the Office of the Prime Minister in Cuba, Castro), and also raises the question of whether Sturgis may have been a source of information to Castro regarding Orta's participation in any assassination plot."

The IG's Report makes the conclusion that this assassination plot using Sturgis came earlier than the sanctioned CIA-mob schemes that took place during the last days of the Eisenhower administration and the early Kennedy years. "The CIA concluded that this October (1960) date is too early for the CIA syndicate operations and that therefore the syndicate may have been acting independently."

Howard Hunt's possible role in the Kennedy assassination has always been of interest to researchers and in 2007, he gave an interview to his son, St. John Hunt, regarding his possible role in the events of November 22, 1963. In the months before Hunt's death, he called St. John to his bedside to tell him what he knew of his life in the CIA and more importantly, his knowledge of the Kennedy assassination. St. John took notes, as well as recording the conversation. Hunt revealed the names of the men whom he alleged took part in the planning of JFK's murder. Most of these men had pivotal roles in the Kennedy administration's secret war against Castro. The names Hunt revealed were: Frank Sturgis, David Morales, David Atlee Phillips, Antonio Veciana, William Harvey, Cord Meyer, a French gunman on the grassy knoll and Lyndon Johnson.

Hunt said that he played no active role in the assassination planning but was just a "benchwarmer" in their discussions. During his confession, Hunt wrote down the names of the people who were involved in the plot like a flow chart, connecting each dot as it went along its natural path. He wrote down "LBJ (Lyndon Johnson) first, followed by lines for each of the other players; Cord Meyer, who became the second highest ranking member of the CIA's Clandestine Service, Bill Harvey, who ran the Cuban plots and nurtured a bitter hatred towards the Kennedy brothers, David Morales, a tough, CIA agent who worked in Havana and later in the CIA's JMWAVE station in Miami, and had numerous connections with the top bosses in organized crime in the U.S., Frank Sturgis of Watergate and the plots to kill Castro, David Phillips, a CIA propaganda officer, who was stationed in Mexico City at the same time that Oswald was supposed to have been in that city, Antonio Veciana, the leader of the militant anti-Castro organization, ALPHA 66, and finally, the so-called French Gunman on the grassy knoll, possibly Lucien Sarti (for further information on the so-called French Connection to the Kennedy assassination, see the author's book *JFK: The French Connectoin*).

The scenario that Hunt laid out was that LBJ ordered the assassination of the president and passed on his instructions to the rest of the group. By implying that Lucien Sarti, a member of the Corsican underworld was on the grassy knoll, firing at JFK, disproves the Oswald as the lone gunman theory into a conspiracy involving at least two people, possibly more. St. John Hunt further states that his father gave him a document that spelled out how the conspiracy unfolded. Cord Meyer discussed the plot with David Phillips, who then met with William Harvey and Antonio Veciana. Oswald had a meeting with the above mentioned men in Mexico City. Veciana then met with Sturgis in Miami who brought David Morales into the plot. There is a change in the location of the assassination plot and it is finally agreed that Dallas is the place where the event will take place.

Hunt goes on to describe his involvement in the assassination planning. In 1963, he met with Morales and Sturgis in a Miami hotel room. Morales took his leave and in comes Frank Sturgis who talks about a "big event" and wants to know if Hunt is willing to go along with their plans. Hunt asked Sturgis what the plan is and Sturgis replies, "killing JFK." Hunt then asks Sturgis why he needs him. Hunt tells them that he wants no part of the deal.

Can Hunt's death be confession be true? If it is, then Hunt was a participant after the fact, knowing just what was going to happen, and did nothing to stop it. Or was it just a made up story that could be used to sell more books? Shortly before his death,

Hunt wrote his memoir called *An American Spy: My Secret History in the CIA.* None of this information was contained in his memoir. St. John Hunt said that prior to his father's death, the elder Hunt was "deeply conflicted and deeply remorseful" that he didn't tell authorities about his foreknowledge of the assassination plot. But can we believe him? Howard Hunt continued by saying that JFK had enemies galore who had the means, motive, and opportunity to kill him.

Hunt's name has also cropped up in another Kennedy assassination related area in documents released by the National Archives and in the possession of the author. Among these documents is a very intriguing file on Hunt called "E. Howard Hunt's Missing Report on the Assassination." This 35-page document tells of a secret report conducted on the Kennedy assassination by Frank Sturgis and fellow Watergate burglar. Bernard Barker.

In part, the document reads as follows, "Barker told of a secret assignment that he and fellow Watergate burglar Frank Sturgis had conducted for their important White House friend and patron, Mr. Hunt. Unfortunately, Barker garbled a key point in the interview, mistakenly referring to the 'death of Bobby Kennedy' rather than the death of John Kennedy, which was the actual subject of this Barker/Sturgis assignment for Hunt. According to the document, Sturgis interviewed a lady who had been at the Castro home when John Kennedy was killed and was telling some 'very strange stories.' This lady was then interviewed by Hunt who took her statement down on tape. Hunt then sent this report to the CIA. This information was never given to the Ervin Committee investigating the Watergate affair." [6]

Frank Sturgis has always been linked one way or another to the Kennedy assassination and he was once thought to be one of the so-called "tramps" who were briefly arrested in Dealey Plaza after the assassination.

The interest in Sturgis's Dallas activities gained momentum when a news article was printed in the Pompano Beach *Sun Sentinel,* written by James Buchanan. According to the writer, Sturgis told him that Oswald was in communication with certain

[6] HSCA Record Number 11210419 and Agency File No. 015106 by Michael Ewing.

members of the Cuban security forces prior to November 22, 1963. When asked for his reaction to the story, Sturgis said that he gave "offhand comments" to Buchanan, and said that they were "guesses, speculation, and rumor."

On the day of the assassination, Sturgis was at his home in Miami and was visited by the FBI. Why the FBI wanted to talk with him is not known, but his year's long activities with the Castro revolution and his associations with CIA people in Havana must have been on their minds. Sturgis later talked of that meeting with the Feds. "They told me I was the one person they felt had the capabilities to do it. If there's anyone capable of killing the president of the United States, you're the guy who can do that."

The late Gaeton Fonzi who was an investigator for the HSCA and a writer on the Kennedy assassination, said, "If you believe that someone other than Oswald had anything to do with the death of the president, then you'd have to look at Frank. A character like Frank Sturgis illustrates some of the dilemmas in investigating the Kennedy assassination. He can't be ignored. He is, by his own admission, a prime suspect. He had the ability and the motivation and was associated with individuals and groups who considered, and even employed, assassination as a method to achieve their goals."

Frank believed that Oswald was a patsy and that Castro was the instigator of the assassination, and that the plot was hatched in Havana before the assassination by Fidel and his brother Raul, and Che Guevera.

The Dallas-Watergate connection links men like Frank Sturgis, Howard Hunt, Bernard Barker, and James McCord to both events that that historical record cannot ignore.

Chapter 37
Booth or Boyd?

One of the most pernicious conspiracy theories surrounding the assassination of President Abraham Lincoln on April 14, 1865 at Ford's Theater in Washington City is that John Wilkes Booth did not die at Garrett's Farm, 12 days after killing the president. The theory goes that he escaped being killed by Union soldiers and that another person's body was substituted in his place. The real Booth then fled to such places as India, Oklahoma, or Texas and lived under assumed identities until his death by natural caused, years later. Over the years, many relatives of John Wilkes Booth say that their infamous relative did indeed escape and that the government was covering up the fact. For example, Joanne Hulme, a distant relative of John Wilkes Booth said that as a young girl her mother told her regarding Booth, "They're gonna say that he died in a barn. He did not die in a barn. He lived for many, many years." One of the conspiracy theories surrounding the Lincoln assassination is that a look alike of Booth, a soldier who fought in the Civil War by the name of Captain James W. Boyd, was the one who was killed at Garrett's Farm and that he was placed there by Secretary of War Edwin Stanton. Is there any validity to the Booth impersonation story? This is what historians say happened.

On Good Friday, April 14, 1865, less than one week after Confederate General Robert E Lee surrendered his Army of Northern Virginia to General Ulysses Grant at Appomattox Court House in Virginia, President and Mrs. Lincoln attended a nighttime performance at Ford's Theater of the play *Our American Cousin* staring Laura Keane. The play was interrupted with applause as the first couple took their seats in the balcony. Accompanying them were Major Rathbone and his fiancé' Clara Harris.

In the middle of the play, the noted actor John Wilkes Booth, stepped into the president's box and pulled out a. 44 caliber Derringer and shot the president in the head, mortally wounding him. Booth then jumped onto the stage, yelling, "sic semper Tyrannis," and, amid the commotion after the assassination, made his way out of the city and met up with his co-conspirator, David Herold in the Maryland countryside.

Booth was a known southern sympathizer and was a low-level agent working for the Confederates as a smuggler during the war. Before the assassination, Booth and a number of his conspirators, planned to kidnap the president while he made his way to a performance in the city and take him to Richmond where he would be ransomed for thousands of Confederate prisoners who were languishing in Union jails. After that plan failed, Booth decided to kill Lincoln at Ford's Theater, in wide ranging plot that also included the Secretary of State, William Seward and Vice President Andrew Johnson (Seward was wounded and no attempt was made to kill Johnson).

After the assassination, Booth and David Herold found their way to the home of Dr. Samuel Mudd whom Booth had previously met on two different occasions. As he jumped onto the stage at Ford's, Booth broke his leg and needed medical treatment. Dr. Mudd administered to Booth's leg and the next day both Herold and Booth left Dr Mudd's home and eventually made their way across the Potomac River into Virginia. With the help of three paroled Confederate soldiers, Booth and Herold found their way to the home of Richard Garrett at Port Royal Virginia, arriving on April 26, 1865. They told the Garrett family that they were Confederate soldiers who were heading home after the war and needed shelter for the night. Richard Garrett allowed them to stay and gave them supper. As the two men were with the Garrett's, twenty-six solders from the 16th New York Cavalry passed by the farm and Booth and Herold grew excited. That night, the men were allowed to stay in the tobacco barn. After midnight, the 16th New York surrounded the farm and Herold came out unharmed. Booth stayed in the barn and when they set fire to the structure, a shot was fired by Boston Corbett, one of Union troops, mortally wounding Booth. Booth died the next day, paralyzed from the waist down.

When Booth was taken out of the barn, David Herold asked Lt. Edward Doherty "Who was that man that was shot in there?"

Doherty replied, "You know who he was."

Herold says, "No, I don't know who that was. His name was *Boyd*. I didn't know it was *Booth*."

This presents a problem, David Herold knew John Wilkes Booth starting back in 1863 when he was performing at Ford's Theater. As a young man he worked as a druggist assistant and was recruited into Booth's kidnap plot against Lincoln. Surely, Herold knew whom he was riding with after Booth shot the president. It wasn't like they'd met only recently. Herold would later be hung after standing trail for his part in the Lincoln conspiracy.

So, if the man killed at the Garrett farm was not John Wilkes Booth was it James W. Boyd?

James Boyd was a real individual, not a made up person. He was born in Hopkinsville, Kentucky in 1822, and made his way to Jackson, Tennessee in the 1840s. He married a woman named Caroline Malone in 1845 and the couple had seven children between 1846 and 1862. When the war began, Boyd enlisted in the Sixth Tennessee Volunteers (CSA), and rose to the rank of Captain. In 1863, James Boyd and two other men were captured by Union troops of the 2nd Iowa Cavalry. The trio led Union troops in a chase by horseback, steamboat, and train, until they were captured. Two of his companions, James Watson and Harry D'Arcy, were tried as spies and sentenced to death. As luck would have it, James Boyd was somehow spared the gallows and taken prisoner. He was sent to various Union prisoner of war camps before being taken to the Old Capitol Prison in Washington City.

The story of James Watson, the traveling companion of James Boyd means telling. R.D. (Robert Daniels) Watson was James' brother. In 1864, R.D.Watson arrived in Montreal, Canada to take care of a business deal. Among the people who took part in this deal were a famous American actor named John Wilkes Booth, and Luke Blackurn, a Confederate doctor who specialized in unconventional warfare, including the use of malaria which he tried to use against Northern targets as the war progressed, and William Browning who was an aide to Governor Andrew Johnson of Tennessee. The men were in Canada to try and broker a meat for-cotton-deal between the North and the South. This was one of the most secret deals that went down during the war, gaining huge profits for a small number of businessmen with the savvy to carry it out.

Jump to 1961 and the work of a noted Civil War buff named

Ray Neff. Neff, a New Jersey chemist, who wrote an article in the old *Civil War Times* magazine in which he reported that he had found a coded message in the National Archives, possibly written by Lafayette Baker, the head of the National Detective Police at the time of the Lincoln assassination. At the same time that the Neff article appeared, another author who was writing a book on the assassination, Vaughn Shelton, came upon the same material as did Ray Neff.

In the archives, Shelton found a note written to John Surratt, the son of Mary Surratt who owned the boarding house in Washington in which the Lincoln conspirators gathered (along with Booth), from New York City dated March 19, 1865 and signed by "R.D. Watson." In the trial of the Lincoln conspirators there is no official mention of anyone by that name. So who was "R.D. Watson?" Neff and Shelton believe it was none other than Lafayette Baker. The brief letter reads as follows, "I would like to see you on important business, if you can spare the time to come to New York. Please telegraph me immediately on receipt of this, whether you can come on or not & oblige,Yours re, R.D. Watson." The address on the note was "Care Demill & Co. 178 ½ Water Street." The R.D. Watson letter was sent to a handwriting expert and the authority said that in his opinion, the letter matched the writing of Baker.

It is possible that the "Demill & Co., located at 178 ½ Water Street, was just a dummy company used to hide the activities of the Lincoln conspirators. While this does not categorically implicate Baker in the pre-assassination planning, it asks questions that still have not been satisfactorily explained.

While in the Old Capitol prison, James Boyd wrote a letter to Secretary Stanton offering a trade; he'd supply information on his confederates in the south in exchange for his freedom. The note from Boyd was delivered by Colonel Wood who was the prison's superintendent. In the letter he asked for a personal interview with Secretary Stanton which was agreed to. Within 24-hours of Body's letter arriving at Stanton's desk, he took an oath of allegiance to the North and had officially changed sides.

James Boyd was now a special detective for Secretary Stanton and he assigned him to go to Mexico on a secret mission. Instead, he showed up at the 178 ½ Water Street address in New York with his controller, William Earle. He then went to Canada for an unspecified mission. Canada was at that time, used by a number of Confederates on behalf of the government in Richmond to plan covert warfare against the North and one of the men who arrived in Montreal was John Wilkes Booth.

James Boyd did secret work for Secretary Stanton but the historical record is bare of exactly what he did. Writing in his book, *Dark Union,* authors Leonard Guttridge and Ray Neff write of Boyd, "Nothing would survive to precisely spell out whose interests he was serving or thought to be serving. So ambiguous was the nature of his allegiance that Lafayette Baker attached a "control" to him, a William Earle, who specialized in liaison with turncoats."`

Stanton is supposed to have sent Boyd undercover to the Johnson Island prisoner of war camp near Sandusky, Ohio. Boyd was supposed to report on any escape plans formed by the Confederate prisoners. With his life in danger at Johnson Island, he was hurriedly transferred to another prison at Point Lookout, Maryland.

According to conspiracy theorists, John Wilkes Booth was told by his mentor and controller, a man named James Barnes who was a Wall Street cotton broker after his return from Canada that he was going to be replaced as the ringleader of the plot to kidnap President Lincoln by a man named, "Captain B" who was once a rebel officer. That rebel officer was James Boyd.

The second conspiracy theory is that Secretary Stanton, who was no friend of Abraham Lincoln, arranged for Boyd to replace Booth and take the fall for the assassination. The other arguments saying that Stanton was involved in the plot, is that he sent only one detective to protect the president at Ford's Theater (the guard left his post and went to a local tavern). The detective involved was John Parker, and his absence let John Wilkes Booth enter the presidential box unmolested. Parker was never punished after the fact. Stanton gave orders to block every escape route out of Washington except the one used by Booth and Herold, following the assassination, and he also failed to send telegrams out of the city to the army notifying them of the shooting. The paper trail on James Boyd ends in February 1865, almost two months prior to the assassination of the president. As mentioned before, James Boyd was a dead ringer for John Wilkes Booth and except for Boyd's hair color, they could have been twins. The children of James Boyd never saw their father again after the person who was found at the Garrett farm was killed. Another interesting fact is that James Boyd had tattooed on his arm, the initials "JWB," the same initials as John Wilkes Booth.

After the assassin was killed at Garrett's Farm, the body was taken aboard the *Montauk* before heading back to Washington. Of all the people who claim to have seen the body on board the ship, no one actually knew John Wilkes Booth prior to the assassination. One of the witnesses who did see the body was Booth's doctor, John May. Dr. May had known Booth for eighteen months and had treated him before. At one point, Dr. May had removed a neck tumor from Booth but upon examination of the corpse on the *Montauk,* he could not observe one. He stated that, "there is no resemblance in that corpse to Booth, nor can I believe it to be him." After turning the body around, Dr. May said that he could not positively identify the body he saw before him as positively being John Wilkes Booth. Also, Boyd had red hair while Booth's was black. In the end, Dr. May reluctantly signed off saying that the body he was examining was indeed John Wilkes Booth. He probably did this so as not to be implicated as an accomplice in the president's murder.

So, what do we have here? Did Booth take on the identity of James Boyd, and if he did, where did he go? There were reports that Booth was living under the alias of John B. Wilkes or John St. Helen. Some researchers say that Booth switched his identity to that of an Englishman called John B. Wilkes from Sheffield, England and lived in India. Wilkes/Booth later returned to the United States and a photograph of him taken in later life was a perfect resemblance of the real Booth.

Another theory is that Booth took on the alias of John St. Helen and that he lived in Franklin County, Tennessee in 1872 where he married a woman named Louisa Payne. He eventually confessed to her that he was really THE John Wilkes Booth and that he'd married her under a false name. Louisa didn't care and they were re-married using Booth's real name. According to the marriage records filed in the Franklin County Courthouse the marriage registry shows John W. Booth's signature on February 24, 1872, seven years after the assassination of the president. John St. Helen finally died in 1903 in Enid, Oklahoma and his identity was confirmed by a friend named Finis Bates who met Booth in Granbury, Texas under the alias of St. Helen.

So, was John W. Boyd replaced as John Wilkes Booth ? It wouldn't be so far-fetched if one ignores the fact that the historical record belonging to Boyd ends in February 1865, two months prior to time whoever was killed at Garrett's farm. Coincidence or conspiracy?

Frank Olson.

Chapter 38
The Death of Frank Olson

On November 18, 1953, ten scientists gathered for a routine meeting in a rustic log cabin in the Appalachian mountain's that took place took place about twice a year. There was nothing out of the ordinary that fateful day, just a few men discussing their latest work for the United States government. What they did not known that day was their activities would set in motion one of the most controversial events of the cold war era and the CIA in particular. One of the men in the room, a well-known American scientist named Frank Olson would be slipped a drug called LSD which he did not know he was taking. The effects were long lasting and within weeks of ingesting the drug he would be dead under very mysterious circumstances. What Frank Olsen took was there result of an experiment that had been going on since World War II and involved experiments on Nazi concentration camp inmates, and more disturbing, innocent American citizens who had no idea what was happening to them.

Frank Olson was an American citizen who was born in 1910 and worked at the U.S. Army's Fort Detrick, Maryland bio warfare lab which was founded in 1943. During that time the scientists working at the facility worked on bacteriological weapons, some of it anthrax spores, which could be used for possible biological warfare purposes.

In 1949, Frank Olson was the Acting Director of the CIA's highly classified Special Operations Division, a man who knew the secrets hidden inside the bowels of Fort Detrick. Some of the work that he did dated back to the end of World War II when the United States undertook a secret operation called Operation Paperclip which secretly brought Nazi scientists back to the United States after the war ended. Some of these scientists experimented in the most ruthless way on death camp inmates and many of them were arrested but spared a trial for war crimes that were being held at Nuremberg. In a quid pro quo with the men, the Nazi scientists agreed to help the United States develop their own germ warfare program. This deal with the devil would not become known to the public until many years later.

While working at Fort Detrick, Frank Olson was associated with a top secret CIA program called MK-ULTRA that was responsible for developing research on various drug related programs. One of these was mind control experiments which the North Koreans had used against captured U.S. soldiers during the conflict. These soldiers sent propaganda to the United States without their knowing what they were doing.

Over the period of twenty-three years, spanning the end of World War II to the beginning of the cold war, the CIA conducted drug experiments including "truth drugs" with cannabis. The first test of this experiment was used against an American citizen named August Del Gracio who was involved with the OSS during the war to enlist the help of Lucky Luciano during the American invasion of Italy and also to help free the New York docks of Nazi sympathizers. He was given cigarettes which were laced with cannabis and he began to talk freely while under the influence of the drug.

The CIA began similar program shortly thereafter called Bluebird that was directed by Sheffield Edwards, the head of the CIA's Office of Security (he would later take part in the CIA's assassination plans against Fidel Castro of Cuba). The Bluebird teams were sent out into the field in October 1950 to Tokyo to experiment on four people, possible double agents who had been captured by the U.S. These tests were successful and they then conducted experiments on captured North Korean soldiers. These experiments were conducted under the direction of Allen Dulles who would serve as the Director of the CIA under both Eisenhower and Kennedy. Bluebird soon morphed into another project called Project Artichoke, which was carried out by CIA's Office of Scientific Intelligence. Project Artichoke, in effect, was a mind control experiment to, "exploit, along operational lines, scientific methods and knowledge that can be utilized in altering the attitudes, beliefs, though processes, and behavior patterns of agent personnel. This will include the application of tested psychiatric and psychological techniques including the use of hypnosis in conjunction with drugs."

In order to keep Project Artichoke secret, experiments were

carried out overseas, in such places as Germany, the Far East, and at a U.S. Naval base in the Panama Canal Zone. It was rumored that some people were actually killed in these experiments.

While Allen Dulles was head of the CIA, the agency proposed a program "for the covert use of biological and chemical materials" on human behavior. In secret, an arrangement was made with a Dr. Harris Isbell, the head of a drug treatment center in Lexington, Kentucky who tested drugs given to him by the CIA. Seven men were given LSD without their knowledge for seventy-seven days. The purpose of the drug was to examine the effect these drugs had to help control people for further testing. [7]

In the 1950s, Frank Olson was part of Operation Artichoke and he traveled to Germany to meet with one of the Nazi scientists working on the project, Kurt Blome. They met at Camp King in Germany where they discussed their work. Olson also witnessed interrogations of Soviet prisoners and other enemy agents while overseas. He also saw similar torture programs carried out by the U.S. on a separate trip to Berlin in 1953 and came home distressed and angry at what he'd witnessed. He had the temerity to protest to his superiors on what he had witnessed and threatened to quit his post if changes weren't made.

It was at the cabin in the Appalachian Mountains that Frank Olson was drugged by his colleagues because the government now believed him to be a security risk and he was interviewed by Military Intelligence officers.

One of the people whom Olson told about his concerns was a colleague at Fort Detrick, Norman Cournoyer. He also told his friend that the believed that the U.S. had used anthrax during the Korean War, despite public denials. In order to find out if Olson had spilled the beans to any other unauthorized persons, the CIA used the same interrogation techniques, truth serums, etc., they used on enemy combatants on Olson. What a way to treat a colleague!

He told Cournoyer about his trip to Europe by saying, "Norm, you would be stunned by the techniques that they used. They made people talk! They brainwashed people. They used all kinds of drugs; they used all kinds of torture. I am getting out of the CIA, Period."

7 Ranelagh, John *The Agency: The Rise And Decline of the CIA,* Simon and Schuster, 1986, Page 205.

Cournoyer later said about what Frank Olson told him by saying, "He was very open and not scared to say what he thought. For that matter, to the contrary. He did not give a damn. Frank Olson pulled no punches at any time. That's what they were scared of, I am sure."

In the early 1950s, before Frank had a change of heart regarding what he was doing, he traveled to England to work on temporary duty status at Porton Downs, a British facility and made frequent trips to "an intelligence facility" in Sussex, England. His passport was stamped "official business for the Department of the Army" and in his travels he toured a number of British military airfields, went to France, Occupied Germany, and Scandinavia, between May and August 1953.

While he was in England, Olson met a fellow scientist named Dr. William Sargent who was sent by the British government to evaluate the MK-ULTRA Program. Sargent, who is now deceased, told author Gordon Thomas that he urged the British government to stay away from the MK-ULTRA program because of the way it was run. It has been postulated that Olson told Dr. Sargent of his serious doubts about the work he was doing and that Sargent might have passed along Olson's doubts to his superiors in the United States.

By late November 1953, Frank Olson was a deeply depressed man. He stayed at home, telling his wife that he had serious doubts about continuing his job. He became moody and depressed and his family began to worry about his mental health. On Monday, November 23, 1953, Olson informed his superior, Lt. Colonel Vincent Ruwet, that he was planning to quit his job. Col Ruwet refused to accept his resignation and both men were now at loggerheads about Olson's future. The next day both men had another meeting and Lt. Col. Ruwet told Olson that he'd be taking him to New York City for treatment of his mental condition. Olson checked into room 1018 at the Hotel Statler with another man on the CIA's payroll, Richard Lashbrook. Lashbrook was in effect, Olson's minder, there to keep an eye on his every move. While in the room, a doctor arrived and gave Olson some medicine for his condition.

In the early morning hours of November 28, 1953, Frank

Olson plunged out of his small hotel room through the plate glass window and fell to his death, landing on the streets of 7th Avenue below. Hearing the noise, the night manager, Armand Pastore rushed out into the street and found Olson lying on the ground. As Pastore held Olson's body in his arms, he died. Pastore saw where the body came from and went up to Olsen's room. He found his companion, CIA agent Richard Lashbrook in the room and told him what happened. Lashbrook didn't seem too concerned that his friend had just died and immediately made a phone call to Dr. Harold Abramson, the same doctor who came to their room earlier to tell him what happened. Lashbrook then used the long distance operator in the hotel to place another call. The operator made the call and listened to the very brief conversation that ensued. Lashbrook said, "He's gone." The reply was, "Well, that's too bad."

When the police were called, they interrogated Lashbrook who told them that he was on the toilet when he heard a loud noise and went to investigate and saw Frank Olson lying on the ground. The police did no further investigation and the case was ruled a suicide.

The CIA maintained that Olson died from a fall from the window (suicide). However, an autopsy that was conducted forty years later on the exhumed body of Olson, revealed that there was an injury to the skull that was most likely caused by a blow to the head. If Frank Olson was hit on the head as the autopsy revealed, then how did he have enough strength to jump out of a very small room, out a plate glass window without help? Furthermore, the autopsy revealed that there were no cuts to his body from broken glass as would happen if someone leaped through any glass window. The findings from this autopsy said that the forensic evidence was "rankly and starkly suggestive of homicide."

This new autopsy was conducted by a forensic scientist named James Starrs, a Professor of Law and Forensic Science at the National Law Center at George Washington University. Working with a number of high-profile scientists, the panel said that the 1953 autopsy was "manipulated" and "totally inaccurate in some very important respects." The official verdict of the Starr team was that Frank Olson died as a result of homicide.

The public did not know anything about the death of Frank Olson or the MK-ULTRA Project until the 1970s when the congress investigated the illegal activities of the CIA and the FBI under the umbrella of the Rockefeller Commission. In its findings, they revealed the use of LSD on unwitting American's and that one of them was Frank Olson. The family of Frank Olson held a news conference and accused the CIA in his death and started their own investigation.

After the death of Frank Olson, the CIA went into cover-up mode. Allen Dulles was informed of the incident by Sidney Gottlieb, who was in charge of the agency's scientific work. Dulles ordered Lyman Kirkpatrick, the CIA's inspector general to make an investigation and report on his findings. Kirkpatrick requested that a reprimand was to be placed in Gottlieb's file and wrote:

> Although Dr. Gottlieb knew all of the individuals who received the drug, he obviously was not aware of their medical records. Therefore, only one individual was excluded from the experiment because of a heart condition. Gottlieb was not aware that over a period of five years, Olson had apparently had a suicide tendency. It was apparent that there is a strong possibility that the drug was a trigger mechanism precipitating Olson's suicide. Uncontrolled experiments as these conducted by TSS could seriously affect the record and reputation of the Agency. The Deputy Chief TSS should be reprimanded for his poor judgement shown in this instance.[8]

John Ranelagh, writing in his book on the CIA called *The Agency: The Rise And Decline of the CIA,* said of the Olson incident, "In retrospect, it is clear that Gottlieb's work lit a fuse to a time bomb that was to explode in the 1970s, destroying a good deal of the agency's image as a proper defender of American values in the public mind."

After the death of Frank Olson, this family filed a lawsuit against the United States government and they received a settlement of $750,000. In the aftermath of the Olson death, the government finally admitted in public that Olson was given LSD

[8] Ibid. Page 209-210.

without his permission.

Eric Olson, Frank's son, led a years-long investigation into his father's death and some help came in an unexpected way. A California history professor, Kathryn Olmstead, found 23 pages of documents in the Gerald Ford library pertaining to the Olson death which showed just how important the Ford White House viewed the fallout from the case. The White House tried to cover up the death of Frank Olsen with two of the president's top aids, Dick Cheney, a senior White House assistant (later vice-president under George W. Bush), and Donald Rumsfeld, who was the White House chief of Staff (and later Defense Secretary to Bush-both men were the architects of the war against Iraq after 9-11).

One of the documents uncovered by Professor Olmstead states, "Dr. Olson's job was so sensitive that it is highly unlikely that we would submit relevant evidence." In another memo, Dick Cheney said, "the Olson lawyers will seek to explore all the circumstances of Dr. Olson's employment, as well as those concerning his death. In any trial, it may become apparent that we are concealing evidence for national security reasons and any settlement or judgment reached thereafter could be perceived as money paid to cover up the activities of the CIA." A further document from the Ford Library written by Cheney and Rumsfeld says that they had to keep the fact of Olson's work secret because, "a drug criminally given him cannot as a matter of law be determined in the course of his official duties." Over the ensuing years, both men refused comment on what role they played in the Olson case.

After all the information concerning the death of Frank Olson was revealed, the Olson family had a private meeting with President Ford in which they received an apology from the president.

The circumstances surrounding the death of Frank Olson are still one of the most perplexing incidents to come out of the cold war era, still begging for final closure.

Chapter 39
William Sebold-Double Agent

In 1940, one year before the United States entered World War II, the German intelligence service, the Abwehr, headed by Wilheim Canaris, and had established a spy ring in the United States located in New York City. The head of the ring was Frederick "Fritz" Joubert Duquesne, an all-around confidence man. Novelist, and reporter, who supervised a 33-man cell that stretched from the city to Long Island. Unlike the submarine spies who arrived in the United States and were quickly rounded up, Fritz Duquesne's men were active in New York, albeit under the watchful eye of J. Edgar Hoover's FBI. However, like the submarine spy ring, one of their members, William Sebold, would eventually pull the plug on their covert activities and inform the United States about what he and his fellow spies were doing. In the aftermath of the spy ring's arrest, the credit would go to the FBI and its mercurial leader, J. Edgar Hoover who basked in its glory, making Hoover the number one spy catcher in the country. The activities of the Sebold-Duquesne spy ring is one of the most underrated espionage operations undertaken by the Germans on American soil and is worth telling for a generation who knew nothing about it.

Even before the United States entered the war, the number one target of Germany was America and its mighty industrial capacity. Germany knew that if the United States ever entered the war on the side of the allies, they would have much harder time defeating both France and Britain. It was in their best interest to keep America out of the war and learn as much intelligence about our war capacity as possible. For that reason, they sent their chief spy to this country, Nichols Ritter whose agents were responsible for the theft of the Norden bombsight. One of Ritter's most trusted American spies was William Sebold, a native of Germany who had lived in the United States for some years and was a law abiding citizen, faithful to Uncle Sam. Before the Sebold affair was over he would be responsible for the total elimination of a prosperous German spy-ring based in New York.

Sebold's real name was George Debowski, a veteran of World War I, and later, a merchant seaman. He was born in Germany but left in 1921 for the United States. He got a job in industrial and aircraft plants in the States and later in South America. During a trip to Galveston, Texas, he jumped ship and sought American citizen ship. In February 1936 he became a naturalized citizen of the U.S, and changed his name to William Sebold. He then moved to San Diego where he got a job with the Consolidated Aircraft Corporation. But what Sebold failed to tell U.S. Immigration officials was that he changed his name and that he was also had a past career as a petty thief.

In February 1939, he returned to Mulheim, Germany to visit his family. As he got off the ship at the port of Hamburg he was met by a group of Gestapo officers who wanted to have a chat with him and told him that he'd be contacted by them in the future. The Gestapo officers, one of whom was Colonel Paul Kraus, told him that they knew of his lying to U.S. authorities about his past before making their pitch. Col. Kraus surprised Sebold by taking out of his pocket a folder containing technical information from the Consolidated Aircraft Company were Sebold worked. The information Colonel Kraus had was a complete file on what was manufactured at the plant. Sebold was stunned. The officer now got to the point. If Sebold did not cooperate with the Gestapo, his family in Germany would be at risk. Col, Kraus went on to tell him that they had a German agent working at the plant If Sebold agreed to spy for Germany they wouldn't notify the Americans about his past. Sebold reluctantly agreed and as they departed, one of the men said, "We need men like you in America." Not knowing what he meant, Sebold arrived at his parent's home, both disturbed angry about what the Gestapo man said.

Sebold spent three days in Mulheim, seeing his family and catching up on old times. He stayed at the Hotel Handelshof and upon returning to the room at night, he found his possessions had been rifled, but nothing taken. A signal had now been sent, one that he could not ignore.

One morning he received a letter telling him to report on July 8 to the Hotel Duisburgerhoff in Berlin. Upon arrival in Berlin, he was met by a man who called himself Dr. Gassner. In reality, Dr.

Gassner was Abwehr Major Nicholas Ritter, alias Dr. Rankin, of the air intelligence corps who was responsible for the theft of the Norden bombsight. Ritter's job was to target Great Britain and the United States for espionage purposes. At age 24, Nicholas Ritter came to the United States and moved to New York where he worked. After twelve years, Nicholas and his wife moved back to Germany at the invitation of the military attache' to Washington, Friedrich von Boetticher who said that Ritter's services were needed by the Armed Forces High. Command. Ritter was fluent in English and he traveled to countries like Holland, Belgium, and Hungary on false passports, recruiting agents who'd make up his spy ring in the United States.

On November 11, 1937, Nicholas Ritter boarded the liner *SS Bremen,* bound for New York. He traveled on his own name and real German passport. His cover identity was that of a textile engineer who was looking for business in New York before heading back to Germany. However, his real mission was to establish a flourishing undercover espionage ring in the city on behalf of the Abwehr. Once in New York, Ritter opened up an office in the Wellington Hotel under the name of "Alfred Landing." He soon met with one of his contacts, Friederich Sohn who worked Carl Norden Inc., the manufacturer of the Norden bombsight which the German's had stolen. One of the men who worked at Norden was Hermann Lange who stole copies of the bombsight and copied them at home. Lange would play an intricate role in the Duquesne spy ring. Ritter sent copies of the bombsight back to Germany via couriers on board the various liners making the route between the United States and Germany.

During his meeting with Dr. Gassner, Sebold was told of the large number of spies that had been planted in various American companies, as well as government agencies. Gassner boasted that Germany was going to take over the United States and that he had plans for Sebold to be part of that operation. Sebold was in a bind, He had to cooperate with Gassner or his family would be in peril.

He spent the next several months undertaking intelligence training in order to prepare for his duties in the United States. But there was one complication. It seems that his passport had been stolen after his visit with Dr. Gassner and he needed a replacement.

Sebold then went to the American Consulate in Cologne, Germany to apply for a new one. In a bold move that could have grave consequences for his safety, he told the security personnel at the consulate that he had been contacted by German intelligence while he visited his family and was being blackmailed into acting as a spy for them. He also said he was willing to work for the FBI in an undercover capacity once he arrived in the States. His offer was accepted and upon completion of his training, Sebold headed for the United States carrying five microphotographs containing instructions for preparing a code and detailing the type of information he was to transmit back to Germany from the United States. He was given the codename "Tramp" by the Abwehr and was given an Abwehr number (A.3549) After getting his final instructions from his Abwehr superiors, Sebold, using the alias "Harry Sawyer," sailed from Genoa, Italy, and arrived in New York on February 8, 1940. He was for all intent and purposes, the Abwehr's main spy in the United States.

Two days after arriving in New York, William Sebold met with sixty-two year old Frederick Duquesne who was Nicholas Ritter's main spy in New York. Duquesne had an office that was used as a front company for his espionage purposes called Air Terminal Associates. Fritz Duquesne was a native of South Africa and harbored a deep hatred toward Great Britain. He served in the German army during World War I and there is evidence that he took part in the destruction of a British merchant ship in 1916 that caused the deaths of a number of British sailors. He worked as a spy for the Germans during the war and he took part in covert operations against British interests in South America from 1914 to 1916. British intelligence did all they could to track him down but had no success. Instead, Duquesne fled to the United States in May 1916 where he was safe from the Brits who put a death sentence on him for his wartime acts. He was arrested by New York City Police for masquerading as an Australian Captain and escaped all extradition requests from the British, faking mental illness. He was put in Bellevue Hospital before escaping. When Nicholas Ritter came to New York, he met with Duquesne and recruited him into his Abwehr network. Duquesne was still wanted by the NYPD and he used a number of aliases to fool the police.

When Sebold came to Duquesne's business, he introduced himself as "Harry Sawyer" the name he took in Germany. Duquesne told Sebold that it was too risky to talk in his office as he believed he was being bugged by the FBI. Instead, they went to a German restaurant in the Yorkville section of Manhattan for their conversation. He regaled Sebold about his plans to wreck-havoc in the U.S., including a plan to blow up the French liner *Normandie,* which was docked in New York harbor (the ship was eventually destroyed by a fire but there is no conclusive proof that the German saboteurs under Duquesne's watch were responsible for its destruction). A few days later, Sebold met with Duquesne in the latter's apartment and handed over to him the four reels of microfilm that he brought with him from Germany. Duquesne had the film developed and found that Sebold had given him a treasure trove of information that had to be sent back to Germany by a secret route. But how was that to be done?

Major Ritter told Sebold that he should set up secret shortwave radio station outside of Manhattan to send his messages. Ritter gave Sebold a large amount of money to finance the project which was deposited in the Chase Manhattan Bank. Sebold's radio station was in the town of Centerport, Long Island which was used to send messages back to Germany. Duquesne was able to get his information from defense plants across the country, including Grumman Aircraft Engineering in Bethpage, Long Island, asking for photos and plans of its emerging technology, posing as a student doing research papers. To his surprise, this information he requested was sent without any follow up by any of the companies he contacted. One of the people who sent him information was Everett Roeder who worked in a high-level position at the Sperry Gyroscope Company in Brooklyn.

What Duquesne did not know was that Sebold had told the FBI about his contact with him and the feds were monitoring their every move. When Duquesne was out of his office, the FBI put in listening devices in the walls and of his office. They also put hidden cameras inside the walls which could not be detected. Anytime Duquesne had meetings regarding his espionage work, the FBI was able to record every word and picture of what transpired.

For his part, Sebold opened up a dummy company in New

York called Diesel Research that was used as his main base of operation. He later operated in the Bronx and on Long Island (his Centerport radio station). Sebold's agents would come to report their activities to him at the

Diesel Research front, but they didn't know that their conversations were being monitored by the undercover FBI sting operation. At his Centerport, Long Island headquarters, Sebold made radio transmissions to Germany, which began in May 1940, giving them mostly bogus information provided by Hoover's G-men. In Berlin, the Abwehr recorded all of Sebold's message traffic and in return, sent back over 200 messages. In their return messages to Sebold and Duquesne, the Abwehr asked him to carry out sabotage and espionage operations inside the United States. They also instructed Sebold to send letters to them with vital information to what was called in spy parlance, an "Accommodation Addresses "in Portugal, and Brazil, which would be carried by special couriers who worked on German liners such as the SS *America*. It was believed that three members of the *America* crew were members of Duquesne's spy network.

The Centerport radio station was run by the FBI, using the money given to Sebold by Major Ritter. The bureau inserted two of their agents to send their secret messages back to Germany, M.H. Price and J. C. Ellsworth. Both men knew how to use shortwave radios and one of them was a "ham," a person who sent private broadcasts to other radio operators across the country. In time, Agent Ellsworth would become Sebold's handler throughout the latter's double life as an FBI informer. In time, both Sebold and Ellsworth would move into separate rooms in a German run boarding house in New York's upper west side and Ellsworth helped Sebold set up his fake business in the city. At one point, Sebold grew so upset about the work he was doing that he threatened to quit. In a long talk with Ellsworth, the agent finally convinced him not to do anything rash and Sebold decided to press on under FBI tutelage.

One of the msot important members of the spy cell was a man called "Paul" who was in reality, a German national named Hermann Lang. Lang met with Major Ritter when Ritter came to the United States to set up his network and he was soon to join

Sebold upon his arrival in the States. Lang came to the United States from Germany in 1927 and was responsible for sending copies of the Norden bombsight, which pilots would use when dropping their bombs on enemy targets with precision accuracy. Lang lived with his wife in the Ridgewood section of Queens and the poor woman had no knowledge of her husband's double life. While in Germany, Lang took part in Hitler's Beer Hall Putsch in 1923, and four years later, moved to the United States where he got a job as a machinist. Lang decided to join the ring due to his longstanding belief in Hitler and what he was trying to do in Germany.

Another person who was part of the Duquesne spy ring was a lovely young woman named Lilly Stein of whom Sebold would have many covert meetings with. With Ellsworth in tow, Sebold went to Miss Stein's apartment at West Eighty-Sixth Street in Manhattan (leaving Ellsworth in the car) on February 19, 1941. Lilly Stein was twenty-four years old, had hazel eyes, brown hair and according to her FBI file, "had better than average looks and a Jewish appearance." Sebold was immediately smitten with Lilly Stein and she turned out to be as good an agent as her appearance. At that meeting in her apartment, Sebold gave Miss Stein the microphotographs he'd brought with him that she immediately read with interest. In another meeting with Lilly that was filmed by the FBI, she told him of her life in Germany, and how she was able to travel to the United States, and most importantly, her contacts in the Abwehr that the FBI was glad to hear about. Lilly Stein was a windfall for Sebold. Over time, she told him the number of planes the British were producing each month (one thousand), information she'd gotten form a British military officer, a Captain Hubert Martineau. It seems that Lilly was getting her information from her lover, a diplomat named Ogden Hammond Jr., who was a vice counsel at the American consulate in Vienna, Austria. In time, she was ordered to end her relationship with Hammond because he was not supplying her with any further information of value.

By the summer of 1941, the FBI had enough information on the Duquesne spy ring to begin the end game. They had hundreds of hours of tape of Fritz Duquesne talking with William Sebold at Sebold's apartment and at Duquesne's office, implicating the

Abwehr in a plot to conduct espionage and sabotage inside the United States. There was even talk of planting a bomb at the Hyde Park home of President Roosevelt. In January 1942, less than a month after the Japanese sneak attack on Pearl Harbor brought the United States into the war, the FBI, under the direct order of J. Edgar Hoover, began a mass arrest of the members of the Duquesne spy ring, using 93 Special Agents to make the arrests. A total of 32 members were arrested, including Lilly Stein, Hermann Lang, and Fritz Duquesne. Three of the spy ring escaped capture as they were en-route to Germany on separate American registered ships. These men were detained on board ship and were arrested at the next port of call.

The Abwehr was surprised to find out that Harry Sawyer (Sebold) was not arrested with the rest of the group. The sent him a final coded message telling him not to make any further contact with Hamburg while they sorted things out. The next time they heard from their prize agent was at the trial of the spy ring members when Sebold testified against them. Most of the spies received sentences ranging from one to sixteen years in January 1942. By the end of 1951, all except one—Fritz Duquesne—had been paroled. With the arrest of the New York spy ring headed by William Sebold, German ability to run espionage operations in the U.S. came crashing down.

After the demise of the spy ring, William Sebold, a.k.a., Harry Sawyer vanished from sight. It is believed he moved to California where he fell on hard times. He went into the chicken business and received unwanted financial help from the FBI. He lived out the rest of his life in obscurity, just the way any good spy would like to be remembered.

Chapter 40
The Pentagon Papers

Six weeks after the death of J. Edgar Hoover, a seemingly minor event took place in Washington, D.C. that would begin the downfall of the presidency of Richard Nixon. The origins of the Watergate scandal had its roots in the paranoia that ran rampant in the Nixon White House. Gearing up for his 1972 re-election run, the Nixon administration put out a full court press against its political enemies. They were mainly concerned with the activities of Senator Edward Kennedy whom they believed posed the greatest challenge for the president's re-election. Other targets of the White House were the liberal media, as well as a number of mostly Democratic Senators who were opposed to Nixon's political agenda.

In order to keep a close watch on their political enemies, and monitor the leaks of important government information, illegal wiretaps were placed on the phones of Morton Halpern, who worked in the office of National Security Advisor Henry Kissinger. Under the direction of Director Hoover, at least thirteen wiretaps were placed on the members of the White House staff, the State and Defense Departments, and a number of journalists. One high-ranking member of the Nixon White House, Colonel Alexander Haig, was believed to be one of the recipients of these bugs. Summaries of these tapes conversations were given to Henry Kissinger by the FBI's William Sullivan. Hoover sent the most sensitive of these messages right to the Oval Office for Nixon's nighttime reading. By the summer of 1970, two years before Watergate, the tape recordings of these conversations were delivered to Nixon's two chief domestic aids, Chief of Staff Bob Haldeman, and John Ehrlichman. No court order was obtained to plant the bugs and they were patently illegal.

The case that generated the use of illegal wiretaps and political retribution from the Nixon administration came in 1971 with the release of the so-called Pentagon Papers by the *New York Times*. The Pentagon Papers was a secret history of United States involvement in the Vietnam War.

The Pentagon Papers was an exhaustive study of U.S. involvement in Vietnam since 1945 and was ordered in early 1971 by then Secretary of Defense Robert McNamara, to see how the war had gone so completely out of control. The study was called "United States-Vietnam Relations, 1945-1967, which was carried out by the Vietnam Study Task Force led by Leslie Gelb, the director of Police Planning and Arms Control for International Security Affairs at the Pentagon. A number of people worked on the study including 36 military personnel, historians, and defense analysts from the RAND Corporation. One of the men who worked at RAND, and who had a major role in the release of the papers was a Harvard educated, ex-Marine named Daniel Ellsberg. In the end, the study was composed of 47 volumes and had 7,000 pages of material. "The study conclusively shows that each US admiration, from Harry Truman through Lyndon Johnson, had knowingly and systematically deceived the American people over the U.S.' involvement and intervention in the region." The Pentagon Papers documents were highly critical of both President's Kennedy and Johnson by whose actions set in motion the most costly war in American history, one that would haunt a generation of Americans and tear the country apart. After reading the Papers, Nixon knew he had leverage over his two predecessors (both of them whom he did not like) and he knew he could use them to his political advantage.

The ire of the Nixon administration centered on Daniel Ellsberg,who ultimately leaked the Pentagon Papers to the *New York Times*. In the wake of the Pentagon Papers case, the Nixon administration would okay a break-in of the office of Ellsberg's psychiatrist, Dr. Lewis Fielding office in Beverly Hills, California to find any derogatory information that Dr. Fielding had on Ellsberg. The break-in would be carried out by some of the same people who broke into the Watergate building in 1972. Ellsberg had previously worked in Vietnam for the CIA on their so-called "pacification" campaign in the 1960s. He also worked for MIT as a research associate, and then moved on to the Nixon White House, under the direction of Henry Kissinger. It was during his time at the Rand Corporation that Ellsberg had access to, and copied the Pentagon Papers. At Rand, Ellsberg consulted with the Pentagon under Secretary of Defense McNamara during the Kennedy administration. He also visited South Vietnam with a research team to look into military strategy. From 1965 to 1966, he served in Vietnam as a civilian on special assignment to the U.S. Department of State, studying counter-insurgency.

In December 1968, Ellsberg met Henry Kissinger who was the National Security Advisor to President Nixon. Part of his job was to advise him on options in the U.S. military action then going on in Vietnam. A friendship soon developed and both men would meet several times during the first two years of Nixon's first term in office. In September 1969, Ellsberg finished reading a copy of Secretary McNamara's Vietnam study and had a change of heart about U.S. policy toward the war. Beginning in October 1969, Ellsberg and his colleague, Anthony Russo, secretly began copying the Pentagon Papers document, secretly giving copies to such anti-war Senators as William Fulbright and George McGovern (McGovern would be the 1972 Democratic presidential candidate against Nixon and would soundly be defeated, running on a peace in Vietnam platform). Ellsberg hoped that these law makers would release the papers but they did not do so. Ellsberg gave a copy of the Pentagon Papers documents to members of the *Washington Post,* including Phil Geyelin, but the paper's owners, Katherine Graham and Ben Bradlee, decided not to publish the report. In an ironic twist, after the break-in at the Watergate office of the DNC, two *Post* reporters, Bob Woodward and Carl Bernstein, would be assigned to investigate the break-in and the *Post* would then be forever linked with the Watergate story. In March 1971, Ellsberg met privately with *New York Times* reporter, Neil Sheehan and showed him the Pentagon Papers report that no one outside of the Pentagon had previously seen. Sheehan, seeing a huge story in the making, shared the report with his fellow reporter Hedrick Smith and their editors. In secret, the members of the *Times,* began to write their bombshell report on the Pentagon Papers which would have a profound effect on the Nixon administration and would ultimately, end up with the Watergate break-in. After the *Times* began publishing the excerpts, the *Washington Post,* despite turning down Ellsberg's initial requests to run the stories, began

341

publishing the secret archive.

When the papers first appeared in print, the Nixon administration did not see any real danger it's in publication. The president believed that the information would hurt the images of LBJ and JFK more than his own. Nixon would say of the papers release, "This is really tough on Kennedy, McNamara, and Johnson. Make sure we call them the Kennedy-Johnson papers. But we need to keep out of it." However, Henry Kissinger held a different view and tried to persuade the president to change his mind about going after the newspapers that ran the stories. He told Nixon that the release of the papers would damage U.S. national security and was especially critical of Daniel Ellsberg, telling the president that Ellsberg was a womanizer and a "known drug user." On June 13, 1971, the government got a court order, temporarily shutting down any further publication of the papers by the *Times,* using the prior restraint rule. After the release of the documents, Ellsberg dropped out of sight, only to reappear on national television, in a CBS interview where he revealed his part in the Pentagon Papers release.

When the *Times* published its third installment of the Papers, Nixon exploded. He said in one of his rants, "I want to know who is behind this and I want the most complete investigation that can be conducted. I don't want excuses. I want results. I want it done, whatever the cost."

The court finally had the last word in the case of the *New York Times Company v. United States,* when they refused to order the *Times* to turn over its copy of the Pentagon Papers for government inspection, saying they would not interfere in a first amendment case. The result of that decision let the Pentagon papers out of the closet (so to speak) and almost every paper in the nation now had complete access to the Ellsberg archive and they began publishing it on a daily basis.

The Nixon administration filed a motion in court stop the release of the papers and the case finally went to the Supreme Court for its final disposition. The court ruled in favor of the newspaper's right to publish, ending the legal battle against the press.

After the bombshell that Ellsberg laid on the Nixon White

House, Henry Kissinger was furious at his one-time employee and urged Nixon to take drastic action against him.

Ellsberg had subsequently been indicted by a grand jury in Los Angeles for disclosing the Pentagon Papers.

The FBI would now be brought into the Ellsberg investigation when William Sullivan suddenly turned over the Kissinger wiretap files to Nixon's assistant attorney general, Robert Mardian. Mardian said that Sullivan told him that Hoover was utilizing these hot files to blackmail Nixon's predecessors. Mardian realized that Hoover might use this information on Nixon and turned the tapes over to Attorney General John Mitchell. The tapes finally wound up in the safe of White House aide John Ehrlichman.

When Nixon found out that part of the Pentagon Papers came from the Washington think tank, the Brookings Institution, he blew his top. The president wanted to retrieve the information and he asked his close White House aide Charles Colson, to develop a plan to get it back. While the plan never took shape, it was ingenious (and illegal), nevertheless. FBI agents were to accompany D.C. Fire Department officers into the Brookings Institution and when the fire alarm suddenly went off, they were to recover the offending material.

The Ellsberg/Pentagon Papers case brought a new urgency to the Nixon White House as far as countering any more leaks of sensitive government information was concerned. With Hoover dead, and no one really at the helm at the FBI, President Nixon took matters into his own hands and created an in-house operation that would be run by the White House to plug any more leaks. The name given to this covert group was the White House Special Investigations Unit, or the Plumbers.

The members of the Plumbers were David Young, an assistant to Henry Kissinger's NSC, Egil Krough, and aide to John Ehrlichman, former FBI agent G. Gordon Liddy, and former CIA agent, and part-time writer, E. Howard Hunt. Hunt worked out of an office in the Executive Office Building across from the White House with an elaborate security and communications apparatus in place.

The Nixon administration put out a full court press on Daniel Ellsberg, even asking the FBI to interview his psychiatrist, Dr. Lewis

Fielding, which he refused, citing doctor/patient confidentiality. Nixon's team even asked the FBI and the CIA to provide them with a detailed profile on Ellsberg, and despite complaints by the CIA, they provided a limited sketch on him. The Plumbers were also disappointed when the FBI refused to give the Ellsberg case its full attention.

The Plumbers were now ready to continue the saga of the Pentagon Papers with a covert break-in of the offices of Ellsberg's psychiatrist, Dr. Lewis Fielding in Beverly Hills, California, looking for any incriminating information on his famous patient. The Fielding break-in was the idea of Howard Hunt who presented his plan to his fellow conspirators, Gordon Liddy and Egil Krough in a meeting at Hunt's office at Room 13 of the EOB. There is evidence that higher ups in the Nixon White House knew and approved the Fielding break-in. Nixon's aide John Ehrlichman gave his written approval for the break-in when he responded to an August 11, 1971 memo about the plan. It seems that Charles Colson had a meeting with Nixon on August 12, 1971 in which he briefed the president on the idea of breaking into the doctor's office. There is still much debate over whether or not the president knew or ordered the Fielding break-in but his quest for any derogatory information on Ellsberg set up the means and motive for the burglary. For example, when Egil Krogh met with the president one week after his resignation in 1974, Nixon was not really sure if he ordered the Fielding break-in or not. Nixon told Krogh that, "If you had come to me I would have approve it." Two years after the president's resignation, he told Bob Haldeman, "Maybe I did order the break-in."

In order to hide the fact that the White House was taking on an illegal operation, the event was farmed out to people who were not then associated with any intelligence agency, i.e., the FBI or the CIA. The men hired to do the job were Bernard Barker, Felipe de Diego, Howard Hunt, Gordon Liddy, and Eugenio Martinez. Hunt and Liddy were, at one time, associated with the CIA and the FBI- Hunt worked for the agency, while Liddy was an ex-FBI agent. Felipe de Diego took part in the Bay of Pigs invasion of Cuba, as well as in U.S. Army intelligence. Martinez was then active with the CIA but it is not known just how deep his cover was.

344

In order to pay for the break-in, and also so it was not traceable to the administration, $10,000 was collected through bribes from executives from the dairy industry, part of a two million payment that had been previously made. On August 25, 1971, Hunt got a Tessina camera which was hidden in a tobacco pouch from his contact in the CIA's Technical Services Division. Liddy was also given a disguise and identification from contacts at the CIA. If the CIA was not actually carrying out the burglary, they were accessories after the fact in helping both Hunt and Liddy.

Before the mission took place, Hunt told Martinez and Diego that they are to burglarize the offices of a "traitor who is spying for the Soviet Union, and that the mission was ordered by the White House. We have to find some papers of a great traitor to the United States, who is a son of a b-tch.," says Hunt. Fake disguises were also obtained by the other men, including disguises used by both Hunt and Diego, voice-altering devices, as well as fake id's Photographic equipment were bought at Sears in order not to leave a paper trail back to the CIA. Hunt used his old CIA identification that he used when he was working on the Bay of Pigs invasion plan, "Edward Hamilton." Martinez would later say of the operation, "The planning is far looser and less meticulous than anything I was used to in the CIA."

On a preliminary visit to Dr. Fielding's office, Hunt and Liddy, masquerading as delivery men, delivered photographic equipment to Dr. Fielding's office. The men encountered a cleaning woman and Hunt told her in Spanish that they were colleagues of Dr. Fielding and they needed to deliver something to him. The lady let them into Dr. Fielding's office and while Liddy took photographs of the place, Hunt had a chat with the woman.

The photographs were then taken back to CIA HQ where they were developed. In a rather strange course of events, the CIA's Deputy Director, General Cushman, told John Ehrlichman that the agency would not have anything more to do with Hunt and his escapades. This was not exactly what happened as Hunt was still allowed somewhat free reign at the agency for his illegal White House activities. It seems that General Cushman was just trying to cover the CIA's backside in case anything public came of Hunt's activities.

The actual break-in took place on the night of September 3, 1972. Hunt's assignment was to watch Dr. Fielding's apartment in case he made an unexpected return to his office (he didn't).At the doctor' s office, Liddy stood watch outside while the other men, Barker, Martinez and De Diego went into the office after business hours were completed. Now, things began to get a little messy. They had a glasscutter to be used to cut a hole in the window but when that didn't work, Martinez broke a window on the ground floor to gain entrance to the doctor's office. They tried to break into Dr. Fielding's file cabinets but could not open them. Instead, in order to cover up their mess the men left the office in shambles, dropping vitamin pills on the floor in order to make it look like a robbery gone bad. In the postmortem that followed the break-in, no incriminating material was found on Daniel Ellsberg's ties to any radical organization or foreign group. After the fact, Dr. Fielding said that, "his notes on the Ellsberg case were indeed in his office at the time and the burglars had obviously found them since the notes were lying on the floor when he arrived at his office on the morning after the burglary."

Once back in Washington, Hunt showed the photographs of the mess in Dr. Fielding's office to John Ehrlichman and wanted to follow up with a burglary attempt on Dr. Fielding's home. Hunt's request was turned down. Martinez told his CIA case officer what had transpired in California, but the man told him to forget about it. Back in California, the police arrested a drug addict who Hunt said, "conveniently confessed to our crime in return for a suspended sentence."

Interesting new material on Hunt's relationship with the CIA while he was working for the Nixon White House sheds new light on his agency ties. When the House Judiciary Committee was investigating Watergate, it showed that Hunt, "was regularly and secretly sending packages to the CIA form the White House." The man who made this statement was Rob Roy Ratliff who was a CIA liaison to the National Security Council. Ratliff said that, "I was aware that Hunt had frequently transmitted sealed envelopes via our office to the Agency." He further stated that Hunt's packages were hand delivered to the CIA, and that Hunt's secret channel to the CIA started at the beginning of Hunt's consultancy at the

White House. Ratliff said that he never opened these packages but that his predecessor had opened one. Ratliff's predecessor said that Hunt's package, "appeared to contain gossip information about an unknown person-he assumed that it had something to do with a psychological study of that person." Another source said that CIA Director Richard Helms had seen the material that Hunt sent to the CIA, giving him a head's upon what the Plumbers were doing vis a vi the Ellsberg/Fielding break-in.[9]

In the end, Egil Krogh, who helped form the Plumbers, plead guilty to violating the civil rights of Dr. Fielding and served six months in jail of his original two-to-six year sentence. On March 7, 1974, Nixon aides John Ehrlichman, Charles Colson, G. Gordon Liddy, and the three Cuban-Americans, Barker, Martinez and De Diego, were charged with the Fielding break-in. Colson reached a plea bargain agreement, cooperated with the prosecution, and plead guilty to one count of obstruction of justice and served seven months in jail. Liddy was also convicted for the break-in and served time for his arrest at the break-in of the DNC headquarters in June 1972.

Fresh from their unsuccessful entry into Dr. Fielding's office, the Plumbers were now ready to make another covert entry on behalf of the Nixon White House's Committee to Re-elect the president (CREEP). Their target was the Democratic National Committee headquarters at the posh Watergate Hotel in Washington D.C. With that event, Watergate was now in full swing.

---

[9] Waldron, Lamar, *Watergate: The Hidden History : Nixon, The Mafia, And the CIA*, Counterpoint, Berkeley, California, 2012, Page 492-493.

Chapter 41
The October Surprise

The name "October Surprise" is a political term used by politicians during a presidential election campaign in which the incumbent president carries out a dramatic foreign or domestic policy incident to enhance his/her chances for re-election. In this case, the October Surprise, if there was indeed one, was initiated by the Reagan-Bush 1980 presidential campaign against President Jimmy Carter. In essence, the October Surprise, according to conspiracy theorists, was a brazen, back door initiative by certain parties in the Reagan campaign and the government of Iran to hold the U.S. hostages until the U.S. presidential race was over (counting on a Reagan campaign victory which was not assured). In return for the release of the hostages, the United States (still assuming a Reagan victory), would guarantee the millions of dollars of arms and equipment bought by the previous government of under the Shah of Iran (who was then in the U.S. undergoing cancer treatment) and embargoed in this country. What has been learned over the past decades is a powerful story of intrigue by certain members of the Reagan campaign, backed up by a group of international arms brokers and intelligence agents who were the backstop for the October Surprise.

However, in order to learn the background of the story, we have to go back to 1979 to the rapidly unfolding political events then taking place in Iran that was the genesis of the October Surprise.

The Shah of Iran ruled his nation with an iron fist during the years of the cold war, serving as a trusted friend and ally of the United States in the Middle East. However, the Shah, who had been placed on the thrown by a CIA backed revolt in the early 1950s, was a corrupt leader who had no intention of giving up power without a fight. By the late 1970s, even the United States had to re-think its commitment to the Shah as his tyrannical rule grew to the extreme. In early 1979, the radical Islamic fundamentalists led by Ayatollah Ruhollah Khomeini took power in Iran, deposing the Shah in a peaceful coup. Upon taking power in Iran, the Ayatollah began a propaganda campaign against the west and the United States in particular, calling us the "Great Satan." Everything that was wrong in the Middle East was laid on the footsteps of the United States and unknown to most people at the time, the revolution headed by the Ayatollah Khomeini was the beginning of the so-called "war on terror" that would culminate in the attack on the World Trade Center on 9-11 and the subsequent wars in Iraq and Afghanistan.

Later in 1979, the Shah of Iran contacted cancer, and President Jimmy Carter allowed him to come to the U.S. for treatment. That decision made by Carter was the last straw as far as Ayatollah Khomeini was concerned. In a decision that was made at the highest levels of the government in Iran, militant "students" attacked the U.S. embassy in Tehran on November 4, 1979, and took over the building, along with 52 American hostages. The siege would last for 444 days and cripple the last days of Carter's presidency.

As Carter was preparing for his re-election in 1980, his administration was obsessed with the release of the hostages which had become his number one priority. His poll numbers were plummeting and the Republican opposition was in a frenzy, attacking the president on a daily basis. In April 1980, the U.S. attempted a military operation in order to rescue the hostages. The rescue mission took place on the night of April 24, 1980, and was made up of 100 members of Delta Force, and other elite members of the U. S. Military (it was called Operation Eagle Claw). The rescue force flew from its base in Egypt using four C-130 cargo planes to its destination in Iran called Desert One, a remote area in eastern Iran. At that location, they were to meet up with eight helicopters which had taken off from an aircraft carrier in the Persian Gulf. The plan called for the troops to board the helicopters and fly to the area called Desert Two, located about fifty miles from Tehran. From there, they were to rendezvous with U.S. agents and Iranian sympathizers who were waiting for them to arrive. They were then to be taken by car and truck to Tehran where the troops would storm the embassy and hopefully, free the hostages.

It was at this point that disaster struck. Two of the helicopters experienced mechanical troubles en route to the sight and one chopper developed a hydraulic malfunction at Desert Two. Since it was now impossible to ferry the soldiers to Tehran, the mission was aborted. However, there was more trouble to come. One of the choppers collided with a cargo plane, leaving many dead and leaving the area with top-secret American military secrets. Back in Washington, President Carter told the nation about the botched rescue operation and American moral plummeted even further.

Soon, a new dimension was added to the hostage crisis. In September 1979, Iran invaded its neighbor Iraq, starting off a war that would last eight years. The Iranians were at a disadvantage because millions of dollars' worth of military spare parts that were previously given to the Shah's government was now embargoed. With Iran in desperate need of military supplies, secret deep cover negotiations began between Washington and Tehran to start the flow of arms once more. Early contacts were conducted using West German intermediaries and it seemed that progress was being made to return the hostages.

It was at this point that a number of back channel, secret negotiations between the parties was started between the Reagan campaign and certain Iranian officials. One of the first sources on these secret dealings were two *Washington Post* reporter, Bob Woodward and Walter Pincus. They said that one meeting took place at the L'Enfant Plaza Hotel in Washington on October 2, 1979. The participants in the meeting were Richard Allen, who would later become President Reagan's first national security adviser, Marine Lt. Col. Robert "Bud" McFarlane, then an aide to Senator John Tower, who would later to become a subsequent National Security Advisor to the president, and Lawrence Silberman an aide to Richard Allen. The person who supposedly served as the intermediary was an Iranian Jewish arms dealer named Hushang Lavie. In later interviews, both Allen and McFarlane said they did not remember the meeting.

According to author Gary Sick who wrote a book on the scandal called *October Surprise: America's Hostages in Iran and the Election of Ronald Reagan,* another secret meeting took place in early March of 1980, involving Reagan campaign manager William Casey, a former OSS operative and later, Reagan's appointee to head the CIA, at the Mayflower Hotel with two

Iranian arms dealers, Cyrus and Jamshid Hashemi. The Hashemi brothers said that it was their understanding that Casey wanted to prevent the Carter administration from gaining political advantage from the freeing of the hostages. Sick said that after the meeting, Cyrus Hashemi told his contacts at the CIA about what had transpired with Casey at the hotel (Cyrus Hashemi died in 1986). Jamshid Hashemi later told the "Frontline" TV show that after the Mayflower meeting, "Casey and an unnamed US intelligence officer met with Mehdi Karrubi, the speaker of the Iranian parliament, in Madrid in late July 1980, promising arms and to unfreeze Iranian assets if release of the hostages were delayed until after the election. The same threesome, Jamshid Hashemi said, met again in Madrid several weeks later, and at that meeting Karrubi agreed to cooperate with the Reagan campaign about the timing of the hostage release."

In the literature on the October Surprise, there have been accounts of other meetings being held in Paris, France between October 15 and 20, 1980. It is believed that William Casey was one of these participants, along with a CIA agent named Donald Gregg, who was then working as an official in the Carter administration's national security aide and then Vice President George H.W. Bush's chief of staff. Gregg said he never took part in any meeting regarding the October Surprise. There were later reports that George Bush attended these meetings but there was no solid proof that he was there. According to sources, one of the Iranian participants in the Paris meeting was Manucher Ghorbanifar, an Iranian born Mossad (Israeli intelligence) agent and arms dealer who played a huge role in Iran-Contra affair during the Reagan administration.

It has also been alleged that one participant in the Paris meetings was Salem bin Laden, the oldest brother of Osama bin Laden. The source of this allegation came from a French intelligence report which said that Salem bin Laden was a close friend of Saudi Arabia's King Fahad who often times took on personal assignments for the king. This meeting was supposed to have taken place in October 1980 and although there are no sources who backed up the story, it places the Bush and bin Laden families together in a highly unusual scheme, years before the 9-11 attacks on the U.S.[1]

[1] Iran-Contra Arms-for-Hostages Scandals: October Surprise-History Com-

It is interesting to note that soon after the Paris meetings ended, Israeli sources said that between October 21 and 23, a shipment of spare parts for F-104s to Iran began, disregarding a ban on US rule that required American approval of any shipments of US-made arms to third parties.

Right after these secret meetings were held, the Iranians suddenly changed their minds and broke off all further negotiations between the American emissaries. For all intents and purposes, the back channel deals between the two parties were now in limbo with the fate of the hostages still in the balance.

Besides the back channel dealings with the Iranians and Reagan campaign intermediaries in Paris and Washington, there is evidence that George Bush used his cadre of ex-CIA people who were loyal to him to work against the Carter administration during this period. This new information came from the diligent work of author and reporter Robert Parry who has done extensive writing and research on the October Surprise story.

While the CIA was not supposed to have anything to do with politics there were a number of then current employees secretly working for Bush's election in in the 1980 election. George Carver, who was a CIA employee, said of the atmosphere at that time, "The seventh floor (where the CIA director had his office) of Langley was plastered with Bush for President signs." For instance, Robert Gambino, who was the CIA's director of security at that time, oversaw the security investigations of senior officials in the Carter administration and was privy to information that could have been detrimental to certain members of Carter's team. One of Gambino's friends was CIA officer Donald Gregg, who served as a CIA representative on Carter's National Security Council.

Another top CIA official who was on Bush's side was the legendary operative, Theodore Shackley. Shackley was a veteran of the CIA's Cuba operations in the 1960s, running the agency's top-secret JMWAVE station in Florida which sent out raids into Cuba against the regime of Fidel Castro, and also operated for the agency in Laos. He would also be linked to the rouge CIA agent, Edwin Wilson who ran his own private intelligence operation around the world, including selling arms to Libya's Qudaffai. George Cave said that Ted Shackley had a cadre of informants in mons website.

353

Germany who were monitoring the hostage negotiations with Iran. Cave said that, "I know he talked to them. I don't know how far it went. Ted was very active on that thing in the winter/spring of 1980."

Another person who knew of the Shackley/Bush connection was author David Corn (now an MSNBC analyst). Corn said, "Within the spook world the belief spread that Shackley was close to Bush. Rafael Quintero was saying that Shackley met with Bush every week. He told one associate that should Reagan and Bush triumph, Shackley was considered a potential DCI," the name for the Director of Central Intelligence.

Another person whom Bush used in finding out information on the on-going hostage situation was the former Democratic governor of Texas, John Connally (Connally was wounded in the assassination of President Kennedy while riding in the car with the president and his wife). According to Richard Allen who was Reagan's foreign policy advisor, Bush called Connally on October 27, 1980 after learning from Connally that "his oil contacts in the Middle East were buzzing with rumors that Carter had achieved the long-elusive breakthrough on the hostages." Allen, on Bush's orders, made inquiries regarding Connelly's information and according to his notes, learned the following information. "Geo Bush already made deal. Israel delivered last week spare parts via Amsterdam. Hostages out this week. Moderate Arabs upset. French have given spares to Iraq and know of JC (Carter) deal with Iran. JBC (Connally) unsure what we should do RVA (Allen) to act if true or not."[2]

Bush then ordered Allen to give that information to Ted Shackley via a person named Jennifer who turned out to be Jennifer Fitzgerald, who was Bush's assistant when Bush was at the CIA.

As mentioned earlier in this chapter, a man named Cyrus Hashemi and his brother were aware of the back channel operations involving William Casey to broker a hostage deal with Iran at the Mayflower Hotel in Washington. During the hostage talks, President Carter turned to Cyrus Hashemi for help. However, it has been learned that Cyrus Hashemi also had links to certain members of the GOP, including a former U.S. intelligence officer

[2] Parry, Robert. *Part 111: The Original October Surprise*, Consortium News, October 29, 2006

named John Shaheen, a Lebanese-born, business man from New York who was a friend of William Casey's. Both men served in the wartime OSS and still had contact over the years. It was Shaheen who first put Hashemi in touch with the CIA with the agency using Hashemi's bank to fund its covert operations. Hashemi helped the CIA in various enterprises involving political dealings in the Middle East, especially during the hostage crisis on 1979-1980.[3]

One of the lingering mysteries of the October Surprise is what role did William Casey play in the affair. This is a complicated story which needs some background information to be provided to the reader.

During the 1980 election campaign between Carter and Reagan, an incident took place that grew heated controversy. Right before one of the televised debates between Reagan and Carter, President Carter's briefing book was stolen by someone in the Reagan campaign thus, allowing them to study the president's strategy and information concerning the administration's policy towards freeing the hostages.

One of top people in the Reagan campaign, William Casey, later to become Reagan's Director of the CIA, studied the topsecret briefing book and knew just what the White House was up to.

If Casey was indeed a part of the secret meetings with individuals seeking to make a deal with Iran for the release of the hostages, this information would be manna from heaven as far as Casey was concerned. But, is there solid proof that Casey traveled to Europe to broker a hostage deal?

Former Representative Lee Hamilton conducted two investigations into Ronald Reagan's secret dealings with Iran and came to the conclusion that he had nothing to do with the operation and that William Casey did not make a trip to Madrid to meet with Iranian representatives. Robert Parry, doing investigative work on the October Surprise, sent a new document that he'd obtained to Rep. Hamilton in 1991 revealing that a deputy White House counsel working for then-President George H.W. Bush was told by the State Department that William Casey, then Reagan's` campaign director, had taken a trip to Madrid in relation to the October Surprise.

The document that Parry received was found at the George

3 Ibid.

H.W. Bush Library in College Station, Texas and was directly related to Casey's trip to Madrid. The contents of the document state that the U.S. Embassy in Madrid passed confirmation of Casey's trip to that country to the U.S. State Department in Washington. The man at State who read the report was Edwin Williamson, the legal adviser to the State Department who passed the report on to Associate White House Counsel Chester Paul Beach Jr., in early November 1991. Williamson said that among the materials found in the State Department files were "materials potentially relevant to the October Surprise allegations was a cable from the Madrid embassy indicating that Bill Casey was in town for purposes unknown."

While this was going on, a meeting was held at the White House on November 6, which was chaired by White House counsel C. Boyden Grey. The topic of the inter-agency meeting was to find a way to control the congressional investigation into the October Surprise case. Parry writes that the reason for the meeting was to control the fallout in order to protect President Bush's re-election chances in 1992. What Grey did not want to happen was to see the congressional committee investigate both the Iran Contra scandal, as well as the October Surprise into one, comprehensive probe.

The push back was now to be coordinated through Grey's office under the direction of associate counsel Janet Rehnquist, the daughter of the late Supreme Court Justice William Rehnquist. At a meeting with his team, Gray laid out their plan. "Whatever form they ultimately take, the House and Senate October Surprise investigation, like Iran-Contra, will involve interagency concerns-and be of special interest to the President."[4]

When Rep. Hamilton was conducting his probe of the October Surprise affair, he was focusing on two important people associated with George H. W. Bush, Robert Gates and the aforementioned, Donald Gregg. In 1991, President Bush appointed Robert Gates as the Director of the CIA and in that post, Gates had ample opportunity to stymy the investigation as head of the agency. Records from the Bush presidential library said that both men were targets of Hamilton's investigation and on May 26, 1992, Rep. Hamilton wrote to the CIA asking for travel records of both

[4] Parry, Robert, *Second Thoughts on October Surprise,* Consortiumnews.com, June 8, 2013.

men from the period from January 1, 1980, through January 31, 1981. When Donald Gregg was interviewed regarding the Iran-Contra scandal in the later stages of the Reagan administration, he was asked by an FBI polygraph expert if he had any connection to the October Surprise, the polygraph expert said that "Gregg was judged to be deceptive in his denials."

The late Lawrence Barcella who was the chief counsel for the congressional probe on the scandal told Robert Parry that "so much incriminating evidence against the Reagan campaign poured in during December 1992 that he asked Hamilton for a three month extension but was rebuffed." Rep. Hamilton said his inquiry was coming to an end and the only thing he could do was to ask the new congress for a reauthorization of the probe but facing so much Republican opposition, he closed down the investigation.

Another unconfirmed report of high-level intervention in the possible release of the hostages comes from author Gary Sick who claimed that former President Richard Nixon met in London with the head of a British helicopter service to discuss the possibility of a Republican-sponsored rescue mission. A person who was associated with the Nixon camp said in regard to this possible meeting, "We will neither confirm nor deny this story. We have nothing to say."

An additional person who had knowledge of the affair was an ex-Israeli military officer by the name of Ari Ben Menache. Ben Menache claimed that he had seen Bush in Paris and that he had been an integral part in the formation of the deal. In time, Ben-Menache's story was punched so full of holes that no one took his charges seriously. He said that the CIA asked Israeli leaders to cooperate with Republican efforts to free the hostages.

Ronald Reagan won the election in 1980 but in the two months remaining in Jimmy Carter's presidency, high-level discussions to free the hostages continued. According to author Gary Sick, by January 15, 1981, a deal was struck between the lame duck Carter administration and the government of Iran that was brokered by Algeria. Soon, the flow of arms to Iran resumed and minutes after the swearing in of Ronald Reagan on January 20, 1981, the hostages were freed after 444 days in captivity. In March 1981, Israel signed an agreement with to ship arms to Iran and one shipment left almost immediately after the release of the hostages. The *Washington Post* said that the shipment was authorized by then Secretary of State Alexander Haig and that it was worth $10 to $15 million. The late Alexander Haig denied the story but said, 'I have a sneaking suspicion that someone in the White House winked." A subsequent congressional investigation (chaired by Rep. Hamilton) found no truth to the October Surprise allegations. But the fact that the hostages were freed so soon after Reagan's swearing in ceremony, makes for tantalizing questions.

Chapter 42
Did Hitler Live?

One of the most intriguing mysteries of World War 2 is whether or not Adolf Hitler committed suicide with his new wife, Eva Braun on April 30, 1945 in his *Fuhrerbunker* in battle-scarred Berlin. The story goes that Hitler and Evan Braun took their own lives by taking cyanide pills. After the deed was done, and upon Hitler's previous instructions, their remains were taken up the stairs through the bunker's exit door, dossed with kerosene, and set afire in the Reich Chancellery garden outside the bunker. The remains of the couple remained in different locations until they were found in 1970, where they were dug up, cremated, and their ashes scattered to the winds. There were also theories that Hitler and Eva shot themselves while they were taking their cyanide pills. In 2009, American researchers performed DNA tests on a skull that was recovered in the bunker that was said to have been Hitler's. The tests revealed that the skull was that of a woman under the age of 40 years old. But what if Hitler and Eva survived the battle of Berlin that fateful day? Over the decades researchers have adopted the conclusion that Eva and Hitler escaped war-torn Europe by submarine and wound up in Argentina under the watchful eyes of the pro-German dictator, Juan Peron? The theory that they fled Germany for Argentina was so plausible that after the end of the war, the FBI took steps to verify if that fact were true and they had agents scouring South America taking the testimony of various people who said that had seen Hitler and writing up reports that went to the desk of J. Edgar Hoover. But if they indeed had survived the battle of Berlin and fled to Argentina, how did they do it and did they have help along the way?

On June 6, 1944, the allies launched the most extensive military operation of World War II, the invasion of France on the coast of Normandy. Troops from the United States, England, Canada, and the other allies sent over 150,000 men ashore at dawn for the decisive battle of the war. A few months later, Paris fell and the City of Light was now in allied hands once more. By early 1945,

Poland had fallen to the allies and Soviet forces were preparing to cross the Oder River near Frankfurt which was only 51 miles from Berlin. It was only a matter of time before Hitler's Thousand Year Reich would come tumbling down. On April 18, 1945, allied troops captured 325,000 German soldiers from Army Group B that left Berlin wide-open. By April 11, 1945, the Americans crossed the Elbe River, only 62 miles from Berlin. Soon, Soviet forces were on the outskirts of the city, shelling Berlin, in the last acts of the war. In his bunker, Adolf Hitler decided to make his last stand and vowed not to be taken alive. When Field Marshall Herman Goring who was head of the Luftwaffe heard from sources that Hitler was planning to take his own life, he sent a telegram to Hitler asking if he could be appointed to take over the leadership of the Third Reich in the event of Hitler's death. Martin Bormann, Hitler's trusted ally in the Nazi leadership, convinced Hitler that Goering's actions were treasonous and Hitler relieved Goering of all his duties and ordered his arrest. To make matters worse for Hitler, Heinrich Himmler offered to surrender his army to the western allies but the offer was turned down. A raging Hitler, seeing treason all around him, ordered Himmler's arrest. By the end of April 1945, Soviet troops were in Berlin, destroying whatever was in their way. They were now near Hitler's *Fuhrerbunker,* and it was only a matter of time before Hitler's headquarters would be fond and overrun.

In his bunker, Hitler and Eva Braun were married on the night of April 29, 1945, only hours before the end came. With Russian soldiers now only 1,600 feet from the bunker, Hitler and Eva went into Hitler's personal study and committed suicide. There are various theories as to just how both of them died, be it by shooting themselves or taking cyanide. Some people in the bunker heard shots and minutes later, Hitler's valet, Heinz Lange, along with Martin Bormann, entered the room and found the two lifeless bodies. Lang said he smelled the taste of burnt almonds which was common in death by hydrogen cyanide. Another version of the events of that night came from Hitler's adjunct, Otto Gunsche who said he saw both Hitler and Eva with blood dripping from their heads, victims of self-inflicted gunshot wounds. The bodies were then taken outside behind the Reich Chancellery where they were doused with oil and set afire. In the aftermath of Hitler's death, Admiral Karl Donitz was appointed as Hitler's successor and he saw the final end to Germany's long war. Hostilities came to an end on May 8, 1945.

In Russia, Joseph Stalin demanded that Germany surrender unconditionally and asked for confirmation that his old nemesis, Hitler, was indeed dead. On May 2, 1945, the Soviet's captured the Reich Chancellery and when Red Army troops entered the area, they found Hitler and Eva dead. There were reports that an elite team of Russian agents from a secret organization called SMERSH, were given the job of locating Hitler's body. SMERSH agents were then said to have exhumed the charred remains and were taken out of Berlin to the town of Magdeburg where they were buried in an unmarked grave.

In the years after the end of World War II, rumors began to fly that Hitler did not die in his bunker and had somehow managed to escape. Among those who doubted the official story was Thomas Dodd, the chief of the U.S. trial counsel at Nuremberg where captured Nazi leaders were standing trial for war crimes. When asked if he thought Hitler was dead, Dodd said, "No one can say he is dead." Soviet leader Joseph Stalin too had his doubts and when asked by President Truman if he believed Hitler was dead, Stalin replied with one simple word, "No." The British also got into the act and in November 1945, they appointed Dick White, then head of counter-intelligence in the British sector of Berlin (he would later become head of both MI5 and MI6 and would also be investigated as being a possible double agent) to look into the matter. White asked a British agent named Hugh Tervor-Roper to investigate the affair in order to discredit Stalin's claims (In later years, Trevor-Roper would become a highly successful historian and writer of World War II). Another reputable person who had doubts about Hitter's demise was none other than General Dwight Eisenhower who led allied forces at the battle of Normandy (he would later become president of the United States). In reporting done regarding the fate of Hitler, author Jerome Corsi, while doing research at the National Archives for a book on the topic of Hitler's death called *Hunting Hitler: New Scientific Evidence That Hitler Escaped Germany,* Corsi found an article in the U.S. military newspaper *The Stars and Stripes,* dated October 8, 1945, in which General Eisenhower said," There is reason to believe that Hitler may still be alive, according to a remark made by General Eisenhower to Dutch newspapermen. The general's statement reversed his previous opinion that Hitler was dead." In his book, Corsi says that Hitler escaped from Berlin and made his way to Argentina with the assistance of members of U.S. intelligence, then the OSS, Office of Strategic Services headed by William Donovan. He makes the claim that members of the OSS were secretly working with various Nazi leaders during the war and that Allen Dulles who was the agent in charge of the OSS Bern office e helped facilitate Hitler's escape. While there is no concrete proof that Dulles aided Hitler, the fact is that Dulles was secretly communicating with anti-Nazi leaders in Germany who were feeding the OSS vital information on what was going on inside the Third Reich.

If Hitler and his henchman did flee to Argentina or other countries in South and Central America, how did they do it? One way was the so-called Nazi ratlines that facilitated the escape of Nazi war criminals as well as leaders of the Third Reich out of the country. It has been estimated that over nine thousand Nazi war criminals fled to South America after World War 2 ended. Many of these people were Croatians, Ukrainians, Russians and other people who had help via certain members of the Vatican hierarchy to flee war-torn Europe. About 5,000 went to Argentina where they were protected by the Nazi leaning Juan Peron and his wife Eva, while an estimated 1,500 to 2,000 went to Brazil, and up to 500 to 1,000 to Paraguay and Uruguay.

One of the main facilitators of the ratline was a German Bishop named Alois Hudal who was a highly placed priest to the German Catholic community in the Vatican. One of Bishop Hudal's Nazi associates was Martin Bormann, one of Hitler's most trusted advisors. Bishop Hudal was a staunch anti-communist, and a Jesuit trained priest. In 1944, he took control over the Austrian division of the Papal Commission of the Episcopate for German-speaking Catholics in Italy. That same year he took command over of the Austrian division of the Papal Commission of Assistance which was set up to aid displaced persons. Bishops Hudal's PCA would form the backbone of the Nazi ratlines used to aid escaping Nazi leaders. Among those whom Bishop Hudal helped escape Europe were SS lieutenant Franz Stangl, the commanding officer at the Treklinka concentration camp, and Gustav Wagner, the commanding officer at the Sobibor camp. When Stangl reached Rome, Hudal found a safe house for him to stay while he made plans for him to leave the country. He arranged for Stangl to receive a Red Cross passport, along with a Syrian visa. Among the other high level Nazi officials whom Bishop Hudal help flee Europe were Joseph Menglele, a doctor who performed experiments on concentration camp victims, as well as Martin Bormann's aide, Alois Brunner. Brunner was responsible for the running of the Drancy internment camp near Paris. In 1947, Hudal's activities were unearthed by a German-language newspaper called *Passauer Neue Presse,* which accused him of running his ratline organization. Despite his being exposed as aiding escaped Nazi war criminals, the bishop continued his secret work, and in August 1948, he contacted President Peron in Argentina asking for 5,000 Argentine visas for German and Austrian soldiers who requested asylum in other countries.

The destination of the ratline was South America, particularly Argentina, Paraguay, Brazil, Uruguay, and Chile. Other endpoints were the United States, Canada, and the Middle East. There were two main routes out of Europe, the first from Germany to Spain, then on to Argentina, the second from Germany to Rome to Genoa, then South America. According to two authors of a book on the Nazi ratline, John Loftus and Mark Aarons, the major Roman ratline was run by a "small but influential network of Croatian priests, members of the Franciscan order, led by Father Krunoslav Dragonovic. He organized a highly sophisticated chain with headquarters at the San Girolamo Seminary College in Rome, but with links from Austria to the final point in the port of Genoa."

In 2006, records declassified at the National Archives regarding these Nazi war criminals show that the United States was aware of the location of Adolf Eichmann, the mastermind of the "Final Solution," more than two years before his capture by Israeli agents in Argentina where Eichmann had been living for years. According to the documents, in 1958, the West German intelligence service told the CIA that Eichmann was living in Argentina under the alias Ricardo Clemens, despite years-long denials from the Argentine government that Eichmann was living in that country. One of the reasons that West Germany did not want to see Eichmann arrested was because they were concerned what he would say about a man named Hans Globke, who was Chancellor Konrad Adenauer's national security adviser. Globke had served in the Jewish Affairs department of the Nazi government in World War II and was involved in writing laws designed to remove Jews from German society. The records said that, "The CIA, which worked closely with Globke, assisted the West Germans in protecting him from Eichmann." In 1960, in an elaborate undercover operation inside Argentina, Eichmann was captured by Israeli agents and smuggle back to Israel on board an El Al flight.

The case that Adolf Hitler and Eva Braun escaped Berlin and made their way to Argentina was spelled out in very controversial book called *Grey Wolf: The Escape of Adolf Hitler* (Sterling, New York, 2011), by Simon Dunstan and Gerrard Williams. The authors write that Hitler had a double who looked just like him, a man maned Gustav Weber and that it was Weber who was inside the bunker in Berlin on the night that Hitler committed suicide. They write that Weber was shot at close range in the bunker by Heinrich "Gestapo" Muller, and that Eva Braun too had a double (who was not identified) and that she also was killed by poison. They also said that two of Hitler's most trusted aides, Martin Bormann and Heinrich Muller, also made their way to Argentina with Hitler and Eva, in an elaborate escape plan by both sea and air.

According to the scenario posited by authors Dunstan and Williams, Hitler's party took off by plane from an airstrip called Rechlin on April 28, 1945, sixty-three miles from Berlin. The Rechlin base was the Luftwaffe's main base that tested new aircraft. It was the home of a secret air unit called KG 200 that was a special-operations unit of the German air force. The captain of the plane was Peter Baumgart who held the rank parallel to that of an SS Captain. He was a South African with British citizenship who left that country for Germany and renounced his citizenship to join the Luftwaffe. His orders were to fly the plane and its secret passengers to an airfield at Tonder in Denmark, near the Elder River. He and his passengers landed at Tender one day later. After he shut down all the engines, Captain Baumgart stood on the tarmac and saw who the passengers were-Adolf Hitler, Eva Braun, and a German general named Roemer and his wife. Captain Baumgart told a court in 1947 that Hitler gave him 20,000 German marks for his efforts. After the party disembarked, Captain Baumgart flew back to Germany. He told the court that had no idea whom he was taking to Denmark and seeing Hitler coming off the plane was something he'd never expected. After the war he was sent back to Warsaw where he stood trial on charges of being an SS member.

Another person who saw Hitler at the Tonder airfield was Frierich von Angelorty-Mackensen, a twenty-four year old wounded SS lieutenant who was being given medical treatment at the airfield. At the base hospital, Hitler spoke to Lt. Mackensen and told him that Admiral Karl Donitz would now be the supreme commander of German forces and that he'd surrender to the allied powers but not to the Soviet Union.

The next leg of the flight took Hitler and his friends (now piloted by a different air crew) to Travemunde on the German coast northeast of Lubeck.

Hitler's next stop was to a Spanish military base at Reus, in the Canary Islands. The German's had constructed a fortified military base there and it was the home of many U-boats that prowled the Atlantic in search of allied ships. The name of the place where Hitler stayed was called Villa Winter which was built in 1943 under the supervision of senior Nazi agents. The man who was responsible for the ultimate construction of the base was Gustav Winter, a German engineer and a senior Abwehr agent who was stationed in the Canary Islands. The island where Winter built his base was called Jandia and was comprised of 44,500 acres of desert like land which was bought via a Spanish front company, Dehesa de Jandia SA. The Villa Winter was a place where the Germans could communicate with their U-boat fleet using a highly sophisticated communications set up. In October 1944, German activities in Spain got the attention of Walter Winchell, a highly read columnist in the United States and a close, personal friend of J. Edgar Hoover. Winchell wrote in one of his columns that, "Hitler has been building air bases in Spain since 1939.Work was supervised by German Army engineers done by Franco's political prisoners who worked at bayonet point, and that Spanish islands off the coast of Villa Garcia were cleared of their civilian population last year. Landing fields, advance Luftwaffe, and three whole regiments of Nazi flyers took over the islands." He also said that there were two major Nazi bases on Gran Garcia, an air base and sub base. All this information was passed on to the FBI which began an intensive investigation of Nazi military bases in the Spanish held territories.

It was from Villa Winter that Hitler and his party now boarded a Nazi U boat called 518 for the dangerous trans-Atlantic trip to their final destination, Argentina. The voyage took fifty-nine days and the U-518 traveled 5,300 miles, under hot, deplorable conditions. They landed in Patagonia which was a safe haven for German immigrants who fled Europe. In Patagonia, German was the language of record and it was protected by the government of Argentina which was a friend of Germany's during the war.

Hitler's U-518 was not the only German U-boat to make shore in that particular region of Argentina. The German U-boat U-880 under the command of SS General Hermann Fegelein arrived off the Argentine coast on the night of July 22-23, 1945, five days before Hitler's U-518 arrived. U-880 was supposed to have off loaded a huge number of supplies for Hitler's use which was transferred to a tug boat. One safely on land, the U-880 was scuttled. Two Nazi submarine's, the U-880 and the U-1235 were spotted along the coast of Argentina near the seaside resort of Mar de Plata about two months after the war ended. There were even unverified reports that the Germans had built a sub base in the Gulf of San Matias and its remains may still be there today.

Hitler was supposed to have found refuge with an old family friend by the name of Walter and Ida Eichhorn of La Falda, Argentina, near the town of Cordoba. The Eichhorn's were German immigrants to Argentina and were friends of Hitler's since he started his Nazi Socialist Party in the early 1930s. They funded his new movement and Hitler was forever in their debt. Whenever the Eichhorn's were in Germany, they stayed at the same residence as Hitler.

One young girl who stayed at the Eichhorn residence at La Falda, was Catalina Gamero. It seems that she suffered a variety of malidies and her parents sent her to live with the couple to recuperate. As Catalina Gamero grew healthier, she took on responsibilities at La Falda, and one day in 1949, she was told that an important visitor was coming to stay with them. Catalina was told to prepare his room and food. That important person, according to Catalina was Adolf

Hitler whom she immediately recognized.

Another person who saw Hitler in Argentina was Mafalda Falcon who was a German nurse during World War II that was run by the Red Cross. While working in a field hospital one day while tending to wounded German soldiers, Adolf Hitler came to visit the wounded men. Falcon did not talk to Hitler but she recognized him nevertheless. After the war ended, Falcon and her husband moved to Patagonia in Argentina where she returned to nursing. While she was working in a hospital in the town of Comodoro Rivadavia, on the Atlantic Coast, she treated a former German soldier who had been sent there for further treatment. One day, three German men came to visit the soldier. One of the men whom she saw that day was Adolf Hitler. [5]

In the United States, reports began circulating in the press that Hitler might have arrived safely in Argentina. On July 18, 1945, an article was published by the Associated Press by writer Vincent De Pascal under the headline "Gov't Probes Rumor Hitler in Argentina." The article went on to say that the U.S. State Department was checking a rumor that Hitler and Eva Braun were hiding in Argentina and asked the U.S. embassy in Buenos Aires to check out the story which appeared in the *Chicago Times*. De Pascal wrote that, "He was virtually certain that Hitler and the woman he is supposed to have married in Berlin's last days are on an immense, German-owned estate in Patagonia. The pair reportedly landed on a lonely shore, from a German submarine which supposedly returned to surrender to the allies."

On September 17, 1945, a memo was sent from the American embassy in London, describing the details of Hitler's landing in Argentina and his relationship with the Eichhorn's. The information was obtained from the War Room through an unnamed OSS representative. Part of the memo says, "If the Fuehrer should at any time get into difficult ties he could always find a safe retreat at LA FALDA where they had already made the necessary preparations."

Another memo from the FBI dated November 23, 1945, goes deeper into the Eichhorn-Hitler relationship. The heading was called: Subject-Hitler Hideout in Argentina-Security Matter." The

[5] Condon, Christopher, *Did Hitler Escaped to South America,* LewRockwell. com, June 21, 2014.

Bureau is in receipt from the Strategic Services Unit of the War Department dated October 23, 1945 concerning the possibility of a "Hitler Hideout" in Argentina. One, Mrs. Eichhorn reported to be a reputable member of Argentine society and the proprietor of the largest spa hotel in La Falda, Argentina, recently made the following observations. That even before the Nazi Party was founded, she made available to Goebbels her entire bank account which, at the time, amounted approximately to thirty thousand marks, which money was to be used for propaganda purposes."

The FBI made another inquiry about the possibility that Hitler landed in Argentina in a long report from the Bureau in Buenos Aires in August 1945. Part of it reads as follows:

> Report Hitler in Argentina. Data available this office contained in report of special Agent [deleted] July 18 entitled Surrender of German sub U-530, Mar del Plata. Concerning rumor re-landing San Julian, Argentina. There now reports he discovered two sets of footprints in one direction only from high water mark then across sand flats to shore proper near San Julian. At point where footprints ended, tire marks found. Indications car had been turned at right angle to shore. Footprints have been made about June 25.While flats covered with floodwaters as area frozen this time of year. Efforts being made to trace car. Inquiries continuing at Veronica.[6]

Whether or not Adolf Hitler escaped to Argentina, the OSS and the FBI had enough plausible leads to follow up on that possibility. When a number of FBI files from the 1940s were declassified many years later, they wrote of the possibility that if Germany lost the war, that Hitler would try and find refuge in South America, i.e., the Eichhorn's. This was such a hot topic that the FBI only closed down its 700-page file on Hitler until 1970.

These reports of Hitler living in Argentina after the war ended should not be taken lightly, as history always has room to fool us in more ways than one.

---

[6] Dunstan, Simon and William, Gerrard, *Grey Wolf: The Escape of Adolf Hitler,* Sterling, New York, 2011, Page 225.

Chapter 43
The FBI and the "Phoenix Memo"

The hot desert of Arizona was not only the home of thousands of retired snow-belt refugees seeking to avoid the cold eastern winters, but the location of a growing Muslim community in the United States. In the events leading up to 9-11, the Phoenix connection would become a huge intelligence blunder for the FBI when it was leanred that a number of 9-11 hijackers were taking flying lessons in Arizona flight schools. As early as 1996, the FBI came across a source in Tucson who had a pipeline not only to militant groups in the Middle East but also Arab men they suspected of taking flying lesson in the area who might be up to no good.

One of the hijackers on 9-11, Hani Hanjour moved to Arizona in the early 1990s and spent much of the decade in the state. The FBI had no idea that he was in Arizona since he had not committed any crime and Al Qaeda was not on their radar at that time. It is reported however that one FBI informant said of Hanjour that "they knew everything about the guy." The first time that the FBI received hard evidence that some radical Muslims were living in Arizona came from one of its agents, James Hauswirth who told his bosses that a group of "heavy duty associates" of al Qaeda leader Sheik Omar Abdul-Rahman had arrived in the state after the 1993 WTC attack. These unidentified men were in Arizona to train someone as a suicide bomber. This person was an FBI informant. The Bureau found out about this incident and ordered one of its agents, Ken Williams, who would later write the famous "Phoenix Memo" to higher ups in the FBI, telling them of the many Muslim men who were taking flying lessons in the area, to monitor the goings on. The Bureau watched as the informant was taken to a deserted area where he is taught how to use explosives. During this test run, a device is planted under a test car but if fails to explode. After this incident, the FBI basically decided not to take any more action regarding these radical Muslims because they viewed them as a low priority. Agent Hauswirth would later explain this reasoning because, "the drug war was the big thing back then, and terrorism was way on the back burner."

The FBI's informer in the car incident was an American convert to Islam, Harry Ellen. Ellen lived in Phoenix in 1994 when he first came in contact with the FBI. Ellen also went by the name of Abu Yusef, and in time he set up a benevolent foundation called al-Sadaqa which aided the poor Palestinians living under Israeli rule. During the 1990s, Harry Ellen came to the West Bank four times, bringing doctors to aid the sick, and even arranged a truce between a number of the various Palestinian groups who were vying for control over anti-Israeli policies. Over time, Ellen made contact with representatives of Yasir Arafat and his PLO.

Back in the United States, the FBI was well aware of Harry Ellen and they decided to make him an asset. They even went so far as to funnel thousands of dollars to Ellen's charity that would then be passed on to the radical terrorist group Hamas which would be used for anti-Israeli operations. Ellen gave permission to the Bureau to bug his home, car, even his foundation in order to gain intelligence on these radical groups. The FBI agent who ran Ellen during this period was Ken Williams, who would later become part of the pre 9-11 story. In the summer of 2001, agent Williams wrote a memo to FBI headquarters warning them that Arab men were taking flight training in U.S. schools.

In October 1996, Ellen told Williams that he had been in contact with a suspicious Algerian pilot who was then training other Middle Eastern men to fly. He later said of this man, "My comment to Williams was that it would be pitiful if the bad guys were able to gain this kind of access to airplanes, flight training and crop dusters. You really ought to look at this. It is an interesting mix of people." He also told Williams to "be very concerned about air schools." Apparently nothing more was done regarding the mysterious Algerian man and Williams told Ellen to "leave it alone." The identity of the Algerian pilot was Lofti Raissi, Rassi was taken into custody in Great Britain but after being questioned by British authorities, was let go. Ellen said that he was asked by Agent Williams to keep an eye out for strange Arab men taking flying lessons and he complied with that request.

Giving testimony before a court case in 2001, Ellen said that,

"Williams wanted the transfer of American funds to some of the terrorist groups for violent purposes." At a time when the U.S. intelligence community had few assets on the ground who were able to infiltrate Arafat's PLO, Agent Williams decided to remove Ellen from further duty. The reason for agent William's decision to pull Ellen out of his orbit was that Ellen was having an affair with a Chinese woman named Joanna Xie whom the Bureau believed was a spy. Whatever grounds Williams had for removing Harry Ellen as a bureau asset also took out a perfect "mole," one that could report on the goings on of Hamas and other radical Middle Eastern terrorist groups.

The identities of these Middle Eastern men who were believed to be taking flying lessons in Arizona five years before 9-11 is a troubling fact indeed. What *is* known is that Hani Hanjour, the suicide hijacker who flew his plane into the Pentagon on 9-11, attended a flight school in Phoenix between January and March 2001. The warning given by Harry Ellen to the FBI five years before 9-11, was yet another missed opportunity on the long road to disaster.

As mentioned before, the Phoenix area rivaled New York as the new hotbed of Islamic militancy in the late 1990s. From the Harry Ellen incident, the FBI leanred that a number of unidentified Arab men were hanging around flight schools in the area. By 1999, new information came to the attention of the FBI concerning another group of possible terrorists who were planning to come to the United States for possible flying lessons. While the FBI did not know the identities of these people, it was felt that it had enough information to warrant an investigation. The FBI's Counter-terrorism Unit in Washington ordered 24 field officers to look into the matter.

In Phoenix, FBI agent Ken Williams was put on alert. Despite these warnings it seems that no organized effort to look for these potential terrorists took place, and in November 2000, FBI headquarters sent a memo to its field offices saying that they had uncovered no leads regarding the recruitment of men taking flying lessons.

In September 1999, FBI agents from their Oklahoma City office arrived at the Airman Flight School in Norman, Oklahoma looking into the backgrounds of Ihab Ali, who once worked as bin Laden's personal pilot. Ali took lessons at the Airman School in 1993 and was later identified as an unidentified conspirator in the Embassy Bombing in Kenya in 1998. FBI agents arrested Ali in Florida in May 1999. It would later be determined that two of the 9-11 hijackers, Mohammed Atta and Marwan Alshehhi traveled to the Airman School but decided not to enroll (they would instead, take lessons in Florida).

By the summer of 2000, the threat level coming from bin Laden's Al Qaeda had reached a fever pitch. Communications intercepts from the NSA, National Security Agency, whose job it is to monitor global communications, began picking up large scale "chatter" suggesting an attack would take place outside the borders of the U.S., although a strike against the U.S. was not discounted.

In Phoenix, FBI Agent Ken Williams was becoming extremely worried regarding the activities of certain Middle Eastern men in his area who he suspected of possible terrorist ties. Agent Williams did not know the identities of these men but he soon learned that a number of these men were taking classes in airport management. He also noticed a contingent of men with possible terrorist ties attending the Embry-Riddle Aeronautical University in Prescott, Arizona. He believed that these men could possibly be terrorists-in-training for some unknown group. On July 10, 2011, Ken Williams wrote up his concerns and sent what is now known as the "Phoenix Memo" to his bosses in Washington.

Ken Williams' Phoenix Memo was sent to the FBI's Radical Fundamentalist Unit in Washington, D.C. that was the repository of all information regarding bin Laden and Al Qaeda. The gist of the memo was his fears that radical Islamic men were taking flight lessons at various schools across the United States for possible use in terrorist attacks. Williams asked the FBI to mount a nation-wide review of Arab-American students going to flight schools in the United States. Nothing of the sort took place because there were too few FBI agents to visit and survey all flight schools in the country.

Agent William's heavily redacted July 10, 2001 memo contains the following information:

Synopsis: UBL (bin Laden) supporters attending civil aviation universities/colleges in the State of Arizona.

Title: Zakaria Mustapha Soubra: IT-OTHER (Islamic Army of the Caucasus-) Soubra was Lebanese attending flight training in Prescott, Arizona who served in Chechnya, and was associated with Al Qaeda.

Details: The purpose of this communication is to advise the Bureau and New York of the possibility of a coordinated effort by Usama bin Laden (UBL) to send students to the United States to attend civil aviation universities and colleges. Phoenix had observed an inordinate number of individuals of investigative nature who are attending or who have attended civil aviation universities and colleges in the state of Arizona.

Despite the specificity of his warnings, the FBI gave his memo the classification of "routine," not "urgent." After 9-11, when Williams's Phoenix Memo hit the fan, the top leaders of the FBI said that Williams' warnings were only speculative and that he had no concrete data that would have prevented the attacks.

Testifying before the Congressional Committee investigating the 9-11 attacks, Ken Williams talked about these events prior to 9-11.

"I cannot sit here and testify today that al Qaeda established a network there. However, looking at things historically in Arizona we have seen persons go to school at the University of Arizona in Tucson who subsequently went on to become rather important figures in the al Qaeda organization. Prior to al Qaeda even coming into existence these people were living and going to school in Arizona. As al Qaeda formed and took off and became operational, we've seen these people travel back into the State of Arizona. We've seen Osama bin Laden send people to Tucson to purchase an airplane for him and it's my opinion that's not a coincidence. These people don't continue to come back to Arizona because they like the sunshine or they like the state. I believe that something was established there and I think it's been there for a long time. We're working very hard to identify that structure. So

I cannot say with a degree of certainty that one is in place there. But, that's my investigative theory."

Another Bureau informant who provided information on certain Islamic men in Arizona was an American Caucasian Muslim named Aukal Collins who informed to the FBI on 9-11 hijacker Hani Hanjour. The FBI paid Collins to monitor the Islamic and Arab communities in Phoenix between 1996 and 1999. He told the Bureau that he was a "casual acquaintance" of Hanjour while the latter was taking flying lessons. He told the FBI that he was concerned about Hanjour because he was associated with a large number of other Arab men taking flying lessons. The FBI later denied that they got any useful information from Collins. Collins was sure that the FBI knew of what these Arab men were doing in Arizona and said regarding the events prior to 9-11. "Just think about it-how could a group of people plan such a big operation full of so many logistics and probably countless e-mails, encrypted or not, and phone calls and messages? And you're telling me that, through all of that, that the CIA never caught wind of it."?

The timing of Ken William's Phoenix Memo came at a time when the FBI was cutting back the number of agents assigned to counter-terrorist duties. In the Phoenix office at the time of William's memo out of total of 230 agents, only 8 focused on domestic and foreign terrorist cases.

The FBI did however ask the CIA to do a name search on a number of those pointed out by Williams but did not give a copy of the memo to the Agency for their perusal. The CIA's response did not match any known person on the list with names in their database.

Despite the fact that Ken Williams had uncovered a possible terrorist cell in Phoenix whose members were interested in taking flying lessons, the top management at FBI HQ did not take his warnings seriously.

In a statement on September 14, 2001, three days after the attacks, FBI Director Robert Muller, who had only been in office for a month, made a most startling observation, despite what William had previously written. "The tragedies quite clearly astonish and shock me and the country. The fact that there were a number of individuals that happened to have received training in flight schools here is *news, quite obviously* (italics by author). If we had understood that to be the case, we would have-perhaps one could have averted this. But beyond that, I and I think everyone else is just astonished at the extent of the tragedy." Three days later, Director Muller made another extraordinary comment. "There were no warning signs that I'm aware of that would indicate this type of operation in the country."

Perhaps Director Muller would not have made that comment if he had been informed of the boast by Abdul Hakim Murad about using hijacked airliners to fly into the CIA, and other high-profile buildings in the U.S.

Unknown to Director Muller and almost everyone else in the U.S. intelligence community, was that one of the 9-11 hijackers Hani Hanjour, took flying lessons in 1997 in Arizona and got his private license. In April 1999, he was able to get his commercial pilots certification and then promptly returned to Saudi Arabia.

On August 6, 2001, one month before Ken Williams' memo was sent to FBI HQ, President George W. Bush received the now famous Presidential Daily Brief (PDB) warning of possible al Qaeda attacks on the United States. A part of the PDB which was titled. "Bin Laden Determined To Strike in US," refers to unusual activities in the United States on the part of al Qaeda. The important portion of the August 6, 2001 PDB that backs up Williams' memo is as follows;

"We have not been able to corroborate some of the more sensational threat reporting, such as that from a (deleted) service in 1998 saying that Bin Laden wanted to hijack a US aircraft to gain the release of "Blind Sheik Umar Abd al-Rahman and other US-held extremists. Nevertheless, FBI information since that time indicates patterns of suspicious activity in this country consistent with preparations for hijackings or other types of attacks, including recent surveillance of federal buildings in New York. The FBI is conducting approximately 70 full field investigations throughout the US that it considers Bin Laden-related. CIA and the FBI are investigating a call to our Embassy in UAE in May saying a group of Bin Laden supporters in the US planning attacks with explosives."

Speaking of Ken Williams, his fellow FBI colleague Ronald

Myers had nothing but praise for his friend. "He is one of the sharpest agents I have ever met. Anyone in FBI management who wouldn't take what Ken Williams said seriously is a fool. It's been my past experienced that the smallest bit of information that comes in could turn out to be the most important piece of the investigation."

It's too bad that the top officials at FBI HQ did not learn of Williams' memo while there was still time to act on it.

Chapter 44
Who Killed Bobby?

$1$968 was the year that rocked America. As the calendar turned on December 31, 1967, and Americans celebrated across the nation, no one knew the explosive nature of what lay ahead. By the time the year ended riots would be common place around the nation, anti-Vietnam War protests would take place on both college campuses and in the streets of cities, large and small, and two beloved political/religious leaders, Senator Robert Kennedy and the Rev. Martin Luther King would be gunned down by assassins, not two months apart. In the political arena, a little known senator from Minnesota, Eugene McCarthy, would challenge the sitting president of the United States, Lyndon Johnson in the New Hampshire primary and almost beat him. The result of the primary election would drive Lyndon Johnson from seeking another term as president of the United States and alter the political climate in the nation on its end. If one had a crystal ball, would things have been different?

As the election year of 1968 began, Senator Robert Kennedy of New York had a decision to make; whether or not to challenge President Johnson for the Democratic presidential nomination or wait four more years. It had been five years since his brother's assassination and that half-decade, many things has changed for Robert Kennedy. Right after the assassination in Dallas, Robert Kennedy secluded himself in his grief, trying to make sense of what happened to his brother Jack. In public, he accepted the results of the Warren Commission that concluded that there was no conspiracy in his brother's murder, but privately he had second thoughts. He believed that John Kennedy had been killed either by some-one in the mob, i.e., Jimmy Hoffa, his old nemesis from his days as a racket buster on the McClellan Committee or that it had something to do with the anti-Castro forces that had been unleashed with the CIA-Mafia plots to kill Castro of Cuba. On the night of the assassination in Dallas, RFK called CIA Director John McCone and asked him point-blank if anyone in the agency was responsible for his brother's assassination. McCone told him no. In the wake of Dallas, Bobby sent his own private investigator to Dallas to look into the assassination. What he found made him more certain that the Warren Commission had been wrong in its lone gunman scenario.

After President Johnson won the Democratic nomination in 1964, he chose Senator Hubert Humphrey of Minnesota as his running mate, leaving Bobby out in the cold. That same year, he decided to run for U.S. Senator from New York amid cries from some who called him a carpetbagger. In Johnson's landslide election, Robert Kennedy defeated the incumbent Republican Senator, Kenneth Keating by a huge margin. It is not a stretch of the imagination to say that Robert Kennedy won his seat on the coattails of the memory of his late brother. The American people were still in shock over the tragic death of their young president and Bobby rode the wave of emotion right into the Senate.

In the Senate, Robert Kennedy was a champion of the poor and disaffected in the nation, trying to make right the wrongs he'd seen as he spoke in New York, as well as across the nation. As the sixties wore on, and the war in Vietnam seemed to go on endlessly, Robert Kennedy had a change of heart as far as the conduct of the war was concerned. He originally supported LBJ's Vietnam policy but as casualties continued to mount and no exit was in site, he began to demand a different approach to the war (He also had to live with the fact that his brother had sent up to 10,000 "advisors" to South Vietnam to help drive out the Viet Cong, only to see a coup to remove the corrupt Nu brothers who ruled the south from power).

Johnson saw Kennedy's new anti-war stance to be treason on his part and Johnson fired back at Kennedy on all fronts. When Senator McCarthy came within a hairs breath of defeating President Johnson in the New Hampshire primary by running on an anti-war platform, the writing was on the wall as far as Johnson was concerned. On March 31, 1968, President Johnson went on national television and made a startling announcement. He said that he was suspending bombing raids against North Vietnam and said he would seek a negotiated settlement to the war. Before his speech was over, he dropped the biggest political bombshell of the year. He said he would not seek another term as president of the United States, saying he wanted to devote the rest of his term to ending the war. LBJ's decision rocked the nation and sent the Democrats in a panic as to who would be the new standard bearer for the election. In the wake of Johnson's decision not to run, Bobby Kennedy made the most important decision of his political career; he'd announce his candidacy for president of the United States, vowing to end the war and bring the nation back together. Only sixteen hours before Kennedy's call for ending the war in Vietnam, Americans were horrified to learn that our soldiers commanded by Lt. William Calley had massacred over five hundred South Vietnamese civilians in a tiny hamlet that would forever be associated with the tragedy of the war in Vietnam called My Lai.

Kennedy's candidacy was not welcome news to many in the country who saw in him a ruthless politician out to regain his brother's fallen dynasty. One of these men was former Vice President Richard Nixon who saw Bobby's announcement on television. Nixon would later say of Kennedy's entry into the race that, "We've just seen some very terrible forces unleased. Something bad is going to come out of this. God knows where this is going to end." Nixon had no idea just how ironic his words actually meant.

Kennedy immediately went on the stump, entering as many primaries as he could. In 1968 there were not as many primaries as there are today and the nomination for president was still in the hands of many of top political bosses in the nation. Kennedy was seen as a usurper by many in the anti-war community who based their hopes on Senator Eugene McCarthy whose showing in the New Hampshire primary forced out LBJ. Before his assassination in June, Kennedy won four primaries; Indiana, South Dakota, Nebraska, and California. He received 2, 305, 148 votes in the primaries and by winning the California primary, he had amassed 393 delegate votes as compared to 561 for Vice President Hubert Humphrey and 258 for Senator McCarthy.

On June 4, 1968, Kennedy and his team celebrated his victory in the all-important California primary by beating Senator McCarthy 46 to 42 percent. Before a cheering crowd at the Ambassador

Hotel, Kennedy thanked his supporters and told them that, "It's on to Chicago and let's win there." Kennedy knew that by winning in California, he was in a good position to win the Democratic nomination that summer at the convention in Chicago. As he walked with this entourage into the kitchen pantry surrounded by two friends who served as security guards, Rafer Johnson who was a former Olympic decathlon champion and Roosevelt, "Rosey" Grier, a pro football player, shots rang out and Kennedy was mortally wounded. The shooter was a Palestinian refugee named Sirhan Sirhan who was immediately subdued. Sirhan had .22-pistol and was able to shoot Kennedy many times, while five other people in the immediate vicinity of the incident were also wounded. Kennedy was rushed to a nearby hospital but his wounds were too severe and he died the next day.

Sirhan Sirhan was born in Jerusalem in 1944, and moved with his family to the U.S. at age 12. He was employed at the Santa Anita racetrack until an accident which took place in 1966 sidelined him. Sirhan was a strange individual who was fixated with the study of hypnosis. In the wake of the assassination, many conspiracy theorists believed that Sirhan had been the subject of a possible mind control experiment a.k.a, Frank Olson, because he had no recollection of ever killing Kennedy. When investigators came to his apartment, they found writings in his hand saying "RFK must die" over and over again, as well as "Robert Kennedy must be assassinated, one saying "pay to the order of," and an entry dated May 18 which said, "Robert F. Kennedy must be assassinated before 5 June 68."

From the beginning of the investigation of the Kennedy assassination by Sirhan, investigators from the LAPD who had jurisdiction in the matter, failed to seek down promising leads and when they did, they often times ignored witness testimony to their own ends. If the LADP did not want another Dallas on their hands, they did a pretty sloppy job of it. If Sirhan had a motive to kill Senator Kennedy they could not fine one (just like Oswald in the JFK assassination). Press reports the following day said that his motive was because Kennedy had supported the sale of 50 Phantom jets to Israel and because of the plight of the Palestinian people. But Sirhan had no previous interest in the cause of his fellow Palestinians and he may have made up the Phantom jet story on the spur of the moment. The LAPD investigated the murder for a year and produced a ten-volume report that said that, "Sirhan fired the shots which killed Kennedy and wounded all five others; that his act was premeditated, that he was not under the influence of any drug or intoxicant; that he was legally sane; and that there was no evidence of conspiracy" (think Warren Commission).

The crime scene was ripe with inconsistencies right from the start as investigators tried to find out what really happened. Sirhan's revolver had eight bullets but a total of seven bullets were recovered from the bodies of RFK and the five people who were wounded in the kitchen pantry, and one bullet was somehow lost in the ceiling interspace of the room. However, when police photographers took pictures of the room, it appeared to show several slugs lodged in doorjambs and one eyewitness named Lisa Urso, said she saw "at least four bullet holes in ceiling tiles." This apparent inconsistency was turned aside by the LAPD when they said that some of the bullets did "double duty" by striking more than one person and possibly ricocheting around the room. In this way, the police investigation could stick to the one gun theory instead of two which would have made the assassination a clear conspiracy. In what would prove to be a masterful cover-up or just sheer malfeasance, the LAPD destroyed the bullet riddled woodwork and tiles in the kitchen pantry which would have been critical to any proper investigation of the crime scene.

There were also a lot of inconsistencies between the official verdict coming from the LAPD involving the actual circumstances of the shooting of Senator Kennedy and what the forensic evidence reveals. The LAPD's version said that Senator Kennedy was killed by a lone gunman, Sirhan Sirhan, who fired a gun from a distance, not at point-blank range, in the kitchen pantry of the Ambassador Hotel. At the autopsy the corner found that Kennedy had been shot three times from behind traversing his body at an upward angle, back to front. The corner said that the kill shot came from directly behind the right ear and at point-blank range. At the time of the shooting, Sirhan was never near enough to Kennedy to have fired the fatal shot and "furthermore, shots from the Defendant could not have left a back-to-front bullet path, because Defendant was in front of the victim. Therefore, bullet trajectory would necessarily have been front-to-back." At the crime scene, Sirhan was not at any time close enough to Senator Kennedy to have fired the fatal shot. The Corner determined that the shot that killed him was fired from within one to three inches away from his left ear. All surviving victims never saw Sirhan that close to RFK. The shooter fired at close range and to the right of Kennedy. One of the most important facts is that Sirhan's gun held only eight bullets but somehow fourteen bullets or bullet fragments were found in the pantry, and in the ceiling. Logic would say that if fourteen bullets were found in the room, then that would mean that another shooter was somewhere in the room when the senator was killed.

After the assassination, independent tests were done to find out exactly what happened that night. One of the people who conducted forensic tests was Dr. Robert Joling, J.D. who was also a professor of Medical Law, as well as a judge and lawyer. He, along with a forensic expert named Phil Van Praag, did an in depth study of all the evidence in the case. They concluded that fourteen bullets were fired at the murder scene. Dr. Joling said of his investigation, "It can be established conclusively that Sirhan did not shoot Senator Kennedy. And in fact not only did he not do it; he could not have done it."

During its investigation, the LAPD was not able to determine just where Sirhan was in the six week period before the assassination. He didn't just disappear and they called it his "White Fog" period.

The LAPD started a task force to investigate the assassination called Special Unit Senator (SUS) after Kennedy was killed. "We took him back for more than a year with some intensity"-where he'd been, what he'd been doing, who he'd been seeing. But there was this ten-or twelve week gap, like a blanket of white fog, we could never penetrate, and which Sirhan himself appeared to have a complete amnesia block about," said Bill Jordan, the night watch commander who was Sirhan's first interrogator."[7]

This so-called 'white fog' period led some researchers to conclude that Sirhan might have been brainwashed at some time before the assassination. A test to determine Sirhan's mental

---

7   Belzer, Richard, and Wayne, David, *Dead Wrong*, Sky-horse Publishing, New York, 2012, Page 193.

stability at the time of the shooting was conducted by Chief Psychiatrist Bernard Diamond and he concluded that he had been programmed under hypnosis. Diamond put Sirhan under a trance, gave him a yellow pad to write on, and told him to write something relating to Senator Kennedy. Sirhan wrote, "RFK" many times, as well as "Robert F. Kennedy" and "RFK must die, RFK must die," until he was told to stop. This incident was witnessed by Dr. Seymour Pollack, director of the University of Southern California's Institute of Psychiatry and Law, who represented the district attorney's office. While still in the trance, Dr. Diamond asked Sirhan if he thought he was crazy and he replied by saying, "no, no, no." Is it possible that Sirhan was a victim of some sort of mind control experiment and that he was what was called at the time a perfect "Manchurian Candidate" who was pre-programed to kill Kennedy? Remember, after his arrest, Sirhan had no recollection of the events of that night and did not recall killing Senator Kennedy. As seen in the chapter on Frank Olson, the CIA had a cold war program that used mind control operations on unsuspecting people. Is it possible that Sirhan was part of that program?

Another person whose conclusion did not match that of the official verdict was coroner Tomas Noguchi, whose autopsy report said that Kennedy had been shot "at point blank range." Noguchi told the *Los Angeles Herald Examiner* that unnamed person in authority urged him to perjure himself during Sirhan's trial but he refused to do so. Noguchi said that when he entered the grand jury room to give his testimony, he was approached by an unnamed deputy DA who urged him to revise his estimate of the firing distances from inches to feet. Once again he refused to do so. In another rather unusual incident, when Noguchi took the stand at Sirhan's trial, the defense cut off his testimony regarding the "gory details" of what angle the shots came from or how close the gun was to Kennedy when he was shot.

One of the most important events that possibly led to a conspiracy in the senator's assassination is the so-called woman in the polka dot dress. At least 25 people who were in the Ambassador Hotel that night, saw a woman about 25-years old, wearing a dress with polka dots on it. One of these witnesses was Sandra

Serrano, a co-chair of the Pasadena-Atladena Youth for Kennedy Committee. She told the police that about 11:30 pm, while she was sitting on a stairwell outside the Ambassador Hotel, she saw the above mentioned woman go by, along with two other men. She remained at that location for about a half hour when she heard what she thought were "backfires" coming nearby. Minutes later, she saw the same three people run by yelling, "We shot him!" Serrano asked them who they shot and they replied, "Kennedy." When she later saw a picture of Sirhan, she said that he was the man who ran past her with the woman, just a few minutes earlier. Her incredible story was backed up by an LAPD officer named Paul Scharaga who was told the same story by an elderly couple in the parking lot behind the hotel. Officer Scharaga then issued an all-points bulletin (APB) on the subjects. The girl was described as having dirty blonde hair, well built, with a crooked nose or "funny nose," wearing a white dress with blue or black polkadots. Other witnesses saw the above mentioned girl in the hotel at various times that night. Just as Officer Scharaga was trying to get clarification of what happened, he encountered a 15-or 20-minute radio blackout before the APB could go out. Minutes later a report from the police came out saying, "Disregard that broadcast. We got Rafer Johnson and Jesse Unruh who were right next to him (Kennedy), and they only have one man and don't want them to get anything started on a big conspiracy." Many years later, Officer Scharaga would say that a claim that he was interviewed by members of the Special Unit Senator were wrong. "That report is phony. No one ever interviewed me, and I never retracted my statement from "We shot him" to "they shot him. This is just how things were done. If they couldn't get you to change your story, they'd ignore you. If they couldn't ignore you, they'd discredit you, and if they couldn't do that, they'd just make something up." All these years later, no one has ever identified the woman in the polka-dot dress.

If there was a second gunman in the hotel pantry when Kennedy was killed, one of the prime suspects was a security guard who was stationed in that location, Thane Eugene Cesar. Cesar was standing directly behind and to the right of Kennedy at the time of the shooting and drew his gun when the shots were fired. Cesar said that when the shots were fired he drew his pistol, an H&R 922 and was subsequently knocked to the floor. An acoustic expert by the name of Van Praag tested Cesar's gun and determined that it had been fired that night. Eyewitnesses said that they heard shots being fired from another gun but Cesar denied that he used his weapon that night. One person who was near Kennedy when he was shot was a CBS News employee named Donald Schulman. He told the following story of what he saw." A Caucasian gentleman (Sirhan) stepped out and fired three times, the security guard (Cesar) hit Kennedy all three times. Mr. Kennedy slumped to the floor. They carried him away. The security guard fired back. Brent: I heard about six or seven shots in succession. Is this the security guard firing back? Schulman: Yes, the man who stepped out fired three times at Kennedy, hit him all three times and the security guard then fired back."[8]

A similar story was in the June 6, 1968 issue of a French newspaper called *France Soir,* which said, "A bodyguard of Kennedy drew his gun, firing from the hip, as in a western."

Cesar said that at the time of the shooing of Kennedy, he drew a .38-caliber revolver. At one point he owned an H&R. 22-caliber nine-shot revolver, of the same type that as Sirhan's pistol with the same ammunition. Cesar told the police that he sold the gun (the .22), three months before the assassination. However, a bill of sale said that Cesar sold the gun on September 6, 1968, three months after the assassination. Another fact that puts Cesar very close to Senator Kennedy is when Kennedy fell to the floor, he was clutching Cesar's necktie in his hands.

One man who thinks that there was another person or persons who killed Kennedy is author David Scheim who wrote a book called *Contract on America,* which had been referenced by this author. He says that the Mafia had a hand in the assassination, just as it is possible that they played some role in his brother's death. He writes that Cesar was assigned to guard the Ambassador Hotel on the night of the assassination by Ace Guard Services. However, he was only employed as a temporary employee by Ace, not a regular employee. Scheim quotes author Alex Bottus as saying that, "According to California records, it had been months and

[8] Scheim, David, *Contract On America: The Mafia Murder of President John F. Kennedy,* Shapolsky Books, New York, 1988, Page 291-292.

months since Cesar had worked for Ace." He also says that Cesar was called on at the last minute to relieve a regular employee who couldn't make it. In an interview with author Dan Moldea, who wrote a book on the assassination, Cesar admitted to having been called earlier that day to come to the Ambassador. Author Bottus claimed that Cesar had long ties to organized crime in the U.S. "You have to trace him either through Missouri, Arkansas, and go down like I said into Chula Vista, you get down in University City, you get down into Tijuana, they all know about Cesar. And this guy's got connections like crazy."

Another interesting story about a possibility conspiracy involves a man by the name of Jerry Owens. Owens told authorities after the assassination that he gave Sirhan and another man a lift, and that they went to the Ambassador Hotel to collect $300.00 for a horse he was going to sell to Sirhan. Owen said he met a blonde girl and two other men. Owen's story was not believed by the police, due to his shady background. Two other authors who wrote on the RFK case, Bill Turner and John Christian, interviewed Bill Powers who were the owner of Wild Bill's Stables near where Owens lived. "Powers told him, before the assassination, about a horse trainer named Sirhan, and further that Powers had seen Sirhan in the back seat of Owen's car during a visit where Owen flashed large bills to pay off a *pickup* truck Powers sold him." The connection between Owens and Sirhan is still a mystery and we don't know if there was any sinister connection between them.

A new, and highly controversial angle to the Robert Kennedy assassination is a possible role of the CIA in the senator's murder This new twist in the story was made by filmmaker Shane O'Sullivan who postulated that there were three CIA agents in the Ambassador Hotel the night Kennedy was killed; David Sanchez Morales, George Joannides, and Gordon Campbell. O'Sullivan said he had photographs of men looking exactly like the three men that were taken at the Ambassador Hotel on night of the assassination. The names of all three men are well-known to Kennedy assassination (JFK) researchers and a brief description of them will be put forth in this chapter. Information on these three men came on November 20, 2008, when the BBC program *Newsnight* aired a program alleging that three CIA operatives were caught on camera at the Ambassador Hotel on the night that Bobby died. All three men had one thing in common besides working for the CIA; they all took part in the CIA's secret efforts to kill Castro and worked out of the CIA's secret location in Miami called JMWAVE. Robert Kennedy was put in charge of Operation Mongoose, the Kennedy administration's secret war to oust Castro from power in Cuba and the younger Kennedy ran rough-shod over agency efforts to destabilize the Castro regime.

Gordon Campbell was a sailor and Army captain who served as a contract agent for the CIA and ferried anti-Castro soldiers across the Florida straits to Cuba, according to Rudy Enders who was a retired CIA officer who knew Campbell during those days. O'Sullivan said that Gordon Campbell was the deputy station chief at the CIA's JMWAVE Miami station. However, research by noted Kennedy assassination writes David Talbot and Jefferson Morley have refuted that claim. Both men wrote that Campbell could not have been at the hotel that night because he had passed away in 1962. Both men interviewed Rudy Enders who told them that Campbell had died of an apparent heart attack at the JM/WAVE station in Miami in his presence. O'Sullivan said that someone who looked like Campbell might have taken over his identity as that was commonplace in the CIA.

David Morales was a noted operative at the CIA in the early 1960s and someone not to be trifled with. He had a reputation as a trained killer would be call upon to take on the most dangerous assignments the agency had to offer. In the late 1950s, Morales was sent to the American embassy in Havana where he and David Atlee Phillips worked on the agency's plans of the Bay of Pigs invasion of Cuba, and later was assigned to the Agency's JMWAVE operation in Miami. In between his Cuba digs, he was sent to such international hot spots as Vietnam and Laos where the CIA had numerous covert operations. According to friends of Morales, "It was on these secret assignments in Southeast Asia, that he took on "Executive Action"-assassination assignments for the CIA. Morales's handiwork as far as assassinations for the Agency was concerned, grew as did his reputation. It was reported that he carried out his assignments in such places as Uruguay, Venezuela, among others.

Morales was deeply outraged against the failure of the Bay of Pigs operation and was very vocal in his criticism of President Kennedy's handling of event. In later years, after his death, his attorney, Robert Walton told a bombshell of a story concerning David Morales and a reference to the Kennedy assassination. In a night of heavy drinking and anti-Kennedy bashing, Walton heard Morales say this about the death of JFK. "Well, we took care of that son of a bitch, didn't we?" Morales' statements was overheard by another CIA veteran of the Castro plots, Ruben Carbajal. Carbajal was Morales' boyhood friend and fellow CIA veteran. When asked for his comments regarding Morale's boast concerning the Kennedy assassination, he just nodded his head. When shown pictures of Morales at the Ambassador Hotel, some of his family members said that the man in the photo looked more like a light-skinned African American than a Mexican-America whom Morales was.

George Joannides name has come to certain prominence in the literature of the Kennedy assassination only in the past years. He served as the chief of the CIA's psychological warfare operations in Miami in 1963 and was the agency's paymaster to the DRE, an anti-Castro group that was located in Miami in that time. It was his job to funnel money to the DRE to the tune of $25,000 a month. Unknown to Joannides at that time was that his role as the liaison between the DRE, would put his Cuban beneficiaries in touch with an ex-Marine named Lee Oswald prior to the assassination of the president in November 1963. Along with giving money to the Miami members of the DRE, Joannides also dispensed funds to DRE members in New Orleans. The CIA's relationship with members of the DRE in New Orleans during the summer of 1963 let them have a unique perspective when Oswald tried to make contact with certain members of the DRE that summer. When the Warren Commission was investigating the Kennedy assassination, the CIA failed to inform them of Joannides's relationship with the DRE, nor the fact that he was aware (or should have been aware) that Oswald had been in touch with certain members of the New Orleans groups. After his retirement from the CIA, he was called back to serve as their liaison with the House Select Committee on Assassinations which was investigating the murders of both

JFK and Martin Luther King. Joannides stalled his work with the committee, only giving them as little information from the CIA files on Oswald as he deemed necessary (Most of the files on George Joannides are still locked up in the CIA's vaults, despite many lawsuits to free them to the public).

When shown pictures of Joannides at the Ambassador Hotel, many people who knew him, including relatives and fellow CIA agents, said it was not the same man. One of these people was Helen Charles, a close friend who knew him in Washington for many years. Others who saw the BBC released picture and who said it was not Joannides, were Mitzi Natsios, the widow of a Greek-American CIA colleague who knew him, along with Timothy Kalaris, a nephew of Joannides.[9]

But why would the agency want to kill Robert Kennedy? He told a number of his closest associates that the only way to re-open the investigation of his brother's death was to gain the presidency, despite his public approval of the findings of the Warren Commission. Once in the White House, Bobby would be unhindered in finding out exactly what the true circumstances were in Jack's assassination. Some members of the CIA might have wanted to keep any possible association with the various intelligence agencies of the U.S. with Oswald a secret. There is more than circumstantial evidence to prove that Oswald was involved in some way either with the CIA, the FBI, or Naval Intelligence prior to his "defection" to the Soviet Union and upon his return to the United States. His time in New Orleans in the summer of 1963 where he associated with both pro and anti-Castro elements is one example of his intelligence ties.

The investigation did not look into the possibility that Kennedy's old nemesis, Jimmy Hoffa, the powerful president of the Teamsters Union, and a man who hated both John and Robert Kennedy with a passion, might have been behind the assassination. RFK and Hoffa began their feud a decade earlier when they butted heads at the rackets committee headed by Senator John McClellan. Over the years, Hoffa had made various threats on Kennedy's life which got back to Bobby. One of these threats took place in August 1962 when Hoffa was talking to his friend Ed Partin at Teamsters

[9] Morley, Jefferson and Talbot, David, *The BBC's Flawed RFK Story,* Mary Ferrell web site.

headquarters. Hoffa then jumped to his feet and asked Partin if he knew anything about plastic explosives. "I've got to do something about that son a bitch Bobby Kennedy. He's got to go." Hoffa then told Partin that he was considering two ways to kill Bobby: one was to use a long range rifle as he drove in his car, and the other was to tourch his home in Virginia. Hoffa told Partin that he knew the layout of Kennedy's home and had no compunction of killing him anyway he could. For his part, Kennedy only had protection from the U.S. Marshalls who guarded his home. He really did not want security but had to bow to the reality that people were out to get him and that he had to keep his family secure.

The RFK assassination inquiry was one that was botched from the start. Numerous eye-witnesses were badgered to change their story, important evidence, i.e. the ceiling tiles that contained bullet fragments at the shooting scene were discarded, allegations that the Greek tycoon, Aristotle Onassis (who later married Jackie Kennedy) might have had a hand in the senator's assassination (see the section in *Dead Wrong* by Richard Belzer and David Wayne), the possibility that Sirhan was under some sort of hypnotherapy at the time Kennedy was killed, and a lack of interest in the possibility that a second gunman was in the kitchen pantry, i.e., Thane Cesar, were never really investigated.

History of full of "what if's," so we'll never know how the story would have been changed if Robert Kennedy had not been assassinated in Los Angeles that fateful night. Would he have gotten the Democratic presidential nomination? Would he have ended the Vietnam War? Would Watergate never have happened? As we contemplate the mysteries surrounding the Senator's assassination, those are things that history cannot reveal.

Chapter 45
What the Warren Commission Got Wrong

The thing I am concerned about, and so is (Deputy Attorney General Nicholas) Katzenbach, is having something issued so we can convince the public that Oswald is the real assassin. Mr. Katzenbach thinks that the President might appoint a Presidential Commission of three outstanding citizens to make a determination.
—Memo from FBI Director J. Edgar Hoover to Walter Jenkins, aide to President Lyndon Johnson, dated November 24, 1963.

It was less than a week after the events in Dealey Plaza when FBI Director J. Edgar Hoover sent this memo to Deputy Attorney General Nicholas Katzenbach. The president's alleged assassin, Lee Harvey Oswald, a 24-year old former Marine, a "defector" to the Soviet Union, a loner with pro-Castro, pro-Marxist leanings, had been brutally murdered in the basement of the Dallas Police Department as he was being transferred to await trial for the murders of the president and of DPD Officer J. D.Tippit. Oswald was shot by a petty gangster with ties to the mob, the owner of a local strip tease club, a man with ties to the FBI, and interests in Cuba, Jack Rubenstein, a.k.a, Jack Ruby.

Oswald was dead, there could be no trial, case closed. But even as Jack Kennedy was laid to rest next to his two young children, questions as to the actual events of November 22, 1963, were beginning to percolate. In Europe, where conspiracies were as common as the change of governments, there was talk of a right wing conspiracy in the assassination of the president.

In the United States, the FBI was given the responsibility of "investigating" the events surrounding the assassination, despite ample warnings by informants in the weeks prior to November 22, 1963, that a plot was afoot.

As far as J. Edgar Hoover was concerned, they had got their man and no further investigation was required. On November 25, the new president, Lyndon Johnson, ordered the FBI Director to prepare a detailed report on the circumstances surrounding Kennedy's death. That same day, Nick Katzenbach wrote a letter to another of Johnson's aides, Bill Moyers going over the details of any assassination study:

1. *It is important that all of the facts surrounding President Kennedy's assassination be made public in a way which will satisfy people in the United States and abroad. That all the facts have been told and that a statement to this effect be made now.*
2. *The public must be satisfied that Oswald was assassin; that he did not have confederates who are still at large, that the evidence was such that he would have been convicted at trial.*
3. *Speculation about Oswald's motivation ought to be cut off, and we should have some basis for rebutting thought that this is a Communist conspiracy.*

At the time of the president's assassination, it was not a federal crime to kill a president of the United States. Since the murder took place in Texas, the inquiry into the event was relegated to a state level. The Lone Star state of Texas would carry out the investigation into John Kennedy's murder, and to that effect, on November 25, Texas Attorney General Waggoner Carr announced his intention to begin an official inquiry.

Not to be outdone by local officials, the United States Congress began plans to start its own investigation into the assassination. On November 26, Republican Senator Everett Dirksen reported that a special Senate panel was being given permission to start up its own plans to look into the events of Kennedy's murder. Heading the special panel was Senator James Eastland who was the chairman of the Judiciary Committee. The House of Representatives too began to make rumblings concerning their part in any investigation.

While Robert Kennedy was not consulted, nor wanted to be, other top men in the new administration began behind the scenes planning to get an official government sponsored inquiry on track. Among those who convinced President Johnson to stop a Texas examination, fearing that it would only convince the public that there was a home grown cover-up taking place, were Yale

Professor Eugene Rostow, Secretary of State Dean Rusk, and the influential columnist Joseph Alsop.

Not known at that time, but revealed years later, was the fact that LBJ himself had doubts about Oswald's true role in the assassination. Johnson would later say that Oswald was a very mysterious young man, who may have had help in planning the murder. Johnson was also very concerned about the possible parts of foreign powers in Kennedy's death, particularly the possible roles of either Cuba or Russia. It was Cuba and the regime of Fidel Castro that most troubled LBJ. Johnson feared that if it were revealed that either country had a hand in Kennedy's assassination, the consequences of such a bombshell might lead to nuclear war.

To finally end such fears and speculation, Johnson, on November 29, 1963, one week after JFK's death, officially appointed a body of distinguished men to officially investigate the death of the president. After all, 54% of the American public, one week after the event, believed that Oswald did not act alone. Thus, the "Warren Commission" was born to seek the "truth" into the crime of the century. But what it turned out to be was not the "truth," nor the full cover-up that conspiracy theorists said it was, but an investigation that was flawed from the start, of men lacking the deep instinct to look wherever the facts could have led them, conspicuously not requiring the testimony of witnesses who were on hand at Dealey Plaza, not pursuing leads and information that would have materially changed the conclusion they reached only nine months later.

The man whom Johnson wanted to chair the committee was Chief Justice of the Supreme Court, Earl Warren. When Johnson breached the possibility of Warren chairing the commission, he wanted no part in it. Warren said it would be unethical for him to chair the commission because he was part of the judicial branch of government and any findings by the committee might be tainted. However, Johnson turned on the charm that had won over so many political opponents over the years and Warren finally accepted the post. Johnson told Warren that public trust in the government's possible role in the assassination was beginning to gel, that there were hints of foreign conspiracies behind the assassination, and more important, that Johnson needed Warren's ok and he would not take no for an answer.

After Johnson's call to the Chief Justice, he issued Executive Order 11, 130 creating the seven-member "Warren Commission."

The members of the Warren Commission were:

*Representative Hale Boggs (D. La.)

*Senator John Sherman Cooper (R. Ky).

*Allan Dulles, who was the former director of the CIA from Eisenhower to Kennedy. JFK fired Dulles after the failure of the Bay of Pigs invasion and he oversaw the secret assassination plans against Fidel Castro of Cuba but never informed the other members of the panel of that important fact.

* Rep. Gerald Ford (R. Michigan). Ford was has been called the "FBI's spy" on the Warren Commission due to his close association with the Bureau during the commission's work. Ford also had a close relationship with the CIA and would later write a book on Lee Harvey Oswald. He was a firm believer in the lone gunman theory and would defend his views the rest of his life. He became president of the United States after the resignation of President Nixon.

* John J. McCloy. He had a long career in government and during World War 2, he served as an assistant secretary of war, was president of the World Bank, and was high commissioner of Germany after the war ended.

*Richard Russell (D. Ga). At the time of the assassination, Russell served as the chairman of the important Senate Armed Services Committee, was much admired by the Pentagon brass, and had wide contacts in the domestic arms industry. By 1970, long after the commission had gone out of business, Russell criticized the Warren Report by saying that he believed that a criminal conspiracy had organized Kennedy's death. Senator Russell was not the only panel member to have certain reservations regarding the final conclusions of the report. Congressman Boggs (who later died under mysterious circustances in a plane crash in the mountains of Alaska), and Senator Cooper only reluctantly signed the final report and would in time, come to criticize parts of the Warren Report.

As the commission got down to work, they divided themselves into working groups. The areas they were to investigate were the following:

*Area One-The Basic Facts of the Assassination.
*Area Two-The Identity of the Assassin.
* Area Three-Oswald's Background.
*Area Four-Possible Conspiratorial Relationships.
*Area Five-Oswald's Death
* Area Six-Presidential Protection.

The commission members themselves did not do much of the day-to-day work and failed to attend a majority of the interviews and meetings. They hired as their General Counsel, attorney, J. Lee Rankin whose views on the assassination mirrored those of J. Edgar Hoover. In fact, the commission relied almost entirely at first on the investigative talents (or lack thereof) of the FBI. Hoover did not want to see the commission established, believing that 1) Oswald was the lone assassin of President Kennedy and 2) if the commission looked deep enough they might uncover the bureau's bumbling in its clandestine contacts with Oswald in Dallas in the months prior to the assassination.

Even more critical of the FBI's pre-assassination performance concerns an FBI teletype dated November 17, 1963 that went out to all FBI offices around the nation. The memo directed all of the bureau's CI's (confidential informants) to find out if a militant revolutionary group had any plans to assassinate the president during his trip to Texas. What is most interesting is that FBI headquarters received no replies to its nation-wide inquiries.

The Warren Commission members were left out in the cold as far as many leads relating to the assassination were concerned and a number of people who might have been prime suspects. Through various bureau informers, Hoover had received reports that Louisianan crime boss Carlos Marcello, had made threats against President Kennedy. Instead of alerting the Secret Service, he filed the information away.

The Warren panel relied heavily in the early stages of their investigation on the work of the FBI after the murder of Oswald by Jack Ruby. It is not too much to say that the FBI under J. Edgar Hoover believed that Oswald was the lone assassin and wanted to make that fact stick as far as the American people were concerned. Hoover had a deep hatred toward both Kennedy brothers and the feeling was mutual. Hoover tried with all his power to hamper the initial investigation of the assassination by the Warren Commission. He bombarded the commission members with daily reports saying that Oswald was the lone assassin, he had no confederates lurking behind hidden walls, and that the FBI was on the case. But for all of Hoover's cajoling, and to the commissioner's credit, they refused to take Hoover's bait. The told the esteemed director that they believed there were serious flaws in the FBI's initial investigation and that their work would continue. But Hoover wasn't done. He had the FBI prepare a 5-volume report on the assassination in December 1963, two months before the first witness appeared before the committee. The account found that Lee Harvey Oswald acted alone in killing the president. In order to cement his power base over the Warren panel, Hoover ordered his agents to dig up dirt, political and otherwise, on the 7 Warren Commissioners. On May 8, 1964, in a probable quid pro quo, President Johnson appointed his good friend J. Edgar Hoover, Director of the FBI for life.

The Warren Commission members had to fend off rumors that Oswald was a possible paid agent of the FBI. If this allegation were proved to be true, then the reputation of the FBI would be in jeopardy, with untold consequences for the nation. Upon hearing the rumors of Oswald being in league with the bureau, Rep. Boggs said that the "implications of this are fantastic." In the end, the WC did not even try to pursue any further into this potentially explosive allegation and let the matter rest.

After what turned out to be a rather selective and perfunctory investigation in which many eyewitnesses to the tragedy in Dealey Plaza who saw or heard events that were in disagreement with the official findings were not called to testify, where eyewitness testimony before the panel members were changed or whose testimony was influenced by counsel, the WC issued its final report on September 24, 1964, two months before the presidential election. The final verdict is as follows. 1) Lee Harvey Oswald alone killed President Kennedy, 2) Lee Harvey Oswald alone killed DPD Officer J.D. Tippit, 3) Jack Ruby alone killed Lee Oswald and neither man had prior knowledge of each other, 4) There was no evidence of a conspiracy, either foreign domestic in the assassination of JFK, 5) All of the shots came from the sixth floor of the Texas School Depository building and came from the rifle owned by Oswald, 6)

Three shots, and three shots only, were fired at President Kennedy, one of which hit him in the neck, which then passed through the body of Gov. John Connolly, the second shot missed the car completely, and the third, and fatal shot, hit the president in the back of the head, killing him instantly. And that was that (There was never any consideration, despite eyewitnesses on the ground in Dealey Plaza that shots came from the front, on the so-called Grassy Knoll).

The WC never looked into the fact that a bullet fragment struck a bystander James Teague who was standing near the triple overpass (the concrete where the bullet landed was taken apart by Dallas city workers but nothing was ever done to thoroughly examine it). What about the dozens of people who saw and heard shots being fired from the area of the grassy knoll? What about Gordon Arnold, a young soldier on leave from the army who was standing near the knoll and felt a bullet come flying over his shoulder? Arnold was never deposed by the commission. And what about the mysterious Secret Servicemen who were deployed around the knoll when all of the real Secret Service Agents were nowhere near Dealey Plaza at the time of the assassination? A young couple named Bill and Gayle Newman and their children were at Dealey Plaza when the shots were fired. They saw the president being hit and in the commotion after the assassination, the saw people running up the knoll toward the railroad tracks. "Bill noticed some men running in the same direction who were carrying what he thinks might have been Thompson submachine guns." He believed the men were either FBI or Secret Service and ran toward the rail yards, not the Texas School Book Depository where Oswald was supposed to have fired the fatal shots. In interviews with a local television station they said they believed the shots came from the top of the hill (grassy knoll). While they were interviewed by the FBI and the sheriff's office, they were never deposed by the WC.

The WC also failed to look into a possible bombshell regarding Oswald and the FBI in the months before the assassination. FBI agent James Hosty who was assigned to the Dallas FBI office, twice visited to the home of Oswald's wife Marina to see if he could locate her husband. Lee was then living in the Dallas suburb of Irving and Marina did not know where he was. When Lee found out of Hosty's visit he went to the Dallas FBI office looking for

Hosty. Hosty was not there when Lee arrived and he left a note for him. The note is supposed to have said, "If you have anything you want to learn about me, come talk to me directly. If you don't cease bothering my wife, I will take appropriate action and report this to the proper authorities." After Oswald was killed, Gordon Shanklin, Hosty's boss, ordered him to destroy the note that Oswald had brought to him. No one really knows what was in the note Oswald left for Hosty but it was evidence that could have been materially useful in any subsequent investigation (Some conspiracy theorists believe that Oswald was handing Hosty a note telling of a possible assassination attempt on JFK's life).

The question of conspiracy was debated among the commission's lawyers one afternoon in early 1964 over lunch in Washington's Monocle restaurant near Capitol Hill. The talk among the attorney's, including David Slawson, who was given the job of searching for foreign plots, lead to a disturbing scenario. What if it were learned that the Russians were responsible for the crime? Would it lead to World War II1? What if it were proven that LBJ had a hand in the plot, (as many conspiracy theorists today believe?) Could they say so in public?

J. Lee Rankin, the Chief Counsel to the committee, had instructed his staff attorney's to look into the role of the CIA in the assassination. As it turned out, they didn't have to look far. The CIA only gave the WC that much information as they were willing to give up, and nothing more. For example, they CIA never reported to the Commission the fact that a high-ranking Soviet defector from the KGB, Yuri Nosenko, had come over to the west shortly after the assassination. It seems that Nosenko had been in charge of the Oswald file while he was in the Soviet Union for over two years. Furthermore, said Nosenko, the Russians had no operational interest in Oswald and that he was not working in any capacity for the Russians at the time of Kennedy's death. That fact would absolve the Russians in any way in Kennedy's murder, leaving the Hoover-Warren theory complete: Oswald was the lone assassin.

The CIA also did not reveal one vitally important fact to the WC that could have eventually changed the entire outcome of the investigation; the fact that the CIA and the American Mafia had put out a contract on the life of Fidel Castro of Cuba and had been trying to kill him, one way or another, since 1959. WC member Allan Dulles was head of the CIA when the secret assassination plots, codenamed ZR/RIFLE/Executive Action, were taking place. Dulles never informed his fellow commissioners of this blockbuster fact and its release to the public would not take place until the mid-1970s when the House Select Committee on Assassinations (HSCA), began their own investigation into the deaths of Martin Luther King and JFK. Dulles also coached certain individuals on how to handle the commission's questions. On April 11, 1964, he met with Agent David Murphy to talk about the allegations that Oswald might have been a CIA or KGB recruit. "Dulles advised Murphy to deny both charges categorically in order to end the debate quickly." When the HSCA ended its inquiry they came to the conclusion that the assassination was "probably the result of a conspiracy" although they did not name the suspected plotters. Richard Helms, who would later become CIA Director and Allan Dulles, knew of the CIA plots to kill Castro, but they successfully kept this knowledge from the full WC, including John McCone, the DCI at the time of the Kennedy murder until August 1963.

The single most controversial fact that the WC concluded was the single bullet theory proposed by Consul Arlen Specter (later a U.S. Senator from Pennsylvania). Specter said that the president and Governor Connally were struck by one bullet "the magic bullet" that caused the wounds (besides the head shot to Kennedy). The magic bullet was supposed to have struck both men mutual times, yet came out in a pristine fashion in Parkland Hospital. Doctors at Parkland Hospital where Kennedy and Connally were taken after being shot described the President's wounds as coming from the front (grassy knoll area), at variance with the report of the doctors who did the autopsy on the president at Bethesda Naval Hospital. The single bullet theory was the most important piece of evidence provided by the WC in explaining what happened to Kennedy but over the past 50 years, photographic and other evidence (the Zapruder film-Abraham Zapruder was the man who filmed the assassination in Dealey Plaza at it took place) have contradicted that theory.

One of the areas where the WC members had a problem solving was Oswald's brief trip to Mexico City in September 1963, two months prior to the assassination. Oswald's Mexico City trip is still one of the unsolved parts of the Kennedy assassination saga that is still being hotly debated even to this day. The Commissioners were highly troubled when it was leanred that Oswald visited both the Cuban and Soviet embassies in Mexico City and met with a high-ranking Soviet official named Valerie Kostikov who was a KGB agent who specialized in assassinations. Ostensibly, Oswald was in Mexico City to get a visa to travel back to Russia via Cuba.

In an rather unusual move, the CIA secretly flew two Commission staffers, David Slawson and William Coleman to Mexico City where they were given a secret briefing from agency officials on information supplied by a CIA asset stationed in the Cuban Embassy. One of the areas that the Commission had a hard time reconciling was the possibility that Oswald, or someone impersonating him, was in Mexico City at the same time. Oswald's trip to Mexico City is filled with confusion and the overt hint of an intelligence operation, i.e., the possibility that the CIA was trying to infiltrate the FPCC (Fair Play For Cuba Committee) in which Oswald was the only member in New Orleans in the summer of 1963. Both men urged the Commission to investigate the anti-Castro angle in the assassination and believed that Oswald was being set up in some way as a tool of these militant groups to take the fall as the pro-Castro "nut" who killed the president. But the Commission ran out of time before they could pursue this matter (Oswald's Mexico trip will be detailed in a later chapter).

Another part of the assassination story that the WC did not look into was the possible Mafia connection to the president's death. The Mafia had ample reason to kill the president because of many factors. The first was the Mafioso's' belief that JFK had reneged on his father's promise that Jack would go easy on them if he was elected, the second was Robert Kennedy's open war on the godfathers, especially Sam Giancana, Jimmy Hoffa, and Santos Trafficante, all of whom, in one way or another, took part in the CIA's plots to kill Castro. Santo Trafficante told a friend that the president would not be re-elected because he was going to be "hit." He later clarified that statement by saying that he would be "hit" by an avalanche of votes in the upcoming election. One theory in the presidents' murder is that the mob was really after Robert

Kennedy but realized that if they killed him, his brother would unleash the full weight of law enforcement upon them. It was then they decided to kill the president instead. With Jack gone, Bobby would be without power, unable to continue his war against them (that's exactly what happened). Carlos Marcello was quoted as saying in regard to the Kennedy brothers, "If you want to kill a dog, you don't cut off the tail. You cut off the head." The HSCA concluded that the Mafia had the means, motive, and opportunity to kill the president but it too did not name names.

One of the most puzzling incidents in the Kennedy assassination saga which the WC had to deal with is the so-called "Odio incident" which took place in late September 1963. Sylvia Odio came from a large, and influential Cuban family. Her father was Amador Odio, one of the wealthiest men in Cuba, who owned the largest trucking business on the island. When Castro first came to power, the Odio's were supporters of his revolution, but as time went on, began to sour on how Castro was running the country.

In September 1963, Amador Odio's daughters Sylvia and Annie were living in Dallas and were highly involved in the anti-Castro cause in that city. On September 26, 1963, an event happened that would change her life and add doubt to the story of Lee Harvey Oswald. On that day, there men came unannounced to her house. Sylvia nor her sisters had ever met the three men before and were wary of letting them in. Instead, Sylvia put up the latch on the door and talked to the men in that fashion. According to Odio, two of the men were Cuban looking, one with more pronounced Mexican heritage than the other. The third man was an American who did not say very much. He was introduced to them as "Leon Oswald."

One of her guests had introduced himself as "Leopoldo" and the other man as "Angel." They said they were friends of Manolo Ray, a leader in the anti-Castro opposition and that they also knew her father. They said that "Leon Oswald' was interested in joining their cause but did not elaborate further and that they said that they had just arrived from New Orleans. Leopoldo told Sylvia that they wanted her to help them to obtain funds for Ray's JURE's activities and asked if she would write a letter to certain anti-Castro businessmen who might be able to help. Sylvia was noncommittal and asked the men to leave. That, as far as Sylvia

Odio was concerned, was the end of the matter.

A few days later, Sylvia received a call from Leopoldo, one of the two Latin men who had been in her house. He began by telling something that Sylvia did not expect to hear. He said that "the American (Leon Oswald) had been in the Marine Corps and was an excellent shot. He said that "the American had said that the Cubans don't have any guts because President Kennedy should have been assassinated after the Bay of Pigs, and some Cubans should have done that because he was the one that was holding the freedom of Cuba actually." Leopoldo said that Leon was "loco," kind of nuts." He asked her if Oswald had made an impression on her and she said that she never gave it much thought.

Both sisters forgot about the incident until the afternoon of November 22, 1963 when they saw the picture of the man accused of killing JFK. Upon seeing the man's photo they tried hard to remember where they had seen him. They both remembered that the man in question was "Leon Oswald," the man who had been to their home, two months before. Upon seeing Oswald's picture, Sylvia had a fainting spell and wound up in the hospital overnight.

Shortly thereafter, Sylvia was interviewed by the FBI who relayed the results of their interview to the Warren Commission. The Commission found their allegations about an Oswald visit credible. However, if what Sylvia and Sarita said were true, the whole basis of the Warren Report of Oswald being the lone assassin, acting alone, might have been put in jeopardy.

The FBI first interviewed Sylvia on December 12, 1963, In August 1964, shortly before the final draft of the report was issued, J. Lee Rankin, the Chief Counsel of the Commission sent the following note to J. Edgar Hoover. "It is a matter of some importance that Mrs. Odio's allegations either be proved or disapproved." The incident did not go away when Staff Counsel Wesley Liebler wrote in a memo, "There are problems. Odio may well be right. The Commission will look bad if it turns out that she is. There is no need to look foolish by grasping at straws to avoid admitting that there is a problem."

And what was the problem? The WC said that at the time of the Odio visit, the real Oswald was in New Orleans on September 26 or 27, 1963, and furthermore, that Oswald was then en-route by bus to

Mexico at that same time. Therefore, Oswald could not have been at the Odio residence as she claimed. But if the real Oswald was at her home in the company of anti-Castro people, then a possible connection between Oswald and anti-Castro, possibly anti-Kennedy people could be ascertained.

The Warren Commission had a real quandary on their hands. Should they take Sylvia Odio at her word and put a huge monkey wrench into the report? Or should they ignore it as being took uncomfortable and let it drop? In the end, the Commission said that while the FBI report was not complete, they concluded that Oswald was not at Mrs. Odio's home in September 1963.

Since its 888-page report was issued in September 1963, the debate concerning the relevancy of the WC has been debated in both print and on television by scholars and laymen alike. One staff member of the WC, David Slawson has recently given an interview to writer and author Philip Shenon describing his doubts about the work done on the commission. At age 33, David Slawson was a young lawyer who, with his fellow colleagues, was given the assignment of looking into whether or not there was a foreign conspiracy in the Kennedy assassination. When the Warren Commission ended its work, Slawson said he was "convinced then-that we had it right," referring to the conclusion that Oswald was the lone assassin. Now, fifty years later, David Slawson is having some real doubts that the WC got its conclusion right. Slawson told author Shenon in an interview with *Politico* Magazine the he was a victim of a "massive cover-up by government officials who wanted to hide the fact that, had they simply acted on the evidence in front of them in November 1963, the assassination, might have been prevented. It's amazing-it's terrible-to discover all of this 50 years late."

Continuing with his interview with Philip Shenon, Slawson elaborated further regarding his doubts about the WC's conclusions regarding whether or not Oswald acted alone. "I now know that Oswald was almost certainly not a lone wolf," said the elderly Slawson.

While Slawson still believes that there was not a far-fetched conspiracy involving the Cubans or the Mafia, he believes that Oswald was the lone gunman in Dealey Plaza. His new concern deals with Oswald's trip to Mexico City in September 1963 where he encountered both Russian and Cuban diplomats. Of Oswald's

Mexico City trip, Slawson said, "I think it's very likely that people in Mexico encouraged him to do this. And if they later came to the United States, they could have been prosecuted under American law as accessories in the conspiracy." [1]

Slawson told Shenon that the CIA knew about Oswald's meetings with the Cubans and the Soviets but hid the evidence from the WC. "It never occurred to me until you interviewed me and I read your book (*A Cruel and Shocking Act: The Secret History of the Kennedy Assassination),* that the commission's investigation had been blocked like this. It never occurred to me that the CIA and other agencies tried to sabotage us like this." In his article for *Politico,* Mr. Shenon wrote the following regarding his talks with Mr. Slawson, "Slawson grew more and more alarmed to discover how much evidence about the assassination-and specifically, about Oswald and the possibility of a conspiracy-had not been shared with him in 1964."

The Warren Commission was a house of cards ready to fall from the start. The two intelligence services who were asked to investigate the circumstances of the president's murder, the CIA and the FBI, were compromised from the start. They gave the WC only the information they wanted them to receive and nothing more. From the beginning of their "investigation," they were compromised in their final verdict of Oswald being the lone gunman, no conspiracy, case closed. The WC members worked in a period of high cold war tensions between the Soviet Union and the United States and the new president, Lyndon Johnson badgered Chief Justice Warren into heading the panel by telling him a nuclear war between the Russians and the U.S. might be unleashed if it were learned that the Russians may have been involved in the president's death. The safety of the nation, President Johnson believed, outweighed the "truth" in the probe of the president's assassination. If the WC had done even a partially thorough job in sifting the evidence in the case, and if they had access to information that were relevant to solving the assassination instead of browbeating and intimidating witnesses, throwing out evidence that they did want to look at, and beginning with a preconceived conclusion that Oswald was guilty, then the verdict might have been different.

[1] Shenon, Philip, *What the Warren Commission Didn't Know,*www. Politico. com/magazine, February 2, 2015.

Chapter 46
The Reasons for the
Watergate Break-In

On the night of June 17, 1972, five well-dressed men in suits with walki-talkies and electronic equipment were arrested in the headquarters of the Democratic National Committee (DNC) located at 2650 Virginia Avenue, NW, in Washington, D.C., the Watergate building by local police after a security guard noticed that a piece of tape had been put over an unlocked door at the offices of Lawrence O'Brien, the DNC's Chairman. The five men arrested were Eugenio Martinez, Virgilio Gonzalez, Frank Sturgis, Bernard Barker, and James McCord. The other two men to be taken into custody were G. Gordon Liddy and E. Howard Hunt. Both Hunt and Liddy had extensive ties to both the CIA and the FBI.

What started out as a routine break-in turned out to be the tip of a very huge iceberg that finally toppled the presidency of Richard Nixon and forced his impeachment and resignation from office.

In the forty plus years since the break-in at the Watergate Hotel, there has been a parlor game to figure out why the burglars broke into the office of DNC Chairman Lawrence O'Brian and who ordered it. Did President Nixon himself order the break-in or did someone else in the White House, acting alone or on orders from others in the Executive Branch order the operation? That answer is still not known, but in the intervening time, both new evidence and old theories still exist.

Little remembered in the saga of Watergate is the fact that the same crew who were captured on June 17, 1972 made an earlier break-in at DNC's headquarters a few weeks back where they installed listening devices and were not caught. The second break-in was to remove these listening devices installed earlier. One of the theories about what the listening devices were for centered on a purported DNC personnel arranging "dates" for VIP's with a call girl ring. The call girl ring was supposed to have been operating near the Watergate complex and was being monitored by the burglar's. There is no evidence to link the break-in with any call girl ring, no matter how salacious such a thing might be.

The first President Nixon himself learned of the break-in was while he was vacationing at his Florida home from his morning paper. He said of his reaction thusly:

> It sounded preposterous. Cubans in surgical gloves bugging the DNC! I dismissed it as some sort of prank. The whole thing made so little sense. Why, I wondered. Why then? Why in such a blundering way. Anyone who knew anything about politics would know that a national committee headquarters was a useless place to go for inside information on a presidential campaign. The whole thing was so senseless and bungled that it almost looked like some kind of set up.

On June 23, Nixon received more information on the break-in from his chief of staff, H.R. Haldeman in an oval office meeting. Haldeman said, "The FBI agents who are working the case, at this point, feel that's what it is. This is CIA."

Nixon, who was no fan of the CIA (and vice versa), had a good idea what Haldeman was talking about. Nixon was the case officer for the aborted Bay of Pigs invasion of Cuba in April 1961 and had been one of its chief proponents. He knew where Haldeman was going and said this in reply:

> Of course, this is a, this is a Howard Hunt operation and exposure of it will uncover a lot
> of things. You open that scab there's a hell of a lot of things we just feel that it would
> be very detrimental to have this thing go any further. This involves these Cubans, Hunt
> and a lot of hanky-panky that we have nothing to do with ourselves. This will open the
> whole Bay of Pigs thing."

But was the Watergate break-in a CIA run operation from the

start? In a June 23 meeting with Haldeman and Nixon which would later become known as the "smoking gun" tape, Haldeman told the president," the way to handle this now is to have (CIA) deputy director Walters call (FBI) interim director Pat Gray and just say, Stay the hell out of this. This is ah, business here we don't want to go any further on it." Nixon agreed. In that same conversation, Haldeman told Nixon that Pat Gray, the acting FBI director, had spoken to Richard Helms and said, "I think we've run right into the middle of a CIA operation."

At the time of their arrests, James McCord and Eugenio Martinez had the closest ties to the CIA. McCord was a veteran of the CIA's Bay of Pigs invasion in 1961, and served as the security chief at Langley. After leaving the CIA, he opened up a private security firm in Maryland. During the hearing process, McCord blew the lid on the rest of his team, saying that the White House was perpetrating a cover up of the Watergate affair, after some of the burglars demanded hush money be paid to them in order to ensure their silence.

Eugenio Martinez was a contract employee at the CIA and at the time of his arrest, was still on the Agency payroll. After the burglary, the CIA lied when it said that Martinez had no relationship with the agency.

Nixon had known of Howard Hunt right from the moment he heard his named mentioned as one of the burglars. Hunt was a long-standing veteran of the CIA dating back to the 1950s and early 1960s and was involved in many covert operations including missions in Cuba and other Central American nations. As far as Nixon was concerned, the fact that three men with CIA ties were arrested in the Watergate must have sent him into a panic. What were these CIA men doing and were they ordered to do so and why?

It was obvious that Nixon was paranoid about getting the CIA off the case and he ordered Haldeman and John Ehrlichman to meet with both Helms and General Walters—the CIA Deputy Director. Helms told Nixon's men that the CIA was not connected to the break-in in any way, and that none of the suspects had worked for the CIA in the last two years. That statement was a lie, as Martinez was a current CIA contract officer.

Under huge pressure from the Nixon White House, Richard Helms reluctantly agreed to Nixon's demand that the CIA pressure the FBI into not going ahead with its investigation of the Watergate burglars. Before leaving the meeting, an infuriated Helms lashed out at Haldeman by saying, "the Bay of Pigs had nothing to do with this. I have no concern about the Bay of Pigs."

Newly released documents from the National Archives obtained by the author describe Howard Hunt's connections to the Cubans involved in the Watergate affair. This document has its origins form the records of the Rockefeller Commission. The memo is from David Bellin to William Schwarzer entitled, "Cuba and the Politicization of Police Power." It reads in part:

"A Cuban explained how the Cubans got into Watergate. They were used to us. When Bay of Pigs operatives like Hunt moved over to Watergate they sent for their old Cubanos. They work like the Mafia. When they want to issue an anti-Communist contract or what looks like an anti-Communist contract, they contact us. We're reliable, intelligent, professional. And we're learning to keep our mouths shut. We're learning to live with this. And we fear the Company. We know the Company. The Company can drop a word and change your life. You don't get a job or a loan for your business, or you're in trouble with police or immigration. To such people the bizarre requirements of Watergate seemed not unusual but SOP."

Nixon used the CIA for his own advantage by ordering Richard Helms to provide him with CIA cables on the Bay of Pigs, information on the assassination of President Diem of South Vietnam, and a file on the Dominican dictator Rafael Trujillo. Nixon wanted these files to find any derogatory information on the Kennedy administrations relationship with these events.

When Richard Helms first learned of the Watergate break-in, he ordered that no one in the agency have anything to do with either McCord or Hunt who obviously had CIA ties. Helms was worried that any leaks of the agency's past relationship with Hunt or McCord would send the wrong message that the CIA had something to do with the break-in. As far as Helms was concerned, Hunt worked for CREEP (Committee to Re-elect the President) at the White House and it was there that any blame would lie. He tasked William Colby to head the agency's investigation of the affair.

The FBI had by now traced the money found on the Watergate burglars to a Mexican bank, and also to a man named Kenneth Dahlberg. The total amount of the cash was $114,000, which had originally been in the possession of CREEP. The money directly tied the Nixon administration to the burglars. The $114,000 had originally been deposited in a Miami bank which was controlled by Bernard Barker, one of the men arrested at the Watergate complex. Unfortunately for the burglars, the money on their persons was sequentially numbered dollar bills which was part of CREEP's operating funds for the break-in. The FBI traced the bills back to Barker, and subsequently, to the offices of CREEP.

By now, Helms decided to end any further CIA involvement in what he obviously saw as a White House cover up and pressed Gray to investigate those already under arrest, and keep out of any further CIA internal business. Helms asked Walters to write to Gray saying, "We still adhere to the request that they (the FBI) confine themselves to the personalities already or directly under suspicion and that they desist from expanding this investigation into other areas which may well, eventually, ran afoul of our operations."

To all concerned, the cover up was now unraveling fast. Patrick Gray wrote President Nixon a letter saying, "Mr. President, there's something I want to speak to you about. Dick Walters and I feel that people on your staff are trying to mortally wound you by using the CIA and FBI and by confusing the questions of CIA interest in, or not in, people the FBI wishes to interview."

Nixon shocked Gray when he said, "You just continue your aggressive and thorough investigation." By this order to Gray, Nixon was sealing his own fate, whether he knew it or not.

There is no smoking gun placing the CIA front and center as the originator of the Watergate break-in, but the fact that McCord, Hunt, and Martinez, all agency employees had an hand in the operation, and that Nixon knew all about Hunt and his secret machinations, makes any Agency participation in the break-in plausible.

In the story of the Watergate scandal, two names are synonymous with the history of the affair; Bob Woodward and Carl Bernstein, two, young *Washington Post* reporters who broke the story over a long period of time. It seems however, that Bob Woodward may have had some relationship with US intelligence, possibly with the CIA. Woodward had no reporting experience when he came to the *Post* but was given a try out due to his recommendations, possibly by someone in the White House.

While in the Navy, Woodward served on the USS *Wright,* specializing in communications, including the White House. Woodward worked on the staff of Admiral Thomas Moorer, chief of Naval Operations and was a briefer in the White House. It was at one of these sessions that Woodward met Mark Felt, later to become famous as "Deep Throat," Woodward's highly placed source in the FBI. Felt would steer both Woodward and Bernstein throughout their Watergate investigation.

A possible CIA connection to Woodward was reported by Nixon's aide Charles Colson when he met with Senator Howard Baker and Fred Thompson, a staff investigator. Colson said that, "The CIA has been unable to determine whether Bob Woodward was employed by the agency. The agency claims to be having difficulty checking personnel files. Thompson says he believes the delay merely means that they don't want to admit that Woodward was in the agency. Thompson wrote a lengthy memo to Baker last week complaining about the CIA's non-cooperation, the fact that they were supplying material piecemeal and had been very uncooperative. The memo went into the CIA relationship with the press, specifically Colby with a cover note and within a matter of a few hours; Woodward called Baker and was incensed over the memo. It had been immediately leaked to him."[2]

Whether or not Woodward had intelligence connections or not, he was given the assignment of covering the arraignment of the Watergate burglars and, along with Carl Bernstein, now had the story of their lives, one which would make them household names.

H.R. Haldeman, one of Nixon's top aides who were deeply immersed in the story of Watergate said of why the break-in took place, "To this day I still don't know why that was done. And I don't know anybody who does. Why they would hit the National

[2] Baker, Russ, *Family of Secrets,* Bloomsbury Press, New York, 2009, Page 207.

Headquarters is beyond me, because nobody in that place knows anything anyway." But if Haldeman did not have any idea who ordered the break-in, another Nixon White House aide said he did. That man was Jeb Stewart Magruder who was sent by Haldeman from the White House to become Attorney General John Mitchell's deputy at the Committee to Re-elect the president. While in that job, he served as a link between Mitchell and Haldeman and some of the members of the break-in team like Hunt and Liddy.

In 1987, Magruder was on a panel discussion at Hofstra University talking about the scandal. He was interviewed by J. Anthony Lukas who wrote a book on the scandal and wrote an article summing up his thesis on Magruder. Lewis wrote that the reason for the break-in was in order to find out if Lawrence O'Brien, the chairman of the DNC, knew about any hanky punky between Nixon and Howard Hughes, particularly $100,000 that was passed from Hughes to Nixon's friend and associate, Charles, "Bebe" Rebozo, some of which was given as personal gifts to Nixon and his wife Pat. Another part of the plan was to dig up dirt on any possible relationship between Nixon and Hughes. Magruder told Lewis regarding his theory of the break-in, "I want to be honest about what happened here. It was a planned burglary. As far as I know the primary purpose of the break-in was to deal with the information that has been referred to about Howard Hughes and Larry O'Brien and what that meant as far as the cash that had supposedly been given to Bebe Rebozo and spent later by the President possibly." He also confirmed that the secondary motive was to keep the Hughes-Rebozo connection "under wraps" during the 1972 presidential election. He also said that during a meeting with John Mitchell, his special assistant Frederick LaRue at Key Biscayne, Florida on March 30, 1972, said the matter was discussed on the phone with Bob Haldeman.

Nixon was paranoid when it came to Howard Hughes and their secret relationship. In 1957, Hughes "loaned" Nixon's brother Donald $250,000 so Donald could save his floundering food business where he sold "Nixonburgers" (the loan was never paid back). Hughes also gave large amounts of money to Nixon's political campaigns ($100,000) which was funneled to Rebozo in 1969 and 1970. After the money was delivered, the Justice

Department's Antitrust Division dropped its objection to Hughes' acquisition of the Dunes Hotel in Las Vegas. Nixon was distrustful of O'Brien because the latter had once served as Hughes's Washington representative from October 1969 to January 1971. O'Brien told Lukas about the Rebozo deal, "If I had, you wouldn't have had to break into my office to get it. I would have told the whole world." At the same Hofstra conference, Lukas met Charles Colson who said he was skeptical of Marauder's theory. "Once when we were in prison, I braced him in a hallway and asked him, What were we doing at the Watergate, Jeb? He turned white as a sheet and wouldn't tell me. Later, on the outside, I asked him again. Still he wouldn't say. I asked, what did he make of Magruder's explanation now? Colson broke into a sly grin. Perhaps Hunt and Liddy were after the Hughes-Rebozo stuff. But they weren't working for Richard Nixon, they were working for Howard Hughes."[3]

Magruder said that Nixon knew about the break-in and that the president got on the line during the March 30, 1972 conversation with Mitchell. Magruder said that he knew it was Nixon "because his voice is very distinct and you couldn't miss who was on the phone." Magruder said he could hear Nixon tell Mitchell, "John, we need to get the information on Larry O'Brien, and the only way we can do that is through Liddy's plan. And you need to do that." Magruder said he heard John Mitchell talk by phone to Maurice Stans who was in charge of finance at CREEP and tell him to give Liddy $250,000 "and let's see what happens."

No one has corroborated Magruder's story and John Dean, Nixon's counsel and the man who testified against the president at the Watergate hearings, did not back up Magruder's story.

"I have no reason to doubt that it happened as he describes it, but I have never seen a scintilla of evidence that Nixon knew about the plans for the Watergate break-in or that the likes of Gordon Liddy were operating at the re-election committee."

There are other theories about what the burglars were looking for in the Watergate 'complex. Howard Hunt believed the break-in occurred in order to find any information that the Castro regime

---

3   Lukas, J. Anthony, *Why the Watergate Break-In?*, ny-times.com, 11/30/1987.

was bankrolling Democratic campaigns. That belief was backed up by fellow burglar Frank Sturgis who said he was recruited into group by Bernard Barker in April 1972 and that Barker was told by Hunt about the Castro-Democratic connection. Barker said that Hunt told him that "they would be acting on behalf a governmental group that had jurisdiction over both the CIA and the FBI." In a 1974 *True Magazine* article, Sturgis said they were looking for a Castro-Democratic connection, and that "they also had been told by Hunt that the FBI suspected there might be a memorandum or other documentation prepared by the Castro regime listing all of the covert actions that had been carried out by the CIA against Castro over prior years. The memorandum purportedly contained a proposal by Castro to reestablish economic ties with the United States in exchange for a promise to stop the covert missions. However, no evidence of this memorandum was found."[4]

When President Nixon was referring to the "whole Bay of Pigs thing," he was possibly referring to the assassination of JFK. That theory was postulated by H.R. Haldeman in his memoir called *The Ends of Power,* said that "he realized in all those Nixon references to the Bay of Pigs, he was actually referring to the Kennedy assassination." In fact, Haldeman suggested to Nixon when first began working for him that he be allowed to look into the facts about the assassination but Nixon told him no.

How Haldeman came to the conclusion of the Kennedy assassination as part of the Watergate story came from a contact he had with CBS correspondent Daniel Shorr who called him seeking information concerning the FBI investigation Nixon mounted against him in August 1971. Shorr told Haldeman that an outgrowth of the Bay of Pigs invasion of Cuba the CIA started an assassination attempt on Castro's life. Castro found out about the CIA's efforts which involved the mob as well as a CIA asset named Rolando Cubela, a.k.a., AMLASH, and took steps to thwart the plot. Castro made a speech on September 7, 1963 in which he said, "Let Kennedy and his brother Robert take care of themselves, since they too, can be the victims of an attempt which will cause their death." In his book, Haldeman wrote that "there was a

---

4   Hunt, Jim and Risch, Bob, *Warrior,* A Forge Book, Tom Doherty Associates, New York, 2011, Page 133.

chilling parallel to their cover-up at Watergate, the CIA literally erased any connection between the Kennedy's assassination and the CIA. No mention of the Castro assassination attempt was made to the Warren Commission by CIA representatives. In fact, Counter-intelligence Chief James Angleton of the CIA called Bill Sullivan of the FBI and rehearsed the questions and answers they would give to the Warren Commission investigators." Haldeman says that since Sullivan was Nixon's top man at the Bureau who was always feeding him information, coming from Hoover's office, Sullivan might have learned of a CIA cover-up coming from Richard Helms who knew about the Castro assassination plots and any possible to the JFK murder. On June 20, three days after the break-in, Nixon called Haldeman and told him, to, "tell Ehrlichman this whole group of Cubans is tied to the Bay of Pigs." Haldeman did not know what Nixon was saying and he asked for clarification. Nixon replied that, Ehrlichman will know what I mean." In another interesting aside concerning Nixon and the Bay of Pigs remark, is the fact that on the day that Nixon made that remark, the taping system in his room which was found at the National Archives years later as part of Nixon's tape collection, had at "least six unexplained erasures."

A theory that has been over looked and ridiculed by mainstream historian and others in the Watergate saga is the possibility that the break-in had to do with a prostitution ring that was run out of the DNC. In the office of the DNC at the time of the break-in was the office of the executive director of the Association of Democratic State Chairman headed by R. Spenser Oliver Jr. Oliver happened to be the nephew of Robert Bennett, the president of the public relations firm called Robert Mullen Co. It so happened that Howard Hunt was employed at the Mullen firm for a while and it is possible that he had two interconnecting jobs at the same time; working at Mullen and also at the Nixon White House. The Robert Mullen Company was a CIA front and that fact was well-known inside the intelligence community and the White House. In his book on Watergate called *Secret Agenda: Watergate, Deep Throat And the CIA,* author Jim Hougan wrote that it was Bob Bennett who was one of Bob Woodward's sources on the unfolding scandal. The CIA knew of Bennett's actions regarding the scandal and in a memo written by Eric Eisenstadt, a case officer he said, "Mr. Bennett said that he has been feeding stories to Bob Woodward of the Washington Post, with the understanding that there be on attribution to Bennett (and the Mullen Company.)" In the same memo, the writer says that the CIA did not instigate the Watergate affair and had nothing do with it. Also, Oliver's father also worked at the Bennett Company, along with Hunt.

The call girl scenario to Watergate goes as follows. Spencer Oliver Jr. was a friend of a lawyer of questionable character named Philip Mackin Bailey who was supposed to have established a DNC connection to a call girl ring run by Heidi Rikin at the Columbia Plaza Hotel. A grand jury and later, an FBI probe was convened to look into the charges of prostitution against Bailey who was charged with violating the Mann Act which prohibited the transport of persons across state lines for immoral purposes. A complaint against Bailey was filed by a girl who attended the University of Maryland who accused him of seducing her with the aid of wine and other drugs. The girl relented to Bailey's actions and he threatened to give the pictures he had taken of her to her parents if she didn't have sex with his various clients. The subsequent FBI probe of Bailey said that he had at least four prostitutes working for him, who, in his own words, said that he was the man "who brought the good times back." He was well connected to highly placed government workers in Washington, including many in the federal government, including, the wife of a powerful senator and unnamed White House attorney. What made the Bailey connection to the Watergate scandal so interesting is the fact that he had many friends at the DNC and that he was familiar with the "comings and goings of DNC worker R. Spencer Oliver. The theory goes that it was Spencer Oliver's phone at the DNC HQ that was bugged by James McCord. Oliver said that he believed his phone was tapped because of his frequent contacts with many Democratic state Chairman's across the country. The use of prostitutes was not new when it came to the men running Nixon's re-election committee. For example, when CREEP was planning its hijinks against the Democrats in the presidential election, Gordon Liddy was in charge of an extra-legal operation called Gemstone. Gemstone called for the use of prostitutes being placed on houseboats across the street from the Fontaineblueau Hotel in Miami Beach, Florida where the Democrats were holding their national convention. The prostitutes were to be used to lure prominent Dem's who would then be ripe for blackmail. However, this part of the operation called Sapphire was scuttled before it could get off the ground. There is no concrete proof that any sort of sexual scheme involving the use of prostitutes was used during the lead up to the Watergate break-in.

There is one more tie-into a possible sexual connection to the break-in. During the Watergate investigation, the assistant U.S. attorney, John Rudy, found in Mackin Bailey's address book which got into the hands of John Dean, contained the name and phone number of "Mo Biner" who was Dean's girlfriend (and later his wife). Next to her name was the reference "clout." It turned out that Mo Biner's roommate, Erika "Heidi" Rikin, was the madam of the call-girl ring and mistress of Washington, D.C, mob boss Joseph Nesline who was associated with the notorious mobster, Meyer Lansky. It has been posturized that the burglars were looking for any information or pictures of an incriminating nature on Dean's girlfriend.

Another overlooked event in the Watergate saga that has gone mostly unexplored was the break-in at the Chilean embassy in Washington on May 13, 1972 by a number of the same men who took part in the break-in at the office of Dr. Lewis Fielding and later at the Watergate complex. Talking about the Chilean operation with Nixon's legal aide, J. Fred Buzhardt, the president told him that the break-in "was part of a cover, a CIA cover, the same rational that was used for the Watergate break-in. The members of the Chilean operation were Hunt, Barker, Frank Sturgis, Eugenio Martinez, and Felipe De Diego (but without Gordon Liddy). It is now known that James McCord took part in the Chilean operation, but he might have given some intelligence information to his pals. A researcher, who worked on Woodward and Bernstein's book *All the President's Men,* Robert Fink, said that he believed the Chilean operation was bugged by the administration (Nixon), a thought that was shared by employees at the embassy. Almost two weeks after the Chilean break-in, CIA Deputy Director Vernon Walters said that John Dean "believed that Barker had been involved in a clandestine entry into the Chilean embassy." A notation in one of Barkers files said that "someone in the *New York Times* believes that Watergate, the break-in at the Chilean Embassy and the attempt to beat up Ellsberg on Capitol grounds are all related and they believe Barker is the key man." Frank Sturgis also discussed his role in the Chilean break-in by saying that his "function was document acquisition, the theft and or duplication of documents." This scenario is eerily similar to what took place on June 17 when the same men broke into the offices of the DNC. If Nixon knew about the Chilean operation, might he have also been aware before of the entry into the DNC Watergate headquarters?

From the available evidence, one can assume that what the Plumbers were really after at the Watergate, among other damaging information on Nixon like his relationship with Howard Hughes, was his belief that somewhere in the files was any reference to his link with the CIA-Mafia plots to kill Fidel Castro and a secret Cuban Dossier that could link the Mafia to his secret anti-Castro operations, beginning at the time that he was Vice President and was the operations officer in the plots to overthrow Castro. It is not inconceivable that he wanted to protect the identities of three of the men involved in the break-in, Hunt, Barker, and Sturgis who took part in both agency and private operations to kill Castro. Nixon also wanted to keep the fact that both Sturgis and Barker had a working relationship with Tampa, Florida mob boss Santo Trafficante Jr. Note-More information on this aspect of the Watergate story is in the book *Watergate: The Hidden History: Nixon, The Mafia, And the CIA* by Lamar Waldron.

While the real reason for the Watergate break-in may never be really verified, all the theories in this chapter have been documented by writers and historians and are open to review and question. Until there comes a time when more information on the event comes to life, there will still be questions about what the burglars were after and "what did the president know, and when did he know it?"

FBI agent Mark Felt.

Chapter 47
Oswald in Mexico City

One of the lingering mysteries surrounding the Kennedy assassination, and the possible role of the president's alleged assassin, Lee Harvey Oswald, is Oswald's trip to Mexico City in the last week of September-first week of October, 1963. After 50 plus years, new information has been shed on Oswald's trip to the Mexican capital, and yet, there is still a genuine puzzlement as to why he was there (if he was there at all, as some Kennedy assassination researchers say), and who may have been impersonating him at that crucial juncture in the entire Kennedy story. Over the decades, new information has come to light that the CIA might have been running some sort of intelligence related mission in Mexico City at the time of Oswald's arrival possibly involving the FPCC (Fair Play for Cuba Committee), and the role of a particular KGB assassin/agent who met Oswald when he showed up at the Russian consulate in that city. Oswald's trip to Mexico City in still a maze within a maze with so many theories and permutations that we still don't really know what he was doing there.

According to the Warren Commission, Oswald went to Mexico City in order to get a visa from the Soviet Embassy to return to Russia via Cuba. According to the Warren Commission, Oswald was eager to get back to the Soviet Union as he was entirely frustrated as to what his life in America had come to.

What is now known is that the CIA was watching Oswald's movements from the time he arrived in Mexico City, to the time he left. Why they were so interested in him probably has to do with an ongoing intelligence mission that was going on at that time, one that is still not revealed to our satisfaction to this day.

At the time of the Kennedy assassination, the CIA had one of the most comprehensive intelligence gathering activities programs running in Mexico City. A CIA analyst named John Whitten, a.k.a, John Scelso who directed an intensive internal report on the Kennedy assassination for the agency and whose identity had been kept secret for years said of these operations, "They were absolutely enormous. We were trying to follow the Soviets and all

419

the satellites and the Cubans. At the same time, the main thrust of the station's effort was to attempt to recruit Russians, Cubans, and satellite people."

Another twist in the CIA's covert espionage game in Mexico City also directly involves Lee Harvey Oswald. Recently discovered documents reveal that a CIA message dated September 16, 1963, informing the FBI that "the agency is giving some consideration to countering the activities of the FPCC, Fair Play for Cuba Committee, in foreign countries. " Oswald was the lone member of the FPCC in New Orleans during the summer of 1963 and was arrested in a scuffle with Carlos Bringuier, an anti-Castro Cuban. Oswald had previously approached Bringuier offering his services in anti-Castro operations, while he was handing out pro-Castro leaflets only a short time later. It is interesting to note that the day after this CIA memo dealing with a covert action against the FPCC, which had a direct Oswald connection, Oswald was applying for a Mexican tourist card. Is there any connection?

One of the many mysterious people with CIA connections who were in Mexico City at the same time Oswald was, was a man named William Gaudet. Gaudet said he was the editor of a small newspaper based in Costa Rica called the *Latin American Traveler.* In reality, Gaudet had been employed by the CIA for over twenty years. Gaudet had known an ex-FBI special agent named Guy Bannister, a rabid ant-Communist, anti-Castro intelligence operative who worked in New Orleans the summer that Oswald was in the city. There were numerous reports that there was a connection between Oswald and Guy Bannister and that Oswald was even working behind the scenes for Banister in one fashion or another. Gaudet said he saw Oswald pass out FPCC flyers in the city and had observed Oswald on various occasions. It has been reported by various writers that Gaudet obtained a visa to follow Oswald to Mexico City on September 17,1963 and that both men had consecutive serial numbers stamped on their visas. Gaudet is long deceased but before he died he said that the thought Oswald was a "patsy," but refused to say why he was in Mexico City at the same time Oswald was there.

One of the first things that Oswald did upon his arrival in Mexico City was to make his way to the Cuban Consulate. There, he showed off his "leftist" credentials; his FPCC card, letters from the American Communist Party, a picture of him being arrested in New Orleans after his "fight" with Carlos Brinquier, and now a disputed membership card for the American Communist Party (it was never proved that Oswald ever belonged to the Communist Party of the U.S). When he asked for a visa to travel to Russia he was told that he had to go to the Russian Embassy. There, he asked for a visa to travel to Russia and was told he had to wait for months in order to get his visa. It is at this time that Oswald is supposed to have made a warning that he would "kill Kennedy," in retaliation for his not being allowed back into the Soviet Union.

But here the story becomes mired in mystery. Was it the real Oswald who came to both the Soviet Embassy and the Cuban Consulate? The answer to that question seems to be NO.

The first person to cast doubt on the real Lee Harvey Oswald as being the man who came to the Cuban Consulate was Sylvia Duran. She was the secretary at the Mexico City Cuban consulate during the time that Oswald (or someone impersonating him) made his brief sojourn to the Mexican capital. She met with Oswald who was desperately trying to get a visa to got to Cuba and then on to the Soviet Union. Sylvia Duran's brief meeting with Oswald caused the CIA a great deal of interest, if not panic, and her testimony regarding Oswald's visit to the consulate would only add to the deepening mystery concerning Oswald's trip, south of the border. She told Oswald that she could not issue him a valid Cuban transit visa until he first got clearance from the Soviet embassy that would approve or disapprove any travel to the Soviet Union. Oswald left and went to the Soviet embassy which was only a short distance away.

A few hours later, he returned to the Cuban Consulate with new passport pictures which he had just taken. Duran accepted Oswald's application and told him to call back in a week. Oswald then said to Duran, "Impossible. I can only stay in Mexico three days." After also speaking with the consul's assistant who explained the same information, Oswald returned later that after they assured him that his visa was going to be processed. He then urgently requested that the Cuban's give him a visa on the spot. Duran then called the Soviet embassy and was told that they had spoken to Oswald and told him that any decision on issuing a visa would take a few months. According to an interview with Sylvia Duran for his book *Conspiracy,* author Anthony Summers told what happened next. Summers said that Duran told him that Oswald "didn't want to listen. His face reddened, his eyes flashed, and he shouted, Impossible. I can't wait that long."

The commotion caused by Oswald got the attention of the chief counsel, Eusebio Azuce. Azuce too had no luck with Oswald and he told him that he (Oswald) was harming the Cuban cause by his outrageous actions. Azuce then ordered Oswald out of the consulate at which point he complied. With the theatrics now over, they closed the office and went home. But that was not the last time the name, nor the face of Lee Oswald, was to surface in the life of Sylvia Duran and Eusebio Azuce.

On the day JFK was shot, Consul Azuce was back in Havana. Days later, he went to the movies and saw a newsreel of Jack Ruby shooting Oswald. Azuce later said that the Oswald whom Ruby shot was "in no way resembled" the Oswald whom he had seen at the consulate in Mexico City. Azuce said the man who came to the consulate and identified himself as Oswald was 35 years old, medium height with dark bond hair. He later said of the real Oswald, was that, "my belief is that this gentleman was not, is not the person or the individual who went to the consulate."

The day after the assassination, the ordeal of Sylvia Duran began. She was arrested by Mexican authorities upon the request of the CIA's Mexico City Station headed by "Winston Scott. The arrest of Sylvia Duran was a hot topic at CIA headquarters as is evident by the cable sent to Scott in Mexico City. "Arrest of Sylvia Duran is extremely serious matter which could prejudice U.S. freedom of action on entire question of Cuban responsibility. With full regard for Mexican interests, request you ensure that her arrest is kept absolutely secret, that no information from her is published or leaked, that all such info is cabled to US, and that fact of her arrest and her statements are not spread to leftist or disloyal circles in Mexican government."

It was evident from the frantic CIA activity after the president's death, that a possible Cuban connection to the events in Dealey Plaza was seriously being considered. It was later revealed that

Cuban president Dorticos pointedly asked the Ambassador to Mexico, Armas, in a phone call on November 26, 1963, about a report that Duran had been questioned about money.

When Duran identified the Oswald that had come into the consulate she had a very interesting observation about what her visitor looked like. She said," that he was blond, short, poorly dressed, that his face gets red when he talks." After being interrogated by Mexican police she was let go. However, her freedom did not last long. She was re-arrested on November 27, 1963 and questioned over the next two days. There were even rumors floating around the CIA that Oswald and Duran had a sexual relationship but that fact was never verified.

Sylvia Duran's story was an important one that could have cleared up any possible Cuban connection to the assassination or her true relationship with Oswald. However, the Warren Commission never questioned her on those important matters.

But the most telling evidence that there was an Oswald imposter in Mexico City was the photo of an "Unidentified Man" that the CIA took of a person that the agency said was the real Lee Oswald. That man, whose picture has been known and seen by researchers, is still a secret and what, if any, his relationship to Oswald and the assassination, is still in doubt.

The origins of the unidentified man photograph goes back to November 23, 1963 when the FBI, after getting it from the CIA, showed it to Marguerite Oswald, Lee's mother. This photograph was said to be the real Lee Oswald but it clearly is not. This man was beefy, with broad shoulders, a receding hairline and older than the 24-year old Oswald. When she testified before the Warren Commission, Mrs. Oswald said that the man was Jack Ruby (clearly not).

It has been learned only in a hugely relevant document called the "Scelso Document," prepared by a CIA analyst by the name of John Whitten who was tasked by the agency to prepare a report on the assassination, that the Warren Commission was not given this photo by the CIA because it concerned a covert intelligence mission in Mexico City that it wanted to keep secret.

Soon, what actions the CIA should take in informing the Warren Commission about this problem spread to the top of the covert action branch of the agency. On March 1, 1964, Ray Rocca wrote an internal memo to Richard Helms stating that "we have a problem here for your determination." The problem was what to do about a photo of a man whom the CIA said was the presidential assassin, but was clearly not. If, as many people suspect, this man was part of some covert operation hinted at by Scelso/Whitten in Mexico City at the time of the Oswald visit, was he in fact a part of the assassination conspiracy? Was he in fact linked in some way with Oswald in a possible framing of the ex-Marine?

During the cold war, Mexico City was one of the hot spots of international espionage. Located between the United States and South America, it was a vital listening post for spies of both NATO and the Warsaw Pact countries. In a book called *Confessions of A Spy: The Real Story of Aldrich Ames,* author Pete Early gives a vivid account of how the spy game was played out in Mexico City. During the 1960s, says Early, the U. S Defense Intelligence Agency (DIA), began flooding the Soviet embassy with dozens of double agents, i.e., volunteer spies to gleam any information that they could get. At that time, the U.S. had over one hundred double agent programs on a world-wide basis with a majority of them taking place in Mexico City. This information, for whatever it is worth, is important to know in light of the obvious Oswald impersonation in that city.

"But the main benefit was that it helped US intelligence identify which Soviets in the embassy (Russian) were KGB or GRU officers, and what procedures the Soviets used when someone volunteered. The constant turnover in volunteers also wasted the Soviets' resources and kept them confused."

Was the "unidentified man" a part of a CIA covert operation that pre-dated the DIA double agent program, twenty years later? It is apparent that this man was not there just for the sights. He was part of some sort of operation, probably in the employ of one of the U.S. intelligence agencies. But which one?

If the CIA knew that the mystery man was not Lee Harvey Oswald, so did the Warren Commission and they took the CIA to task over it. In late March 1964, William Coleman wrote a memo on this subject:

"As you know, we are still trying to get an explanation of the photograph which the FBI showed Marguerite Oswald soon after the assassination. I hope that. Memorandum of March 24, 1964, sent by Mr. Rankin by the CIA is not the answer which the CIA intends to give us as to this inquiry."

What the Warren Commissioners did not know in relation to the investigation of the CIA's sensitive sources and methods concerning the mystery man was that the CIA had three sources of covert intelligence coming from the Soviet Embassy; a human mole inside the building, hidden microphones and surveillance cameras outside the building, taking pictures of everyone who entered and left. The only time that the cameras were not working was when the real Oswald (if he was there at all1) paid a visit.

Years later, the late CIA Director, William Colby, would comment on the unidentified man, "To this day, we don't know who he is."

In the wake of the Kennedy assassination, the Warren Commission, among others, tried to link Lee Oswald to either the Cubans or the Russians. As described above, in September-October 1963, Oswald, or someone who was impersonating him, traveled to Mexico City where "Oswald" tried to get a visa to return to Russia via Cuba. It was common practice for the CIA to bug the Cuban Consulate and the Russian Embassy where "Oswald" went, in order to get the necessary travel documents.

Oswald made contact with Valery Kostikov in the Russian Embassy. Kostikov was a high level KGB agent who had been serving in the Soviet's Mexican compound since 1960. As described by recent CIA documents, it is believed that Kostikov was a member of the top secret Soviet 13th Department which was responsible for assassination activity in the Western Hemisphere. Certain members of the CIA tried to paint Oswald as a member of the Communist Party (which he was not) and more importantly, as a Soviet agent in touch with Kostikov. Thus, they tried falsely to link the Soviet Union somehow with the president's assassination.

The history of Department 13 dates back to 1936 when the old Soviet Union, under the brutal reign of Joseph Stalin, decided that it needed a terror organization that would carry out political assassinations outside the country. During World War II, Department 13 sabotaged German forces in the Ukraine and killed hundreds of Russians who collaborated with the Germans.

Over the years, the CIA has linked Department 13 to assassination attempts on the late President of Yugoslavia, Marshall Tito and General Eisenhower during his visit to Korea during that war. Only the top members of the Central Committee could give approval to any assassination attempt, and in 1963 would have had to have the approval of then Premier Nikita Khrushchev. Recent declassified CIA files reveal that the main job of Department 13 was sabotage against enemy targets. Specially trained KGB agents were tasked to carry out such assassinations, but sometimes the Russians hired foreigners to do the job.

According to CIA files, Department 13 would have put Oswald under close surveillance during the time he spent in the Soviet Union, may not have actually had any interest in him, but kept him under close observation. The files reveal that the CIA believed that Oswald could possibly have been recruited by the Soviets after his return to America because of something in Oswald's past that they could use against him. In the CIA's assessment, it is possible that Oswald was told to meet with his handlers in the Soviet Union but the KGB usually debriefed their agents in a secret location. "It does seem plausible that if Oswald was meeting with the KGB, it would let him make these calls. There would have been no trace of contact with the KGB. The CIA knows a great deal about KGB's Mexico City operations and Oswald's activities don't fit the normal pattern."

After the president's murder, CIA bugs in the Soviet Embassy picked up an unusual conversation between Kostikov and Mirabil, the Cuban ambassador to Mexico. Mirabil called to speak to a Soviet named Yatskov, a KGB counter-intelligence officer, but spoke instead to Kostikov. Their conversation centered on a "suitcase." Mirabil asked Kostikov if he wanted to go on a "picnic" but he refused. The CIA's reaction to this conversation was that the two men were talking in some sort of code but "doesn't understand the conversation." In relation to the Oswald-Kostikov connection, the CIA files reveal that if Kostikov was involved in any way in the Kennedy assassination, he would have been immediately sent out of the country. Instead, he stayed in Mexico City until 1965, and "It is unlikely that he was involved in Kennedy's death."

At the center of the Mexico City controversy is an alleged intercept by CIA electronic surveillance of a phone call on October 1, 1963 from a person who said he was "Lee Oswald." The call was placed to the Soviet Embassy in Mexico City of which the caller, Oswald, "described his contact with Valery Kostikov. It has been long rumored by researchers that the person who made this call was impersonating the real Oswald. On October 8, 1963, the CIA's Mexico City station, regarding the phone call, gave a physical description and six photographs of the person in mention. The description said the person was 35-years old, six foot tall, with an athletic build, and had a receding hairline. This discerption did not fit Oswald's physical profile in any way. So, then, who was this person? Oswald was 24 and had a slight build, nothing resembling the person the CIA described.

During the same October 1, 1963, conversation, the CIA surveillance of the Soviet Embassy picked up a conversation in broken Russian between a person identifying himself as Lee Oswald and his talk of his conversation with Kostikov. This person was most likely an imposter because the real Lee Oswald was fluent in the Russian language and in fact, his wife Marina, said that when she first met Lee his Russian was so good that she thought he came from a different part of the Soviet Union than she did (Also remember that Marine Oswald was supposed to have taken courses in Russian at the Monterey Language School).

In fact, the FBI took very seriously the implications of a possible Oswald imposter in a letter they wrote to the Secret Service dated November 23, 1963, one day after the assassination. It was based in part upon information received by CIA HQ on October 9, 1963, referring to the goings on at the Soviet Embassy on 10-1-63. It read:

> The Central Intelligence Agency has advised that on October 1, 1963, an extremely sensitive source had reported that an individual identified as Lee Oswald contacted the Soviet embassy in Mexico City inquiring as to any messages. Special Agents of this bureau, who have conversed with Oswald in Dallas, Texas, have observed photographs of the individual referred and have listened to

a recording of his voice. These Special Agents are of the opinion that the above-referred-to individual was not Lee Harvey Oswald.[5]

This brings up two important points; who was the person impersonating Oswald and where are the tapes of the conversation that the Bureau was referring to? In its investigation of the Kennedy assassination in the mid-1970s, the HSCA said of this missing tape. "Finally on the basis of an extensive review and detailed testimony by present and former CIA officials and employees, the committee determined that CIA headquarters never received a recording of Oswald's voice. The committee concluded, therefore, that the information in the November 23, 1963 letterhead memorandum was mistaken and did not provide a basis for concluding that there had been an Oswald impersonator?" So, who was right, the HSCA? Or did the CIA have a tape of the Oswald conversation and destroy it or lose it in some way?

CIA documents on Oswald's Mexico City trip were opened many years ago and are referred by researchers as the "Lopez Report." Some interesting questions in this regard are as follows:

"Question: Could Oswald have met KGB in Mexico City under cover of visa application?

Answer-It is possible. In an unusual case, KGB will meet agents at Embassy or Consulate where there is a natural reason for meeting there. However, normally KGB meets agents and takes them, under heavy security, to a safe house.

Question: What is your assessment of Oswald's telephone calls in Mexico City?

Answer: They seem to indicate only that he was applying for a visa. It does not seem plausible that if Oswald was meeting KGB, it would let him make these calls. There would have been no trace of contact with KGB. CIA knows a great deal about KGB Mexico City operations and Oswald's activities don't fit the normal pattern.

Question: Do Oswald's telephone conversations seem unusual?

Answer: Only with regard to the fact that he was asked to return to the Consulate to give them his address.

Question: Were any of the employees of the Cuban Embassy who Oswald contacted or might have contacted members of the

[5] *The Final Assassination Report,* New York Times Edition, 1979, Page. 321.

428

DGI-such as Duran, Calderon or Azuce?

Answer: The CIA has no evidence that these individuals were DGI.

Question: If Oswald had any contact with a DGI agent, would the government of Cuba be aware of it?

Answer: Yes, However, there have been no reports from Cuba that Oswald contacted DGI. [6]

One of the most important persons in the CIA who took part in the Oswald-Mexico City episode was Winston Scott, a poet, and a writer, and was the Station Chief in Mexico City from 1956-1969. He also wrote a personal memoir of his life in the CIA which mysteriously disappeared within days of his sudden and premature death.

On the day of the assassination, a high level meeting took place at the United States Embassy in Mexico City. In attendance were Winston Scott, the U.S. Ambassador to Mexico, Thomas Mann, and Clark Anderson, who was the FBI's legal attache.' Their discussion concerned new information that Oswald visited the Cuban and Russians embassies. Clark Anderson fumed at Scott because Scott had not told him of the Oswald visit. Anderson was given the photos and tapes of Oswald's visit to the two embassies. These materials were then flown immediately to Dallas where FBI agents were in the process of interrogating Oswald. The agents were surprised to learn that the photos of the man who visited both embassies were not Oswald. "The photographs depicted a man about forty years old, around six feet tall, with a stocky, muscular build, and sporting a receding hairline and a square jaw." This was the picture of the so-called "Unidentified Man" who was impersonating Oswald.

Scott, as well as Ambassador Mann, also tried to tie Oswald with pro-Castro forces. They championed a version of events that centered on Gilberto Alvarado, a Nicaraguan intelligence agent who said that he had seen Oswald meeting in Mexico City with a "tall, thin Negro with reddish hair" and a "blonde girl with a Canadian passport named Maria Luisa." Alvarado said that the Negro gave Oswald $6,500 as a payment to kill JFK.

When President Johnson was preparing to organize a

[6] CIA Briefing on (Alleged) Soviet-Cuban Assassination. Date 1/15/76. Record Number: 157-10011-10029.

commission to look into the president's assassination, he ignored pleas from Scott and others to at least consider the fact that Oswald might have been involved with Cuba.

In his testimony to the HSCA, former Ambassador Mann gave his reservations about what took place in Mexico City on the weekend of the assassination. He said that "instructions were received from Washington to stop investigative efforts to confirm or refute rumors of Cuban involvement in the assassination. Mann said his instructions came from Dean Rusk and he believed that Scott, "CIA Station Chief, and Anderson, FBI Legate, had received similar instructions from their respective directors."

When Scott retired from the CIA in 1969, he remained in Mexico City and went into private business, creating a firm called Diversified Corporate Services. He also kept most of his private files that he had accumulated over the years. He told his friends that he was going to write an autobiographical "novel" about his life, including his time in the OSS in World War II and the working title of the book was called *Foul Foe*. The manuscript, which was never released to the public has numerous, candid references to the CIA's relationship with Oswald during the September-October 1963 time period. Furthermore, after Scott's death, his manuscript was seized, along with his personal papers.

Scott's death was sudden and tragic and has been a matter controversy for many years. He fell from a ladder in his home, fell off the roof, and received a number of cuts and bruises. He didn't seem too fazed with the injury and resumed his normal activities. On April 26, 1971, one day after his fall, his wife found him dead in their home.

In the wake of Scott's mysterious death, the CIA, which had been notified of the event shortly after it happened, moved quickly. In circumstances that are still unknown today, James Angleton, the agency's legendary counterintelligence chief, made a hurried trip to Mexico City to retrieve all of Scott's personal papers, including the cryptic manuscript he had written. What could have made Angleton go to Mexico in such a hurry? Could it have been Scott's very knowledgeable information that the learned about Oswald's visit to Mexico, and any potential CIA involvement?

In the immediate aftermath of the assassination, the CIA came across a report concerning the statement by Luisa Calderon, an employee of the Cuban Embassy in Mexico City at the time of the president's death. The CIA received information from a "reliable source" that Luisa Calderon, who was believed to be a possible agent of the Cuban intelligence service, the DGI, had made possible incriminating statements concerning the assassination of the president before the news of the assassination took place. The CIA report on Calderon says that when she was asked if she heard of the news of the assassination, she replied to the effect that, "Yes, of course I knew almost before Kennedy." She also reported that her colleagues in the Cuban Embassy learned about the assassination, "a little while ago."

When Calderon's supposed remarks hit the fan at CIA HQ shortly after the assassination, Ray Rocca wrote a memo stating that this was, "Latin hyperbole. Boastful ex post facto suggestion of foreknowledge. This is the only item in the (sensitive operation) coverage of the Cubans and Soviets after the assassination that contains the suggestion of foreknowledge or expectation."

The first official account of Calderon's remarks from the U.S. government's standpoint came on November 27, 1963, four days after the assassination, in a cable sent by Ambassador Thomas Mann to the State Department. Mann wrote, "Washington should urgently consider feasibility of requesting Mexican authorities to arrest for interrogation, Eusebio Azuce, Luisa Calderon, and Alfredo Mirabal. The two men are Cuban nationals and Cuban consular officers. Luisa Calderon is a secretary in the Cuban Consulate here."

The unofficial reason for this request was to forestall a return trip to Cuba by the above mentioned people in order to escape interrogation by either Mexican or American officials in the Kennedy assassination investigation. They may have been right concerning Calderon who made reservations to go back to Cuba via Cubana Airlines on December 11, 1963.

If the Luisa Calderon confession was bizarre enough, events from a CIA secret source would only tend to complicate the matter even more. In May 1964, the CIA received information from one of its sensitive and reliable sources codenamed "A-1," a defector who once worked for the DGI, the Cuban intelligence service.

A-1's debriefing was conducted by Joseph Langosch, the Chief of Counterintelligence for the Special Affair Staff (SAS) in Jim Angleton's department. Langosch reported that A-1 said that he had no direct knowledge of Lee Oswald or his activities in Mexico City.

However, he did say that he had information about the assassination coming from various members of the DGI. Among the most important information from A-1 was the following concerning Oswald and his possible association with the Cuban's: "Prior to October 1963, Oswald visited the Cuban Embassy in Mexico City on two or three occasions. Before, during and after these visits, Oswald was in contact with the DGI, specifically with Luisa Calderon, Manuel Vega Perez, and Rogelio Rodriguez Lopez."

Langosch said that he wasn't sure what, if any relationship Luisa Calderon had with the DGI. A-1 was later to tell Langosch concerning Oswald and the DGI, "Luisa Calderon, since she returned to Cuba has been paid a regular salary by the DGI even though she had not performed any services."

Clearly, A-1's allegation about a possible Oswald connection with Luisa Calderon fit the category of a "sensitive source and method" which the agency was reluctant to discuss in public.

In June 1964, a member of Rocca's CI Staff gave Howard Willens of the Warren Commission access to information regarding the possible Oswald-Calderon connection. The WC wrote of this possible association, "The precise relationship of Luisa Calderon to the DGI is not clear. She spent about six months in Mexico from which she returned to Cuba in early 1964. "Willens was not supplied with any of the detailed reports to the CI branch by A-1 concerning Calderon, her possible relationship with Cuban intelligence and possibly, with Oswald.

In the end, the mystery of Luisa Calderon's statement about a possible link with the Cuban government and the president's alleged assassin, was not clearly determined. What is beyond doubt is that the CIA had, for whatever reason, i.e., an on-going covert operation in Mexico City possibly using Luisa Calderon, or someone else, deliberately withheld certain pertinent information on her activities to the Warren Commission. The CIA countered by saying that they gave the WC its information that possibly linked Calderon to the Cuban DGI, and potentially, to their own government. When the HSCA wrote their report they concluded that Luisa Calderon had no CIA connections.

In one of the most interesting aspect s of the Oswald-Mexico City adventure is a report involving Attorney General Robert Kennedy and the Oswald trip in September-October 1963. The first person to report on the covert visit of Robert Kennedy to Mexico City was author and former military intelligence officer John Newman in his book *Oswald and the CISA*. Robert Kennedy's visit to Mexico City is full of intrigue as his trip coincided with the ongoing CIA internal investigation of alleged assassin, Lee Oswald's time spent in that city. According to released CIA files, the person who brought to light RFK's trip to Mexico City was a CIA officer named June Cobb.

In 1960, Cobb worked at the Ministry Office of Fidel Castro in Havana and was one of Castro's closets aids. Her name was brought to the attention of the CIA who was monitoring Castro after the overthrow of the Batista regime in 1959. When Miss Cobb came to New York she was approached by CIA officer Henry Hermsdorf. In time, Hemsdorf was able to "turn" Miss Cobb into an American double agent, reporting on Castro and his inner circle. According to Cobb's account, Robert Kennedy made a secret trip to the Mexican capital in either September or October 1964, in conjunction with the CIA's investigation of his brother's death. The CIA's own files confirm that RFK was in Mexico City at the time.

The Robert Kennedy-Mexico City story was confirmed by Winston Scott who wrote in a "memo for the file, that, "She (Elana Garro), who met Oswald in Mexico City in September 1963), wanted to tell him (RFK) she had met with him and two friends at the home of Horacio and Silvia Duran."

In doing the research for his book, Newman conducted an interview with former FBI agent James Hosty who was keeping tabs on Oswald and his wife in Dallas, Texas in the months preceding the assassination. Hosty said that Thomas Karamessines, then the CIA's deputy director for plans, was also in Mexico City to "call off the investigation."

433

After leaving the city, the U.S. Ambassador to Mexico, Thomas Mann, called off the inquiring into Oswald's alleged southern sojourn. Hosty went further and said that his CIA contacts inside the American Embassy in Mexico City heard Robert Kennedy ordering that any future probes be stopped: they weren't.[7]

Why Robert Kennedy went to Mexico City is still not known, but his visit might have been a reaction to his war against organized crime and its then secret collaboration with the CIA in their plots to kill Castro.

After the assassination of his brother, RFK was nagged by the thought that if he hadn't gone after the mob so ruthlessly (the HSCA said that organized crime had the "means, motive, and opportunity "to kill JFK), his brother might still be alive.

Maybe RFK wanted to stop the inquiry before any more damaging information concerning his brother and any other elements connected to the CIA or the mob in the aftermath of the assassination would be exposed. RFK's trip to Mexico City needs further clarification in the files still classified by the government.

---

[7] Newman, John, *Oswald And The CIA*, Carroll & Graf Publishers, New York, 1995, Page, 382.

Chapter 48
Spies in the Roosevelt Administration

Prior to and during World War II, the United States was riddled with hundreds, possibly thousands of spies working for the Soviet Union. The Soviets were our ally's against Germany, but Stalin saw the United States as one ally worth cultivating. Under the direction of the American Communist party (CPUSA) headed by Earl Browder, communist agents burrowed into every facet of the American nation, including various departments of the U.S government. All this information was not known to the public at the time due to wartime constraints and the need for secrecy. This chapter will describe the many men and women who worked secretly for the Russians in the Roosevelt administration and whose identities have only been revealed in the recent past by the release of the so-called Venona papers which gave a detailed description of who these spies were and what they did.

To the general reader, the name Venona may not mean much. But to the dozens of American cryptographers who worked diligently to break the coded messaged dispatched to Moscow by its agents in the United States, the Venona Project would yield vital information that proved the vast extent of Soviet espionage against its ally, the United States.

The project was located in a little-known girls' school called Arlington Hall, where talented linguists, code breakers and mathematicians analyzed over 25,000 secret wartime Soviet messages that came into the United States. The first batch of Venona materials was made public in 1995 and changed the way we understood Soviet-American relations during that era.

Some of the people who penetrated our government at the highest levels of the Roosevelt administration included Alger Hiss, Harry Dexter White, Lauchlin Currie, Whittaker Chambers, and Duncan Lee, positioned in such important agencies as the

Treasury, State, the OSS (the United States' secret spy agency) and even inside FDR's White House.

One of these spies was a rather plain woman named Elizabeth Bentley who was one of the major players in the Soviet espionage establishment in the U.S. during the war. She was a graduate of Vassar College with an M.A. from Columbia University, who had joined the Communist Party USA (CPUSA) in 1930. Her lover recruited her into spying, a man named Jacob Golos, who headed one of the most important Soviet spy rings in Washington during the war years. Following Golos's sudden death, Bentley assumed leadership of the Golos network.

It was assumed that Bentley was merely a courier for Golos, but that was not the case. She was privy to all vital information and knew every employee's name. One of Bentley's primary jobs was as liaison between Golos and another Soviet spy group in D.C. headed by Gregory Silvermaster. Itzhak Akhmerov, the head of Soviet espionage in Washington, called Bentley an "intelligent, sober-minded, quiet woman."

Bentley did all she could to separate her American communist cell from that controlled by the NKVD, which was the secret police of the Soviet Union from 1935 to 1943, and a forerunner of the KGB. Bentley withheld vital information from her Soviet handlers and kept much of the material gleamed from American sources for her own use.

Despite the fact that Akhmerov referred to Bentley as "one hundred percent our woman," she was undergoing a dramatic change of heart about Russia. When its government discovered her affairs with both a man and a woman in her organization, any confidence they might have had in her soured.

According to the Venona tapes, Soviet bosses said of Bentley, "Taking into account that Bentley won't go anywhere voluntarily, and may damage us here very seriously, only one remedy is left-get rid of her."

Bentley went to the FBI in November 1945 and told them her story. She exposed all of the agents she worked with in Washington: men in top posts in the Roosevelt administration-Lauchlin Currie, one of FDR's closest advisors, Harry Dexter White, Assistant Director of the Treasury, and dozens of Washington officials.

The defection of Elizabeth Bentley was a devastating blow to the Soviet spy operation in the United States. Many spies named by Bentley fled to Russia, breaking down a widespread espionage ring in the country. After the war, Bentley would testify before the House Un-American Activities Committee (HUAC), which was investigating communist penetration of American government by the Soviet Union. That investigation led to the 1950s McCarthy witchhunts that would dominate the American political scene for years.

Jacob Golos was one of the most important spymasters for the Soviet Union in Washington and his name would not have become known to historians and writers if it were not for the Venona papers. He was born in the Ukraine, and after spending some time in a labor camp he immigrated to the U.S. where his parents had already taken up residence.

He soon became a member of the CPUSA and took up the Russian cause in his new home. He returned to the Soviet Union in 1919 and worked for the Bolshevik regime in a Siberian coal mine. It is also believed that during his stay in Russia, he joined the Cheka, or secret police.

He returned to the United States in the 1920s and worked as a party organizer in Detroit and Chicago. In 1927, Golos took on an assignment that would last until his death in 1943 and root him firmly in the United States. He was one of the founders of a Soviet front organization called World Tourists, a travel agency composed of workers who were members of the CPUSA.

Another part of Golos's operation was faking U.S. passports. The names on these passports were taken from the files of the deceased, and persons who had permanently left the United States. In a federal investigation, 16 people were exposed using fake credentials. The FBI kept a careful watch over their operations and as it became obvious that World Tourists was working for the CPUSA, the federal government swooped down, charging them as an unauthorized agent of a foreign government. In a plea bargain, World Tourists pled guilty on the foreign agent charge and was fined a partly $500. Golos received a suspended sentence.

By the 1930s, Golos was working under the control of the GRU in New York. His main contact was Gaik Ovakimian, the

Soviet Consul.

Golos and Bentley became lovers, but that posed a complicated situation for Golos. He was married, but in 1935, he sent his wife and son back to Russia. Soon, Bentley moved in with him. Bentley served as an intermediary between her many high-level contacts in Washington and Golos. In time, she would head the operation.

Soon, Bentley took on more important assignments for her boss. She serviced a number of mail drops for Golos, who received messages from his widespread contacts. Golos also sent Bentley to Washington where she brought back sensitive data from his sources. Among Golos's Washington channels were Nathan Silvermaster and Harry Dexter White, who was the number-two official in the U.S. Treasury Department.

Ever since the fiasco with Golos's World Tourists, and his subsequent imprisonment, the FBI had been keeping a watch on his activities. In a deciphered letter concerning Golos's activities, the writer said, "If something happens to them (referring to other agents), much of what has been created will be reduced to ashes. Some operatives believe that Golos has become a virtual chief in the U.S. He provides people for different kinds of services and missions in every field of our work. Yet Golos is on the books of American counterintelligence as a major NKVD agent. Therefore, his presence in the station becomes dangerous for business."

There is also a fleeting connection between Golos and Julius Rosenberg. After Elizabeth Bentley defected to the FBI, she told them a man named Julius contacted Golos to offer the services of a number of unnamed engineers willing to work for the Russians. Bentley did not know who this Julius was, but she was able to meet with him and provide the bureau with a description. The "Julius" who offered his services to the Golos network was Julius Rosenberg.

By 1942, the strains of operating his network took a terrible toll on Golos's health. After the Germans attacked Russia, once their ally, Golos even talked about returning to Russia to join the army. The final straw in Golos's relationship with the Russians came when they ordered him to turn over the web of American contacts that he had cultivated for so many years.

On November 25, 1943, Jacob Golos died of a heart attack.

Elizabeth Bentley took over the reigns of his organization but within two years would become an informant for the FBI. The death of Jacob Golos and the loss of Elizabeth Bentley deprived the Soviet Union of one of their most effective espionage rings operating in the United States.

Judith Coplon was one of the most important of the Russian spies who worked in the U.S. during the war. She was born in Brooklyn, New York, attended Bernard College and took courses in Russian studies. The more she studied Russian culture, the more she became enamored if the Soviet system and soon became active in the communist student group. It was from these roots that Judith would grow into a Russian spy.

In 1943, she got a job with the Department of Justice. Although a background check was required, they failed to notice her Russian political leanings. She worked in the Foreign Agents Registration section of the Justice Department and had access to FBI files.

Friend, and fellow communist, and KGB spy Floria Wovachin pointed out Coplon's potential to ringleader Pavel Mikhailovich Fitin, the Soviet Union's top spymaster working in America. In 1944, the New York KGB office gave permission to take on Coplon. Vladmir Pravdin, a KGB agent working undercover for the Soviet news service *Pravda,* said Coplon, "Was a serious person, politically well developed... there is no doubt of her sincere desire to help us. She had no doubts for who she is working."

The Venona tapes on Coplon applaud her work but that did not permit her to steal top-level documents until she was firmly established in her Justice Department job. Coplon warned the KGB of FBI counterintelligence operations directed against them.

As part of her job in the Foreign Agents Section, Coplon had knowledge of all foreign agents operating inside the United States. These people had to register with her section, thus, the FBI knew all potential spies inside the country. Coplon was able to accumulate a large dossier of names, which she used to her advantage.

Coplon had her own KGB contact/agent, Valentine Gubitchev. On trips to New York, she passed on FBI materials to him. By now, the FBI knew that its most guarded secrets were finding their way to the Soviet government, and traced the leak to Judith Coplon. She was put under surveillance and subsequently arrested in 1949 in the process of passing counterintelligence files to Gubitchev.

Gubitchev claimed diplomatic immunity and was returned to Russia. Coplon was sentenced to 75 years. However, she never spent a day in jail, as her case was appealed on the grounds that the FBI had used an unauthorized wiretap while gathering evidence against her.

The name of Rep. Samuel Dickstein is probably not known by many of the readers of this book, but he was a secret spy for the Russians during the early 1940s and had the distinction of being one of the few (if any spies for a foreign government while in congress). Rep. Dickstein served as a leading member of a powerful congressional committee called the McCormick-Dickstein Committee which began operations in 1934. The purpose of the committee was to probe allegations of widespread activities of the pro-Nazi German American Bund and other domestic fascists groups allegedly operating in the U.S. Dickstein really had no room to stand on as far as the fascist threat to America; there was none. He tried desperately to link domestic fascists to the government in Germany and stirr up resentment of the American public to Germany. He was also a corrupt politician who, as Chairman of the House Committee on Immigration and Naturalization, sold his high-ranking position in order to get visas for people to enter the U.S. or to get permanent residence status for these people. The KGB first approached Rep. Dickstein in 1937, when Leo Helfgott, who was an Austrian KGB operative, paid him a $1,000 bribe to obtain a permament residence visa.[1]

KGB files on Rep. Dickstein tell of whom they were working with. "We are fully aware of whom we are dealing with. Crook (his codename) is completely justifying his codename. This is an unscrupulous type, greedy for money, consented to work because of money, a very cunning swindler. Therefore it is difficult to guarantee the fulfillment of the planned program even in the part he proposed to us himself. He demands nothing for himself, because of his ideological affinity to the USSR."

Over the years, Rep. Dickstein provided the Russians with materials on U.S-based fascists and gave the name of a Russian

---

[1] Haynes, John Earl, Klehr, Harvey, and Vassillev, Alexander, *Spies: The Rise And Fall of the KGB in America,* Yale University Press, New Haven, 2009, Page 286.

defector to the U.S. named Walter Krivitsky. Krivitsky was subsequently found dead in a Washington D.C. hotel room of an apparent, "suicide" (this event sounds eerily familiar with the death of CIA officer Frank Olsen).

Dickstein also had a hidden past that his colleagues in the House, as well as his constituents at home did not know; he had formerly worked in secret for both the British and Polish intelligence services, a fact that he eventually shared with the Russians.

During his time as a secret Russian spy, the influence and the information that he promised the Russians eventually dried up. He was beginning to supply less and less intelligence to his Russian handlers and in February 1940, they decided to officially cut ties with him. While on the Soviet payroll, Rep. Dickstein earned $12,000, about $200K in today's money.

Rep. Dickstein served in congress until 1946 and then served as a judge in the New York Supreme Court until his death in 1954. Who knows what would have happened if his identity as a covert Russian spy had been revealed during his tenure in congress.

When World War II broke out, the United States did not have any professional intelligence agency to combat the Nazi threat and had to scramble in order to form such an agency. What we came up with was the OSS, the Office of Strategic Services headed by a Wall Street lawyer and World War I hero, William Donovan. In time, the OSS was staffed with some of the most brilliant and talented people the nation had. Poets, writers, librarians, soldiers, all flocked to Washington to enter Donovan's lair. With so many people entering the ranks, Donovan and his team did not have the time or the resources to vet all these newcomers into their ranks. If they were willing to fight, they were hired, no questions asked.

One of these men was Duncan Lee who came from a well-established family from Virginia. He was a Rhodes Scholar and got a law degree from Yale in 1935. After graduation, Lee joined the New York law firm headed by William Donovan called Donovan, Leisure, Newton and Lumbard. When Donovan took over the OSS, he asked Duncan Lee to come aboard and the young man jumped at the chance. What none of the members of the OSS knew was that Lee was a secret communist, something he did very well from his new bosses. While he was in his last year at Yale, the FBI got a tip that Lee was a communist but the bureau only filed a report on the accusation and did little else. On his own time, Lee joined the CPUSA, once again fooling the FBI.

Jacob Golos learned from his sources in the CPUSA, that Lee had joined the OSS and he now had a mole inside our top intelligence service, one he could exploit. Elizabeth Bentley was asked to meet with Lee in Washington and she cultivated him as a source for Golos. Bentley said of her meeting with Lee that, "After my initial meeting with Lee, he began to supply me with OSS information of a varied nature. These data were always given by him orally, and he would never furnish anything in writing, nor would he allow me to make notes of the information he gave me."

In time, Lee gave Bentley information on OSS operations in Europe that might affect Soviet interests and identified OSS agents who operated in foreign nations. He also gave Bentley such information as the names of OSS agents who were parachuted into Hungary and Yugoslavia, and the secret meetings then going on between certain OSS officers and some disaffected Axis nations who were interesting in seeking a peace deal with the west. When he later testified to the accusations against him, Lee said he had only known Bentley as "Helen" and did not know her last name. He denied all charges of spying for the Russians and told an incredulous congress that he met Jacob Golos whom he knew as "John."

The Venona tapes revealed the huge extent of Lee's espionage for the Russians. As a member of the OSS, he gave away such secrets as American and British strategy in discussions with Joseph Stalin over post-war relations with Poland, American diplomatic activities in Turkey and Romania, and OSS operations in both France and China. After the war ended, Lee left the United States on a semi-permament basis but returned from time to time to visit old friends and colleagues who would still talk with him. The revelations made again st him by Elizabeth Bentley sent shockwaves across the bow of old OSS hands who had no idea that one of their trusted friends would be a traitor in their midst.

Another top Soviet mole hidden inside the American military establishment was William

Weisband, who worked in the Army's Signals Security Agency, an earlier version of the NSA. In 1944, Weisband worked in the Venona Project as a "language consultant." While Weisband did not officially work on the Venona Project, he was allowed to read some of their decrypts and knew all about the secret project.

The Venona files narrowed down a suspect whom they called "LINK." One Venona message said that "Link had completed a language course in Italian in Arlington, Virginia, (the home of the Venona operations) and was expected to be sent overseas shortly." The reference to LINK fit Bill Weisband to a tee. He had been at Arlington Hall taking foreign language lessons and went to Britain in July 1943, and then on to North Africa.

Weisband was only outed via the Venona files when it was revealed that the KGB had been working with an agent called "Nick." Nick turned out to be Amadeo Sabatini who was filmed by the FBI exchanging materials with Grigory Kheifers, a KGB agent who worked out of the Soviet consulate in San Francisco. When the FBI finally tracked down Kheifers and brought him in for interrogation, he denied being a Soviet agent but led them to another contact of his named James York. Under questioning by the FBI, York admitted to being a Soviet spy when he worked for Douglas Aircraft in California. One of his contacts was a man named Bill whom he gave information on the design of motors for the experimental aircraft called the XP-58. The Bill mentioned by York was in fact, William Weisband. The FBI brought in Weisband but he refused to admit to being a spy and he refused to sign an affidavit to that effect. He also declined to obey a grand jury subpoena. At trial, he was sentenced to one year in prison for contempt of court and was fired from the NSA. While Bill Weisband's name is not that wellknown in intelligence history, he did a considerable amount of damage by revealing NSA' secrets to the Russians from 1944 to 1945.

Gregory Nathan Silvermaster was one of the top Soviet agents who operated in the United States during the war and ran one of its most extensive espionage rings, whose members included a number of high-ranking members of the Roosevelt administration. He was born in Russia in 1898 and came to the U.S.in 1914. He graduated from the University of Washington in 1920 and joined the communist party. After getting his doctorate at the University of California, Berkeley, he got a job with the Resettlement Administration, which was associated with the Department of Agriculture. He later had positions in the U.S. Maritime Labor Board and the Farm Security Administration, until 1944. He then transferred to the War Assets Division at Treasury, and then the Commerce Department. There were rumors in the Roosevelt administration that he was a covert communist and he denied all the charges levelled against him. He lobbied Under Secretary of War Robert Patterson to overrule his detractors so he could be given a promotion in the government. Silvermaster called on Harry Dexter White, the assistant secretary of the Treasury to lobby on his behalf and he saw Secretary Patterson to put in a good word for him. Not known to anyone was that White was part of Silvermaster's covert spy network in Washington. Another person who vouched for Silvermaster was presidential aid Lauchlin Currie who was also a secret member of the Russian espionage service operating in the upper levels of government.

While Silvermaster ran his espionage ring in Washington the FBI knew that he was a contact with Gaik Ovakimian, a KGB officer who ran Soviet espionage operations from 1933 to 1941. The top levels of government also did not know that Whittaker Chambers told Assistant Secretary of State Adolf Berle that both he and Silvermaster had been members of the CPUSA movement in Washington in the 1930s. The KGB had been getting first hand reports on the FBI's interest in Silvermaster from Lauchlin Currie but since they (the FBI) had no concrete proof that he was a Russian spy, they had no authority to arrest him and the Russians let him continue with his covert work. The top members of Russian intelligence in Moscow had such a strong belief in his work that they wrote a memo stating that, "It is doubtful whether we (the KGB) could get same results as Robert" (Silvermaster's codename). Silvermaster's wife, Helen was an active member of her husband's spy network and did everything from copy material from their sources to being a courier in Washington. The Venona files say that the Russians paid them a regular salary and gave them a bonus in 1944 of three thousand dollars. The Venona files reported that the Silvermaster network handed over to the Russians a huge amount of secret material from its members inside the government, including information on weapons, aircraft production, tank, artillery, and shipping news, copies of U.S. diplomatic cables, OSS reports, and even the feud between President Roosevelt and Secretary of State Cordell Hull about British intentions in the Balkans after the war ended. Nathan Silvermaster's spy network went undetected during the war, despite some misgivings about him by the FBI which were not followed up by the relevant intelligence bodies in the United States.

If Nathan Silvermaster was the best Soviet spy in Washington during the 1940s, another highly placed Russian agent was working directly in the White House as an aide to President Roosevelt, Lauchlin Currie. He entered White House service in 1939 as a senior administrative assistant to the president. The president trusted Currie so much that he sent him on missions to China in 1942 as his personal representative, and as the head of an American economic mission to the Nationalist government. In 1943, he was appointed to run the day-to-day operations of the Foreign Economic Administration, a powerful agency that oversaw spending for foreign nations.

Currie was part of the Soviet underground in Washington but never served as a bona fide agent. The Russians gave Currie the cover name of "Page" and he did provide the KGB with a limited amount of information that came across his desk. Currie was able to provide the KGB with tantalizing information on the administration's foreign policy decisions, particularly as it concerned foreign leaders, both allied and enemy.

The decrypted Venona files show that Currie was in contact with Anatoly Gromov, a KGB officer who worked out of the Soviet Embassy in Washington. The FBI learned that Currie met with Gromov often and sent messages to each other. In 1947, Currie told the FBI that he had met with Gromov in early 1945. Intelligence reports later confirmed that Currie also met with Vasily Zubilin, who was Gromov's predecessor as KGB station chief in 1943. Elizabeth Bentley said she met with Currie as a cutout but that she did not know if he met directly with Gregory Silvermaster during his work in D.C.

After the war, Currie got caught up in the red scare investigations going on in congress and his name kept coming up as a possible Russian spy. In order to get away from the frenzy surrounding him, Lauchlin Currie left the United States for Columbia and some years later, renounced his American citizenship.

The highest-ranking Soviet spy in the Roosevelt administration was Harry Dexter White who served as the assistant secretary of the Treasury and was the man most responsible for the founding of the World Bank and the International Monetary Fund (IMF). He joined the Treasury department in 1934 and was one of Treasury Secretary Henry Morgenthau's most trusted advisors when it came to monetary matters. Both he and the noted economist John Maynard Keynes were the chief architects of the historic Bretton Woods monetary agreement that was signed in 1944 that formed international monetary policy for years to come. In an interesting aside, Vice President Henry Wallace who was replaced by Harry Truman as the vice-presidential candidate by FDR in the 1944 presidential election of 1944, told White that he was the first choice to become the new secretary of the Treasury and would have been so if FDR had died one year earlier and Wallace had become president.

Whittaker Chambers said that White was not a member of CPUSA but was a member in good standing with the Soviet network in Washington. One of the pieces of evidence provided by Chambers against Alger Hiss that was found in his pumpkin farm was a long memo that was written by Harry White. Elizabeth Bentley said about White that Silvermaster told her that "White had been giving information to the Russians during the thirties but ceased abruptly when his contact turned sour in 1938." Silvermaster later told Bentley that White renewed his ties with the CPUSA's underground soon thereafter. White was not the only spy in the Treasury Department at that time. Some of his colleagues were Frank Coe, Harold Glasser, Victor Perlo, Sonia Gold, Gregory Silvermaster, Solomon Adler, among others.

Chambers produced evidence of White's complicity in Soviet espionage activities by producing the so-called "White Memorandum," a four-page document that he wrote regarding a number of Treasury department's financial matters relating to Japan.

The Venona tapes reveal that the U.S. had deciphered fifteen KGB messages concerning White from 1944 to 1945 in which he discussed or gave them information. Some of the material related to FDR's foreign policy on the Polish government-in-exile in which the U.S. said they'd agree to allow Russia, after the war was over, to acquiesce to their annexation of Latvia, Estonia, and Lithuania. In 1945, White as also a member of the U.S. delegation to the founding of the United Nations where he met with Soviet intelligence officers to report on U.S. negotiating strategy. When White told his Soviet controllers that he was thinking about leaving the espionage business for the private sector in order to pay for his daughter's college education, the Russians said they could provide him with two thousand dollars for her expenses. The New York KGB station agreed to pay the money but it is not known, via Venona, if the money was ever paid.

The name of Elizabeth Bentley is frequently mentioned throughout this chapter as it relates to the unmasking of Soviet spies in the Roosevelt administration. When she defected to the FBI, Bentley gave up the name of Harry Dexter White as a communist agent upon her appearance in the summer of 1948 before the House Committee on Un-American Activities. White testified at the committee hearings but died suddenly of a heart attack at his home in Fitzwilliam, New Hampshire.

The KGB assigned a number of codenames for Harry White, among them "Jurist," "Lawyer," and "Richard. One of the most damaging reports concerning White's espionage was documented in a July 31, 1944 decrypt of a meeting in White's apartment where he met with a high-ranking Soviet official named Koltsov. White passed along information to Koltsov which he sent to the Soviet underground, and said that he and his wife were "willing to endure any self-sacrifice for the cause of Soviet-American cooperation" and that he'd be willing to meet with his Soviet handlers every 4-5 months, provided that "they would last no longer than half-an-hour and that they would take place while White was driving his automobile."

If we play the game of "what if" in history, and Harry White had become the Secretary of the Treasury under the presidency of Henry Wallace (who, was suspected himself of being a Soviet sympathizer), can you imagine just how much history would have changed in the cold war years? Even if this did not happen, the fact of the matter is that Harry Dexter White was the highest ranking member of the Roosevelt administration to spy for the Soviet Union and, like the other moles inside the government, was not unmasked until years later.

Chapter 49
The Spy in the Pentagon

One year before the Watergate break-in, the Nixon administration went to war against some of their old enemies, as well as new ones. The scenario that unfolded was right out of a good spy novel featuring a vindictive president out to get his old nemesis, who was a well-known Washington newspaper man (whom he once targeted for assassination), an insignificant Navy Yeoman who worked in the office of the office of the Joint Chiefs of Staff inside the National Security Council who was stealing top secret, classified material right out of his office in the Pentagon, as well as stealing material from Henry Kissinger, President Nixon's top foreign policy advisor. Throw in the White House Plumbers who took part in the Watergate break-in one year later and you have quite a story, one, that most historians have never heard of or refused to write about it.

The story began in December 1971 when Jack Anderson, one of the most respected and feared reporters in Washington wrote a column under his byline regarding the deployment of American warships in the Indian Ocean. This took place just at the time that hostilities were underway between India and Pakistan, two old rivals who were seeking hegemony in East Asia. The conflict took place just as the United States was still in Vietnam and the public had no stomach for another United States presence in that area of the world. The title of Anderson's article was called "U.S. Tilts to Pakistan" and the material quoted by Anderson could only have come directly from classified material in the possession of the Pentagon via its Special Action Group in meetings that took place on December 3 and 4 in which it was discussed the topic that Pakistan was being used as a conduit for top secret talks the Nixon administration was carrying on with China which would eventually lead to an historic settlement of both nation's animosity toward each other. It was obvious from the material in the article that someone who had knowledge of the meetings had leaked the material to Jack Anderson. But who was he and how did he get the information? What the movers and shakers in Washington and the interested public did not know at the time was that this was a spy affair that took place inside the Pentagon with the cooperation of two of the military's top commanders, Admiral Thomas Moorer, the chairman of the Joint Chiefs of Staff and Rear Admiral Robert Welander. Another person on the periphery of the scandal was Rear Admiral Rembrandt Robinson, who, along with Admiral Welander, were the liaisons between the JCS and the White House's National Security Council and were spying on behalf of the NSC.

The main culprit of the Anderson leaks was an unnoticed Navy Yeoman named Charles Radford who was a clerk/typist in the Pentagon, as well as an aide to both Robinson and Welander. For thirteen months, Charles Radford stole and copied NSC documents from burn bags inside his office as well as any other relevant top-secret material that came across his desk. Two of the men whom Radford pilfered this material from were well-known people inside the Nixon administration, and names that are well-known to both Kennedy assassination researchers and historians of the time, Henry Kissinger, later to become Nixon's Secretary of State and General Alexander Haig, who would serve as Nixon's Chief of Staff after the firing of H.R. Haldeman and in the Reagan administration as his Secretary of State.

When the Anderson article hit the stands, the Nixon administration went into overdrive (and panic mode) to find out who the leaker was. Nixon aide John Ehrlichman ordered the second in common of Plumbers, David Young, to look into the Anderson leak. A second person to join the hunt was Pentagon investigator W. Donald Stewart who joined forces with Young to find the culprit. Donald Stewart knew immediately that the administration now had a huge scandal on their hands. In essence, it involved a military spy ring that was targeting the White House, something unpresented in American history. The Moorer-Radford affair, as it was being called at the time was non-fiction but the brewing scandal was being compared to a best-selling book at the time called *Seven Days in May* (later to become a movie of the same name, starring Michael Douglas and Burt Lancaster) written by Fletcher Knebel and Charles Bailey about a military takeover of the United States government. David Stewart, the Pentagon sleuth, told writer James Hougan who wrote a book called *Secret Agenda:*

Watergate, Deep Throat and the CIA, regarding the analogy to *Seven Days in May,* "Did you see that film *Seven Days in May?* That's what we were dealing with, and the Senate Whitewashed it. Moorer should have been court-martialed."

As the investigation of the Anderson leak progressed, John Ehrlichman briefed the president and told him that "there were only two men in that office (Joint Chiefs), and one's an admiral, and one's a yeoman." The yeoman turned out to be petty officer Charles Radford. Radford, and it turned out that he knew Jack Anderson, and it would subsequently become known that he was the one who supplied Anderson with the material that he used for his column. They were both Mormons and spent time with each-others families during off hours. When Radford was stationed in India with the Navy, he met Jack Anderson's parents who were in that nation and befriended them. After Radford's arrest, the Nixon administration tried to tie Anderson and Radford as if they were long-standing friends-they were not. Radford met Anderson one time before December 1971. This took place at an Anderson family reunion in late 1970, in which Radford had been invited to attend by Anderson's parents. They also met once at a Chinese restaurant called the Empress which was just a social affair, nothing more, nothing less.

Charles Radford was the perfect man to act a spy for the JCS. He was 27 years old, and worked in the secret liaison office between the National Security Council which was run by Henry Kissinger, and the Joint Chiefs of Staff. He sported a top-secret clearance and part of his job was to take secret messages back and forth between the Pentagon and the White House.

When Anderson found out that Radford had entrée to the inner sanctum of Henry Kissinger's office, and the wealth of information that lay there, Anderson began to cultivate Yeoman Radford to the hilt. Anderson said of his new relationship with Radford by saying, "Suddenly, I began to view our dinner guest as he main course."

He told Anderson that Kissinger did not like India and had an animus toward that nation. Radford told Anderson that in his opinion, the U.S. dispatching of the naval fleet to the Bay of Bengal was one that would lead to the United States being involved in another war in Asia. With Anderson's article about the dispatching of the U.S. Fleet to the area, any chance of war between the United States and Pakistan ended before it began.

Shortly after the publication of Anderson's India-Pakistan article, Radford was called into the office of his commanding officer, Admiral Robert Welander who wanted to know if it was Radford who gave the compromising information to Anderson. Radford denied the allegation. b He in turn, spoke to his boss Admiral Thomas Moorer, the Chairman of the JCS. The next day, Pentagon security officers changed the combination of thirteen file cabinets that were stuffed with top-secret material that was in Radford's office. One day later, he was relieved of his duties.

Radford was then given days on end of polygraph interviews regarding the leak to Anderson. He denied giving any classified material to the writer but his denials were not believed. Radford said of the polygraph examination he had to take by saying, "I was very suspicious of the polygraph, but I felt that I had no alternative and that I had to do it. I felt that if I refused, that would make me look even guiltier." When H.R. Haldeman heard the tapes of Radford's sessions he told the president that, "Radford's polygraph makes clear that he did it." Donald Stewart was so incensed of what both Radford and Anderson had done, that he made up plans to arrest the two men if they tried to leave the country. Stewart also said that what Radford had done was more detrimental to the security of the nation as anything that Daniel Ellsberg had done during the Pentagon Papers case.

Newly released Nixon tapes shed a broader light on the Radford-Moorer affair than had previously been known. The tapes showed that Radford "broke down and cried" during his polygraph sessions and further dropped a huge bombshell when he implied that Admiral Welander gave his approval for his espionage activities. Steward believed that Radford's actions were "a hanging offense" for the military to be spying on the president and Bud Krough, who was Ehrlichman assistant, believed his actions were just the beginning of a military coup against the government, thus, the mention of the Seven Days in May scenario.

Charles Radford was also able to get secret material of the type he gave to Jack Anderson when he accompanied Henry Kissinger on his foreign trips on behalf of the Nixon administration. At the end of each day's sessions, Radford pilfered the waste paper baskets that contained the top-secret material that was supposed to be burned or discarded and either made copies for himself or kept the originals. Radford was such a trust worthy person, it seems, that he accompanied Henry Kissinger on his secret trips to China when the Nixon administration decided to begin the first phase in developing official relations with Beijing. He also accompanied General Alexander Haig to Southeast Asia on numerous occasions. Upon his return to the United States, Radford gave his material to Admiral Welander who in turn, passed it on to Admiral Moorer. Why would someone who worked in the Pentagon under Admiral Welander, not Kissinger's NSC staff, is allowed to make such sensitive trips with so much on the line? When he was questioned by the Senate committee that investigated the affair, Welander said that Radford was requested to make these trips at the request of General Haig. This was contradicted by Radford when he said that he was asked by Kissinger to accompany him to Paris because, "it was felt, a male stenographer could also run errands and handle baggage—which a female stenographer could not do." [2]

Admiral Moorer later said that he was able to get the same type of information that Radford brought back from "conventional channels," and that Radford did not have to get it for him. Moorer, it seems, had first-hand knowledge of Kissinger's planned visit to China in preparation for establishing foreign relations between the two nations, even before the CIA knew about it.

Jim Hougan writes in his book *Secret Agenda,* that Radford admitted to spying on the NSC while he worked for Admiral Welander's predecessor, Admiral Rembrandt Robinson. "When Welander took over the liaison office between the NSC and the Joint Chiefs of Staff, said Radford, he indicated to me that he knew what I had done for Admiral Robinson. He indicated he wanted me to do the same type of thing for him. He said," I understand that you have gone on these trips and brought back information of interest, and he asked me if I would do the same thing for him." (*Secret Agenda,* Page 72).

The newly released Nixon tapes paint General Alexander Haig in a rather bad light in the Radford spy scandal. Admiral Welander admitted his role in the surveillance operation, and in a bombshell

[2] Hougan, *Secret Agenda,* Page 69.

statement, implicated General Haig, who was Kissinger's aide and the intermediary between the Pentagon and the White House. Seeing that things were not going right for him, Haig called Fred Buzhardt, the general counsel to the Defense Department and asked that Admiral Welander be interviewed once again to ensure that nothing detrimental to Haig be released to the public. Haig was able to keep his side of the story quiet and he kept that secret for many years. In an interview in 1996, he said that the "spy ring was nothing more than the normal kind of internal espionage that goes on all the time among executive branch departments."

The tapes also reveal that President Nixon did not really trust either Haig or Kissinger when it came to the scandal. Nixon said of Kissinger that, "Henry is not a good security risk," and that he was "convinced that Haig must have known about this operation. It seems unlikely he wouldn't have known." Nixon was nothing but a crafty politician (hence, the moniker "Tricky Dick") and he appointed Haig as his chief of staff after the resignations of Haldeman and Ehrlichman. The president knew enough not to sacrifice Haig to the wolves after he fired Haldeman and Ehrlichman in order to keep some semblance of order in his crumbling White House, after the revelations of Watergate continued to pour out. The president knew he could not afford another scandal on his hands involving Haig in a military spying operation against his administration. He wisely let the Haig matter drop as he continued to try and save his crumbling presidency.[3]

For Nixon's part, once he found out about the Moorer-Radford affair, the president's paranoia left to center stage. He fumed over how a lowly clerk like Radford could have privy to so much secret material and began to ponder the ways to break both Radford and Anderson. Nixon was so paranoid about the entire episode that he even asked his aides to find out if there was any homosexual relationship between the two men. Pentagon sleuth Stewart said that David Young had asked him "to develop and prove that there was a homosexual relationship between Jack Anderson and Radford." To the administrations chagrin, Stewart did not pursue that angle and when David Young found out what Stewart had said, Young said, "Damn it, damn it, the President is jumping up and down and he wants this and we're always telling him everything can't be

---

[3] Hoff, Joan, *The Nixon Story You Never Heard,* Counterpunch, 10/7/2001.

done. The president is mad at us and we're telling him it can't be done." To his credit, Stewart refused to adhere to Nixon's demand and was backed up by his own boss in the Pentagon. Ehrlichman called Defense Secretary Melvin Laird who told him that he could find no evidence of any homosexual relationship between the two men and the matter was dropped.

The Radford-Moorer affair took place during increasing tensions between the Nixon administration and the military that saw in Nixon a man who was weakening the safety of the nation by pulling out our troops from Vietnam and the opening toward China at the expense of the long-standing American ties to Nationalist China. One of these military men who objected to Nixon's policies was Admiral Elmo Zumwalt who, in 1976, wrote of his misgivings in his book called *On Watch: A Memoir.* In the book he wrote of the spy ring that, "I had first completely distorted the incident and exposure would have done damage to the military at time when it was already under heavy attack." John Ehrlichman even told Nixon that Admiral Zumwalt had been given some of the purloined documents given to Anderson by Radford and both Attorney General John Mitchel and Ehrlichman believed (wrongly) that Admiral Zumwalt was somehow involved in the scandal. Nixon fumed at what he saw as a betrayal by the military against him and he railed that," The Joint Chiefs are all a bunch of shits, and Zumwalt was the biggest shit of all."[4]

For his part, President Nixon was in a damned if he did and damned if he didn't position regarding the scandal. If he went public with the facts of the scandal, there would be no telling what the ramifications would have been from the public as far as his presidency was concerned. If he couldn't control the military, how safe would the country really be?

The president met with Attorney General John Mitchel, John Ehrlichman, and Nixon aide, Egil "Bud" Krough to plan strategy. After much heated debate, Mitchell told the president that the "important thing is to paper this thing over, because this Welander thing is going to get right into the middle of Joint Chiefs of Staff." Another factor that played into Nixon's mind was that 1972 was an election year and he could not afford a disgrace that would jeopardize his chances for re-election. Nixon would not have to

[4] Feldstein, Mark, *Poisoning The Press*, Page 189.

worry on that front. The Democrats nominated Senator George McGovern who ran on an anti-Vietnam war plank and was too liberal for the nation and Nixon won in a massive landslide. While the new Nixon tapes show the president showing his anger at being blindsided by the affair, saying at times that the JCS activities was "wrong. Understand? I'm just saying that's wrong. Do you agree?" He also-called it a "federal offense of the highest order. "However, cooler minds interceded and the president decided it was best just to drop the entire matter, and pretend it never happened.

Nixon sent John Mitchell to talk with Admiral Moorer about the affair and the JCS chairman denied any knowledge of the stolen papers and said that if he had indeed seen any such papers, the fault would lie with Admiral Welander.

In the aftermath of the scandal, President Nixon re-appointed Admiral Moorer to another term as chairman of the JCS, a move that would have been unheard of if the president had decided to reveal all he knew to the public. The re-appointment of Admiral Moorer must have sent tongues wagging inside the Pentagon, as many top military leaders now recognized that they had the president over a barrel when it came to military matters. If the president would cave on the Moorer matter, what other concessions could they wrangle from him in the future?

In their seminal book on Watergate and the Moorer-Radford affair called *Silent Coup: The Removal of A President* buy Len Colodny and Robert Gettlin, the authors write that Nixon had to handle NSC advisor Henry Kissinger with kid gloves regarding the aftermath of the scandal. While the volatile Kissinger was basically kept under wraps, he asked Kissinger to shut down the JSC liaison office at the NSC. In his notes on the affair, John Ehrlichman wrote of the president's order," Don't let K blame Haig." They write that "the president's instruction was a very explicit injunction from Nixon intended to protect Haig, and at the time Ehrlichman dismissed the action as a simply logical one; Nixon didn't want Kissinger blaming his chief military aide because the espionage had been conducted by the military." So, it seems that for some reason or another, Nixon went all out to protect Haig from any future harm that might come out of the affair. Nixon was probably doing this to protect his flank from any future blackmail on Haig's part, if and when the general needed to pursue such a course.

In the end, Admiral Moorer was re-appointed chairman of the JCS. Admiral Welander was fired from his position and was given sea duty. In 1972, he was sent to Vietnam and was killed when his helicopter crashed in the Gulf of Tonkin.

Charles Radford was suspended from his Pentagon job and was sent to a new assignment at a Naval Reserve Training base in Oregon where he'd be out of the limelight and where he wouldn't be able to make any more problems than he already had.

As far as Jack Anderson was concerned, a phone tap that was in place Radford's home for six months after his transfer, revealed that he made to calls to Anderson. One of these calls was to congratulate him on winning the Pulitzer Prize for his articles on the "tilt to Pakistan."

The next year, 1972, David Young and his Plumbers would set their sights on a new target; the Watergate Apartment Complex that housed the DNC, the Democratic National Committee Headquarters. However, this affair wouldn't go the same route as that of the Radford-Moorer spy affair. In the end, the perfidy of Young and the Plumbers would unseat President Nixon, while one of the biggest scandals of the Nixon era, the plot to spy on the United States military, went hardly noticed.

Chapter 50
Nixon and the Vietnam Peace Talks

Like the Moorer-Radford affair, there was another scandal that concerned Richard Nixon during the 1968 presidential election campaign against Vice President Hubert Humphrey that the public did not know of at that time. Like the Moorer-Radford affair, the circumstances of the affair did not reach the public until years later with the release of documents that were in the records at the Lyndon Johnson library in Austin, Texas that shed light on Richard Nixon's efforts to thwart the Paris Peace talks that were going on in order to end the war in Vietnam. This secret effort by candidate Nixon involved the government of South Vietnam, and a woman who was in league with the Nixon campaign to blunt the efforts to give the government of South Vietnam a better deal when the war finally came to an end.

By 1968, there were two wars going on; one in Southeast Asia where the United States was bogged down in a seemingly endless war with casualties mounting daily, and one at home where student protests against the war were mounting on college campuses and in the streets of the nation in an ever growing intensity to end the conflict. By that time, almost 30,000 U.S. troops had been killed in the jungles of Vietnam, with no end in sight. The Vietnam War took center stage as the nation prepared for a presidential election that year. On the Democratic front, Senator Eugene McCarthy entered the race for president as a peace candidate and almost beat President Johnson in the New Hampshire primary. Robert Kennedy too entered the race for president after McCarthy's impressive showing in New Hampshire in order to seek an end to the war. After his humiliating showing in New Hampshire, President Johnson shocked the nation when he told a national audience that he was not going to run for re-election in order to try to end the war. For his part, Richard Nixon, who won the Republican nomination, stayed pretty mute in order to let the president try and end the war. But that stand would not last for long. As the campaign got down to the last weeks, and with Hubert Humphrey now in the lead in most of the polls, Nixon knew he was in trouble and took matters into his own hands in order to stop a potential defeat that was looming on the horizon.

In the weeks prior to electionday, President Johnson decided to try to end the war by convincing the North Vietnamese, the Viet Cong, and the South Vietnamese government run by President Nguyen Van Thieu, to come to the peace table in Paris, France, to see if they could end the conflict. This was no mean feat as both sides had been at war with each other for years and each side distrusted the other. It would take a huge effort to bring all three parties to the bargaining table but LBJ knew he had to take a chance, no matter the outcome. In order to prepare for conditions that would aid the peace effort, LBJ ordered a halt to the bombing of North Vietnam on October 31, 1968, only one week before the November election. No sooner had LBJ's bombing halt was announced, when a major obstacle was placed in the president's way. South Vietnamese President Thieu told his nation and the world that he would not take part in any negotiation with the north.

President Thieu was taking a huge risk in turning down his participation in the peace talks. The United States was his major benefactor in both men and military supplies and he knew that if the U.S. pulled the plug, his regime would probably collapse. He was taking a chance, no doubt, one that he was convinced was in the best interest of his nation. As the American election wound down, President Thieu had to decide who would be the best ally for his nation, Hubert Humphrey or Richard Nixon. The Vice President said publicly that if elected, he'd stop the bombing and that future U.S. combat operations would not be unlimited. For his part, Nixon said he had a secret plan to end the war (which he never revealed, and after he won the election, he resumed the bombing of the North, and invaded Cambodia), and told President Thieu he was on his side. However, in public, he said that he would not play politics with the war and would support the president in any way he could. On the side however, Nixon took another, secret track when it came to the prospect of peace talks with the North Vietnamese. Using intermediaries, he contacted the government of President Tieu and encouraged him not to relent to LBJ's pressure and told him, in secret, that if he were elected president, he'd resume the bombing and do all he could to win the war (this would be called "peace with honor").

Nixon first leanred of the LBJ peace initiative from Henry Kissinger, who, during the Nixon administration, would play in intricate role in negotiating the final peace treaty to end the war in Vietnam, and also, Nixon's secret breakthrough with China, serving as both the president's national security advisor and as Secretary of State (under both Nixon and Ford). Writing in his book on Richard Nixon called *Nixonland,* author Rick Perlstein said of this regarding the secret dealing with South Vietnam, "The Johnson team trusted Kissinger implicitly. They shouldn't have. Kissinger was a double agent feeding the intelligence to Nixon that let him scotch the peace deal before the election."

Another person who wrote about the Nixon peace initiative was the late historian Stephen Ambrose, who taught at the University of New Orleans, who wrote a biography of Richard Nixon. He wrote that, "In private, Nixon made contact with President Thieu in an effort to scuttle the peace prospects. Clark Clifford, who had replaced McNamara as secretary of defense, thought Nixon's action probably decisive in convincing President Thieu to defy President Johnson." Nixon heard that Johnson found out about his double dealing and asked Senator George Smathers of Florida to send a message to the president saying that, "there was not any truth at all in this allegation."[1]

Nixon's intermediary in the Pairs Peace talks fiasco was a well-known woman by the name of Anna Chennault, called the "Dragon Lady." She was forty-three years old at the time and was an anti-communist to the bone. Her husband was General Claire Chennault who was a World War II hero who commanded the Flying Tigers air unit that was made up of pilots from various nations who attacked Japanese troops in Southeast Asia during the war. At that time, she was living in the Watergate apartment complex and was well-known in both American and foreign diplomatic circles as someone who was influential with some of the most notable American allies in Asia at the time, namely the president of the Philippines, Ferdinand Marcos and Chiang Kai-shek of National-

[1] Summers, Anthony, *The Arrogance of Power: The Secret World of Richard Nixon,* Viking Books, New York, 2000, Page 298.

461

ist China (Taiwan). In 1968, Mrs. Chennault was active in Nixon's election campaign and served as the vice-chairman of the Republican National Finance Committee and co-chairman of Women for Nixon-Agnew. She was a friend of Nixon's for many years and considered him both a personnel and political friend.

Anna Chennault was one of the most influential women in post-war Washington even though she did not hold any elective office. She was part of the so-called "China Lobby" who advocated on behalf of the Nationalist Chinese government on Formosa and was anti-communist in its political philosophy. The members of the China Lobby blamed the Democrats for the loss of China after the war, especially blaming President Harry Truman, General George C. Marshall and Dean Acheson for "losing" China to the forces lead by Mao Zedong. Nixon knew of Mrs. Chennault and cultivated her during his days when he was out of political power. She was the only Chinese American to attend the 1968 GOP convention and using her persuasive political talents, managed to raise a quarter million dollars for the Nixon campaign. In Washington, her friends and adversaries called her "the Dragon Lady" whose name was taken from a then popular comic strip character called *Terry and the Pirates*. In a conversation with Senator Richard Russell about her, the president said, "She's young and attractive. I mean, she's a pretty good-looking girl. And she's around town and she is warning them to not get pulled in on this Johnson move."

So, it was no coincidence that Nixon reached out to Anna Chennault to act as his back channel to the government of President Thieu at this critical moment in the Paris Peace talk's initiative.

Mrs. Chennault contacted the ambassador of South Vietnam to the United States at Nixon's behest, Bui Diem. In July 1968, during the height of the presidential campaign, in a private arrangement, she introduced Nixon to Ambassador Diem at Nixon's home in New York City. Mrs. Chennault later said of that meeting that Nixon told Bui Diem that, "if elected, I will have a meeting with Thieu and find a solution to winning the war." He also told her that she would be his private contact in any future conversations concerning this matter. Records of that meeting that was released years later stated that an internal Nixon staff memo sent to "DC," Nixon's campaign pseudonym said that, "It would have to be absolute top secret. Should be," Nixon wrote, but I don't see how-with the SS (Secret Service). If it can be secret RN would like to see."

Anna Chennault met a number of times with President Tieu of South Vietnam and he told her that he "would much prefer to have the peace talks after your (the U.S.) elections," and asked her to convey this message to Nixon. President Diem also used the services of Ambassador Diem when reaching out to candidate Nixon.

She also had covert contacts with one of Nixon's most trusted political and personal friends, John Mitchell in this secret back channel deal. Mitchell served as Nixon's campaign manager during the election and would later serve as his attorney general and took part in the cover-up of the Watergate affair. She met at one time with both Nixon and Mitchell in New York City where the men told her to tell President Thieu that he would get "a better deal" if Nixon were elected. Speaking of this matter, Anna said that "they worked out this deal to win the campaign" and said, "Power overpowers all reason." During the hectic last days of the presidential campaign when Vice President Humphrey was overcoming Nixon's lead, Mrs. Chennault met a number of times with John Mitchell to discuss strategy. Mitchell told her not to call him on his private phone because he believed it was being tapped. In the forefront of all their calls was the fact that John Mitchell always told her that if and when President Johnson announced a call for peace talks, that President Thieu not participate.

John Mitchell was not paranoid when it came to believing that his phone might have been tapped. Newly discovered documents relating to the Nixon peace talks initiative, show that the National Security Agency had put wiretaps on the South Vietnamese Embassy in Washington and surveillance operations was conducted on Anna Chennault. The information gleamed from the NSA led President Johnson to conclude that Nixon was colluding with South Vietnamese President Thieu in order to block any peace initiatives. The NSA was not the only covert agency in the act. It seems that the CIA had placed a bug in the office of President Thieu.

One NSA intercept was from Ambassador Diem to President Thieu. In the message, Ambassador Diem said that time was on their side when it came to the peace talks and that, 'I am still in contact with the Nixon entourage, which continues to be the favorite despite the uncertainty provoked by the news of an imminent bombing halt."

Johnson was alarmed and bitter about Nixon's possible complicity and one of his presidential recordings makes it clear just how much he distrusted Nixon in the matter:

> Well, I've got one this morning that's pretty rough for you. We have found our friend, the Republican nominee, our California friend, has been playing on the outskirts with our enemies and our friends both, our allies and the others. He's been doing it through rather subterranean sources here.[2]

The man who was behind this secret information to LBJ was Alexander Sachs who was an economist on Wall Street, working for Lehman Corporation (later Lehman Brothers). Sachs was an old New Dealer who worked for FDR and wrote campaign speeches for him. On October 28, 1968, Sachs received information from a trusted source saying that Nixon was playing politics with the peace talks and that he wanted to make Sachs aware of what he knew. Sachs then told his friend, Under Secretary of State for Political Affairs Eugene Rostow that, "The speaker said he thought the prospects for a bombing halt or a cease fire were dim, because Nixon was playing the problem as he did the Fortas affair-to block. He was taking public positions intended to achieve that end. They would incite Saigon to be difficult, and Hanoi to wait. These difficulties would make it easier for Nixon to settle after January.

Sachs immediately told LBJ of what he had learned and the president was livid. He told him that the government of South Vietnam was "going to be difficult" and President Thieu said that the three day time period in which the bombing over the north

---

[2] Hughes, Ken, *Chasing Shadows: The Nixon Tapes, the Chennault Affair, And the Origins of Watergate,* University of Virginia Press, Charlottesville, Va., 2014, Page 5.

was halted by the U.S. and the beginning of the Paris Peace talks was not enough time to send a diplomatic party to Paris. In reality, President Thieu had no intention of sending a delegation to Paris. He had been in touch with Nixon via Anna Chennault and Ambassador Diem and knew that Nixon would hold out for a better deal for Thieu if and when he was elected president.

President Johnson now faced a huge dilemma; whether to release the scant but powerfully incriminating information he had on Nixon's perfidy as far as the peace talks were concerned. If the American public found out what Nixon was doing, then the election most likely would have swung in Humphrey's favor. But what would Nixon's reaction be? Publically, he backed Johnson's bombing halt but as we see, in private he was doing all he could to scuttle the deal. Secretary of State Dean Rusk echoed Johnson's distrust of Nixon and his team. "He said he wouldn't put it past him at all to do something like this, but he didn't have any real knowledge of him" (speaking of John Mitchell). He also said that, "I feel that this thing could blow up into the biggest mess we've ever had if we're not careful here."

Walt Rostow also took the same position about releasing the information on Nixon. He said to reveal this information are so explosive since "the materials are so explosive that they could gravely damage the country whether Mr. Nixon is elected or not. If they get out in their present form, they could be the subject of one of the most acrimonious debates we have ever witnessed."

The NSA was not the only covert agency looking for information on the Nixon-Chennault affair. One week before the election, the president ordered the FBI to find out what was going on. He told them to place a wiretap on the South Vietnamese Embassy, tell who entered and left the building, put a tail on Anna Chennault and report on her comings and goings, and place a phone tap on her apartment in the Watergate complex. The FBI obliged the president on the first three items but did not place the bug in her home. The surveillance of Mrs. Chennault paid off handsomely as the FBI saw her enter the South Vietnamese embassy in Washington on October 30, most likely to meet with her contacts in the building.

The NSA wiretaps on the office of President Thieu in Saigon

alerted the Johnson administration to the fact that Thieu was monitoring the political situation in Washington as far the upcoming elections were concerned. One intercept quoted President Thieu as saying that the Johnson administration "might halt the U.S. bombing of North Vietnam as part of a peace maneuver that would help Humphrey's campaign but that South Vietnam might not go along." Another intercept had the South Vietnamese leader as saying," It appears that Mr. Nixon will be elected as the next president and that any settlement with the Viet Cong should be put off until the new president was in place."

President Johnson now wanted to reach out to his political adversaries in the Republican Party to inform them of what Nixon was up to. One of these calls went to the Senate Republican Leader Everett Dirksen. Dirksen was one of the most powerful and respected lawmakers in Washington and despite his party affiliation, Johnson considered him someone whom he could talk with in confidence. The president phoned Dirksen on November 2, three days before the election and told him the latest details of what was going on and asked Dirksen to intervene on his behalf. Nixon told Dirksen that, "The agent (Chennault) says she's just talked to the boss in New Mexico and that he said that the South Vietnamese must hold out, just hold on until after the election. Johnson said, "We know what Thieu is saying to them out there. We're pretty well informed at both ends. Johnson believed the boss in New Mexico, was Nixon's running mate, Spiro Agnew, who was there on a campaign trip." Johnson then told Dirksen that, "I don't want to get this in the campaign. They oughtn't be doing this. This is treason." Dirksen replied by saying, "I know."[3]

The president further told Sen. Dirksen that the public would be outraged if it found out what Nixon was doing but didn't want to publicize the fact that he knew what was going on. Dirksen than said he'd get in touch with Nixon and would get back to the president. LBJ told Dirksen to tell Nixon that, "You just tell them that their people are messing around in this thing, and if they don't want it on the front pages, they better quit it."

Dirksen called Nixon and relayed what Johnson told him. Nixon was probably angered that the administration had somehow

[3] Parry, Robert, *How Richard Nixon Sabotaged 1968 Vietnam Peace Talks to Get Elected President,*www.truth-out.org, January 18, 2013.

found out about his double dealing, but he wouldn't come out and admit it. On November 3, Nixon called the president and told him that he just gone on TV and said that he'd do nothing to undermine the president's efforts for a peace deal with Hanoi. He lied to the president by saying, "I feel very strongly about this. Any rumblings around about somebody trying to sabotage the Saigon government's attitude, there's absolutely no credibility as far as I'm concerned." The president, who by now had received all the tapes from the NSA bugging, snapped back at the candidate by telling him in no uncertain terms, "I'm very happy to hear that Dick, because that is taking place. Here's the history of it. I don't want to call you but I wanted you to know what happened." In the same taped conversation, Nixon, told the president once again that, "My God, I would never to anything to encourage Saigon not to come to the table. Good God, we want them over in Paris, we got to get them to Paris or you can't have a peace. The war apparently now is about where it could be brought to an end. The quicker, the better. To hell with the political credit, believe me." LBJ ended the conversation by warning Nixon that, "You just see that your people don't tell the South Vietnamese that they're going to get a better deal out of the United States government than a conference."

There was however, a stone that could have blown the whole Nixon-peace deal to shreds. It seemed that a reporter from the *Christian Science Monitor,* named Beverly Deppe who was in Saigon, got word from her sources that something was in the wind concerning Nixon's outreach to President Thieu. She was going to write a story regarding Nixon's influence on President Thieu and the president's refusal to send a delegation to the Paris peace talks until the election was over. Another *Monitor* reporter named Saville Davis checked out her story with Ambassador Diem but he knocked down the story, saying there was no truth to it. The Deppe/Davis story reached President Johnson's desk and after consulting with Clark Clifford and Walt Rostow, they decided not to go public with the Nixon bombshell story.[4]

On November 5, 1968, the American people went to the polls, and in one of the closets presidential elections in years, elected Richard Nixon over Hubert Humphrey by only 500,000 votes, unaware of the back channel shenanigans that the new president-elect

[4] Ibid.

was doing.

After the election, Johnson telephoned Nixon and threatened to release the peace talks story if Nixon didn't cooperate. Nixon told the president that he'd call President Thieu and ask him to take part in the Paris negotiations. However, nothing of the sort took place and as the day of Nixon' s inauguration got closer, the president ordered Walt Rostow to remove the incriminating papers from the White House safe were it was being held.

When Nixon entered office, he took steps to find Johnson's file on him at all costs. He ordered H.R. Haldeman, his chief of staff, to find and destroy Rostow's file so no one could get their hands on it. In their conversations, Haldeman told Nixon that Rostov's file was being held at the Brookings Institution in Washington and the president proposed that they use E. Howard Hunt to enter Brookings and find the file. Remember, that Nixon asked his Plumbers unit, which included Hunt, to break into Brookings and get back the Pentagon Papers which were leaked by Daniel Ellsberg. Haldeman recalled that on June 30, 1971, the president told him that, "I want the break-in. Hell, they do that. You're to break into the place, rifle the files, and bring them in. Just go in and take it. Go in around 8:00 or 9:00 o'clock." Just like the proposed raid of Brookings to find the Pentagon Papers, this plan never took place.

But this was not the end of the story. Upon the death of President Johnson on June 22, 1973, Walt Rostow now had to decided what to do with what he called the "X" Envelope containing the Nixon pace file. He wrote a three-page summary of what was in the files called a "memorandum for the record," in which he outlined some of his thoughts on the scandal. He wrote, "I am inclined to believe the Republican operation in 1968 relates in two ways to the Watergate affair of 1972. Second, they got away with it. Despite considerable press commentary after the election, the matter was never investigated fully. Thus, as the same men faced the election of 1972, there was nothing in their previous experience with an operation of doubtful propriety to warn them off, and there were memories of how close an election could get and the possible utility of pressing to the limit-and beyond."

On June 26, 1973, at the height of the Watergate affair, Rostow finally decided what to do with the "X" Envelope. He wrote in pen a "Top-Secret" note that said, "To be opened by the Director, Lyndon Baines Johnson Library, not earlier than fifty (50) years from this date."

Luckily for historians and others interested in the Nixon years, the curator at the LBJ Library did not wait fifty years to open Rostow's file. On July 22, 1994, the envelope was opened and the archivists began their painstaking process of going through all the papers and audio files contained inside.

No one knows why President Johnson did not publically reveal the contents of the "X" Envelopes in the waning days of the 1968 election. If he did, most likely the shocking news that Nixon was colluding with the government of South Vietnam to hinder the peace talks would have thrown the election to Vice President Humphrey. Maybe Johnson believed such revelations would cause a tremendous amount of harm to the nation in the midst of the war and possibly tarnish his reputation as well. During Nixon's time in office, 20,000 more American soldiers died in Vietnam whose lives may have been saved if the Paris peace talks had succeeded in 1969 after Nixon took office.

Anna Chennault may have put the whole sordid affair in perspective when she gave an interview to the *Shanghai Star* in 2002. In the interview she said of the Nixon peace deal affair, "To end the war was my only demand. But after Nixon became president, he decided to continue the war. Politicians are never honest."

Chapter 51
Searching for the Octopus

Independent journalist Danny Casolaro was on the trail of the biggest story of his life. For years he had been investigating a host of national scandals that dominated the Reagan-Bush years from the October Surprise, Iran-Contra, the mob and other lesser tales of corruption. It was in search of the "Octopus," as he began to call these conspiracies that he was trying to unravel, that brought him to his uncertain demise in a hotel room in Martinsburg, West Virginia on August 10, 1991.But the death of Danny Casolaro, ruled a suicide by the local medical examiner, is still hotly debated among writers and other interested parties who believe that he was done in just as he was about to expose the truth concerning the "Octopus" and its many and varied links to recent American history.

Daniel Casolaro was born in McLean, Virginia on June 16, 1947. He had a rather harsh upbringing with one of his siblings dying shortly after being born, and a sister named Lisa, dying of an apparent drug overdose. His father was a doctor and Danny came from a well-to-do family. He attended Providence College and dropped out at age twenty, never graduating. He married a girl named Terrill Pace and they had a son, but divorced after thirteen years of marriage.

He made a living as a freelance writer, and some of his articles were published in such magazines such as, *The Washington Crime News Service, The Globe, The National Star, The National Enquirer, The Washington Star, The Providence Journal,* and *Home and Auto.* He also cofounded a magazine called *Computer Age,* and later sold it, taking a loss. He was also a poet and a songwriter.

As he was doing his research he would often tell his friends that he had a lucrative contract with a major publisher who was funding his work; no such contract existed. In this regard, while he was engaged in the Octopus research, he told his friend Bill McCoy who was a retired CID (Criminal Investigative Division) officer who was then a private detective, that he had been given an assignment by *Time* Magazine to do a story on his work. He also said he was working with the noted Washington reporter, Jack

Anderson on the story, and that he had been given assurances by publishers, Little Brown and Time Warner who said they'd finance his work (no such assurances were ever given). McCoy later said of his friends claims that it was "misplaced exuberance. He wasn't getting to the nub of it."

It was in 1990 after Danny sold his share in his *Computer Age* magazine that he turned his full attention to tracking down the Octopus. It was during that year that a friend steered him to the Inslaw case, a story that was just starting to break in the national press.

Inslaw was a software company that was run by Bill Hamilton and his wife. Hamilton was an ex-employee of the National Security Agency, the top-secret U.S. government agency that keeps track of foreign communications and codes. The Hamilton's were developing a powerful computer system called PROMIS (Prosecutors Management Information System) for the U.S. Justice Department. PROMIS would allow prosecutors to follow the track of criminals through the labyrinth of the justice system, telling the interested party such information as the offenders criminal past, known associates, aliases, and pending court cases, etc. In 1982, for $10 million, Hamilton was going to set up this massive software system for the Justice Department, headed by President Reagan's Attorney General, Edwin Meese. PROMIS was supposed to have been installed at the offices of 42 U.S. Attorney across the nation. But then things began to go very wrong, very fast. The Justice Department then decided not to pay the Hamilton's for the PROMIS software and in February 1985 the government withheld payments of $1.77 million in costs and fees, and took action to bankrupt the company. The Hamilton's took the U.S. government to court and won two reversals of the Justice Department decision before their case was thrown out by the U.S. Court of Appeals.

Now, a new twist entered the Hamilton-PROMIS deal. A man named Earl Brain, who was a friend of Attorney General Meese, and the owner of United Press International, had a controlling interest in a software company called Hadron Inc. Brain was able to get the rights to PROMIS software and won a U.S. government contract. Previously, Dominic Laiti, the Hadron Chairman, tried to buy PROMIS but Hamilton refused to sell. Brain was now able to get the software by intervention by the Justice Department. Brain however, had a secret side to him, and had been linked to covert operations with U.S. and Israeli intelligence agencies, and was said to have once worked for the CIA. A former Israeli intelligence agent named Ari Ben-Menashe, said that Brain "contacted Rafi Eitan, a former Mossad agent and counter-terrorism adviser to Israel with the intent that the software be sold to intelligence agencies around the world. Ben-Menashe further claims that it was Rafi Eitan who initiated the idea of installing a "trap door" into the software, which would permit the Mossad to secretly enter the database after it was sold, thus allowing them to spy on countries that purchased the program. Deciding that the trap door be installed outside Israel, Ben-Menashe contracted Yehuda Ben-Haman, who owned Software and Engineering Consultants based in Chatsworth, California, and for a fee of $5,000 contracted him for the job." [5]

Brain then sold the software with the "Trap Door" installed, to the government of Jordan to be used by their intelligence services. The CIA now got right into the program and asked Earl Brain to help them out. They developed their own software like that of PROMIS and asked Michael Riconosciuto, who was the director of Research for Wakenhut Corporation, a private security company, to help them out. The work on the CIA's new software took place at the Cabazon Indian Reservation near Indio California. It was at this hideaway location that Riconosciuto set up the CIA's trap door on PROMIS. Riconosciuto further said that the implementation of the PROMIS software would eventually be used by other nations' intelligence services.

He said that PROMIS had been used by two departments of the Canadian government and that Bill Hamilton did not authorize the sale. In the wake of the illegal sale of the software to Canada, Inslaw hired former attorney general Elliot Richardson to defend the company and he filed a legal suit saying that Inslaw was a victim of a conspiracy led by the Justice Department. In court, the bankruptcy judge George Bason, ruled in favor of Inslaw and they were given a settlement of $6.8 million in compensation. However, in the aftermath of the bankruptcy trial Judge Bason was not re-

[5] Bixman,Karen, *Obstruction of Justice: Exposing the Inslaw Scandal and Related Crimes*, Media Bypass Magazine, No date.

appointed to the bench, only to be replaced by one of the attorneys who argued the Inslaw case for the government. That was not to be the end of the legal case as far as Inslaw was concerned. In 1991, the U.S. District Court of Appeals reversed the original decision saying that the bankruptcy courts had no jurisdiction in taking on the case in the first place. The U.S. Congress not got into the act and the Senate formed a Permanent Subcommittee was conducted to look into the facts surrounding the loss of PROMIS from Bill Hamilton. After their investigation, the members of the committee said that their inquiry was hampered by a lack of cooperation by the Justice Department and said, "It found employees who desired to speak to the subcommittee but chose not to out of fear for their jobs." The Chief Investigator for the Senate Judiciary Committee told Bill Hamilton that a source of his in the Justice Department told him "that Inslaw was a lot dirtier for the Department of Justice than Watergate had been, both in its breath and depth." The committee said that they could find no proof that any employees at Justice had been intimidated and no action was taken against them.

In the late 1980s, Bill Hamilton got a call from a friend who told him to call a man named Michael Riconosciuto who had information related to the PROMIS controversy. According to Riconosciuto, Edwin Meese had given the software to one of his business associates (Earl Brain) who then sold it to police departments in foreign countries such as Canada, South Korea, Israel and Iraq (Hadron Inc.).

Hamilton, who had also been a friend of Danny Casolaro, told him of his call from Riconosciuto and the reporter immediately got in touch with him. The two men met and Riconosciuto began to regale Casolaro with a myriad tale of deception and spy stories that would boggle the mind. He told Casolaro that he knew "Carlos the Jackal," the infamous terrorist who attacked French police and aided the PLO which was headed by Yasir Arafat, taped a phone conversation with then CIA Director William Casey, said he was responsible for the collapse of the CIA funded Nugan Hand Bank, and other speculative tales. He also told Casolaro that the Canadian Royal Mounted Police were using PROMIS in their work, and more importantly, that he had proof that the Reagan administration had used the software during the so-called "October Surprise" in which it was alleged that the U.S. hostages were kept in jail in Iran in a secret deal between the Reagan campaign and the government of Iran. Riconosciuto told Hamilton that both he and Earl Brain had traveled to Iran in 1980 and paid $40 million to certain Iranian officials in order to persuade them not to release the hostages before the presidential election of 1980 between Reagan and President Carter. It was reported that in the aftermath of the Brain-Riconosciuto trip to Iran that Brain profited from the illegal pirating of the PROMIS software.[6]

Riconosciuto said the research for PROMIS took place on the Cabazon Indian Reservation near Indio, California. Casolaro said he had a reliable witness who told him that he had seen both Riconosciuto and Brain on different occasions at the Cabazon Reservation. David Corn, who covered the Inslaw story, wrote that, "Hamilton discovered that Wackenhut had indeed entered into the venture with the Cabazons to produce arms and equipment on their sovereign territory for U.S. agencies and that Riconosciuto was somehow involved." (David Corn, (The *Nation,* 1991).

Riconosciuto also made a wild claim that he was entangled with the development of chemical and biological weapons development with a company called Park-O-Meter which was owned by Seth Ward. He said that the weapons were destined for transfer to the Contras and were to be taken to them via C130 transport planes that were being flown out of a secret airstrip located in Mena, Arkansas. He also asserted that he developed a computer software system to help launder money coming from the Mena site for the Contra operation. Located near the Rich Mountains in the beautiful Ouachita Mountains, Mena would become one of the hot spots in the U.S. government's covert supply of military equipment to the Sandinista rebels fighting the government of Nicaragua during the administration of President Reagan. But what transpired was not just the secret supplying of arms to the U.S. backed rebels; it also involved the trans-shipment of illegal drugs from South America in exchange for arms from the U.S.

Riconosciuto did not fear well in the long run. He was arrested in March 1991 in Washington, D.C. on charges of selling methamphetamines. At his trial in January 1992, he said that he was being

[6] Casolaro's death and his investigation into the Inslaw case, www.apfn.org.

set up by the Justice Department but he was not believed and a jury convicted him on 7 counts of distributing drugs.

The facts of this huge conspiracy that was now starring Danny Casolaro in the face was all he needed to devote all his time to exposing what he saw as an all-encompassing government tale of misdeeds and corruption. If he had any idea of what lay ahead, he might have had second thoughts.

It was at this point that Danny Casolaro wound up in Martinsburg, West Virginia in search of the Octopus but he probably went there in search of a source that was going to reveal to him the mastermind of the conspiracy. After Casolaro's death, his housekeeper, Olga, said that she received many threatening phone calls from people who would not identify themselves.

Before leaving for Martinsburg, Casolaro told his family that if anything happened to him they should threat his death as "unordinary." While in Martinsburg he met with a friend named William Turner at the Sheraton Hotel at about 2:30 in the afternoon. Turner said he gave Danny a bunch of documents, and then departed. While at the Sheraton, Danny met with a man who had the appearance of being an Arab. He also saw a man named Mike Looney who rented a room next to Danny's. Casolaro told him that he was going to meet a source who would help him "solve the case." Whoever this "source" was, he never showed up.

In the early afternoon of August 10, 1991, a maid, going into Casolaro's room, found him dead in the bathtub, his wrists slit, and a suicide note near hid bed. According to the medical examiner, there were three or four wounds on the right wrist and seven or eight on the left. When the local law enforcement and medical teams arrived at the hotel, they found a note which read:

> To those who I love the most.
> Please forgive me for the worst possible thing I could
> have done. Most of all, I'm sorry to my son. I know
> deep down that God will let me in.

The local coroner did an autopsy and then, without the permission of the Casolaro family, embalmed the body. In an interesting note to the story, a few days after Casolaro was found dead, an agent of the FBI named Thomas Gates, who knew Danny, arrived in Martinsburg to look into the matter.

At his funeral, the family was surprised to see strange military men at attendance, one man, who put a medal on the casket. What were these men doing there?

Elliot Richardson, the attorney for Inslaw told reporters after the death of Danny Casolaro that, "The significant thing about Danny's death is that he was just seeking confirmation of what he believed he already knew. He said that if the informers Mr. Casolaro had already talked to were to be believed, it involved a conspiracy far worse that Watergate." Richardson wrote an opinion piece in the *New York Times* in defense of Bill Hamilton and Inslaw. He wrote, "When the Watergate special prosecutor began his investigation, indications of the President's involvement were not as strong as those that now point to a widespread conspiracy implicating government officials in the theft of Inslaw technology. " Richardson, who himself would resign in the wake of the so-called "Saturday Night Massacre" during the height of the Watergate scandal when he was ordered by President Nixon to fire Special Prosecutor Archibald Cox (he refused). By all accounts, Elliot Richardson, a man with a long and distinguished service to his country, was not by any means a conspiracy theorist. Rather, he was a man who did the right things and was not intimidated by anyone in authority. For him to say that the circumstances of Casolaro's death were suspicious, were high praise indeed.

Just like the mysterious deaths of witnesses after the assassination of President Kennedy, there were a number of unexplained deaths surrounding the Casolaro case. For example, Paul Morasca, who was a roommate of Michael Riconosciuto in San Francisco, was murdered in January 1982 after he began to expose CIA activities, partly which involved the Wakenhut Company. Private investigator Larry Guerrin, who worked for Riconosciuto on the Inslaw case, was found dead in Mason County, Washington, in February 1987. An important source for Casolaro in his investigation was Alan Standorf, was found shot to death shortly before he was to meet with Casolaro on January 31, 1991 in the car he owned at Washington National Airport. Standorf worked for the NSA as an electronic employee and provided Danny with information on the Justice Department. Another suspicious death was that of a lawyer named David Eisman who was killed only 24-hours before he was scheduled to meet with Riconosciuto. It was believed that Eisman was involved in some capacity with the CIA. Peter Sandvugen, who was helping Riconosciuto in his case against the Justice Department, was found dead on December 2, 1992. He once worked for the CIA in the 1980's, although what he did for the agency is not known.[7]

Following Casolaro's death, Elliot Richardson called for an official probe into Danny's death but that request was denied. However, a congressional subcommittee on Economic and Commercial Law of the Committee on the Judiciary had hearings on the Inslaw affair and Casolaro's death. Their report, which was released on September 10, 1992, accused some Justice Department officials with criminal misconduct and asked that a special prosecutor be appointed. Attorney General William Barr declined to appoint one, but asked that Chicago attorney Nicholas Bua, a former U.S. District Judge, and five Justice Department prosecutors take on the case. In June 1993, after a perfunctory investigation, the Bua Report was released and absolved the Justice Department officials of any malfeasance in the affair.

Whatever Danny Casolaro was investigating went to the grave with him. But to this day, the questions surrounding the activities of the "Octopus," still linger.

---

[7] Karen Bixman, Media Bypass Magazine.

Chapter 52
Who Killed Martin Luther King?

The year 1968 would prove to be one of the most eventful times in American history. By the time the year was over, two of the most important figures of the day, Senator Robert Kennedy and Dr. Martin Luther King would die of assassins bullets, the city of Chicago would be rocked by anti-Vietnam War riots during the Democratic National Convention, and Richard Nixon would be elected president of the United States that November in one of the closets national elections in years. It was a time that most of those who were living would never forget and by the time the calendar crossed into 1969, it was one that we'd be happy to see gone.

The first of our national tragedies was the assassination of Dr. Martin Luther King on the evening of April 4, 1968 while he was in Memphis, Tennessee to give support to striking sanitation workers who were demanding better wages and working conditions. At 6:01P.M, as the Rev. King stood on the balcony of the Lorraine Motel, he was felled by a shot that came from a motel that was directly across the street. Dr. King was hit in the jaw then lodged into his spine. He was immediately taken by his aides to St. Josephs Hospital were doctors were unable to save his life and died at 7:05 P.M. Two months later, a white man by the name of James Earl Ray was arrested in London for the death of Dr. King and was brought back to Memphis to stand trial. At his trial, James Earl Ray pleaded guilty in order to be spared the death penalty and was given a ninety-nine year jail term. No sooner had he plead guilty, then he changed his plea, saying he had been railroaded into taking the fall for killing Dr. King and that he had no role in the assassination. In the early 1970s, the United States Congress (HSCA) began a public investigation into the deaths of both President John F. Kennedy and Dr. Martin Luther King. The Kennedy assassination probe got most of the attention, while the King case was put on the national backburner. In the end, the committee said that JFK was probably killed as a result of a conspiracy but were unable (or unwilling) to name the possible suspects. In their findings in the King case, the committee believed that James Earl Ray was the sole assassin of Dr. King, that he had fired one shot that killed him, that Ray had stalked King in the months leading up to the assassination in Memphis, and that the shot that killed him had come from the bathroom window of the boarding house across the street from the Lorraine Motel.

However in the decades following the assassination of Dr. King, new evidence that was not available at the time puts a new light on the events in Memphis on April 4, 1968, including a number of white-wingers who had the means, motive and the opportunity to kill Dr. King, a shadowy figure whom Ray called "Raoul" who was supposed to have guided Ray on his trail to Memphis, the fact that there were certain U.S. military units in Memphis at the time of the King assassination who were monitoring conditions in the city, the possibilities that his brother, Jerry Ray had been deceptive when questioned by the HSCA about certain aspects of his brother's actions in the assassination story (including that about Raoul), and the fact that in 1999 a trial involving a wrongful death lawsuit brought by the King family against a man named Loyd Jowers, a former Memphis café owner, who claimed in 1993 that he conspired with others unknown to kill King while he was staying in Memphis, found that a conspiracy had indeed existed in the death of Dr. King.

The death of Dr. King was not only a personal tragedy for this family but for the nation and the world at large. He was the prime figure in the civil rights movement in the United States, preaching non-violent action to break the barriers of prejudice that had been inflicted upon the African-American population of the United States since the beginning of the civil rights movement in the early 1960s. During his time as the preeminent civil rights leader in the country, Dr. King had accumulated many enemies who saw him as a person who was inspired by the communist movement and who posed a danger to the nation. Among those whom hated Dr. King were those in the white supremacist movement, and members of the FBI, led by J. Edgar Hoover who had put Dr. King under surveillance for years in order to discredit him and ruin his life. He was also a vocal opponent of the War in Vietnam and attacked both the Johnson and Nixon administration's policies on the war, which led to animosity between both sides. All of these challenges to the status quo made Dr. King a force that the establishment in the country had to be wary of. So, it was in this highly volatile setting that Dr. King made his trip to Memphis in April 1968 and his tragic death.

James Earl Ray was born on March 10, 1928 in Alton, Illinois. His family had little roots and made many moves over the years. Ray held many menial jobs which led him nowhere and in December 1945he enlisted in the Army. He was stationed in West Germany and continued to get into trouble and after a while, the Army decided to discharge him due to "ineptness and lack of adaptability for service" in December 1948. He then traveled the country in seek of employment, going to Chicago, Los Angeles and in between and was arrested for numerous crimes. Back in Illinois, Ray robbed a cab driver, was found guilty at trial, and was sentenced to the State Prison farm in Pontiac, until his release in March, 1954. He then went to Florida where he was arrested for the robbery of a Post Office in Illinois and on July 1, 1955, was sentenced to 45 months at the Federal penitentiary in Leavenworth, Kansas. His crime spree continued and he was arrested again in March 1956 for the robbery of grocery stores in St. Louis, Missouri and back in Alton, Illinois. He was then sentenced to begin a 20-year jail term at the Missouri State Penitentiary but tried to escape in November 1961, and again in March 1966.

His next attempt at escape was successful when, on April 23, 1967, he fled from the prison and eluded state and federal authorities for the next 11½ months. He managed to wind up in such cities as Montreal, Canada, Chicago, Birmingham, Los Angeles, and Atlanta, one step ahead of the law. While in he was in Birmingham, Ray bought a high-powered .243-caliber Winchester rifle, but days later, he returned to the store and exchanged it for a. 30.06 caliber Remington. The store clerk said that he had changed the rifle on the advice of his brother but Ray later said he exchanged the rifle on the advice of the shadowy man called Raoul. On April 4, 1968, Ray arrived in Memphis, Tennessee and, under the alias of "John Willard," rented a room at the Lorraine Motel, across the street from where Dr. King and his party were staying. The owner of the rooming house, Mrs. Bessie Brewer, offered Ray a certain room but he turned it down in favor of another one that faced the Lorraine Motel. The official version of the events say that Ray stood in the second floor bathroom of the hotel and fired one shot that killed Dr. King. But here was where things began to get murky. There were no actual eyewitnesses who saw James Earl Ray kill King or anyone else from the bathroom window. A man who lived in the rooming house, Charles Stephens, heard the shot and ran out of his room to see what happened and said he said he saw a man running out of the hotel with a bundle in his arms. The man he identified was James Earl Ray. Two other witnesses, Harold Carter, who was drinking near the motel, said he saw a man fleeing in the direction the bushes near the motel. Solomon Jones Jr. who was the chauffeur to Dr. King, also said he saw someone running away from the motel but both men could not identify who he was.

After the assassination, authorities found a bundle that was wrapped up in a bedspread near the motel. The bundle contained a rifle in a box, a radio, a pair of binoculars, tools, and some clothing. The rifle and binoculars were purchased by Ray, but why would he leave such incriminating evidence on the ground in front of the shooters nest for the police to find? If he indeed did do the shooting, that evidence would be directly tied to Ray and could have been used in a court of law. The HSCA said that Ray dropped the bundle as he made his escape from the Lorraine Motel and headed for his white Mustang for his getaway from the city.

In 1997, new information came to light regarding the arrival of certain Army intelligence units to Memphis only days before the arrival of Dr. King in the city. The unit, the 111th Military Intelligence Group came from Fort McPherson in Atlanta and contained at least 10 undercover agents after a riot took place on March 28, 1966 during a protest march King led in support of striking sanitation workers in the city. Many of these soldiers' arrival and departure in Memphis coincided with Dr. King's arrival and departure from the city. Col. Edward McBride, the commander of the 111th Group said that, "We were never given any mission to keep King under surveillance."

A man named Jimmy Locke, who lead the Memphis task force and as there when King was shot said, "We took note when he was in Memphis in his public moves. We knew he was speaking, we knew he was going to march in the parade. We weren't particularly concerned except that he might be the catalyst for an event of some kind." None of the agents who were part of the 111th Military Intelligence Group said they took any action against Dr. King while they were in the city, nor did they bug his hotel room as many have speculated. Speaking to these charges, Colonel McBride said, "That's the most ridiculous thing I ever heard." The agents said they were there to monitor public meetings, using civilians and other undercover assets and to report when Dr. King and his people attended these rallies.[1]

Fleeing the scene of the shooting, Ray drove his white Mustang to Atlanta and then somehow managed to flee to Canada. During his travels, James Earl Ray used a number of aliases to hide his true identity. He purchased his rifle under the name "Harvey Lowmeyer" and it was with that identity that the Memphis Police began looking for him. When the FBI got into the investigation of King's assassination, they centered on a man who called himself "Eric S. Gault," a name used on a registration card found at the New Rebel Motel in Memphis. Ray began using the alias of "Eric S. Gault" beginning in late July 1967 when he went to Canada. William Pepper, a lawyer who was a family friend of the King's and an author on the King assassination, wrote in his book, *Act of State :The Execution of Martin Luther King,* said, that in his investigation of the assassination, a source showed him a picture of Eric St. Vincent Gault, the same identity that Ray assumed while on the run between July 18, 1967 and April 4, 1968. Pepper wrote that the picture of Eric St. Vincent Gault came from a file that belonged to the NSA, the National Security Agency. The real Eric Gault worked for Union Carbide's factory in Toronto, Canada and that he had a top-secret clearance. Why did James Earl Ray pick a real name of a person who had a high-security clearance and more to the point, how did he find Gault in the first place? Was it just coincidence, or were there other people helping him along the way?

Pepper also wrote that Union Carbide worked in high-security research for its U.S. parent company. According to William Pepper,

---

[1] "Retired agents say they monitored King in Memphis." Associated Press, November 30, 1997.

the NSA took part in the investigation of the King assassination by putting certain people on a watch list. The Watch List was given to Frank Raven, who worked in the NSA and that he was given the names to be put on the watch list by other intelligence agencies. The granting authority to put people on the watch list came from the Secretary of Defense, Clark Clifford, who said he had no recollection of issuing such an order. Raven said he objected to having been ordered to use the watch list but said that, 'You couldn't argue with it-it came from the highest level.'[2]

During his flight from the law, Ray used other aliases other than that of Eric Gault. He used the names of real people such as Raymond George Sneyd, Paul Bridgeman, both of whom were real people who lived in Toronto. It is possible that Ray found these names by using the public records of that time, either the phone book, or other open source material that he could locate. However, before going to Toronto, there was never any proof that Ray had previously been to Canada.

Fingerprints found on the rifle that was taken from the bundle left at the scene, soon matched that of James Earl Ray, and a nation-wide alert went out for his capture. He then traveled to East St. Louis for some time before heading to Chicago where he bought an old Chrysler for $100.00. He then headed to Detroit and then on to Canada. According to Ray, it was during this time that he met a man who called himself "Raoul" who gave him money in exchange for his help in importing certain amounts of contraband of which he had no knowledge of. Due to vigilant police work, on June 1, 1968, the Royal Canadian Mountain Police found a potential photographic match between two individuals and Ray and a man named George Raymond Sneyd. On June 8, 1968, Ray was arrested at Heathrow Airport in London, England, as he was making further travel plans to Rhodesia. He was then extradited back to the U.S.to stand trial for the murder of Martin Luther King. At trial, he was represented by Arthur Hanes but was soon replaced by the flamboyant lawyer, Percy Forman. Ray plead guilty in order to be spared the death penalty and was given a 99-year sentence. On the day of his trial, Ray told the judge that in his opinion, there was a conspiracy at foot in the King assassination.

[2] Pepper, William, *Act of State: The Execution of Martin Luther King*, Verso Books, New York, 2003, Page 78.

He said that he did not totally agree with the findings of Attorney General Ramsey Clark that he alone killed King and three days later he changed his plea to innocent and asked for a new trial in a letter to the presiding Judge, Battle. The judge did not act on his request and in a highly improbably set of circumstances, he was found dead of an apparent heart attack while in his chambers. But how did a loner with little education, very little money and no infrastructure to aide him on his journey, make it across the Atlantic and wind up in London? Here, according to Ray's story is where the mysterious Raoul came in.

According to Ray's account, the mysterious Raoul gave him money for his use and in February of 1968, he sent Ray funds for him to travel to Los Angeles, but then told him to go to New Orleans. Instead, both Ray and Raoul traveled together to Atlanta, but then their itinerary changed, and they were scheduled to go to Miami, but the trip never took place. In late March 1968, Raoul told Ray that they were now heading to Memphis for some kind of work. On April 4, 1968, the day that King was killed, Raoul told Ray to go to a movie but he said no. Raoul then sent Ray to get the tires of his car changed and when he returned to the Lorraine Motel he found it surrounded by police. Ray then made his escape from Memphis in his white Mustang and it was only when he was on the highway going to out of the city that he heard of the killing of Dr. King. When he was questioned by the members of the HSCA regarding his escape from Memphis, the staff counsel asked him if he ever had any thought in his mind that the events that had just taken place in Memphis (the King killing) had anything to do with the orders that Raoul had given him earlier that day. Ray responded by saying, "No, no there was no connection that day whatever."

Ray said that minutes after he heard of the killing of Dr. King, he wanted to call some of Raoul's associates to find out what to do. He now realized that the police were seeking a man driving a white Mustang and believed he was now wanted in the assassination of Martin Luther King. Ray now headed for Atlanta and had become convinced that Raoul was somehow involved in the assassination of King and that he'd be caught up in the middle of the manhunt. When questioned by the HSCA another time, he was asked again about the possible role of Raoul in the assassination. He told the staff members that, "I think it was his association with the Mustang, he was in the general area, and, of course, the guns." He continued by saying, "If they were looking for me, then the next assumption was that they might have been looking for this Raoul, and there may have been some offense committed in this area." Ray told the committee that while he was with Raoul, that the latter never said anything bad about Dr. King and made no mention of killing him. The HSCA made a full-fledged attempt to find out who Raoul was and never could come up with any definite conclusion of his true identity. In their report, they wrote regarding this elusive person, "Ray's story of his flight assumes, as a necessary ingredient, Raoul's presence in the Memphis rooming house. The committee, however, found no evidence to support the existence of Raoul on April 4, 1968, or any other time."

Ray told many different versions of the Raoul story and some of it made no sense. He told his first lawyer, Arthur Hanes, that around 6 P.M. on April 4, 1968, he was sitting in front of the rooming house when Raoul came running into the car, put a covering over his head and told him to drive away. After a few blocks, Raoul jumped out of the car and Ray never saw him again. The consensus among those historians and writers who have looked into the King assassination, believe that the elusive Raoul was a combination of a number of people who aided Ray during his time on the lamb. In the ensuing years since King was assassinated, there has been no verifiable identification of just who Raoul really was. However, that may have changed due to the research of attorney William Pepper and may shed new light on just who Raoul was.

In 1991, William Pepper had filed a civil law suit against Loyd Jowers, and the unnamed Raoul and one of the people whom he was preparing to depose was Glenda Grabow who told him that while living in Houston, Texas in the 1960s, she had met a person by the name of Raoul and that she subsequently found out that this man had some part in the killing of Dr. King. Pepper met with Glenda Grabow at her Memphis, Tennessee home and she proceeded to tell him her story. In 1962, Glenda, who was then a teenager, met a man who called himself "Drago." Many years later she found out that his real name was Raoul (In his book,

Pepper used the pseudonym of "Pereria" as Raoul's last name). After Glenda married at a young age, she met with Drago many times and she oftentimes drove him around the city. She also met a man named Armando who subsequently told the Grabow's that Drago was his cousin and that his real name was Raoul Pereria and that Pereria came from Brazil or Portugal to the United States. As they became closer, Armando and another man whom they knew named Torrino, told them that Raoul had killed Dr. King and related some of the same facts, i.e., talking about trees near the rooming-house where Ray was supposed to have shot King. In the 1970s says Grabow, she assisted both Armando and Torrino in a number of illegal activities such as gunrunning, making false passports, and making X-rated films. She said that at one time, a shipment of guns had arrived from New Orleans via boat and were unloaded at the Houston docks, and that she took possession of these items.

The story now gets murkier when it was learned from Peppers research, that a British merchant seaman named Sid Carthew, while living in Montreal in 1967-68, met a man named Raoul in a bar in the city called the Neptune Tavern (remember, that Ray spent some time in Montreal one year before the King assassination). In their conversations, Raoul tried to get Carthew interested in buying certain guns but he told him he was not interested. Carthew described Raoul as having dark hair and was probably of Mediterranean-like appearance (possibly from Portugal). Glenda said that Raul Pereira lived in Houston for a while and that at times, she drove him and Armando across the city to do their work. One time she dropped Raoul off at a movie theater where he met an associate of Louisiana mob boss Carlos Marcello. Glenda also said that she saw Raoul and Armando meet with Marcello in Houston a few times. Glenda recalled a meeting of the men-Raoul-Armando-at Torrino's house in the early 1970s. Glenda had a key ring that had the pictures of JFK, RFK and Martin Luther King on it, and when Raoul saw it, he became highly agitated. He (Raoul) then said, "I killed that black son of a bitch once, and it looks like I'll have to do it again."

But the story does not end there. In the late 1970s, Percy Forman represented James Earl Ray's brothers who had gotten in a scrape with the law. Glenda got to know Foreman and at one point he told her that Ray had to be "sacrificed" for their welfare. He also told her that Ray was innocent. Foreman also told Glenda that he had known Raoul for some time but would not elaborate further on their relationship.

As the years passed, Pepper learned that a man named Raoul Pereria was living in the United States but after many months of futile efforts to get either him or his family to talk to him, he ran into a dead end.[3]

We now turn to the events of what James Earl Ray did while he was in Canada in 1967 after his escape from prison. His original story was that he wanted to go to Montreal in order to sign onto a merchant ship that would take him to another country. However, there is new evidence that points to the fact that while he was in Canada, Ray was engaged in heroin smuggling between Canada and the U.S. One of Ray's brothers told a reporter that the real reason he was in Canada was to "make money in dope. (James) told me he had a contact, made it in prison, in Montreal. Some guy who had been in the same prison as Ray. Guy would supply Ray with dope. Ray had contact in Detroit-ran it back and forth. Detroit-Montreal."

Ray's brother said that James made about $7,000 for running drugs during a seven-month period (*Legacy of Secrecy,* Lamar Waldron and Thom Hartman). He also told reporter Dan Rather that he went to Montreal to, "meet with some people. I thought they were possibly narcotics smugglers." The man who ran the heroin network of which Ray was a small part of was Carols Marcello, the mob boss of Louisiana who possibly played an intricate role in the assassination of JFK. Some researchers say that while Ray did not ever meet in person with Marcello, that the mobster used Ray as a patsy in taking the fall for killing Dr. King.

In their book, *Legacy of Secrecy: The Long Shadow of the JFK Assassination,* authors Lamar Waldron and Thom Hartman, spell out how Carlos Marcello was involved in the King assassination. They quote a previously unpublished 1968 U.S. Justice Department memo that linked the Marcello organization which was based in New Orleans and two men, Frank Liberto, a Memphis racketeer and an associate of Marcello and Joe Carameci, who was called

[3] Ibid, Page 53-60.

a "professional killer." After the assassination, the FBI denied having any knowledge of Joe Carameci, but did however, have in its files an open criminal investigation on Frank Joseph Caracci (different spelling). He was called in that memo "as an associate of Carlos Marcello, New Orleans La Cosa Nostra leader."

The Justice Department memo on this case reads as follows:

> The Cosa Nostra (Mafia) agreed to broker or arranged the assassination of Martin Luther King for an amount somewhat in excess of three hundred thousand dollars, after they were contacted by representatives of 'Forever White,' an elite organization of wealthy segregationists in the Southeastern states. The Mafia's interest was less the money than the investment-type opportunity presented, i.e. to get in a position to extract government or other favors from some well-placed Southern white persons, including the KKK, and White Citizens' Councils. Quitman was said to be a possible base for 'Forever White's operations.[4]

Five months after King's assassination, this JD memo was sent to the Assistant Attorney General of the Civil Rights Division. The genesis of the story came from a journalist named William Sartor who was a "contact" writer for *Time* magazine. Apparently, Sartor was investigating the possible link between Marcello and the King assassination when he was murdered in Texas (it took *only* twenty-one years for the Waco, Texas DA to call Sartor's death a homicide).

The HSCA did not have access to the JD memo at the time of their investigation and might have taken a different tack if they'd been aware of it. The Committee wrote in their final report that, "While the Committee concluded that there was a likelihood of conspiracy in the assassination of Dr. King, and that James Earl Ray assassinated Dr. Martin Luther King as a result of a conspiracy," it did not have access to material that is now in the historical record that might have led to naming others involved.

While Ray was on the lamb in Montreal acting as drug smuggler, he somehow managed to elude the manhunt for him back

---

[4] Waldron, Lamar, and Hartman, Thom, *Legacy of Secrecy,* CounterPoint, Berkeley, California, 2008, Page 513.

in the States and in 1967, made his way to Mexico for unspecified work (probably drug or gun smuggling). In the fall of 1967, James Earl Ray entered Mexico from Laredo, Texas and stayed at the Nuevo Laredo motel thtat was a hideaway for the criminal type who was in Mexico. Ray smuggled contraband hidden in the tire of his car and was paid $2,000 for his services. Ray revealed that his sponsors in Mexico told him that they'd provide him with travel documents so that he could get to another country, as well as money to finance his travels. Ray also said that while he was in Mexico, he was involved in running guns and other materials. In November, 1967, he left Mexico bound for Los Angeles where he delivered dope to his contacts (he also took advantage of the good life and took dance lessons and had plastic surgery).

In 1993, a new wrinkle in the King assassination case was brought forward. This involved a man named Loyd Jowers who owned Jim's Grill which was located near the boarding house in Memphis where the shots were fired that killed Dr. King. That year, Jowers appeared in a nation-wide television show on ABC called *Prime Time Live*. Jowers told the audience that a Mafia associated produce dealer named Frank Liberto gave him $100,000 to hire a hit man to kill Dr. King and that he kept the rifle used in the assassination in his place of business and that the money had come from a person in New Orleans whom he did not reveal. Jowers was told that at the appointed time, someone would come and pick up the rifle, that there would be a patsy who would be chosen to be blamed for the assassination, and the some members of the Memphis police department would be involved in the assassination, and that furthermore, that there would be little if any Memphis policemen on duty near the Lorraine Motel that day. Jowers further said that shortly before the assassination, a man came to see him who identified himself as either "Raoul" or "Royal, "and that this person told him that his job was to keep the rifle in his possession until someone would come to pick it up. Jowers went on to say that about 4: P.M. on April 4, 1968, Raoul came to pick up the rifle and subsequently left the bar. He said that right after the shots were fired at Dr. King, he retrieved the gun from the bushes. The next day, Raoul arrived to retrieve the gun and then left.

Years later, William Pepper, on behalf of the King family, sued

Jowers in wrongful death lawsuit. In 1999, a civil trial went forward which garnered national publicity (by then, James Earl Ray had died and was not part of the proceedings). When the trial was over, the judge read the jury's verdict to the waiting court. He said, "In answer to the question did Loyd Jowers participate in a conspiracy to do harm to Dr. Martin Luther King, your answer is yes." He then asked the jury if others were involved in the assassination, including government agencies, the answer was "yes." The jury awarded the plaintiffs (the King family) one hundred dollars.

Despite the guilty verdict in the civil lawsuit, there has been no definite evidence that points to Jowers as being part of the King conspiracy. His statements were too murky and were not backed up in court beyond a reasonable doubt.

Many conspiracy theorists say that the FBI, under J. Edgar Hoover, set up King for assassination. Since King's rise to fame as the leader of the civil rights movement, Hoover tried everything in his power to discredit King and his followers. The FBI put wiretaps on certain King's aides whom they believed had ties to the communist party, and even infiltrated agents into his inner circle. After King's "I have a dream speech," Robert Kennedy authorized full electronic surveillance of King. Hoover's agents placed bugs in King's hotel rooms when he traveled and at his own home in Atlanta. The Bureau was now able to listen in to King's policies regarding the civil rights movement, as well as more, juicer information; that King was having sexual relations with other women.

Hoover exacerbated the situation regarding King, when, in a press conference, he called King, "the most notorious liar," and "one of the lowest characters in the country, " in response to King's attack on the FBI that it did not have enough African-American agents. The FBI also wrote a bogus letter, suggesting that for the good of the nation, he kill himself.

Like the JFK and RFK assassinations, there are still a number of unanswered questions regarding the circumstances surrounding the murder of Martin Luther King on April 4, 1968. In hindsight, one can only hope that if the legal team that took Ray's case in 1968 had the new information we now have, the verdict might have been different.

LBJ looks at JFK.

Chapter 53
The LBJ Connection

In Oliver Stone's hit movie called *JFK*, New Orleans District Attorney Jim Garrison, when summing up his case against New Orleans businessman Clay Shaw who was on trial for his participation in the conspiracy to kill President John Kennedy, told the jury that the two men who would profit most from the killing of the president were the former president, Lyndon Johnson and the current president, Richard Nixon. Both men were corrupt politicians and while there is no evidence that Nixon had any foreknowledge of the Kennedy assassination; the same cannot be said of the Lyndon Johnson. Over the years many assassination researchers have made the case that LBJ was warned beforehand (along with J. Edgar Hoover) that JFK was going to be killed and did nothing to stop it. It is not too much of a stretch to say that JFK liked his arch rival in the political realm, Richard Nixon, more than he did Lyndon Johnson. Both Kennedy and Nixon came to the congress fresh from serving in World War II and even though their political philosophy was not in sink, they had a grudging respect for one another.

When JFK picked Lyndon Johnson as his vice-presidential running mate in the 1960 election, he had no idea of how much that decision would play out in the historical record. Kennedy picked Johnson not because he liked him, but because of the electoral map. He needed Texas in order to win the election and since Johnson was the Senator from Texas, he believed that by putting him on the ticket, it would help his election chances. Kennedy's gamble proved right and he beat Nixon by the slimmest of margins. Once he was in the White House, Kennedy left Johnson in the wind, basically keeping him out of the most important decisions of the day. No more did LBJ, once the powerful Senate majority leader be the power player he once was, he was now relegated to the backbench, an afterthought in the corridors of power. Kennedy sent him overseas to see foreign leaders and he did an admirable job in that respect. Among Kennedy's top aids, Johnson was referred to in the most derogatory way, most of which the president did not know about. Robert Kennedy was one of the most vocal opponents of LBJ's, and the feeling was mutual. Bobby never liked the idea that his brother had picked Johnson for the vice-presidency in 1960 and he let Johnson know about it on numerus occasions.

Throughout his presidency, JFK knew all about Johnson's sordid past but he never used it against him until the last months of his presidency when one of Johnson's top aides, Bobby Baker, was being investigated for political corruption charges (more about Bobby Baker in this chapter). JFK's secretary, Evelyn Lincoln said in later years that the president was going to replace Johnson as his vice-presidential candidate in the 1964 election with North Carolina Governor Terry Sanford. The Bobby Baker scandal which was by then threatening to get out of control and bring Johnson down with him, ended abruptly with the president's assassination in Dallas on November 22, 1963.

Throughout his political career, Lyndon Johnson had been linked to a number of suspicious deaths that resulted from his year's long membership in the Senate and his powerful position of Majority Leader. He also had close associations with a number of men of questionable reputation such as Bobby Baker and Billie Sol Estes. It was from these two men that Johnson's secret ties would be investigated, only to be swiped aside when he became the 37th president of the United States.

In order to learn all about the alleged crimes of LBJ, the reader has to understand the man behind all the stories that link him to his to this sordid tale. The man in question was Bllie Sol Estes, a corrupt wheeler-dealer in the decades from the 1940s to the 1960s who was very close to Lyndon Johnson and who was alleged to have information that LBJ was behind the Kennedy assassination.

Billie Sol Estes was born on a rural farm near Clyde, Texas on January 10, 1925. He was one of six children of John and Lillian Estes and as a young man, the Estes family found hard times in the depression years. He had a talent for making deals and money and as a teenager, was able to make a $3,000 profit in the buying and selling of sheep. By age 18, he had made a profit of $38,000, a forte of what he would accomplish in later years. He then moved to Pecos, Texas where he began to sell irrigation pumps to local farmers who were having a hard time keeping up their farms. Estes sold ammonia as a fertilizer to local farmers who then began to have better luck selling their crops. Through the selling of the irrigation pumps, he soon made a large profit and was on his way to becoming a man to be reckoned with in the Texas business community. However, his luck soon turned when the Department of Agriculture began to control the production of the cotton crop. Agricultural allotments were given out by the federal government, telling local farmers how much cotton they could grow during each season. It was during this time that Estes made contact with Senator Lyndon Johnson, then a mover and shaker in the world of politics both in Washington and Texas. Through Johnson's work on his part, by 1958, Estes ran a scam allowing him to get federal agricultural subsidies which he was not entitled to get. By his own account, he got $21 million a year for growing and storing cotton crops that did not exist.

The Agriculture Department soon found out what Estes was up to and they mounted an investigation on him. The man who was sent to probe Estes' dealings was Henry Marshall, an Investigator for the Agriculture Department. Over a two year period, Marshall found out that Estes had bought 3,200 acres of cotton allotments from over one hundred different farmers. Marshall told his superiors in Washington on August 31, 1960, (during the height of the presidential election of which LBJ was running as Kennedy's vice presidential candidate) that," The regulation should be strengthened to support our disapproval of every case." It was alleged that a large amount of money that came from the Estes scam would up in the coffers of LBJ's political campaigns. Soon, word of Marshall's investigation of Estes wound up on Johnson's desk and he took active measures to stop his probe. Johnson contacted the Department of Agriculture and asked that Henry Marshall be given a promotion to a higher-ranking job in order to get him away from his Estes probe. However, Marshall would not bow to LBJ's harsh tactics and he refused any promotion and instead, re-doubled his investigation into Estes' illegal activities. By taking that course of action, Henry Marshall was signing his own death warrant.

Fearing that time was not on his side, Bille Sol Estes had his lawyer, John P. Dennison, meet with Marshall in Robertson County, Texas to hash things out. The meeting took place on January 17, 1961, (three days prior to JFK's inauguration) and Marshall told Dennison that his client was involved in a "scheme or device to buy allotments, and will not be approved, and prosecution will follow if this operation is ever used." One week after the meeting between Marshall and Dennison, A. B. Foster, who ran Billie Sol Enterprises wrote a letter to Clifton Carter, who was a friend of LBJ.'s, describing in detail all that Marshall had alleged that Estes was doing, and asking for his help in rectifying the on-going situation. Estes later said that on that same day (January 17, 1961), he had a meeting with Johnson, Cliff Carter, and Ed Clark, regarding Marshal's allegations. At the meeting, Johnson was said to have made this remark regarding Marshall, "It looks like we'll just have to get rid of him." At the same meeting, it was alleged that the person who was to "get rid" of Henry Marshall was a notorious hit man named Malcom "Mac" Wallace, who was said to be in cahoots with Johnson.

On June 8, 1961, Henry Marshall was found dead on his farm next to his Chevy Fleetside pickup truck. Police found his rifle next to his body, with five gunshot wounds in his torso (just how a person was able to fire five gunshots into his body is beyond belief). The local County Sheriff Howard Stegall ruled that Marshall had committed suicide and in their investigation, no forensic examination of the crime scene was conducted. Later, the undertaker, Marley Jones, who examined Marshall's wounds said of the circumstances surround in his death that, "To me it looked like murder. I just do not believe a man could shoot himself like that." In 1986, Raymond Jones, Marley's son, told writer Bill Adler that, "Judge Farmer told him he was going to put suicide on the death certificate because the sheriff told him to." In the end, Judge Lee Farmer ruled that Henry Marshall's death was "death by gunshot, self-inflicted."[5]

One man who had serious doubts about the circumstances surrounding the death of Henry Marshall was Texas Ranger Clint Peoples had had an exceptional career in Texas law enforcement and was no one to be trifled with. It was during the latter stages of

[5] Famous Crimes: Billie Sol Estes, Spartacus-eductional.com/JFKestes.htm.

his career that he was appointed to be a U.S. Marshall and began a thirty-year investigation that started in 1962 on the case against Malcolm Wallace and his associations with Lyndon Johnson and Cliff Carter.

Another of the cases that Ranger Peoples was associated with was the unexplained murder of George Krutilek in August 1962. George Krutilek was the accountant for Billie Sol Estes and the fraudulent scam that he was running. Estes later testified that LBJ ordered that Krutilek be killed at the hands of Mac Wallace. One day after he was questioned by the FBI regarding the Estes matters, he was found dead from carbon monoxide poisoning. Besides ingesting carbon monoxide, there was a large bruise found on his head indicating that some sort of violent struggle had taken place.

In the early part of 1962, Billie Sol Estes and two other men, Harold Orr and Coleman Wade were arrested by the FBI and charged with fifty-seven counts of fraud and conspiracy. Both Orr and Wade would late die in suspicious circumstances and it was believed at the time that both men had died by suicide (there's that suicide ruling again). However, in later year, Estes claimed that both men were killed by Mac Wallace under the direction of LBJ.

Agriculture Secretary Orville Freeman believed that Henry Marshall had died under mysterious circumstances and said he was a man "who left this world under questioned circumstances."

In congress, the Senate Permanent Subcommittee on Investigations began a probe into Billie Sol Estes and his corrupt practices. In time, it was revealed that three officials of the Agricultural Adjustment Administration in Washington, Red Jacobs, Jim Ralph and Bill Morris took bribes from Estes and were fired. In September 1961, Estes was fined $42,000 for his illegal cotton allotments. However, in a rather unusual move that shook Washington, Estes was appointed by Secretary of Agriculture Freeman to the National Cotton Advisory Board.

It was also revealed that Billie Sol Estes told Wilson Tucker, who was the deputy director of the Agriculture Department's cotton division on August 1, 1961, that he "Threatened to embarrass the Kennedy administration if the investigation were not halted." Tucker later testified that, "Estes stated that this pooled cotton allotment matter had caused the death of one person and then asked me if I knew Henry Marshall." This meeting took place at least six months before questions about the circumstances of Marshall's death began to spread.

At the time that Peoples began investigating the death of Henry Marshall, he reported to Colonel Homer Garrison who was the director of the Texas Department of Public Safety. Peoples interviewed Nolan Griffin, who worked in a gas station in Robertson County. Griffin told Peoples that on the day that Marshall died, he came across a man who asked him for directions to Henry Marshall's farm. Mr. Griffin was asked by the Rangers to provide a description of the man whom he saw and after the sketch artist made a reproduction, the man whose picture he drew resembled that of Mac Wallace. Mac Wallace was a suspect in the murder of Doug Kisner in 1951. Mac Wallace was tried for the death of Doug Kisner but the outcome of the trial was less than satisfactory. Mac Wallace was sentenced to five years in jail but then, suddenly and unexpectedly, he was given a suspended sentence and put on probation. The court stipulated that his probation centered on the stipulation that he stay out of trouble for the next five years. (This was what local people at the time called "Texas Justice"). A number of people at that time said that a corrupt bargain went down in the sentence of Mac Wallace between the prosecutor and the judge and that the hidden had of Lyndon Johnson was in the background.

With the heat coming from Washington in the form of Secretary Freeman, the body of Henry Marshall was removed from his grave and an autopsy was performed by Dr. Joseph Jachimczyk. The doctor's findings revealed that Marshall did not commit suicide and further said that only as much as 30 percent of carbon monoxide was found in his body. Dr. Jachimczyk also said that after viewing the body, that the believed the bruise on Marshall's head had been caused by "a severe blow to the head." He also cast doubt on the suicide verdict by saying that if he had used the rifle to kill himself there would have been traces of soot on his clothes but none were found.

Billie Sol Estes was sentenced to prison for his participation in the cotton allotment scheme and while if he wanted to incriminate Vice President Johnson, he didn't say a word. However, all that changed when he was released from jail in 1984. Estes met with Clint Peoples and the Ranger was able to persuade Estes to talk, and he appeared before the Robertson Country officials that had previously looked into the death of Henry Marshall. In a session that probably made the grand jurors blush, Estes told them of his participation in the cotton allotment scheme and much more. He told them that Johnson, Cliff Carter, and Malcolm Wallace had met to discuss what to do with Henry Marshall and his allegations of wrong doing against Estes. Estes said that Mac Wallace followed Marshall to a secluded place near his farm and almost beat him to death and then shot Marshall five times.

By 1984, the U.S. Justice Department wanted to know more about what Estes knew and he was contacted via his lawyer, Douglas Caddy. Attorney Caddy wrote a letter to Justice requesting that his client be granted immunity for further prosecution and if he did that, he was willing to provide them with further incriminating information that he had in his possession. However after much back and forth, Caddy said that Estes would not testify regarding his bombshell information.

The Estes story might have died on the vine if not for new information that came from a writer named Glen Sample who wrote a book on the Kennedy assassination called *The Men On the Sixth Floor.* Mr. Sample gained possession of a letter written to Douglas Caddy from Stephen Trott, then the Assistant Attorney General of the Criminal Division which was dated May 29, 1984. Trott told Caddy that he'd be interested in hearing what Estes had to say only if he cooperated fully and gave the Justice Department all relevant information, including the extent of his participation in the crimes, as well as the name of his sources. On August 9, 1984, Douglas Caddy wrote Attorney General Trott and gave him some startling information. Parts of his letter are as follows. "My client, Mr. Estes, has authorized met to make this reply to your letter of May 29, 1984. Mr. Estes was a member of a four-member group, headed by Lyndon Johnson, which committed criminal acts in Texas in the 1960s. The other two, besides Mr. Estes and LBJ were Cliff Carter and Mac Wallace. Mr. Estes is willing to disclose his knowledge concerning the following offenses:

I. Murders

The killing of Henry Marshall. The Killing of George Krutilek, The killing of Ike Rogers and his secretary. The killing of Harold Orr. The Killing of Coleman Wade. The killing of Josefa Johnson. The Killing of John Kinser and the killing of President John F. Kennedy.

In addition, Mr. Estes is willing to testify that LBJ ordered these killings, and that his orders through Cliff Carter to Mac Wallace, who executed the murders. In the cases of murders no. 1-7, Estes' knowledge of the precise details concerning the way the murders were executed stems from conversations he had shortly after each event with Cliff Carter and Mac Wallace. Mr. Estes declares that Cliff Carter told him the day Kennedy was killed, Fidel Castro also was supposed to be assassinated and that Robert Kennedy, awaiting word of Castro's death, instead received news of his brother's killing. Mr. Estes, states that Mac Wallace, whom he describes as a 'stone killer' with a communist background, recruited Jack Ruby, who in turn recruited Lee Harvey Oswald. Mr. Estes said that Cliff Carter told him that Mac Wallace fired a shot from the grassy knoll in Dallas, which hit JFK from the front during the assassination.

II. The Illegal Cotton Allotments.

Mr. Estes desires to discuss the infamous illegal cotton allotment schemes in great detail. He has recordings made at the time of LBJ, Cliff Carter and himself discussing the scheme. These recordings were made with Cliff Carter's knowledge as a means of Carter and Estes protecting themselves should LBJ order their deaths.

III. Illegal Payoffs.

Mr. Estes is willing to disclose illegal payoff schemes, in which he collected and passed on to Cliff Carter and LBJ millions of dollars. Mr. Estes collected payoff money on more than one occasion from George and Herman Brown of Brown and Root, which was delivered to LBJ."[6]

These were mind-boggling accusations and if proven to be

[6] The Estes Documents: home.earthlink.net.sixthfloor/estes.htm.

true, would have led to a major scandal in American history. However, by the time the Estes allegations were made to Justice, a number of the major players in the drama were dead, including LBJ, Cliff Carter, Henry Marshall, etc. As for Billie Sol Estes, he died on May 14, 2013, taking his secrets (and more, to his grave).

But who was Mac Wallace, the other major player in the drama? If one is to believe the standard story of Mac Wallace's life, he was the henchman of Lyndon Johnson from the time LBJ was a congressman, senator, Vice President and President of the United States. He was supposed to have killed between eight and seventeen people and said to have killed Doug Kinser. Mac Wallace first met Lyndon Johnson when he was the president of the student body at the University of Texas and asked the young congressman to talk to the students. The two men soon bonded and a relationship soon was started that would last for years to come. In 1939, he joined the Marines but was soon discharged when he hurt his back. During World War 2, he was not eligible for service and instead, entered the University of Texas where he was an A student. In 1949, he a got a job at the Department of Agriculture, got married, and soon was having an affair with the sister of LBJ, Josefa. Soon thereafter, Josefa had a relationship with a golf pro named Douglas Kinser. To add to the drama, Wallace's wife, Mary Andre, started a relationship with Doug Kinser and when Wallace found out, he returned to Texas and killed the poor man. As mentioned before, Wallace was found guilty of murder, but somehow had his sentence suspended and served no time in jail.

Soon after his trial, Wallace somehow managed to get a job with two aircraft companies, one called Temco, a defense contractor owned by David Harold Boyd. In order to join the company, one needed to have a security clearance but miraculously Wallace, who was accused of having killed Doug Kinser, got one without any problem (It was believed at the time that Johnson helped him get the security clearance).

New information on the life of Mac Wallace has been gleamed from the work of the noted writer Joan Mellen who revealed that the Office of Naval Intelligence had conducted five investigations concerning the activities of Mac Wallace. According to Mellon's research, "these Navy files proved that Wallace had been enlisted as a hit man in a chain of murders of which Lyndon Johnson was the sponsor." The ONI knew that Wallace was allowed to work in a company that required its employees to have a security clearance despite his sordid background and did not object, makes one believe that they had no trouble with that fact. In an aside, Temco's owner, David Boyd, owned the building that housed the Texas School Book Depository, the place where it was said, Lee Oswald fire the shots that killed JFK.[7]

The ONI investigation of Mac Wallace began in 1951 and continued until 1964. They wanted to know if he was still working for Temco and later for a company called Ling Electronics in 1961. During their investigation of Wallace, the ONI recommended that Wallace's security clearance of SECRET be revoked and denied. Another part of their probe on Wallace was the allegation that he was associated with two Communists, a classmate named Elgin Williams, who was indeed a Communist, and Stuart Chamberlin, another friend.

The FBI undertook two security investigations of Mac Wallace, one when he protested the trustees' firing of the president of the University of Texas, Homer Rainey, and the other time when he was hired for his job at Agriculture. In 1964, ONI reduced his clearance from Secret to Confidential, limiting the amount of classified information he could use while at work.

There were also rumors in recent years that a latent fingerprint belonging to Mac Wallace was found in the Texas School Book Depository at the time of the Kennedy assassination, leading many to believe that Mac Wallace was somehow involved in the president's killing. However, after a number of tests were performed by fingerprint experts, no positive match was made regarding Mac Wallace's alleged participation in the events in Dallas in 1963.

At the end of her lecture in Canterbury, England where I got the above mentioned information on Wallace and the ONI, Joan Mellen said, "I have not yet completed my work on Malcolm Wallace. Nor am I through with Lyndon Johnson and his crimes and misdemeanors. I will say, for now, that they rise to the highest and most vicious crime of which a person may be found guilty,

[7] Mellen, Joan, *The Canterbury Lectures-Lecture Two: Lyndon Johnson and Mac Wallace, Sunday April 27, 2014*. Canterbury Christ Church University.

a crime that goes far beyond a simple murder." (She is referring to LBJ's participation in the attack of the *USS Liberty* by Israeli forces on June 8, 1972).

Another wheeler-dealer whom Johnson relied heavily on, and who almost brought down his political career was Bobby Baker who was the Secretary of the Senate during the time of LBJ's heyday in congress. He was called by the senators whom he gave favors for, including lobbying for their bills, and procuring some of them "dates" when their wives weren't around, the "101st Senator." During his time as Secretary of the Senate, Baker was associated with a number of mob figures such as Meyer Lansky, Sam Giancana, Ed Levinson, among others and gained a fortune on his meager congressional salary.

Bobby Baker was born in Pickens, South Carolina in 1929 and at the tender age of fourteen, was a page at the Senate. During this time, Lyndon Johnson took a liking to the young man and as time went on, Johnson turned Baker into his protégé, teaching him the ins and outs of the Senate, whose palms to grease and in time, making him one of the most influential, unelected members who worked the Hill. In the 1950s, Baker used his influence to help the Intercontinental Hotel chain to establish casinos in the Dominican Republic. Using his influence, Baker tried to get mobsters like Ed Levinson, as associate of Meyer Lansky and Sam Giancana to become partners in the deal and the first casino opened in 1955. One of the invited guests to show up was LBJ. When Johnson was elected vice president in 1960, Baker became LBJ's secretary and his most trusted political advisor. Baker's deal with the mobsters went south when Rafael Trujillo, the dictator of the Dominican Republic, was killed in a CIA sanctioned attack by dissidents in that country.

Seeking new avenues of opportunity, Baker, in 1962, started a company called Serve-U-Corporation with his colleague, Fred Black, and two mobsters, Ed Levinson and Benny Sigelbaum. The company provided vending machines for companies that operated on federally granted programs. The vending machines were produced by a business that was owned by Sam Giancana, the mob boss of Chicago. As time went on, Baker somehow managed to rake in $3.5 million from profits from Serve-U Company on a salary of $20,000 a year. As time went on, the Baker problem caught the attention of Attorney General Robert Kennedy who had heard rumors about Baker's mob ties and his sudden fortune. Bobby had the Justice Department start an investigation of Baker and soon the probe had its sights on the vice president himself. It seems that not only was Baker involved with certain mobsters whom Bobby was targeting, including Sam Giancana, but that possibly Johnson was involved in the outskirts of the scandal. This involved the awarding of a $7 million contract for a new jet fighter plane, the F-111 to the General Dynamics Company which was based in Texas. There were rumors on Capitol Hill that Johnson was possibly involved in the awarding of the contract to General Dynamics, although it couldn't be proven. Soon, the heat was getting too much for Baker to bear and on October 7, 1963, Baker was forced to resign his powerful senate post. Another casualty of the F-111 scandal was Fred Korth, the Navy Secretary.

Another scandal that involved Baker was the operation of the so-called Quorum Club, a private club on Capitol Hill that Baker created. The club operated out of the Carroll Arms Hotel near the Senate offices and it provided girls (prostitutes, in some cases), to influential Senators and some people in the Kennedy administration.

One of the girls who were part of Baker's Quorum Club was an East German refugee named Ellen Rometsch, who had come with her husband, a West German army sergeant who worked at the West German mission in Washington to the United States in 1961. Through Baker's intersession, Ellen Rometsch was invited to the White House to see President Kennedy and an affair soon took place. Soon, the FBI found out about the Rometsch-Kennedy affair and it turned out that the beautiful Ellen Rometsch had come from East Germany and had once been member of a Communist youth organization. The rumor going around Hoover's bureau was that she was possibly an East German spy who had now bedded the president of the United States. Very quietly, Ms. Rometsch and her husband were hustled out of the country and sent back to West Germany.

During the FBI's investigation of Bobby Baker, the Rometsch affair took center stage and in an FBI memo dated October 26, stated, "That pertains to possible questionable activities on the part of high government officials. It was also alleged that the President and the Attorney General had availed themselves of services of playgirls." The news of the Rometsch affair soon got into the hands of Senator John Williams, (R-Delaware) and he threatened to hold hearings in the Senate Rules Committee, the same one that was investigating the Bobby Baker affair. Robert Kennedy now got into the act and he called J. Edgar Hoover to discuss the problem. Hoover then briefed Senators Mike Mansfield and Everett Dirksen and in a private session, told them about the Baker-Kennedy-Rometsch affair. To the relief of the administration, the Rometsch affair was hushed up and never saw the light of day. It is not a stretch of the imagination to believe that Bobby Baker told LBJ all about the President's affair with Mrs. Rometsch. This would have been fodder for Johnson (and, of course, J. Edgar Hoover), if they at some time, wanted to reveal to the public what they knew about the scandal.

By November 1963, the Baker scandal was about to get ripped wide open. It seems that *Life Magazine* in an issue dated November 8, 1963, was doing an in depth report on Baker's illegal activities, including a report on the Quorum Club and the activities of Ellen Rometsch, and more importantly, Baker's secret relationship with Vice President Johnson. The headline in the magazines story read as follows: "Capital Buzzes Over Stories of Misconduct in High Places: The Bobby Baker Bombshell." The publication featured a picture of LBJ and the caption underneath which said, "That Baker was an indispensable confidant" of LBJ. The magazine was about to reveal how Baker had gotten rich on his government salary and his ties to Johnson.

Life's editors were now setting their sights on LBJ himself, digging into his past, wondering how he had accumulated so much money from his humble beginnings in Texas to his million dollar fortune in 1963. The reporter who took on the job of looking into Johnson's past was William Lambert whose previous reporting broke the story of the Teamsters Union's association with the mob in the U.S.

A second *Life* article which was dated November 22, 1963 (the day Kennedy was shot in Dallas), went even further in tackling the

Johnson-Baker relationship. The main writer was Keith Wheeler who had nine other members of *Life's* staff on hand to assist him in his research. The article went even further in exploring Baker's control of the Quorum Club, the use of girls as prostitutes for certain members of congress, and at the center of his work, the relationship of LBJ to the Baker scandal. The reporters wrote that, "In a very real sense, the present Establishment is the personal creation of Lyndon Baines Johnson who, from the day he took over as majority leader until he went to the Vice Presidency, ruled it like an absolute monarch."

The managing editor of *Life,* George Hunt, took an active interest in his reporters work and he scheduled a meeting with both William Lambert and Keith Wheeler for the morning of November 22, 1963. As the meeting progressed, word came that the president had been killed in Dallas and the session was adjourned. At the time of the conference, *Life's* editors were planning to release a third bombshell report on the Baker affair but with the death of Kennedy and the rise to the presidency of LBJ, the man whom they were looking into, the Baker-Johnson story was ended. Thus, with one fell swoop LBJ's presidency was now free of any further scandal as the country tried to figure out what happened to JFK and move on from the nightmare that we'd all been through.

Many Kennedy assassination researchers believe that Lyndon Johnson was the man responsible for the president's death. Taken together, of all the people who would benefit the most with JFK gone, it was LBJ. He would now be president of the United States, instead of being investigated by a possible congressional committee on the Bobby Baker scandal and his relationship to him, and if he survived the scandal, possibly being dumped by the JFK in the upcoming 1964 election. By the fall of 1963, Johnson saw the inevitable end of his powerful political career and he was helpless to do anything about it. Now, all that had changed. The political gods had made their move and Johnson could now go on to move his own, national agenda.

One week after the Kennedy assassination, the new president created the Warren Commission to investigate his predecessor's assassination. Johnson cajoled Chief Justice Earl Warren to chair the commission, despite his reluctance to take on the position. The

Warren Commission did not do its job carefully, in the end, leaving more questions than answers in the circumstances surrounding Kennedy's death. He changed JFK's Vietnam policy, creating a war which tore the nation apart and resulted in his decision not to seek re-election in 1968, paving the way for Richard Nixon and Watergate. All of LBJ's work on civil rights which profoundly changed the way the United States operated took second stage to his Vietnam catastrophe.

Robert Kennedy, who himself disliked Johnson to the point of hatred, (the feelings were mutual), summed up his thoughts on the Vice President by telling his friend Arthur Schlesinger, "And my experience with him since then (1960) is that he lies all the time. I'm telling you, he just lies continuously, about everything. In every conversation I have had with him, he lies. As I've said, he lies even when he doesn't have to."[8]

---

[8] Guthman, Edwin, and Shulman, Jeffrey, Editors, *Robert Kennedy In His Own Words,* Bantam Books, New York, 1988, Page 26.

Chapter 54
What Happened to Marilyn?

On the night of August 4, 1962, an ambulance was called to the Los Angeles home of actress Marilyn Monroe, one of the nation's most admired film stars and sex icons. There have been conflicting rumors about just what happened to Marilyn Monroe and the circumstances surrounding her untimely death at age thirty-six. Unknown to the public at the time of her death was that Monroe was having an affair with President John F. Kennedy whom she had met when Kennedy was running for the Democratic presidential nomination in 1960. It was also rumored that she had some sort of relationship with Robert Kennedy, the president's brother and the Attorney General of the United States. Some of the theories surrounding Monroe's death lead to the Mafia who was supposed to have bugged the stars home in order to have blackmail on Robert Kennedy in his long-standing war against the mob, i.e., Santos Trafficante, Jimmy Hoff, and Carlos Marcello. Another theory is that the Kennedy's, either Bobby or the president himself, ordered that Monroe to be silenced because she was about to reveal her relationship with the president (and, or Bobby) that would have ruined his presidency. One of the stories goes that Marilyn was going to tell the world some of the juiciest pieces of information that she'd gotten from either Bobby or the president, involving the plans to kill Fidel Castro of Cuba. Among the interesting facts about Marilyn's death is that she had a diary that she kept in her home regarding her relationship with friends and colleagues. The diary is supposed to have revealed her affair with the president as well as her other secrets. The person who told of Marilyn's diary was her friend Jean Carmen with whom she confided many of her secrets. A person who worked in the LA's corners office, Lionel Grandison, said that the diary arrived at the corners office after her death, was put in a safe, but it then went missing.

Marilyn Monroe was born Norma Jean Mortenson on June 1, 1926. She came from what we would call today a dysfunctional family with her mother being put in a home for mental illness and her father leaving when she was a child. She was sent to a number of foster families which had a lasting impress on her as she grew up. Unlike countless number of people who flocked to Los Angeles seeking fame in the movie business, Norma Jean was one of the lucky ones. Her striking good looks and hour glass figure made her an instant success in an industry where looks were paramount for someone's future. Soon, her figure would grace any number of young men's rooms where her pinup looked down at them while they dreamed unrealistic fantasies. Soon, she got her big break in the movie business and was signed by 20th Century Fox and proceeded to change her name to Marilyn Monroe. Shen then earned roles in her career in such films as *All About Eve, Gentlemen Prefer Blondes, The Seven Year Itch, Bus Stop* and *Some Like It Hot.* She also had an up-and-down married life, hitching up with two powerful men, the famous playwright, Arthur Miller (1956-61) and the super-star of the New York Yankees, "Joltin-Joe"Dimaggio (1954).

From the time that LA county officials found Marilyn Monroe dead in her Los Angeles home, the circumstances surrounding her demise took a strange turn. Among them were the exact times that Marilyn succumbed and when her body was found. The official story is that on August 4, 1962, she had declined to attend a party given by the actor Peter Lawford (and JFK's brother-in-law) because she felt tired. Later that night, Monroe's housekeeper, Eunice Murray, saw a light on in Monroe's room but went to bed, thinking all was well. At about 3:30 A.M. Miss Murray awoke and saw that the light was still on and knocked on the door. She then went outside and looked into Marilyn's room and saw her naked in the bed. Thinking that something was wrong, she immediately called Dr. Ralph Greenson, Monroe's psychiatrist. Dr. Greenson came to the house, broke the window and found Marilyn unresponsive in her bed. He then called Dr. Hyman Engelberg, Monroe's physician. At 4:25. A.M., Dr. Engelberg called the emergncy number and said that Monroe was dead. The answering officer was Sgt. Jack Clemmons of the West LA Police Department who, upon arriving at the home, found her unresponsive. The corner came to the home, looked at the body and later said that Monroe had died from "acute barbiturate poisoning due to ingestion of overdose,,a probable suicide."

Here is where the discrepancy's start to mount up. To start off, the time of Marilyn's death is inconsistent with some of the witness statements. Murray told the police that she called Dr. Greenson at midnight but later changed her story to around 3:30 in the morning. Stg. Clemmons said that both Doctor Engelberg and Greenson said they called emergency services at midnight or shortly thereafter. However, in their official testimony, the doctors insist that they were called at 3:30 a.m. Peter Lawford, who was a friend of Marilyn's, said in a 1982 interview that he learned of her death around 1:30 a.m. by her lawyer, Milton Rudin. The writer, Anthony Summers who wrote a book about Monroe called *Goddess,* said that Monroe's agent, Arthur Jacobs might have been told about her passing around 11:00 pm, while they were attending a concert at the Hollywood Bowl. Also, when the ambulance attendants arrived at the Monroe home, they said that, in their observation that her body was in "advanced rigor mortis," postulating that she had been dead at least 4-6 hours.[9]

Thomas Noguchi, the Deputy Medical` Examiner, said that Monroe might have digested 50 Nembutal pills, which is a barbiturate, but found, "No visual evidence of pills in the stomach or the small intestine. No residue, No retractile crystals." However, in his book *Coroner,* he wrote that the toxicological reports of Monroe's blood found "confirmed his suspicions of an overdose." Some conspiracy theorists say that the overdose was given via a suppository that would leave no trace of barbiturates in her stomach.

Non-conspiracy theorists point out that Monroe was a long time user of drugs and pills and that she might have overdosed on purpose. She was also in a depressed mood on the day of her death, partly due to the fact that a short time before, she had been fired by 20th Century Fox from her movie, *Something's Got To Give.* On the day she died, she reportedly called actor Peter Lawford who later said that Monroe sounded drugged and told him, "Say goodbye to Jack (President Kennedy), and say goodbye to yourself, because you're a nice guy."

In their final analysis, the "Suicide Investigative Team" from

[9] Litchfield, Michael, *It's A Conspiracy!,* Earth Works Press, Berkeley, California, 1992, Page 131.

the Los Angeles medical examiner's office, issued their report on her psychological state that verified the verdict of suicide. They cited her year's long state of depression and drug use, and mood swings to justify their ruling.

Another issue to be answered is what happened to Monroe's phone records after her death. A reporter from the *Los Angeles Herald Tribune* sought her phone records and was told by someone in the phone company that other people were looking for her phone records and that the tape of her calls had disappeared. In 1985, an unnamed FBI agent who had knowledge of the phone records said that he heard that certain people in the Bureau's LA office had removed some of Monroe's phone records. "Bureau personnel, who normally wouldn't have been there-agents from out of town. They were on the scene immediately, as soon as she died, before anyone realized what had happened. It had to be on the direction of somebody high up, higher than Hoover... either the Attorney General or the President." (Ibid, Page 132).

It seems that Miss Monroe had kept a diary of her personal thoughts which was confirmed by her friend, Robert Slatzer. Slatzer said that among the notations in her diary was information on Robert Kennedy, among others. He said that Monroe and Kennedy had spoken about politics and that Bobby was supposed to have been mad at her because she didn't remember what he'd told her. After her death, the Coroners Aide Lionel Grandison said that her diary had been seen in his office with other evidence that had been brought into the office but the diary mysteriously disappeared one day later.

Another inconsistency is what happened to the police files on Monroe's death. Twelve years after her death (1974), Captain Kenneth McCauley of the LAPD, contacted the Homicide Division and asked that he been allowed to see the files they had on the actress's death. He was told that the department had none of the files in their possession. In 1966, LA Mayor Sam Yorty asked for a copy of the same file from the police department and they told him that it did not exist. LA Police Lieutenant Marion Phillips said that in 1962, a high-ranking police official, "had taken the file to show someone in Washington. That was the last we saw of it."

There also have been persistent reports over the years that

Monroe's home was wire-tapped by people unknown in order to get incriminating information on the Kennedy brothers. One theory is that the Mafia, either Sam Giancana or Jimmy Hoffa ordered the wiretaps be placed in her home and were monitored off site. The story goes is that they hired a man named Bernard Spindel to collect incriminating information on RFK. One tape is said to contain a heated confrontation between RFK and Marilyn on August 4, in which the Attorney General demanded that he be given her diary. No one knows what happened to the diary (if it even existed) but in an unrelated matter, the New York County DA's office was investigating Spindel for illegal wiretapping and his home in New York was raided. Conspiracy theorists believe that during the raid, the police found the Monroe tapes and confiscated them.

In his book *Official and Confidential: The Secret Life of J. Edgar Hoover,* Anthony Summers revealed that the FBI also bugged the home of Peter Lawford on the direct orders of Director Hoover. The name of the person who installed the bug is not named but he said that the bugs were placed in Lawford's living room and bedrooms. He said that an intermediary of Hoover's met with this person to arrange the installations of the bugs. The reason for the installation of the bugs was because Hoover wanted "information on the organized crime figures coming and going at the Lawford place. Sam Giancana was there sometimes. But of course, the Kennedy's, both John and Robert, went there too." The same source told Summers that Bobby Kennedy told the Bureau that Lawford's home was not to be bugged but Hoover overruled him and was in constant receipt of the bug transcripts. The source also said that Hoover gave the tapes to Jimmy Hoffa apparently for blackmail purposes. Summers writes that one of the men who monitored the bugs at the Lawford home was an investigator by the name of John Danoff. He recalled hearing the voices of both JFK and Monroe having a sexual encounter.

Robert Kennedy first met Monroe on February 1, 1962 at Peter Lawford's home. During the meeting, Monroe asked Robert Kennedy if it was true that the administration was going to fire Hoover. Robert was said to reply that, "he and the president didn't feel strong enough to do so, though they wanted to."

It is a fact that Robert Kennedy and his family arrived in San Francisco on Friday afternoon, August 4, 1962 and were in town to meet with friends in Gilroy, California. There have been persistent rumors over the years that Robert Kennedy was at Monroe's home on the night of her death and that fact was covered up to protect the Attorney General. The general story is that the president sent his brother to see Miss Monroe to tell he that her affair with the president was over and that she should have no further contact with him. That entreaty failed and Bobby too succumbed to Marilyn's charms and they both entered into a sexual relationship.

All this is related to the fact that President Kennedy had an affair with Marilyn Monroe prior to his becoming president in 1961. They supposedly first met in the 1950s and had an on again-off again relationship that culminated in the 1960s while Kennedy was campaigning in California. They were supposed to have met at various times at the home of Peter Lawford and his wife Patricia Lawford (Kennedy's sister) at their Santa Monica home. The president saw Monroe off and on when he was president, with, or without Jackie Kennedy's knowledge. They met once in March 1962 while JFK was in California and on May 19 in New York. This was the last time that JFK would meet with Marilyn as things were now heading to the breaking point between them. Monroe told friends that she was in love with the president had that she wanted to marry him. This fantasy was probably due to her continuing mental state and her use of drugs. She also threatened to go public with her affair with the president if he didn't change his mind about seeing her again.

Peter Lawford said that Hoover warned the president that Lawford's home "had very likely been bugged by the Mafia." It was at this point in the Kennedy-Monroe saga that Jack Kennedy sent his brother Bobby out to California to confront Marilyn and calm her down. It seems however that Bobby's trip to Monroe's home had the opposite effect and he was soon having a sexual relationship with her. According to FBI sources, they were monitoring Bobby's visits to Monroe when he was in California and the reports of these meetings wound up on Hoover's desk. According to Peter Lawford's account of the incident, both he and Robert Kennedy went to Monroe's home on the afternoon of her death. During that session, Marilyn threatened to call a press conference detailing her relationship with both Kennedy brothers. Lawford further said that Monroe was hysterical and that they had to call Dr. Ralph Greenson who gave her a sedative to calm her down. There is another scenario as to what happened that day at Monroe's home. A number of people familiar with the account say that after Kennedy, Lawford and Dr. Greenson left her home, Marilyn frantically called Lawford and Bobby and his brother-in-law returned to her home to find her either dead or dying in bed. They then called an ambulance and when it arrived, they went with Marilyn to the hospital but before they arrived, they told the ambulance driver to return to her home. By this time, Marilyn was dead and the two men put her back in her bed and both men left as quickly as they came. Years later, Dr. Greenson said that he knew for a fact that Robert Kennedy was in Marilyn's home the day she died. Kennedy then returned to northern California to reunite with his family. An added touch to the drama of what happened at Monroe's home came from LA Chief of Detectives Thad Brown who said he was summoned back to headquarters because of a "problem." The problem, it seems was that a piece of paper was found in her home with the phone number of the White House on it. The president was notified at 6:04.A.M. of the death of Monroe in a phone call from Peter Lawford. We can only speculate what the reaction of JFK might have been when he heard the news. In those days, it was a standing order among newspapermen and women that if they had any idea of a secret relationship between the president and Miss Monroe that they'd keep it to themselves (as hard as that may seem). On one hand, he would have been saddened to hear of the death of Monroe whom he apparently liked as a person. But, on the other hand, he must have been relieved that her death would keep whatever potential scandal from coming to the forefront. Some conspiracy theorists say that the Kennedy's had Monroe killed. Why? The Kennedy family was ruthless when it came to dealing with their enemies, political and otherwise. But they did not have to resort to murder in order to silence their opponents. If Monroe was killed, as is a possibility, then others unknown were more than ready and willing to carry out the deed.

When Monroe was found dead, the LA Corner said that she had died from "acute barbiturate poisoning due to ingestion of overdose." In a sensational book called *Double Cross* (1992) which was written by Sam Giancana's half-brother Chuck, said that Sam Giancana had Monroe murdered in that exact fashion. "By murdering her, Bobby Kennedy's affair with the starlet would be exposed. It might be possible to depose the rulers of Camelot."

The most famous public photo of Jack Kennedy and Monroe together came when the actress was on stage at New York's Madison Square Garden to sing Happy Birthday to President Kennedy. Marilyn was decked out in such a tight fitting dress that left nothing to the imagination. A number of Kennedy advisors as well as a number of Democratic politicians asked the president not to appear with Monroe at the Garden event so as not to raise any eyebrows. Arthur Schlesinger Jr, one of Kennedy's most trusted advisors, said that the president did not have any relationship with Monroe, this coming from one of Kennedy's stalwarts who didn't know or want to know anything adverse affecting his friend, the president. Anyone who was at the event in Madison Square Garden that night and saw the way Monroe was signing to the president, knew just by her body language that something was going on between them. Those who were in the know, and those who only had an inkling of what was supposedly going on between the president and Monroe, had the good sense not to go public with their beliefs.

The "Kennedy did it" conspiracy in the death of Marilyn Monroe is not a new theory and it was given new life in a book by Jay Margolis, an investigative reporter and Richard Buskin, the author of thirty books called *The Murder of Marilyn Monroe: Case Closed.* Their book, which came out in 2014, places the blame for her murder on Robert Kennedy, Peter Lawford, and Dr. Ralph Greenson, her psychiatrist who was responsible for giving her a fatal dose of pentobarbital into her heart. Another witness to the event was supposed to have been the ambulance driver, James Hall. The three men were at her Brentwood home on the night of August 5, 1962, pleading with Marilyn to give them her diary that held the hidden secrets of her affair with both Jack and Bobby. The authors say that later that night, Bobby came back to Monroe's home with a bodyguard from the Los Angeles Police Department who injected her with a powerful sedative. Then, two LAPD "Gangster Squad" officers held her down, took off her clothes, and gave her an enema that contained a large amount of Nembutal's pills as well as seventeen chloral hydrates. They then departed the home and later that night, Monroe's maid, Eunice Murray, found her dead. Mrs. Murray then called an ambulance and when they arrived at her home, Monroe was barely alive. They put her on a breathing device and took her to the hospital. Dr. Greenson was there the whole time and he told the attendant to take her off the breathing machine and when no one was looking, he injected some fatal substance into her heart, causing her death. [10]

This is just one of the many theories surrounding the death of Marilyn Monroe and cannot be verified to an absolute extent.

Non conspiracy theorists say that Monroe was deeply depressed at the time of her death (she had once before tried to commit suicide), and that she accidentally overdosed while taking her pills.

The Marilyn Monroe death, like so many other tragic losses that have been depicted in this book, will be debated as long as people are interested in learning the truth.

---

[10] No Author, *Bobby Kennedy ordered murder of Marilyn Monroe, new book claims,* Al Arabiya News, May 17, 2014.

Chapter 55
The Vatican Bank Scandal

By the late 1970s, the world woke up to a financial scandal that would soon be front page news across both the United States and Europe. By the time it all ended, the affair would engulf the Vatican, which was by all accounts was one of the most trustworthy institutions in the world, the CIA, the Mafia, certain high-ranking prelates who managed the Vatican's finances, shadowy characters who would come to dominate the headlines, and the failure of certain banks in both the United States and Italy. At the heart of the affair was a high-ranking Priest from Cicero, Illinois, Archbishop Paul Marcinkus, who was the present of the Institute for Religious Works, or the Vatican Bank.

The history of the Vatican Bank dates back to 1929 during the reign of the Italian dictator Benito Mussolini. During the 1920s, the Vatican did not have its own bank and was essentially broke. All this changed dramatically when in February 1928, the Lateran Treaty was signed by the Vatican and Mussolini and the Vatican became its own separate state, along having full diplomatic rights as would any other nation. The Vatican was now given a huge fortune that amounted to three-quarters of a billion lire and another billion in negotiable bonds in compensation for the lands it lost when it became a nation-state. With the Vatican now cash rich, it set up an organization to administer it called the Patrimony of the Holy See' and the funds were administered by the Bank of Rome who was more than happy to look after the Vatican's finances. Soon though, the Pope changed the name of its banking organization to The Institute for Religious Works, or IOR. He did this because he didn't want the Vatican to be seen a banking institution that lent and borrowed money. In another deal with Mussolini, it was agreed that the IOR would not pay tax on its dividend income and the Vatican would now be cash full and not have to rely on other institutions for its money.

By the 1960s, the banks' power and influence grew to the point where it controlled interests in thousands of local companies and owned considerable real estate in Rome. The Vatican bank also heavily invested its money in the U.S., Germany, and Switzerland. But by the early 1970s, bad investments caused the Vatican Bank to go broke, and the man most responsible for the collapse was an Italian-American banker named Michele Sindona, who by 1974, had squandered away somewhere between $120 million and $1 billion dollars. Besides Michele Sindona, the other main players in the Vatican Bank drama were Bishop Paul Marcinkus, Roberto Calvi and Lico Gelli who headed a Masonic Lodge in Italy. The Masonic Lodge was also-called P-2, or Propaganda 2, made up of Freemasons, people who throughout the centuries took part in revolutionary activities against existing governments. P-2 was one of Italy's most secretive organizations and was banned by the Italian parliament when an investigation revealed that it was linked to some of the highest members of the Italian parliament, the military, and the press. There were also allegations that P-2 took part in assassinations, kidnappings, and illegal arms trading across the world. It was also rumored that P-2 was somehow involved in the death of Roberto Calvi in London. Gelli was well connected in Vatican circles due to his friendship with Cardinal Paolo Bertoli who worked in the Vatican's Diplomatic Corps. Cardinal Bertoli even introduced Gelli to Bishop Paul Marcinkus. Once the Vatican scandal erupted in plain sight, Gelli did not fare well. After the collapse of the Banco Ambrosiano, the Italian police raided Gelli's private offices on March 17, 1981, and confiscated a large amount of vital information which included lists of the names of the P-2 members, which included members of parliament, the armed forces, and heads of the Italian secret services, and information on both Roberto Calvi and Michael Sindona. Other members of the P-2 which were revealed were some high-ranking members of the Vatican who allied themselves with Gelli. P-2 was shut down by Italian prosecutors and after its fall, Gelli went on the run and was captured in Cannes, some years later. Another participant which would play in intricate part in the scandal was the Banco Ambrosiano of Milan who owned by the Vatican Bank and became involved in a massive financial scandal causing a $790 million run on "Ambro funds". Some conspiracy theorists and other mainstream writers, who covered the Vatican Bank scandal, came to the conclusion that either one or more of the above mentioned people had something to do with the sudden death of Pope John Paul 1, Alberto Luciani who died in in papal chambers after serving as Pontiff for only one month. During his brief tenue, the Pope had serious doubts about how the IOR was running and he even sold one bank controlled by the Vatican called Banca Cattolica di Veneto, or "the priest's bank" to Robert Calvi. Pope John Paul had no idea that the bank was laundering money and before his death he had a talk with both Roberto Calvi and Bishop Marcinkus to discuss possible changes in the way the bank was run and who would oversee it. It was rumored that the Pope was thinking of replacing Marcinkus with Cardinal Giovanni Benelli of Florence. In an interesting plot twist, many members of the Vatican staff, some priests, nuns, and others, organized a lottery to see which day Bishop Marcinkus would be fired.

The man most responsible for the collapse of the Banco Ambrosiano was Michele Sindona who is central to this story. Michele Sindona was born from poor roots in Patti, Sicily, where he was raised by his grandmother Nunziata along with his brother Enio. Nunziata knew the local bishop and she would take young Michele to see him often. The bishop would ply the boy with stories of the Church that Michele relished.

In 1938, he attended the University of Messina and graduated four years later with a degree in tax law. After school he got a job as a bookkeeper and also worked in real estate. But with the allied invasion of Italy during World War II, young Michele's life would be forever changed.

On July 10, 1943, as allied armies landed on Italian soil, the local Mafia aided British and American troops in securing the beachhead. Michele Sindona drove a produce truck for the arriving Americans and British, and also supplied the local populace with food. All of this was done under the direction of mob boss Vito Genovese. Four years later, Michele moved to Milan where he was given an introduction to the pro-secretary of State for the Vatican, Giovanni Battista Montini, later to be named Pope Paul V1. Michele quickly won over the prelate and he was appointed as the Vatican's first chief fundraiser, later to become the chief financial director of the Vatican.

His first venture was to buy Milan's Banca Privata Finanzaria, or BPP for the Vatican, but he had to hide the Vatican's ownership of the bank and used his connections in Switzerland to hide the transaction. Soon he had invested the Vatican's money in both legal and illegal enterprises, most of them not known to the Pope.

In 1963, Sindona had made his first American purchase; the Libby, McNeil, Libby Company, a food processing company that had international distribution sales. Later that year, Sindona began his partnership with a secret society in Italy called the Masonic Lodge headed by a right-wing nationalist named Lico Gelli. Also called P-2, or Propaganda 2, and made of up Freemasons, people who throughout the centuries, took part in revolutionary activities against existing governments. P-2 was one of Italy's most secretive organizations.

As time went on, Sindona would invest some of the Vatican's money in P-2. By 1974, and using P-2's cash, Sindona had bought 6 banks in 4 countries, including the United States. From all his Vatican investments, many of whom the Pope and his top aides did not know about, Sindona got the nickname as "God's Banker."

In the summer of 1974, he enlarged his financial empire by establishing an-international money Brokerage Company called Moneyrex. Using Moneyrex as a cover, he transferred millions of lira out of Italy and placed them in secret Swiss accounts. He also transferred money from P-2's drug business into his personal accounts.

Soon, Sindona would form an alliance with the powerful American Genovese and Gambino crime families; laundering money for the Gambino's who were forever in his debt. As Sindona's name became more familiar with the international powers that be, his services were sought after by the secret services of a number of countries who used him as a middle man when they wanted discretion in their endeavors. He was used as a conduit for a number of covert CIA missions, passing funds, for example, to the Greek colonels before they took power in 1967. He also gave millions of dollars to centrists and right-wing political parties in Italy, including the ruling Christian Democrats. He now set his sights on America and bought his first American bank, New York's Franklin National Bank. He paid $40 million for one million shares of the bank. Once in control of Franklin, Sindona transferred millions of dollars of Franklin's assets to his Swiss account, causing Franklin to collapse. Franklin's demise soon lead to the collapse of Sindona's other European financial holdings.

Sindona also had ties with the CIA when he bought the Rome *Daily American,* a newspaper which the Agency covertly funded. Later, Sindona said that he bought the paper at the request of American Ambassador Graham Martin who feared that the paper would "fall into the hands of the leftists." Later, Ambassador Martin denied the charges and called Sindona "a liar." To say that Michele Sindona was well connected in business and financial circles is an understatement. He had on his side, Mafia dons, banking leaders such as the Hambros of London, Continental Illinois, the Rothschild family, David Kennedy, President Nixon's Treasury Secretary, the Vatican Bank and its president, Bishop Paul Marcinkus. He once said of his relationship with these powerful people thusly, "I prefer to deal with men like Somoza. Doing business with a one-man dictatorship is much easier than doing business with democratically elected governments. They have too many subcommittees, too many controls. They also aspire to honesty, that's bad for the banking business."

In 1972, Sindona met with Maurice Stans who was President Nixon's chief fund raiser for the upcoming presidential election. Sindona wanted to ingratiate himself with the president and he offered Stans a suitcase which contained $1 million in cash as a campaign gift. Unfortunalty, Stans had to refuse the offer because of a new law that said that anonymous gifts were illegal.

By 1973, however, Sindona's luck was beginning to run thin. In Rome, Bishop Marcinkus wrote a check for $307,000 for losses accrued by the Vatican Bank by Sindona as a result of illegal dealings on the American stock exchange in shares from a company called Vetco Industries. The Security and Exchange Commission found out that an investment broker in LA had acquired on behalf of Sindona and Marcinkus some 27 percent of Vetco. "The Vatican paid the fine, then sold its shares at a profit."

Things were about to get worse for Michele Sindona when, in 1974, the Italian judiciary setup a secret investigation of him, his links to the Vatican and his other nefarious operations worldwide. The man who was put in charge of the Sindona probe was Giorgio Ambrosoli who, by March 21, 1975, sent a secret report on Sindona's actions to the attorney general of Italy. He soon had proof that Sindona was using a myriad of offshore lending institutions to launder his money, many which belonged to the Vatican Bank. As his investigation went on, Ambrosoli was able to make a list of seventy-seven names of people who were doing illegal business with Sindona, including a number of people inside the Vatican Bank. During his investigation, Ambrosoli was threatened by unknown persons who hinted that if he did not end his investigation than bad things were going to happen to him. Instead of surrendering to the threats, he continued to purse his leads wherever they took him. A banker colleague of Sindona's, Enrico Cuccia, overheard Sindona tell a friend while he was in New York that, "he wanted everyone who had done him harm killed, in particular Giorgio Ambrosoli." Unfortunalty for Ambrosoli, that horrible event was about to take place.

On July 11, 1978, after Ambrosoli was leaving his office for his Milan home, he was approached by three men who stopped him abruptly on the street. They asked him if he was Doctor Ambrosoli and without any fanfare, they shot him three times into his chest, He was rushed to a hospital but was dead within hours. Before he died he managed to say that the person who shot him had an American-Italian accent. In the day following the death of Mr. Ambrosoli, two other Italian officials who were investigating the case were killed. One was Lt. Colonel Antonio Varisco, who was responsible for the investigation into Gelli's P-2. The other victim was Boris Guiliano, the chief of the Flying Squad who was killed as he left a local restaurant in Palermo. The man who took over Ambrosoli's job, Emanuele Basile, was killed the next year while walking with his family on a crowded street.

In the wake of the killings, the Italian government made a cursory investigation into the affairs of the looting of the Banca Privata Italiana, and the allegation that Sindona, Roberto Calvi, and Bishop Marcinkus might have diverted $6.5 million among themselves. However, no further investigation was conducted and the matter died on the vine.

On March 9, 1979, Sindona was indicted on 29 counts of perjury, fraud, and misappropriation of bank funds. His trial was set for August 1, but on September 1, 1979, he was kidnapped from his New York hotel and taken to Palermo. After being interrogated by men in hooded masks, he was taken out of Italy to Salzburg, Munich, Frankfurt and back New York. On October 6, 1979, Sindona's attorney, Marvin Frankel, received a phone call from Sindona himself saying that he'd been released and was in New York at 42nd Street and Tenth Avenue. He was picked up, and eight days later, he was in the courtroom of Judge Thomas Griesa. He told the judge that he'd been kidnapped by "leftists" and that he was supposed to be tried for "economic crimes."

In a huge twist that no one expected, the Italian police arrested John Gambino during a visit to Rome. When they searched him, they found a piece of paper on his person that read, "741, Saturday, Frankfurt." All this had to do with an FBI investigation of a TWA flight with that number which left Frankfurt for New York's Kennedy Airport on October 13, three days before Sindona suddenly reappeared. One of the passengers on the plane was a man who said his name was Joseph Bonamico of Brooklyn. It turned out that the street address he wrote on his customs declaration did not exist, and the agents sent the customs form to their forensics lab. The results of the exam were shocking; the handwriting on the form belonged to Sindona but his fingerprints were on the customs form that belonged to Bonamico. Is it possible that Sindona was lying about his own kidnapping and that it was all a hoax? That is a possibility that we have to consider when looking into Sindona's absence during that time.[11]

Sindona was so eager to get the United States authorities off his back that he even put out feelers to a professional hit man named Luigi Ronsisvalle to assassinate John Kenney who was the Assistant U.S. District Attorney who was heading his extradition case while he was still in Europe. Much to Sindona's displeasure, Ronsisvalle turned down Sindona's generous offer of $100,000 for the Kenney hit. Ronsisavlle knew too much about how the U.S. judicial system worked to be suckered into Sindona's wild and impractical scheme.

In October 1979, he surrendered to U.S. authorities. On March 27, 1980, he was convicted of 68 counts of perjury and mishandling

---

[11] Posner, Gerald, *God's Banker: A History of Money And Power At The Vatican,* Simon & Schuster, New York, 2015, Page 295.

bank funds. He was sentenced to a 27-year jail term at the Federal Correctional Center in Otisville, New York.

The other person of interest in the Vatican Bank scandal was Roberto Calvi, the former head of the powerful Banco Ambrosiano who had long-standing covert contacts with both Sindona and Bishop Marcinkus. The life of Roberto Calvi was one that would have made any Hollywood producer proud and the facts surrounding his death on London was even more bizarre. On June 12, 1982, Roberto Calvi, left his home in Rome and using a false passport, fled to London. Six days later, a passerby walking along the Blackfriars Bridge in that city, noticed a body hanging from one of the pillars. The police were called and the body was cut down. What the police found left hem confused. The name on the man's passport read Glan Robert Calvini. The body was weighed down with 7,400 British pounds and large amounts of Swiss and U.S. currencies.

As the investigation proceeded, British and Italian authorities began to uncover one of the largest baking and political scandals in recent memory, and one that would reach into the portals of the Vatican. They very idea of a Vatican Bank is a strange phenomenon, yet such an operation had been going on just beyond the pastoral halls of the Pope's balcony. By the 1960s, the banks power and influence grew to the point where it controlled interests in thousands of local companies in Italy and owned considerable real estate in Rome. The Vatican Bank also heavily invested its money in the U.S., Germany, and Switzerland. But by the early 1970s, bad investments caused the Vatican Bank to go broke, and the man most responsible for the collapse was Michele Sindona, who by 1974, had squandered away somewhere between $120 million and $1 billion. But the story does not end there. Back in Italy, the Banco Ambrosiano of Milan owned by the Vatican Bank became involved in a massive financial scandal causing a $790 million run of cash.

The president of the Vatican Bank, Archbishop Paul Marcinkus (more about him later) asked the Secretary of State to open an investigation of Banco Ambrosiano's dealings. The focus of the investigation centered on the bank's president, Roberto Calvi who was eventually tried and found guilty of taking $27 million out of

Italy and was given a four year prison term (Banco Ambrosiano closed down on August 6, 1982).

Roberto Calvi was the intermediary for the Vatican as it began to invest its money in various offshore shell companies, some legal, some not, and began taking in a rich horde of cash. Bishop Marcinkus sat on the Board of the Banco Ambrosiano's subsidiary in Nassau, Bahamas and he controlled the cash that flowed out of the Caribbean,-Lichtenstein-Luxembourg network. Calvi was responsible for these undercover connections-including those that were funneled from dummy corporations in such places as Panama and other places around the globe. In 1963, Calvi and Banco Ambrosiano had acquired Banca del Gottardo in Lugano, Switzerland that, due to Calvi's illegal efforts, made Banca del Gottardo one of the key conduits for laundering Mafia money. Another bank that Calvi ran was called Banco Ambrosiano Overseas, Nassau that was founded in 1971 and in a rather unusual circumstance, had Bishop Paul Marcinkus as one of its board of directors. Not known to financial authorities in Italy and elsewhere during that time was that Calvi arranged that the Vatican Bank and Banco Ambrosiano were interconnected in their illegal money laundering activities. One example of their cooperation was when, in November 1976, Calvi bought 53.5 percent of Banco Mercantile of Florence and hid the fact that the purchase was made on behalf of the Vatican Bank. Throughout Calvi's wheeling's and dealings, he made purchases on behalf of the Vatican bank who gave a wink and a nod to his corrupt activities.

Calvi's downfall came when Italian authorities arrested Luci Gelli in March 1981 when they arrived at his home looking for evidence surrounding the kidnapping of Michele Sindona. They found a list that Gelli kept of 962 members of his P-2 organization as well as many government documents. The Gelli scandal resulted in the down fall of the Italian government and the new prosecutors renewed their case against Calvi, and two months following the Gelli raid, the police arrested Calvi. Calvi's family turned to Bishop Marcinkus for help but the priest had no intention of helping his fellow crook and turned down all their entireties. The Vatican Bank was not going to be brought into a scandal of their own making and Calvi, for all intents and purposes was on his own. Bishop Marcinkus told Calvi's son Carlo that, "If we do, it's not only the IOR and the Vatican's image that will suffer. You'll lose as well, for our problems are your problems, too." To make matters more problematic for the Vatican, while Calvi was in his Lodi prison, he somehow continued as present of Banco Ambrosiano, leaving the banking world shaking their heads.

The Calvi-Sindona link was more than anyone could imagine and after Sindona was charged with ordering the murder of Giorgio Ambrosoli, who was investigating Sindona's illegal activities, Calvi tried to commit suicide by taking an overdose of barbiturates.

On July 20, he was sentenced to four years in jail for taking $27 million out of Italy and fined 16 billion lira. His lawyers managed to get him released on bond and to everyone's surprise (or not), the board of Banco Ambrosiano unanimously reconfirmed Calvi as chairman. One wonders how many hands he had to pay off in order to make that happen.

The circumstances of just how Roberto Calvi died are as mysterious as his life and entire books have been written on that subject. Here are the basic facts. Now out on bail but not out of the clutches of the law, Calvi sought out his contacts in the Mafia, most notably the arms smuggler and Mafia don, Falvio Carboni. Carboni got Calvi a false passport in the name of Gian Roberto Calvini. Calvi went to Austria and finally to London where he met his fate. The official coroner's inquest in London ruled that Calvi had committed suicide by strangulation. But if so, how could he have climbed down a busy London bridge, attached a rope to his head, and committed the final act without anyone seeing him? To make matters more confusing for the police, they found on Calvi's body four pieces of brick and concrete and a separate piece had been lodged in the front of his pants, all of these items weighing twelve pounds. Did they just happen to be on his person when he died? Sounds fishy to, don't you think? The likelihood of Calvi's death being ruled a suicide is impractical. For instance, he had to climb down a paraphet to a scaffold and then onto a ladder to a level where he could then somehow, weightd down with twelve pounds of rock, hang himself. The most likely alternative is that he was killed by persons unknown, and then taken in the pre-dawn hours and left on the bridge for others to find him.

Deputy Superintendent John White of the London police told writer Edward Jay Epstein in an interview that, "We don't even know how he got from his hotel, for and one half miles away, to Blackfriars Bridge." After his death, the London police canvased taxi drivers in the city and no one admitted to have taken Calvi anywhere near the Blackfriars bridge that day, nor could they find anyone who could tell them about his activities in the city in the three days prior to his death. "Calvi had been smuggled to London by a conspiracy that involved arranging three false identities, eight separate private plane flights around Europe, a speed boat, four different cars and 14 temporary residences including The Baur Au Lac and Holiday Inn in Zurich, the Amstel in Amsterdam, the George in Edinburgh and the Hilton, Sheraton and Chelsea in London. The conspirators included Flavio Carboni, a Sardenian contractor, Silvano Vittor, a cigarette smuggler and their girl-friends, the Austrian sisters Manuela and Micheala Klienszig. They all denied seeing Calvi the night he disappeared."[12]

For conspiracy theorists the type of Calvi's death is important. Death by handing is one of the penalties used by the Masons for someone who had violated their oath. Was Caliv's death a warning by Mason's not to fool with them in any way? In another unusual circumstance, Calvi's secretary, 55-year old Graziella Teresa Corrocher, threw herself out of a window to her death. Later, a note was found in her room attacking Calvi. She wrote, "He should be twice-damned for the damage he did to the group to all of us who were at one time proud of it."

There were two official inquests into Cavli's death, one conducted by David Paul who conveniently left out important information relating to the incident and the jury only took nine hours to decide that Calvi's death was a suicide. A second jury was impaneled and this time they voted to overthrow the first verdict. The experts said that a certain amount of drugs could have been used to put Calvi to seep before his was hung.

Who was the most likely to have taken part in Calvi's death? The major culprits most likely were Bishop Paul Marcinkus and/or Michele Sindona or their henchmen. Both men had no love for Calvi and it is entirely possible that that they may have pulled

---

[12] Epstein, Edward Jay, "Query: The First Calvi Mystery: Was his death suicide or murder? www.edwardjayepstein.com.

strings with their Mafia associates to have Calvi rubbed out.

Who was the American who took part in the Vatican Bank scandal and was associated on a close level with both Calvi and Sindona?

Paul Marcinkus was at times the papal bodyguard called "the Gorilla" and an Archbishop of the church at the time the Vatican Bank scandal erupted. He was born on January 15, 1922 in Cicero, Illinois, the center of Al Capone's criminal network. He came from a Lithuanian family who were working class and spoke poor English. He studied to become a priest and was ordained in 1947. He then went to Rome where he studied at the same school as that of the future pope, Albino Lucian, called Gregorian. He later got his doctorate in cannon law and his star in the church was now on the rise. He was a large man, over six feet tall, and weighted over 220 pounds, not your typical looking priest. He later went back to Chicago where he worked as a parish priest and a member of the local diocese. He caught the attention of Cardinal Samuel Stritch who was the head of the archdiocese in Chicago and he had Marcinkus transferred to the English section of the Vatican secretary of state's office 1952. He also served the church in Bolivia and Canada before returning to Rome. One of Marcinkus' most notable fans was New York's Cardinal Spellman who often told Pope Paul V1 that Marcinkus was someone who could aid the church in the future. He saved the Pope from harm when the Pontiff was in Rome and an overeager crowd suddenly barred his way. Marcinkus elbowed the Pope to safety and his star was immediately born. When the Pope travelled on overseas trips such as to India and the United Nations, it was Paul Marcinkus who served as his official bodyguard.

In 1971, the Pope made a decision that would have a profound effect on how the Vatican Bank would be run for years; he appointed his trusted advisor, Paul Marcinkus as head of the IOR, or the Institute for Religious Works (he would stay in that position until 1989). One of Marcinkus' favorite phrases was, "You can't run a church on Hail Marys.""

In 1971, the year that Marcinkus was appointed to head the IOR, first met Roberto Calvi through Michele Sindona and from that first introduction, the seeds of the Vatican Bank scandal with all three men participating were laid, with fatal consequences for all of them. By his own admission, Marcinkus had no knowledge of banking and it was only by his intimate friendship and support of the Pope that he was selected to become head of the IOR. If he had to do it over again by the Pope might have had second thoughts about his appointment of Marcinkus to such a high-caliber post in the Vatican.

Another thing that the Pope did not know was that Bishop Marcinkus was involved up to his neck with members of the Mafia. According to a mobster named Vincenzo Calcara who was being investigated by the Italian police, he said that when Marcinkus ran the IOR, the institution helped to launder $6.5 million in Mafia cash. He told investigators that he flew from Sicily to Rome carrying two large suitcases containing $100,000. When he landed at the Rome airport, he was met by Marcinkus and an unnamed cardinal and was driven to a lawyer's office in the city where Calacra turned over the cash. The money eventually wound up as "clean" money with the IOR taking a service fee for their work. A second mafia member named Rosario Spatola, testified that he heard Marcinkus "bragging" that he had high contacts in the Mafia.[13]

Marcinkus also made a secret deal with Roberto Calvi when it came to the IOR's relationship and loans to various other banks with whom they did business (mostly undercover). In August 1981, Marcinkus met with Calvi at IOR's headquarters and gave him what was called "letters of patronage" or "letters of comfort," which assured their parties that the Vatican stood behind Banco Ambrosiano. The letters went onto say that the IOR "directly or indirectly" controlled banks in Panama, Luxembourg, and Liechtenstein. The letters were so vaguely written that the receiver would be led to understand while the IOR would not assume the debt, it would however, let the precipitant know that it was endorsing the loan. Marcinkus also asked Calvi to give him a counter-letter which was backdated to August 26-absloving the Vatican of any obligation to repay the loans. For a man who had no knowledge or interest in banking, Bishop Marcinkus was learning fast.

---

[13] Posner, Gerald, *God's Banker: A History of Money And Power At The Vatican,* Simon and Schuster, New York, 2015, Page 377.

While Marcinkus was involved with Calvi and Sindona in their money laundering schemes using the IOR as their conduit, he was making friends with high-level American officials in Washington, providing them with valuable information coming from the Vatican. Marcinkus's contact in Rome was the U.S. envoy to the Hole See, William Wilson, a friend and advisor of President Ronald Reagan. Upon arriving in Rome in February 1981, Ambassador Wilson counted Marcinkus as a close friend and the two men met many times officially and unofficially. Soon, Marcinkus was providing Ambassador Wilson with classified information on the activities of the Pope and he even tried to persuade the Pontiff to take pro-American position when it came to foreign relations. Marcinkus's information was passed on to other American ambassadors with the warning that, "Please be sure to protect the source." The State Department soon leanred of Marcinkus's illegal involvement with Calvi and Sindona but they did not press Wilson for further information on what he was up to. The thought in Washington was the less they knew about what Marcinkus was up to, the better.

The Bishop was now in the cross hairs of an FBI investigation relating to the possible defrauding of the United States government centering on a company called American Trading Services "by concealing millions of dollars in the Institute of Religious Works" (the Vatican bank). A total of $7.7 million dollars was supposed to have been concealed in two accounts owned by the Institute Per Le Opera di Riligione that had been opened five years previously by the ATS. The matter got the attention of U.S. Deputy Presidential Envoy to the Holy See delivered a three-page telex to Marcinkus by Benjamin Civiletti, the Deputy Attorney General. Calvetti asked Marcinkus for details of the American Trading affair and he replied one month later saying that he had gone through the facts of the case but could not find anything wrong that the Vatican bank might have been accused of. He had the nerve to tell Civiletti that, "The IOR is not a bank in the ordinary sense of the word." Speaking of the questionable $7.7 million he said, "Ours is a modest organization and any operation involving large sums would not go unnoticed."

In 1973, two FBI agents and a federal prosecutor visited Marcinkus in the Vatican as part of their investigation into counterfeit bonds and securities and believed that he had some part in running it. He said that the Vatican was not responsible in any way for the sale of $900 million worth of stocks and bonds which were made of up of counterfeit money. The IOR, he said, had gotten involved "because of the stories told by some confidence people." The FBI came away from that meeting confidant that Marcinkus was somehow involved in the scheme but had no solid evidence to prove their point beyond a reasonable doubt.[14]

In a stunning development Ambassador Wilson told the U.S. Attorney General that the accusations against the Bishop were "based on innuendo and possibly, even by association." He also had the timidity to ask the Justice Department to allow Marcinkus to be able to read the contents of any FBI files they had on him (his request was refused). It seemed that certain high-level members of the Reagan administration were trying to protect the bishop at all costs, even if it meant covering up his crimes.

While all this was going on, Marcinkus was facing further scrutiny from a book that was to be released by the noted crime writer, Richard Hammer, "with the first ever account of the 1973 fraud and counterfeit investigation that prompted the FBI to interview Marcinkus at the Vatican." Wilson even got former New York Mayor Robert Wagner to intercede on behalf of Marcinkus and he approached the publisher, Holt Reinhart to allow Marcinkus the opportunity to read the manuscript before publication (it was refused). The book, called *The Vatican Connection,* was released early, due to the major publicity it received in the press. The publisher wrote of the books contents as, "The astonishing account of a billion-dollar counterfeit stock deal between the Mafia and the Church."

In the end, Marcinkus was forced to resign his job as head of the IOR. The Vatican paid out $224 million to its creditors of the Banco Ambrosiano in what it called "recognition of moral involvement" in the bank's default.

Paul Marcinkus died on February 22, 2006, age 84, in Sun City, Arizona.

Roberto Calvi was found dead hanging from Blackfriars Bridge in June 1982.

Michele Sindona died in prison while serving a life sentence

[14] Ibid, Page 284-285.

under unusual circumstances (why not). After eating breakfast in his private cell, he suddenly collapsed yelling, "I've been poisoned." He was in a coma, dying two days later.

Chapter 56
America At War with Itself

While the United States was fighting the North Vietnamese and the Viet Cong in the jungles of Southeast Asia in what seemed like a never ending war, the flames of discord and discontent at home were beginning to burn. From the college campuses in California to New York, to the massive street demonstrations that went on across the nation in protest to the Vietnam War, it seemed like the old order was crumbling fast. Hard hats battled with student war protesters, demonstrations against college administrators seemed to crop on an almost weekly basis and demonstrators seemed to live outside the gates of the White House. Thomas Jefferson once said that a little revolution was necessary some of the time, and by the late 1960s and early 1970s, it seemed that his dictum had become reality. By the time the decade of the 1970s had ended, the American people came to know the names of certain radical groups like the Weather Underground, the Black Panthers, and the Symbionese Liberation Army as well as they knew the names of their family. They'd also come to know the name of an unknown girl named Patricia Hearst, the heir to the publishing fortune founded by her relative, William Randolph Hearst, By the time that the Hearst story was over, Patty would adopt the revolutionary name of "Tania" and renounce all of her wealth of privilege.

The road to violence and destruction started very meekly when, in 1964, eight hundred students were arrested in a confrontation with the administration of the University of California-Berkeley over the right to have protests on that campus. This was the beginning of the so-called Free Speech Movement which would soon spread across the nation's campuses. On February 21, 1965, the radical African-American political leader, Malcolm X was killed at the Audubon Ballroom in Manhattan where he was about to deliver a speech. Three gunmen climbed the stage and shot him 15 times at point-blank range. He later died at Columbia Presbyterian Hospital. The men responsible for his death were members of the Nation of Islam, a radical African-American group who espoused violence against the government and had broken apart from the more moderate groups led by Martin Luther King. When JFK was killed, Malcolm X said that the "chickens had come home to roost," a phrase that meant that Kennedy had got what he deserved. From August 11-16, 1965, riots broke out in the black neighborhood of Watts in Los Angeles after the police stopped a black motorist. Three days later, when the riots were finally put down, 30 people were dead, and 1,000 wounded. On October 15, more than two million people across the nation attended a Peace Moratorium protesting the Vietnam War. In 1968 Senator Robert Kennedy, who was running for president, was killed in Los Angeles (allegedly) by a Palestinian named Sirhan Sirhan. That same year, Rev. Martin Luther King was killed in Memphis, Tennessee, by an ex-convict by the name of James Earl Ray. That same year, a group calling itself the Black Panther Party called for violent revolution in the nation and would soon turn against police, nation—wide.

In June 1969, the nation-wide anti-war organization called the Students for a Democratic Society (S.D.S.), splintered off from its leadership and formed the Weather Underground Organization and began advocating extreme violence against the established order in the country. The Weather Underground was originally established by financially well-off white, college-age students who based their political ideology on socialism and communism. Over time, the most radical of these people began a campaign of bombing and attacks against such institutions as police departments, a bombing at the U.S. Capital and attacks against New York City Police Department headquarters. Their slogan was "We are your mother's worst nightmare."

By January 1970, the core group of the Weather Underground had about one hundred dedicated revolutionaries who split up into three groups, one in San Francisco, New York, and in the Midwest like Detroit and Pittsburgh. A small group of Weathermen met in Michigan in the latter days of 1969 to plot strategy. One of the leaders of the band, Howard Machtinger, aided by a few of his most trusted soldiers, decided that they would begin targeting police forces across the nation. In rationalizing their decision to attack police they said, "If your definition of terrorism is you don't care who gets hurt, we agreed we wouldn't do that. But as to causing damage, or literally killing people, we were prepared to do that."

The three most important leaders of the group were Howard Machtinger in San Francisco, Bill Ayers (a friend of President Obama) in the Midwest, and Terry Robbins in New York. They made the most basic decisions as to just what type of targets to attack, were and when. Howard Machtinger and his party decided to attack targets in the San Francisco Bay area. One of their targets was the Hall of Justice complex in Berkeley. They placed two pipe bombs that were connected to an alarm clock. A second attack took place on February 12, 1970, when about six Weathermen took up positions around the Berkeley police department complex. Right before midnight, when the shifts were changing, two Weathermen took up positions near the police cars and planted a bomb near one of them. As the cops went to their respective cars, the bomb exploded, causing 30 plate glass windows in the municipal building to shatter. More than two dozen officers were injured in the attack. Seconds after the first bomb went off; a second explosion rocked the parking area, injuring six cops who had to be taken to a nearby hospital for treatment. Three weeks later, the faction led by Bill Ayers and the Detroit cell, tried to set off an explosion near a police precinct but the bomb failed to detonate.

The most audacious attack took place on March 6, 1970 in New York's Greenwich Village area that shattered the stillness of the night and put the Weather Underground on Page 1. Prior to the attack in the Village, the group tried to bomb the residence of Judge Murtagh by throwing Molotov cocktails but it did little damage. The leader of the Village attack was Terry Rollins who organized the plot. They set up shop at the vacated home of Cathy Wilkerson's father's that had become vacant when he took a trip to the Caribbean. The home was located at 18 West 11th Street in the trendy section of New York that catered to young people of all stripes. As preparations for the attack took place, a number of people who were most responsible for the planning took up residence. They were Cathy Wilkerson, Terry Robbins, Kathy Boudin, and Ted Gold, who was once a student at Columbia University. They decided to use dynamite in their upcoming attack, as the other paraphernalia they used in previous bombings attempts did not work. While none of them had any technical abilities to make a bomb, their enthusiasm took over, rather than trying to figure out just how to assemble the bomb. One of their targets was supposed to have been the army base at Fort Dix in New Jersey where an officer's club dance was supposed to have been held. The reason they chose Fort Dix was to "bring the war home" to the people of the United States. The attack was to be carried out on March 6, just as the crowd of people was descending on the base. Not all of the top leadership of the underground knew of the pending attack, but among those who knew and approved of it were Robbins, Bill Ayers, and Mark Rudd, one of the founding radicals of the radical cause of the time. Robbins told Rudd that, "We're going to kill the pigs at a dance at Fort Dix." Years later, two members of the cadre, Bernardine Dohrn and Jeff Jones, said they had relatively no knowledge of the attack. On March 5, one day prior to the attack, another participant came to the townhouse to take part in the planning. Her name was Diana Oughton, who was Bill Ayer's girlfriend. Many years later, when speaking about the Greenwich Village attack, she said her group "viewed those they planned to kill only as an abstraction."

That night, the group gathered to make their crude bomb but did not know how much destruction it might cause or really how to safety assemble the bomb; their indecision would prove to be costly. As the bomb was being assembled, it suddenly exploded, killing Ted Gold, Diana Oughton, and Terry Robbins. Kathy Boudin and Cathy Wilkerson fled the scene, naked and took refuge at a neighbor's home where they cleaned themselves up and left the area before the police arrived. Boudin would be on the lamb for the next ten years and took part in the 1980 botched attempt to rob a Brink's Armored Car in New York.[15]

Soon, a new name would become front and center in America's war with itself-the SLA-the Symbionese Liberation Army and their star, Patricia Hearst.

Patricia Hearst was the middle daughter of the newspaper tycoon, Randolph Hearst, the chairman of the board of the Hearst Corporation, which owned many newspapers and magazines and his wife Catherine. She attended Menlo College in California and

[15] Burrough, Brian, *How Ron Fliegelman Became The Weather Underground's Bomb Guru*, Vanity Fair, 3/2015.

when she met a man named Steven Weed, they moved in together in Berkeley, California where Weed was granted a graduate fellowship and teaching grant at the University of California, Berkeley. On the morning of February 4, 1974, Patty's idyllic life changed when she was abducted from her apartment by members of the Berkeley based SLA-Symbionese Liberation Army. She was forcibly put in the back of a truck and taken north of San Francisco. The nineteen-year old Patty would now be a pawn in the clutches of the SLA and her story would become front page news for months to come.

Soon her kidnappers were heard from and they demanded in exchange for her release, the freedom of two SLA members who were convicted of the 1973 murder of Marcus Foster, Oakland's fist black school superintendent (there demands were refused). They also demanded that the Hearst family give millions of dollars to feed the needy in California. The Hearst family and the Hearst Foundation then gave over $2 million in food aid for the needy in the San Francisco Bay area. This was not enough for her kidnappers who demanded an additional $4 million be put in the pot. Further talks failed and it seemed that both groups were now at an impasse.

One of the SLA leaders who kidnapped Patty Hearst was Donald DeFreeze who called himself General Field Marshal Cinque Mutume. DeFreeze had been in and out various jails including Vacaville where he organized a black inmate self-help group but whose real goal was to start a black revolt in the United States. The SLA kept Patty held hostage in a closet for 57 days, where she suffered abuse at their hands.

Eventually, Patty was given an ultimatium; join the SLA or be killed. Patty decided to join the SLA and take on their revolutionary cause, changing her name to "Tania."

Twelve days later, the SLA robbed a bank in San Francisco and surveillance cameras later showed Patricia Hearst carrying a carbine, taking part in the robbery. The incident caused the U.S. Attorney General to label her a "common criminal," while her supporters said she'd been brainwashed into taking part in the robbery. The FBI now put out flyers naming her as a "material witness" in the robbery.

But Patty's acts of violence were just getting started. The SLA now moved to Compton, California, a poor suburb of L.A, where they began to stockpile guns and ammunition for later use. On May 16, 1974, two SLA members, William and Emily Harris, were seen trying to steal ammunition from a sporting goods store, Patty was their lookout person, carrying a machine gun. The Harris's soon fled the scene but in their escape, Patty opened fire on local authorities. Soon, the police, using stolen cars as their lead, traced the Harris's and Patty to an apartment in Compton.

Soon, hundreds of police surrounded the house and a large firefight began, with police lobbing tear gas canisters into the house in order to flush them out. The house was now on fire and when two SLA members left the burning building, they were shot by the police. In the ensuing chaos, De Freeze and two others were dead. However, Patty and the Harris's managed to flee the scene and went on the lamb for over a year.

They lived for a time in both Pennsylvania and New York before heading back to California. While on the loose, they took part in bank robberies in Sacramento and put bombs under police cars.

Patty's luck ran out when she was arrested by the FBI in San Francisco on September 18, 1975.

The "trial of the century" (long before the OJ Simpson case) began two years later in a federal court in San Francisco where she faced charges of armed bank robbery, and use of a fire arm in the robbery of the bank in Hibernia. She was defended by the noted criminal defense attorney F. Lee Bailey who used brainwashing by the SLA as her defense. In the end, the jury found her guilty on two counts and was sentenced to seven years in jail. She served only two years when in a lucky break on her part, President Jimmy Carter commented her sentence in 1979. For their part, Emily and William Harris served six years in jail for kidnapping Patty. In 2002, they, along with others, were convicted of killing a man during a SLA robbery in 1975.

Shortly after her sentence was commuted, Patty Hearst married her bodyguard, Bernard Shaw. She later had a new career in acting, wrote a bestselling autobiography in 1982, and wrote a murder mystery called *Murder at San Simeon.*

Besides the activities of the Weather Underground and the kidnapping of Patricia Hearst, another incident that challenged the status quo took place in a small town called Media, Pennsylvania which would shake the foundations of the FBI to its roots, hasten the downfall of its powerful director, J. Edgar Hoover, and expose just how far the Bureau went in its war against home-grown radicals.

On the night of March 8, 1971, while most of the nation was watching the heavyweight championship fight between Muhammad Alli and Joe Frazier, a team of ordinary Americans broke into the little known FBI office located in the small town of Media, Pennsylvania. By the time their illegal break-in had ended, and in the days and months to follow, the burglars would read some of the most revealing and disturbing top-secret files that the Bureau had in their coffers. What they read was nothing less than a huge, illegal operation targeting Americans because of their political views, including many in the antiwar left, a large section of the African-American population. The files also revealed a secret FBI covert program that covered all these groups, codenamed COINTELPRO.

The burglary was the brainchild of William Davidon, a professor of physics at Haverford College and a regular attendee at anti-war protests in Philadelphia. After the Nixon administration invaded Cambodia in the summer of 1970, Mr. Davidon assembled a few of his most trusted friends who shared his political views, to meet in his apartment. There, they devised as audacious plan to break into the FBI office in Media, Pennsylvania and steal whatever files they could get their hands on. The group was made up of ordinary people who were fed up with the status quo in American, who were left leaning in their politics and who were adamantly opposed to the war in Vietnam. If they couldn't use their silent protests to end the war, then maybe their intrusion into the FBI building might be a better alternative. The members of the burglary team were made up of William Davidon, Keith Forsyth, and John and Bonnie Raines. Keith Forsyth was single, age, early 20's, and was a cab driver in Philadelphia. John and Bonnie Raines was a married couple who had a family to care for. John worked as a religion professor at Temple University in Philadelphia and Bonnie had a job at a day care center in the city. For months on end, the team met at Raines' apartment going over the floor plans of the building that housed the FBI office in Media. It was a perfect location for such a robbery; the building was located in an out of the way area that had little car or pedestrian traffic.

Bonnie Raines played an integral part in the preparations for the break-in. Posing as a student from Swarthmore College who was supposed to be studying job opportunities for women in the FBI, got access to the inside of the building and left with a knowledge of just about every nook and cranny of the inside of the office, including the fact the building did not have a security system. All was now ready for the break-in; the only time was when.

As Alli and Frazier were punching each other to bits, Mr. Forsyth, the designated lock picker, opened the door to the FBI office and the gang entered and began looking for the most important documents they could find. They managed to fill several large suitcases with their treasure trove and safely escaped the area without being seen. They stopped at a farmhouse about one hour's drive from Media where they began to study what they'd pilfered. What they found only confirmed what they'd believed for years; the FBI had been conducting a large scale, covert investigation of the radical right, on dissident political groups who opposed the war and others whom they believed would pose a threat to the nation. Calling themselves the Citizen's Committee to Investigate the FBI, the burglars began sending the documents to various newspapers around the nation. Soon, as these papers began to publish the documents stolen from Media, other national news outlets such as the *New York Times* began their own investigations of the Bureau's activities. Two of the groups whom the FBI targeted were antiwar activists and members of the dissident student groups. One document said of these organizations, "It will enhance the paranoia endemic in these circles and will further serve to get the point across there is an FBI agent behind every mailbox." One document had the title called "COINTELPRO" which had no meaning to them at the time. Sometime later, newsman Carl Stern who worked for NBC, filed a suit under the FOIA to get information on COINTELPRO, also known as Counterintelligence

Program. He soon found out just what it meant. COINTELPRO began in 1956 and included an exhaustive campaign to spy on civil rights leaders, political organizers and suspected members of the Communist Party. Other revelations were the systematic FBI spying on Dr. Martin Luther King and their efforts to discredit him and his civil rights organizations.

The fallout of the FBI's COINTELPRO program was looked into when the Congress set up an investigation of the nation's intelligence agencies headed by Senator Frank Church of Idaho. The Church Committee looked into the goings on of the FBI and the CIA, and also included a House panel that investigated both the King and Kennedy assassinations.

The burglars of the Media headquarters went on the lamb and were never caught. The FBI assigned over 200 agents to look for leads into the case but they came up empty. It wasn't until years later when a writer named Betty Medsger wrote a book called *The Burglary* that the entire story of what happened that night in Media, came to light. Sometimes one insignificant event causes a ripple that reverberates and changes the way we look at things in our nation's history. The Burglary of the FBI office in Media certainly fit that case to a tee.

THE END

BIBLIOGRAPHY

Aron, Paul, *Unsolved: Mysteries of American History,* John Wiley &Sons, New York, 1997.

Backless, John, *Turncoats, Traitors & Heros: Espionage in the American Revolution,* Da Capo, Press, New York, 1998.

Baker, Russ, *Family of Secrets,* Bloomsbury Press, New York, 2009.

Balsiger, David & Sellier, Charles, *The Lincoln Conspiracy,* Schick Sun Classics Books, Los Angeles, California, 1977.

Belzer, Richard, & Wayne, *Dead Wrong,* Skyhorse Press, New York, 2012.

Bernstein, Carl & Woodward, Bob, *All The President's Men,* Simon and Schuster, New York, 1974.

Bamford, James, *Body of Secrets: Anatomy of the Ultra-Secret National Security Agency,* Doubleday, New York, 2001.

Benson, Michael, *Who's Who In The JFK Assassination: An A To Z Encyclopedia,* Carol Publishing, New York, 1993.

Breuer, William, *Hitler's Undercover War,* St. Martin's Press, New York, 1989.

Cantor, George, *Bad Guy's in American History,* Taylor Publishing Co, Dallas, Texas, 1999.

Douglas, James, *JFK And the Unspeakable: Why He Died and Why It Matters,* Orbis Books, Maryknoll, New York, 2008.

Duffy, Peter, *Double Agent,* Charles Scribner, New York, 2014.

Dunstan, Simon & Williams, Gerrard, *Grey Wolf: The Escape of Adolf Hitler,* Sterling, New York, 2011.

Edsel, Robert, *The Monuments Men: Allied Heros, Nazi Thieves, And The Greatest Treasure Hunt in History,* Little Brown & Co, New York, 2009.

Eisenschmil, Otto, *Why Was Lincoln Murdered?,* Grossett &Dunlap, New York, 1937,

Epstein, Edward Jay, *Legend:The Secret World of Lee Harvey Oswald,* McGraw Hill & Co, New York, 1978.

Feldstein, Mark, *Poisoning The Press: Richard Nixon, Jack Anderson, and the Rise of Washington's Scandal Culture,* Farr, Strauss and Giroux, New York, 2010.

Fonzi, Gaeton, *The Last Investigation,* Thunders Mouth Press, New York, 1993.

Fulsom, Don, *Nixon's Darkest Secrets,* St. Martin's Press, New York, 2012.

American Conspiracy Files

Garment, Leonard, *In Search of Deep Throat,* Basic Books, New York, 2000.

Gentry, Curt, *J. Edgar Hoover: The Man And the Secrets,* W.W. Norton & Co, New York 1991.

Guttridge, Leonard, & Neff, Ray, *Dark Union,* John Wiley and Sons, Hoboken, NJ, 2003.

Hayes, John Earl, Klehr, Harvey & Vassilev, Alexander, *Spies: The Rise And Fall of the KGB in America,* Yale University Press, New Haven, Ct., 2009.

Horn, James, *A Kingdom Strange: The Brief and Tragic History of the Lost Colony of Roanoke,* Basic Books, New York, 2010.

Hughes, Ken, *Chasing Shadows,* University of Virginia Press, Charlottesville, Va., 2014.

Israel, Peter, & Jones, Stephen, *Others Unknown: Timothy McVeigh and the Oklahoma City Bombing Conspiracy,* Public Affairs, New York, 2001.

Janeczko, Paul, *The Dark Game: True Spy Stories From Invisible Ink to CIA Moles,* Candlewick Press, Somerville, Mass, 2010.

Kilmeade, Brian & Yaegar, Don, *George Washington's Secret Six: The Spy Ring That Saved the American Revolution,* Penguin Group, New York, 2013.

Kneece, Jack, *Family Treason: The Walker Spy Case,* Stein & Day Publishers, New York, 1986.

Kross, Peter, *Spies, Traitors and Moles: An Espionage and Intelligence Quiz Book,* Illuminet Press, Lilburn, GA, 1998.

Ibid, *The Secret History of the United States: Conspiracies, Cobwebs And Lies,* Adventures Unlimited Press, Kempton, IL, 2013.

Ibid, *New Jersey History,* Middle Atlantic Press, Wilmington, DE, 1987.

Ibid, *Oswald, the CIA and the Warren Commission: The Unanswered Questions,* Bridger House Press, Hayden, ID, 2011.

Ibid, *The Encyclopedia of World War 2 Spies,* Barricade Books, Fort Lee, NJ, 2001.

Ibid, *Target Fidel: A Narrative Encyclopedia on the US Government's Plots to Kill Fidel Castro-1959-1965,* Privately Printed, 1999.

Lance, Peter, *1000 Years For Revenge,* Regan Books, New York, 2003.

Lane, Mark, *Plausible Denial: Was the CIA Involved in the Assassination of JFK?,* Thunders Mouth Press, New York, 1991.

Litchfield, Michael, *It's A Conspiracy: The National Insecurity Council,* Earth Works Press, Berkeley, California, 1992.

Mappen, Mark, *Murders And Spies, Lovers, and Lies,* Avon Books, New

York, 1996.

Marrs, Jim, *Alien Agenda,* Harper Collins Publishers, New York, 1997.

Ibid, *Crossfire: The Plot that killed Kennedy,* Carroll & Graf, New York, 1989.

Martin, A.G. D., *Mafia: Inside The Dark Heart,* St. Martin's Press, New York, 2008.

Michel, Lou, & Herbeck, Dan, *American Terrorist: Timothy McVeigh and the Oklahoma City Bombing.*

Mellen, Joan, *Our Man in Haiti,* Trine Day Publishers, Waterville, Oregon, 2012.

Nelson, Philip, *LBJ: From Mastermind to the Colossus,* Skyhorse Press, New York, 2014.

Newman, John, *Oswald And the CIA,* Carroll & Graf, New York, 1995.

Ibid, *Where Angels Tred Lightly: The Assassination of President Kennedy, Volume 1,* Create Space, 2015.

Newark, Tim, *Mafia Allies,* Zenith Press, St. Paul, MN. 2007.

Parry, Robert, *Trick or Treason: The October Surprise Mystery,* Sheridan Square Press, New York, 1993.

Pepper, William, *An Act of State: The Execution of Martin Luther King,* Verso, New York, 2003.

Polmar, Norman & Allen, Thomas, *Spy Book: The Encyclopedia of Espionage,* Random House, New York, 1997.

Posner, Gerald, *God's Bankers: A History of Money and Power At the Vatican,* Simon and Schuster, New York, 2015.

Rose, Alexander, *Washington's Spies: The Story of America's First Spy Ring,* Random House, New York, 2006.

Russell, Dick, *The Man Who Knew Too Much,* Carroll & Graf Publishers, New York, 1992.

Sayer, Ian & Botting, Douglas, *Nazi Gold: The Story of the World's Greatest Robbery and Its Aftermath,* Cangdon & Weed, Inc., New York, 1984.

Scheim, David, *Contract on America: The Mafia Murder of President John F. Kennedy,* Shapolsky Press, New York, 1988.

Shenon, Philip, *The Commission: The Unanswered History of the 9-11 Investigation,* Twelve Books, New York, 2008.

Sick, Gary, *October Surprise,* Three Rivers Press/Times Books, New York, 1992.

Sullivan, Shane, *Who Killed Bobby? The Unsolved Murder of Robert F. Kennedy,* Union Square Press, New York, 2008.

Steers, Edward, Jr., *The Lincoln Assassination Encyclopedia,* Harper

Books, New York, 2010.

Summers, Anthony, *An Arrogance of Power: The Secret World of Richard Nixon,* Viking, New York, 2000.

Ibid, *Conspiracy,* McGraw Hill Books, New York, 1980.

Ibid, *Official and Confidential: The Secret Life of J. Edgar Hoover,* G. P. Putnam, Sons, New York, 1993.

Swanson, James, *Manhunt: The 12-Day Chace for Lincoln's Killer,* William Morrow & Co, New York, 2006.

Sulick, Michael, *Spying In America,* Georgetown University Press,, Washington, D.C., 2012.

Talbot, David, *Brothers: The Hidden History of the Kennedy Years,* Free Press, New York, 2007.

Tannenhaus, Sam, *Whitaker Chambers,* Random House, New York, 1997.

Tidwell, William, with Hall, James & Gaddy, David, *Come Retribution: The Confederate Secret Service and the Assassination of Lincoln,* University Press of Mississippi, Jackson, MS, 1988.

Thomas, Evan, *The War Lovers: Roosevelt, Lodge, Hearst, And the Rush to Empire,* Little Brown & Co., New York, 2010.

Thompson, Paul, *The Terror Timeline,* Ragan Books, New York, 2004.

Vise, David, *Spy: The Bureau and the Mole: The Unmasking of Robert Hanssen, The Most Dangerous Double Agent in FBI History,* Atlantic Monthly Press, New York, 2002.

Walker, Dale, *Legends, and Lies: Great Mysteries of the American West,* Forge Books, New York, 1997.

Weinstein, Allen & Vassiliev, Alexander, *The Haunted Wood,* Random House, New York, 1999.

Wise, David, *Spy: The Inside Story of How the FBI's Robert Hanssen Betrayed America,* Random House, New York, 2002.

Woodward, Bob, and Bernstein, Carl, *The Secret Man: The Story of Watergate's Deep Throat,* Simon and Schuster, New York, 2005.

Yallop, David, *In God's Name: An Investigation into the Murder of Pope John Paul,* Bantam Books, New York, 1984.

Magazines and Other Sources:

Anderson, Ross, *The Bug that Poisoned the President,* Food Safety News, Feb. 21, 2011.

Bates, Daniel, *Is this the face of Butch Cassidy and proof he DIDN'T die in 1908 shootout with the Bolivian army?,* Mail Online, August 16, 2011.

Bernstein, Adam, *Paul Marcinkus Indicted in Bank Scandal,* Washington Pose, 2-22-06.

Bixman, Karen, "Obstruction of Justice. Exposing the Inslaw Scandal and Related Crimes, *Media Bypass Magazine,*" no date.

Burris, Charlie, *It's the 70th Anniversary of the Watergate Conspiracy,* Lew Rockwell.com.

Burrough, Brian, "Meet the Weather Underground Bomb Guru," *Vanity Fair*, March 20, 2015.

Corn, David, *How Mark Felt Fooled the FBI,* The Nation, July 4, 2005.

Ibid, "The Double Side of 'I Have a Dream.' The FBI's War on Martin Luther King," *Mother Jones*, March 8, 2013.

Craig, R. Bruce, *Setting the Record Straight: Harry Dexter White and Soviet Espionage,* History News Network, April 30, 2012.

Dowling, Kevin & Knightly, Philip, *The Olson File: A Secret that could destroy the CIA,* www.seredipity.li/cia/olson.

Curtis, Gregory, *Should We Care!,* Texas Monthly, March 2000.Curtis, Richard, *Reprieve of the October Surprise: It's The Worst Surprise Still to Come?.*WRMEA- May-June 1991.

Condon, Christopher, *Did Hitler Escape to South America?* Lew Rockwell.com, 6-21-14.

Danini, Carmen, *De La Mena Diary Paper Authenticated.* San Antonio Express, 1998.

Epstein, Edward Jay, *The first Calvi Mystery: Was his death suicide or murder?* Edwardjayepstein.com/questions.

Fazio, John, *Confederate Complicity In the Assassination of Abraham Lincoln: Part 3.* The Cleveland Civil War Roundtable, 2008.

Glasser, Jeff, *Secrets Cheap: John Anthony Walker,* US News and World Report, Jan 27-Feb 3, 2003. Pages, 68-69.

Gawalt, Gerard, *The Thomas Jefferson Papers: America and the Barbary Pirates.* World-wide web.

Hoff, Joan, *The Nixon Story You Never Heard,* Counterpunch.org. 1-7-2001.

Hogan, James, *Throat,* Mary Ferrell Foundation.

Havill, Adrian, *The Arrest of Spy Robert Hanssen,* www.commandpost.com, Feb 18, 2013.

Hitchens, Christopher, "To the Shores of Tripoli," *Time Magazine*, July 5, 2004, Page 56-61.

Holley, Joe, *Jimmy Charga; Smuggler Linked to Judge's Death,* Washington Post, July 28, 2008.

Jaskaw, *Vatican's role in saving Nazi war criminals comes to a new light,* atheistnews blog, 3-21-12.

Kross, Peter, *The Plumbers And The Torrijos Assassination Plot,* Back Channels, Vol. 4, No. 1, Page, 12-14.

Ibid, *The Conundrum of Alger Hiss,* Trenton Times, 5-21-2000.

Ibid, *De Mohrenschildt & Oswald,* Back Channels, Vol 1 No. 3, Spring 1992, Page 2-3.

Ibid, *Hitler's Gold,* Back Channels, Vol. 1. No. 3, Spring 1992, Page 3-4.

Ibid, *The John Wood Murder Case,* Back Channels, Vol. 1, No. 3, Spring 1992, Page8-11.

Ibid, *Lost Colony remains a mystery,* Trenton Times, November 26, 2000.

Lee, Martin, *Banking for God, The Mob And The CIA,* www.motherjones.com/politics, July 1, 83.

Longo, Mark, *To The Shores of Tripoli,* Military Heritage, June 2005, Page 39-49.

Lukas, Anthony, *Why the Watergate Break-in?,* www.nytimes.com, 7-27-03.

Mazetti, Mark, *Burglars Who Took on FBI Abandon Shadows,* International NYT, Jan. 7, 2014.

Mellen, Joan, *The Canterbury Lectures-Lecture Two—Lyndon Johnson & Mac Wallace,* April 2, 2014, joanmellen.com.

Marriott, Michael, *President Zachery Taylor's Body To Be Tested for Signs of Arsenic,* New York Times, June 15, 1991.

Mc Sherry, Patrick, *USS Maine-Mission in Havana, world-wide web.*

Mc Morrow, Edward, *What Destroyed the USS Maine-An Opinion,* www.spanamwar.com.

Mc Greal, Chris, *MLK friend and photographer was FBI informant,* The Guardian, September 14, 2010.

Morley, Jefferson, & Talbot, David, *The BBC's Flawed RFK Story,* The Mary Ferrell Foundation.

Noah, Timothy, *Did Nixon really order the Watergate-break-in?,* msnbc.com, 8-9-14.

No author, *Magruder: Nixon personally gave order for Watergate break-in,* usatoday.com, 7-27-03.

No author, *Did the CIA Kill Bobby Kennedy?,* The Guardian.com, 11-19-2006.

No author, *Duquesne Nazi Germany Spy Ring FBI Files,* www.paperlessarchives.com.

No author, *America's Spies,* USS WestPoint.com.

No author, *Shocking Evidence Hitler Escaped Germany,* wnd.com, 1-5-14.

No author, *Retired agents say they monitored King in Memphis,* Associated Pres, November 30, 1997.

No author, *Famous Crimes: Billie Sol Estes,* www.spartacus-educational.

No author, *The Estes Documents:* home.earthlinks.net.

No author, *Church, Benjamin, Revolutionary War Surgeon,* Encyclopedia of Biography, Page 250-51.

No author, *Biographies of Dr. Benjamin Church.* Dictionary of American Biography (Scribner's), Page 100-101.

No author, *The Barbary Pirate Wars: The Life and times of William Eaton,* world-wide web.

No author, *History of Butch Cassidy, LeRoy Parker,* Utah.com.

No author, *David Crockett (1786-1836) Biography,* world-wide web.

No author, *Sundance Kid,* Spartacus-educational. Com.

No author, *Jesse James Poisoned Lincoln's Assassin,* henrymarkow.com.

No author, *Zachary Taylor/The White House,* world-wide web.

No author, *U.S. Entry into World War I, 1917-1926,* Milestones, Office of the Historian, US Department of State.

No author, *The Zimmerman Telegram: Teaching with Documents, The Zimmerman Telegram.*

No author, *The Zimmerman Telegram,* Cryptographic Quarterly, No date.

No author, *Saudi Arabia and the 9-11 Terrorist Attacks,* The Wire, 2-6-13.

Parry, Robert, *Second Thoughts on October Surprise,* Consortium news, June 8-2013.

Ibid, *Part 3: The Original October Surprise,* Truth-out-.org, 10-29-06.

Ibid, *How Richard Nixon Sabotaged 1968 Vietnam Peace Talks to get Elected President,* www.truth-out. Org.

Ibid, *LBJ's "X" File on Nixon's Treason,* Consortiumnews. 3-3-12.

Pressley, Sue Anne, *Conspiracy Found in MLK Killing,* Washington Pose, Dec. 9- 1999.

Prados, John, *The John Walker Spy Ring and the U.S. Navy's Biggest Betrayal,* USNI News, September 2, 2014.

Ridgeway, James, *Did the FBI Bury Oklahoma City Bombing Evidence?* Mother Jones, July 21, 2011.

Simpich, Bill, *Lee Harvey Oswald's First Intelligence Assignment,* 9-20-2010.

Stelzer, C.D, *The trial of MLK's assassin leads to St. Louis,* Riverfront Times, April 8, 1999.

Seybert, Tony, *The Strange Death of Zachary Taylor,* world-wide-web, May 29, 2005.

Shenon, Philip, "What The Warren Commission Didn't Know," *Politico Magazine*, 2-2-15.

Skemp, Shelia, "William Franklin: His Father's Son," *Pennsylvania Magazine of History*
& Biography, April 1985, Volume. 109, Issue 2, Page 145-178.

Ibid, *Benjamin Franklin, Patriot, and William Franklin, Loyalist,* Pa. History, January 1998, Volume 65, Issue 1, Page 35-45.

Summers, Anthony & Swan, Robbyn, *Lee Harvey Oswald: A Simple Defector,* Nov. 19, 2013.

Swords, Michael, *The University of Colorado UFO Project: The Scientific Study of UFO's,* Journal of UFO Studies, New Series, Vol. 6, 1995/1996.

Thornton, Richard, *America Unearthed: At Roanoke Island the Dare Stones controversy,* www.examiner.com.

Thomas, Gordon, *US Vice President Dick Cheney & Secretary of Defense Donald Rumsfeld Linked to Murder of CIA Scientist,* www.rernse.com.

Van Gelder, Lawrence, "Joseph Charga, 50, Lawyer linked to assassination, Dies," *New York Times*, December 15, 1996.

U.S. Department of Energy-*The Manhattan Project-Espionage And the Manhattan Project,* History Commons.org.

Watson, Paul, *Confirmed: FBI Got Warning Day Before OKC Bombing,* Infowars, Feb. 8, 2011.

Weiner, Tim, "W. Mark Felt, Watergate Deep Throat Dies at 95," *New York Times*, June 1, 2005.

Wright, Lawrence, "The Twenty-Eight Pages," *The New Yorker*, September 9, 2014.

Zymanski, Greg, *New Lead in Vatican Bank Scandal Surfaces,* www.motherjones.com/politics, July 1, 1983.

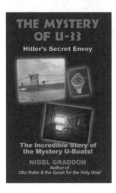
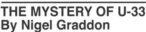

SECRETS OF THE UNIFIED FIELD
The Philadelphia Experiment, the Nazi Bell, and the Discarded Theory
by Joseph P. Farrell

Farrell examines the now discarded Unified Field Theory. American and German wartime scientists and engineers determined that, while the theory was incomplete, it could nevertheless be engineered. Chapters include: The Meanings of "Torsion"; Wringing an Aluminum Can; The Mistake in Unified Field Theories and Their Discarding by Contemporary Physics; Three Routes to the Doomsday Weapon: Quantum Potential, Torsion, and Vortices; Tesla's Meeting with FDR; Arnold Sommerfeld and Electromagnetic Radar Stealth; Electromagnetic Phase Conjugations, Phase Conjugate Mirrors, and Templates; The Unified Field Theory, the Torsion Tensor, and Igor Witkowski's Idea of the Plasma Focus; tons more.
340 pages. 6x9 Paperback. Illustrated. Bibliography. Index. $18.95. Code: SOUF

NAZI INTERNATIONAL
The Nazi's Postwar Plan to Control Finance, Conflict, Physics and Space
by Joseph P. Farrell

Beginning with prewar corporate partnerships in the USA, including some with the Bush family, he moves on to the surrender of Nazi Germany, and evacuation plans of the Germans. He then covers the vast, and still-little-known recreation of Nazi Germany in South America with help of Juan Peron, I.G. Farben and Martin Bormann. Farrell then covers Nazi Germany's penetration of the Muslim world including Wilhelm Voss and Otto Skorzeny in Gamel Abdul Nasser's Egypt before moving on to the development and control of new energy technologies including the Bariloche Fusion Project, Dr. Philo Farnsworth's Plasmator, and the work of Dr. Nikolai Kozyrev. Finally, Farrell discusses the Nazi desire to control space, and examines their connection with NASA, the esoteric meaning of NASA Mission Patches.
412 pages. 6x9 Paperback. Illustrated. References. $19.95. Code: NZIN

ARKTOS
The Polar Myth in Science, Symbolism & Nazi Survival
by Joscelyn Godwin

Explored are the many tales of an ancient race said to have lived in the Arctic regions, such as Thule and Hyperborea. Progressing onward, he looks at modern polar legends: including the survival of Hitler, German bases in Antarctica, UFOs, the hollow earth, and the hidden kingdoms of Agartha and Shambala. Chapters include: Prologue in Hyperborea; The Golden Age; The Northern Lights; The Arctic Homeland; The Aryan Myth; The Thule Society; The Black Order; The Hidden Lands; Agartha and the Polaires; Shambhala; The Hole at the Pole; Antarctica; more.
220 Pages. 6x9 Paperback. Illustrated. Bib. Index. $16.95. Code: ARK

MIND CONTROL, WORLD CONTROL
The Encyclopedia of Mind Control
by Jim Keith

Keith uncovers a surprising amount of information on the technology, experimentation and implementation of Mind Control technology. Various chapters in this shocking book are on early C.I.A. experiments such as Project Artichoke and Project RIC-EDOM, the methodology and technology of implants, Mind Control Assassins and Couriers, various famous "Mind Control" victims such as Sirhan Sirhan and Candy Jones. Also featured in this book are chapters on how Mind Control technology may be linked to some UFO activity and "UFO abductions.
256 Pages. 6x9 Paperback. Illustrated. $14.95. Code: MCWC

LOST CITIES & ANCIENT MYSTERIES OF THE SOUTHWEST
By David Hatcher Childress

Join David as he starts in northern Mexico and searches for the lost mines of the Aztecs. He continues north to west Texas, delving into the mysteries of Big Bend, including mysterious Phoenician tablets discovered there and the strange lights of Marfa. Then into New Mexico where he stumbles upon a hollow mountain with a billion dollars of gold bars hidden deep inside it! In Arizona he investigates tales of Egyptian catacombs in the Grand Canyon, cruises along the Devil's Highway, and tackles the century-old mystery of the Lost Dutchman mine. In Nevada and California Childress checks out the rumors of mummified giants and weird tunnels in Death Valley, plus he searches the Mohave Desert for the mysterious remains of ancient dwellers alongside lakes that dried up tens of thousands of years ago. It's a full-tilt blast down the back roads of the Southwest in search of the weird and wondrous mysteries of the past!

486 Pages. 6x9 Paperback. Illustrated. Bibliography. $19.95. Code: LCSW

TECHNOLOGY OF THE GODS
The Incredible Sciences of the Ancients
by David Hatcher Childress

Childress looks at the technology that was allegedly used in Atlantis and the theory that the Great Pyramid of Egypt was originally a gigantic power station. He examines tales of ancient flight and the technology that it involved; how the ancients used electricity; megalithic building techniques; the use of crystal lenses and the fire from the gods; evidence of various high tech weapons in the past, including atomic weapons; ancient metallurgy and heavy machinery; the role of modern inventors such as Nikola Tesla in bringing ancient technology back into modern use; impossible artifacts; and more.

356 PAGES. 6x9 PAPERBACK. ILLUSTRATED. BIBLIOGRAPHY. $16.95. CODE: TGOD

VIMANA AIRCRAFT OF ANCIENT INDIA & ATLANTIS
by David Hatcher Childress, introduction by
Ivan T. Sanderson

In this incredible volume on ancient India, authentic Indian texts such as the *Ramayana* and the *Mahabharata* are used to prove that ancient aircraft were in use more than four thousand years ago. Included in this book is the entire Fourth Century BC manuscript *Vimaanika Shastra* by the ancient author Maharishi Bharadwaaja. Also included are chapters on Atlantean technology, the incredible Rama Empire of India and the devastating wars that destroyed it.

334 PAGES. 6x9 PAPERBACK. ILLUSTRATED. $15.95. CODE: VAA

LOST CONTINENTS & THE HOLLOW EARTH
I Remember Lemuria and the Shaver Mystery
by David Hatcher Childress & Richard Shaver

Shaver's rare 1948 book *I Remember Lemuria* is reprinted in its entirety, and the book is packed with illustrations from Ray Palmer's *Amazing Stories* magazine of the 1940s. Palmer and Shaver told of tunnels running through the earth—tunnels inhabited by the Deros and Teros, humanoids from an ancient spacefaring race that had inhabited the earth, eventually going underground, hundreds of thousands of years ago. Childress discusses the famous hollow earth books and delves deep into whatever reality may be behind the stories of tunnels in the earth. Operation High Jump to Antarctica in 1947 and Admiral Byrd's bizarre statements, tunnel systems in South America and Tibet, the underground world of Agartha, the belief of UFOs coming from the South Pole, more.

344 PAGES. 6x9 PAPERBACK. ILLUSTRATED. $16.95. CODE: LCHE

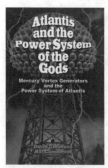

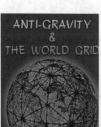
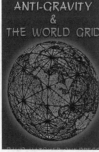

MAPS OF THE ANCIENT SEA KINGS
Evidence of Advanced Civilization in the Ice Age
by Charles H. Hapgood

Charles Hapgood has found the evidence in the Piri Reis Map that shows Antarctica, the Hadji Ahmed map, the Oronteus Finaeus and other amazing maps. Hapgood concluded that these maps were made from more ancient maps from the various ancient archives around the world, now lost. Not only were these unknown people more advanced in mapmaking than any people prior to the 18th century, it appears they mapped all the continents. The Americas were mapped thousands of years before Columbus. Antarctica was mapped when its coasts were free of ice!

316 PAGES. 7x10 PAPERBACK. ILLUSTRATED. BIBLIOGRAPHY & INDEX. $19.95. CODE: MASK

PATH OF THE POLE
Cataclysmic Pole Shift Geology
by Charles H. Hapgood

Maps of the Ancient Sea Kings author Hapgood's classic book *Path of the Pole* is back in print! Hapgood researched Antarctica, ancient maps and the geological record to conclude that the Earth's crust has slipped on the inner core many times in the past, changing the position of the pole. *Path of the Pole* discusses the various "pole shifts" in Earth's past, giving evidence for each one, and moves on to possible future pole shifts.

356 PAGES. 6x9 PAPERBACK. ILLUSTRATED. $16.95. CODE: POP

SECRETS OF THE HOLY LANCE
The Spear of Destiny in History & Legend
by Jerry E. Smith

Secrets of the Holy Lance traces the Spear from its possession by Constantine, Rome's first Christian Caesar, to Charlemagne's claim that with it he ruled the Holy Roman Empire by Divine Right, and on through two thousand years of kings and emperors, until it came within Hitler's grasp—and beyond! Did it rest for a while in Antarctic ice? Is it now hidden in Europe, awaiting the next person to claim its awesome power? Neither debunking nor worshiping, *Secrets of the Holy Lance* seeks to pierce the veil of myth and mystery around the Spear. Mere belief that it was infused with magic by virtue of its shedding the Savior's blood has made men kings. But what if it's more? What are "the powers it serves"?

312 PAGES. 6x9 PAPERBACK. ILLUSTRATED. BIBLIOGRAPHY. $16.95. CODE: SOHL

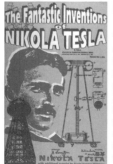

THE FANTASTIC INVENTIONS OF NIKOLA TESLA
by Nikola Tesla with additional material by
David Hatcher Childress

This book is a readable compendium of patents, diagrams, photos and explanations of the many incredible inventions of the originator of the modern era of electrification. In Tesla's own words are such topics as wireless transmission of power, death rays, and radio-controlled airships. In addition, rare material on a secret city built at a remote jungle site in South America by one of Tesla's students, Guglielmo Marconi. Marconi's secret group claims to have built flying saucers in the 1940s and to have gone to Mars in the early 1950s! Incredible photos of these Tesla craft are included. •His plan to transmit free electricity into the atmosphere. •How electrical devices would work using only small antennas. •Why unlimited power could be utilized anywhere on earth. •How radio and radar technology can be used as death-ray weapons in Star Wars.

342 PAGES. 6x9 PAPERBACK. ILLUSTRATED. $16.95. CODE: FINT

REICH OF THE BLACK SUN
Nazi Secret Weapons & the Cold War Allied Legend
by Joseph P. Farrell

Why were the Allies worried about an atom bomb attack by the Germans in 1944? Why did the Soviets threaten to use poison gas against the Germans? Why did Hitler in 1945 insist that holding Prague could win the war for the Third Reich? Why did US General George Patton's Third Army race for the Skoda works at Pilsen in Czechoslovakia instead of Berlin? Why did the US Army not test the uranium atom bomb it dropped on Hiroshima? Why did the Luftwaffe fly a non-stop round trip mission to within twenty miles of New York City in 1944? *Reich of the Black Sun* takes the reader on a scientific-historical journey in order to answer these questions. Arguing that Nazi Germany actually won the race for the atom bomb in late 1944,

352 PAGES. 6x9 PAPERBACK. ILLUSTRATED. BIBLIOGRAPHY. $16.95. CODE: ROBS

THE GIZA DEATH STAR
The Paleophysics of the Great Pyramid & the Military Complex at Giza
by Joseph P. Farrell

Was the Giza complex part of a military installation over 10,000 years ago? Chapters include: An Archaeology of Mass Destruction, Thoth and Theories; The Machine Hypothesis; Pythagoras, Plato, Planck, and the Pyramid; The Weapon Hypothesis; Encoded Harmonics of the Planck Units in the Great Pyramid; High Freqquency Direct Current "Impulse" Technology; The Grand Gallery and its Crystals: Gravito-acoustic Resonators; The Other Two Large Pyramids; the "Causeways," and the "Temples"; A Phase Conjugate Howitzer; Evidence of the Use of Weapons of Mass Destruction in Ancient Times; more.

290 PAGES. 6x9 PAPERBACK. ILLUSTRATED. $16.95. CODE: GDS

THE GIZA DEATH STAR DEPLOYED
The Physics & Engineering of the Great Pyramid
by Joseph P. Farrell

Farrell expands on his thesis that the Great Pyramid was a maser, designed as a weapon and eventually deployed—with disastrous results to the solar system. Includes: Exploding Planets: A Brief History of the Exoteric and Esoteric Investigations of the Great Pyramid; No Machines, Please!; The Stargate Conspiracy; The Scalar Weapons; Message or Machine?; A Tesla Analysis of the Putative Physics and Engineering of the Giza Death Star; Cohering the Zero Point, Vacuum Energy, Flux: Feedback Loops and Tetrahedral Physics; and more.

290 PAGES. 6x9 PAPERBACK. ILLUSTRATED. $16.95. CODE: GDSD

THE GIZA DEATH STAR DESTROYED
The Ancient War For Future Science
by Joseph P. Farrell

Farrell moves on to events of the final days of the Giza Death Star and its awesome power. These final events, eventually leading up to the destruction of this giant machine, are dissected one by one, leading us to the eventual abandonment of the Giza Military Complex—an event that hurled civilization back into the Stone Age. Chapters include: The Mars-Earth Connection; The Lost "Root Races" and the Moral Reasons for the Flood; The Destruction of Krypton: The Electrodynamic Solar System, Exploding Planets and Ancient Wars; Turning the Stream of the Flood: the Origin of Secret Societies and Esoteric Traditions; The Quest to Recover Ancient Mega-Technology; Non-Equilibrium Paleophysics; Monatomic Paleophysics; Frequencies, Vortices and Mass Particles; "Acoustic" Intensity of Fields; The Pyramid of Crystals; tons more.

292 pages. 6x9 paperback. Illustrated. $16.95. Code: GDES

THE FREE-ENERGY DEVICE HANDBOOK
A Compilation of Patents and Reports
by David Hatcher Childress

A large-format compilation of various patents, papers, descriptions and diagrams concerning free-energy devices and systems. *The Free-Energy Device Handbook* is a visual tool for experimenters and researchers into magnetic motors and other "over-unity" devices. With chapters on the Adams Motor, the Hans Coler Generator, cold fusion, superconductors, "N" machines, space-energy generators, Nikola Tesla, T. Townsend Brown, and the latest in free-energy devices. Packed with photos, technical diagrams, patents and fascinating information, this book belongs on every science shelf.
292 PAGES. 8x10 PAPERBACK. ILLUSTRATED. $16.95. CODE: FEH

THE ENERGY GRID
Harmonic 695, The Pulse of the Universe
by Captain Bruce Cathie

This is the breakthrough book that explores the incredible potential of the Energy Grid and the Earth's Unified Field all around us. Cathie's first book, *Harmonic 33*, was published in 1968 when he was a commercial pilot in New Zealand. Since then, Captain Bruce Cathie has been the premier investigator into the amazing potential of the infinite energy that surrounds our planet every microsecond. Cathie investigates the Harmonics of Light and how the Energy Grid is created. In this amazing book are chapters on UFO Propulsion, Nikola Tesla, Unified Equations, the Mysterious Aerials, Pythagoras & the Grid, Nuclear Detonation and the Grid, Maps of the Ancients, an Australian Stonehenge examined, more.
255 PAGES. 6x9 TRADEPAPER. ILLUSTRATED. $15.95. CODE: TEG

THE BRIDGE TO INFINITY
Harmonic 371244
by Captain Bruce Cathie

Cathie has popularized the concept that the earth is crisscrossed by an electromagnetic grid system that can be used for anti-gravity, free energy, levitation and more. The book includes a new analysis of the harmonic nature of reality, acoustic levitation, pyramid power, harmonic receiver towers and UFO propulsion. It concludes that today's scientists have at their command a fantastic store of knowledge with which to advance the welfare of the human race.
204 PAGES. 6x9 TRADEPAPER. ILLUSTRATED. $14.95. CODE: BTF

THE HARMONIC CONQUEST OF SPACE
by Captain Bruce Cathie

Chapters include: Mathematics of the World Grid; the Harmonics of Hiroshima and Nagasaki; Harmonic Transmission and Receiving; the Link Between Human Brain Waves; the Cavity Resonance between the Earth; the Ionosphere and Gravity; Edgar Cayce—the Harmonics of the Subconscious; Stonehenge; the Harmonics of the Moon; the Pyramids of Mars; Nikola Tesla's Electric Car; the Robert Adams Pulsed Electric Motor Generator; Harmonic Clues to the Unified Field; and more. Also included are tables showing the harmonic relations between the earth's magnetic field, the speed of light, and anti-gravity/gravity acceleration at different points on the earth's surface. New chapters in this edition on the giant stone spheres of Costa Rica, Atomic Tests and Volcanic Activity, and a chapter on Ayers Rock analysed with Stone Mountain, Georgia.
248 PAGES. 6x9. PAPERBACK. ILLUSTRATED. BIBLIOGRAPHY. $16.95. CODE: HCS

ORDER FORM

One Adventure Place
P.O. Box 74
Kempton, Illinois 60946
United States of America
Tel.: 815-253-6390 • Fax: 815-253-6300
Email: auphq@frontiernet.net
http://www.adventuresunlimitedpress.com

ORDERING INSTRUCTIONS

✓ Remit by USD$ Check, Money Order or Credit Card

✓ Visa, Master Card, Discover & AmEx Accepted

✓ Paypal Payments Can Be Made To:

   info@wexclub.com

✓ Prices May Change Without Notice

✓ 10% Discount for 3 or More Items

SHIPPING CHARGES

United States

✓ Postal Book Rate { $4.50 First Item / 50¢ Each Additional Item

✓ POSTAL BOOK RATE Cannot Be Tracked!
   Not responsible for non-delivery.

✓ Priority Mail { $6.00 First Item / $2.00 Each Additional Item

✓ UPS { $7.00 First Item / $1.50 Each Additional Item

   NOTE: UPS Delivery Available to Mainland USA Only

Canada

✓ Postal Air Mail { $15.00 First Item / $2.50 Each Additional Item

✓ Personal Checks or Bank Drafts MUST BE US$ and Drawn on a US Bank

✓ Canadian Postal Money Orders OK

✓ Payment MUST BE US$

All Other Countries

✓ Sorry, No Surface Delivery!

✓ Postal Air Mail { $19.00 First Item / $6.00 Each Additional Item

✓ Checks and Money Orders MUST BE US$ and Drawn on a US Bank or branch.

✓ Paypal Payments Can Be Made in US$ To:
   info@wexclub.com

SPECIAL NOTES

✓ RETAILERS: Standard Discounts Available

✓ BACKORDERS: We Backorder all Out-of-Stock Items Unless Otherwise Requested

✓ PRO FORMA INVOICES: Available on Request

✓ DVD Return Policy: Replace defective DVDs only

ORDER ONLINE AT: www.adventuresunlimitedpress.com

Please check: ✓

☐ This is my first order   ☐ I have ordered before

Name

Address

City

State/Province   Postal Code

Country

Phone: Day   Evening

Fax   Email

Item Code	Item Description	Qty	Total

Please check: ✓

	Subtotal ▶	
☐ Postal-Surface	Less Discount-10% for 3 or more items ▶	
	Balance ▶	
☐ Postal-Air Mail (Priority in USA)	Illinois Residents 6.25% Sales Tax ▶	
	Previous Credit ▶	
☐ UPS	Shipping ▶	
(Mainland USA only)	Total (check/MO in USD$ only) ▶	

☐ Visa/MasterCard/Discover/American Express

Card Number:

Expiration Date: Security Code:

✓ SEND A CATALOG TO A FRIEND: